ARRANGEMENT OF MATERIAL

STYLE

ANALYZED ESSAYS

J. Keiser

KUTZTOWN STATE COLLEGE
KUTZTOWN, PA

CLASSICAL RHETORIC FOR THE MODERN STUDENT

CLASSICAL RHETORIC
for the Modern Student

SECOND EDITION

EDWARD P. J. CORBETT
THE OHIO STATE UNIVERSITY

NEW YORK OXFORD UNIVERSITY PRESS 1971

This book is gratefully dedicated to my family

PREFACE to the Second Edition

The first edition of *Classical Rhetoric for the Modern Student* had a more favorable reception and a wider classroom use than I had dared hope for when the book was published in 1965. Part of the success of the book was due undoubtedly to the revival of interest in formal rhetoric at the time. That wave of interest has ebbed somewhat since then—or at least leveled off—but rhetorical activity has increased at an astounding rate in the last five years. Not all of this rhetorical activity has exemplified the kind of persuasive tactics taught by the ancient rhetoricians. In an article entitled "The Rhetoric of the Open Hand and the Rhetoric of the Closed Fist" in the December 1969 issue of *College Composition and Communication*, I contrasted the old style of rhetorical activity ("the open hand") with the new style ("the closed fist"), which came into prominence in the second half of the 1960's. I characterized this newer style as being increasingly (1) *non-verbal*, a kind of "body rhetoric" that seeks to communicate with and influence an audience by muscular demonstrations of various kinds—marches, boycotts, sit-ins, take-overs, riots; (2) *gregarious*, in the sense that instead of a solitary speaker or writer addressing an audience, a group of like-minded people band together to communicate their message; (3) *coercive*, depending more on aggressively presented "demands" than on persuasively formulated "requests"; (4) *non-conciliatory*, in the sense that the persuaders, instead of attempting to ingratiate themselves with an audience, deliberately attempt to shock, to exasperate, even to alienate an audience.

If this new style of rhetoric is to predominate in the 1970's, it would seem to be the height of folly to reintroduce into this context a style of rhetoric as old-fashioned as classical rhetoric. (As one wag suggested, maybe I should by publishing a Modern Rhetoric for the Classical Student.) But if we conceive of rhetoric as Aristotle conceived of it—namely, as the art dealing with the discovery and use of "all the available means of persuasion in any given case"—the old-style rhetoric still has some pertinence to the social and political purposes of our age and, of course, stands to gain from a study of the new strategies of persuasion that have been developed. Moreover, despite the recent resort to bombings, there are encouraging signs that the exercise of the more extreme varieties of close-fisted rhetoric is abating. Young people are beginning to see that they are more likely to create a brave new world by working within "the system" than by working from the outside to destroy it. Although increasing attention will indubitably be paid to those emotional, psycho-physical springs that trigger men's responses and actions, it does not seem likely that men will entirely abandon the strategy of appealing to the rationality, the reasonableness, of their fellowmen. One of the most salutary lessons that has come down to us from the Greek rhetoricians and philosophers is that unless we treat man as an integrated complex of intellect, will, passions, and physicality, we shall not produce whole men.

A number of changes and additions have been made in this second edition. For one thing, I have replaced some of the readings with more contemporary selections, not only to engage student interests but to illustrate that many of the strategies of ancient rhetoric are still operative today. I was disposed to replace more of the readings, but in response to pleas from teachers and students who used the first edition, I have retained most of the readings which were subjected to an extensive analysis. Another change is that I have prefaced most of the major reading selections with an orienting headnote.

I have attempted to enhance the reference value of the text by providing a more detailed table of contents, by putting some terminology in boldface type, and by setting up on the endpages a reference chart to key sections of the book. Most of the illustrations of the schemes and tropes in the chapter on Style have been replaced with examples from contemporary prose. The section on reference books in External Aids to Invention has been updated and somewhat expanded. Since the book continues to be used in some upper-division and graduate courses in rhetoric, I have expanded the Survey of Rhetoric to include a treatment of some of the developments in rhetoric during the nineteenth and twentieth centuries, and I have expanded the Bibliography with a listing of the many new books on rhetoric that have appeared since 1965.

I owe a great debt of gratitude to the many teachers and students who wrote me or buttonholed me at meetings, offering suggestions for the improvement of the book. I am especially indebted for detailed critiques from A. M. Tibbetts of the University of Illinois and from Ned Hedges and his freshman staff at the University of Nebraska. And I am profoundly grateful to the editorial staff of the Oxford University Press for their consistently wise counsel and for their continuing faith in the book. Whatever short-comings still remain in this new edition must be attributed solely to my stubbornness or myopia.

E. P. J. C.

Columbus, Ohio
January 1971

PREFACE to the First Edition

This book endeavors to present a coherent, realistic art of composition— an adaptation of classical rhetoric. The men from whom we inherited the classical system—Aristotle, Cicero, and Quintilian—firmly believed that some of the skills involved in the process of composition could be taught. Having studied the practice of successful speakers and writers, they brought together a set of precepts to aid their students in acquiring those skills, but they were sensible enough to recognize that one does not acquire a skill simply by studying rules; one must also submit to the discipline provided by imitation and practice. And they recognized too that in order to derive the maximum benefit from precept, imitation, and practice, the student had to be fired with a desire to learn as much as his natural endowments permitted.

So stated, the subject matter of this book would not seem to be revolutionary, for the methods of learning how to write have not changed very much since the Sophists first set up their schools of rhetoric in fifth-century Athens. In a sense, however, it is a new approach that is presented here, for the kind of rhetoric set forth in this book has been absent from American classrooms for about a century and has been replaced by other systems of teaching whatever is teachable about composition. In writing this book, the author believes that the elaborate system of the ancients, which taught the student how to find something to say, how to select and organize his material, and how to phrase it in the best possible way, is still useful and effective— perhaps more useful and effective than the various courses of study that replaced it. No system, classical or modern, has been devised that can change students suddenly and irrevocably into masters of elegant prose, but the ancient teachers of rhetoric, refusing to be impressed by the notion of "creative self-expression" until the student had a self to express and a facility for expressing it, succeeded in large part in developing a method which, when well taught, could help students to write and speak effectively.

Classical rhetoric is a positive discipline. Rather than tell the student what not to do, it instructs him in what should be done. Schoolboys of Shakespeare's time crept as unwillingly to class as students do today, but because classical rhetoric prevailed in Renaissance schools, they were not as much intimidated by a blank sheet of paper as their modern counterparts are.

The first chapter of this book gives a brief explanation of the kind of rhetorical training that flourished in the schools of the West for over two thousand years. The next three chapters develop the three vital parts of classical rhetoric: Chapter II, Discovery of Arguments; Chapter III, Arrangement of Material; Chapter IV, Style. The Appendix provides a history of rhetoric and a bibliography for those who will pursue their interest in the subject.

The present order of the chapters does not have to be the order followed in the classroom. In one sense, the order observed here is a natural one: we first must find something to say, then organize our material, and then put it into words. However, long before the student reads his way through the second chapter, he will be writing themes, an activity that involves all three processes. He must know something about all three processes when he sits down to write, but he cannot be instructed in all three at once. Every teacher makes his own adjustment to this fact. Since style is the most teachable of the skills involved in composition, some teachers will find it more convenient to start with Chapter IV. Others may prefer to begin with the chapter on arrangement.

Some explanation should be offered for the heavy emphasis on argumentative discourse. The bias is partly historical; rhetoric, throughout the ages, was primarily concerned with the means of argument. But a more important reason for concentrating on it in this text is that argumentative discourse is the form of rhetoric that students will be most exposed to in their lives. And they will exercise their power of argumentative discourse, more than any other, if they speak or write formally at all. However, only a few of the rhetorical principles presented in this book are peculiar to persuasive prose. Most of the principles of invention, arrangement, and style are equally applicable to exposition, description, and narration.

Because the bulk of this book is taken up with instruction in the principles of rhetoric, only a limited number of readings could be provided. Hopefully, by the time the student has worked his way through them, he will be able to apply the rhetorical principles he has learned to any reading matter available to him. He will begin to see classical rhetoric operating in any prose he hears or reads, whether it be an editorial or a letter-to-the-editor in the local newspaper, a clever advertisement in a current magazine, a campaign speech, a television commercial, a "begging letter" that comes in the morning mail, or a classmate's impassioned plea in the student council.

I am indebted to Wilbur Samuel Howell of Princeton University, Marvin T. Herrick of the University of Illinois, Dudley Bailey of the University of Nebraska, and Wayne C. Booth of the University of Chicago, who read various portions of the manuscript and offered helpful criticism. I am sure that wherever I have followed their advice the book has been improved. I am grateful also to the editorial staff of the Oxford University Press for their persistent confidence in the book and their judicious guidance. Finally, I must profess my gratitude to my wife, whose patience and encouragement did much to bring the book to completion.

E.P.J.C.

Omaha, Nebraska
January 1965

CONTENTS

IV/ STYLE 414

V/   A SURVEY OF RHETORIC   594

BIBLIOGRAPHY   631

INDEX   643

CLASSICAL RHETORIC FOR THE MODERN STUDENT

I fear, however, that I may be regarded as setting too lofty an ideal for the orator by insisting that he should be a good man skilled in speaking, or as imposing too many subjects of study on the learner....I would ask the skeptical to consider how great are the powers of the mind of man and how astonishing its capacity for carrying its desires into execution. For has not man succeeded in crossing the high seas, in learning the number and the courses of the stars, and almost measuring the universe itself—all of them accomplishments of less importance than oratory but of far greater difficulty?

QUINTILIAN

For the rules in textbooks of rhetoric cannot by themselves make expert those who are eager to dispense with study and practice.

DIONYSIUS OF HALICARNASSUS

Of all skill, part is infused by precept, and part is obtained by habit.

SAMUEL JOHNSON

It is foolish to suppose that you can teach anybody to write, but it is equally foolish to suppose that you cannot teach people a great deal about writing.

ROLFE HUMPHRIES

The more extensive a man's knowledge of what has been done, the greater will be his power of knowing what to do.

BENJAMIN DISRAELI

I / INTRODUCTION

Rhetoric is the art or the discipline that deals with the use of discourse, either spoken or written, to inform or persuade or move an audience, whether that audience is made up of a single person or a group of persons. Broadly defined in that way, rhetoric would seem to comprehend every kind of verbal expression that man engages in. But rhetoricians customarily have excluded from their province such informal modes of speech as "small talk," jokes, greetings ("Good to see you"), exclamations ("What a day!"), gossip, simple explanations or directions ("Take a left at the next intersection, go about three blocks to the first stoplight, and then . . ."). Although informative, directive, or suasory objectives can be realized in the stop-and-go, give-and-take form of the dialogue, rhetoric has traditionally been concerned with those instances of formal, premeditated, sustained monologue in which a single person seeks to exert an effect on an audience. This notion of "an effect on an audience" —a notion which gets at the very essence of rhetorical discourse—is implicit in such definitions of rhetoric as Marie Hochmuth Nichols's: "a means of so ordering discourse as to produce an effect on the listener or reader"; Kenneth Burke's: "the use of language as a symbolic means of inducing cooperation in beings that by nature respond to symbols"; or Donald Bryant's: "the function of adjusting ideas to people and of people to ideas." The classical rhetoricians seem to have narrowed the particular effect of rhetorical discourse to that of persuasion. Aristotle, for instance, defined rhetoric as "the faculty of discovering all the available means of persuasion in any given situation." But when one is reminded that the Greek word for *persuasion* derives from the Greek verb "to believe," one sees that Aristotle's definition can be made to comprehend not only those modes of discourse which are "argumentative" but also

3

those "expository" modes of discourse which seek to win acceptance of information or explanation.

But whether we are seeking, as the eighteenth-century rhetorician George Campbell put it, "to enlighten the understanding, to please the imagination, to move the passions, or to influence the will," we must adopt and adapt those strategies that will best achieve our end. *Strategies* is a good rhetorical word, because it implies the *choice* of available resources to achieve an end. It is no accident that the word *strategy* has military associations, for this word has its roots in the Greek word for *army*. Just as a general will adopt those resources, those tactics, which in his judgment are best calculated to discomfit the enemy, so the marshaller of language will seek out and use the best arguments, the best arrangement, and the best style to "win" his audience.

Let us look at a modern piece of written discourse in which the author is seeking to confirm or to change the attitude of his unseen audience about a complex issue and ultimately to induce his audience to act in accord with that attitude.

Ronald Dworkin: On Not Prosecuting Civil Disobedience

1 How should the government deal with those who disobey the draft laws out of conscience? Many people think the answer is obvious: The government must prosecute the dissenters, and if they are convicted it must punish them. Some people reach this conclusion easily, because they hold the mindless view that conscientious disobedience is the same as lawlessness. They think that the dissenters are anarchists who must be punished before their corruption spreads. Many lawyers and intellectuals come to the same conclusion, however, on what looks like a more sophisticated argument. They recognize that disobedience to law may be *morally* justified, but they insist that it cannot be *legally* justified, and they think that it follows from this truism that the law must be enforced. Erwin Griswold, the Solicitor General of the United States, and the former Dean of the Harvard Law School, appears to have adopted this view in a recent statement. "[It] is of the essence of law," he said, "that it is equally applied to all, that it binds all alike, irrespective of personal motive. For this reason, one who contemplates civil

From the *New York Review of Books,* June 6, 1968, pp. 14-21. This essay was reprinted in a collection of *New York Review* articles entitled *Trials of the Resistance* (Random House). By permission of the *New York Review of Books* and Ronald Dworkin.

disobedience out of moral conviction should not be surprised and must not be bitter if a criminal conviction ensues. And he must accept the fact that organized society cannot endure on any other basis."

2 *The New York Times* applauded that statement. A thousand faculty members of several universities had signed a *Times* advertisement calling on the Justice Department to quash the indictments of the Rev. William Sloane Coffin, Dr. Benjamin Spock, Marcus Raskin, Mitchell Goodman, and Michael Ferber, for conspiring to counsel various draft offenses. The *Times* said that the request to quash the indictments "confused moral rights with legal responsibilities."

3 But the argument that, because the government believes a man has committed a crime, it must prosecute him is much weaker than it seems. Society "cannot endure" if it tolerates all disobedience; it does not follow, however, nor is there evidence, that it will collapse if it tolerates some. In the United States prosecutors have discretion whether to enforce criminal laws in particular cases. A prosecutor may properly decide not to press charges if the law-breaker is young, or inexperienced, or the sole support of a family, or is repentant, or turns state's evidence, or if the law is unpopular or unworkable or generally disobeyed, or if the courts are clogged with more important cases, or for dozens of other reasons. This discretion is not license—we expect prosecutors to have good reasons for exercising it—but there are, at least *prima facie,* some good reasons for not prosecuting those who disobey the draft laws out of conscience. One is the obvious reason that they act out of better motives than those who break the law out of greed or a desire to subvert government. If motive can count in distinguishing between thieves, then why not in distinguishing between draft offenders? Another is the practical reason that our society suffers a loss if it punishes a group that includes—as the group of draft dissenters does—some of its most loyal and law-respecting citizens. Jailing such men solidifies their alienation from society, and alienates many like them who are deterred by the threat. If practical consequences like these argued for not enforcing prohibition, why do they not argue for tolerating offenses of conscience?

4 Those who think that conscientious draft offenders should always be punished must show that these are not good reasons for exercising discretion, or they must find contrary reasons that outweigh them. What arguments might they produce? There are practical reasons for enforcing draft laws, and I shall consider some of these later. But Dean Griswold and those who agree with him seem to rely on a fundamental moral argument that it would be unfair, not merely impractical, to let the dissenters go unpunished. They think it would be unfair, I gather, because society could not function if everyone disobeyed laws he disapproved of or found disadvantageous. If the government tolerates those few who will not "play the game," it allows

them to secure the benefits of everyone else's deference to law, without shouldering the burdens, such as the burden of the draft.

5 This argument is a serious one. It cannot be answered simply by saying that the dissenters would allow everyone else the privilege of disobeying a law he believed immoral. In fact, few draft dissenters would accept a changed society in which sincere segregationists were free to break civil rights laws they hated. The majority want no such change, in any event, because they think that society would be worse off for it; until they are shown this is wrong, they will expect their officials to punish anyone who assumes a privilege which they, for the general benefit, do not assume.

6 There is, however, a flaw in the argument. The reasoning contains a hidden assumption that makes it almost entirely irrelevant to the draft cases, and indeed to any serious case of civil disobedience in the United States. The argument assumes that the dissenters know that they are breaking a valid law, and that the privilege they assert is the privilege to do that. Of course, almost everyone who discusses civil disobedience recognizes that in America a law may be invalid because it is unconstitutional. But the critics handle this complexity by arguing on separate hypotheses: If the law is invalid, then no crime is committed, and society may not punish. If the law is valid, then a crime has been committed, and society must punish. This reasoning hides the crucial fact that the validity of the law may be doubtful. The officials and judges may believe that the law is valid, the dissenters may disagree, and both sides may have plausible arguments for their positions. If so, then the issues are different from what they would be if the law were clearly valid or clearly invalid, and the argument of fairness, designed for these alternatives, is irrelevant.

7 Doubtful law is by no means special or exotic in cases of civil disobedience. On the contrary. In the United States, at least, almost any law which a significant number of people would be tempted to disobey on moral grounds would be doubtful—if not clearly invalid—on constitutional grounds as well. The constitution makes our conventional political morality relevant to the question of validity; any statute that appears to compromise that morality raises constitutional questions, and if the compromise is serious, the constitutional doubts are serious also.

8 The connection between moral and legal issues is especially clear in the current draft cases. Dissent has largely been based on the following moral objections: (a) The United States is using immoral weapons and tactics in Vietnam. (b) The war has never been endorsed by deliberate, considered, and open vote of the peoples' representatives. (c) The United States has no interest at stake in Vietnam remotely strong enough to justify forcing a segment of its citizens to risk death there. (d) If an army is to be raised to fight that war, it is immoral to raise it by a draft that defers or

exempts college students, and thus discriminates against the economically underprivileged. (e) The draft exempts those who object to all wars on religious grounds, but not those who object to particular wars on moral grounds; there is no relevant difference between these positions, and so the draft, by making the distinction, implies that the second group is less worthy of the nation's respect than the first. (f) The law that makes it a crime to counsel draft resistance stifles those who oppose the war, because it is morally impossible to argue that the war is profoundly immoral, without encouraging and assisting those who refuse to fight it.

9 Lawyers will recognize that these moral positions, if we accept them, provide the basis for the following constitutional arguments: (a) The constitution makes treaties part of the law of the land, and the United States is a party to international conventions and covenants that make illegal the acts of war the dissenters charge the nation with committing. (b) The constitution provides that Congress must declare war; the legal issue of whether our action in Vietnam is a "war" and whether the Tonkin Bay Resolution was a "declaration" is the heart of the moral issue of whether the government has made a deliberate and open decision. (c) Both the due process clause of the Fifth and Fourteenth Amendments and equal protection clause of the Fourteenth Amendment condemn special burdens placed on a selected class of citizens when the burden or the classification is not reasonable; the burden is unreasonable when it patently does not serve the public interest, or when it is vastly disproportionate to the interest served. If our military action in Vietnam is frivolous or perverse, as the dissenters claim, then the burden we place on men of draft age is unreasonable and unconstitutional. (d) In any event, the discrimination in favor of college students denies to the poor the equal protection of the law that is guaranteed by the constitution. (e) If there is no pertinent difference between religious objection to all wars and moral objection to some wars, then the classification the draft makes is arbitrary and unreasonable, and unconstitutional on that ground. The "establishment of religion" clause of the First Amendment forbids governmental pressure in favor of organized religion; if the draft's distinction coerces men in this direction, it is invalid on that count also. (f) The First Amendment also condemns invasions of freedom of speech. If the draft law's prohibition on counseling does inhibit expression of a range of views on the war, it abridges free speech.

10 The principal counterargument, supporting the view that the courts ought not to hold the draft unconstitutional, also involves moral issues. Under the so-called "political question" doctrine, the courts deny their own jurisdiction to pass on matters—such as foreign or military policy—whose resolution is best assigned to other branches of the government. The Boston court trying the Coffin, Spock case has already declared, on the basis of this

doctrine, that it will not hear arguments about the legality of the war. But the Supreme Court has shown itself (in the reapportionment cases, for example) reluctant to refuse jurisdiction when it believed that the gravest issues of political morality were at stake and that no remedy was available through the political process. If the dissenters are right, and the war and the draft are state crimes of profound injustice to a group of citizens, then the argument that the courts must refuse jurisdiction is considerably weakened.

11   We cannot conclude from these arguments that the draft (or any part of it) is unconstitutional. If the Supreme Court is called upon to rule on the question, it will probably reject some of them, and refuse to consider the others on grounds that they are political. The majority of lawyers would probably agree with this result. But the arguments of unconstitutionality are at least plausible, and a reasonable and competent lawyer might well think that they present a stronger case, on balance, than the counterarguments. If he does, he will consider that the draft is not constitutional, and there will be no way of proving that he is wrong.

12   Therefore we cannot assume, in judging what to do with the draft dissenters, that they are asserting a privilege to disobey valid laws. We cannot decide that fairness demands their punishment until we try to answer the further question: What should a citizen do when the law is unclear, and when he thinks it allows what others think it does not? I do not mean to ask, of course, what it is *legally* proper for him to do, or what his *legal* rights are—that would be begging the question, because it depends upon whether he is right or they are right. I mean to ask what his proper course is as a citizen, what, in other words, we would consider to be "playing the game." That is a crucial question, because it cannot be unfair not to punish him if he is acting as, given his opinions, we think he should.[1]

13   There is no obvious answer on which most citizens would readily agree, and that is itself significant. If we examine our legal institutions and practices, however, we shall discover some relevant underlying principles and policies. I shall set out three possible answers to the question, and then try to show which of these best fits our practices and expectations. The three possibilities I want to consider are these:

(1)   If the law is doubtful, and it is therefore unclear whether it permits someone to do what he wants, he should assume the worst, and act on the assumption that it does not. He should obey the executive authorities who command him, even though he thinks they are wrong, while using the political process, if he can, to change the law.

[1] I do not mean to imply that the government should always punish a man who deliberately breaks a law he knows is valid. There may be reasons of fairness or practicality, like those I listed in the third paragraph, for not prosecuting such men. But cases like the draft cases present special arguments for tolerance; I want to concentrate on these arguments and therefore have isolated these cases.

(2) If the law is doubtful, he may follow his own judgment, that is, he may do what he wants if he believes that the case that the law permits this is stronger than the case that it does not. But he may follow his own judgment only until an authoritative institution, like a court, decides the other way in a case involving him or someone else. Once an institutional decision has been reached, he must abide by that decision, even though he thinks that it was wrong. (There are, in theory, many subdivisions of this second possibility. We may say that the individual's choice is foreclosed by the contrary decision of any court, including the lowest court in the system if the case is not appealed. Or we may require a decision of some particular court or institution. I shall discuss this second possibility in its most liberal form, namely that the individual may properly follow his own judgment until a contrary decision of the highest court competent to pass on the issue, which, in the case of the draft, is the United States Supreme Court.)

(3) If the law is doubtful, he may follow his own judgment even after a contrary decision by the highest competent court. Of course, he must take the contrary decision of any court into account in making his judgment of what the law requires. Otherwise the judgment would not be an honest or reasonable one, because the doctrine of precedent, which is an established part of our legal system, has the effect of allowing the decision of the courts to *change* the law. Suppose, for example, that a taxpayer believes that he is not required to pay tax on certain forms of income. If the Supreme Court decides to the contrary, he should, taking into account the practice of according great weight to the decisions of the Supreme Court on tax matters, decide that the Court's decision has itself tipped the balance, and that the law now requires him to pay the tax.

14 Someone might think that this qualification erases the difference between the third and the second models, but it does not. The doctrine of precedent gives different weights to the decisions of different courts, and greatest weight to the decisions of the Supreme Court, but it does not make the decision of any court conclusive. Sometimes, even after a contrary Supreme Court decision, an individual may still reasonably believe that the law is on his side; such cases are rare, but they are most likely to occur in disputes over constitutional law when civil disobedience is involved. The Court has shown itself more likely to overrule its past decisions if these have limited important personal or political rights, and it is just these decisions that a dissenter might want to challenge.

15 We cannot assume, in other words, that the Constitution is always what the Supreme Court says it is. Oliver Wendell Holmes, for example, did not follow such a rule in his famous dissent in the *Gitlow* case. A few years before, in *Abrams,* he had lost his battle to persuade the court that the First Amendment protected an anarchist who had been urging general strikes

against the government. A similar issue was presented in *Gitlow,* and Holmes once again dissented. "It is true," he said, "that in my opinion this criterion was departed from [in *Abrams*] but the convictions that I expressed in that case are too deep for it to be possible for me as yet to believe that it . . . settled the law." Holmes voted for acquitting Gitlow, on the ground that what Gitlow had done was no crime, even though the Supreme Court had recently held that it was.

16 Here then are three possible models for the behavior of dissenters who disagree with the executive authorities when the law is doubtful. Which of them best fits our legal and social practices?

17 I think it plain that we do not follow the first of these models, that is, that we do not expect citizens to assume the worst. If no court has decided the issue, and a man thinks, on balance, that the law is on his side, most of our lawyers and critics think it perfectly proper for him to follow his own judgment. Even when many disapprove of what he does—such as peddling pornography—they do not think he must desist just because the legality of his conduct is subject to doubt.

18 It is worth pausing a moment to consider what society would lose if it did follow the first model or, to put the matter the other way, what society gains when people follow their own judgment in cases like this. When the law is uncertain, in the sense that lawyers can reasonably disagree on what a court ought to decide, the reason usually is that different legal principles and policies have collided, and it is unclear how best to accommodate these conflicting principles and policies.

19 Our practice, in which different parties are encouraged to pursue their own understanding, provides a means of testing relevant hypotheses. If the question is whether a particular rule would have certain undesirable consequences, or whether these consequences would have limited or broad ramifications, then, before the issue is decided, it is useful to know what does in fact take place when some people proceed on that rule. (Much anti-trust and business regulation law has developed through this kind of testing.) If the question is whether and to what degree a particular solution would offend principles of justice or fair play deeply respected by the community, it is useful, again, to experiment by testing the community's response. The extent of community indifference to anti-contraception laws, for example, would never have become established had not some organizations deliberately flouted those laws.

20 If the first model were followed, we would lose the advantages of these tests. The law would suffer, particularly if this model were applied to constitutional issues. When the validity of a criminal statute is in doubt, the statute will almost always strike some people as being unfair or unjust, because it will infringe some principle of liberty or justice or fairness which

RONALD DWORKIN: ON NOT PROSECUTING CIVIL DISOBEDIENCE **11**

they take to be built into the Constitution. If our practice were that whenever a law is doubtful on these grounds, one must act as if it were valid, then the chief vehicle we have for challenging the law on moral grounds would be lost, and over time the law we obeyed would certainly become less fair and just, and the liberty of our citizens would certainly be diminished.

21 We would lose almost as much if we used a variation of the first model, that a citizen must assume the worst unless he can anticipate that the courts will agree with his view of the law. If everyone deferred to his guess of what the courts would do, society and its law would be poorer. Our assumption in rejecting the first model was that the record a citizen makes in following his own judgment, together with the arguments he makes supporting that judgment when he has the opportunity, are helpful in creating the best judicial decision possible. This remains true even when, at the time the citizen acts, the odds are against his success in court. We must remember, too, that the value of the citizen's example is not exhausted once the decision has been made. Our practices require that the decision be criticized, by the legal profession and the law schools, and the record of dissent may be invaluable here.

22 Of course a man must consider what the courts will do when he decides whether it would be *prudent* to follow his own judgment. He may have to face jail, bankruptcy, or opprobrium if he does. But it is essential that we separate the calculation of prudence from the question of what, as a good citizen, he may properly do. We are investigating how society ought to treat him when its courts believe that he judged wrong; therefore we must ask what he is justified in doing when his judgment differs from others'. We beg the question if we assume that what he may properly do depends on his guess as to how society will treat him.

23 We must also reject the second model, that if the law is unclear a citizen may properly follow his own judgment until the highest court has ruled that he is wrong. This fails to take into account the fact that any court, including the Supreme Court, may overrule itself. In 1940 the Court decided that a West Virginia law requiring students to salute the Flag was constitutional. In 1943 it reversed itself, and decided that such a statute was unconstitutional after all. What was the duty, as citizens, of this people who in 1941 and 1942 objected to saluting the Flag on grounds of conscience, and thought that the Court's 1940 decision was wrong? We can hardly say that their duty was to follow the first decision. They believed that saluting the Flag was unconscionable, and they believed, reasonably, that no valid law required them to do so. The Supreme Court later decided that in this they were right. The Court did not simply hold that after the second decision failing to salute would not be a crime; it held (as in a case like this it almost always would) that it was no crime after the first decision either.

24 Some will say that the flag-salute dissenters should have obeyed the Court's first decision, while they worked in the legislatures to have the law repealed, and tried in the courts to find some way to challenge the law again without actually violating it. That would be, perhaps, a plausible recommendation if conscience were not involved, because it would then be arguable that the gain in orderly procedure was worth the personal sacrifice of patience. But conscience was involved, and if the dissenters had obeyed the law while biding their time, they would have suffered the irreparable injury of having done what their conscience forbade them to do. It is one thing to say that an individual must sometimes violate his conscience when he knows that the law commands him to do it. It is quite another to say that he must violate his conscience even when he reasonably believes that the law does not require it, because it would inconvenience his fellow citizens if he took the most direct, and perhaps the only, method of attempting to show that he is right and they are wrong.

25 Since a court may overrule itself, the same reasons we listed for rejecting the first model count against the second as well. If we did not have the pressure of dissent, we would not have a dramatic statement of the degree to which a court decision against the dissenter is felt to be wrong, a demonstration that is surely pertinent to the question of whether it was right. We would increase the change of being governed by rules that offend the principles we claim to serve.

26 These considerations force us, I think, from the second model, but some will want to substitute a variation of it. They will argue that once the Supreme Court has decided that a criminal law is valid, then citizens have a duty to abide by that decision until they have a reasonable belief, not merely that the decision is a bad law, but that the Supreme Court is likely to overrule it. Under this view the West Virginia dissenters who refused to salute the Flag in 1942 were acting properly, because they might reasonably have anticipated that the Court would change its mind. But if the Court were to hold the draft laws constitutional, it would be improper to continue to challenge these laws, because there would be no great likelihood that the Court would soon change its mind. This suggestion must also be rejected, however. For once we say that a citizen may properly follow his own judgment of the law, in spite of his judgment that the courts will probably find against him, there is no plausible reason why he should act differently because a contrary decision is already on the books.

27 Thus the third model, or something close to it, seems to be the fairest statement of a man's social duty in our community. A citizen's allegiance is to the law, not to any particular person's view of what the law is, and he does not behave unfairly so long as he proceeds on his own considered and reasonable view of what the law requires. Let me repeat (because it is crucial) that this is not the same as saying that an individual may disregard what the courts have said. The doctrine of precedent lies near the core of our legal system, and no one can make a reasonable effort to follow the law unless he grants the courts the general power to alter it by their decisions. But if the issue is one touching fundamental personal or political rights, and it is arguable that the Supreme Court has made a mistake, a man is within his social rights in refusing to accept that decision as conclusive.

28   One large question remains before we can apply these observations to the problems of draft resistance. I have been talking about the case of a man who believes that the law is not what other people think, or what the courts have held. This description may fit some of those who disobey the draft laws out of conscience, but it does not fit most of them. Most of the dissenters are not lawyers or political philosophers; they believe that the laws on the books are immoral, and inconsistent with their country's legal ideals, but they have not considered the question of whether they may be invalid as well. Of what relevance to their situation, then, is the proposition that one may properly follow one's own view of the law?

29   To answer this, I shall have to return to the point I made earlier. The Constitution, through the due process clause, the equal protection clause, the First Amendment, and the other provisions I mentioned, injects an extraordinary amount of our political morality into the issue of whether a law is valid. The statement that most draft dissenters are unaware that the law is invalid therefore needs qualification. They hold beliefs that, if true, strongly support the view that the law is on their side; the fact that they have not reached that further conclusion can be traced, in at least most cases, to their lack of legal sophistication. If we believe that when the law is doubtful people who follow their own judgment of the law may be acting properly, it would seem wrong not to extend that view to those dissenters whose judgments come to the same thing. No part of the case that I made for the third model would entitle us to distinguish them from their more knowledgeable colleagues.

30   We can draw several tentative conclusions from the argument so far: When the law is uncertain, in the sense that a plausible case can be made on both sides, then a citizen who follows his own judgment is not behaving unfairly. Our practices permit and encourage him to follow his own judgment in such cases. For that reason, our government has a special responsibility to try to protect him, and soften his predicament, whenever it can do so without great damage to other policies. It does not follow that the government can guarantee him immunity—it cannot adopt the rule that it will prosecute no one who acts out of conscience, or convict no one who reasonably disagrees with the courts. That would paralyze the government's ability to carry out its policies; it would, moreover, throw away the most

important benefit of following the third model. If the state never prosecuted, then the courts could not act on the experience and the arguments the dissent has generated. But it does follow that when the practical reasons for prosecuting are relatively weak in a particular case, or can be met in other ways, the path of fairness lies in tolerance. The popular view that the law is the law and must always be enforced refuses to distinguish the man who acts on his own judgment of a doubtful law, and thus behaves as our practices provide, from the common criminal. I know of no reason, short of moral blindness, for not drawing a distinction in principle between the two cases.

Analysis of "On Not Prosecuting Civil Disobedience"

It should be pointed out that we are dealing here with only part of the full text of Ronald Dworkin's essay. In the original source, the author went on for another ten pages to develop his argument. But the selection reprinted here is enough of a self-contained unit to permit us to study the author's strategies of persuasion.

The author is dealing with a contemporary issue of vital concern to a number of people in the United States, especially to the young men of draft age. It is the kind of issue that lends itself to rhetorical discourse, because there is no simple right-or-wrong answer to the question raised by the issue. Aristotle observed that men never argue about situations over which they have no control. We never argue, for instance, about whether men should assume their share of child-bearing or about whether the sun should be allowed to rise tomorrow (although we do argue about whether our community should adopt daylight-saving time). We argue only about those human affairs that operate in the realm of the uncertain, the contingent, the probable. We may argue about whether a particular event (a murder, for instance) took place or about the consequences of an event (whether, for instance, a proposed new tax will produce the benefits promised by its advocates). Most questions about human affairs—like this one about whether those who refuse to be drafted into the army should be prosecuted—are exceedingly complex and therefore do not admit of simple answers. There are usually plausible arguments to be offered on both sides of such complex questions. In such matters, that man will win others to his point of view who presents, not the "truth" necessarily—because in such matters the "truth" is often not ascertainable—but the stronger argument, the higher probability, for his case. One of Plato's objections to rhetoric was that rhetoricians, unlike philosophers, were not interested in the truth but were interested only in the opinion of the many, in what most men *believed* to be true. But lacking Plato's optimism that the truth was always discoverable, Aristotle saw that men had frequently to make crucial decisions, especially in those areas of human affairs that he comprehended under the terms *politics* and *ethics,* on the basis of mere probabilities. Rhetoric, for him and for most later rhetoricians, was the discipline that guided men in making wise decisions in the area of the contingent.

Even in the title of his essay, Ronald Dworkin indicates which side he takes in the controversy about whether those who disobey the draft laws should be prosecuted, but in the essay itself, he presents fairly the arguments of the opposition and acknowledges graciously the plausibility of those arguments. The poles of the argument are not represented in black-and-white, good-and-bad terms. He concedes points to the opposition wherever he can; he acknowledges the limitations of his own arguments. These concessions and confessions are, as we shall see later, part of his strategy of persuasion, but for now we can view them as evidence of his recognition that the question being discussed is highly arguable and eminently complex. Accordingly, if he is to persuade his readers to take the same position on the draft issue as he has taken, he must present arguments stronger, more convincing, than those advanced by the opposition.

The ancient rhetoricians taught that there were three kinds of rhetorical argument—*logos,* the appeal to reason; *pathos,* the appeal to emotions; *ethos,* the appeal of the speaker or writer's character or personality. This essay is remarkably free of appeals to the emotions of the audience. Dworkin might have decided to avoid emotional appeals either because of the kind of person he is or because of the nature of the subject matter; but the chief determinant was probably his estimate of the kind of audience he was dealing with. He viewed the likely readers of his essay as highly literate, sophisticated people, who, while they might be, on certain occasions, just as much creatures of emotion as the next man, would, in the discussion of this issue, be tolerant of, more impressed by, rational argument. There are some effective emotional appeals that Dworkin might have used and that other speakers and writers have used in discussing this issue, but he chose not to use them. Another audience—extreme "hawks," for instance, or extreme "doves"—might be less patient with an exclusively rational approach, might be more prone to respond to emotional appeals, but for his audience, Dworkin elected to forgo the available emotional appeals.

By choosing to concentrate on the legal and prudential aspects of the question—because those are the aspects he estimates his audience will be most impressed by—Dworkin commits himself to the pursuit of those arguments which appeal primarily to the reason, the intellect, of his audience. So we should expect him to resort frequently to facts, laws, propositions, documentary evidence, testimony of authorities—in short, to much of the machinery of inductive and deductive logic; and when inferences or conclusions cannot be shown to "follow necessarily" from the facts or premises, he will be urging the *probable* or *plausible* conclusions that can be drawn from his line of argument.

We might start out by looking at the general outline of these first thirty paragraphs of his argument:

Introduction (paragraphs 1 and 2)

    Question to be dealt with: "How should the government deal with those who disobey the draft out of conscience?"

    Answer that many people give to this question: "We must prosecute and punish all dissenters."

I. Refutation of the view that the government must prosecute every instance of law-breaking (para. 3–7)

    A. On practical grounds (para. 3)

    B. On grounds of fairness (para. 4–7)

II. Consideration of the question whether the validity of the draft law is doubtful (para. 8–11)

III. Consideration of the question of what a citizen should do when the law is unclear or doubtful (para. 12–29)

    A. Three possible courses of action (para. 13–16)

    B. Refutation of the first course (para. 17–22)

    C. Refutation of the second course (para. 23–26)

    D. Arguments for accepting the third course (para. 27–29)

Conclusion: Summary of the arguments and reaffirmation of his recommendation (para. 30)

What we are exposing when we lay out an outline like this is the choice that a speaker or writer has made about the disposition or arrangement of his material. In classical rhetoric, disposition or arrangement was the second of the main processes involved in the exercise of persuasive discourse. The first process was the invention or discovery of arguments; the third was style or the verbalization of the arguments; the fourth was memory, the memorizing of the composed speech; the fifth was delivery, the pronunciation of the composed speech before a live audience. Chapter II of this book will deal with the first of these processes, Discovery of Arguments; Chapter III will deal with Arrangement of Material; Chapter IV will deal with Style. Memory and Delivery will not be treated in this book.

Each of the subsequent chapters of the book will deal in some detail with the principles guiding the most judicious choices from among the available means for composing a discourse which is intended to work some kind of effect on an audience. In the outline presented above, we observe the result of the choice that one author, writing for a certain kind of audience, has made from among the possible ways of organizing his arguments on the question of whether those who disobey the draft law should be prosecuted and punished. In the final evaluation, we might judge that the author had not made the *best* choice of his options. We might judge, for instance, that it would have been more effective if he had first presented a strong case for the course of action he would recommend and then had refuted the arguments for other courses of action; or if, instead of designating the three possible courses of actions all at once and then arguing for or against each course, he had revealed each course of action one by one, refuting it and then arguing for the one he advocated.

But if we take a close look at the order that Dworkin has imposed on his presentation, we will see that his arrangement is at least defensible, that it has indeed a discernible logic or coherence to it. Having presented in the introductory paragraphs two reasons that people advance for the necessity of punishing all dissenters, Dworkin sees that a natural next step is to refute the general principle that a government must prosecute every instance of law-breaking. And that is what he does in the first major division of the body of the essay (para. 3–7), and he attempts to refute that general principle from two points of view—on practical grounds (para. 3) and on grounds of fairness (para. 4–7). But in a series of transitional sentences in paragraph 7, the author suggests that perhaps we cannot really decide the question of fairness until we discuss whether the draft law is valid or not, either on moral or on constitutional grounds. And so in the next major section of the essay (para. 8–11), the author pursues the question of whether the validity of the draft law is at least doubtful. Having established a plausible, if not conclusive, argument that the draft laws are of doubtful validity, Dworkin sees that the next step is to consider what it is proper for a citizen to do when a law is of doubtful validity. So he proposes three possible courses of action and then considers in turn each of these courses of action. Rejecting the tenableness of the first two courses of action, he then argues for the tenableness of the third course of action. In paragraph 30 he summarizes the arguments he has pursued up to this point. (In the original source, he went on to develop further his argument and ended up, in the final paragraph of the full text, with the general conclusion "that we have a responsibility toward those who disobey the draft laws out of conscience, and that we may be required not to prosecute them, but rather to change our laws or adjust our sentencing procedures to accommodate them.")

What we have been examining is the progress or sequence of Dworkin's argument. If we were to examine now the individual arguments within that framework, we would be making observations about the kinds of arguments he uses, both for confirmation of his own position and for refutation of the opposing positions, and making judgments about the fairness, cogency, or validity of those arguments. We might see that his argument generally takes this syllogistic form:

> The government should not prosecute citizens who disobey a law that they believe to be of doubtful validity.
> Draft-resisters are citizens who disobey a law they believe to be of doubtful validity.
> Therefore, the government should not prosecute draft-resisters.

Paragraphs 13–29, in which the author is considering the three possible courses of action, might be regarded as arguing for the tenableness of the first premise. The arguments presented in paragraphs 8–11 have at least an indirect bearing on the second premise, since they deal with the grounds upon which the draft-resisters base their resistance to the draft. In making a judgment about the validity of this general syllogistic argument, we would have to know whether Dworkin, in the second premise, means to say *"all* draft-resisters" or only *"some* draft-resisters," because if he means only *some,* then according to one of the rules about the distribution of terms—rules that will be discussed in the section on the syllogism in the next chapter—the conclusion would be invalidly drawn. But the author deals with the problem of the extension of this term in paragraphs 28–29, where he argues that no distinction need be made between those draft-resisters who explicitly believe, and those who only implicitly believe, that the draft laws are invalid.

In studying the various building blocks in the edifice of his argument, we would analyze and evaluate the truth, relevance, and cogency of testimony, examples, precedents, facts, and the validity of his inferences from these. The author, it might be noted, does not document his evidence, in the sense that he provides footnote references for his quotations, citations, and allusions, but in the text itself he does reveal in a general way the sources of his evidence. Only if we had reason to doubt the reliability or accuracy of the author would we feel the need for more specific documentation. What might be harder for us to assess would be whether and to what extent the author distorts the "whole truth" by what he leaves unsaid. One of the questions we might ask, for instance, is whether the three courses of action he considers are the only courses of action possible in this situation. If we could show that he neglects to consider some model of behavior that fits his criterion of "our legal and social practices," he might be accused of "begging the question" or "stacking the cards." Or someone might be able to demonstrate that a quotation or an example cited as a supporting argument was meant to say something quite different in the context in which it originally appeared.

What it is particularly important for us to discern is that most of his arguments do not lead—nor does he claim that they lead—to conclusive proof of his thesis. But in most rhetorical discourse, the author seeks to establish only a high degree of probability for his thesis. One instance where the author is careful to point out the limitations of his argument is in the summary paragraph 11: "We cannot conclude from these arguments that the draft (or any part of it) is unconstitutional. . . . But the arguments of unconstitutionality are at least plausible, . . ." We do not demand absolute proof; we expect only that the author will *persuade* us, will make us *believe,* that the course of action he recommends is a reasonable and prudent one. That will be our ultimate test of how well he has managed his "appeal to reason."

But there is one other mode of rhetorical proof yet to consider—the ethical proof. How much persuasiveness is exerted by the image of himself that the author projects in his essay? Since most of those who read this essay will not have any prior knowledge of Ronald Dworkin, their estimate of his qualifications and character will have to be based on what they can infer about him from what he has written here. Sometimes an author or a speaker comes to us with an antecedent reputation that disposes us to react to him either favorably or unfavorably. But while recognizing this fact, Aristotle insisted in his *Rhetoric* that the ethical appeal depends ultimately and crucially on what is said and how it is said in the discourse itself. Aristotle maintains that a speaker or writer will establish his credibility with us—that is, his persuasiveness—if he projects an image of himself as being a man of good sense, good moral character, and goodwill.

What kind of "person" emerges from the prose of this essay? The answer to that question will differ, in some particulars, from reader to reader, but it seems safe to assert that most readers will get the impression of a man marked by temperateness, fairness, and reasonableness. He shows himself to be capable of making nice distinctions, of making gracious concessions, of drawing conclusions that do not grossly exceed what the evidence warrants. If he is not a professional lawyer, there is ample evidence that he has some knowledge of the law and of legal procedures.* Expressions like "it does not follow," "we cannot assume," "begs the question," suggest that he has some formal knowledge of the principles of logic. The coherent structure of his argument seems to indicate that he has an orderly and tidy mind.

A good deal of the *ethos* of the author is established by his style. Chapter IV of this book will outline and exemplify the kinds of things we look at when we study someone's style. In general, we analyze someone's style by noting the choices an author makes from among the lexical and syntactical

---

* As a matter of fact, Mr. Dworkin is a graduate of the Harvard Law School, was a Professor of Law and Master of Trumbull College at Yale University, and now occupies the Chair of Jurisprudence at University College, Oxford.

resources of the language in which he writes. Most readers would probably not regard Dworkin's style to be eloquent or even particularly unique, but despite the close-knit argument that is developed in the essay, they probably would judge it to be commendably lucid. A close look at his choice of diction and sentence patterns might reveal how he achieves this lucidity. If the "tone" of the essay strikes the reader as being calm and dispassionate, that impression can probably be accounted for by an examination of his diction. We have already noted the infrequent occurrence of extreme or emotional language (one of the rare instances of tendentious language is the "mindless view" in the second sentence of the first paragraph). It is notable too how much the author keeps himself in the background, thus avoiding any damaging impression of egoism or arrogance. There are about a dozen uses of the first-person pronoun in the essay, but the "I" intrudes only when the author wants to indicate clearly to his readers that what he is saying is a personal opinion or to signal what he has done or is going to do.

If the author establishes his credentials with us, if he establishes himself with us as a person whom we can trust and admire, the traits of character outlined in these last two paragraphs have undoubtedly helped to create that impression. And if he has created a favorable impression of himself, he has considerably enhanced the persuasiveness of his discourse.

It is impossible to calculate just how persuasive this example of rhetorical discourse has been for everyone who read it. Those who *strongly* believed, before reading the essay, that all draft-resisters should be prosecuted, probably still believe that they should be prosecuted—but maybe they do not believe so strongly now. Those who believed that draft-resisters should not be prosecuted are probably fortified in their opinion by Dworkin's arguments. Maybe the only ones who were really persuaded to *change* their position were those who were wavering or uncertain before they read the essay. Even the most convinced reader, however, would not suggest that Dworkin has said the "last word" on this complex question, but perhaps the valuable service that the author has rendered with his essay is to make all of us reexamine and maybe readjust our positions on this vital issue.

Lest we think, however, that this display of deliberative rhetoric is another of the glorious products of our technological age, let us look at one more example of this kind of persuasive effort. The example is taken from one of the world's great masterpieces, written many centuries before the art of rhetoric was even formulated. It is the famous scene in Book IX of Homer's *Iliad* in which Odysseus, Phoinix, and Ajax come to Achilles' camp and plead with him to return to battle. Achilles has been sulking in his tent ever since Book I, when Agamemnon, the leader of the Greek forces besieging the city of Troy, affronted Achilles by taking the girl Briseis, one of his prizes of war. After Achilles withdrew his troops from the front lines, the fortunes of war went from bad to worse for the Greeks. Agamemnon's army is now desperate. The envoys must succeed in persuading Achilles to return to battle.

We will look at only the first two speeches in this scene—Odysseus' plea to Achilles, and Achilles' reply to Odysseus.

Homer: The Envoys Plead with Achilles

1 "Your health, Achilles! With all these appetizing dishes to dispose of, we cannot complain of our rations, either in my lord Agamemnon's hut or here again in yours. But at the moment the pleasures of the table are far from our thoughts. We are confronted by a disaster, your highness, the magnitude of which appals us. Unless you rouse yourself to fight, we have no more than an even chance of saving our gallant ships or seeing them destroyed. The insolent Trojans and their famous allies are bivouacking close to the ships and wall. Their camp is bright with fires. They are convinced that there is nothing left to stop them now from swooping down on our black ships. Zeus the Son of Cronos has encouraged them, with lightning flashes on the right. Hector has run amuck, triumphant and all-powerful. He trusts in Zeus, and fears neither man nor god in the frenzy that possesses him. His one prayer is for the early coming of the gracious Dawn, for he is itching to hack the peaks from the sterns of our ships, to send up the ships themselves in flames, to smoke us out and to slaughter us by the hulls. And indeed I am terribly afraid that the gods may let him carry out his threats—that it may be our fate to perish here, far from Argos where the horses graze. Up with you then, if even at this late hour you want to rescue the exhausted troops from the Trojans' fury. If you refuse, you yourself will regret it later, for when the damage has been done there will be no mending it. Bestir yourself, before that stage is reached, to save the Danaans from catastrophe.

2 "My good friend, when your father Peleus sent you from Phthia to join Agamemnon, did he not admonish you in these words: 'My son, Athene and Here, if they wish you well, are going to make you strong. What *you* must do is to keep a check on that proud spirit of yours; for a kind heart is a better thing than pride. Quarrels are deadly. Be reconciled at once; and all the Argives young and old will look up to you the more"? Those were the old man's precepts—which you have forgotten. Yet even so, it is not too

From *The Iliad*, trans. E. V. Rieu. The Penguin Classics. Book IX, pp. 167-72.

late for you to yield. Give up this bitter animosity. Agamemnon is ready to make you ample compensation the moment you relent. If you will listen, I will enumerate the gifts he destined for you in his hut. Seven tripods, untarnished by the flames; ten talents of gold; twenty cauldrons of gleaming copper; and twelve powerful, prize-winning race-horses. He said that with nothing more than the prizes they had won for him, a man would not be badly off or short of precious gold. In addition, he will give you seven women, skilled in the fine crafts, Lesbians whom he chose for their exceptional beauty as his part of the spoils when you yourself captured the city of Lesbos. These you shall have from him, and with them the woman he took from you, the daughter of Briseus. Moreover, he will give you his solemn oath that he has never been in her bed and slept with her, as a man does, your highness, with a woman. All these gifts shall be put in your hands at once. Later, if the gods permit us to sack the great city of Priam, you must come in with us when we are sharing out the spoils, load your ship with gold and bronze to your heart's content, and pick out twenty Trojan women for yourself, the loveliest you can find after Argive Helen. And if in due course we get back to Achaean Argos, the richest of all lands, you can become his son-in-law, and he will treat you as he does Orestes, his own beloved son, who is being brought up there in the lap of luxury. He has three daughters in his palace, Chrysothemis, Laodice and Iphianassa. Of these you shall choose for your own whichever you like best and take her to Peleus' house without making the usual gifts. In fact, he will pay *you* a dowry, a generous one, bigger than anybody has ever given with his daughter. Not only that, but he will give you seven fine towns, Cardamyle, Enope and grassy Hire; holy Pherae and Antheia with its deep meadows; beautiful Aepeia, and Pedasus rich in vines. They are all near the sea, in the farthest part of sandy Pylos. Their citizens are rich in flocks and cattle. They would do homage and pay tribute to you as though you were a god, acknowledging your sceptre and prospering under your paternal sway. All this he will do for you, if you relent. But if your hatred of Atreides, gifts and all, outweighs every other consideration, do have some pity on the rest of the united Achaeans, lying dead-beat in their camp. They will honour you like a god. Indeed, you could cover yourself with glory in their eyes, for now is the time when you could get Hector himself. He fancies that he has no match among all the Danaans whom the ships brought here, and he may even venture near you, in his insensate fury.'

3   "Royal son of Laertes, Odysseus of the nimble wits," replied Achilles the great runner; "to save you from sitting there and taking it in turns to coax me, I had better tell you point-blank how I feel and what I am going to do. I loathe like Hell's Gates the man who thinks one thing and says another; so here I give you my decision. You can take it that neither my lord Agamem-

non nor the rest of the Danaans are going to win me over, since it appears that a man gets no thanks for struggling with the enemy day in, day out. His share is the same, whether he sits at home or fights his best. Cowards and brave men are equally respected; and death comes alike to one who has done nothing and one who has toiled hard. All I have suffered by constantly risking my life in battle has left me no better off than the rest. I have been like a bird that brings every morsel she picks up to her unfledged chicks, however hard it goes with *her*. I have spent many a sleepless night and fought through many a bloody day—against men who, like us, are fighting for their womenfolk. I have captured twelve towns from the sea, besides eleven that I took by land in the deep-soiled realm of Troy. From each I got a splendid haul of loot, the whole of which I brought back every time and gave to my lord Agamemnon son of Atreus, who had stayed behind by the ships, and who, when I handed it over, gave a little of it out, in bits, but kept the lion's share. What he did give to the princes and kings in recognition of their rank is safe in their possession; and I am the only one he has robbed. It is not as though he had no wife. He *has* one, of his own choice. Let him sleep with her and be content.

4 "For that matter, what drove the Argives to make war on Troy? What did Atreides raise an army for and bring it here, if not for Helen of the lovely hair? And are the Atreidae the only men on earth who love their wives? Does not every decent and right-minded man love and cherish his own woman, as I loved that girl, with all my heart, though she was a captive of my spear? But now that he has snatched her from my arms and swindled me, don't let him try his tricks on me again. I know him too well. He will not succeed.

5 "No, Odysseus, he must look to you and the other kings if he wants to save the ships from going up in flames. He has already done marvels without me. He has built a wall, I see, and dug a trench along it, a fine broad trench, complete with palisade. But even so he cannot keep the murderous Hector out! Why, in the days when I took the field with the Achaeans, nothing would have induced Hector to throw his men into battle at any distance from the city walls. He came no farther than the Scaean Gate and the oak-tree, where he took me on alone one day, and was lucky to get home alive. But things have changed, and now I do not choose to fight with my lord Hector. So to-morrow I am going to sacrifice to Zeus and all the other gods, then lade and launch my ships. The very first thing in the morning, if you have the curiosity to look, you will see them breasting the Hellespont where the fishes play, and my men inside them straining at the oar. And in three days, given a good crossing by the great Sea-god, I should set foot on the deep soil of Phthia. I left a rich home there when I had the misfortune to come here; and now I shall enrich it further by what I bring back, the

gold, the red copper, the girdled women, and the grey iron that fell to me by lot—everything, in fact, but the prize of honour that was given me and insultingly withdrawn by one and the same man, his majesty King Agamemnon son of Atreus.

6 "Tell him all I say, and tell him in public, so that the rest may frown on any further efforts he may make to overreach a Danaan prince, unconscionable schemer that he always is. And yet he would not dare to look me in the eye, for all his impudence. No; I will help him neither by my advice nor in the field. He has broken faith with me and played me false: never again shall I be taken in by what he says. So much for him. Let him go quietly to perdition. Zeus in his wisdom has already addled his brains.

7 "As for his gifts, I like them just as little as I like the man himself. Not if he offered me ten times or twenty times as much as he possesses or could raise elsewhere, all the revenues of Orchomenus or of Thebes, Egyptian Thebes, where the houses are stuffed with treasure, and through every one of a hundred gates two hundred warriors sally out with their chariots and horses; not if his gifts were as many as the grains of sand or particles of dust, would Agamemnon win me over. First he must pay me in kind for the bitter humiliation I endured.

8 "Again, I will not have any daughter of Agamemnon son of Atreus for my wife. She could be lovely as golden Aphrodite and skilful as Athene of the Flashing Eyes, and yet I would not marry her. He can choose some other Achaean, someone more royal than me and on a level with himself. If the gods allow me to get safely home, Peleus will need no help in finding me a wife. Up and down Hellas and Phthia there are plenty of Achaean girls, daughters of the noblemen in command of the forts. I have only to choose one and make her my own. There were often times at home when I had no higher ambition than to marry some suitable girl of my own station and enjoy the fortune that my old father Peleus had made. For life, as I see it, is not to be set off, either against the fabled wealth of splendid Ilium in the peaceful days before the Achaeans came, or against all the treasure that is piled up in Rocky Pytho behind the Marble Threshold of the Archer-King Apollo. Cattle and sturdy sheep can be had for the taking; and tripods and chestnut horses can be bought. But you cannot steal or buy back a man's life, when once the breath has left his lips. My divine Mother, Thetis of the Silver Feet, says that Destiny has left two courses open to me on my journey to the grave. If I stay here and play my part in the siege of Troy, there is no home-coming for me, though I shall win undying fame. But if I go home to my own country, my good name will be lost, though I shall have long life, and shall be spared an early death.

9 "One more point. I recommend all the rest of you to sail home too, for you will never reach your goal in the steep streets of Ilium. All-seeing Zeus has stretched out a loving hand above that city, and its people have taken heart. So leave me now and report to the Achaean lords in open council, as you seniors have the right to do—they must think out some better way of saving the ships and all the troops beside them, now that these overtures to me have met with blank refusal. But Phoenix can stay here and spend the night with us. Then he could embark for home with me in the morning— that is to say, if he wants to. There will be no compulsion."

Analysis of "The Envoys Plead with Achilles"

The situation dramatized in this scene from the *Iliad* is one that we see enacted frequently today, possibly in our own lives, certainly in public life: one man or a group of men trying to persuade another man to do something or to assent to something. Today it may be a young man begging his father to let him use the family car for a Saturday night date, or it may be, as it was in 1952, the party leader trying to convince an indifferent General Eisenhower or a reluctant Governor Stevenson to run for the office of the President. This rather common situation calls for uncommon rhetorical powers.

Viewed from the standpoint of narrative, this is an intensely dramatic scene that Homer has posed in the ninth book of his epic; viewed from the standpoint of rhetoric, this is a situation that will call upon all the resources of the men sent on this crucial mission. Agamemnon chose his ambassadors shrewdly: Odysseus, "the man who was never at a loss"; Ajax, reputed to be the mightiest Greek warrior after Achilles; Phoinix, Achilles' beloved old tutor. Each of them will work on the aggrieved and disgruntled Achilles in his own way.

The Homeric heroes took as much pride in their skill with words as in their skill with arms. When Phoinix rose to plead with Achilles, he reminded his former pupil of how he had schooled him to be "both a speaker of words and a doer of deeds." And throughout the *Iliad*, Achilles boasts of, and his companions acknowledge, his skill in oratory. Odysseus knows that he is not as great a warrior as Achilles, but he is conscious that he is superior to Achilles in rhetorical prowess. In Book III of the *Iliad*, Antenor described Odysseus when he came to the Trojan court to negotiate for the return of Helen: "But when he uttered his great voice from his chest, and words like unto snowflakes of winter, then could no mortal man contend with Odysseus." And it was Odysseus, remember, who in Book II restrained the Greeks, by the power of his rhetoric, from rushing off to their ships and sailing home. Phoinix too is on his mettle in this scene. As Quintilian said, "The teacher should therefore be as distinguished for his eloquence as for his good character, and like Phoinix in the *Iliad* be able to teach his pupil both how to behave and how to speak" (*Institutio Oratoria*, II, iii, 12).

It is no wonder that rhetoricians found Homer a rich mine for quotations and illustrations, for the *Iliad* and the *Odyssey* are filled with models of almost every kind of eloquence. Quintilian remarked that the magnificent speeches in the first, second, and ninth books "display all the rules of art to be followed in forensic or deliberative oratory" (*Institutio Oratoria*, X, i, 47). Today we find it almost laughable to read about warriors pausing in the heat of battle, as they do in some of the scenes of the *Iliad,* to hurl long speeches at one another. But the tradition of oratory was already well established—if not yet well formulated—in Homer's time, and this tradition persisted and grew stronger throughout the Golden Age of Athens. So we must take the oratory displayed in this scene as seriously as the participants took it, and we must savor the relish with which they indulged in this battle of words.

The participants in this battle of words are clearly engaged in what the classical rhetoricians called *deliberative* discourse. In classifying the three kinds of oratory, Aristotle pointed out that deliberative oratory is concerned with *future* time; that the means used in this kind of oratory are *exhortation* and *dissuasion;* and that the special topics that figure most prominently in this kind of discourse are the *expedient* and the *inexpedient,* or the *advantageous* and the *injurious.* In other words, when we are trying to persuade a man to do something, we try to show that the recommended course of action is either a good in itself (and therefore worthy of pursuit for its own sake) or something that will benefit him. The envoys are trying to exhort Achilles to undertake an action in the future (on the morrow, if he will) that will be advantageous both to himself and to the Greeks. Achilles is engaged in refuting the exhortations.

Our selection from this scene reproduces only Odysseus' plea to Achilles and Achilles' reply to Odysseus. Let us look at the strategies of argument in these two speeches.

We have already remarked that Odysseus was reputed to be the most accomplished speaker among the Greeks. And indeed his speech here is a model, in miniature, of the well-organized oration. It has an exordium, a narration, a proof, and a peroration. None of these parts is developed to the extent that it would be in a full-fledged deliberative oration, but the speech does conform to the standard *dispositio* or arrangement laid down by the teachers of rhetoric.

Odysseus begins his speech by offering a toast to Achilles. Here he is doing what is often done in the exordium or introduction to a discourse: attempting to ingratiate himself with his audience, to conciliate his audience that is indifferent or reluctant or hostile (whichever term best describes Achilles' mood at the moment). All the rhetoricians emphasize the importance of putting the audience in a receptive frame of mind, especially if the audience is suspicious or hostile. The need to dispose an audience favorably explains why so many speakers begin their talk with a joke or a humorous anecdote.

Odysseus then proceeds to the *narratio*, or the exposition of the state of affairs at the moment (paragraphs 2 and 3). He describes for Achilles the desperate straits in which the Greeks now find themselves. In doing this, he employs the device of *enargeia*, which, as Quintilian puts it, "makes us seem not so much to narrate as to exhibit the actual scene, while our emotions will be no less actively stirred than if we were present at the actual occurrence" (*Institutio Oratoria*, VI, ii, 32). Thus Odysseus pictures for Achilles the countless watch-fires burning in the Trojan bivouac outside the line of the Greek ships; the favorable omen given by Zeus's lightning; and the "devouring flame" that threatens to engulf the ships. All these fire images are subtly calculated to arouse Achilles' anger, since to the Greek mind fire was intimately associated with the emotion of anger. By picturing Hector in his frenzied, arrogant, triumphant assault on the ships, Odysseus seeks to touch Achilles' pride and envy. He is needling Achilles. Are you going to let Hector make good his boast that he will chop down our ensigns and smother our ships with fire and smoke? If an appeal like this does not touch Achilles' pride, perhaps it will touch his sense of loyalty and patriotism.

Odysseus then launches into that part of his speech that the Latin rhetoricians called the *confirmatio*—the proof of one's case. It is in this section that the speaker brings to bear "all the available means of persuasion" to support the cause he is espousing.

Odysseus first tries to influence Achilles by reminding him of his father Peleus' warning that he should restrain his proud temper and avoid quarrels. Not only is restraint of temper a good in itself, but it disposes a man to fight more effectively, and it disposes the gods, in whose hands our fortunes rest, to look with favor on our cause. Odysseus is here appealing to filial piety. Achilles is not as distinguished for *pietas* as was that later epic hero Aeneas, but in a strongly patriarchal society such as existed in ancient Greece, a son would not be entirely impervious to the advice of his father. If this reminder of a forgotten warning does not prevail with Achilles, it is only because Achilles feels that there is an over-riding justification for his anger.

After this, Odysseus catalogues for Achilles all the gifts that Agamemnon is prepared to give him if he will return to battle. Aristotle pointed out in his *Rhetoric* that exhortation and *dissuasion* turn ultimately on considerations of happiness or, more generally, the Good. Whenever we try to persuade someone to do something, we try to show him the benefits that will result from his action. Some of the goods that most men agree upon as contributing to happiness are such external goods as a respected family, loyal friends, wealth, fame, honor, and such personal excellences as health, beauty, strength. Of all these goods, Odysseus comes down heaviest on wealth. He entices Achilles with the list of all the gold, the horses, the servant women, and the property that Agamemnon will bestow on him. Not only will he get back the girl Briseus, the object of the quarrel with Agamemnon in the first place, but he will be honored with one of Agamemnon's daughters as a bride.

Odysseus is plainly appealing to Achilles' self-interest here. Achilles could not help being tempted by the king's generous offerings, for in this aristocratic society one of the marks of honor for a hero was abundant possessions. And, besides, these generous offerings would be a manifestation of Agamemnon's humiliating capitulation to Achilles. We shall see, when we consider Achilles' rebuttal, why it is that he was able to resist the tempting offer of these goods.

Odysseus did not, of course, have to *invent* these appeals. He is merely repeating, verbatim, the offer that Agamemnon had made, at the beginning of Book IX, before the council that immediately preceded this embassy. Odysseus was using the available means of persuasion, but he didn't have to discover these means.

One point needs to be made, however, about this verbatim retailing of Agamemnon's offer. The shrewd Odysseus did leave out one part of Agamemnon's council speech. At the very end Agamemnon had said: "All this will I accomplish so he but cease from wrath. Let him yield; Hades I ween is not to be softened neither overcome, and therefore is he hatefullest of all gods to mortals. Yea, let him be ruled by me, inasmuch as I am more royal and avow me to be the elder in years." Odysseus knew that if he were to repeat these words he would only increase Achilles' anger. For these words reveal that Agamemnon's capitulation is grudging and half-hearted. And certainly the king's insistence that he is still the superior man would have antagonized rather than conciliated Achilles.

Odysseus concludes his appeal by playing a slightly different note. If Achilles cannot rise above his hatred of Agamemnon, let him consider the honor he can win for himself by destroying Hector and rescuing the Greeks. This is another appeal to self-interest, but it is self-interest on a higher plane than the previous reminder of material rewards. For the Homeric hero, personal glory was the highest good. Odysseus has reserved the strongest appeal for the climax of his argument.

Achilles' reply is immediate and impulsive. There is no reflective pause to weigh the arguments. One gets the impression that Achilles had given only half an ear to Odysseus' plea and that he has been waiting impatiently for Odysseus to stop speaking so that he can have his say. One is not surprised then to find Achilles' speech emotionally charged—and, as a consequence, disorganized.

Achilles seems not so much to answer Odysseus as to express, vigorously and repeatedly, his scorn of Agamemnon's offer and to declare his determination not to fight. At first he talks as though he had not listened to Odysseus at all. He says he won't fight any more because he gets no thanks or reward for risking his life. But Odysseus has just told him of the thanks and reward he will get if he returns to battle. He will get not only what he had before the quarrel but additional rewards in superabundance.

As Achilles' torrent of speech tumbles on, however, it is clear that he *has* heard Odysseus. Achilles shows himself to be aware of all the details of Agamemnon's offer. But he spurns the offer. He is not just holding out for a higher price. No, he would reject the offer even if it were infinitely greater than it is. Some other considerations are now influencing Achilles.

Something has happened to Achilles while he has been brooding in his tent. He has been evaluating the rationale of war in general and this war in particular. Why have they been fighting here for ten years? To rescue Helen? But that is an inane cause to fight and die for. Why should hundreds of wives be widowed so that the king's brother can recover his wife? The sheer stupidity of the war and the egregious arrogance of Agamemnon in marshalling so many noble warriors to fight such a war magnifies the insult that Achilles has sustained. Does Agamemnon really think that he can compensate for all this with his paltry gifts?

Nor has Achilles been deaf to Odysseus' plea on the grounds of personal honor. As we have pointed out, the prospect of winning personal glory exercised a strong attraction for the Greek heroes. But having seen this war in proper perspective, Achilles no longer finds the attraction of personal honor as potent as it once was for him. There is something more dear to him now than honor and wealth—life. Achilles says, "For life, as I see it, is not to be set off, either against the fabled wealth of splendid Ilium in the peaceful days before the Achaeans came, or against all the treasure that is piled up in Rocky Pytho behind the Marble Threshold of the Archer-King Apollo." And a little later on he says, "But if I go home to my own country, my good name will be lost, though I shall have long life, and shall be spared an early death." Achilles has decided at this point that life is a higher good than fame or wealth.

In making this decision, Achilles has employed one of Aristotle's common topics—the topic of degree. When men deliberate about a course of action, the choice is not always between a good and an evil; sometimes the choice is between two or more goods. In making a choice from among several goods, men decide on the basis of degree: which of these goods is the greater good or the greatest good? And that is the topic that Achilles resorts to here. As readers of the *Iliad* know, Achilles later changes his mind and elects honor over life. But at the moment and in answer to Odysseus' persuasive appeals, he declares his preference for life over wealth and honor.

This is all the argument that one can make out of Achilles' rebuttal. Most of his speech is taken up with impassioned but eloquent ranting. One thing is clear, though, at the end of his speech: he will not fight. And it appears that Odysseus, the renowned orator, the man who was never at a loss, has utterly failed to move Achilles. It is now Phoinix's turn to appeal to him, and then Ajax's. But we have not reproduced these two speeches in our selection. If the student is interested in observing the rhetorical appeals made by Phoinix and Ajax, he can read them in the ninth book of the *Iliad*.

What lessons about rhetoric can the modern student learn from a study of this episode, which constitutes a dramatic scene in a narrative poem but which is presented in the form of an oratorical debate? He learns for one thing that, despite the hundreds of years that separate his society from Homer's, men acted and responded then in much the same way that they do today. Men still sulk because of a real or supposed affront to their dignity; other men try to salve the wounds of the insult. The dominant ideals of a society change with the passage of time—today, for instance, we put more of a premium on actions that contribute to the common welfare than on actions that contribute only to a man's personal honor—but the basic human passions and motivations are the same today as they were in Homer's day.

In this episode, we see men arguing in much the same way as we argue today. What do we do when we want to change someone's attitude or get someone to do something? We appeal to him in much the same way that Odysseus, Phoinix, and Ajax appealed to Achilles. We try to show a man how a proposed course of action will benefit him, how it will contribute to his happiness. The material rewards we offer him may not be fancy tripods and swift race horses, but they will be similar lures—deep-freezes and Cadillacs. Or we may try to show him how much honor or power he will reap for himself. Or we may try to show him how foolish or how dangerous his failure to act will be.

If these appeals to his understanding fail to move him, we try other approaches. We try to induce such emotions as anger, fear, pity, shame, envy, contempt. Since it is the will that controls whether a man will act or not and since an appeal to the emotions is one of the most potent means of moving the will, we may find that in some circumstances the emotional appeal is the most effective tactic. We would hope too that the ethical appeal of our speech would help to influence our reluctant man. If the man perceives from our persuasive efforts that we are men of intelligence, good character, and good will, he will be disposed to listen and respond to our logical and emotional appeals.

In short, what we learn from this display of rhetoric is that in similar circumstances we employ the same strategies of appeal that the envoys did. We make use of "all the available means of persuasion in any given case."

We may find and employ *more* arguments, we may arrange them differently, we may use a more temperate or a more florid style in which to convey our arguments; but fundamentally our strategies will be the same as those used by the envoys.

It is with the strategies of discourse directed to a definite audience for a definite purpose that this text will be concerned.

A Brief Explanation of Classical Rhetoric

The student has just seen two examples of persuasive discourse. The analyses of these two pieces introduced some terminology that may be completely unfamiliar to him. The terminology is strange because it belongs to an art that was formulated many centuries ago and that ceased to be a vital discipline in our schools sometime in the nineteenth century. Although the student may often have heard the term *rhetoric* used, he probably does not have a clear idea of what it means. His uncertainty is understandable, because the word *rhetoric* has acquired many meanings. Rhetoric may be associated in his mind with the writing of compositions and themes or with style—figures of speech, flowery diction, variety of sentence patterns and rhythms—or with the notion of empty, bombastic language, or rodomontade (to use a bombastic word), of "sound and fury, signifying nothing," of "sounding brass and tinkling cymbals." Perhaps tucked away somewhere in his consciousness is the notion of rhetoric as the use of language for persuasive purposes.

What all these notions have in common is that rhetoric implies the use or manipulation of words. And, indeed, a look at the etymology of the word *rhetoric* shows that the term is solidly rooted in the notion of "words" or "speech." The Greek words *rhēma* ("a word') and *rhētor* ("a teacher of oratory"), which are akin, stem ultimately from the Greek verb *eirō* ("I say"). Our English noun *rhetoric* derives from the Greek feminine adjective *rhetorikē,* which is elliptical for *rhetorikē technē* ("the art of the rhetor or orator"). English got its word immediately from the French *rhétorique.*

This investigation of the etymology of the term brings us somewhat closer to the original meaning of rhetoric: something connected with speaking, orating. From its origin in fifth-century Greece through its flourishing period in Rome and its reign in the medieval *trivium,* rhetoric was associated primarily with the art of oratory. During the Middle Ages, the precepts of classical rhetoric began to be applied to letter writing, but it was not until the Renaissance, after the invention of printing in the fifteenth century, that the precepts governing the spoken art began to be applied, on any large scale, to written discourse. Today, curiously enough, the principles of classical rhetoric are more likely to be studied in Speech classes than in English classes: we have come full circle.

Although the etymology of the word does not imply it, rhetoric was associated primarily with persuasive discourse, as in the examples we read at the beginning of this chapter. From its beginnings and throughout its history, classical rhetoric was thought of as the art of persuasive speech. Its end was to convince or persuade an audience to think in a certain way or to act in a certain way.

Rhetoric as persuasive discourse is still very much exercised among us, but American students no longer receive any extensive training in the art of persuasion. Frequently, the only remnant of this training in the modern college is the attention paid to argumentation in a study of the four forms of discourse—Argumentation, Exposition, Description, and Narration. But this study of argumentation usually turns out to be just an accelerated course in logic. For the classical rhetorician, logic was an ancillary but distinct discipline. Aristotle, for instance, spoke of rhetoric as being "an offshoot" or "a counterpart" of logic. The speaker might employ logic to persuade his hearers, but logic was only one among many "available means of persuasion." So the student who studies argumentation in his Freshman English class today is not really exposed to the rich, highly systematized discipline that earlier schoolboys submitted to when they were learning the persuasive art.

Although classical rhetoric has largely disappeared from our schools, there was a time when it was very much alive. For extended periods during its two-thousand-year history, the study of rhetoric was the central discipline in the schools. Rhetoric enjoyed this eminence because, during those periods, skill in oratory or in written discourse was the key to preferment in the courts, the forum, and the church. One of the reasons why the study—if not the practice—of rhetoric has declined in our own times is that in an industrial, technological society like our own there are avenues to success other than the communication skills. It is part of the folklore of America that in the years from about 1870 to 1910 some barely literate men became millionaires—some of whom, happily, eventually founded libraries and endowed universities.

One fact that emerges from a study of the history of rhetoric is that there is usually a resurgence of rhetoric during periods of violent social upheaval. Whenever the old order is passing away and the new order is marching—or stumbling—in, a loud, clear call goes up for the services of the man skilled in words. One needs only to hearken back to such historical events as the Renaissance in Italy, the Reformation in England, and the Revolution in America to find evidence of this desperate reliance, in times of change or crisis, on the talents of men skilled in the persuasive arts. As Jacob Burckhardt has pointed out in *The Civilization of the Renaissance in Italy,* the orator and the teacher of rhetoric played a prominent role in the fifteenth-century humanistic movement that was casting off the yoke of the medieval church. After Henry VIII broke with Rome, the Tudor courts resounded with the arguments of hundreds of lawyers engaged to fight litigations over confiscated monastic properties. Students of the American Revolution need recall only Tom Paine's incendiary pamphlets, Patrick Henry's rousing speeches, Thomas Jefferson's daring Declaration of Independence, and Hamilton's and Madison's efforts to sell constitutional democracy in the *Federalist Papers* to be convinced that in time of upheaval we rely heavily on the services of men equipped with persuasive tongues and pens. Something of the same kind of rhetorical activity is raging today among the nationalists fighting for independence in African and Asian countries.

The student who wants to learn something about the history of rhetoric can read the Survey of Rhetoric in the Appendix of this book, and he can further pursue his interest by reading some of the primary and secondary texts on rhetoric listed in the Bibliography in the Appendix. Before getting into the study of rhetoric in the next chapter, however, the student may want to gain some general knowledge of the classical system of rhetoric and its terminology. By the time Cicero came to write his treatises on rhetoric, the study of rhetoric was divided, mainly for pedagogical convenience, into five parts: *inventio, dispositio, elocutio, memoria,* and *pronuntiatio.* Since this text professes to be an adaptation of classical rhetoric, the student may appreciate an explanation of these terms and other key terms so that he might better understand the kind of rhetoric presented in the next three chapters.

The Five Parts of a Discourse

Inventio is the Latin term (*heuresis* was the equivalent Greek term) for "invention" or "discovery." Theoretically, an orator could talk on any subject, because rhetoric, as such, had no proper subject matter. In practice, however, each speech that he undertook presented him with a unique challenge. He had to find arguments which would support whatever case or point of view he was espousing. According to Cicero, the speaker relied on native genius, on method or art, or on diligence to help him find appropriate arguments. Obviously, that man was at a great advantage who had a native, intuitive sense for proper arguments. But lacking such an endowment, a man could have recourse either to his dogged industry or to some system for finding arguments. *Inventio* was concerned with a system or method for finding arguments.

Aristotle pointed out that there were two kinds of arguments or means of persuasion available to the speaker. First of all, there were the non-artistic or non-technical means of persuasion (the Greek term was *atechnoi pisteis*).

These modes of persuasion were really not part of the art of rhetoric; they came from outside the art. The orator did not have to *invent* these; he had merely to use them. Aristotle named five kinds of non-artistic proofs: laws, witnesses, contracts, tortures, oaths. Apparently, the lawyer pleading a case in court made most use of this kind of proof, but the politician or the panegyrist could use them too. The councilman today, for instance, who is trying to persuade the citizens to adopt a sales tax quotes statistics, legal contracts, existing laws, historical documents, and the testimony of experts to bolster his case. He does not have to invent these supporting arguments; they already exist. True, there is a sense in which he has to find such supporting arguments. He has to be aware that they exist, and he has to know what departments or records to go to in order to discover them. (One of the sections in the next chapter will provide expositions of some of the standard reference books which can supply the student with the facts, figures, testimonies to support his arguments.) But the councilman does not have to imagine these arguments, to think them up—to invent them, in the classical sense of that term.

The second general mode of persuasion that Aristotle spoke of included artistic proof—"artistic" in the sense that they fell within the province of the art of rhetoric: *rational* appeal (*logos*), *emotional* appeal (*pathos*), and *ethical* appeal (*ēthos*). In exercising the rational appeal, the speaker was appealing to his audience's reason or understanding. He is "arguing," in other words. When we argue, we reason either *deductively* or *inductively*—that is, we either draw conclusions from affirmative or negative statements (e.g. No man can attain perfect happiness in this life; John is a man; therefore John cannot attain perfect happiness in this life) or make generalizations after observing a number of analogous facts (e.g. Every green apple that I bit into had a sour taste. All green apples must be sour.) In logic, the deductive mode of arguing is commonly referred to by the term that Aristotle used, the *syllogism*. In rhetoric, the equivalent of the syllogism was the *enthymeme*. The rhetorical equivalent of *full induction* in logic is the *example*. Since the next chapter will provide an elaborate explanation of syllogism, enthymeme, induction, and example, we will not dwell on them here.

A second mode of persuasion is the emotional appeal. Since man is by nature a rational animal, he should be able to make decisions about his private and public life solely by the light of reason. But man is also endowed with the faculty of free will, and often enough his will is swayed more by his passions or emotions than by his reason. Aristotle expressed the wish that rhetoric could deal exclusively with rational appeals, but he was enough of a realist to recognize that man is often prompted to do something or accept something by his emotions. And if rhetoric was, as he defined it, the art of discovering "all the available means of persuasion," then he would have to give a place in his *Rhetoric* to an investigation of the means of touching the emotions. Accordingly, he devoted the major portion of Book II of his *Rhetoric* to an analysis of the more common human emotions. This was the beginning of the science of human psychology. If the orator was to play upon man's emotions, he must know what those emotions were and how they could be triggered off or subdued.

A third mode of persuasion was the ethical appeal. This appeal stemmed from the character of the speaker, especially as that character was evinced in the speech itself. A man ingratiated himself with his audience—and thereby gained their trust and admiration—if he managed to create the impression that he was a man of intelligence, benevolence, and probity. Aristotle recognized that the ethical appeal could be the most potent of the three modes of persuasion. All of an orator's skill in convincing the intellect and moving the will of an audience could prove futile if the audience did not esteem, could not trust, the speaker. It is for this reason that politicians seeking election to public office take such great care to create the proper image of themselves in the eyes of the voters. It was for this reason also that Cicero and Quintilian stressed the need for high moral character in the speaker. Quintilian defined the ideal orator as "a good man skilled in speaking." In his *Nicomachean Ethics,* Aristotle explored the *ēthos* proper for the individual; in his *Politics,* the *ēthos* proper for individuals living together in a society.

The method that the classical rhetoricians devised to aid the speaker in discovering matter for the three modes of appeal was the *topics*. *Topics* is the English translation of the Greek word *topoi* and the Latin word *loci*. Literally, *topos* or *locus* meant "place" or "region" (note our words *topography* and *locale*). In rhetoric, a topic was a place or store or thesaurus to which one resorted in order to find something to say on a given subject. More specifically, a topic was a general head or line of argument which suggested material from which proofs could be made. To put it another way, the topics constituted a method of probing one's subject in order to discover possible ways of developing that subject. Aristotle distinguished two kinds of topics: (1) the special topics (he called them *idioi topoi* or *eidē*); (2) the common topics (*koinoi topoi*). The special topics were those classes of argument appropriate to particular kinds of discourse. In other words, there were some kinds of arguments that were used exclusively in the law courts; some that were confined to the public forum; others that appeared only in ceremonial addresses. The common topics, on the other hand, were a fairly limited stock of arguments that could be used for any occasion or type of speech. Aristotle named four common topics: (1) more and less (the topic of degree); (2) the possible and the impossible; (3) past fact and future fact; (4) greatness and smallness (the topic of size as distinguished from the topic of degree). In the text itself we shall see how the topics are put to work.

All of the considerations reviewed in the last two or three pages fell within the province of *inventio*. Chapter II, entitled "Discovery of Arguments," will be concerned with this aspect of rhetoric—how to "discover" something to say on some given subject, which is the crucial problem for most students. The chief reason for the student's inarticulateness on certain subjects is the lack of experience or reading background that can stock a student's reservoir of ideas. At other times, his inarticulateness stems from his inability to look into a subject to discover what he already knows about the subject. Since *inventio* is a systematized way of turning up or generating ideas on some subject, the student may find this rhetorical approach helpful.

The second part of rhetoric was *dispositio* (Greek, *taxis*), which may be translated as "disposition," "arrangement," "organization." This was the division of rhetoric concerned with the effective and orderly arrangement of the parts of a written or spoken discourse. Once the ideas or arguments are discovered there remains the problem of selecting, marshalling, and organizing them with a view to effecting the end of the discourse.

In the simplest terms, one might say that any discourse needs a beginning, a middle, and an end; but this is self-evident and not much help. Rhetoricians spelled out the division of a discourse more specifically and functionally. Aristotle held that there were really only two essential parts of a speech: the statement of the case and the proof of the case; but he was ready to concede that in practice orators added two more parts: an introduction and a conclusion. Latin rhetoricians, like the author of the *Ad Herennium,* further refined these divisions, recognizing six parts: (1) the introduction (*exordium*); (2) the statement or exposition of the case under discussion (*narratio*); (3) the outline of the points or steps in the argument (*divisio*); (4) the proof of the case (*confirmatio*); (5) the refutation of the opposing arguments (*confutatio*); (6) the conclusion (*peroratio*).

Such a division may strike the student as being arbitrary, mechanical, and rigid. Two things may be said in defense of this conventional pattern. It did set forth clear principles of organization, and inexperienced writers need nothing so much as simple, definite principles to guide them in arrangement of material. Then too the rhetoricians allowed for some adjustments in this scheme. Accepting the Aristotelian notion of the "available means of persuasion," they acknowledge that on some occasions it was expedient to omit certain parts altogether (for instance, if one found it difficult to break down the opposing arguments, it might be advisable to omit the stage of *confutatio*) or to re-arrange some of the parts (for instance, it might be more effective to refute the opposing arguments *before* advancing one's own arguments).

Unquestionably, there is a close inter-relation between *inventio* and *dispositio,* and in many rhetoric books these two divisions were treated under one head. Disposition was looked upon as just another aspect of invention; *inventio* was the originative aspect, and *dispositio* was the organizing aspect. As the student may learn from the history of rhetoric in the Appendix, Peter Ramus and his followers, like Francis Bacon, wanted to relegate invention and disposition to the province of logic and to limit rhetoric to considerations of style, memory, and delivery. Chapter III of this text, entitled "Arrangement," will deal with this aspect of rhetoric.

The third part of rhetoric was *elocutio* (Greek, *lexis* or *hermēneia* or *phrasis*). The word *elocution* means something quite different to us from what it meant to the classical rhetorician. We associate the word with the act of speaking (hence, the elocution contest). This notion of speaking is, of course, implicit in the Latin verb from which this word stems, *loqui*, "to speak" (cf. Greek, *legein*, "to speak"). We have a number of English words based on this Latin verb: *loquacious, colloquial, eloquence, interlocutor*. It was after the revival of interest in delivery in the second half of the eighteenth century that the word *elocution* began to take on its present meaning. But for the classical rhetorician, *elocutio* meant "style."

Style is a difficult concept to define, although most of us feel we know what it is. Famous definitions of style, like Buffon's "style is the man," Swift's "proper words in proper places," Newman's "style is a thinking out into language," and Blair's "the peculiar manner in which a man expresses his conceptions," are apt, but they are just vague enough to tease us out of thought and just general enough to give us a sense for style without giving us a clear definition of it. None of the major rhetoricians attempted to give a definition of style, but most of them had a great deal to say about it; in fact, some of the Renaissance rhetorics were devoted exclusively to a consideration of style.

One of the points that elicited a great deal of discussion was the classification of styles. Various terms were used to name the kinds of style, but there was fundamental agreement about three levels of style. There was the *low* or *plain* style (*attenuata, subtile*); the *middle* or *forcible* style (*mediocris, robusta*); and the *high* or *florid* style (*gravis, florida*). Quintilian proposed that each of these styles was suited to one of the three functions that he assigned to rhetoric. The plain style was most appropriate for instructing (*docendi*); the middle for *moving* (*movendi*); and the high for *charming* (*delectandi*).

All rhetorical considerations of style involved some discussion of *choice of words,* usually under such heads as correctness, purity (for instance, the choice of native words rather than foreign words), simplicity, clearness, appropriateness, ornateness.

Another subject of consideration was the composition or arrangement of words in phrases or clauses (or, to use the rhetorical term, *periods*). Involved here were discussions of correct syntax or collocation of words; patterns of sentences (e.g. parallelism, antithesis); proper use of conjunctions and other correlating devices both within the sentence and between sentences; the euphony of sentences secured through the artful juxtaposition of pleasing vowel and consonant combinations and through the use of appropriate rhythmical patterns.

A great deal of attention was paid, of course, to *tropes* and *figures* (Greek, *schēmata,* hence the English term *schemes,* which was often used in place of *figures*). Since the concept of tropes and schemes is very complex, it is better that we defer any definition and illustration of these terms to the appropriate section of the text.

Also involved in considerations of style were arguments about (1) the functional vs. the embellishing character of style; (2) Asianism vs. Atticism; (3) the written style vs. the spoken style; (4) economy of words vs. copia of words. These points of discussion are rather peripheral matters, but it is remarkable how much time and energy the rhetoricians devoted to such controversies. The final chapter of this book will be devoted to consideration of style.

The fourth part of rhetoric was *memoria* (Greek, *mnēmē*), concerned with the memorizing of speeches. Of all the five parts of rhetoric, *memoria* was the one that received the least attention in the rhetoric books. The reason for the neglect of this aspect of rhetoric is probably that not much can be said, in a theoretical way, about the process of memorizing; and after rhetoric came to be concerned mainly with written discourse, there was no further need to deal with memorizing. This process did receive, however, some attention in the schools of rhetoric set up by the sophists. The orator's memory was trained largely through constant practice (just as professional actors today acquire an amazing facility in memorizing a script), but the rhetors did suggest various mnemonic devices that facilitated the memorizing of speeches. The courses that one sometimes sees advertised in newspapers or magazines—"I Can Give You a Retentive Memory in Thirty Days"—are modern manifestations of this division of rhetoric. There will be no consideration in this book of this aspect of rhetoric.

The fifth division of rhetoric was *pronuntiatio* (Greek, *hypokrisis*) or delivery. As in the case of *memoria,* the theory of delivery was conspicuously neglected in the rhetoric texts until the elocutionary movement began about the middle of the eighteenth century. But most rhetoricians would acknowledge the importance of effective delivery in the persuasive process. When Demosthenes, the greatest of the Greek orators, was asked what he considered to be the most important part of rhetoric, he replied, "Delivery, delivery, delivery." Despite the neglect of delivery in the rhetoric books, a great deal of attention was devoted to this aspect in the Greek and Roman schools of rhetoric. Skill in delivery can best be acquired, of course, not by listening to theoretical discussions of this art but by actual practice and by analyzing the delivery of others. Understandably enough, discussions of delivery, as well as of memory, tended to be even more neglected in rhetoric texts after the invention of printing, when most rhetorical training was directed primarily to written discourse.

Involved in the treatment of delivery was concern for the management of the voice and for gestures (*actio*). Precepts were laid down about the modulation of the voice for the proper pitch, volume, and emphasis and about pausing and phrasing. In regard to action, orators were trained in gesturing, in the proper stance and posture of the body, and in the management of the eyes and of facial expressions. What this all amounted to really was training in the art of acting, and it is significant that all the great orators in history have been great "hams."

There is no denying the importance of delivery in effecting the end that one sets for oneself. Many speeches and sermons, however well prepared and elegantly written, have fallen on deaf ears because of inept delivery. The writer lacks the advantage a speaker enjoys because of his face-to-face contact with an audience and because of his vocal delivery; the only way in which the writer can make up for this disadvantage is by the brilliance of his style.

The Three Kinds of Persuasive Discourse

All rhetoricians distinguished three kinds of orations, and this tripartite classification is well-nigh exhaustive. First of all, there was *deliberative* oratory, also known as *political, hortative,* and *advisory,* in which one deliberated about public affairs, about anything that had to do with politics, in the Greek sense of that term—whether to go to war, whether to levy a tax, whether to enter into an alliance with a foreign power, whether to build a bridge or a reservoir or a temple. More generally, however, deliberative discourse is that in which we seek to persuade someone to do something or to accept our point of view, as in the two pieces we considered at the beginning of this chapter. According to Aristotle, political oratory was always concerned about the *future* (the point at issue is something that we shall or shall not do); its special topics were the *expedient* and the *inexpedient;* and its means were *exhortation* and *dehortation.*

Secondly, there was *forensic* oratory, sometimes referred to as *legal* or *judicial* oratory. This was the oratory of lawyers in the courtroom, but it can be extended to cover any kind of discourse in which a person seeks to defend or condemn someone's actions. (Richard Nixon's famous "Checkers" speech before a nationwide television audience can be considered as an example of forensic rhetoric; and Newman's *Apologia Pro Vita Sua* is another example of forensic discourse.) Forensic oratory, according to Aristotle, was concerned with *past* time (court trials are always concerned with actions or crimes that took place in the past); its special topics were *justice* and *injustice;* and its means were *accusation* and *defense.*

Thirdly, there was *epideictic* oratory. This species has had a variety of other titles: *demonstrative, declamatory, panegyrical, ceremonial.* It is the oratory of display, the kind of oratory exemplified in the *Gettysburg Address* and in the old-fashioned Fourth of July speeches. In this kind of discourse, one is not so much concerned with persuading an audience as with pleasing it or inspiring it. *Ceremonial* discourse—the term we shall use in this text— is the most "literary" and usually the most ornate of the three kinds of discourse. Aristotle had to strain to fit a proper time-province to this form of oratory, but in the interests of neatness he laid it down that ceremonial oratory was concerned primarily with the *present*. Its special topics were *honor* and *dishonor,* and its means were *praise* and *blame.* The ancients made no provision in their rhetorics for sermons or homiletics. But later, when rhetoric was studied in a Christian culture, the art of preaching was usually considered under the head of epideictic oratory—even though preachers are also concerned with man's past and future actions.

The Relevance and Importance of Rhetoric for Our Times

After reading the foregoing explanation of some of the key terms of classical rhetoric, the student might be prompted to say: "This is all very interesting. But what does it have to do with me? This kind of rhetoric may have had a long and honorable tradition in Western culture, but this rather stodgy and highly formalized approach to composition seems to be quite useless in our technological age. And as for myself, I don't see that I'll ever have any use for rhetoric, since I am going to be an electrical engineer."

The student's doubts about the usefulness and relevance of the kind of rhetoric that will be presented in this text deserve an answer. In reply, one might say first of all that the student cannot escape rhetoric, no matter what his vocation in life is. Every day of his life, he either uses rhetoric or is exposed to it. Every half-hour that he spends in front of his television set he is subjected three or four times to somebody's efforts to get him to buy something. And he himself employs rhetoric countless times every day. Perhaps he has to convince his father to let him use the car or to induce his girl friend to go bowling with him instead of working on her term paper or to inveigle his friend into changing shifts with him at the parking lot where they work after school. He is not aware, of course, that the announcer in the TV commercial (nor is the announcer aware probably) may have been wooing him with the common topic of degree; nor is he aware that in the debate with his father over the use of the family car he may have been using an enthymemic chain of arguments. No, he was using persuasive devices that come naturally, instinctively to human beings. Just as men immediately acknowledge the validity of the logical principle that a thing cannot at the same time be and not be, so they readily use or respond to those verbal strategies that men have always used to induce attitudes in others or to prompt others to action.

Rhetoric, like grammar or logic or poetics, is not an *a priori* science. Aristotle did not sit in his cubicle and dream up a set of principles for convincing other men. Rather, he observed the practice of effective orators, analyzed their strategies, and from that observation and analysis codified a body of precepts to guide others in the exercise of the persuasive art. Aristotle believed, as did every other rhetorician who composed a treatise on the persuasive art, that what men did instinctively they could do more effectively if they consciously schooled themselves in the *art* of that activity. Many jazz pianists never took a lesson in their life; they just "picked it up," as they will tell you. None of these accomplished performers would deny, however, that they might improve their performance if they were to take a course in, say, harmonics at some music school.

Rhetoric then is an inescapable activity in our lives. Of the four conventional forms of spoken or written discourse—exposition, argumentation, description, and narration—we indulge in, or are exposed to, argumentation most often. Everyone living in community with other men is a rhetorician. A mother constantly uses rhetoric on her child; a teacher, on his students; a salesman, on his clients; a foreman, on his workers. So if our student thinks that he will have no use for rhetoric when he becomes an electrical engineer, he is mistaken. If nothing else, he will have to convince his assistants to be orderly, precise, and thorough in the experiments they conduct for him.

Grammar, logic, and rhetoric are the three arts of language. Skill in the language arts is more important today than it used to be. Technological improvements in communication and transportation have brought us into more frequent and crucial converse with the inhabitants of our own country and with the peoples of other nations. It is important to our welfare that we learn how to ingratiate ourselves with others, how to express our thoughts and desires, how to allay their fears, and how to conciliate our differences. Rhetoric can help here. With the invention of the "ultimate weapon," the hydrogen bomb, science has brought us to the brink of annihilation. It behooves us now to withhold this means of settling the tensions that exist in the world and exploit the possibilities of settling those tensions by the use of the power-ful weapons of words. Rhetoric is the art that shows us how to hone that weapon and to wield it most effectively.

Many public activities today rely heavily on the art of rhetoric. Advertis-ing, that vast, ubiquitous industry in twentieth-century life, is perhaps the best example of an activity that practices what Aristotle preached. Adver-tising certainly makes use of all the "available means of persuasion" to in-duce people to buy things, and while questions are sometimes raised about the ethics of advertising, there is no denying that specialists in advertising are remarkably effective rhetoricians.

Many other fields of endeavor in modern life rely on rhetoric in varying degrees. The diplomat is a traveling rhetorician with portfolio. The public-relations man is a practitioner of ceremonial rhetoric, that variety which is not so much interested in effecting persuasion as in reflecting credit on a person or an institution. Law is such a many-faceted profession today that many lawyers never get a chance to exhibit the forensic brand of rhetoric in the courtroom; but even those lawyers whose principal function is to prepare briefs for the Clarence Darrows of the courtroom can be said to be engaged in the *inventio* and *dispositio* aspects of rhetoric. Insurance men and salesmen (especially the door-to-door salesmen) practice deliberative rhetoric, often very effectively, every day. Preachers, candidates for public office, and par-liamentary speakers are as actively exercising their rhetorical skills today as they ever were.

There are some forms of rhetoric practiced today that we regard with sus-picion, and even disdain. One of these is propaganda. The term *propaganda* was once a neutral word, signifying the dissemination of truth. But because some men have used propaganda for unscrupulous purposes, *propaganda* has taken on decidedly unfavorable connotations. Closely allied to this dis-reputable form of rhetoric is demagoguery. The names of the most successful of the twentieth-century demagogues are etched so painfully into our memo-ries that they need not be specified here. These were the exploiters of specious arguments, half-truths, and rank emotional appeals to gain personal ad-vantage rather than to promote the public welfare. The newest variety of dangerous rhetoric is *brainwashing*. A definitive analysis of this diabolical technique has yet to be written, but a beginning has been made in the terri-fying final chapters of George Orwell's *1984*. A good argument for an in-tensive study of rhetoric is that citizens might thereby be put on their guard against the onslaughts of these vicious forms of persuasion.

One of the chief values of rhetoric, conceived as a system of gathering, arranging, and expressing our material, is that it represents a *positive* ap-proach to the problems of writing. Students have too often been inhibited in their writing by the negative approach to composition—don't do this, beware of that. Classical rhetoric too had its negative prescriptions, but, in the main, it offered positive advice to help the student in the composition of a specific kind of discourse directed to a definite audience for a particular purpose. Rhetoric cannot, of course, tell the student what he must do in any and every situation. No art can do that. But rhetoric can lay down the general principles that the student can adapt to fit the particular situation. At least it can provide the student with a set of procedures and criteria that can guide him in making strategic decisions in the composition process.

Rhetoric was primarily a synthetic art—an art for "building up" something. But it can also be used as an analytical art—an art for "breaking down" what has been composed. As such, the study of rhetoric can make us better readers. Once we are made aware of all the artifice that goes into the composition of a discourse, we are better equipped to analyze what other speakers and writers have done to achieve their effects. As Malcolm Cowley pointed out a few years ago, the New Criticism of men like Cleanth Brooks and Robert Penn Warren represented an application of rhetorical principles to the close reading of poetic texts. Mortimer Adler's *How to Read a Book,* which became a surprising bestseller during the 1940's, presented a rhetorical technique for the reading of expository and argumentative prose. Wayne C. Booth, in his book *The Rhetoric of Fiction* (1961), has shown us how "rhetoric" operates in the short story and the novel. And in recent years, hardly an issue of the professional journals in Speech or English appears without someone's rhetorical analysis of some piece of didactic or non-didactic literature.

The student will be amazed at the new dimensions revealed when he uses the rhetorical approach for the study of satire, to name just one of the literary genres. Satire is essentially an exercise in rhetoric—rhetoric in the classical sense of persuasive discourse. The satirist is engaged either in deliberative rhetoric or in ceremonial rhetoric: either the satirist is seeking to influence the attitude of his audience, often with the ultimate purpose of moving his audience to do something, or he is seeking, through the medium of praise or blame, to induce his audience to accept or reject some person or group of persons. Jonathan Swift's "A Modest Proposal" is a display of deliberative rhetoric. For examples of ceremonial rhetoric, we can hearken back to those devastating portraits of political and literary enemies that we get in John Dryden's "Absalom and Achitophel" or "Mac Flecknoe" or in Alexander Pope's "Epistle to Dr. Arbuthnot" or "The Dunciad." Today the eighteenth-century brand of satire seems to be enjoying a revival, especially among young people of college age. Whether it is the satire in *Mad Magazine* or the satire of the stand-up comedians who reach their audience through television or records, all of the techniques have their roots in Aristotelian rhetoric.

The student may fear that an elaborately systematized approach to composition will inhibit rather than facilitate writing. There is no denying that formula can retard and has retarded inventiveness and creativity. But to admit that formula can inhibit the writer is not to admit that it invariably does inhibit him. Almost every one of the major English writers, from the Renaissance through the eighteenth century—Chaucer, Jonson, Shakespeare, Milton, Dryden, Pope, Swift, Burke—had been subjected to an intensive rhetoric course in their grammar school or university. If one cannot claim that the study of rhetoric made them great writers, one might yet venture to say that rhetoric made them better writers than they might have been on genius alone.

Lest we raise any false hopes, however, we hasten to warn the student that this adaptation of classical rhetoric offers no magic formula for success in writing. The student will have to work hard in order to profit from the instruction offered in this book, for it is not all easy to understand, and what is learned must be applied.

The road to eloquence is a hard road and a lonely road, and the journey is not for the faint-hearted. But if, as we are told, the ability to use words to communicate thoughts and feelings is man's most distinctively human accomplishment, there can be few satisfactions in life that can match the pride a man feels when he has attained mastery over words. As Quintilian said, "Therefore let us seek wholeheartedly that true majesty of expression, the fairest gift of God to man, without which all things are struck dumb and robbed both of present glory and the immortal acclaim of posterity; and let us press on to whatever is best, because, if we do this, we shall either reach the summit or at least see many others far beneath us."

II / DISCOVERY OF ARGUMENTS

Formulating a Thesis

The beginning of all discourse is a subject. Subject is the *res* of the *res-verba* combination that rhetoricians talked about. *Res* (*what* is said) was the province of rhetoric called "invention." *Verba* (*how* it is said) was the concern of two other parts of rhetoric, "style" and "delivery." Obviously, no decisions about expression can be made until one's subject matter has been clearly defined.

Frequently, our subject matter is assigned to us. The teacher announces in class, "For next Friday I want you to write a 500-word letter to the editor of the school newspaper, giving your views on the proposed increase in tuition." Or the editor of a magazine writes to one of his authors and asks him whether he will do a 3000-word piece on the civil rights demonstrations in his community. Or the president of a corporation asks one of his junior executives to prepare a report for the next business meeting on the success of the latest advertising campaign. In such instances, our subject is given to us. At other times, of course, an author chooses his own subject.

But the choice or designation of a subject is only a beginning; in fact, it can be a dead-end if something further is not done to define the subject. It is not enough to decide that one is going to write on "democracy." Before "democracy" can become a real subject for a discourse, something must be *predicated* of it. The subject must be converted into a theme; it must, to use a term from logic, be stated in the form of a *proposition*. So our vague subject "democracy" must become something like "Democracy is the form of government which best allows a man to realize his potentialities as a human being" or "Democracy functions best when the people are educated." Now

45

we have a theme; now we have a more precise notion of what we are going to write about.

John Henry Newman, in a section called "Elementary Studies" in his *Idea of a University,* points out the importance of stating a subject in the form of a proposition. His fictitious Mr. Black is commenting on a composition written by a boy named Robert:

> "Now look here," Mr. Black says, "the subject is *'Fortes fortuna adjuvat'* [Fortune favors the brave]; now this is a *proposition;* it states a certain general principle, and this is just what an ordinary boy would be sure to miss, and Robert does miss it. He goes off at once on the word *'fortuna.' 'Fortuna'* was not his subject; the thesis was intended to *guide* him, for his own good; he refuses to be put into leading strings; he breaks loose, and runs off in his own fashion on the broad field and in wild chase of 'fortune,' instead of closing with a subject, which, as being definite, would have supported him.
>
> "It would have been very cruel to have told a boy to write on 'fortune'; it would have been like asking him his opinion 'of things in general.' Fortune is 'good,' 'bad,' 'capricious,' 'unexpected,' ten thousand things all at once (you see them all in the Gradus), and one of them as much as the other. Ten thousand things may be said of it: give me *one* of them, and I will write upon it; I cannot write on more than one; Robert prefers to write upon all."

Hundreds of Roberts are defeated every year in their composition classes because they will not or cannot define their subject. The Latin rhetoricians used a formula for determining the point of issue in a court trial that might help students decide on a thesis. The formula consisted of three questions that were asked about the subject of dispute or discussion:

> *An sit* (whether a thing is)—a question of fact
> *Quid sit* (what it is)—a question of definition
> *Quale sit* (what kind it is)—a question of quality

In a murder trial, for instance, the case for the prosecution and the defense could turn on one of three issues:

> 1. Did Brutus, as has been alleged, kill Caesar? (whether a thing is)
> 2. If it is granted that Brutus *did* kill Caesar, was the act murder or self-defense? (what it is)
> 3. If it was in fact murder, was Brutus justified in murdering Caesar? (what kind it is)

The application of this formula settles the issue in a trial and in turn suggests the topics that the lawyers resort to in arguing their case.

The use of this formula will not establish the thesis of a discourse, but it can help the student determine what aspect of the subject he is going to treat, and then he is in a position to formulate a thesis. Let us suppose that his instructor has asked him to write a letter to the editor about the increase in tuition. What aspect of the subject is he going to talk about? Is there actually going to be an increase in tuition next term? Or has an increase only been proposed? Perhaps the student knows that the Board of Trustees has been considering an increase in tuition but has not yet formally voted on the proposal. If so, that could very well be the burden of the letter he writes: "The students of this university have been in an uproar about something that is not yet a fact. If they had taken the trouble to investigate the facts, they would know that they do not yet have any just cause for complaint."

Suppose that the report about the cost per credit-hour has been confirmed. What aspect is there left to talk about? Well, he might become involved in a question of definition. Is the change from $15 to $17 per credit-hour really an *increase* in tuition costs? Not if one considers that the Board of Trustees has also voted to reduce the number of credit-hours that students will be allowed to take in any one semester. So although the cost per credit-hour will go up, the total cost of tuition per semester will remain the same. It is apparent that in this instance a discussion of the definition of *increase* could turn into a mere quibble on words, but with other subjects, like "democracy" or "socialized," there would be more of an opportunity to deal with a definition of terms.

But suppose that a change in tuition has been approved and that this change does constitute a substantial increase in the cost of tuition. Now the third question (*quale sit*) can disclose the area of discussion. Was the increase necessary? Can it be justified? In comparison with the general rise in the cost of living, does the increase in tuition become minimal? Will the increase in tuition ensure the continuance of or even an improvement in the quality of our education? Or will the increase prevent many students from continuing their education? The application of the third question to this particular subject turns up a number of areas of discussion.

The subject matter considered in relation to the current situation or occasion and to the audience often dictates which of the three questions is most applicable. In any case, however, the application of the pertinent question does help to define the aspect of the subject that is to be discussed. Once that aspect has been determined, the student should be prepared to formulate a thesis sentence. Once the subject has been narrowed down, what does he want to say about his subject?

The cardinal principle is to *state the thesis in a single declarative sentence*

It is important that the thesis be formulated in a *single* sentence. As soon as the student launches into a second sentence, he introduces foreign or subsidiary matter which is likely to violate the unity of his thesis. It is equally important to formulate the thesis in a *declarative* sentence. Hortatory sentences like "Let us fight to preserve the integrity of our democracy" and interrogatory sentences like "Is democracy a feasible form of government?" leave the subject fuzzy; both kinds of sentence have a tentative or uncertain air about them. The thesis will be clearly and firmly stated if the predicate *asserts* or *denies* something about the subject: "The integrity of our democracy can be preserved only if we fight to maintain it"; "Democracy is (is not) a feasible form of government."

The thesis sentence is a good starting-point in the composition process because it forces the writer to determine at the outset just what it is that he wants to say about his chosen or designated subject. Moreover, it lays the foundation for a unified, coherent discourse. Then, too, it often suggests some of the *topics* that can be used for the development of the discourse.

Say that a student took as his thesis this proposition: "Democracy is a feasible form of government for the newly emergent countries of South Africa." That statement precisely defines what the student wants to say about his subject: he is going to argue that a democratic form of government will work in South Africa. If the student keeps that objective constantly in mind, there is a good chance that his discourse will have a tight unity. The mere verbalization of the thesis also suggests some lines of development. Will he not, for instance, have to define at the beginning of his essay at least two of the key terms in his proposition, *democracy* and *feasible?* Will it not be advisable also to specify which countries of South Africa he is talking about? Is it possible that in arguing the feasibility of a democratic government in certain countries of South Africa he could compare the situation in these countries with the situation in other countries where democracy proved successful? The statement of his thesis has already suggested the topics of definition and comparison as possible lines of argument and has also suggested a possible organization of his essay that will be conducive to coherence.

Defining the thesis in a single declarative sentence will also help the student determine whether he can adequately handle the given or chosen subject within the word limit set for him. The subject "democracy" is so broad that the student could not forecast how much development would be necessary. A proposition like "Democracy is the best form of government" is still somewhat broad and vague, but at least it fixes some limits to the subject. The student could perhaps not do justice to such a thesis in 500 words; but he might be able to treat it satisfactorily in 1500-2000 words. On the other hand, a proposition like "Representative democracy allows each citizen to exercise some voice in the conduct of his government" might very well be satisfactorily treated in 500 words.

Simple as the principle is, many students have difficulty in framing their thesis in a single declarative sentence. Part of their difficulty stems from the fact that they do not have a firm grasp on their ideas before they sit down to compose a thesis sentence. Thought and language interact upon each other. Hugh Blair once said, "For we may rest assured that whenever we express ourselves ill, there is, besides the mismanagement of language, for the most part, some mistake in our manner of conceiving the subject. Embarrassed, obscure, and feeble sentences are generally, if not always, the result of embarrassed, obscure, and feeble thought."

It often takes considerable practice before the student acquires the ability to define his thesis sharply. He can foster the development of this ability if he will make a habit of formulating a thesis sentence for any formal prose he reads. Sometimes the author helps him by stating his thesis somewhere in the essay, and in that case his job is to detect that thematic sentence. In some cases, however, the central idea of an essay is nowhere explicitly stated, and he must be able to abstract the central idea from the whole essay. The ability to generalize in this way is often the last ability the student acquires in learning how to read. If he cannot abstract a thesis from what he reads, it is not likely that he will have much success in formulating his own thesis sentences.

He must acquire this ability if he hopes to be able to communicate clearly and coherently with others through the medium of written prose. Failure to sharply define one's subject is the chief cause of fuzzy, disunified discourse. Vague beginnings invite chaotic endings. The audience for a discourse, whether written or spoken, can achieve no firmer grasp of the thesis than the writer or speaker himself has. As a matter of fact, if we make allowance for what is inevitably lost in the process of transmission, the audience's grasp will always be *less* firm than the writer's or speaker's.

So we round back to what was said earlier in this chapter: the beginning of coherent, unified writing is a sharply defined thesis. But as soon as that general principle is enunciated, it invites some qualification. Someone once said, "I don't really know what I want to say until I have said it." And indeed there may be times when it may be advantageous for one to start writing *before* he has a clear, firm idea of what his thesis is. In such cases, the act of writing out his as yet unfocused thoughts could become part of the invention process, could lead to the discovery of what he finally wanted to say about the subject he had chosen, or been delegated, to write on. The articulation of his thesis would not come until *after* he had written his rough draft. We could still say, however, that even in those cases the articulation of the thesis would be the starting point, the catalyst, the focusing device for the writing of the final product,

The Three Modes of Persuasion

The thesis we formulate serves as an objective for the discourse we intend to compose. It specifies the idea that we would like to "put across" to others. In argumentative discourse, the thesis indicates the truth or proposal that we want our audience to accept or act upon. But how do we get others to accept our point of view? How do we get others, in Kenneth Burke's terms, "to identify" with us?

Aristotle said that we persuade others by three means: (1) by the appeal to their reason (*logos*); (2) by the appeal to their emotions (*pathos*); (3) by the appeal of our personality or character (*ēthos*). We may use one of these means exclusively or predominantly, or we may use all three. Which of these means we use will be partly determined by the nature of the thesis we are arguing, partly by current circumstances, partly (perhaps mainly) by the kind of audience we are addressing. All men develop some instincts for adapting means to fit the subject, occasion, and audience, but by experience and education some men so refine these instincts that their success in dealing with others can be attributed to an art rather than to a mere knack. And when persuasive activities approach the condition of art they can be said to fall within the province of rhetoric.

Before we discuss the *topics,* the system that the classical rhetoricians devised to help one find something to say on any given subject, we will consider the strategies of these three modes of appeal.

The Appeal to Reason

Rationality is man's essential characteristic. It is what makes man human and differentiates him from other animals. Ideally, reason should dominate all of man's thinking and actions, but actually, man is often influenced by passions and prejudices and customs. To say that man often responds to irrational motives is not to say that he never listens to the voice of reason. We must have faith not only that man is capable of ordering his life by the dictates of reason but that most of the time he is disposed to do so. Because the rhetoricians had that faith in their fellow men, they thought of rhetoric as an offshoot of logic, the science of human reasoning. "Rhetoric is the counterpart of dialectics," Aristotle said in the first sentence of his *Rhetoric.* Aristotle had dealt with strict logic in the six treatises that collectively have been called the *Organon,* and in two of these treatises, the *Prior Analytics* and the *Posterior Analytics,* he had dealt primarily with deductive and inductive reasoning. Dialectics was the popular form of "analytics" or logic, in the same way that rhetoric was the popular form of the strict demonstration that took place in the sciences. Plato's *Dialogues,* with their give-and-take of question and answer, are good examples of the informal way in which men argue logically with one another. Similarly, rhetoric is the practical art by which we learn how to manipulate all the available means of persuading a large, heterogeneous, perhaps uneducated audience. The appeals to reason that an orator might use do not violate the principles of strict logic; they are merely adaptations of logic. So, whereas the syllogism and induction are the forms that reasoning takes in logic, the enthymeme and the example are the forms that reasoning takes in rhetoric.

Whenever formal deductive or inductive logic is "an available means of persuasion," we should, of course, make use of it. In literary and scientific journals, we often find the authors of articles presenting masses of evidence or employing full-fledged deductive reasoning in order to convince their professional colleagues of the soundness of their experiments or theses. Even in popularized articles on abstruse subjects, where we do not expect to get the full panoply of logical demonstrations, those authors who are jealous of their professional reputations will take care not to violate the principles of logical reasoning.

As a foundation for the discussion of the rhetorical appeals to reason, we will review some of the principles of logic. First, let us consider the matter of definition.

Principles of Definition

Exposition and argumentation often turn on definition. Exposition, in fact, is a form of definition. In order to *explain* something, we have to tell what a thing is or describe it or enumerate its parts or demonstrate its operation. A dictionary is an expository work—a work that defines, not things, but words which stand for things. All "how to" books are primarily expository, because, by showing how something works or operates, these books are in a sense explaining or defining that thing. Discourses that analyze or classify things are also instances of expository definition.

In the *Topica,* one of his treatises on logic, Aristotle lays down the principles governing what is commonly referred to as an "essential definition." An essential definition is one that designates that which makes a thing what it is and distinguishes that thing from all other things; in other words, it is one that spells out a thing's fundamental nature. For instance, the widely accepted essential definition of *man* is as follows: "A man is a rational animal." The predicate term "rational animal" designates a man's essence and cannot be used of any other creature.

One of the tests by which we can determine whether we have arrived at an essential definition is to see whether we can *convert* the proposition—that is, interchange the subject and predicate terms without destroying the truth of the proposition. The proposition "A man is a rational animal" can be converted to "A rational animal is a man." The proposition is as true in its second form as it is in its first. Let us apply the test to another definition of man, "Man is a biped animal." When we convert the proposition to "A biped animal is a man," we can readily see that the "truth" has been upset, because while it is true that every man is a biped animal, it is not true that every biped animal is a man. "Two-footedness" is a characteristic of man, but it does not designate the essence of man. "Rationality" does designate man's essence, not only because it is characteristic of man, but because it "belongs" exclusively to man.

In an essential definition, the subject and predicate are equivalent terms. In a loose sense, an essential definition sets up an equation: *man* equals *rational animal; rational animal* equals *man.* To use another analogy, the subject term in an essential definition must "weigh" as much as the predicate term. We must be able to interchange the weights on the scale and still keep the scale in balance. That's the trouble with the terms *man* and *biped animal*—they do not "weigh" the same.

It was Aristotle, with his biologist's passion for classification, who showed us how to formulate an essential definition. We put the "thing to be defined" (the *definiendum*) into a *genus* or general class and then give the *differentiae* or the specific differences that distinguish this thing from every other thing comprehended in the same general class. In the essential definition that we used, "animal" is the *genus,* and "rational" is the *differentia* that distinguishes man from every other creature that can be classified as an animal.

The student must not get the idea that the *differentia* will always be given in a single word, as in our definition of man. Sometimes we have to designate several differences in order to distinguish the thing from other things in the same class. Consider this definition for instance: "An automobile is a vehicle that runs on four wheels." We have the *genus* (vehicle) and a *differentia* (runs on four wheels), but obviously this *differentia* is not sufficient to distinguish an automobile from other vehicles that run on four wheels. The etymology of the word suggests another *differentia* that would help to distinguish an automobile—*auto,* "self-," and *mobilis,* "movable." So we would add that this four-wheeled vehicle is propelled by an internal engine. If this were not sufficient to distinguish an automobile we could add *differentiae* which specify the kind of engine that propelled it, the material the vehicle is made of, its shape, and what it is used for.

The *differentiae* in a definition often specify one or more of the four causes of a thing: the *material,* the *formal,* the *efficient,* and the *final.* For instance, if one were explaining a table, one might say that a table is a piece of furniture (the *genus*) made by a carpenter (efficient cause) from wood (material cause) with a broad, flat top resting horizontally on four legs (formal cause) on which one puts things, often dishes for a meal (final cause, the end or purpose of the thing). It goes without saying that the *differentiae* will change as we attempt to define various kinds of tables. Some tables are made of metal or stone by metalworkers or stonemasons; some tables rest on three legs, others on six; people use tables for a variety of purposes, e.g. to sit or stand at while they are writing or drawing or cutting cloth.

The student will find it instructive to open his dictionary at random and look at the definitions of nouns on the page to which he opens. He will find that most definitions of nouns follow the Aristotelian pattern: the substantive is assigned to a general class and then differentiated in one or more ways. He will also find that a dictionary does not often attain or even strive for an essential definition. For practical purposes, we do not often need the precision or exclusiveness of an essential definition. And besides, it is extremely difficult to arrive at, or to know when we have arrived at, an essential definition. Most of us would find it frustrating to specify the essence of a typewriter (even though we would be able to pick out a typewriter from a group of other artifacts), and unless we have desperate need of an essential definition, we do not take the trouble to seek one. We will settle for a serviceable definition of a typewriter. On the other hand, philosophers have sought an essential definition of *man* because it has seemed important to determine just what a man's essence is.

Definitions of anything will vary, of course, according to the definer's point of view and his particular basis of classification. In fact, one of the ways to distinguish the various branches of knowledge is to note the methods and bases of definition used by each science. A biologist, for instance, might define a man as "an erect, bipedal, giant mammal relatively unspecialized in body form." Or if he were attempting an operative definition, he might define man as "the only creature capable of modifying his evolutionary future." A behavioral scientist might define man as a "social animal" or a "tool-making creature" or "a creature that prepares its food with fire." A theologian might define man as "an adopted son of God." Each of these definitions is true in its own way, and each of them tells us something useful to know about man. For some purposes, we will find the biologist's definition of man more useful than the logician's definition. (In Vercors's fascinating novel *You Shall Know Them,* a murder trial turns on whether the strange creatures that a scientist has discovered in the jungle and brought back to civilization can be classified as human. In our space age, we may be faced with a similar problem if we find some form of primate life on other planets.) A rhetorician is especially interested in the fact that words admit of a variety of valid definitions.

Other Methods of Definition

Synonyms

There are other ways to define words besides the Aristotelian method of giving the genus and the specific differences. One of the common ways is to cite synonyms. We often resort to this method in the case of adjectives, nouns, and verbs. So if we want to convey the meaning of *inflexible,* we might cite such synonyms as *adamant, implacable, obdurate, stiff, unbending;* to clarify the meaning of *infer* we might offer such synonyms as *deduce, conclude, judge, gather.* Aristotle questioned this method of definition; he maintained that a real definition could be rendered only in a phrase. And he was probably right, for although a synonym can illuminate the meaning of a strange word, it does not really inform us about the mode of being of that word. Still and all, synonyms do play a useful part in clarifying the words used to convey ideas or feelings.

Etymology

Closely allied to definition by synonyms is definition by reference to etymology. One might explain the meaning of *inflexible* by pointing out that the word derives from the Latin prefix *in-,* meaning in this case "not," the Latin verb *flectere,* meaning "to bend," and the suffix *-ible,* meaning "able to be"—hence "not able to be bent." A study of etymology can throw light on the meaning of words, can suggest subtle shades of meaning, and can serve as a mnemonic device—especially for those who have some knowledge of the parent languages. But there is one caution about relying on etymology for the meaning of words: the meanings frequently drift far from the etymological roots. The English word *police,* to take only one example, has strayed considerably from its root in the Greek word *polites,* meaning "citizen." Citing the etymology of *democracy* might stir up more arguments than it would settle.

Description

Another method of definition, frequently used to convey a notion of a complex organization or mechanism, is the extended description. These descriptions often mention the *genus* and several of the *properties* and *accidents* of the thing to be defined, but the definition is presented in discursive prose rather than in the tight, unitary phrases that a dictionary uses. Comparisons, analogies, metaphors, and similes are frequently employed to facilitate definitions by description.

Example

A method especially useful in defining abstractions is giving an example. The dubious syntax, "Honesty is when..." is usually a signal that we are about to get a definition by this method. A definition by example might run something like this:

> You ask me what *honesty* is. Well, I'll tell you. One night about 10:30 while a rather elderly man was walking to the subway after work, he spied a black purse lying in the gutter. Some woman must have dropped it as she was getting into a cab. He looked about him. There was no one else on the street at the moment. He picked up the purse and opened it. Inside the purse was a bundle of ten-dollar bills bound with a rubber-band. Riffling through the bills, he estimated that there was 150 to 200 dollars in the bundle. The only identification in the purse was an envelope bearing the name and address of a lawyer. What should he do? Nobody had seen him pick up the purse. The woman who had dropped the purse obviously didn't need the money as desperately as he did. The money could solve a lot of his financial problems at home. He was tempted. But he knew he wouldn't sleep at night if he took the purse home. He snapped the purse shut and walked two blocks out of his way to turn the purse in at the police station. You ask me what honesty is. *That* is honesty.

Defining by example has long been a favorite device of preachers, orators, and teachers. The *exemplum,* an anecdote or short tale with a moral, once played a prominent part in literature. Aesop's *Fables* and Chaucer's *Pardoner's Tale* are just two instances of this genre.

In conclusion, here are three rules which should govern our attempts to define terms:

> 1. The defining terms should be clearer and more familiar than the term to be defined.

This principle is so self-evident that it hardly needs to be enunciated, yet it does need some qualification. Dr. Johnson's notorious definition of a *network* as a "reticulated fabric, decussated at regular intervals, with interstices at the intersections" is not very enlightening to someone who has no notion of a network—although this much-ridiculed definition is remarkably accurate and precise. By using more familiar words, modern dictionaries succeed in conveying a clearer notion of a network. The real difficulty in observing the first rule presents itself when one has to define a relatively simple, everyday object. How does one define an *egg?* Will not the defining terms necessarily be "harder" words than the term to be defined?

2. The definition should not repeat the term to be defined or use synonymous or derivative terms.

As we said above, synonyms do not really define; they are merely similar, perhaps more familiar words, which may illuminate the meaning of an unknown word. Nor can the repetition of the same word or of an inflectionally derivative word do much to clarify the meaning of the *definiendum*. So we should avoid definitions like these: "Justice is a virtue which prompts a man to deal justly with another man"; "Man is a creature possessing a human nature"; or definitions like Bardolph's in *King Henry IV*, Part Two, Act III, scene ii: "Accommodated: that is, when a man is, as they say, accommodated; or when a man is, being, whereby 'a may be thought to be accommodated—which is an excellent thing."

3. The definition, wherever possible, should be stated positively, not negatively.

The phrase "wherever possible" has to be inserted here because sometimes a concept is so obscure or ambiguous that it is difficult to define it positively; in such cases we realize some gain if we are told at least what the concept is *not*. Of course, concepts that are themselves negative in meaning can hardly be defined positively. So a concept like *darkness* has to be defined negatively as "the absence of light." There can be a rhetorical advantage also in the use of negative definitions—for instance, a series of statements telling what a thing is *not* before one comes forth with the statement of what a thing is. The kind of definition that the third rule cautions against is one like this: "Democracy is that form of government which does not deprive its citizens of their civil liberties." If this is the *only* definition of democracy offered, no one is going to have much of an idea about what democracy *is*.

The Syllogism

The syllogism was a schematic device that Aristotle invented to analyze and test deductive reasoning. People in real life rarely argue in a strict syllogistic form, but the syllogism is a useful device for analyzing the method or form that people observe when they reason deductively. We cannot give a full course in logic here, but we can set down some of the basic principles governing this form of deductive reasoning.

The syllogism reasons from statements or propositions. These propositions are called *premises*. The reasoning follows this course: if *a* is true, and *b* is true, then *c* must be true. Before we consider the syllogism itself, we should say something about the kinds of propositions that appear in categorical syllogisms. Let us start out with the *square of opposition,* a device that logicians invented mainly for mnemonic purposes (see figure on page 46).

The square of opposition presents schematically the four kinds of *categorical propositions*—that is, propositions that either assert or deny something, without conditions or alternatives proposed.

> The A-proposition (All men are mortal beings) is a *universal affirmative.*
>
> The E-proposition (No men are mortal beings) is a *universal negative.*
>
> The I-proposition (Some men are mortal beings) is a *particular affirmative.*
>
> The O-proposition (Some men are not mortal beings) is a *particular negative.*

The letters attached to these propositions happen to be the first four vowels in the English alphabet, but these letters were chosen to label the propositions because they are the first two vowels in two pertinent Latin verbs:

> *AFFIRMO* (I affirm)—so the A and I are attached to the affirmative propositions.
>
> *NEGO* (I deny)—so the E and O are attached to the negative propositions.

All men are mortal beings.   No men are mortal beings.

Some men are mortal beings.   Some men are not mortal beings.

In argument, it is frequently necessary that one be able to classify propositions as to their *quantity* and *quality.* When we ask about the quantity of a proposition, we are seeking to determine whether the proposition is *universal* or *particular*—that is, whether a statement is being made about a whole class or about only part of a class. When we ask about the quality of a proposition, we are seeking to determine whether the proposition is *affirma-*

tive or *negative*—that is, whether the predicate asserts something about the subject or denies something about the subject. Notice that the two propositions above the horizontal line drawn through the square of opposition are *universal* propositions; the two below the line are *particular* propositions. The two propositions to the left of the vertical line are *affirmative* propositions; the two propositions to the right of the vertical line are *negative* propositions.

Each language has its own lexical and grammatical devices for indicating the quantity and quality of propositions. In English, universal propositions are signalled by such words as *every, all, no* before the subject term of the propositions. Particular propositions are signalled by such words as *some, most, many, a few, the majority of.* The presence of the adverb *not* in the predicate indicates that a proposition is negative. But propositions can also be rendered negative in English by the presence of *no, none, none of the, not all, not any of the* in the subject.

In classifying propositions, one never has any difficulty determining whether a proposition is affirmative or negative. One does have difficulty at times, however, determining the quantity of a proposition. What is the quantity, for instance, of a proposition with a proper name as the subject, e.g. "John Smith is mortal"? It seems that since we are asserting something about a particular person, the proposition must be particular. Most logicians, however, would classify this as a universal affirmative, because mortality is being predicated of the entire subject in the same way as in the proposition, "All men are mortal," mortality is being predicated of the whole class of men. By the same reasoning, "John Smith is not mortal" would be classified as a universal negative.

How does one classify the quantity of a proposition like "Men are more stable emotionally than women"? If one is arguing face to face with someone, he can stop his opponent and ask him to clarify the quantity of his statements:

> "Look, you just said that men are more stable emotionally than women. Do you mean *all* men or just *some* men?"
>
> "I mean *some* men ... no, I'll go so far as to say the *majority* of men."
>
> "All right, go on—but remember now what limits you have placed on the extension of your term."

Whenever we are engaged in discussions or arguments with someone present before us, we frequently stop him to ask for clarifications of statements. But when we see a categorical statement in print we cannot call upon the author for clarification. The common practice in such circumstances is to assume, especially if the assertion has the air of a general statement—e.g.

"Quakers are zealous, sincere pacifists" or "Birds are feathered creatures"—that the author meant the statement to be taken as a universal. In reconstructing his argument for the purpose of analysis, we would put an "all" in front of the subject term.

How does one classify a proposition like "All men are not mortal"? It is clearly a negative proposition, but despite the "All" in front of the subject term, this proposition does not have the same meaning as the E-proposition, "No men are mortal." "All men are not mortal" is the contradictory form of "All men are mortal." In the square of opposition, contradictory propositions are opposed diagonally. So "All men are not mortal" is really an O-proposition, equivalent in meaning to "Some men are not mortal." The same would be true if the statement took the form of "Not all men are mortal." The final test must always be the *meaning*, not the *form*, of the statement.

It is customary and useful to put categorical statements in the following form:

(Quantity word)   (substantive)   (copulative verb)   (substantive)
Example: All   men   are   mortal beings

Oftentimes, statements put in this form will be awkward and unidiomatic. "All men are mortal" is certainly more idiomatic than "All men are mortal beings." Frequently, too, assertions are made with transitive or intransitive verbs—e.g. "Men run faster than women" and "Most men can hit a golf ball farther than most women can." Putting such categorical statements into the prescribed form frequently results in some very awkward locutions:

"Men run faster than women." > "All men are faster runners than women." "Most men can hit a golf ball farther than most women can." > "Some men are athletes capable of hitting a golf ball farther than most women can."

The reason for putting statements into the prescribed form is that when these statements occur in syllogisms it is easier for the beginner to pick out terms. As we shall see, some of the rules for a valid syllogism involve the distribution of terms. So it is important that we be able to ascertain the terms. Substantives with their cluster of modifiers are easier to pick out than terms hidden in predicate adjectives or action verbs. After the student has had practice analyzing arguments, he can dispense with this conversion process and deal with statements in their natural form.

One can learn a great deal about the process of deductive reasoning from studying the relationships of propositions in the square of opposition. Here are the valid deductions we can make from the various propositions:

1. If the A-proposition is true, the I-proposition must be true; likewise, if the E-proposition is true, the O-proposition must be true.

   If it is true that *all* men are mortal, it logically follows that *some* men are mortal. And if it is true that *no* men are mortal, it is equally true that *some* men are not mortal.

2. If the I-proposition is true, no deduction can be made about the A-proposition; likewise, if the O-proposition is true, no deduction can be made about the E-proposition.

   If we determine that *some* men are mortal, we cannot infer from that fact that *all* men are mortal. In other words, we cannot *infer* the truth of the universal proposition from the particular proposition; we have to *prove* the truth of the universal.

3. If the A-proposition is true, the E-proposition is false; likewise, if the E-proposition is true, the A-proposition is false.

   We know *a priori* that if one of a pair of *contrary* propositions is true, the other is necessarily false. Common sense tells us that if *all* men are mortal, the contrary proposition "No men are mortal" must be false.

4. If the A-proposition is false, no deduction can be made about the E-proposition; likewise, if the E-proposition is false, no deduction can be made about the A-proposition.

   Although, as we saw in (3), contrary propositions cannot both be true, they both may be false. So if the proposition "No men are mortal" is false, we may not conclude that all men are mortal. That proposition may also be false.

5. In the case of contradictory propositions (A and O; E and I), one of them must be true and the other false. Accordingly, these are the valid deductions we may make about the propositions opposed diagonally in the square of opposition:

   a. If A is true, O must be false.
   b. If A is false, O must be true.
   c. If O is true, A must be false.
   d. If O is false, A must be true.
   e. If E is true, I must be false.
   f. If E is false, I must be true.

g. If I is true, E must be false.
h. If I is false, E must be true.

The law of contradiction is based on the principle that a thing cannot at the same time be and not be. This law plays an important part as one of the means of logical proof in persuasive discourse.

6. If the I-proposition is true, no deduction can be made about the O-proposition; likewise, if the O-proposition is true, no deduction can be made about the I-proposition.

If the I-proposition is false, the O-proposition is true; likewise, if the O-proposition is false, the I-proposition is true.

In the case of subcontraries (the propositions opposed horizontally at the bottom of the square of opposition), both of them can be true, but both of them cannot be false (compare this with the relationship between contrary propositions). It is easier to see that both the subcontraries could be true if we take the propositions "Some men are Republicans" and "Some men are not Republicans." But we cannot deduce the truth of one from the truth of the other. We can, however, infer the truth of one from the falsity of the other.

We are now ready to look at a syllogism. The following syllogism has become Exhibit A in almost every elementary book of logic:

All men are mortal beings.
Socrates is a man.
Therefore, Socrates is a mortal being.

This syllogism sets forth the full chain of reasoning that is implicit in a statement like this: "Socrates is bound to die too, because he is, like the rest of us, a human being." The syllogism is made up of three categorical propositions, the first two of them being called *premises,* the last one being the *conclusion* drawn from these premises. The categorical syllogism is built on three terms: a major term, a minor term, and a middle term. Here are the simple criteria for picking out these terms:

The *major term* is the predicate term of the conclusion ("mortal beings").
The *minor term* is the subject term of the conclusion ("Socrates").
The *middle term* is the term that appears in both of the premises but does not appear in the conclusion ("men" and its singular form "man").

The syllogism is made up of three propositions: a major premise, a minor premise, and a conclusion. The major premise is the proposition that contains the major term ("All men are mortal beings"). The minor premise is the proposition that contains the minor term ("Socrates is a man"). In constructing a syllogism, we usually put the major premise first—although it should be understood that in actual deductive reasoning the major premise could occur in any order and, in fact, need not be expressed at all (see the later discussion of the enthymeme).

It is not so easy to define the conclusion. We could say that the conclusion is the proposition deduced from the two premises or that the conclusion is the proposition that contains both the major term and the minor term but not the middle term. But such definitions involve us in a circular argument. We cannot determine the major and minor premises unless we know the major term and the minor term, and we cannot determine the major and minor terms unless we know which proposition is the conclusion. If we were to remove the word *Therefore* from the third proposition in our model syllogism and if we were then to scramble the order of the propositions, it would be impossible to tell which of the propositions was the conclusion. Any one of the propositions could serve as the conclusion, although only one combination—the combination in our model—would produce a valid syllogism.

The main point of this is that we cannot reconstruct a syllogism from deductive reasoning as we are likely to find it in argumentative discourse unless we can pick out the conclusion. In the enthymeme, "Socrates is bound to die too, because he is, like the rest of us, a human being," the first clause is clearly the conclusion; *because* signals one of the reasons or premises for the conclusion. In argumentative discourse, conclusions are often signalled by the use of such function words as *therefore, thus, hence, consequently, so.* The context of an argument will also serve as a guide to the conclusion.

So much for the form of the syllogism. Before we set down the rules for a valid syllogism, we need to establish two important points. The first is the distinction between *truth* and *validity.* Truth has to do with the *matter* of the syllogism; validity has to do with the *form* of the syllogism. When we inquire about the truth of a syllogism, we are asking whether a proposition is true or false. "All men are mortal beings." Is that a true statement? Do you agree? When we inquire about the validity of a syllogism, we are not at all concerned about whether the propositions are true; we are concerned only with whether the inferences are justifiable, whether we can logically draw this conclusion from those premises. All the rules for the syllogism concern the form, the validity, of the syllogism.

It is extremely important that the student keep this distinction in mind. If he withholds his assent to a conclusion, he must know whether he is objecting to the truth of the premise or the validity of the reasoning. If he detects an invalid argument, he can utterly destroy his opponent's argument in a matter of minutes. If he objects to the truth of a proposition, he has a harder task on his hands, for it may take a long time to demonstrate that his opponent's statement is false. We must be satisfied about *both* the truth of the premises and the validity of the reasoning before we will give our assent to a conclusion. But the peculiar force of a syllogistic argument resides in this: *if* we assent to the truth of the premises and *if* we agree that the reasoning is valid, we *must* grant the conclusion. Under these conditions, rational people cannot resist the conclusion.

The second point we need to establish is the meaning of the term *distribution*. In logic, distribution signifies the full extension of a term to cover all the objects or individuals in the class denoted. In the phrase "all men," the term *men* is said to be distributed because the *all* designates the total number of individuals in the class of *men*. In the phrase "some men," *men* is undistributed because the *some* designates something less than the total number of individuals in the class. Sometimes we speak of a distributed term as being a *universal term* and of an undistributed term as being a *particular term*.

In the syllogism, we usually have no difficulty determining whether the subject term of propositions is distributed, because the quantity words (*all, every, no, some, most*), if present, will tell us. Since, as we have pointed out, most logicians regard a proposition that has a proper name as the subject as being a universal proposition ("Socrates is a rational animal"), the proper name may be regarded as a distributed term (the predicate applies to the *entire* subject).

It is a little more difficult to determine—or at least to recognize—whether predicate terms are distributed. For the beginning student, it is just as well that he use this simple formula:

1. The predicate terms of all *affirmative* propositions (all A- or I- propositions) are *undistributed*.
2. The predicate terms of all *negative* propositions (all E- or O- propositions) are *distributed*.

Let us see why this is so. When we assert "All men are mortal beings," it is clear that "mortal beings" is predicated of every member of the class of men. At the same time, however, we are not saying, "All men are all the mortal beings that are." Perhaps this can be clarified with a system of circles. Let one circle represent the entire class of men and another circle represent the entire class of mortal beings. Now here is a picture of the proposition "All men are mortal beings":

The proposition asserts that the entire class of men is "in" the class of mortal beings, but as the circles make clear, the class of men does not have as wide an extension, does not cover as much area, as the class of mortal beings. There are other mortal beings (birds, animals, fish) that are not men. We have then made an assertion about the entire class of men but not about the entire class of mortal beings. So the term *men* is distributed, but the term *mortal beings* is undistributed.

Now here is a picture of the proposition "No men are mortal beings":

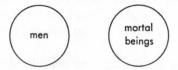

We have asserted that *none* of the class of men is "in" the class of mortal beings: or, to put it another way, the entire class of men is excluded from the entire class of mortal beings. Both terms are being used in the widest possible extension, and therefore both the subject term and the predicate term of an E-proposition are distributed.

The scheme of circles can also illustrate the distribution of the predicate terms in I- and O-propositions:

I-proposition: O-proposition:

Some men are mortal beings.   Some men are not mortal beings.

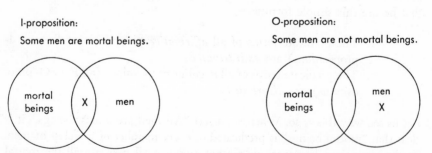

In the I-proposition, part of the *men* circle (the checkmarked area) overlaps part of the *mortal being* circle, and so it is clear that neither the subject term nor the predicate term is distributed—in neither case is the entire class involved. In the O-proposition, part of the *men* circle (the checkmarked area)

falls outside the *mortal being* circle; consequently, the subject term *men* is undistributed (a predication is made about something less than the whole class of men), but the predicate term *mortal beings* is distributed (the "some men," represented by the checkmark, is wholly outside the entire class of mortal beings).

The distribution of predicate terms is not an easy concept to grasp. If the circle diagrams have not clarified this concept, it would be well for the student to rely, until the light strikes him, on the simple formulas that the *predicate terms of all affirmative propositions are undistributed* and that the *predicate terms of all negative propositions are distributed.* This matter of distribution is important, because two of the rules for a valid syllogism involve distribution of terms and because many of the fallacies in deductive reasoning are the result of an inference being drawn from undistributed terms.

We are ready now to look at the rules for a valid syllogism. Remember that these rules concern the form or the logic of the argument, not the truth of the propositions:

1. There must be three terms and only three terms.
2. The middle term must be distributed at least once.
3. No term may be distributed in the conclusion if it was not distributed in the premise.

Most invalid syllogisms will be detected by the application of these three rules. Occasionally, however, a syllogism will pass the test of these three rules and yet will not be a valid syllogism. So we must add three more rules:

4. No conclusion may be drawn from two *particular* (as opposed to *universal*) premises.
5. No conclusion may be drawn from two negative premises.
6. If one of the premises is negative, the conclusion must be negative.

Let us apply these six rules to our model syllogism and see whether the reasoning is valid. Here is the syllogism again:

All men are mortal beings.
Socrates is a man.
Therefore, Socrates is a mortal being.

The first rule is that there must be *three terms and only three terms.* In the elementary stages of testing syllogisms, the student must actually count the terms. Once he has counted three terms, he may not stop there; he must go on to make sure that there are *only* three terms. In the first proposition, there are two terms, *men* and *mortal beings.* In the next proposition, there are two terms, *Socrates* and *man*. Since *Socrates* is a term clearly distinct from the *men* and *mortal beings* of the first proposition, we have now determined that there are three terms in this syllogism. But we must now go on to check that the syllogism has no more than three terms. What about *man* in the second proposition? Is it not a fourth term? Is it not different from *men* in the first proposition? *Men* does differ grammatically from *man*, being the plural form of the singular noun, but lexically the two terms do not differ, since they both have the same referent. Terms are the "same"— are *univocal*, to use the logician's term—if the referent of the terms is identical. If, for instance, we substituted *He* for *Socrates* in the conclusion, we would not be introducing a fourth term into the syllogism because the referent or antecedent of *He* is, presumably, *Socrates*. (We would, of course, be introducing another term if the antecedent of the pronoun were not *Socrates*.) Sometimes in arguing with someone we call for a clarification of the ambiguity of pronoun reference. "Who is *they?*" we ask our opponent, just to make sure that he hasn't shifted referents. Likewise we can use synonyms or periphrasis without introducing a new term. If in the conclusion we were to substitute "a man who will die" for *mortal being*, we would not be introducing another term. In such cases, of course, we must be satisfied that the synonym or periphrasis means the same as the term for which it is substituting.

What we must be especially on our guard against is the use of the same term with different meanings. To do this is to be guilty of what the logician's call *equivocation*. Let us look first at an obvious example of equivocation:

> All men have hearts.
> All celery plants have hearts.

No native speaker of English would be deceived by the shift of meaning in the two uses of the word *hearts*. The second *hearts* is clearly a new term. It is subtle shifts of denotation that can trap us. We must be alert enough to catch a subtle shift like this:

> All draftsmen are designing men.
> All politicians are designing men.

The point might be made here that from the logician's point of view shifts in denotation will result in fallacious reasoning, but that from the rhetorician's point of view shifts in denotation can be used for certain stylistic effects, in which case the audience is aware of both meanings. The pun, the figure of speech that rhetoricians called *paronomasia*, is an example of this kind of shift in denotation. One of the famous examples of paronomasia was Christ's promise to the chief of his apostles: "Thou art Peter [Greek, *petra*, rock], and upon this rock I will build my church." Rhetorical effects are also achieved by shifts in the connotation of words. We shall discuss this further in the chapter on style.

Let us go back now to counting the terms in our model syllogism. We had gone through the two premises and discovered that we had three distinct terms and decided that *man* in the second premise was not a fourth term. In the conclusion, *Socrates* is a repetition of a term in the minor premise, and *mortal being* is a repetition, in singular form, of a term in the major premise. So our model syllogism passes the first test: it has three terms and only three terms.

Now to test the syllogism by the second rule: *the middle term must be distributed at least once.* The middle term, we said, was the term that occurred in both premises but not in the conclusion. Our middle term here is *men (man).* We must determine whether it is distributed, whether it is used, at least once, to include the whole class. "All men are mortal beings" is our major premise. The middle term *men* is distributed. We can tell that it is distributed by noting the *All.* Is the middle term distributed in the minor premise, "Socrates is a man"? No, it is not; here it is the predicate term of an affirmative proposition, which, as we have said, is never distributed. But since our middle term is distributed *once,* our syllogism passes the test of the second rule. Later on, we shall see examples of the fallacy of the undistributed middle—one of the commonest fallacies in deductive reasoning.

According to the third rule for a valid syllogism, *no term may be distributed in the conclusion if it was not distributed in the premises.* The conclusion of our model syllogism is "Therefore, Socrates is a mortal being." If, as we observed, propositions with a proper noun as subject must be regarded as universal propositions, *Socrates* is a distributed term. So we must check to see whether this term was distributed in the premise. *Socrates,* we find, is the subject term of the same kind of proposition in the minor premise and is therefore a distributed term. *Socrates* is distributed in the conclusion, but *Socrates* is also distributed in the premise; hence our third rule is satisfied. The predicate term (*mortal being*) of the conclusion is undistributed (remember, the predicate term of affirmative propositions is undistributed). If we find any term in the conclusion to be undistributed, we can stop right there; we do not have to check to see whether the term is distributed in the premise.

Our model syllogism has passed the test of the first three rules, and generally this indicates that the reasoning is valid. But, just to be sure, we have to apply the fourth, fifth, and sixth rules. We can do that hurriedly. The fourth rule is that *no conclusion may be drawn from two particular premises.* Both of the premises in our model syllogism are universals. The fifth and sixth rules do not apply at all because neither of the premises is negative.

So the reasoning in our model syllogism is unshakably valid. We are satisfied about the *form* of the argument. Now before we assent to the conclusion, we must be satisfied about the *matter* of the argument—that is, about the truth of the premises. Is it true that all men are mortal, that all men are destined to die? Do we agree that Socrates is a man, that Socrates is a species of the genus *man?* If we answer "yes" to both of those questions, we must grant the conclusion.

If, on the other hand, we deny the truth of either premise, we will have to settle down to demonstrating that the premise is false or to listening to our opponent's arguments that the premise is true. Arguments about the truth of premises can go on for a long time and even then not be settled. Usually, arguments that go on and on are arguments about the truth or falsity of propositions. Even those arguments that are stalemated by the lack of agreement about the definition of terms are arguments about the matter and not about the form of the argument. Whenever it can be shown that the mode of arguing is illogical, the dispute can be settled very quickly. The rules for a valid syllogism were derived inductively from a study of the way in which the human mind reasons, and no one has successfully challenged the validity of these rules. Even one who has no formal training in logic and its technical terminology can be shown very quickly, in layman's terms, that his reasoning is invalid, if it is.

Once the student has been instructed about the form, the terminology, and the rules for the syllogism, it is simply a matter of practice with sample syllogisms before he acquires a proficiency in detecting fallacies in deductive reasoning. A number of syllogisms have been provided in the exercises immediately following this section. In the beginning stages, the student may have to apply the rules, one by one, in a mechanical fashion. After he has had some practice in dealing with syllogisms, he will be able to tell at a glance whether the syllogism is valid or not. For instance, any time he finds a syllogism taking this form, he will detect the Fallacy of the Undistributed Middle:

> All A is B.
> All C is B.
> ∴ All C is A.

Whenever the middle term (B) is the predicate term of two affirmative premises, the middle term will be undistributed, and consequently no conclusion can logically follow from those premises.

Since the arguments based on the topic of antecedent and consequent often take the form of a hypothetical or conditional proposition, we should consider the principles that govern validity of reasoning in the hypothetical syllogism. When we argue in the form of a hypothetical proposition, we are proposing that the truth of the antecedent (the *if* clause) implies the truth of the consequent (the main clause). So we say, "If he has leukemia, he will die." The truth of the consequent, however, does not necessarily imply the truth of the antecedent: "If he dies, he has leukemia" is not necessarily true.

If we construct a deductive argument from the hypothetical proposition, we can detect, from another angle, that the truth of the antecedent does not follow from the truth of the consequent. First let us look at a valid deductive argument:

> 1. If he has leukemia, he will die.
>   He has leukemia.
>   Therefore, he will die. (VALID)

Here the second premise affirms that the antecedent is true. If it is confirmed that a man has leukemia and if everyone afflicted with leukemia invariably dies, then it logically follows that this man will die.

Now let us see what happens to the validity of the argument when the second premise affirms the consequent:

> 2. If he has leukemia, he will die.
>   He will die.
>   Therefore, he has leukemia. (INVALID)

Confronted with this argument, most of us would be prompted to say, "Somehow I don't feel that the conclusion follows from the premise." Our feeling about the conclusion would be right. A logician labels this form of argument "the fallacy of affirming the consequent." Common sense tells us that from this sequence of propositions one may not validly infer that the man has leukemia from the affirmation that the man is going to die.

If the consequent is *denied,* a valid conclusion may be drawn. We can use the same sort of propositions to illustrate this form of argument:

> 3. If he has leukemia, he will die.
>   He will not die.
>   Therefore, he does not have leukemia. (VALID)

The validity of this conclusion may not be immediately apparent, but if we reflect a moment on what the premises say, we are forced to agree to the conclusion. If a man afflicted with leukemia inevitably dies and if a doctor affirms that this man is not in apparent danger of death, the one thing we can assert definitely is that this man does not now have leukemia.

Let us look at an example of "the fallacy of denying the antecedent":

> 4. If he has leukemia, he will die.
>   He does not have leukemia.
>   Therefore, he will not die. (INVALID)

Common sense tells us that even if both premises are true, the conclusion does not follow, because we recognize that a man could die from something other than leukemia.

Here is a simple table of criteria for testing the validity of hypothetical syllogisms:

> If the minor premise (that is, the second premise)
> (1) affirms the antecedent—the conclusion is valid (see syllogism 1 above)
> (2) affirms the consequent—the conclusion is invalid (see syllogism 2)
> (3) denies the consequent—the conclusion is valid (see syllogism 3)
> (4) denies the antecedent—the conclusion is invalid (see syllogism 4)

Since arguments based on the topic of contradiction sometimes take the form of "either/or," or disjunctive, propositions, we might take a look at some of the principles governing this kind of deductive reasoning.

The issue in an argument might take this form: "Either he committed the murder, or he did not commit the murder." We recognize that these are the only two possibilities. Therefore, if one of the possibilities is disproved, the other one must be true. As anyone knows who has witnessed a fictional or real-life courtroom drama, it sometimes takes a protracted trial to prove or disprove one of the alternatives posed in our sample disjunctive proposition. But once we have proved one of the alternatives to be true, we automatically prove the other to be false.

In setting up the disjunctive proposition, however, we must take care to set up *mutually exclusive* alternatives. The proposition "He is either a student or a teacher" has the form of a disjunctive proposition, but the alternatives, the matter of the disjunctive statement, are not mutually exclusive. For he could be a teacher and a student in any one period. However, if we were to say, "Either he is a teacher, or he is not a teacher," we have set up mutually exclusive alternatives, for being a teacher and not being a teacher are the only two possibilities in this instance.

Exercise

Test the following syllogisms for validity. Wherever necessary, convert the propositions into the form of substantive terms on both sides of a copulative verb. Where no quantity word is expressed, presume that *All* precedes the subject term if the proposition is affirmative or that *No* precedes the subject term if the proposition is negative—e.g. *Men are not happy > No men are happy people*. Since the student should not be at all concerned with the truth of the propositions when he is testing a syllogism for validity, nonsense words or symbols will occasionally be used for the terms of the propositions.

1.   No out-of-state students are taxpayers.
      Some freshmen are out-of-state students.
      ∴ Some freshmen are taxpayers.

2.   All Catholics are Protestants.
      All Protestants are Baptists.
      ∴ All Catholics are Baptists.

3.   All typhoons are destructive windstorms.
      All cyclones are destructive windstorms.
      ∴ All cyclones are typhoons.

4.   All college graduates are potential wage-earners.
      No high-school graduates are college graduates.
      ∴ No high-school graduates are potential wage-earners.

5.   No Russians are democratic.
      All Americans are democratic.
      ∴ All Americans are Russians.

6.   All those who contribute to the Community Chest are charitable.
      John Smith does not contribute to the Community Chest.
      ∴ John Smith is not charitable.

7.   All horse-race betting is gambling.
      Some gambling is illegal.
      ∴ Some horse-race betting is illegal.

8.   Some Marines have been awarded the Distinguished Service Cross.
      No civilians have been awarded the Distinguished Service Cross.
      ∴ Some civilians are not Marines.

9.   Those who get good grades study diligently.
      All students are anxious to get good grades.
      ∴ All students study diligently.

10.   All brilligs are slithy toves.
      No slithy toves are borogoves.
      ∴ No borogoves are brilligs.

11.   No planets are suns.
        No planets are satellites.
        ∴ No satellites are suns.

12.   All cosmonauts are highly trained men.
        Some test pilots are not highly trained men.
        ∴ Some cosmonauts are not test pilots.

13.   All A is B.
        Some B is C.
        ∴ Some C is A.

14.   Some A is B.
        All B is C.
        ∴ Some C is A.

15.   Anything I possess is mine.
        I possess your pen.
        ∴ Your pen is mine.

16.   All contracts are based upon an agreement between two parties. The United Nations is based upon an agreement among several countries.
        Therefore the United Nations can also be classified as a contract.

17.   Because most Americans are industrious and all of them love free-dom, most industrious people love freedom.

18.   Since robins are two-legged creatures and since all birds are two-legged creatures, it follows that all robins are birds.

19.   Since only radicals want to subvert the duly constituted government of a country, this man can't be a radical because he wants to preserve the government of the country.

20.   Prabusks are certainly not panbuls. I know that because plocucks are panbuls and prabusks are plocucks.

The Enthymeme

Our treatment of the categorical, hypothetical, and disjunctive syllogisms was sketchy, but all the fundamentals were touched on. These fundamental principles should provide us with sufficient guidance for the construction or analysis of deductive reasoning according to the laws of formal logic. We have by no means exhausted all the facets and complexities of Aristotelian or scholastic logic, nor have we touched on symbolic logic, which has developed from the mathematical studies of men like Gottlob Frege, Alfred North Whitehead, and Bertrand Russell and from studies in semantics by men like C. K. Ogden, I. A. Richards, and Alfred Korzybski. But our primary concern is with rhetoric, and we can linger in the province of logic only long enough to gather some useful basic principles.

We turn now to a consideration of the enthymeme, which is the rhetorical equivalent of the syllogism. In modern times, the enthymeme has come to be regarded as an abbreviated syllogism—that is, an argumentative statement that contains a conclusion and one of the premises, the other premise being implied. A statement like this would be regarded as an enthymeme: "He must be a socialist because he favors a graduated income-tax." Here the conclusion (He is a socialist) has been deduced from an expressed premise (He favors a graduated income-tax) and an implied premise (either [a] Anyone who favors a graduated income-tax is a socialist or [b] A socialist is anyone who favors a graduated income-tax). Incidentally, the student who has developed some skill in analyzing the validity of syllogisms will detect that if the implied premise is [b], the conclusion (He is a socialist) is invalidly drawn because the middle term (anyone who favors a graduated income-tax) is undistributed in both of the premises of the fully reconstructed syllogism.

The modern notion of the enthymeme as a truncated syllogism is probably implicit in Aristotle's statement, "The enthymeme must consist of few propositions, fewer often than those which make up normal syllogism" (*Rhetoric,* I, 2). But according to what Aristotle said in the *Prior Analytics* (Bk. II, Ch. 27), the essential difference is that the syllogism leads to a necessary conclusion from universally true premises but the enthymeme leads to a tentative conclusion from probable premises. In dealing with contingent human affairs, we cannot always discover or confirm what is the truth. Think of how difficult it often is to prove that the defendant is guilty of the crime with which he is charged; how much more difficult it is to prove the wisdom or advantage of a future course of action—for instance, that a proposed tax cut will contribute to the general prosperity of the country. But frequently, in the interests of getting on with the business of life, we have to make decisions on the basis of uncertainties or probabilities. The function of rhetoric is to persuade, where it cannot convince, an audience. And in matters where the truth cannot be readily ascertained, rhetoric can persuade an audience to adopt a point of view or a course of action on the basis of the merely probable—that is, on the basis of what usually happens or what people believe to be capable of happening.

We can illustrate the difference by looking at a syllogism and an enthymeme. Our model syllogism is a good example of the kind of deductive reasoning that can lead to an irresistible conclusion. The major premise of that syllogism—"All men are mortal"—states a universal truth. Both history and the evidence of our own senses tell us that all men must die. The minor premise—"Socrates is a man"—is a truth that can be unmistakably verified. From these two "truths" then we can arrive at the infallible conclusion that Socrates too will die.

But suppose someone argues this way: "John will fail his examination because he hasn't studied." Here we have an enthymeme, both in the sense of a truncated syllogism and in the sense of a deductive argument based on probable premises. The truth of the minor premise here—"John hasn't studied"—could be confirmed. The probable premise resides in the unexpressed proposition—"Anyone who doesn't study will fail his examination." We all know that the latter proposition is not universally true. But we also know that those who do not study usually fail their examinations. It is, in other words, probable that those who do not study will fail. For all practical purposes, that probability is enough to persuade us that next week we will see John's name on the Dean's list of failures.

Aristotle was shrewd enough to see that we base persuasive arguments not only on what usually or generally happens but also on what people believe to be true. For that reason, the man who seeks to persuade a select audience must apprise himself of the generally held opinions of that group. If it is known, for instance, that a certain group of people believe that the Fire God causes the rainfall, someone could use that received opinion to persuade his audience that it is their failure to propitiate the Fire God that is responsible for the protracted drought. Every civilization has a body of accepted opinions that influence the conduct of its affairs—a body of "truths" which have never really been demonstrated but in which the people have faith, almost to the point of accepting them as self-evident.

The enthymeme then—"a kind of syllogism," as Aristotle puts it—is the instrument of deductive reasoning peculiar to the art of rhetoric. It often suppresses some of the links in the chain of argument because the audience is impatient with, or incapable of attending to, the kind of closely reasoned, full-scale argument associated with formal logic. And the audience can be satisfied with probable conclusions because it recognizes the contingent nature of the things that rhetoric deals with.

Since the enthymeme partakes of the nature of the syllogism, its mode of inference is similar to that of the syllogism. One of the premises may be missing, but the missing premise is as readily supplied as the missing parts of an elliptical grammatical structure. When we are seeking to refute someone else's enthymeme, it may be the missing premise that we should attack, because the implied proposition may be the vulnerable spot in the other man's argument.

For instance, take the enthymeme, "He must be a Communist because he advocates civil rights for minority groups." We cannot really judge the validity of the conclusion ("He must be a Communist") until we look at the implied premise. We might *sense* that the conclusion is unwarranted, but until we exposed the implied proposition, we could not demonstrate that the conclusion was unwarranted. We cannot determine, in other words, whether the conclusion follows logically until we study the conclusion in relation to the expressed premise *and* the implied premise.

What is the implied premise in this instance? In the discussion of the syllogism, we said that if we can determine which proposition in a deductive argument is the conclusion we can reconstruct the full syllogism. The minor term, we learned, is the subject of the conclusion; the major term is the predicate of the conclusion. Since "he" is the subject term of the conclusion, we know that the expressed premise (he advocates civil rights for minority groups) is the minor premise of the full syllogism. We also know that the major premise of the full syllogism will contain the predicate term of the conclusion ("a Communist"). But although we know that the implied premise will contain this term, we do not know for sure whether this major term is the subject term of the major premise or the predicate term of the major premise. The implied premise could take either of these forms:

> All Communists are advocates of civil rights for minority groups.
> All advocates of civil rights for minority groups are Communists.

It is important that we be able to determine which form the implied premise takes, because until we do so, we cannot determine whether and where the argument is vulnerable. If the person who advanced the enthymeme meant to imply that "all Communists advocate civil rights for minority groups," we would not have to spend our time discussing whether that proposition was true; we could very quickly point out that this argument is invalid because the middle term ("advocates of civil rights"), being the predicate term of two affirmative propositions, is undistributed. If our opponent did not understand what it meant to say that a term was "undistributed," we could point out to him that his argument had not established that only Communists advocate civil rights for minority groups. At bottom, this is the fallacy behind all assertions of guilt by association.

If, on the other hand, the implied premise is "All advocates of civil rights for minority groups are Communists," the reasoning will be valid, because now the middle term is distributed (*"All"* advocates). Hence we can impugn only the truth of the implied proposition. Is it true that anyone who advocates civil rights is a Communist? Whether we judged this proposition from the viewpoint of what is necessarily true (the province of strict logic) or from the viewpoint of what is probably true (the province of rhetoric), we would have to deny that this proposition is true. So although the argument in this case is valid, we would not grant the conclusion because the implied premise is patently false.

Aristotle said that the materials of enthymemes are *probabilities* and *signs*. We have already treated of the probable propositions, which constitute the premises of an enthymeme and which constitute, in Aristotle's eyes, the essential distinction between enthymemes and syllogisms. A sign is an indication or concomitant of something else; it may occur before or simultaneously with or after something else. Smoke, for instance, is a sign of fire; lightning is a sign that thunder is about to rumble; thunder is a sign that lightning has flashed. A sign is not a cause or reason for something else happening; it is merely an indication that something has happened, is happening, or will happen. Signs, like probabilities, can constitute the premises of an enthymeme.

Aristotle distinguished two kinds of signs that figure in an enthymeme—*infallible* and *fallible*. An infallible sign is that which invariably accompanies something else. It is said, for instance, that smoke invariably accompanies fire. Accordingly, whenever we see smoke or smell smoke we conclude that there is a fire someplace. And if it was really smoke we saw or smelled, there will of course *be* a fire someplace. Now, what makes a conclusion drawn from this kind of sign infallible is not only that smoke invariably accompanies fire but that smoke accompanies fire exclusively. If what we commonly know as smoke sometimes accompanied something else besides fire, we could not conclude infallibly that the presence of smoke was a sign of the presence of fire.

If a sign does not invariably and exclusively accompany something else, it is fallible—that is, any conclusion drawn from a sign of this kind will always be open to refutation. For instance, fast breathing is often a sign that a man has a fever. But because fast breathing does not always accompany a fever and because fast breathing sometimes attends other physical conditions, we cannot conclude infallibly that a man has a fever from the fact that he breathes rapidly. The condition of fast breathing would justify us in concluding that the man probably has a fever, but no more than that. The probability of his having a fever increases, of course, if the fast breathing is accompanied by other signs or symptoms of fever—high temperature, flushed cheeks.

Circumstantial evidence in a court trial is usually based on a series of fallible signs. The prosecuting lawyer reminds the jury of a number of suspicious circumstances: the accused was discovered with blood on his coat; his face was badly scratched; his shirt was torn; there was an ugly purplish bruise on his skin. "Are these not signs," the prosecutor asks the jury, "of a fierce physical struggle?" The prosecutor hopes that the jury mentally answers "yes" to his rhetorical question. Circumstantial evidence can never prove absolutely that a man is guilty, and for this reason many states will not allow the death penalty to be imposed on a man convicted by this evidence alone. But circumstantial evidence, especially when it has acquired cumulative force from the citation of a large number of incriminating particulars, can have great persuasive power with a jury.

So the rhetorician will use infallible signs for his enthymemes whenever such signs are available to him. But he will also use fallible signs, because he knows that they can have persuasive force. He will remain aware, however, that arguments built upon fallible signs are always open to challenge. Fallible signs are like analogies: they never prove, but they can persuade.

Let us stress again two points about the use of the rhetorical enthymeme: (1) it is important to ascertain the implied premise of an enthymeme, because the implied premise or assumption may be the vulnerable spot in the argument; (2) the probable propositions and the fallible signs used in rhetorical enthymemes do not lead to necessarily and universally true conclusions, but they can be effectively persuasive.

How may the student recognize an enthymeme when he meets one in ordinary discourse? Fortunately, enthymemes assume a fairly common syntactic pattern accompanied by a limited number of function words. Enthymemes often take the form of a compound sentence, the two clauses being joined by co-ordinating conjunctions *for* or *so* or linked logically by such conjunctive adverbs as *therefore, hence, consequently;* or they take the form of a complex sentence, the clauses being joined by such subordinating conjunctions as *since* or *because.*

Let us illustrate the syntactic form of the enthymeme by taking two propositions and linking them grammatically in a variety of ways to form an enthymeme. These are the two propositions:

> John Smith would not make a good governor. He has Communist leanings.

These two independent clauses, juxtaposed paratactically, could constitute an enthymeme. The context in which those two sentences occurred might suggest to the hearer or reader a logical relationship between the two statements: the second statement gives the grounds for the first assertion. An alert, sophisticated audience will readily detect the connection between these two statements. Rather than rely on the implied relationship, however, most speakers or writers will tie the two statements together explicitly. Note the various ways in which they could do this:

John Smith would not make a good governor, *for* he has Communist leanings.
　　　　　　　　　　　　　　　 because he has Communist leanings.
　　　　　　　　　　　　　　　 since he has Communist leanings.

John Smith has Communist leanings, *so* he would not make a good governor.

John Smith has Communist leanings; *therefore* he would not make a good governor.
　　　　　　　　　　　　　　　 consequently he would not make a good governor.
　　　　　　　　　　　　　　　 hence he would not make a good governor.

But not every sentence employing linking words like *for, because,* and *therefore* will constitute an enthymeme. Take, for instance, a statement like this: *He didn't go to the lecture last night, because he had a headache.* Here the *because*-clause merely gives a *reason* for his not going to the lecture; it is not a premise from which the conclusion is deduced. If we link the first statement with a different statement, however, we will have an enthymeme: *He didn't go to the lecture last night, so he must differ ideologically with the guest speaker.* Now the first statement becomes the ground or the premise for the inference stated in the second clause.

Sometimes there will be an ambiguity about the relationship of the clauses. Take this statement for instance: *He did not kill his mother because he loved her.* What is the import of this statement? Is this statement merely denying the reason given for the murder? It may mean something like this: he did not kill his mother because he loved her and wanted to relieve her of any further agony from her incurable disease; no, he killed her because he wanted to collect on her insurance. Or it may mean this: he loved his mother; therefore it is ridiculous to suggest that he killed her. If the statement means the latter, we would have a true enthymeme. The import of the statement depends upon whether the *because*-clause is *restrictive* or *non-restrictive*. If the clause is restrictive, we are denying the reason alleged for the crime. If the clause is non-restrictive, we are stating a premise upon which we have based our conclusion that he did not murder his mother. If we were speaking this sentence, we would indicate whether the clause was restrictive or nonrestrictive (and therefore the import of the entire statement) by some phonemic device of intonation. If we were writing that sentence, we could clarify the meaning by one of two courses: (1) recasting the sentence to remove the ambiguity; (2) putting a comma before *because* if the clause is non-restrictive or leaving the comma out if the clause is restrictive. Unless we *wanted* the statement to be ambiguous, it would probably be better to reword the sentence so that our meaning would be clear.

Speakers and writers will sometimes deliberately leave statements of this kind ambiguous. They sometimes seek to discredit someone by innuendo. If they render the relationship between statements vague, they may trap the audience into accepting an implication that is unwarranted by the facts. We must be alert enough to detect such chicanery and scrupulous enough not to employ such devious means ourselves. This is not to deny that ambiguity can be an effective and legitimate literary device, as in a poem, for instance.

Exercise

Expressions of deductive reasoning in practical discourse will most often take the form of the statements in the following Exercise—that is, the form of the enthymeme. In order to test the *truth* and the *validity* of the reasoning, convert these statements into a full syllogism, supplying the missing, implied premise. Sometimes the implied premise may take two forms, and in those cases, you will have to consider both forms of the premise. For instance, in the enthymeme "That must be a sour apple, because it's hard and green," the implied premise may be either (a) All hard and green apples are sour, or (b) All sour apples are hard and green. If the implied premise was (b), you would reject the conclusion because the reasoning is invalid (the middle term "hard and green" is undistributed in both premises). If the implied premise was (a), you might reject the conclusion because you did not agree that all hard, green apples are sour. Sometimes in reconstructing the full syllogism, you may have to rephrase the propositions, but if you do, be sure to preserve the sense of the original statement. For example, the enthymeme "Where would our country be today if it were not for our long tradition of free enterprise?" might be recast in this fashion:

> Anything which promotes prosperity is good.
> The free-enterprise system is something that promotes prosperity.
> Therefore, the free-enterprise system is good.

1. He must be happy, because he's smiling all the time.

2. A nuclear war is inevitable, for our sworn enemy, Communist China, now has the hydrogen bomb.

3. He would not take the crown. Therefore 'tis certain he was not ambitious. —Shakespeare, *Julius Caesar*, III, ii, 118.

4. Because 29.8 per cent of Thurber's sentences are simple sentences, we can say that a good part of his essay is easy to understand. —Student theme

5. Since you didn't speak up in my defense at the meeting, you must be as much against me as the rest of them are.

6. John definitely didn't drive the car home last night. He never puts the car in the righthand side of the garage.

7. No, the fuse isn't blown. It's the light bulb that is bad. When you flip the wall-switch, all the other lights in the room go on, don't they?

8. In your statement you assert that our actions, even though peaceful, must be condemned because they precipitate violence. —Martin Luther King, Jr., "Letter from Birmingham Jail"

9. Since the bullet obviously entered through his back, we have to rule out suicide; quite certainly he was murdered.

10. We must conclude that she's not a natural blonde. Otherwise, how do you explain those clearly visible black roots in her hair?

11. Blessed are the poor in spirit, for they shall see God.

12. The most convincing evidence that cigarette-smoking causes lung cancer is that the number of non-smokers who die from lung cancer is so minimal as to be negligible.

13. The Civilization of the Dialogue is the only civilization worth having and the only civilization in which the whole world can unite. It is, therefore, the only civilization we can hope for, because the world must unite or be blown to bits. —Robert M. Hutchins, "Morals, Religion, and Higher Education"

14. You've come a long way, baby. You can't deny that all those electrical appliances have freed you from slavery to your household.

15. My girl doesn't love me anymore. The last three times I called her for a date, she said she had to stay in and catch up on her schoolwork.

16. It is better to die, for death is gentler than tyranny. —Aeschylus, *Agamemnon*, lines 1450–51.

17. She must have lost her car keys somewhere between the check-out counter and the parking lot, because she remembers taking the keys out of her purse when she was paying her bill and laying them on the counter.

18. You say he's a great hitter. Hogwash! A great hitter doesn't strike out 113 times a season.

19. Since cultivation of mind is surely worth seeking for its own sake, there is a knowledge which is desirable, though nothing come of it. —John Henry Newman, *The Idea of a University*

20. How do I know that the "silent majority" is indeed a majority? Well, they elected a conservative President, didn't they?

The Example

All knowledge is acquired and all proof is achieved through either deduction or induction. The syllogism is the formal device that Aristotle invented to analyze and systematize deductive reasoning. The enthymeme, as we have just seen, is a kind of imperfect syllogism, which produces, not the conclusive demonstration that we get in science and logic, but belief or persuasion.

Just as deductive reasoning has its rhetorical equivalent in the enthymeme, so inductive reasoning has its rhetorical equivalent in the *example*. In induction we proceed from the particular to the general. Hence in a scientific demonstration or in logic we arrive inductively at a generalization through observation of a series of particulars. The validity and truth of the generalization will be in direct proportion to the *number* of pertinent particulars studied. The generalization, "Women are more careful drivers than men," will be "truer" and will be more validly derived if it was based on a study of the driving habits of a million men and women than if it was based on a study of only 100,000 men and women—presuming, of course, that the same criteria for carefulness were used in both studies.

The reason for the greater reliability of the generalization made from a number of instances is that there is less of an "inductive leap." Both deduction and induction make use of inference. The difference is that deduction makes inferences from *statements,* while induction makes inferences from *verifiable phenomena.* Induction leaps from known, observed facts, over an area of unknown, unobserved instances, to a generalization. The more facts or instances that are observed, the narrower will be the gap of the unknown that has to be leaped and accordingly the more reliable will be the generalization.

Aristotle realized that an orator addressing an audience could not adduce a whole series of particular instances to substantiate his generalization. A scientist of course must offer the supporting evidence of hundreds, even thousands, of experiments if he is to convince his colleagues of the validity of his generalization. But an orator has only a limited amount of time, and a writer has only a limited amount of space, to present their case to an audience, and they cannot risk boring their audience with an exhaustive catalogue of supporting evidence. Normally they will offer only one or two cogent examples to support their generalizations.

Let us illustrate the use of the rhetorical example by imagining the kind of argument that a senator might employ in trying to persuade his colleagues not to declare war against a neighboring country. The point that he wants to make, the generalization that he seeks to establish, is that waging war against a neighbor will prove disastrous for the country initiating the war. If he had time, he could recite from world history dozens of instances of how wars waged against neighbors proved to be disadvantageous to the country precipitating the conflict. Instead he cites a single example, analogous to the present situation, preferably one from American history and recent enough to be impressive. He might, for instance, cite the example of the Spanish-American War or the Mexican War. We can imagine his saying something like this:

> Look, it's true that we won this war, but consider the price we paid for waging war on a neighboring country. We disrupted our economy by expending millions of dollars to finance the invasion. We sent ten thousand young men to an early death, at a time when the labor market at home was ominously sparse. Millions of dollars worth of American property was damaged or destroyed. Besides, we alienated the good will of the dominant European powers. And instead of retaining an unaggrieved buffer state on our southern border, we produced at our threshold a hostile, vindictive nation that at the first opportunity would gladly enter into an alliance with any major power that sought to invade us. The price we paid for that war far exceeded the benefits we reaped. Gentlemen, I tell you that a war now against neighboring ——— would have equally disastrous consequences.

One of the strategies open to those senators who advocate going to war against the neighboring country would be to offer examples of other wars waged against neighbors which did *not* prove disastrous for the aggressor. Many considerations would determine which of these conflicting examples would produce more belief in the audience, but one of the considerations certainly would be the degree of similarity in the past and present situations.

An argument by example does not really prove anything, for like the rhetorical enthymeme, the example leads, most of the time, to a mere probability. But because a probability is what usually happens or what is believed to happen, the example has persuasive value. The example, of course, is always exposed to challenge and refutation. The opposition can counter with the reminder that on the grounds of strict logic a single example does not *prove* anything—no more than a single swallow makes a summer. Another way for the opposition to counteract the persuasive force of the example is, as we have pointed out, to cite another similar example where the outcome was just the opposite of the one cited. In such cases, the issue will be decided by a complex of attendant considerations: (1) the relative impressiveness and pertinence of the conflicting examples; (2) the persuasiveness of the other arguments offered in support of the contention; (3) the persuasiveness of the styles of the discourses; (4) the "ethical appeal" of the two men offering examples; (5) the force of the "emotional appeals"; (6) the emotional climate of the times. (See treatment of Example under topic of Testimony, pp. 144-45.)

The Fallacies

Before we quit this section on the logical modes of appeal, we should consider, at least briefly, the common fallacies in deductive and inductive reasoning. An awareness of these fallacies can be of help to us when we are seeking to refute arguments that oppose the position we maintain, and it can also prevent us from indulging in specious reasoning in our own discourses.

In common parlance, the word *fallacy* has two meanings: (1) a false, erroneous statement, an untruth; (2) invalid, specious, or deceptive reasoning. The first of these meanings has to do with the *matter* of the argument; the second, with the *form* or *mode* of argument. Formal logic is concerned primarily, although not exclusively, with the form of argument, but since *fallacy* denotes for most people a "false statement," we should say a few words about fallacious matter.

Fallacies of Matter

A false statement can be detected and refuted only if one knows what the truth is. The claim that the earth was the center of our solar system was not detected as a falsehood until Copernicus discovered the corrective fact: that the sun was the center of our universe. We may suspect a statement—as Copernicus must have suspected the Ptolemaic view of the universe—but we cannot disprove the statement until we have discovered the facts. One of the cardinal principles of argument is that the burden of proof rests upon the one who challenges the generally accepted view of things. Since most astronomers hold that human life as we know it does not exist on the other planets in our solar system—in other words, since the testimony of experts concurs—the burden of proof that there *is* life on these other planets rests on those who make the counterclaim. Man's exploration of outer space may turn up the "facts" that will either confirm or correct the generally received view.

Since truth is the only corrective of falsity, it is extremely important that all of us learn, through experience or education, as many facts about our world as are necessary for our effective and purposeful existence, or at least learn how and where to acquire facts. The man of inferior or inadequate knowledge will always be at a disadvantage in his dealings with other men. How often all of us have been frustrated in an argument by having to admit, "I can't discredit your assertion because at the moment I don't know the facts." If in the course of an argument about the rate of economic growth someone makes the telling point that at least a third of the families in the country have a total annual income of less than $2000, we cannot discredit that claim by saying simply, "That's not so." We can call for and challenge the source of a man's information, but we will most effectively undermine an assertion by adducing evidence that a claim is false. The next best thing to having the refutative information at our fingertips is to know where we might find the facts that will discredit our opponent's statement.

One point needs to be made very strongly here: mere assertion, on either side of an argument, does not constitute proof. It is amazing how often argument is conducted solely with assertions and counterassertions. Conducting an argument in this fashion is like two young boys standing toe to toe and shouting at one another, "My pa can lick your pa," "No, he can't," "Yes, he can," "Oh, yeah!" An argument like this gets nowhere, but a surprising number of people seem to think that it does. (Just take a look at the letters-to-the-editor column of your local newspaper.)

This is not to say that every time we make a categorical statement we need to substantiate our statement. There are some statements that most men regard as being self-evident—e.g. a whole is equal to the sum of all of its parts. The writers of the Declaration of Independence made some statements in the opening paragraphs of that document that they asserted were self-evident: "that all men are created equal," "that they are endowed by their Creator with certain unalienable rights." A self-evident proposition has been defined as a statement that all men or most men would immediately assent to once they understand the terms of the statement. Being self-evident, such statements do not have to be proved.

Another kind of statement that normally does not have to be proved is the statement regarded as "true by definition": "Two plus two equals four"; "Democracy is government of the people, by the people, and for the people"; "A majority is any plurality in excess of 50 per cent of the total number." Such statements are "true" in the sense that a consensus has defined them. Sometime in the future, consensus could establish that a majority was a plurality of 60 per cent of the total number. Most laws and statutes, for instance, can be regarded as "true by definition."

The third kind of statement that does not demand proof is the statement about matters that even the minimally informed person should know: "There are fifty states in the United States"; "All wage-earning adults in America must file an income-tax report once a year"; "A vast body of water separates North America from Europe." The nature of the subject matter and the composition of the audience will largely determine which statements of this kind need to be substantiated. Many statements about physics that might need to be substantiated for an audience of laymen would not have to be proved for an audience of physicists.

Nor should we demand more precision and accuracy in statements than the occasion demands. When our opponent claims that "150,000 home owners defaulted on their mortgage payments last year," we make ourselves appear silly by countering, "According to the Government Bureau of Statistics only 146,987 home owners defaulted on their mortgage payments last year." A corrective statement like this is mere punctilio and does nothing to advance our own argument or to weaken our opponent's argument. There are occasions, of course, when strict accuracy should be insisted on. When someone, in order to advance his argument, claims that the successful candidate for the office of the President received a clear majority of the electoral votes, it might be useful for our purposes to point out that the successful candidate had a margin of only 345,330 votes, a bare 0.1 per cent of the total popular vote, and that therefore he did not receive an overwhelming mandate from the people.

Beware also of the fallacy of the half-truth, which can be a particularly vicious but surprisingly effective tactic in argument. In the half-truth everything that is said is true, that is, verifiable as a fact; but because not enough is said, the total picture is distorted. Such omission of details conceals or distorts the context of a situation. Imagine someone seeking to impugn the loyalty of a nuclear scientist with a narrative like this: "For years Professor X carried on an active correspondence with top Soviet scientists. He subscribed to at least six Russian scientific journals. In 1956 he was observed having lunch in a New York restaurant with four Soviet scientists. In 1958 he took a trip to Moscow. A strange pattern of affinity with Soviet ideology, is it not?" Professor X did, and would admit that he did, everything ascribed to him here; but he would not admit the implications drawn from these facts. He would not admit the implications because a number of relevant facts that would put his relationship with Soviet scientists in the proper perspective have been omitted. He did correspond with Soviet scientists, but all of these letters were cleared by the State Department. He did subscribe to six Russian journals, but every scholar who wanted to keep up on the developments in science had to read the periodical literature from other countries. He did have lunch with four Russian scientists, but also present at that luncheon were four other American physicists, including Professor Y, whose loyalty no one called into question. The trip he took to Moscow in 1958 was sponsored by the Atomic Energy Commission after he had been cleared by an intensive investigation by the FBI.

This is a bald example of the fallacy of the half-truth, but its very obviousness helps to illustrate how more subtle examples of this fallacy operate. It shows how what is left unsaid can distort the total picture. It is for this reason that witnesses in court are made to swear that they will tell "the *whole* truth and nothing but the truth."

Because every categorical statement is, in a sense, unique, we can hardly do more here than lay down the general cautions and principles in regard to fallacies of matter. Each statement of a purported fact must be examined on its own terms and in its own context. The falsity of a statement—if the statement is false—can be detected and exposed only by one's knowledge of the facts. Mere assertion does not constitute proof, but not every statement needs to be substantiated. Nor should punctilious accuracy be insisted on where such precision is irrelevant or inconsequential. We should, however, bear in mind that by indulging in the half-truth we can, paradoxically, tell lies by speaking "nothing but the truth."

Fallacies of Reasoning

All fallacies of reasoning, whether inductive or deductive, could be classified as *non sequiturs*—that is, as conclusions or generalizations that "do not follow" from the premises. A logical fallacy is, at bottom, an instance of incoherence—the chain of reasoning does not link together.

Since we have dealt at length in previous sections with inductive and deductive *non sequiturs,* we will here merely list the fallacies, with a minimum of comment and with cross references to the sections where these fallacies have been elaborated on.

A. Fallacies of Reasoning in Deduction

1. *Equivocation:* This is the fallacy of using the same term with two or more meanings or referents. In syllogistic reasoning, equivocation introduces a fourth term into the process. No conclusion can be validly drawn from premises that have four terms. Equivocation could also invalidate inductive reasoning. If the referent of the term used to specify the particulars keeps shifting, no valid generalization can be made about the series of particulars. (See SYLLOGISM, pp. 65-67.)

2. *Undistributed Middle Term:* This common fallacy results basically from a failure to supply a link in the chain of arguments, a failure to establish that the major term and the minor term coincide. A diagram of one form of this fallacy will point up the missing link.

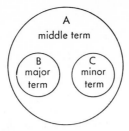

This arrangement of circles could be a schematic representation of an argument like the following:

> All Communists are people.
> All Americans are people.
> Therefore, all Americans are Communists.

The B and C circles are shown to be comprehended within the larger A-circle, but the C-circle does not fall inside the B-circle, nor does it even overlap the B-circle. In other words, the two premises have not established that there is any connection between B and C. That failure to establish a connection is the missing link in this kind of argument, and until the link is supplied, we cannot arrive at any conclusion. (See SYLLOGISM, p. 67.)

3. *Illicit Process:* This is the fallacy in which a term in the conclusion has a wider extension than it has in the premises; or, to put it another way, a term is distributed or universal in the conclusion, but was undistributed or particular in the premise. It stands to reason that we cannot draw any conclusion about *all men* if in the premises we have been talking only about *some men.* Such a conclusion simply "does not follow." (See SYLLOGISM, p. 67.)

4. *Conclusion from Two Negative Premises:* Because two negative premises establish no relationship among all three terms in a syllogistic chain of reasoning, no conclusion, either affirmative or negative, can be drawn. Negative premises exclude relationships. Unless one of the premises is affirmative so that it can include a relationship, we cannot validly arrive at any conclusion. (See SYLLOGISM, p. 65.)

5. *Affirmative Conclusion from a Negative Premise:* Since a negative premise excludes a relationship between two of the terms in a syllogism, the only kind of conclusion that can be arrived at logically is a proposition that excludes any relationship between one of these terms and a third term.

This is a diagrammatic representation of the following two premises, the X indicating the area specified by the second premise:

> No Russians are free men.
> Some Russians are atheists.

It should be apparent from the diagram that it is logically impossible to get the terms *free men* and *atheists* together in any kind of affirmative predication. There *may be* an affirmative relationship between *free men* and *atheists* (for instance, the area of the *atheist* circle that is outside the *Russian* circle could fall inside the *free men* circle). But that relationship has to be demonstrated; it cannot be inferred from this set of premises. From this set of premises, we can logically deduce only this conclusion: *Some atheists are not free men.* (Since the X-area is inside the *Russian* circle and since no part of the *Russian* circle is in the *free men* circle, it stands to reason that the X-area cannot be in the *free men* circle.) The moral of this explication: do not allow anyone, including yourself, to draw an affirmative conclusion from a negative proposition. (See SYLLOGISM,   p. 65.)

6. *"Either/Or" Fallacy:* This is a common fallacy of those who tend to judge life by a two-valued rather than a multi-valued system. Psychologists designate this tendency as the "black-or-white syndrome." There are some either/or situations from which we may draw valid inferences; the condition for valid inference is that the alternatives be exhaustive. If we start from the premise, "Either he voted for the candidate or he didn't vote for him," we can legitimately infer one alternative from the proof or disproof of the other alternative. We can make this inference validly because one or the other of the situations *must* exist. As the premise is phrased, no other situation is possible. But if we start from the premise, "Either he voted for the candidate or he voted for the candidate's opponent," we have not posed alternatives which take all the possible actions in the case into account. Voting for this or that candidate is not the only possibility; the man might not have voted at all or might have voted for a third candidate. So if we prove that he didn't vote for the candidate, we may not infer that he must have voted for the candidate's opponent; we have to go on to prove that he voted for the candidate's opponent. (See DISJUNCTIVE SYLLOGISM,   p. 70.)

7. *Fallacy of Affirming the Consequent:* This is the fallacy occurring in deductive reasoning that starts out with a hypothetical proposition. For example:

> If he makes concessions to the Russian ambassador, the prestige of the United States will decline.

The consequent is affirmed: "The prestige of the United States has declined." The fallacy now is the conclusion drawn from this affirmation of the consequent: "He must have made concessions to the Russian ambassador." That conclusion is clearly a *non sequitur.* (See HYPOTHETICAL SYLLOGISM, pp. 69-70.)

8. *Fallacy of Denying the Antecedent:* This is another fallacy that can occur in reasoning from hypothetical propositions. For example:

> If he captures the undecided votes, he will win the election.

The antecedent is denied: "He did not capture the undecided votes." The fallacy now is the conclusion drawn from this denial: "He did not win the election." This conclusion would follow if it had been established that the *only* way to win the election is to capture the undecided votes. We would have to start out with, and secure agreement on, this premise: "Only if he captures the undecided votes, will he win the election." (See HYPOTHETICAL SYLLOGISM, pp. 69-70.)

B. *Fallacies of Reasoning in Induction*

1. *Faulty Generalization:* We are liable to this fallacy when we "jump to a conclusion" from inadequate evidence. Evidence can be inadequate in a number of ways: (1) the particulars may be irrelevant; (2) the particulars may be unrepresentative; (3) the particulars may not be numerous enough to warrant the conclusion. All of these inadequacies concern evidence gathered by observation or study. Sometimes our generalizations are based on evidence derived from authority. Generalizations based on evidence derived from authority can be faulty when the authority quoted is (1) biased or prejudiced, (2) incompetent, (3) outmoded. Even when the authority quoted is objective, competent, and reliable, a generalization from the evidence supplied by this authority can be faulty if the authority is (1) inaccurately quoted, (2) misinterpreted, (3) quoted out of context. (See COMMON TOPICS, pp. 137-38.)

2. *Faulty Casual Generalizations:* These are fallacies to which all cause-and-effect inferences are liable. These fallacies can occur when we argue (1) from an effect to a cause or (2) from a cause to an effect. We offend in the first way (1) when we assign an inadequate cause to an effect; (2) when we

fail to take into account the fact that there could be more than one cause for the same effect. We offend in the second way (1) when we fail to establish that a potential cause of an effect could and did operate in a particular situation; (2) when we fail to take into account that the same cause can produce diverse effects. One of the commonest instances of faulty causal generalization is the fallacy commonly referred to as *post hoc, ergo propter hoc* ("after this, therefore because of this"). This fallacy results from the assumption that because there is a temporal relationship between events (something happened *after* something else) there is also a causal relationship—e.g. "Our sales shot up 25 per cent after we started using that musical jingle in our advertising campaign." The use of the musical jingle *may* have been a cause for the increase in sales. But we may not assume that it was a cause; we must prove that it was a cause. (See COMMON TOPICS, pp. 124-25.)

3. *Faulty Analogy:* Argument by analogy is always the most vulnerable of all modes of argument. It is always exposed to the charge, "The analogy does not hold." But some analogies are more vulnerable than others. They are especially vulnerable when they concentrate on irrelevant, inconsequential similarities between two situations and overlook pertinent, significant dissimilarities. The analogical argument, "Where there is smoke, there is fire," commonly used to throw suspicion on someone's character or activity, is frequently open to the objection that the persuasiveness of the similarities is weakened, if not entirely nullified, by the dissimilarities. While it is true that argument by analogy always rests on shaky ground, it is possible for someone to become so niggling in his attitude toward all analogy that he is liable to strain at a gnat and swallow a camel. Perhaps we can avoid this carping habit by remembering that an analogy never proves anything; at best, it persuades someone on the grounds of probability. It is the *degree* of probability that will be susceptible to challenge.

C. *Miscellaneous Fallacies*

A number of fallacies will be grouped here under the heading "Miscellaneous" because they are not peculiar to either inductive or deductive reasoning and because they are a blend of material fallacies, formal fallacies, and emotional fallacies.

1. *Begging the Question:* This fallacy (labelled *petitio principii* by the Scholastic logicians) is found more often in deductive reasoning than in inductive reasoning. Basically, this is the fault of circular reasoning. In syllogistic reasoning, for instance, this fallacy occurs when we assume in the premise the conclusion that we are trying to prove. A lawyer would be guilty of "begging the question" if he pleaded before a jury, "My client

would not steal because he is an honest man." We can more readily detect the *petitio principii* if we reconstruct the full chain of reasoning from the lawyer's enthymeme:

> Any man who is honest will not steal.
> My client is honest.
> Therefore, my client would not steal.

The second premise and the conclusion say the same thing in different words, because of the tautological definition set up in the first premise. The argument eddies around in a circle; it doesn't go anywhere. We get this same kind of circular argument in a sequence like this: "God exists." "How do you know that God exists?" "The Bible says so." "Why should I put my credence in what the Bible says?" "Because it's the inspired word of God." God is worthy of a more cogent argument than this.

One of the commonest and subtlest forms of this fallacy is the question-begging epithet: "This *murderer* should be put away for life." "We don't want any *controversial* figures as lecturers in this state." "This *creeping socialism* won't fool the American people." The occurrence of certain formulas should alert us that an instance of question-begging may be lurking in the verbiage. We should be on our guard whenever we meet expressions like "obviously," "of course," "as everyone knows," "really," "unquestionably." (Whenever you see one of these expressions in this textbook, take another look at the sentence in which these expressions occur to see whether what the author has said *is* obvious or unquestionable.)

2. *Argument* Ad Hominem *("to the man")*: This is a form of emotional argument, the fallacy of switching the argument from a discussion of issues to a discussion of personalities. If we find that we cannot refute a man's argument, we might attack his character. "My opponent's arguments are very impressive, but remember, this is the man who deserted his faithful wife and family after he had won his first political victory." Judged by its prevalence throughout history, this tendency to denigrate the character of one who espouses a cause or argument rather than to evaluate the cause or argument on its own merits seems to be natural to man. We sometimes see this sort of thing in literary criticism. Attention is diverted from the literary work itself to a discussion of the vicious character of the author; the work is assumed to be foul because the author is a notorious rake. As Alexander Pope said,

> Some judge of authors' names, not work, and then
> Nor praise nor blame the writings, but the men.
>
> *An Essay on Criticism,* II, 412-13.

A man's character can have some relevance to an argument—when, for instance, we are attempting to assess the reliability of his testimony or the likelihood of his having done something—but a discussion of a man's character becomes an irrelevancy—and thereby a form of fallacy—when such a discussion is used merely to distract attention from the issue at hand. Beware of the "poisoned spring" tactic.

3. *Argument* Ad Populum (*"to the people"*): This is another devious emotional appeal, similar to the argument *ad hominem*. This is the tactic of appealing to irrational fears and prejudices in order to prevent audiences from squarely facing the issues. Honorific terms—*Americanism, patriotism, motherhood, rugged individualism*—are used to stir up a favorable emotional climate; pejorative terms—*socialism, godlessness, radical, reactionary*—are used to arouse hostile reactions. None of these terms are "good" or "bad" in themselves. They become "weasel words" when they so color the emotional atmosphere of a discussion that men are disposed to accept as proven what has only been asserted. Appeals to emotions are legitimate—in fact, rhetoricians maintained that men often could not be moved to action unless their emotions were touched—but appeals to emotions are reprehensible when they cloud the issue, when they anesthetize men's rational faculties, when they move men to do things or accept things which they would not do or accept if their conscience or reason were allowed to operate.

4. *The "Red Herring"*: This is another diversionary tactic. "Red herring" is a term adopted from hunting and refers to the practice of dragging a herring across the trace in order to lead the hounds astray from their pursuit of the prey. The classical term for this fallacy is *ignoratio elenchi* (literally, "ignorance of the refutation"). This is another device, like the *ad hominem* or *ad populum* arguments, of ignoring or avoiding the issue. Backed into a corner in an argument, all of us are prone to steer the discussion to a side issue. "You accuse me of cheating on my income tax, but doesn't everybody cheat a little bit?" "So what if the general did lose that battle? Think of all his glorious victories in the past." The disputant who allows his opponent to "change the subject," to dodge the main issue, may soon find himself losing the argument because his opponent has shifted his position to safer ground.

5. *The Complex Question*: An oft-quoted example of this is the question, "When did you stop beating your wife?" It is impossible to give a simple answer to such a question without incriminating oneself. What is wrong here is that a question like this has two parts. It combines these questions:

"Do you beat your wife?" and "When did you stop beating her?" It is a form of question-begging. Just as a defending lawyer would jump to his feet to protest the prosecutor's question, "Why did you steal the diamond ring?" so anyone confronted with a two-pronged question should insist that the implicit question be dealt with first. "Wait a minute. Let's determine first whether I ever beat my wife." A familiar legislative practice is to attach riders to an important bill. When the bill is brought up for a vote, the legislator is faced with a dilemma. He may favor the main bill but object to the riders, or vice versa. But he is now placed in a situation where he has to accept or reject the whole package. In an argument, fortunately, we can insist that a complex question be dealt with part by part.

The Ethical Appeal

In the previous section we dealt at some length with the logical *pisteis,* the materials and methods of proof or persuasion that appeal to the reason. Ideally, men should be able to conduct a discussion or argument exclusively on the level of reason. But the rhetoricians were realistic enough to recognize that men are creatures of passion and of will as well as of intellect. We have to deal with men as they are, not as they should be. If we conceive of rhetoric as the art of discovering all the available means of persuasion, we will be disposed to make use of whatever effective (and, one would hope, legitimate) means lie open to us. As was pointed out earlier, Aristotle recognized a second means in the ethical appeal, the persuasive value of the speaker's or writer's character.

The ethical appeal can be the most effective kind of appeal; even the cleverest and soundest appeal to the reason could fall on deaf ears if the audience reacted unfavorably to the speaker's character. The ethical appeal is especially important in rhetorical discourse, because here we deal with matters about which absolute certainty is impossible and opinions are divided. Quintilian felt that of the three kinds of rhetorical discourse, deliberative oratory had the most need for the ethical appeal (he called it *auctoritas*). As Quintilian said, "For he who would have all men trust his judgment as to what is expedient and honourable, should possess and be regarded as possessing genuine wisdom and excellence of character."—*Institutio Oratoria,* III, viii, 13.

The ethical appeal is exerted, according to Aristotle, when the speech itself impresses the audience that the speaker is a man of sound sense (*phronēsis*), high moral character (*aretē*), and benevolence (*eunoia*). Notice that it is *the speech itself* which must create this impression. Thus a man wholly unknown to his audience (and this is often the case when we listen to a speech or read an article in a magazine) could by his words alone inspire this kind of confidence. Some men, of course, already have a reputation familiar to an audience, and this reputation, if it is a good one, will favorably dispose an audience toward a man, even before he utters a word. In the last analysis, however, it is the discourse itself which must establish or maintain the ethical appeal, for what a man says in any particular discourse could weaken or destroy his previously established reputation.

How does a man create the impression by his discourse that he is a man of sound sense, high moral character, and benevolence? The question is crucial; unfortunately, the answer must be couched in rather general terms. An obvious answer, of the general sort, is that a man must truly possess these qualities. "No one gives what he does not have," as the Latin maxim puts it. It is not the province of rhetoric, however, to form such a character—except perhaps in an indirect way. While it is true that the *whole* man is engaged in any communicative discourse, rhetoric can train only those faculties involved in the discovery, arrangement, and expression of ideas.

If we grant that a man strongly imbued with good sense, good moral fiber, and good will toward others will be disposed to conduct a discourse in a manner that will exert a strong ethical appeal, can we lay down any other positive precepts? Positive precepts, yes, but no more specific than the one just proposed. If a discourse is to exhibit a man's good sense, it must show that the speaker or writer has an adequate, if not a professionally erudite, grasp of the subject he is talking about, that he knows and observes the principles of valid reasoning, that he is capable of viewing a situation in the proper perspective, that he has read widely, and that he has good taste and discriminating judgment. If a discourse is to reflect a man's moral character, it must display a man's abhorrence of unscrupulous tactics and specious reasoning, his respect for the commonly acknowledged virtues, and his adamant integrity. If the discourse is to manifest a man's good will, it must display a man's sincere interest in the welfare of his audience and his readiness to sacrifice any self-aggrandizement that conflicts with the benefit of others.

It will help too if the discourse displays a man's sound knowledge of human psychology and his nice sense of appropriate style. He must be aware of the kind of *ēthos* that Aristotle talked about in Book II, Chapters 12-17 of the *Rhetoric*—the nature of various forms of government and the character of different periods of life (youth, middle age, old age) and of different conditions of life (wealth, poverty, education, illiteracy, health, sickness). Aware of the disposition of people at various ages and in various conditions of life, the speaker or writer will adapt his tone and his sentiments to fit his audience. Old men, for instance, do not think and act and view things in the same way that adolescents do. Young men are, by and large, quick-tempered, fickle, impetuous, idealistic; old men tend to be phlegmatic, conservative, deliberate, and pragmatic. Women react to certain things differently from men. Rich men and poor men view things in different ways. Men accustomed to a democratic way of life respond to certain sentiments and arguments in a different way from men brought up in a dictatorship.

The *whole* discourse must maintain the "image" that the speaker or writer seeks to establish. The ethical appeal, in other words, must be pervasive throughout the discourse. The effect of the ethical appeal might very well be destroyed by a single lapse from good sense, good will, or moral integrity. A note of peevishness, a touch of malevolence, a flash of bad taste, a sudden display of inaccuracy or illogic could jeopardize a man's whole persuasive effort.

But although the ethical appeal must be maintained by the discourse as a whole, there may be places in the discourse where the author will make a special overt attempt to establish his credit with his audience or to ingratiate himself with his audience. The two places in the discourse where authors commonly make such explicit overtures are the introduction and the conclusion. The author does not explicitly call attention to the fact that he is seeking to impress or conciliate his audience, but his effort to impress his audience is nonetheless obvious and calculated. The following quotation, from the opening paragraph of one of Benjamin Franklin's speeches, exemplifies just such an overt attempt:

> It is with reluctance that I rise to express a disapprobation of any one article of the plan, for which we are so much obliged to the honorable gentleman who laid it before us. From its first reading, I have borne a good will to it, and, in general, wished it success. In this particular of salaries to the executive branch, I happen to differ; and, as my opinion may appear new and chimerical, it is only from a persuasion that it is right, and from a sense of duty, that I hazard it. The Committee will judge of my reasons when they have heard them, and their judgment may possibly change mine. I think I see inconvenience in the appointment of salaries; I see none in refusing them, but on the contrary great advantages.

From Benjamin Franklin, *Speech in the Constitutional Convention on the Subject of Salaries*, June 2, 1787.

Franklin is about to argue against a proposal made to the Constitutional Convention, but he must dispose his audience to listen to his counterarguments. So he tries to show that he harbors no ill will toward the man who made the proposal ("for which we are so much obliged to the honorable gentleman who laid it before us"; "I have borne good will to it"); that he is motivated in his objection, not by partisan considerations but by principle ("from a persuasion that it is right, and from a sense of duty"); that he is not so cocksure of his own views that he is impervious to correction ("their judgment may possibly change mine"). The overall impression created by this brief overture is that of a modest, magnanimous, open-minded gentleman. Even his opponents in the assembly would be disposed to listen to his counterarguments.

Here is an example of a special attempt to exert an ethical appeal in the closing paragraph of a discourse:

> In this work, when it shall be found that much is omitted, let it not be forgotten that much likewise is performed; and though no book was ever spared out of tenderness to the author, and the world is little solicitous to know whence proceeded the faults of that which it condemns; yet it may gratify curiosity to inform it, that the *English Dictionary* was written with little assistance of the learned, and without any patronage of the great; not in the soft obscurities of retirement, or under the shelter of academic bowers, but amid inconvenience and distraction, in sickness and in sorrow. It may repress the triumph of malignant criticism to observe that if our language is not here fully displayed, I have only failed in an attempt which no human powers have hitherto completed. If the lexicons of ancient tongues, now immutably fixed, and comprised in a few volumes, be yet, after the toil of successive ages, inadequate and delusive; if the aggregated knowledge and cooperating diligence of the Italian academicians did not secure them from the censure of Beni; if the embodied critics of France, when fifty years had been spent upon their work, were obliged to change its economy and give their second edition another form, I may surely be contented without the praise of perfection, which, if I could obtain, in this gloom of solitude, what would it avail me? I have protracted my work till most of those whom I wished to please have sunk into the grave, and success and miscarriage are empty sounds: I therefore dismiss it with frigid tranquillity, having little to fear from censure or from praise.

> From Samuel Johnson, Preface to the *English Dictionary,* 1755.

Here a good deal of the ethical appeal is being exerted by the style, for this is certainly a magnificent piece of English prose. But Dr. Johnson is also making a deliberate effort to say those things about himself and his work that will leave his audience with a favorable opinion of him. Throughout the long discourse that preceded this final paragraph, Johnson had been explaining what he hoped to do in his *Dictionary,* what difficulties he faced in effecting his purpose, and what his successes and failures were. That elaborate exposition itself helped to create the impression of an intelligent, self-sacrificing, high-minded scholar. Here now in this final paragraph he makes an overt effort to reinforce the impression of himself. What comes through to the audience is a suitable blend of modesty and confidence, of regrets and self-gratulations, of animus and forgiveness.

It would be easy to find illustrations, in contemporary speeches, articles, and letters, of discourse that failed to create favorable impressions of the men who composed them. But since there is something uncharitable about publicly exposing someone, whether living or dead, as an example of an unprincipled, stupid, malevolent, or generally unprepossessing person, let us take as our example some fictitious person. Here is an excerpt from *Pride and Prejudice* in which Mr. Collins proposes marriage to Elizabeth Bennet:

> "My reasons for marrying are, first, that I think it a right thing for every clergyman in easy circumstances (like myself) to set the example of matrimony in his parish; secondly, that I am convinced it will add very greatly to my happiness; and thirdly—which perhaps I ought to have mentioned earlier—that it is the particular advice and recommendation of the very noble lady whom I have the honor of calling patroness. Twice has she condescended to give me her opinion (unasked too!) on this subject; and it was but the very Saturday night before I left Hunsford—between our pools at quadrille, while Mrs. Jenkinson was arranging Miss de Bourgh's footstool, that she said, 'Mr. Collins, you must marry. A clergyman like you must marry. Choose properly, choose a gentlewoman for *my* sake; and for your *own,* let her be an active, useful sort of person, not brought up high, but able to make a small income go a good way. This is my advice. Find such a woman as soon as you can, bring her to Hunsford, and I will visit her.' Allow me, by the way, to observe, my fair cousin, that I do not reckon the notice and kindness of Lady Catherine de Bourgh as among the least of the advantages in my power to offer. You will find her manners beyond anything I can describe; and your wit and vivacity, I think, must be acceptable to her, especially when tempered with the silence and respect which her rank will inevitably excite. Thus much for my general intention in favor of matrimony; it remains to be told why my views were directed to Longbourn instead of my own neighbourhood, where I assure you there are many amiable young women. But the fact is that being, as I am, to inherit this estate after the death of your honoured father (who, however, may live many years longer), I could not satisfy myself without resolving to choose a wife from among his daughters, that the loss to them might be as little as possible, when the melancholy event takes place—which, however, as I have already said, may not be for several years. This has been my motive, my fair cousin, and I flatter myself it will not sink me in your esteem. And now nothing remains for me but to assure you in the most animated language of the violence of my affection. To fortune I am perfectly indifferent, and shall make no demand of that nature on your father, since I am well aware that it could not be complied with; and that one thousand pounds in the four per cents, which will not be yours till after your

mother's decease, is all that you may ever be entitled to. On that head, therefore, I shall be uniformly silent; and you may assure yourself that no ungenerous reproach shall ever pass my lips when we are married."

From Jane Austen, *Pride and Prejudice,* Chapter 19.

There is certainly a rhetorical situation set up here in this scene from an early nineteenth-century novel: a man seeking to induce a young woman to marry him. Though an appeal to reason is hardly negligible at a time like this, emotions probably play a more important part in bringing two people to such a decision. And if there is ever a time when a man's ethical appeal must be strong, it is the moment when he proposes. Presumably, a man has been exerting an ethical appeal throughout the relationship, but when he comes to the moment of actually proposing marriage he can hardly wish to say anything that will destroy the girl's good opinion of him.

This speech provides a classic example of a man who intends to convey a favorable impression of himself but succeeds only in discrediting himself by what he says and the manner in which he says it. There are two audiences for Mr. Collins's speech: Elizabeth and the reader. Jane Austen clearly intends to reveal Mr. Collins for the pompous, self-righteous, egocentric timeserver that he is, but we cannot presume that Elizabeth will react in exactly the same way as we do to Mr. Collins's speech. We must make some allowances for the mores of the age and for the kind of person Elizabeth herself is. A young girl of that time would expect a man to propose to her in the highly formal language that Mr. Collins uses, and she would probably not have been as unfavorably impressed as we are by Mr. Collins's mercenary considerations.

But even when all these allowances are made for the differences in the reactions of the two audiences for the speech, we cannot believe that after this exposure of Mr. Collins's motives Elizabeth could regard him as a man of "good sense, good will, and high moral character." She had developed an antipathy for him before this moment which this display of rhetoric could do nothing but confirm. Hence, we are not at all surprised at the firmness and forthrightness of her rejection of Mr. Collins: "I am perfectly serious in my refusal. You could not make *me* happy, and I am convinced that I am the last woman in the world who would make you so." And if we the readers needed any further confirmation of our unfavorable impression of him we could turn to that delightfully obnoxious letter of condolence that he sends to the Bennet family in Chapter 48 upon the occasion of Lydia's elopement.

There is no denying the role that the ethical appeal plays in the persuasive process. In a sense, the ethical appeal is the "hidden persuader." In our world, such enterprises as public relations, motivational psychology, market research, and advertising, are engaged in searching for effective stimuli and in creating the proper "image." The groundwork for all of this activity was laid by Aristotle two thousand years ago.

Aristotle discussed the ethical appeal, not only because he recognized how vital it was in persuasion but also because he wanted to answer the enemies of rhetoric, like Socrates, who complained that rhetoricians sanctioned any kind of shallow knowledge, sophistical reasoning, and unscrupulous tactics that would gain the end of persuasion. If persuasion depends greatly, even pre-eminently, on ethical appeal, the persuader cannot afford to create the impression by his discourse that he is superficial, immoral, or malicious. Cicero and Quintilian, with their insistence on "the good man speaking," may have given greater emphasis to the importance of the ethical image than Aristotle did, but they were not supplying a note that Aristotle had entirely neglected.

The Emotional Appeal

The third mode of persuasion specified by Aristotle and recognized by all later rhetoricians is the appeal to the emotions of the audience. People are rather sheepish about acknowledging that their opinions can be affected by their emotions. They have the uneasy feeling that there is something undignified about being stirred to action through the emotions. And indeed, in some cases, there is something undignified about a rational man being precipitated into action through the stimulus of his aroused passions. All of us at one time or another have been ashamed of something we did under the pressure of strong emotion. The source of our shame was not so much that we had been prompted to action by our emotions as that we had done something regrettable. We are not ashamed of falling in love, even though the act of falling in love is prompted by strong emotion. But we are ashamed of hurling a vase against the wall in a fit of anger. What makes the difference here is the consequences of our emotional stress. Because falling in love was "good," we felt no compunction; because smashing the vase was "evil," we were ashamed of our impulsive act.

There is nothing necessarily reprehensible about being moved to action through our emotions; in fact, it is perfectly normal. Since it is our will ultimately that moves us to action and since the emotions have a powerful influence on the will, many of our actions are prompted by the stimulus of our emotions. When it is not pure emotion that prompts our will, it is a combination of reason and emotion. This fact has a great bearing on the strategies of rhetoric. George Campbell, the eighteenth-century Scottish rhetorician, made a strong claim for the important part that emotions play in the persuasive process: "So far, therefore, is it from being an unfair method of persuasion to move the passions, that there is no persuasion without moving them."—*Philosophy of Rhetoric,* Book I, Ch. VII.

Richard Whately, the nineteenth-century English rhetorician, analyzed the persuasive process this way: "For in order that the Will may be influenced, two things are requisite: (1) that the proposed Object should appear desirable; and (2) that the Means suggested should be proved to be conducive to the attainment of that object."—*Elements of Rhetoric,* Part II, Ch. I. It is argument (the appeal to the understanding) that produces conviction about the conduciveness of the means to the desired end; it is the appeal to the emotions that makes the end seem desirable. In order to whip up a people into a mood for war, one would have to do two things: (1) remind the people that the freedom and security of a nation is a desirable end; (2) convince them that going to war is the best means of securing this end. The order of these two activities can vary. Sometimes it will be better to excite the desire first and then show that there is some connection between the proposed action and the end; at other times, it will be more expedient to convince the understanding first and then stir up the emotions.

Do not some men play on people's emotions for unscrupulous purposes? Of course they do. All of us could tick off a half dozen examples from history without much strain on the memory. The fact that some men exploit the emotions for unscrupulous purposes may constitute a caution about the use of emotional appeal, but it does not constitute a condemnation of emotional appeal. Some men use sophistical arguments, but we do not therefore condemn all argument as a means of effecting conviction.

An important consideration for rhetoric is that our emotions are not under the direct control of volition. We cannot *will* ourselves into being angry against someone. On the other hand, our intellectual faculties, reason and memory, are under the direct control of our will. We can, by an act of the will, force ourselves to recall historical facts, to engage in calculation, to analyze a whole, or to synthesize parts.

There are two consequences for rhetoric from the fact that our will does not have direct control of our emotions. The first consequence is that it is perilous to announce to an audience that we are going to play on the emotions. As soon as we apprize an audience of such an intention, we jeopardize, if we do not entirely destroy, the effectiveness of the emotional appeal. It is not so with appeals to the understanding. It is frequently advantageous to announce to an audience that we are about to embark upon a course of reasoning. Accordingly, we have no hesitation about calling attention to the conclusion we hope to establish, to the steps we will take in proving our point, or to our method of arguing.

The second consequence for rhetoric is that we must get at the emotions indirectly. We cannot arouse an emotion, either in ourselves or in others, by thinking about it. We arouse emotion by contemplating the object that stirs the emotion. So if we seek to arouse the anger of an audience, we must describe a person or a situation of a sort that will make the audience angry. The anger can be enkindled even when the description is quite dispassionate. Horace's precept that if you want me to feel an emotion, you must first feel that emotion yourself (*si vis me flere, dolendum est primum ipsi tibi*) is basically sound, but it is possible to feel an emotion without displaying it extravagantly. In fact, there will be times when the more dispassionate the emotion-provoking description is, the more intense will be the emotion aroused.

Here is a good example of how to stir an emotional response in the audience by describing a scene. Appealing to the patriotism of his English audience, Macaulay wants to arouse their righteous indignation against the arrogant, cruel, despotic Surajah Dowlah, so that he can subsequently justify the punitive expedition that Lord Clive led against the Indian colony. He might have described this same scene in such a way as to stir an Englishman's pride in the bravery of the colonial troops. But here he describes the scene in such a way as to arouse the audience's anger against the native troops and their commander. Here is Macaulay's account of the infamous episode of the Black Hole of Calcutta:

> Then was committed that great crime, memorable for its singular atrocity, memorable for the tremendous retribution by which it was followed. The English captives were left to the mercy of the guards, and the guards determined to secure them for the night in the prison of the garrison, a chamber known by the fearful name of the Black Hole. Even for a single European malefactor, that dungeon would, in such a climate, have been too close and narrow. The space was only twenty feet square. The air-holes were small and obstructed. It was the summer solstice, the season when the fierce heat of Bengal can scarcely be rendered tolerable to natives of England by lofty halls and by the constant waving of fans. The number of the prisoners was one hundred and forty-six. When they were ordered to enter the cell, they imagined that the soldiers were joking; and, being in high spirits on account of the promise of the Nabob to spare their lives, they laughed and jested at the absurdity of the notion. They soon discovered their mistake. They expostulated; they entreated; but in vain. The guards threatened to cut down all who hesitated. The captives were driven into the cell at the point of the sword, and the door was instantly shut and locked upon them.
>
> Nothing in history or fiction, not even the story which Ugolino told in the sea of everlasting ice, after he had wiped his bloody lips on the scalp of his murderer, approaches the horrors which were recounted by the few survivors of that night. They cried for mercy. They strove to

burst the door. Holwell, who, even in that extremity, retained some presence of mind, offered large bribes to the gaolers. But the answer was that
nothing could be done without the Nabob's orders, that the Nabob was
asleep, and that he would be angry if anybody woke him. Then the prisoners went mad with despair. They trampled each other down, fought
for the places at the windows, fought for the pittance of water with which
the cruel mercy of the murderers mocked their agonies, raved, prayed,
blasphemed, implored the guards to fire among them. The gaolers in the
meantime held lights to the bars, and shouted with laughter at the frantic
struggles of their victims. At length the tumult died away in low gaspings
and moanings. The day broke. The Nabob had slept off his debauch, and
permitted the door to be opened. But it was some time before the soldiers
could make a lane for the survivors, by piling up on each side the heaps
of corpses on which the burning climate had already begun to do its
loathsome work. When at length a passage was made, twenty-three
ghastly figures, such as their own mothers would not have known, stag-
gered one by one out of the charnel-house. A pit was instantly dug. The
dead bodies, a hundred and twenty-three in number, were flung into it
promiscuously and covered up.

From Thomas Babington Macaulay, "Lord Clive," *Critical and
Historical Essays,* 1843.

The kind of description calculated to stir emotion in the audience must
appeal to the imagination, and the imagination can be seized in this kind of
word-painting by the use of sensory, specific detail. Macaulay makes generous use of sensory detail in his description, and characteristically, he drama-
tizes the scene in order to increase its emotional impact. But unfortunately
he is not content to let a vivid reporting of the scene create the desired emotional effect. He tries to excite an extra pulse of emotion by editorializing on
the scene ("Nothing in history or fiction...") and loading his description
with hyperbolic, provocative words ("great crime," "singular atrocity,"
"loathsome work," "ghastly figures"). By contrast, note how Mark Antony
speaking after Caesar's assassination arouses the anger of his audience:

You all do know this mantle. I remember
The first time ever Caesar put it on.
'Twas on a summer's evening, in his tent,
That day he overcame the Nervii.
Look, in this place ran Cassius' dagger through.
See what a rent the envious Casca made.
Through this the well-beloved Brutus stabbed,
And as he plucked his cursed steel away,
Mark how the blood of Caesar followed it,
As rushing out of doors, to be resolved

If Brutus so unkindly knocked, or no.
For Brutus, as you know, was Caesar's angel.
Judge, O you gods, how dearly Caesar loved him!
This was the most unkindest cut of all,
For when the noble Caesar saw him stab,
Ingratitude, more strong than traitors' arms,
Quite vanquished him. Then burst his mighty heart,
And, in his mantle muffling up his face,
Even at the base of Pompey's statue,
Which all the while ran blood, great Caesar fell.

William Shakespeare, *Julius Caesar*, III, ii.

Mark Antony does not bid the mob, "Be angry, ye citizens of Rome!" Nor does he seek to arouse the anger of the mob by calling the assassins "scoundrels" and "traitors." Rather, he makes the people contemplate the bloody, dagger-rent mantle that Caesar wore the day he was killed. It is the sight of this object, dramatically displayed, its significance evoked by Antony's pathetic comments, and followed by Antony's incendiary comments on the brutality and ingratitude of the deed, that whips the people up into a frenzy of vindictive anger.

We have just seen two examples of how to arouse an emotional response in an audience by a vivid description of a scene. There's another method that speakers and writers use to stir emotions, which is not as dependable as the method we have been describing. This second method does not so much "earn" an emotional response as it "begs" for it. This is the method that relies for its effect mainly on the use of emotion-laden words. The author makes use of those honorific or pejorative terms, of those favorable or unfavorable connotations of words, that will touch an audience. Here is how Edmund Burke tried to stir his reader's resentment against the revolutionary mob that stormed the royal palace at Versailles at the beginning of the French Revolution in 1789 and seized the Queen, Marie Antoinette:

It is now sixteen or seventeen years since I saw the queen of France, then the dauphiness, at Versailles; and surely never lighted on this orb, which she hardly seemed to touch, a more delightful vision. I saw her just above the horizon, decorating and cheering the elevated sphere she just began to move in—glittering like the morning-star, full of life, and splendor, and joy. Oh! what a revolution! and what a heart must I have, to contemplate without emotion that elevation and that fall! Little did I dream when she added titles of veneration to those of enthusiastic, distant, respectful love, that she should ever be obliged to carry the sharp antidote against disgrace concealed in that bosom; little did I dream that I should have lived to see such disasters fallen upon her in a nation of

gallant men, in a nation of men of honour and of cavaliers. I thought
ten thousand swords must have leaped from their scabbards to avenge
even a look that threatened her with insult.—But the age of chivalry is
gone.—That of sophisters, economists, and calculators, has succeeded; and
the glory of Europe is extinguished forever. Never, never more, shall we
behold that generous loyalty to rank and sex, that proud submission, that
dignified obedience, that subordination of the heart, which kept alive,
even in servitude itself, the spirit of an exalted freedom. The unbought
grace of life, the cheap defence of nations, the nurse of manly sentiment
and heroic enterprise is gone! It is gone, that sensibility of principle, that
chastity of honour, which felt a stain like a wound, which inspired courage whilst it mitigated ferocity, which ennobled whatever it touched, and
under which vice itself lost half its evil, by losing all its grossness.

From Edmund Burke, *Reflections on the Revolution in France*, 1790.

Edmund Burke starts to picture the Queen so that the audience can contemplate her and feel the same emotion that he feels for her. But her picture never emerges through the blaze of Burke's "rhetoric." She glitters
on the horizon "like the morning-star," but we never really get to see her.
Instead, Burke takes over and stirs up our emotions with the grandiloquent
rhythm of his prose and with his litany of honorific terms ("titles of veneration," "men of honour," "gallant men," "age of chivalry," "generous loyalty,"
"proud submission," "dignified obedience," "chastity of honor," etc.). It is
somewhat unfair to pluck this purple patch out of its context, because when
one sees it in its setting in the long pamphlet that Burke wrote, it does not
strike the reader as being so blatantly sentimental as it appears in isolation.
But the passage does illustrate very well what a man skilled in the choice
and manipulation of words can do to the emotions of his audience.

When Aristotle turns to a consideration of the emotions in Book II, Chap
ters 2-17 of the *Rhetoric*, he intends to supply the student of rhetoric with
topics for an appeal to the emotions of an audience. Taking some of the
common emotions, in pairs of opposites—e.g. anger and meekness, love and
hatred, fear and boldness, shame and shamelessness—he analyzes these emotions from three angles: (1) their nature; (2) their object—that is, the kind
of people toward whom we experience the emotion; (3) their exciting causes.
Aristotle claims that we must know all three things about an emotion if we
hope to arouse it in others.

This analysis is one of the earliest attempts at psychology. Admittedly,
Aristotle's psychology is primitive and inchoate. John Locke and such eighteenth-century Scottish philosophers as David Hume, Thomas Reid, Francis
Hutcheson, and Lord Kames made great advances over Aristotle's primitive
psychology; and of course the major modern advances in psychology were

begun by Sigmund Freud. But Aristotle's analysis of the emotions can be of value to the student who is not professionally trained in psychology, because his analysis was sound as far as it went and was based on the kind of commonsense observation of people that even the amateur is capable of making. From our knowledge of our own emotional mechanism and from our observation of the emotional reactions of others, we are familiar enough with the common emotions to be able to manipulate them for persuasive purposes.

The student should read Aristotle's analysis of the emotions in Book II of the *Rhetoric*. What we can do here is quote some excerpts from Aristotle's analysis of anger to show the elementary level and astuteness of Aristotle's non-professional observations about human emotions. As the student reads these excerpts, he should pause occasionally to ask himself how well these observations accord with his own observations of angry people.

> Anger may be defined as an impulse, accompanied by pain, to a conspicuous revenge for a conspicuous slight directed without justification towards what concerns oneself or towards what concerns one's friends. If this is a proper definition of anger, it must always be felt towards some particular individual, e.g. Cleon, and not 'man' in general.... It must always be attended by a certain pleasure—that which arises from the expectation of revenge. For since nobody aims at what he thinks he cannot attain, the angry man is aiming at what he can attain, and the belief that you will attain your aim is pleasant.... It is also attended by a certain pleasure because the thoughts dwell upon the act of vengeance, and the images then called up cause pleasure, like the images called up in dreams.
>
> [A discussion of slighting follows, since it is the slight that excites anger.] Now slighting is the actively entertained opinion of something as obviously of no importance.... There are three kinds of slighting— contempt, spite, and insolence. (1) Contempt is one kind of slighting: you feel contempt for what you consider unimportant, and it is just such things that you slight. (2) Spite is another kind; it is a thwarting another man's wishes, not to get something yourself but to prevent his getting it.... (3) Insolence is also a form of slighting, since it consists in doing and saying things that cause shame to the victim, not in order that anything may happen to yourself, or because anything has happened to yourself, but simply for the pleasure involved.... The cause of the pleasure thus enjoyed by the insolent man is that he thinks himself greatly superior to others when ill-treating them.... A man expects to be specially respected by his inferiors in birth, in capacity, in goodness, and generally in anything in which he is much their superior: as where money is concerned a wealthy man looks for respect from a poor man; where speaking is concerned, the man with a turn for oratory looks for respect from one who cannot speak: the ruler demands the respect of the ruled,

and the man who thinks he ought to be a ruler demands the respect of the man whom he thinks he ought to be ruling....

... The persons with whom we get angry are those who laugh, mock, or jeer at us, for such conduct is insolent. Also those who inflict injuries upon us that are marks of insolence.... Also those who speak ill of us and show contempt for us, in connexion with the things we ourselves most care about: thus those who are eager to win fame as philosophers get angry with those who show contempt for their philosophy; those who pride themselves upon their appearance get angry with those who show contempt for their appearance; and so on in other cases.... Again, we are angrier with our friends than with other people, since we feel that our friends ought to treat us well and not badly. We are angry with those who have usually treated us with honour or regard, if a change comes and they behave to us otherwise: for we think that they feel contempt for us or they would still be behaving as they did before.... Further, with those who slight us before five classes of people: namely, (1) our rivals, (2) those whom we admire, (3) those whom we wish to admire us, (4) those for whom we feel reverence, (5) those who feel reverence for us: if anyone slights us before such persons, we feel particularly angry....

The persons with whom we feel anger, the frame of mind in which we feel it, and the reasons why we feel it, have now all been set forth. Clearly the orator will have to speak so as to bring his hearers into a frame of mind that will dispose them to anger, and to represent his adversaries as open to such charges and possessed of such qualities as do make people angry.

Rhetoric, Book II, Chapter 2, trans. W. Rhys Roberts. Reprinted by permission of the Clarendon Press, from *The Works of Aristotle,* ed. W. D. Ross, Volume XI.

The point to make about Aristotle's analysis of the emotions—or any other analysis of emotions for that matter—is that after the student has read the analysis he should "forget" about it. He should "forget" about it in the same sense that someone who has read a "how-to" book about batting should forget what he has read when he takes a bat in hand and starts swinging at the ball. The student will not really forget what he has read; he will unconsciously incorporate what he has learned about the emotions into his appeal. This is just another way of urging the student to "be natural." All of us, to one degree or another, continually appeal to the emotions of others. From our dealings with our fellow men and from our experience with our own emotional reactions, we develop certain instincts about the emotions. It is upon these instincts that we draw when we make an emotional appeal.

Some people's instincts along these lines are more fully developed than other people's. When we say of someone that he has "quite a line" or that he is a "smooth operator," we are probably paying tribute to his natural or developed talent for producing the right emotional touch at the right time.

Making a conscious study of the emotions and being aware that we are appealing to someone's emotions will not necessarily make us more adept at this kind of appeal. But a conscious knowledge of any art makes it more *likely* that we will practice the art skillfully. The man who learned to play the piano by ear will not be hurt by studying music; but he might very well be helped to play better.

To sum up what we have said about the emotional appeal: Be aware that the emotional appeal plays a vital part in the persuasive process; intellectual conviction is often not enough to move people's will to act. Be alert for emotional appeals from others; don't allow your heart to prompt you to do something that your reason or conscience would later regret. Be natural; let the nature of the subject matter, the occasion, or the audience elicit the appropriate kind and the right amount of emotional appeal. Remember that you cannot command yourself or others to feel emotions; you must conjure up the scene or situation or person that will make people experience the emotions you want to rouse in them. Be aware—as will be pointed out again in the chapter on Arrangement—that people sometimes have to be put into the right emotional mood before they will listen to appeals to reason; at other times it is better to start out with appeals to reason and then rouse the audience to the proper emotional pitch in a grandiloquent peroration.

The Topics

Once the student has a subject and has converted it into a sharply defined thesis, he is faced with the task of developing that subject. If he is engaged in persuasive discourse, he must find "arguments" to develop his subject. In the preceding section we saw that anyone bent on persuading others makes use of one or more of the three modes of appeal—the appeal to reason, the appeal to emotions, the appeal of character. If he decides to make use of the appeal to reason, he will develop his arguments inductively or deductively. If he argues deductively, he will resort to the syllogism or, more likely, the enthymeme. If he argues inductively, he will resort to full induction or the example. But for any of these modes of appeal, whether it be logical, emotional, or ethical, he must either *have* something to say or *find* something to say.

Sometimes, from his experience, his education, or his reading, the student will already have something to say. On many of the subjects he is asked to write about in college classes, the student is able to write a 500- to 800-word theme quite readily, for he has a sufficient stock of ideas on those subjects to be able to write, as it were, "off the top of his head." He is most likely to have a great deal to say when he feels very strongly about something, for then ideas seem to come to him unbidden.

In this chapter, however, we are concerned with the problems of the student who does not have, or thinks he does not have, something to say on some given subject. A student can be said to have "nothing to say" when he has (1) no ideas at all on a subject, (2) only a few ideas or not enough ideas to develop a subject adequately, or (3) a mass of vague, jumbled, inaccurate, or untenable ideas. Such a student has to *find,* to *discover,* or, to use the rhetorical term, to *invent* his material. Some measure of *invention* will be involved in all four forms of discourse—exposition, argumentation, description, and narration. But invention figures most prominently in expository and argumentative discourse, because in description or narrative discourse the writer has more occasion to "create" his material than to "invent" it.

What are the student's resources when he has to find his material? His chief resources will always be the fruits of his education, his reading, his observation, and his reflection. Both Cicero and Quintilian maintained that the most valuable background for an orator was a liberal education, because they recognized that such a broad education was best calculated to aid a man faced with the necessity of inventing arguments on a wide variety of subjects.

But wide and varied experience, reflection, education, and reading come only with time and effort. What about the student who has not yet reaped the benefits of experience and study? Is he condemned to be inarticulate? Is there some system that can supply the deficiencies of his resources? The rhetoricians thought that there was such a system in the *topics.*

As we saw in the section of Chapter I devoted to definitions of key terms, the topics were the general heads under which were grouped arguments for a particular subject or occasion. They were the "regions," the "haunts," the "places" where certain categories of arguments resided. There was some sense to the attempt by Peter Ramus and his followers in the seventeenth century to relegate the topics to the province of logic, for the system of the topics is really an outgrowth of the study of how the human mind thinks. The human mind, of course, does think about particular things, but its constant tendency is to rise above the particulars and to abstract, to generalize, to classify, to analyze, and to synthesize. The topics represented the system that the classical rhetoricians built upon this tendency of the human mind.

The rhetoricians saw, for instance, that one of the tendencies of the human mind is to seek out the nature of things. So they set up the topic of Definition. Another tendency of the human mind is to compare things, and when things are compared, one discovers similarities or differences—and the differences will be in kind or in degree. When one is presented with a subject, one then looks at it to find out whether, for one's specific purpose, it presents an opportunity for definition or comparison.

Perhaps the student will gain a clearer notion of the function of the topics if he will think of the topics as "suggesters," as "prompters," as "initiators," as a "checklist," of ideas on some subject. Being general heads or categories, the topics "prime the pump," as it were; by suggesting general strategies of development, they help to overcome inertia. Just as the starter on an automobile turns the motor over until the compression system takes over, so the topics initiate a line of thought, which then moves forward on its own momentum.

One of the terms we used in the previous paragraph to clarify the function of the topics was "checklist." The term "checklist" suggests that one goes through the list of topics, one by one, asking oneself whether this particular topic will turn up any material for the development of our subject. In the beginning stages, the student may very well have to do just this. He will eventually discover, however, that some of the many available topics will not be suitable for certain situations. The football coach does not go to his bench indiscriminately when he needs a substitute. He calls from the bench the man who has been trained for a particular position and who can best serve the particular situation that has developed on the field. As Quintilian said, "I would also have students of oratory consider that all forms of argument which I have just set forth cannot be found in every case and that when the subject on which we have to speak has been propounded, it is no use considering each separate type of argument and knocking at the door of each with a view to discovering whether they may chance to serve to prove our point, except while we are in the position of mere learners."—*Instit. Orat.,* V, x, 122. Quintilian envisioned the time when, as the result of study and practice, the student would acquire that "innate penetration" and "power of rapid divination" which would lead him directly to those arguments suited to his particular case. Eventually, he would arrive at the happy condition in which the arguments would "spontaneously follow the thought."

In the remaining portion of this chapter, we are going to consider the aids to invention under three main heads: (1) the common topics; (2) the special topics; (3) external aids to invention. The common topics will provide the student with a stock of general lines of argument that can be used in the development of any subject. The special topics will provide him with lines of argument especially pertinent to the particular kind of persuasive discourse in which he is engaged—deliberative, judicial, or ceremonial. The external aids to invention will direct the student to some of the standard reference books which will provide him with the facts and figures he may need to substantiate his own arguments or to refute opposing arguments. These aids to invention, it will be noted, are arranged on an ascending scale of specialization: the common topics yield arguments on virtually any subject; the special topics yield arguments for a particular kind of discourse; and the external aids to invention yield data for a specific case. As Aristotle pointed out, the common topics are the aids belonging most properly to rhetoric; as we move up the scale and rely on more specialized knowledge for our arguments, we are moving out of the province of rhetoric and invading the provinces of other disciplines, such as law, history, ethics, politics, science.

The Common Topics

Before we consider the common topics in detail, let us set forth, in outline form, the common topics and their sub-topics:

DEFINITION
    A. Genus
    B. Division

COMPARISON
    A. Similarity
    B. Difference
    C. Degree

RELATIONSHIP
    A. Cause and Effect
    B. Antecedent and Consequence
    C. Contraries
    D. Contradictions

CIRCUMSTANCE
    A. Possible and Impossible
    B. Past Fact and Future Fact

TESTIMONY
    A. Authority
    B. Testimonial
    C. Statistics
    D. Maxims
    E. Law
    F. Precedents (Examples)

Definition

We have already discussed definition at some length in an earlier section of this chapter, where we were reviewing some of the basic principles of logic. Here we will confine our discussion to the uses that rhetoricians made of the topic. Definition is a way of unfolding what is wrapped up in a subject being examined. One of the rhetorical uses of this topic is to ascertain the specific issue to be discussed. Opponents in a dispute may be arguing at cross-purposes if they do not clearly establish just what the point at issue is. Therefore, after we have formulated our thesis, we may find it necessary to define the key terms in our thematic proposition so that our audience will clearly understand what we are talking about.

In law trials also it is frequently necessary to define the point at issue. In the court trial, for instance, held in London's Old Bailey in October, 1960, against Penguin Books Ltd. for publishing D. H. Lawrence's *Lady Chatterley's Lover,* it was extremely important that both the prosecution and defense determine at the outset just what was the issue at stake. Was Penguin Books being prosecuted for violating the provisions of the Obscene Publications Act of 1959? If so, in what way specifically had Penguin Books offended against this law? Had it offended by publishing an obscene book? If so, what was to be the definition of "obscene book" used in this trial? If an obscene book is one that tends to "corrupt or deprave those who read it," what is the meaning of the terms "corrupt" and "deprave"? And should there not be some determination of *who* it is that is likely to be depraved or corrupted? And did *Lady Chatterley's Lover* fall under the provisions of Section 4 of the Act, which exempt from the charge of obscenity any book judged to be in the interests of "science, literature, art, or learning"? (For the transcript of this interesting trial, see *The Trial of Lady Chatterley: Regina v. Penguin Books Limited,* ed. C. H. Rolph. A Penguin Special, 1961.)

All these questions of definition were important in the trial and had to be posed and resolved at the outset. The student can well imagine how many words were expended to settle these questions. He can learn from this example how useful the topic of definition can be to him when he is faced with the problem of developing a subject. Judging from the frequency with which students begin their themes with a definition from the dictionary ("As Webster says, ..."), they would seem to realize instinctively the value of definition as a springboard for the development of a subject. The trouble with most "As Webster says" gambits in student themes, however, is that they serve no useful function. The definitions are there in the introduction because the student does not know how to get into his subject. They are a stalling tactic which the student uses while he is trying to work up momentum for the main push.

A definition becomes really functional when it is used as Matthew Arnold does in refutation of Thomas Henry Huxley's "Science and Culture," one of the essays reproduced among the readings at the end of this chapter.

> Let us, I say, be agreed about the meaning of the terms we are using. I talk of knowing the best which has been thought and uttered in the world; Professor Huxley says this means knowing *literature.* Literature is a large word; it may mean everything written with letters or printed in a book. Euclid's *Elements* and Newton's *Principia* are thus literature.

All knowledge that reaches us through books is literature. But by literature Professor Huxley means *belles lettres*. He means to make me say,
that knowing the best which has been thought and said by the modern
nations is knowing their *belles lettres* and no more. And this is no sufficient equipment, he argues, for a criticism of modern life. But as I do
not mean, by knowing ancient Rome, knowing merely more or less of
Latin *belles lettres*, and taking no account of Rome's military, and political, and legal, and administrative work in the world; and as, by knowing
ancient Greece, I understand knowing her as the giver of Greek art, and
the guide to a free and right use of reason and to scientific method, and
the founder of our mathematics, and physics and astronomy and biology
—I understand knowing her as all this, and not merely knowing certain
Greek poems, and histories, and treatises, and speeches—so as to the
knowledge of modern nations also.

When we are seeking to clarify some of the important terms in a discussion, we can quote definitions from a dictionary. But the dictionary definitions will suit our purpose only when these accepted definitions agree with
our notions. Sometimes, however, we have to devise our own definitions,
either because the accepted definitions are too vague or because we believe
them to be erroneous or inadequate. In such cases, we *stipulate* the meaning
we will attach to certain terms in our discussion. Because Coleridge found
that existing definitions of a poem did not accord with his notions of this
genre, he formulated a definition which he felt was accurate:

> The final definition then, so deduced, may be thus worded. A poem is
> that species of composition which is opposed to works of science by pro-
> posing for its *immediate* object pleasure, not truth; and from all other
> species (having *this* object in common with it) it is discriminated by
> proposing to itself such delight from the *whole* as is compatible with a
> distinct gratification from each component *part*.
>
> From Samuel Taylor Coleridge, *Biographia Literaria*, Chapter XIV, 1817.

Genus

The topic of definition can be used not only for clarifying the point at issue
but also for suggesting a line of argument. In the *Apology*, which is reproduced among the readings at the end of this chapter, we see Socrates using
the topic of definition to defend himself against the charge of being an atheist.
Asking what was meant by the "divine," Socrates proposed that it must refer
either to the gods or to the works or agencies of the gods. He then goes on
to argue from this definition that he could not be considered an atheist:

> But then you swear in the indictment that I teach and believe in divine
> or spiritual agencies (new or old, no matter for that); at any rate, I be-

lieve in spiritual agencies—so you swear in the affidavit; and yet if I
believe in divine things, how can I help believing in spirits or demigods;
—must I not? To be sure I must; and therefore I may assume that your
silence gives consent. Now what are spirits or demigods? are they not
either gods or the sons of gods?

In the last sentence of this quotation, Socrates is resorting to an argument
based on the first sub-topic under definition—the sub-topic of genus. Whenever the predicate of a proposition puts the subject into a general class of
things—"Americans are lovers of freedom," "Suicide is a crime against society"—the subject is, in a sense, being defined, because limits are being fixed
to the term. But such propositions can also pose an argument. The rhetorical
force of the topic of genus derives from the principle that what is true (or
untrue) of the genus must be true (or untrue) of the species. If all men are
mortal, then John Smith, if he is a man, must be mortal too. Cicero in his
Topica gives this example of an argument from Genus. If a man, he says,
bequeathed all the silver in his possession to his wife, a lawyer could argue
that the man intended to leave his wife not only all his silver plates and
statues and candlesticks but also all the coin in his coffers, for coin is just as
much a species of silver as are plates and statues and candlesticks.

Simply predicating a genus of some subject term will constitute a "proof,"
however, only when the audience is disposed to grant the truth of the classification. The preacher who declares from the pulpit, "Murder is a grievous
sin," can safely presume that his congregation will agree with him. Whenever a speaker or writer cannot presume such ready assent, he must, of course,
go on to justify his classification.

Perhaps the commonest use of definitions in argument is as a premise for
a further argument. One form of this is the proposal of a definition as a
norm and then the demonstration that something else either conforms or
does not conform to this standard. We see another form of this in *The Federalist, No. 10,* reproduced among the readings at the end of this chapter.
In paragraph 13 of this discourse, James Madison defines "a pure democracy"
as "a society consisting of a small number of citizens, who assemble and administer the government in person." After pointing out in the remainder of
the paragraph the shortcomings of such a system of government, Madison
goes on to indicate in the next two paragraphs the direction that his argument will take in the rest of the discourse:

> A republic, by which I mean a government in which the scheme of
> representation takes place, opens a different prospect and promises the
> cure for which we are seeking. Let us examine the points in which it
> varies from pure democracy, and we shall comprehend both the nature
> of the cure and the efficacy which it must derive from the Union.

> The two great points of difference between a democracy and a republic
> are: first, the delegation of the government, in the latter, to a small num-
> ber of citizens elected by the rest; secondly, the greater number of citizens,
> and greater sphere of country, over which the latter may be extended.

Madison is going to use the differences between the nature of a republic and
the nature of a pure democracy as the means of proving his thesis that a
confederation of states is the best way to control factions.

Division

We do in effect define something when we enumerate the parts that go to
make it up and when we designate the species of a genus. We would be
illuminating the nature of the state if we were to designate, as Socrates did
in the early books of *The Republic,* the various occupations needed to make
it function. So too the analysis of government into its various species—monarchy, democracy, oligarchy, tyranny, etc.—helps to throw some light on the
concept.

One rhetorical use of the topic of division is to lay out the organization of
the exposition or argument that is to follow. We see an example of this in
the opening paragraphs of Francis Bacon's discourse on the Idols of the
Mind:

> The idols and false notions which are now in possession of the human
> understanding and have taken deep root therein, not only beset men's
> minds that truth can hardly find entrance, but even after entrance ob-
> tained, they will again in the very instauration of the sciences meet and
> trouble us, unless men being forewarned of the danger fortify themselves
> as far as may be against their assaults.
>
> There are four classes of Idols which beset men's minds. To these for
> distinction's sake I have assigned names, calling the first class *Idols of the
> Tribe;* the second, *Idols of the Cave;* the third, *Idols of the Marketplace;*
> the fourth, *Idols of the Theatre.*
>
> From Francis Bacon, *Novum Organum,* 1620.

Bacon takes up each of these idols in turn, explains what they are, and shows
how they inhibit clear thinking. For another example of this kind of
division, see paragraph 6 of Martin Luther King's "Letter from Birmingham
Jail," in which the author specifies the four basic steps in a nonviolent campaign. Subsequent paragraphs of the letter develop each of these basic steps
in turn.

Besides this use of division as an organizing principle, it can also be used
to establish the grounds for an argument. We see an example of this use in
paragraph 13 of Matthew Arnold's essay reproduced among the readings at
the end of this chapter:

Deny the facts altogether, I think, he hardly can. He can hardly deny that when we set ourselves to enumerate the powers which go to the building up of human life, and say that they are the power of conduct, the power of intellect and knowledge, the power of beauty, and the power of social life and manners—he can hardly deny that this scheme, though drawn in rough and plain lines enough, and not pretending to scientific exactness, does yet give a fairly true representation of the matter. Human nature is built up by these powers; we have the need for them all. When we have rightly met and adjusted the claims of them all, we shall then be in a fair way for getting soberness and righteousness with wisdom. This is evident enough, and the friends of physical science would admit it.

From Matthew Arnold, "Literature and Science."

Arnold then uses this division into four "powers" to argue that an education in the humanities is superior to an exclusively scientific education, because the humanities can administer to the development of all of these powers in man, whereas an education in the natural sciences alone cannot.

Division can also be used to set up an argument by elimination. One can set up alternatives—"A man is a citizen either by birth or by naturalization" —and then by proving (or disproving) one alternative, he disproves (or proves) the other. Or one can enumerate a series of possibilities and eliminate them one by one. For instance, a defense attorney might argue like this:

A man in these circumstances might steal for any one of these reasons: (A). . . ; (B). . . ; (C). . . ; (D). . . . Now, we have firmly established that A and B could not possibly have been my client's motives. Furthermore, not even the prosecution has suggested in this trial that C or D could have been my client's motives. Since none of the possible motives are applicable in this case, it is clear that my client is innocent of the charge of stealing.

If the defense attorney has taken care to consider *all* the possible motives for this crime, a jury would find this to be a rather persuasive argument.

We have shown how division can be useful as a principle of organization and as the basis for an argument. In conclusion, we might point out that since explanation is sometimes managed by analysis of a whole into its parts, division can be as useful in expository writing as in argumentative discourse.

Comparison

The second common topic that we will consider is comparison. For the purposes of learning, explaining, or arguing, we frequently resort to the strategy of bringing two or more things together to study them for similarities, differences, superiority, or inferiority. This tendency to compare things is as natural for man as the tendency to define things. Man in his most primitive state must early have turned to comparison in an attempt to fathom the bewildering world about him and to establish a scale of values. He discovered that the familiar often helped him to understand the unfamiliar, and he learned that by measuring one thing against another he could discriminate the "more" from the "less." In this section we shall investigate some of the ways in which we can use the topic of comparison in order to discover something to say on a given subject.

Similarity

One possible result of comparing things is the detection of similarity, the likeness of two or more things. Similarity is the basic principle behind all inductive argument and all analogy. In induction, we note similarity among a number of instances and make an inference about a further unobserved or unconfirmed instance. Analogy argues that if two things are alike in one or two characteristics, they are probably alike in another characteristic. The rhetorical form of induction, as we have seen, is the example—drawing a probable conclusion from a single instance of similarity. Perhaps the simplest way to differentiate analogy from induction by example is to say that whereas analogy argues from the similarities of dissimilar things, example argues from the similarities of similar things.

The following is the simplest and commonest form of argument from similarity: "If self-control is a virtue, so is abstinence." Here, noting the similarity in kind between self-control and abstinence and observing that virtue can be predicated of self-control, one infers that abstinence too must be a virtue. The ordinary person resorts to this kind of argument every day: "The student who copies from his neighbor in an examination and the student who allows or encourages his neighbor to copy from him are equally culpable. Both actions are forms of cheating." "The last time we attempted prohibition of the sale of liquor all kinds of abuses resulted. If the present proposal to prohibit the sale of narcotics is passed, we'll experience the same kind of legal and moral chaos."

The student will find many arguments from similarity among the readings in this book. We will look at only one example—the one from paragraph 25 of Martin Luther King's "Letter from Birmingham Jail," in which Dr. King answers the charge that the demonstrations of his group should be proscribed because they tend to encourage violence:

> In your statement you assert that our actions, even though peaceful, must be condemned because they precipitate violence. But is this a logical assertion? Isn't this like condemning a robbed man because his possession of money precipitated the evil act of robbery? Isn't this like condemning Socrates because his unswerving commitment to truth and

his philosophical inquiries precipitated the act by the misguided populace in which they made him drink hemlock? Isn't this like condemning Jesus because his unique God-consciousness and never-ceasing devotion to God's will precipitated the evil act of crucifixion? We must come to see that, as the federal courts have consistently affirmed, it is wrong to urge an individual to cease his efforts to gain his basic constitutional rights because the quest may precipitate violence. Society must protect the robbed and punish the robber.

Here, in a series of rhetorical questions, Dr. King is arguing on the basis of the similarity in comparable situations existing in the *same* order of being. When, however, we draw our comparisons between similar things existing in *different* orders of being—as, for instance, when we compare the structure of a society to the organization of a beehive—we are moving over into the province of another variety of the topic of similarity, *analogy*.

We might have treated analogy along with some of the basic principles of logic, but analogy, like most rhetorical arguments, produces only probable proof. Hence we will give here some of the principles governing it. Analogy revolves around the principle that two things which resemble one another in a number of respects resemble one another in a further, unconfirmable respect. This principle might be graphically represented by this scheme:

$$A \quad 1 \; 2 \; 3 \; 4 \; \longrightarrow \; 5$$
$$B \quad 1 \; 2 \; 3 \; 4 \; \longrightarrow \; (5)$$

Two things, A and B, resemble one another in four known, confirmable respects. From these points of resemblance, we argue that B resembles A in a fifth respect (5 being known and confirmable in the case of A but not in the case of B). As in inductive argument, there is a leap from the known to the unknown. It is because of this inductive leap that analogy achieves probability rather than certainty.

Let us look at an example of argument by analogy:

There is only one cure for the evils which newly acquired freedom produces; and that cure is freedom. When a prisoner first leaves his cell he cannot bear the light of day: he is unable to discriminate colours or recognise faces. But the remedy is, not to remand him into his dungeon, but to accustom him to the rays of the sun. The blaze of truth and liberty may at first dazzle and bewilder nations which have become half blind in the house of bondage. But let them gaze on, and they will soon be able to bear it. In a few years men learn to reason. The extreme violence of opinion subsides. Hostile theories correct each other. The scattered elements of truth cease to contend, and begin to coalesce. And at length a system of justice and order is educed out of the chaos.

From Thomas Babington Macaulay, *Essay on Milton,* 1825.

Macaulay states his thesis in the first sentence of this passage: he contends that the cure for the evils that attend newly won emancipation is freedom. Noting similarities in the condition of a nation which has won its independence and that of a man who has just been released from prison, he elaborates that similarity to support his contention.

As we have already pointed out, an analogy does not really prove anything, but it can have persuasive value. Sometimes the nature of one's audience will determine how effective an argument by analogy will be. In most cases, however, the persuasiveness of the analogy will depend largely on adherence to these two principles:

1. The similarities between two things must concern pertinent, significant aspects of the two things.
2. The analogy must not ignore pertinent dissimilarities between the two things being compared.

For instance, an anthropologist might try to prove that a certain island in the Pacific was once inhabited by comparing it with another Pacific island known to have been inhabited. He might point out that both islands had palm trees, sandy beaches, placid lagoons, mild climate, and shelter from high winds. However, by ignoring the fact that the questionable island had a very low annual rainfall and that the island was too far from any mainland or other island to make it likely that people could have reached it by sailboat or canoe, he would be ignoring factors that are important to the issue at hand—namely, could people have reached the island, and once they reached it, could they have survived? Most of the time when someone says, "Your analogy doesn't hold," he is exposing an analogy that has avoided consideration of important differences. For instance, in the example quoted above, Macaulay has pointed out a number of similarities between the situation of a released prisoner and the situation of an emancipated nation. But are there not some relevant dissimilarities between the two situations? Is there not a significant difference between a nation of people and a single person—a difference that might justify a difference of treatment?

Analogy is often used too for purposes of exposition. By comparing something unfamiliar or abstruse with something familiar, one can facilitate his explanation. Here is an example of this use in an essay by Dr. J. Robert Oppenheimer, in which he uses the analogy of a tree to show how knowledge tends to ramify:

> How then does it go? In studying the different parts of nature, one explores with different instruments, explores different objects, and one gets a branching of what at one time had been common talk, common sense. Each branch develops new instruments, ideas, words suitable for

describing that part of the world of nature. This tree-like structure, all growing from the common trunk of man's common primordial experience, has branches no longer associated with the same question, nor the same words and techniques. The unity of science, apart from the fact that it all has a common origin in man's ordinary life, is not a unity of deriving one part from another, nor of finding an identity between one part and another, between let us say, genetics and topology, to take two impossible examples, where there is indeed some connection.

From J. Robert Oppenheimer, "On Science and Culture."

In paragraph 19 of Edmund Burke's "Letter to a Noble Lord," reproduced among the readings in this chapter, we see another use being made of analogy. By comparing his present situation with that of a fallen oak tree, Burke is seeking to stir the emotions of his audience:

> But a Disposer whose power we are little able to resist and whose wisdom it behooves us not at all to dispute, has ordained it in another manner and (whatever my querulous weakness might suggest) a far better. The storm has gone over me; and I am like one of those old oaks which the late hurricane has scattered about me. I am stripped of all my honours, I am torn up by the roots and lie prostrate on the earth! There, and prostrate there, I most unfeignedly recognize the Divine justice and in some degree submit to it.

Difference

Another possible result of comparing two or more things is a detection of differences. At some time in his academic career, the student must have been asked to answer an essay-question that begins with the formula, "Compare and contrast...." The "compare" part of that formula is asking the student to set forth the similarities between things; the "contrast" part of the formula is asking the student to note the differences between things. In the eighteenth century, it was common for those critics who were influenced by John Locke's psychology of knowledge to define *wit,* the imaginative faculty, as the faculty that saw resemblances between things and to define *judgment,* the rational faculty, as the faculty that saw differences between things. Wit, in other words, was the synthetic faculty, and judgment was the analytic faculty. It would be well to develop both judgment and wit.

Rhetoricians made use of the topic of difference to gather arguments for confirmation or refutation. Edmund Burke's essay at the end of this chapter, "Letter to a Noble Lord," is a good essay for the student to study for an illustration of the operation of the topic of difference. In this *apologia,* Burke bases most of his defense on difference. He spends a great deal of time, for instance, contrasting the pension that he has received from the government with the pension that the Duke of Bedford's family received many years ago. Here is just one example, from paragraph 3 of the essay, of Burke's argument from differences:

> I really am at a loss to draw any sort of parallel between the public merits of his Grace, by which he justifies the grants he holds, and these services of mine, on the favorable construction of which I have obtained what his Grace so much disapproves. In private life, I have not at all the honour of acquaintance with the noble Duke. But I ought to presume, and it costs me nothing to do so, that he abundantly deserves the esteem and love of all who live with him. But as to public service, why truly it would not be more ridiculous for me to compare myself in rank, in fortune, in splendid descent, in youth, strength, or figure, with the Duke of Bedford, than to make a parallel between his services and my attempts to be useful to my country. It would not be gross adulation, but uncivil irony, to say that he has any public merit of his own to keep alive the idea of the services by which his vast landed pensions were obtained. My merits, whatever they are, are original and personal; his are derivative. It is his ancestor, the original pensioner, that has laid up this inexhaustible fund of merit, which makes his Grace so very delicate and exceptious about the merit of all other grantees of the Crown. Had he permitted me to remain in quiet, I should have said, 'tis his estate; that's enough. It is his by law; what have I to do with it or its history? He would naturally have said on his side, 'tis this man's fortune.—He is as good now as my ancestor was two hundred and fifty years ago. I am a young man with very old pensions; he is an old man with very young pensions—that's all.

The student can study the topic of difference as it occurs in the readings reproduced at the end of this chapter. In paragraph 15 of *The Federalist, No. 10,* for instance, James Madison, after defining the terms "pure democracy" and "republic," goes on to contrast the efficiency of these two forms of government. Matthew Arnold makes frequent use of the topic of difference in his essay "Literature and Science"; in paragraph 11, to pick out only one example, we see Arnold marking the differences between the physical sciences ("knowledge of things") and the humanities ("knowledge of words"). In paragraph 16 of "Letter from Birmingham Jail," Dr. King points out the crucial differences between a just law and an unjust law. A study of these and other examples should convince the student of how common the topic of difference is in discourse and of how useful this topic can be for purposes of exposition or persuasion.

Degree

More and less—the topic to which we have attached the label "degree"—was one of the four common topics that Aristotle discussed in his *Rhetoric.* Aris-

totle perceived that in comparing things we sometimes discover, not a difference *in kind,* as in the previous topic, but a difference *in degree.* One thing
will be better than another; or it will be worse. The relevance of this fact
for rhetoric is that sometimes when we are seeking to persuade others to do
something or to accept something, we have to show our audience that the
choice before them is not between a good and an evil but between a greater
good and a lesser good—or between a greater evil and a lesser evil.

Questions of degree are not easy to settle, mainly because judgments about
such a difference are usually relative and subjective. To help orators find
arguments to decide questions of degree, Aristotle provided a set of criteria
in Book I, Chapter 7 of his *Rhetoric.* Here are some of his criteria:

> 1. A greater number of things can be considered more desirable
>   than a smaller number of the same things.

Deciding questions of degree by numerical superiority must be attended with
certain cautions. Numerical superiority, first of all, must be reckoned in regard to things of the same species. Ten one-dollar bills are obviously a greater
good than five one-dollar bills; but ten one-dollar bills are not a greater good
than five ten-dollar bills. Then too numerical superiority becomes a helpful
determinant of degree only when all other things are equal. A congressman
might argue that a tax bill which will bring in four billion dollars of revenue
is a better proposal than the tax bill which will bring in only three billion
dollars. But the congressman's argument will persuade his colleagues only if
a number of other considerations are equal: if both bills are equally just; if
both bills are equally enforceable; if both bills can be administered at relatively equal cost. Numerical superiority would also be qualified by the quality of the things involved. It might be argued, for instance, that the football
coach who recruited twenty players had done a better job than the coach
who recruited only fifteen players. But the coach who had recruited only
fifteen players might actually have engaged a greater number of superior
athletes or have recruited two or three players who are worth more to a team
than the entire twenty players hired by the other coach.

> 2. That which is an *end* is a greater good than that which is only
>   a *means.*

The principle underlying this criterion is that a *means* is desirable only for
the sake of something else; but an *end* is desirable for its own sake. Health,
for instance, is a greater good than exercise, because we indulge in exercise
for the sake of acquiring or maintaining health. Exercise is a means to a
good outside itself; but in relation to exercise, health is an end, something
which is desirable for its own sake.

3. What is scarce is greater than what is abundant.

This principle is the basis of most monetary systems. Silver coins are of greater value than copper coins because silver is a scarcer metal than copper; gold is more valuable than silver for the same reason. We should be aware, however, that in some circumstances the opposite principle could be used as a criterion of superior value. We could argue that what is abundant is a greater good than what is scarce because the abundant is more useful. Thus although water is more abundant than gold, in some circumstances water would be judged the greater good because it was more useful.

4. What men of practical wisdom would choose is a greater good than what ignorant men would choose.

Plato's many arguments about the "one" and the "many" were examples of the application of this criterion. What is involved here is the impressiveness of authority. As a practical matter, we all rely on the judgments of experts. Where judgments about value conflict, the antecedent probability is that the judgment of the expert is more reliable than that of the amateur. Under the fifth of the common topics, we shall discuss at some length the part that testimony or informed opinion plays in exposition and argument.

5. What the majority of men would choose is better than what the minority would choose.

This criterion, the opposite of the previous one, smacks very much of the nose-counting method of determining worth. "If you want to find out what the most worthwhile current novels are, consult the best-seller lists." "The better candidate is the one the people elect." This criterion will have persuasive value with people who conceive of the *good* in the Aristotelian sense of that which is desirable for its own sake. Desirability is a quite different thing from worth. We all know that what all men or most men desire is not always a good in the moral or aesthetic sense. But if, in any given discussion, people are thinking of good in terms of what is desirable, then the preference of the majority will be persuasive.

Advertisers make great use of this criterion. "More people smoke Camels than any other cigarette." Sometimes of course what all men or most men choose *is* the worthiest good. There is a certain presumptive evidence that the product most people buy is the best product. Other factors, of course, influence the popularity of a product—its price, its prestige value, its advertising—but if there is any validity to the maxim "You can't fool all of the people all of the time," one is inclined to believe that it is the quality of the product that maintains sales at a high level.

6. What men would really like to possess is a greater good than what men would merely like to give the impression of possessing.

In *The Prince,* Machiavelli said that a reputation for virtue was so important to the image a ruler needs to create that if he was not *really* a virtuous man he must at least give the *appearance* of being a virtuous man. Tested by this sixth criterion, Machiavelli's view suggests that power is a greater good than virtue, because power is what the ruler really wants and in order to get it he is ready to assume a mask of virtue. Aristotle uses a similar example: one could argue that health is a greater good than justice, because while men can be content with the mere reputation for being just, men prefer being healthy to only seeming healthy.

7. If a thing does not exist where it is more likely to exist, it will not exist where it is less likely to exist.

This is a line of argument to which logicians commonly assign the Latin label *a fortiori* ("from the stronger"). John Donne, in the sonnet that depreciates the power and dreadfulness of death, used an *a fortiori* argument to develop his thesis. Here are the first six lines of that sonnet:

Death, be not proud, though some have called thee
Mighty and dreadful, for thou art not so,
For those, whom thou think'st thou dost overthrow,
Die not, poor Death, nor yet canst thou kill me.
From rest and sleep, which but thy pictures be,
Much pleasure, then from thee much more must flow,

A paraphrase of the elliptical syntax in lines 5 and 6 will clarify the *a fortiori* argument implicit in those lines. In line 5, Donne says that rest and sleep are like death, are "imitations" of death. We all know that we derive a great deal of pleasure from rest and sleep; therefore, we should derive even more pleasure from that which they imitate, from death. If so much pleasure from the *lesser* thing, how much more pleasure from the *greater* thing. Therefore death cannot be as dreadful as we have been led to believe.

An *a fortiori* argument can work in two directions: (1) from the greater to the lesser, or (2) from the lesser to the greater. Donne starts out with a consideration of the lesser and then makes an inference about the greater. An *a fortiori* argument that works in the other direction would take a form like this: "If a man would steal from a friend, he would steal from a stranger."

An *a fortiori* argument sets up two possibilities, one of which will be more probable than the other. Whatever can be affirmed about the less probable can be affirmed with even greater force about the more probable. Like most rhetorical arguments, an *a fortiori* argument does not lead to certainty; it leads to a more or less strong probability.

A number of arguments from the topic of degree are pointed out in the analyses of whole essays in this and the following chapter. Here are two leads to arguments from degree in some of the readings that are not analyzed:

> I have almost reached the regrettable conclusion that the Negro's great stumbling block in his strike toward freedom is not the White Citizen's Councilor or the Ku Klux Klanner, but the white moderate, who is more devoted to "order" than to justice; who prefers a negative peace which is the absence of tension to a positive peace which is the presence of justice; who constantly says: "I agree with you in the goal you seek, but I cannot agree with your methods of direct action"; who paternalistically believes he can set the timetable for another man's freedom; who lives by a mythical concept of time and who constantly advises the Negro to wait for a "more convenient season." Shallow understanding from people of good will is more frustrating than absolute misunderstanding from people of ill will. Lukewarm acceptance is much more bewildering than outright rejection.

> From paragraph 23 of Martin Luther King's "Letter from Birmingham Jail"

> If then there is to be separation and option between humane letters on the one hand and the natural sciences on the other, the great majority of mankind, all who have not exceptional and over-powering aptitudes for the study of nature, would do well, I cannot but think, to choose to be educated in humane letters rather than in the natural sciences. Letters will call out their being at more points, will make them live more.

> From final paragraph of Matthew Arnold's "Literature and Science."

Relationship

Cause and Effect

The first sub-topic that we will consider under the general head of relationship is cause and effect. Just as men have always exhibited a desire to know the nature of things and a curiosity about likenesses and differences, so they have always felt the urge to discover the "why" of something. A child exhibits the first glimmerings of rationality when he passes from the stage of asking the question "what" about the world around him to the stage of asking the question "why." "What is that, Daddy?" "That's rain, son. It's water that falls from those dark clouds." "Why, Daddy?" Having noted an effect, the child begins to ask questions about the cause.

Men have traditionally accepted as axiomatic the principle that every effect must have a cause. Many of the arguments for the existence of God, for instance, have been based on this principle. Having observed the universe in its wonderful immensity, harmony, and complexity, men have postulated that this world had its beginnings in God, the Prime Mover, the Uncaused Cause.

Cause-and-effect relationships constitute one of the most fruitful sources of arguments. But before we explore the rhetorical uses of cause and effect, we should review a few principles governing this kind of reasoning.

First of all, we must recognize that an effect could have a number of possible causes. In the case of a broken window, for instance, we know that a number of things could account for that broken window. Someone could have thrown a rock at the window; the wind could have broken the window; tremors in the earth could have broken the window; a sonic boom from a passing jet airplane could have broken the window. Although these are all possible causes of the broken window, only one of these will be the cause of *this* broken window. The task is to determine *which* cause. Most detective stories start out with a murder. The detective must sort out, from all the possible or probable causes, *the* cause of this particular murder; he must discover the murderer.

Secondly, the cause that we assign for an effect must be capable of producing the effect. It must, in other words, be an *adequate* cause. If a detective discovers that a robust man was strangled to death, he immediately rules out as a suspect the little old maiden aunt, the twelve-year-old nephew of the deceased, and the 114-pound chambermaid. All of these people are capable of murdering someone, even by strangling a person, but they could not have strangled the powerful man stretched out on the carpet in the library. Now, there is the ju-jitsu artist who had been paying court to the victim's daughter....

Thirdly, once we have a probable and adequate cause for something, we must consider whether there are other adequate causes for the effect. Yes, there was that ju-jitsu artist, but there was also that tall, gangly butler and that wiry, irascible gardener. They too could have strangled the man.

Fourthly, we must consider whether the conditions or circumstances were such that the potential cause could operate. In a controlled experiment—like those that a chemist conducts in the laboratory—such conditions as time, temperature, humidity, proportions, can be stabilized or varied to test whether the hypothetical cause is the real cause. In the case of human beings acting as efficient causes, such conditions as opportunity and motivation must be considered.

Lastly, we must also consider whether the hypothetical cause always produces an effect and whether it invariably produces the same effect. In short, we must establish not only that a putative cause *could* produce a particular effect but also that it *would* produce the effect.

One of the commonest errors in cause-and-effect reasoning is the fallacy usually referred to by the Latin label *post hoc ergo propter hoc* ("after this, therefore because of this"). This is the error of supposing that where there is a time relationship between two events there is also a cause-and-effect relationship. A number of supersititons are built upon this fallacy. John Smith got hit by a car at the intersection of Fifth and Main Streets because five minutes before, he had walked under a painter's ladder. It is understandable, of course, why men tend to suppose that when one event chronologically follows another event the later event was caused by the earlier event. But we must *prove* the cause-and-effect relationship; we cannot *presume* relationship. Try proving that John Smith's having walked under a ladder resulted in his being hit by a car. On the face of it, the action does not seem to be a suitable or adequate cause for the effect. His walking under the ladder could indicate general carelessness, and that carelessness could explain why he was hit while crossing a busy intersection. But there was no direct relationship between the two events.

The principles we have been reviewing in connection with cause-and-effect relationships are the principles normally discussed in a logic class. Nevertheless, a conscientious rhetorician must be aware of these principles too and must observe them in his presentation of arguments. He must be especially careful to observe these principles when he is addressing a sophisticated audience that will not accept slipshod causal reasoning.

In persuasive discourse, arguments based on causal relationships work in two directions. We can argue from an effect back to a cause, or we can start with a cause and argue that it will produce a particular effect or effects. We see an instance of an argument from cause to effect in Jonathan Swift's *A Modest Proposal*. After making his "modest proposal" that the poor people of Ireland should sell their year-old infants as table fare for the wealthy, he points out that the implementation of his proposal would have these effects:

> I have too long digressed, and therefore shall return to my subject. I think the advantages by the proposal which I have made are obvious and many, as well as of the highest importance.
>
> For first, as I have already observed, it would greatly lessen the number of Papists, with whom we are yearly overrun, being the principal breeders of the nation, as well as our most dangerous enemies....
>
> Secondly, the poorer tenants will have something valuable of their own, which by law may be made liable to distress and help to pay their landlords rent, their corn and cattle being seized, and *money a thing unknown.*
>
> Thirdly, Whereas the maintenance of an hundred thousand children, from two years old, and upwards, cannot be computed at less than ten shillings a piece *per annum,* the nation's stock will be thereby increased fifty thousand pounds *per annum,* besides the profit of a new dish, intro-

duced to the tables of all gentlemen of fortune in the kingdom, who have
any refinement in taste, and the money will circulate among ourselves, the
goods being entirely of our own growth and manufacture.

Swift goes on to name a fourth, fifth, and sixth effect of his proposal, but
this is enough to illustrate our point. As any schoolboy knows who has read
this famous ironical essay, Swift was not seriously offering a proposal that
he expects the government to adopt, but the point is that he was using the
terminology and the kind of argument that a hard-headed mercantilist of
the eighteenth century might have used in trying to persuade others that
"people represent the riches of a nation." If it is fairly self-evident, as in
this instance, that the cause will produce the proposed effects and if the
proposed effects seem desirable to the audience, the mere recital of the effects
will be persuasive.

If, on the other hand, it is not self-evident that the proposed effects will
follow from a particular cause, then one must prove his claims. Before Dr.
Jonas Salk, for instance, won approval from the U.S. Department of Health,
Education, and Welfare to put his vaccine on the market, he had to present
ample evidence that it would, as he claimed, prevent polio. With something
as crucial as a vaccine one would have to present proof sufficient to create
virtual certainty about its effects. In many affairs of state, however, such as a
proposal that a reduction in occupation taxes would attract dozens of new
industries to a community, a legislator would have to produce only a high
degree of probability in order to persuade his colleagues.

The other way to argue causally is from effect back to a cause. We see
James Madison arguing from effect to cause in paragraph 7 of *The Federalist,
No. 10:*

> But the most common and durable source of factions has been the various
> and unequal distribution of property. Those who hold and those who
> are without property have ever formed distinct interests in society. Those
> who are creditors and those who are debtors fall under a like discrimina-
> tion. A landed interest, a manufacturing interest, a mercantile interest, a
> moneyed interest, with many lesser interests, grow up of necessity in
> civilized nations, and divide them into different classes, actuated by dif-
> ferent sentiments and views. The regulation of these various and interfer-
> ing interests forms the principal task of modern legislation and involves
> the spirit of party and faction in the necessary and ordinary operations
> of the government.

Again it may be well to point out that in human affairs it is not always necessary to demonstrate, with the same rigorous certainty that we expect in logic
or science, that a particular effect was produced by a certain cause and no
other. It is often sufficient that we produce a high degree of probability.

Antecedent and Consequence

Closely allied to the topic of cause and effect is the topic of antecedent and consequence. In fact, the latter may be regarded as merely a looser form of the cause-and-effect arguments practiced in logic. The etymology of the term *consequence* (the Latin verb *sequi,* to follow) is the key to an understanding of the way in which rhetoric used this topic. The persuader pursues this line of argument: given this situation (the antecedent), what follows (the consequence) from this? If he can detect a cause-and-effect relationship between the antecedent and consequence, he will avail himself of the relationship to strengthen his case. But he will also make use of less compelling kinds of consequences (things that follow). For instance, he might argue that since Jane Smith was not the legal wife of John Smith at the time of his death, it follows that she is not entitled to his possessions. Here there is no cause-and-effect relationship, but some judgment does follow from the existent situation.

We frequently use this kind of antecedent-consequence argument in our everyday affairs. "If girls are admitted to the university as full-time students, they must be accorded the same rights and privileges as the male students." "If these students violated the university's regulations about drinking at school-sponsored gatherings, they must be suspended." "If this man is a natural-born citizen, he has the right to vote." Sometimes the consequence follows from the definition of the antecedent term. For example, "If this figure is a square, it has four right-angles" or "If this creature is a man, he is a rational animal."

The student should note that there is usually an implied premise whenever an argument takes this form. When we say, "If girls are admitted to the university as full-time students, they must be accorded the same rights and privileges as the male students," we imply that all full-time students are entitled to the same rights and privileges. Oftentimes it is this unexpressed premise, this assumption, that is the vulnerable spot in an argument. So when one is looking for an opening to refute such an argument, he would do well to search for the assumption.

The student will recall that in the earlier section of this chapter, where some of the main principles of logic were reviewed, the antecedent-consequence proposition often served as the major premise of the hypothetical syllogism. ("If this man is a natural-born citizen, he has the right to vote." "This man *is* a natural-born citizen." "Therefore, he has a right to vote.") The student should review the rules governing the validity of such deductive reasoning so that he may be guided in formulating his own antecedent-consequence arguments and in detecting fallacies in the arguments that others present.

Here are a few examples of arguments from antecedent and consequence from the readings at the end of this chapter:

> We cannot know all the best thoughts and sayings of the Greeks unless we know what they thought about natural phenomena. We cannot fully apprehend their criticism of life unless we understand the extent to which that criticism was affected by scientific conceptions. We falsely pretend to be the inheritors of their culture, unless we are penetrated, as the best minds among them were, with an unhesitating faith that the free employment of reason, in accordance with scientific method, is the sole method of reaching truth.
>
> From paragraph 30 of Thomas Henry Huxley, "Science and Culture."

> If one recognizes this vital urge that has engulfed the Negro community, one should readily understand why public demonstrations are taking place. The Negro has many pent-up resentments and latent frustrations, and he must release them. So let him march; let him make prayer pilgrimages to the city hall; let him go on freedom rides—and try to understand why he must do so. If his repressed emotions are not released in nonviolent ways, they will seek expression through violence; this is not a threat but a fact of history. So I have not said to my people: "Get rid of your discontent." Rather, I have tried to say that this normal and healthy discontent can be channeled into the creative outlet of non-violent direct action. And now this approach is being termed extremist.
>
> From paragraph 30 of Martin Luther King's "Letter from Birmingham Jail"

Contraries

At first sight the topic of contraries may seem very much like the topic of difference. But there is a subtle difference between the two topics. Difference involves unlike or dissimilar things, things which differ *in kind;* contraries on the other hand, involve opposite or incompatible things of the same kind. Differences become apparent when we compare things: contraries become apparent when we relate things. *Liberty* and *license* would be an example of difference; *liberty* and *slavery* would be an example of contraries.

Before discussing the rhetorical uses of the topic of contraries, we will briefly consider some of the logical principles governing contraries. Contrary terms are terms opposed to one another in the same order or genus. *Cold* and *loud* are different terms, but they are not contrary terms, because *cold* concerns the order of temperature, and *loud* the order of sound. *Cold* and *hot,* and *loud* and *quiet,* would be contrary terms. So if one person said, "This book is bad" and the other person said, "This book is good," we would say that the propositions are opposed as contraries.

These are the things we know about contrary propositions *a priori*—that is, before examination or analysis: (1) If one of the propositions is true, the other one is false; in other words, contrary propositions are incompatible; (2) If one of the propositions is false, the other one is not necessarily true; in other words, both of the propositions could be false. (See the "Square of Opposition" in the section on logic.)

In an argument, then, if it has been agreed upon that contrary assertions have been made about the same subject, one can discredit the other assertion by proving that his assertion is true; in that case, one doesn't have to *prove* that the other assertion is false (if I prove that the book is red, I don't have to prove that the book is not green). On the other hand, if one proves that his opponent's proposition is false, his own proposition is not automatically true; one must go on to *prove* that his own proposition is true. (If I prove that the book is not green, I cannot assume that the book is red; after all, the book might be blue.)

In rhetoric, arguments involving contraries or opposites sometimes take a form in which the subject terms and the predicate terms are both contrary. In Book II, Chapter 23, of the *Rhetoric,* Aristotle gives an example of an argument based on the topic of contraries: "Self-control is beneficial because licentiousness is harmful." Here the subject terms *self-control* and *licentiousness* are contraries; and the predicate terms *beneficial* and *harmful* are contraries too. We establish the truth of the first proposition ("Self-control is beneficial") by showing that the opposite of *beneficial* (namely, *harmful*) can be predicated of the opposite of *self-control* (namely, *licentiousness*). If someone were to argue, "If war is the cause of our misery, peace is the way to promote our happiness," he would be advancing the same kind of argument, for he would in effect be saying, "Peace must be a good because war is an evil."

In the following excerpt, Henry David Thoreau argues from contraries— diligence (exertion) versus sloth (sluggishness), purity (chastity) versus impurity (sensuality), and wisdom versus ignorance—contending that whereas sloth makes a man ignorant and impure, diligence will make him wise and pure:

> All sensuality is one, though it takes many forms; all purity is one. It is the same whether a man eat, or drink, or cohabit, or sleep sensually. They are but one appetite, and we only need to see a person do any one of these things to know how great a sensualist he is. The impure can neither stand nor sit with purity. When the reptile is attacked at one mouth of his burrow, he shows himself at another. If you would be chaste, you must be temperate. What is chastity? How shall a man know if he is chaste? He shall not know it. We have heard of this virtue, but we know not what it is. We speak conformably to the rumor which we have heard. From exertion come wisdom and purity; from sloth, igno-

rance and sensuality. In the student, sensuality is a sluggish habit of mind. An unclean person is universally a slothful one, one who sits by a stove, whom the sun shines on prostrate, who reposes without being fatigued. If you would avoid uncleanness and all the sins, work earnestly, though it be at cleaning a stable.

From "Higher Laws," *Walden,* 1854.

Contradictions

In the previous discussion, we saw that propositions like "the water is hot" and "the water is cold" are contrary propositions. Contradictory propositions would be opposed this way: "the water is hot"; "the water is not hot." In studying the square of opposition in the section on logic, we saw also that A and O propositions are contradictory—"all fathers are members of the male species" and "some fathers are not members of the male species"—and that E and I propositions are contradictory—"no fathers are members of the male species" and "some fathers are members of the male species." Contradiction is built on the principle that a thing cannot at the same time and in the same respect be and not be.

As in the case of contraries, there are some things we know *a priori* about contradictory propositions: (1) one of the propositions must be true, and the other must be false; (2) if one of the propositions is true, the other is false; (3) if one of the propositions is false, the other is true. So if one group of medical men says that cigarette-smoking causes lung cancer and another group says that it does not cause lung cancer, we know, before we ever investigate the facts, that one of these groups is right and the other is wrong. As we know from the heated controversy about this question in the press, it has been difficult for either group to prove conclusively that its claim is the correct one. But still we know that one of these groups has to be right, and someday scientists and doctors may be able to prove beyond doubt which group is right. Until such time, people will be guided in their decision about whether to smoke or not by the group which presents the most persuasive or probable arguments.

In preparing arguments, either for confirmation or for refutation, we will recognize contradictions as a helpful topic whenever we see two propositions related in such a way that the truth of one entails the falsity of the other. So we might begin a section of our discourse in this fashion: "Some people maintain that the Constitution guarantees the right of every citizen to vote; others maintain that the Constitution states no such right." From these two contradictory propositions, we could go on to argue for one or the other claim. Sometimes we will start out by setting up an either/or situation: "Either he is willing to take a loyalty oath, or he is not willing"; "One thing we know for certain is that this mysterious cousin of his in Australia is either a man or a woman." And if the alternatives in the disjunctive proposition are indeed mutually exclusive, we know that if we can prove one of the alternatives to be true we will have proved that the other is necessarily false. Sometimes the contradiction between two related statements is implicit rather than explicit, and in that case our line of argument will be to point up the inconsistency or, as we say, "the contradiction in terms." So we might launch a refutation in this fashion: "My opponent claims that he is a fervent advocate of democracy. But has he not made it abundantly clear that he would deny the vote to certain citizens solely on the basis of color?" By showing that the two positions are incompatible, we would in effect be proving that our opponent is *not* a fervent advocate of democracy.

Circumstance

The Possible and the Impossible

The first sub-topic to be considered under the general head of circumstance is the possible and the impossible. Often when we are seeking to persuade others to do something, we have to show them that the proposed course of action is possible; likewise, when we are seeking to discourage others from doing something, we may want to show them that the proposed course of action is impossible. Even when people recognize that a course of action is desirable, they will sometimes hesitate to embark on it because they doubt that it is feasible.

A common way to inspire an audience with confidence in the practicality of a proposed course of action is to cite examples of people who have accomplished a similar or identical thing. The examples will be persuasive in proportion to the similarity of the actions and the circumstances.

One can also argue deductively about the possible. In his *Rhetoric,* Aristotle proposed some lines of arguments about the possible. He did not lay down another set of arguments for the impossible, but suggested at the end of the action on the possible, "As for the impossible, the speaker will obviously have his stock of arguments in the opposites of the foregoing." The student will recognize that in arguing the possible one frequently employs some of the other topics that we have already discussed. Here are some of the lines of argument that Aristotle poses:

> 1. If one of a pair of contraries is possible, then the other is possible too.

The assumption here is that any two contraries, from their nature as contraries, are possible. For instance, if a man can get well, he can fall sick. It should be pointed out, however, that in some cases the pair of contraries may not be *equally* possible. For instance, in some cases we may not be able to argue that if a man can fall sick, he can get well, because he may be suffering from an incurable disease. As always in rhetoric, one must seize on the arguments that are available for the particular case in question.

2. If one of a pair of similar things is possible, the other thing is possible too.

For instance, if it is possible for a man to play an organ, it is possible for him to play a piano. The fact that men have always argued for the possibility of one thing by pointing to the possibility of a similar instance suggests that the principle involved here is self-evident.

3. If the more difficult of two things is possible, then the easier is possible too.

For instance, a spokesman for the National Aeronautic and Space Administration may one day be arguing before Congress that if it is possible to rocket a single man to Mars, it is possible to rocket several men to the moon. The student may recognize here the operation of the *a fortiori* argument that we discussed in connection with the topic of degree.

4. If something can have a beginning, it can have an end; and conversely, if something can have an end, it can have a beginning.

The principle upon which this argument is based is that no impossibility comes, or begins to come, into existence. Aristotle's classic example of an impossibility—of something that cannot have a beginning and therefore cannot have an end—is squaring a circle. Aristotle is not suggesting that everything that has a beginning will necessarily be finished. What he is suggesting is that every beginning implies an end and that every end implies a beginning. The man who uses this topic to win acceptance for his proposal is arguing for the feasibility or facility of his plan rather than for its mere possibility. He argues, in effect, that "well begun is half done," that what has been begun can with faith, perseverance, and hard work be brought to fruition.

5. If the parts of a thing are possible, then the whole is possible; and conversely, if the whole is possible, the parts are possible.

One can imagine a group of space scientists using this line of argument to convince members of Congress that it is possible to put a man into orbit. By showing that all the component parts of a launching vehicle have been manufactured or can be manufactured, they could argue that a rocket capable of putting a man into space could, if adequate appropriations were made by Congress, be constructed. The writers of the *Federalist* papers used an argument like this when they proposed that a confederation of states was possible because the components of such a confederation already existed. The persuasiveness of an argument in the other direction—from whole to part—is self-evident. If a functioning unit exists, then all the parts necessary for that functioning unit must exist.

> 6. If a thing can be produced without art or preparation, it certainly
> can be done with the help of art or planning.

This is a kind of *a fortiori* argument, but it differs slightly from the line of argument suggested in (3) above. Principle (3) is concerned with an argument about whether a thing can be done at all; (6) is concerned with whether a thing can be done well.

In paragraph 24 of his essay "Literature and Science," Matthew Arnold asks, "Have humane letters, then, have poetry and eloquence, the power here attributed to them of engaging the emotions?" To substantiate his claim that the humanities *can* engage the emotions, he refers to the common experience of men. "The appeal," Arnold says, "is to experience. Experience shows that for the vast majority of men, for mankind in general, they have the power." The assumption behind all appeals to experience or historical example is that if something *has* been done, it can be done again.

One of the advantages that James Madison attaches to a confederation of states is that there is less chance of unworthy men seizing control of the government. He does not say that it is *impossible* for unworthy men to seize power in a confederation of states, but he does say that it is *more difficult* for such men to seize power. He puts it this way in paragraph 18 of *The Federalist, No. 10:*

> In the next place, as each representative will be chosen by a greater
> number of citizens in the large than in the small republic, it will be more
> difficult for unworthy candidates to practise with success the vicious arts
> by which elections are too often carried; and the suffrages of the people
> being more free, will be more likely to center in men who possess the
> most attractive merit and the most diffusive and established characters.

The student will discover many other examples of arguments from the possible and impossible in the readings reproduced in this book.

Past Fact and Future Fact

The topic of past fact is concerned with whether something has or has not happened. In ancient rhetoric it played an important part in forensic oratory, since for the definition of the issue in a court trial it was important to determine whether an act had been done or not. Future fact—or, more accurately, future probability—was concerned with whether or not something would happen; this topic was used most often in deliberative oratory.

Wherever evidence or testimony is available to prove that something has happened, it should of course be presented to substantiate the claims that have been made about past events. But frequently in human affairs it is not easy, sometimes impossible, to discover the evidence or testimony that could confirm the occurrence of an event. In such cases, one must resort to arguing the *probability* of something having occurred. As we have said repeatedly, the *probable* is the main province in which the rhetorician operates; after all, there can be no room for argument about what is certain.

Where past fact cannot be established empirically, deductive reasoning takes over and, arguing from probable premises, draws more or less probable conclusions. Here are some lines of arguments that one can use to persuade others about a past fact:

> 1. If the less probable of two events has occurred, the more probable event is likely to have occurred too.

Here is the *a fortiori* argument again. Statisticians, among others, make use of this line of argument to establish the probability of past occurrences. If a number of triplets have been born, then a proportionate number of twins have been born too. Imagine a prosecuting lawyer using this line of argument to persuade a jury about the guilt of the defendant: "If, as has been admitted, this man has been guilty of stealing money from his father, do you find it too far-fetched to believe that he was capable of embezzling money from his employer?" The degree of probability would increase of course with the frequency of occurrence.

> 2. If something that naturally follows something else has occurred, then that something else has happened too; and conversely, if the antecedents were present, then the natural consequences occurred too.

Men instinctively reason this way. If we hear thunder, we presume that lightning has flashed, even though we may never have seen the flash of lightning. Or if lightning flashed, then thunder followed. If a man has forgotten something, we presume that he once knew it. If a man has a fever, we suppose that he has been seized by some illness. If a man shows up with a black eye and a swollen lip, the natural supposition is that he has been in a fight or walked into a door.

3. If someone had the power and the desire and the opportunity to do something, then he has done it.

The principle supporting the probability here is that men will gratify their desires when they have the chance, either through lack of self-control or through a natural appetite for what they perceive as a good. Prosecuting lawyers have employed this line of argument in trying to convince a jury that the defendant was guilty. Such arguments of course can legally establish nothing more than a strong suspicion of guilt, but combined with other incriminating evidence, they do have great persuasive power.

Arguments *against* the probability of something having occurred can be found in the opposites of the foregoing lines of argument.

One must more often rely on probable arguments to establish future fact than to establish past fact, because where something has occurred there is always the chance of discovering the proof that it has indeed occurred; but there is always a note of uncertainty about future events. Here are some suggestive lines of argument for persuading others about the likelihood of a future event:

1. If the power and the desire to do something are present, then that something will be done.

One of the strong arguments that have been advanced in support of nuclear disarmament is that the mere possession of atomic weapons poses a constant temptation to a nation to use them against an enemy. Some pacifists go so far as to argue that the use of the nuclear bomb is not only probable but inevitable.

2. If the antecedents of something are present, then the natural consequences will occur.

"If dark clouds have gathered, it is going to rain." (Even the weatherman will admit that this event is just a probability.) "If a raging mob has gathered in the public square, violence will follow." Some consequences, of course, occur so regularly, that high probability verges on virtual certainty. When a tightly closed room is filled with gas fumes, it is virtually certain that if someone strikes a match in that room an explosion will occur.

3. If the means are available, the end will be accomplished.

The odds-makers at Las Vegas are certainly going to pick as the winner of the World Series the baseball team that appears to be stronger on paper. But as everyone knows, the team with the "best means" does not always win the World Series. This line of argument is a familiar one in political debate. Now that the legal machinery has been set up to protect civil rights, it appears likely that some time in the near future everyone in the United States will enjoy the rights and privileges of first-class citizenship.

In paragraph 44 of "Letter from Birmingham Jail," Dr. King, making use of a skillful blend of the topic of future fact and the topic of past fact, supports his contention that the Negro will eventually triumph in his struggle for freedom and equality:

> I hope the church as a whole will meet the challenge of this decisive hour. But even if the church does not come to the aid of justice, I have no despair about the future. I have no fear about the outcome of our struggle in Birmingham, even if our motives are at present misunderstood. We will reach the goal of freedom in Birmingham and all over the nation, because the goal of America is freedom. Abused and scorned though we may be, our destiny is tied up with America's destiny. Before the pilgrims landed at Plymouth, we were here. Before the pen of Jefferson etched the majestic words of the Declaration of Independence across the pages of history, we were here. For more than two centuries our forebears labored in this country without wages; they made cotton king; they built the homes of their masters while suffering gross injustice and shameful humiliation—and yet out of a bottomless vitality they continued to thrive and develop. If the inexpressible cruelties of slavery could not stop us, the opposition we now face will surely fail. We will win our freedom because the sacred heritage of our nation and the eternal will of God are embodied in our echoing demands.

Testimony

Under the general head of testimony, we shall consider six sub-topics—authority, testimonial, statistics, maxims, law, precedent. Unlike the other topics, which derive their material from the nature of the question under discussion, testimony derives its material from external sources. In the next section of this chapter, entitled "External Aids to Invention," the student will be advised about some of the standard reference works that can provide additional supporting material for exposition or argumentation.

Authority

The first sub-topic to be considered under the topic of testimony is authority. It is probably true that informed opinion or authority carries less weight today than it once did. In an age characterized by a scientific attitude and a democratic spirit, men are temperamentally not as disposed as they once were to be impressed and swayed by the voice of authority and the pronouncements of men "in the know." In situations where facts are recoverable

—and modern technology has greatly extended the realm of the empirical—men prefer facts to opinions. They are not as ready to accept something as true merely because someone says it is true. For them, it is "facts" which carry the persuasive force.

Although modern man is not as disposed to accept authority as his grandfather was, he is frequently forced by circumstances to rely on authority. Informed opinion does indeed still play a prominent part in the conduct of human affairs. For one thing, knowledge is so diversified and specialized in our age that no man can claim, as Francis Bacon once did, to take all knowledge for his province, and since the day-to-day affairs of a society cannot wait for all its citizens to catch up with the latest discoveries, men are obliged to take the "word" of some expert about the facts. For another thing, since men dispute mainly about uncertain, unpredictable matters, they frequently must turn to informed opinion to guide them in settling issues or making decisions.

Although informed opinion is not infallible, it has great persuasive force. We tend to grant more credence to the testimony of experts than to the testimony of amateurs; we place more faith in the opinions of those who pronounce on matters connected with their field of knowledge than in the opinions of those speaking outside their field of competence. A Congressional committee investigating the potential danger from nuclear fall-out will pay more attention to the renowned physicist than to the ordinary citizen, however interested and well-read the citizen may be. There have been instances, of course, where the expert turned out to be wrong and the amateur to be right, but there is always greater probability that the expert will be right.

Sometimes experts offer conflicting opinions. In evaluating conflicting testimony from equally competent experts, we must rely on other criteria in deciding which opinion to accept. In such cases, we ask questions like these:

1. Is there anything inconsistent, contradictory, or illogical in the expression of the opinion itself?
2. Do the experts harbor any prejudices that might influence or color the proffered opinion?
3. Do any of the experts have an axe to grind? an advantage to gain? a score to settle?
4. Is one expert's opinion based on more recent, more reliable information than the other's is?
5. Is one expert's opinion accepted by more experts? by the more authoritative experts?
6. What are the basic assumptions behind the expressions of opinion? Are any of these assumptions vulnerable? Does the exposure of these assumptions reveal that the conflict between the experts is more apparent than real because they are viewing the same matter from different points of view?

Answers to probing questions like these will determine which of the conflicting opinions will have the greater persuasive force for a particular occasion and a particular audience.

Testimonial

Similar to the topic of authority is the strategy of the testimonial, which takes many forms: the letter of recommendation, the advertising "puff," the "blurb," the character-witness appraisal, the opinion-poll, the best-seller list, the audience-rating. All of these represent attempts to influence opinion, action, or acceptance. The testimonial does not have to come from an impartial, expert source to be persuasive. Sometimes the persuasive force of a testimonial stems from the esteem we have for the person or the achievements of the one offering the recommendation. "Roger Ruth smokes Olympic cigarettes." An advertising slogan like that could influence thousands of people to buy Olympic cigarettes because Roger Ruth is a renowned athlete. What a slogan like this attempts to do is to transfer the esteem we have for the person to the product he recommends. In rhetorical terminology, the testimonial has "ethical appeal"—the kind of appeal that Aristotle says is often more effective in persuading an audience than appeals to reason or appeals to emotions. People tend to forget that Roger Ruth's skill as a ballplayer does not especially qualify him to be a good judge of cigarettes; that Roger Ruth is being paid to give his recommendation; that Roger Ruth's testimonial does not necessarily prove anything about the quality of Olympic cigarettes.

Two general observations can be made: (1) the testimonial can be remarkably persuasive in certain circumstances and with certain audiences; (2) the testimonial is remarkably vulnerable to refutation. Not every testimonial, of course, is to be discounted as dishonest, insincere, or irrelevant. The important caution is that the testimonial must not be used or accepted uncritically.

Statistics

Similar to the testimonial is the citation of statistics. "Five million people last year bought Humbug Products." "Fifty-eight per cent of the new homes built last year were equipped with Leakproof Appliances." Sometimes this strategy is referred to as the "bandwagon technique." Everybody's doing it, so it must be good. Now, there is no denying that the preference for one product over another could be an indication that the preferred product is superior in quality to the other products. Most people have faith that superior quality, all other things being equal, will in the long run win out over the second-rate and the meretricious. So statistics can be a useful and an effective topic in many discussions.

What we must guard against in the use of statistics is making unwarranted inferences. Statistics, if accurate and if legitimately gathered, confirm a fact;

but they do not always support an inference made from that fact. The fact that a book has been at the top of the best-seller list for twelve months or more supports the fact that many people have bought this book. That fact, however, will not necessarily justify the further assertion, "This best-selling novel is the best novel published last year" or "You too will thrill to the drama of this runaway best-seller."

In the previous paragraphs we have been considering comparative statistics —pairs or groups of figures and percentages which help to decide questions of *more* and *less*. But statistics can be used in argument for purposes other than deciding superiority. Statistics can be used, for instance, to settle contrary and contradictory assertions. Suppose that one party in a dispute maintains, "Most Americans own their homes," and that the other party maintains, "Most Americans do not own their homes." If the two disputants agree upon the meaning of *own*, these two statements are directly contradictory. As we saw in the discussion of the topic of contradiction, one of these statements is true, and the other is false. An obvious way to determine which assertion is true is to cite statistics: "The 1960 Census reveals that (number) Americans or _____ per cent of citizens over twenty-one years of age have completely paid off the mortgage on the house in which they dwell."

Statistics can be used to support or discredit all kinds of assertion. The chief caution to be observed in regard to the use of this topic is that one should not accept statistics uncritically. Statistics are always liable to the challenge of questions like these:

1. What is the source of these statistics?
2. Is this a qualified, unbiased source?
3. How were these figures arrived at?
4. Was the sampling a reliably representative survey?
5. When were these figures gathered?
6. Are these figures contradicted or superseded by figures from other sources?

Polls and surveys are playing an increasingly prominent role in modern life. The better polling agencies, by devising scientific formulas for extrapolating sample findings, have achieved an amazing record of accuracy. Electronic computing machines too have increased the reliability of the interpretations and predictions made from statistics. We should be aware, however, that polling techniques, especially those that depend for their findings on personal interviews with people, have certain built-in limitations. The wording of a question put to the man in the street influences his response. Any time a question-begging word gets into a question the response will be biased. The responses to a question like "Do you favor the abolition of excessive taxes?" cannot be interpreted to mean that most people favor the abolition of taxes. Sometimes the juxtaposition of questions can bias the responses. If the question "Should subversive organizations be outlawed in America?" were followed by the question "Should the Communist Party be outlawed in America?" the response to the second question would undoubtedly be prejudiced by the response to the first question.

Another weakness inherent in the personal interview stems from two assumptions that pollsters make: (1) that people always know their own mind on questions put to them; (2) that people will give truthful answers to questions put to them. Does the man in the street always know, at any given stage in a presidential campaign, which candidate he favors? If he is undecided or confused, he will sometimes give an answer, any answer, because he is ashamed to admit to the pollster that he does not really know which candidate he favors at the moment. When the question concerns a matter that is more complex, the likelihood increases that the interviewee does not know his own mind. Pollsters make provision for this uncertain state of mind by permitting the interviewee to answer "Undecided," but sometimes a person is undecided even about whether he is undecided. As for the other assumption, for one reason or another, some people deliberately mislead the questioner, by not giving a truthful answer. Recognizing this fact, pollsters include a discount-factor in their formulas for extrapolating the information they have gathered.

All of the above observations about the cogency and weaknesses of statistics suggest the ways in which we can use statistics to support our own arguments or to refute the arguments advanced by the opposition. Employed discreetly, statistics can be a valuable topic in expository and argumentative writing.

Maxims

We shall use the term *maxims* (Greek, *gnomai;* Latin, *sententiae*) to cover precepts, proverbs, famous sayings, epigrammatic pronouncements, self-evident truths, sententious generalizations—all kinds of charismatic statements that people introduce into an argument. In the *Rhetoric,* Book II, Chapter 21, Aristotle treated maxims as a prelude to his discussion of the enthymeme, because, as he observed, maxims often constitute one of the premises of a syllogistic argument. For instance, in an argument about financial matters, one can imagine a disputant saying, "A fool and his money are soon parted." The full argument suggested by this proverb would run something like this:

> A fool and his money are soon parted.
> John Smith is undeniably a fool when it comes to money matters.
> John Smith is sure to lose out on his investment.

Maxims are statements, not about particular matters, but about universal matters. So the statement "Yon Cassius has a lean and hungry look" would not be a maxim, but it would take on the air of a maxim if it were changed to "One should be wary of lean and hungry men." It is not all general statements, however, that can be considered maxims. "A straight line is the shortest distance between two points" would not be one. Maxims are general statements about human actions, about things that are to be chosen or avoided in human action.

The value of maxims, according to Aristotle, is that they invest a discourse with "moral character," with that ethical appeal so important in persuading others. Because maxims touch upon universal truths about life, they win ready assent from the audience, and because of their air of hoary wisdom, they are endowed with a peculiar sanctity. Because maxims strike this note of ancient, sanctified wisdom, they are more appropriate, as Aristotle observed, when they come from the lips of older, experienced men. A maxim is just as true when uttered by a young man as when uttered by an older man, but, in certain circumstances, a maxim issuing from a callow youth will sound pretentious, even ridiculous. Alexander Pope was fortunate that many of his readers did not know that the author of the collection of wise and witty precepts in *The Essay on Criticism* was barely twenty-one years of age.

Maxims should not be avoided merely because they are well known. Their very familiarity may be an asset. The familiar often seems self-evident and for that reason wins an uncritical acceptance. Herein lies a danger however. The familiar quotation, the slogan, the platitude, the bromide have a way of acquiring immunity from criticism. For this reason, we often resort to the sanctified truism when we are seeking acceptance for our cause. Instead of earning assent, we bribe it. Besides running the danger of being unethical, such a practice can induce lazy habits. When the maxim upon which we are basing an argument is challenged, we may be unprepared to defend its truth. Sometimes too we wrongly concede an argument because we have not taken the trouble to question the apparently "truthful" premise.

These reminders are not intended to discourage the use of the topic of maxims; they are intended merely to alert us to the dangers of uncritical acceptance of "what oft was thought." The student should bear in mind Plato's salutary observation, "The unexamined life is not worth living."

Law

Under the topic law will be comprehended all statutes, contracts, testaments, records, and documents which can be drawn on to substantiate or refute a claim. Recorded evidence has a compelling force in any argument. An argument about the date of a man's birth, for instance, can usually be settled summarily by a birth certificate or a baptismal record. Producing a bona fide will can silence rival claimants to a man's inheritance. When a critic adduces a statement from diaries or letters about an author's intention in a literary work, he does not necessarily clinch his interpretation, but he certainly strengthens it.

People have a great awe of the written or printed word. How often we have heard the statement, "But it says so, right here in the book." Respect for the recorded word is in many ways a good thing. We could hardly conduct the affairs of daily life if society did not maintain respect for what is recorded "in black and white." Without deeds and contracts, all property rights, for one thing, would be tenuous. A verbal contract between a car-owner and a dealer will not stand up in court; but a written warranty, duly signed by both parties, gives a judge something concrete and definite upon which to decide a litigation.

What we must remember, however, is that documentary evidence does not necessarily foreclose all further debate; recorded words are open to challenge and to interpretation. We can protest, for instance, that a document produced in evidence is not an authentic document. Challenges like the following can also be brought forward to test the authenticity of a document:

1. There is no proof that the document in question actually issued from the hand of the alleged author.
2. The document was not duly witnessed.
3. This document is only a transcription or reproduction of an allegedly extant original.
4. In the process of transmission, the wording of the document was altered.
5. Those authorities who could attest to the authenticity of the document are not available.
6. Another or a later document invalidates this one.

Then too the wording of documents is always open to interpretation. The Constitution of the United States, for instance, is the bona fide document upon which our government is based. But one of the chief functions of the Supreme Court is to interpret the already authenticated wording of the Constitution. In our own time, we have seen what heated disputes have developed over the doctrine of separation of church and state in Article 1 of the Bill of Rights ("Congress shall make no law respecting an establishment of religion, or prohibiting the free exercise thereof") and over the doctrine of states' rights in Article 10 of the Bill of Rights ("The powers not delegated to the United States by the Constitution, nor prohibited by it to the States are reserved to the States respectively, or to the people."). The meaning of statute laws too is constantly being argued in courts.

Precedent (Example)

The last of the sub-topics to be considered under testimony is precedent or example. Etymologically, *precedent* stems from a Latin verb which meant "to go before"; hence the modern sense of "something that has happened before." In one of its modern senses, *precedent* is a technical term in law, designating a judicial decision in the past that can be used as a standard in making judgments about subsequent similar cases. Because judges are often guided by previous decisions, lawyers, in preparing briefs for a case, will search out decisions that other judges have made in similar cases. The task of the lawyer is to convince the judge that the case under consideration is indeed similar to the previous case. In effect, the lawyer's argument runs something like this:

> Your honor, I have shown that the case under consideration has a precedent in the case of New York vs. John Smith, No. 2435, tried on October 29, 1919 before Judge Harry Snodgrass. In that case, Judge Snodgrass returned a judgment that the defendant did not have to pay taxes to the plaintiff on property that had been confiscated before the due date of the tax payments. The judge ruled that although John Smith continued to occupy the property for three months, he ceased to be the owner of the property on the date that he signed the confiscation papers, and he was no longer liable for taxes once he transferred ownership, even though he continued, per agreement, to occupy the property rent-free for three months. Since the circumstances of this case are similar to those in the New York case and since the tax laws in this state are similar to those that prevailed in New York at that time, I respectfully propose that a similar ruling be made in this case.

The opposing lawyer, of course, will try to prove that the two cases are not similar or that an important difference has been overlooked or that an important consideration has been distorted. Or he will cite, if available, other precedents in which a quite different judgment was returned. When opposing precedents are presented, the lawyers will contend that one precedent should supersede the other. Each lawyer will try to show that his precedent is more relevant or more logical or more recent or more reliable (because it comes from a more reputable source) or more cogent (because there are more precedents of this kind than of the other kind).

So much for precedent in its legal sense. In a broader sense, precedent or example is the bringing to bear on a present case what has been done in a similar case in the past. Aristotle considered example to be the rhetorical equivalent of full induction in logic or in scientific demonstration, because in practical discourse the speaker or writer does not have the leisure to present, nor does the audience have the patience to listen to, the whole string of particulars which confirm a generalization arrived at through the inductive process; there is time and patience for the citation of only one or two examples. When there is a dispute, for instance, about how to finance the building of a bridge, the parties in the dispute will cite a few examples of how other states financed such a project and how successful the methods proved to be. The inference that the persuader hopes his audience will draw from the analogous case is that such-and-such a method of financing will be equally successful (or unsuccessful) in the case under consideration. The examples can be historical (and therefore verifiable by, or familiar to, an audience), or they can be, as in the case of the parables that Jesus Christ invented so frequently during his public ministry, fictional. The External Aids to Invention, discussed earlier in this chapter, are the resources to consult for apt historical examples, if such examples are not ready to hand.

It happens that the sub-topics we have considered under Testimony do not figure prominently in the readings reproduced at the end of this chapter. There are no uses, for instance, of Statistics in any of the readings in this chapter. (There are instances of this sub-topic, however, to be found in paragraphs 11, 12, 21, and 40 in George Wald's "A Generation in Search of a Future" in the next chapter.) But although there are not many examples of the use of Testimony in the readings in this chapter, such examples are not entirely absent. Students can consult the following places to observe how the various sub-topics of Testimony have yielded arguments for the authors:

> Authority: Huxley, ¶ 2, 20; Arnold, ¶ 11, 18, 21; King, ¶ 15, 32.
> Testimonial: Huxley, ¶ 14; Arnold, ¶ 5, 17, 19, 24; King, ¶ 31, 46.
> Maxims: Huxley, ¶ 39; King, ¶ 12, 16.
> Law: Burke, ¶ 6, 15; King, ¶ 18, 47.
> Precedents (Examples): Burke, ¶ 19; Arnold, ¶ 27, 28; King, ¶ 6, 7, 14, 21, 43, 45.

In our technological age, where knowledge is becoming more and more specialized and where the storage and retrieval of information have become highly sophisticated, the topic of Testimony is likely to be increasingly resorted to for both professional and popular discourse.

Special Topics

As pointed out in the introductory remarks of the previous section, rhetoricians commonly divided the topics into two general kinds—common topics and special topics. Common topics were depositories of general arguments that one could resort to when discussing virtually any subject. Special topics on the other hand, were more particular lines of argument that one could resort to when discussing some particular subject. In the three main kinds of rhetorical activity—deliberative, judicial, and ceremonial—we tend to rely, fairly regularly, on certain topics which are more particular than common topics and yet more general than specialized knowledge. In a case at law, for instance, the teacher of rhetoric could not be expected to instruct his students in the points of law peculiar to this case; but he could point out to his students that most law cases turned on a limited number of recurring topics.

The value of the special topics in the composition process is that once the student has determined which of the three kinds of rhetorical discourse he is committed to, he knows immediately what his general objective is and also the more or less special kinds of arguments that he must pursue to attain that objective. His composition will not therefore write itself, but he has in the special topics a springboard to launch him in the right direction. And once he has his general direction fixed, he will more readily detect which of the common topics and what specialized knowledge are pertinent and therefore especially useful.

Let us look now at the special topics for each of the three kinds of persuasive discourse.

Special Topics for Deliberative Discourse

Are there some common denominators among the appeals that we use when we are engaged in exhorting someone to do or not to do something, to accept or to reject a particular view of things? There are indeed. When we are trying to persuade someone to do something, we try to show him that what we want him to do is either good or advantageous. All of our appeals in this kind of discourse can be reduced to these two heads: (1) the worthy (*dignitas*) or the good (*bonum*) and (2) the advantageous or expedient or useful (*utilitas*). The English terms do not express fully and precisely what the Latin terms denoted, but perhaps the English terms do convey the general idea of "what is good in itself" (and therefore worthy of being pursued for its own sake) and "what is good for us" (a relative good, if you will, one that would be expedient for us to pursue because of what it can do for us or what we can do with it). John Henry Newman used somewhat the same distinctions in his *Idea of a University* when he was trying to show us the difference between "liberal knowledge" and "useful knowledge." There are some subjects or disciplines, Newman maintained, that we cultivate for their own sakes, irrespective of the power they give us or the use to which they can be put. There are other subjects or disciplines that we cultivate primarily, if not exclusively, for the use to which we can put them.

If we were trying to convince someone to study poetry, for instance, we might urge that the cultivation of poetry is a good in itself and therefore worthy of pursuit for its own sake and that it is no depreciation of the worth of poetry to admit that the study of poetry cannot be put to any practical uses. On the other hand, we might conduct our appeal on a less exalted level by showing that the study of poetry can produce practical results. The study of poetry can teach us, for instance, how to be more intensive readers, how to be more precise writers, how to be keener observers of the world about us.

Whether we lean heaviest on the topic of the worthy or the topic of the advantageous will depend largely on two considerations: (1) the nature of our subject, (2) the nature of our audience. It should be obvious that some things are intrinsically more worthy than others. It is easier to demonstrate, for instance, that the study of poetry is a good in itself than to demonstrate that the building of a bridge is a good in itself. In the latter case, it would be the wiser course—because it is the easier and more cogent course—to exploit the topic of the advantageous. When one is trying to convince a group of taxpayers that they should vote for a bond issue to finance the building of a bridge, one is more likely to impress the taxpayers by demonstrating the usefulness of such a bridge than by showing its aesthetic value.

So too the nature of our audience will influence our decision about the special topic to emphasize in a particular deliberative discourse. Because the audience is the chief determinant of the best means to effect a given end, we should have at least a general sense of the temper, interests, mores, and educational level of our audience. If we discern that our audience will be more impressed by appeals based on the topic of the worthy, then our knowledge of the audience will have to be a little fuller and a little more accurate, because now we must have, in addition to a general sense of the temper of the audience, some knowledge of just what things are regarded as "good" by this audience and what the hierarchy of good things is. Men being what they are, however, it is probably true, as Cicero and the author of the *Ad Herennium* observed, that the topic of advantage will appeal more frequently to more people than will the topic of worth.

All deliberative discourses are concerned with what we should choose or what we should avoid. Aristotle observed that the end which determines what men choose and what they avoid is happiness and its constituents. Happiness then may be looked upon as the ultimate special topic in deliberative discourses, since we seek the worthy and the advantageous because they are conducive to our happiness. Unquestionably, men differ in their concept of happiness. Aristotle presented some of the commonly accepted definitions:

> We may define happiness as prosperity combined with virtue; or as independence of life; or as the secure enjoyment of the maximum of pleasure; or as a good condition of property and body, together with the power of guarding one's property and body and making use of them. That happiness is one or more of these things, pretty well everybody agrees.
>
> *Rhetoric,* I, 5.

Even today, most people, if asked, would say that happiness was one or other of these conditions or perhaps some combination or modification of these.

They would probably agree too with Aristotle's specifications of the constituent parts of happiness: "good birth, plenty of friends, good friends, wealth, good children, plenty of children, a happy old age, also such bodily excellences as health, beauty, strength, large stature, athletic powers, together with fame, honor, good luck, and virtue." One of the recurring themes in fantasies is the situation in which a good fairy allows a man three wishes. Presented with that opportunity, the man chooses the three things which he believes will make him happiest; and usually his choices will be some of those things enumerated in Aristotle's list. The student might ask himself what *he* would specify if he were allowed three choices. His choices would reveal not only a great deal about his scale of values but also how little his view of what constitutes happiness differs from the views that men have held down through the ages.

In summary then, let us say that when we are engaged in any kind of deliberative discourse, we are seeking to convince someone to adopt a certain course of action because it is conducive to his happiness or to reject a certain course of action because it will lead to unhappiness. The two main special topics under the general head of happiness are the worthy and the advantageous. In developing these special topics, we will sometimes have occasion to use some of the common topics, such as the possible and the impossible (when urging the advantage, for instance, of a certain course of action, we may have to show that the course we are advocating is practicable or easy) and the topic of more and less (when seeking to direct a choice from among a number of goods, for instance, we have need of criteria to help us discriminate degrees of good). In developing the special topics, we will also need a fund of specialized knowledge pertinent to the subject we are debating. In discussing matters of public polity, for instance, we need a great deal of accurate and specific knowledge about kinds of government, the laws and constitution of a state, the mechanism of legislation. In addition, we must have at our fingertips, or know where to find, a sufficient number of facts, precedents, or statistics to support our assertions. It is not the special province of rhetoric to supply this specialized knowledge, but a rhetoric text like this can direct the student to the sources of such information. In a later section of this chapter, the student will be apprised of the standard reference works which can supply him with the specialized knowledge he may need to develop his discourse.

For an analysis of the special topics, as well as common topics, in a deliberative discourse, see the analysis of "Xenophon Talks to the Soldiers" at the end of this chapter.

Special Topics for Judicial Discourse

Anyone reading the classical rhetorics soon discovers that the branch of rhetoric that received the most attention was the judicial, the oratory of the courtroom. Litigations in court in Greece and Rome were an extremely common experience for even the ordinary free citizen, and it was a rare citizen who did not go to court at least a half dozen times during the course of his adult life. Moreover, the ordinary citizen was often expected to serve as his own advocate before a judge or jury. The ordinary citizen did not possess the comprehensive knowledge of the law and its technicalities that the professional lawyer did, but it was greatly to his advantage to have a general knowledge of the strategies of defense and prosecution. As a result, the schools of rhetoric did a flourishing business in training the layman to defend himself in court or to prosecute his offending neighbor. In defending the usefulness of the art of rhetoric, Aristotle said, "It is absurd to hold that a man ought to be ashamed of being unable to defend himself with his limbs, but not of being unable to defend himself with speech and reason, when the use of rational speech is more distinctive of a human being than the use of his limbs."—*Rhetoric, I,* 1.

In our time, the majority of citizens—except perhaps for traffic offenses—rarely if ever make an appearance in court. If they do have to go to court, they may, technically, serve as their own counsel, but usually they will hire a professional lawyer to serve them. Some of the students who are reading this text will become lawyers, and before they graduate from law school, they will have received an intensive training in the technicalities of the law and in the conduct of trials. For most men today, however, there is no need to become conversant with the subtleties of the law or to train themselves to become shrewd, eloquent pleaders before a judge or jury.

Training in this kind of rhetoric is, however, not entirely dispensable. All of us have occasion to indulge in this kind of persuasive discourse. We may never have to face the full panoply of the courtroom, but we do sometimes have to defend our actions or views, to impugn the actions of others, or to dispute the wording, interpretation, and application of texts of all kinds.

The special topics for judicial discourse developed from the efforts to ascertain the *status* of a case. As we saw in the initial section of this chapter devoted to the formulation of the thesis, the rhetoricians set up a useful formula for determining precisely the issue that was to be discussed. In order to pinpoint the issue or thesis, they asked three questions about the general subject: whether a thing is (*an sit*), what it is (*quid sit*), of what kind it is (*quale sit*).

Once the issue has been settled—and only then—the pleader, either for the defense or for the prosecution, can determine the special topics that will be pertinent to the development of the case. The ultimate special topics for all judicial discourse are justice and injustice. The terms right and wrong can serve as substitute terms if we take them in their legal, not moral sense.

The sub-topics that can be used to develop the special topics of justice and injustice may be grouped under the three questions which serve to establish the issue:

A. Whether Something Happened

The major sub-topic here is *evidence.*
In developing this topic we pursue questions like these:
   1. What is the evidence?
   2. How, when, where, and by whom was the evidence gathered?
   3. What about the reliability of the evidence?
      a. Is it accurate?
      b. Is it relevant?
      c. Is it consequential?
      d. Is it merely circumstantial?
   4. What about the credibility of the witnesses adducing the evidence?
      a. Are they prejudiced?
      b. Are they reliable?
      c. Are they competent?
      d. Are they consistent?
   5. What about the conflicting evidence?

B. What It Is

The major sub-topic here is *definition.*
In developing this topic we pursue questions like these:
   1. What specifically is the charge being made?

2. What is the legal definition of the alleged injustice?
3. What law is supposedly violated?
   a. a written, promulgated law?
   b. an unwritten, natural law?
      (E.g. in Sophocles' play, Antigone pleads that although she had violated the written law of the community by burying her brother Polynices she was thereby obeying a higher law.)
4. Who was harmed by the alleged injustice?
   a. an individual?
   b. the community?
5. Did the victim suffer the harm against his will?
6. What was the extent of the harm?

C. The Quality of What Happened

The major sub-topic here is *motives* or *causes of action*.
In developing this topic we pursue questions like these:
   1. Was the alleged injustice done intentionally or unintentionally?
   2. If unintentionally, what was the cause of action?
      a. chance?
      b. compulsion?
      c. natural inclination?
   3. If intentionally, what was the cause of action?
      a. habit?
      b. deliberation?
      c. passion?
      d. appetite?
   4. If intentionally, what was the wrong-doer's motive?
      a. profit?
      b. revenge?
      c. punishment?
      d. pleasure?
   5. What kind of person was the doer of the act?
   6. What kind of person was the victim of the alleged injustice?
   7. Were there extenuating circumstances?

The topics we have just reviewed are the things that we invariably discuss when we are seeking to exculpate ourselves or to inculpate someone else. These topics are especially useful in courtroom trials, involving felonies and other violations of civil law. But they are useful also in discussions of the justice and injustice of human acts which are something less than crimes— misdemeanors, errors of judgment, incompetency, neglect of duties, malevolence, etc. The questions set down under the various sub-topics can serve as "suggesters" or "prompters" of the direction our discussion might take when we are engaged in this kind of persuasive activity. For the development of the special topics, pertinent common topics will present themselves as other resources. The nature of the case under consideration will in every instance determine which of the special topics and common topics are relevant.

For an analysis of the special topics, as well as the common topics, in a judicial discourse, see the analysis of Socrates' *Apology* at the end of this chapter.

Special Topics for Ceremonial Discourse

The nature of ceremonial discourse is perhaps easier to grasp than its distinction from the other two kinds. Ceremonial discourse sometimes shades off into deliberative discourse, sometimes into judicial. The ceremonial orator did indeed seem to be more intent on impressing the audience with the eloquence of his laudatory efforts than he did on persuading his audience to adopt a certain course of action. But in praising a great man, he was suggesting, indirectly at least, that his audience go and do likewise; and in thus suggesting a course of action he was moving over into the realm of deliberative discourse. Likewise, when he praised or censured a man, he encroached on the province of judicial discourse, because like the lawyer in the courtroom he seemed to be engaged in exonerating or discrediting someone.

Ceremonial discourse differs from deliberative discourse in that its primary object is to praise or censure someone, not to persuade men to do or not to do something. It differs from judicial discourse in that it does not deal primarily or exclusively with the characters of men charged with crime or misconduct. Unless we recognize this third category, we have no place to put such discourses as Fourth of July speeches, funeral orations, nominating speeches at political conventions, sermons, memoirs, obituaries, profiles, letters of reference, citations, and those remarks that masters of ceremony make in introducing a featured speaker. These forms are clearly distinct from deliberative or judicial discourse.

What then are the special topics relevant to this kind of discourse? All the rhetoricians agreed that the general aim of ceremonial discourse is praise or censure of someone. This being the aim, the obvious special topics would be virtue and vice or, more generally, the noble and the base. We praise a man because of his good qualities; we censure him because of his bad qualities. Whereas judicial discourse is concerned primarily with a man's *legal* innocence or guilt, ceremonial discourse is concerned primarily with a man's *moral* goodness or badness.

Although there are some virtues, like justice and courage, which have been universally acknowledged and esteemed by all people in all ages, certain other virtues enjoy a higher esteem in one civilization than they do in others. Humility, for instance, seemed not to have been a prized virtue in the civilization that Homer portrayed in the *Iliad* and the *Odyssey;* but in most Christian cultures, humility is regarded as one of the supreme virtues. So once again we are reminded of the importance of the audience as a determinant of what is done in a persuasive discourse. The age and sex of an audience, its economic and educational level, its political and religious affinities, its interests and its values—all of these will have a great influence on the virtues that we tend to stress for a particular audience. A man's gentleness might be a virtue to stress before an audience made up exclusively of women; a man's courage might be the virtue to stress before an audience of laboring men.

The following are the virtues that people commonly discuss when they are seeking to praise someone (in parentheses are the corresponding vices— those bad qualities that people mention when they are seeking to discredit someone):

1. *Courage (Cowardice)*:—*fortitude* is sometimes used as a synonym for this virtue, but fortitude is a broader term, signifying imperturbability in the face not only of dangerous situations but of all trying situations.

2. *Temperance (Incontinence)*:—the virtue (and vice) connected with physical pleasures of all kinds.

3. *Justice (Injustice)*:—these terms are to be taken in a somewhat narrower sense than they had as special topics in judicial discourse. For example, we might define justice as the virtue that respects the natural and legal rights of other men.

4. *Liberality (Illiberality)*:—*generosity* or even *charity* might be other words for the virtue which disposes us to expend time, money, or effort for the good of others.

5. *Magnanimity (Meanness of spirit)*:—akin to liberality but carries the implication of good one does for others on a large scale or in reversal of expectations.

6. *Prudence (Rashness)*:—an intellectual virtue which disposes a man to make wise decisions about means and ends.

7. *Gentleness (Brutality)*:—*kindness,* because a broader, might be a better term.

This list does not exhaust the virtues (and vices) by any means. It will merely suggest the sort of qualities of character that people of all ages and cultures value in a man and that contribute to the esteem in which a man is held. In general, those virtues which produce benefits for others will be more highly regarded than the virtues which are good mainly for the person who possesses them. It is noteworthy that many of the Beatitudes that Christ mentioned in his famous Sermon on the Mount are social virtues—virtues that result in benefits for others. It is true that we do laud a man for his personal saintliness (and personal sanctification must be each man's primary goal), but it is easier to praise the man whose virtues benefit others besides himself. It was for this reason that St. Paul designated charity as the greatest of the virtues.

While virtue is the special topic that we most exploit in praising a man, there are other attributes and circumstances that we mention when we are seeking to convince others of a man's worthiness. For instance:

1. *Physical attributes*—agility, strength, beauty, health
2. *External circumstances*—family background, education, economic status, political, social, religious affiliations
3. *Actions and achievements*
4. *Sayings*
5. *Testimony of others*

The student may have noted how many of the resources that one uses in ceremonial discourse are the devices that novelists, dramatists, and short-story writers use to characterize the people in their fictions. The writer of narrative uses dialogue (what a man says and how he says it), action (what a man does and how he does it), descriptions of physical appearance, testimony of other characters in the story, and straight exposition of personality to give his readers an idea of the characters that figure in his story. The narrative writer has one more resource, however, that is not available to the writer or speaker engaged in praising or censuring someone: he can reveal the *thoughts* of his characters—the truest index of a man's moral bent.

Aristotle observed that the common topic of amplification and depreciation is most suitable for ceremonial discourse, for when we seek to praise a man it is natural that we should try to magnify or amplify his virtues and to minimize or extenuate his vices; and when we intend to censure a man, we do just the opposite—we magnify his vices and minimize his virtues. Aristotle pointed out some of the useful ways of heightening the effect of praise:

1. Show that a man is the first one or the only one or almost the only one to do something.

2. Show that a man has done something better than anyone else, for superiority of any kind is thought to reveal excellence.
3. Show that a man has often achieved the same success, for this will indicate that his success was due not to chance but to his own powers.
4. Show the circumstances under which a man accomplished something, for it will redound more to his credit if he has accomplished something under adverse conditions.
5. Compare him with famous men, for the praise of a man will be magnified if we can show that he has equalled or surpassed other great men.

Variations of these points can be used to *depreciate* a man. If we can show, for instance, that many men have done the same thing, we can minimize a man's achievements.

For an analysis of the special topics, as well as common topics, in a ceremonial discourse, see the analysis of Pericles' "Funeral Oration" at the end of this chapter.

In this section, we have reviewed the topics that we usually resort to when we are seeking to convince an audience that a man is great or noble or virtuous or competent (or the opposite—that he is insignificant or base or vicious or inept). Not all of these topics will be available to us on every occasion. If a man does not possess a particular virtue or does not possess it to a pre-eminent degree, we cannot, obviously, extol that virtue in the man. If a particular virtue has no special appeal for a particular audience, it would be unwise of us to dwell on it. And if a particular virtue is not especially pertinent to the occasion, we do little to enhance the praise of a man by expatiating on that attribute. As in most rhetorical activities, we must develop instincts for what is most appropriate and most effective. Because such instincts are among "the nameless graces beyond the reach of art," rhetoric cannot equip the student with those instincts; it can only point the way.

Manuel Bilsky, McCrea Hazlett, Robert E. Streeter, and Richard M. Weaver: Looking for an Argument

Up to this point, we have been discussing the topics abstractly, with occasional brief illustrations of the operation of the topics in actual discourse, and later in

From *College English*, XIV (January, 1953), 210–16. Reprinted by permission of the National Council of Teachers of English and the authors.

this chapter, we will provide analyses of the operation of the topics in whole discourses. Such illustrations and analyses provide evidence of how the topics have yielded matter for discourse that is already composed. But in ancient rhetoric, the topics were regarded as devices for generating matter for discourse that had yet to be composed. In the following article, the authors report how they made use of four of the topics in a composition class at the University of Chicago to help their students find something to say in their assigned themes.

I

1   It is widely believed that courses in composition should deal with argumentation; and few question that argumentation is related to logic. Many teachers of English stress the importance of "clear" or "straight" thinking and implement their convictions by giving their students more or less systematic training in the labyrinthine ways of the syllogism. This is clearly valuable. Because logic provides the form of good argument, it should be treated with some thoroughness.

2   However, most modern discussions of argumentation assume that the whole problem can be solved by means of logic. Students will be able to argue well, it is believed, if they are lectured on the principles of logic, trained in the detection of fallacies, and earnestly exhorted to think honestly. For the teaching of composition, such a point of view is not completely satisfactory, because logicians deliberately exclude subject matter. If this is not amply demonstrated by pointing to the complex sets of nonlinguistic symbols which they have concocted, it can be clearly established by a nonsense syllogism:

> If Gilbert and Sullivan wrote *Iolanthe,* then the fall of Napoleon was largely brought about by his invasion of Russia.
> Gilbert and Sullivan wrote *Iolanthe.*
> Therefore, the fall of Napolean was largely brought about by his invasion of Russia.

This is formally a valid hypothetical syllogism. But it must be emphasized that it is unexceptionable only in a formal sense. A single reading reveals that the argument is ridiculous. Clearly, teachers and students of composition cannot stop where the logician does.

3   We are primarily concerned with teaching our students to write well. While the development of skill in logical analysis is a valuable means to this end, we need other techniques and tools which will assist in the process of creation. We need to discover ways to help students to find relevant and effective arguments. Because it is formal in its nature and analytic in its use,

THE COMMON TOPICS 157

logic, though basic to the study of argumentation, cannot entirely fulfill this need. Recognizing this problem, the English Staff of the College of the University of Chicago has recently been exploring one concrete solution. What follows is a summary account of the theory and practice of this experiment.

4 We may begin by recalling our implication that the student who is instructed in logic is only half-instructed in rhetoric. He has been told to write an argument, but the syllogism is only the frame of an argument. The sense of vague frustration over the syllogism not infrequently shown by students may be accounted for by the fact that the "argument" is still but a formula. In the argumentative process there is still wanting what the traditional rhetoricians call *invention,* and that means simply the discovery of content—of relevant supporting material.

5 All this points to the truth that, to have any power to move, an argument must say something intelligible about the actual world. Because real arguments are made up of such predications, we find most of our substance for argument by interpreting and classifying our experiences. The most fundamental of these categories of interpretation are being, cause, and similarity. To deny these is to deny all possibility of argument. But in actual practice no one denies them, for we no sooner begin to talk about the world than we find ourselves saying that such and such a thing exists as a member of such and such a class, or that it is the known cause of a certain effect (or the known effect of a certain cause), or that it has certain points of similarity with some other thing. These recognized aspects of phenomena provide examples of what the classical writers called the *topoi* or "regions," and what have come to be translated as the "topics."

6 They are so called because they constitute regions of experience from which the substance of an argument can be drawn. It is a matter of everyday observation that arguments are made by saying that X is a kind of thing, or that X has a known definite effect, or that X has important points of similarity with a thing better understood than itself. The "topics" represent only an analysis of these kinds of predicables that may appear in arguments. Let us suppose, for illustration, that you are accosted one night by a robber, who threatens you with a pistol and demands your money. Assuming that you could get him to listen to argument, you might find yourself ranging over the following "regions" or possibilities:

1. You could tell him that what he is attempting is a crime. This would be an argument from *genus.*
2. You could tell him that his act will result in his having to spend years in the penitentiary. This would be argument from *consequence.*
3. You could tell him that this is the sort of thing he would dislike

if he were the victim of it himself. This would be argument from *similarity*.

4. You could tell him that this sort of thing is forbidden by the Bible. This would be argument from *authority*.

Although you may think that we have here overestimated the patience of our hypothetical gunman, you will have to admit that each of these arguments has a certain degree of force, which the abstract syllogism cannot have. That is why we say that we have now invented arguments. The areas from which they can be drawn here start to emerge with some distinctness, and so we have the beginning of a "topic."

7   In our teaching we have commonly referred to these topics as the "sources" of argument, which is another way of indicating their nature. To return to the classroom for illustration: suppose now the student is given the assignment of writing an argument about freedom of expression or democracy or world federation. With these sources outlined for him, he can begin to develop his case by consulting such recognized areas of experience and observation as genus, consequence, similarity, etc. Even the student of limited ability now finds that he has more to say about the subject than he had first supposed.

II

8   Naturally, introducing the topical approach into a college composition course calls for some practical decisions. One of the more important of these concerns the choice of specific topics to be presented. When we undertook to teach the topics as part of the Chicago composition course, we decided to deal with only a few topics but to choose them so that they could be related, sometimes explicitly but more often by implication, to a much longer list. This gives the teacher latitude; it enables him to emphasize one or another aspect of any one of the topics. Next we kept in mind that we wanted topics useful in the art of teaching composition. The result has been a relatively limited and pedagogically useful list, with a considerable degree of flexibility.

Genus

9   The argument from genus or definition comprises all arguments made from the nature of a thing. In presenting this type of argument, we merely take whatever fact or idea is the subject of our deliberation and refer it to its class. If our audience is sufficiently impressed with the actuality of that class (i.e., with its reality as a class containing this member among others), it will grant that whatever is true of that class is true of this fact or idea in question, which is the point we are seeking to make by our argument.

10 For example: suppose someone is seeking to argue that a certain fiscal policy of the government is undesirable. What he may do, if he is using the argument from genus, is to take this single policy and put it in the class "inflation." Now if he is successful in doing that, he transfers the significance of (presumably the feeling about) inflation to the fiscal policy of the government which he is attacking. We are assuming here that the speaker says no more than "This is inflation." If he goes into the consequences of inflation, he is leaving his argument from genus for a further argument from consequences. The same analysis holds for "This is treason," "This is a betrayal of the working class," "This is true Americanism," and for any other argument which seeks to find its motivation through a fixed predicable constituting a genus. It may be pointed out here, incidentally, that training in the critical and precise use of genera is the best possible safeguard against irresponsible "name-calling."

11 In teaching the topics, it may be necessary at some point to take into account the empirical fact that arguments employ two types of definition (and it may be possible to distinguish these as [1] *genus* and [2] *definition*). The first type employs a universally accepted convention for which the speaker does not feel that description, analysis, or "proof" is required. It is, so to speak, one of the established categories of the public mind, and one feels that nothing more is needed than to name it. Probably for a minister with a rather orthodox congregation, "sin" is such a term. Therefore, when he has categorized, either flatly or through extended exposition, such and such an action as "sin," he has made his argument. The genus is so well established that it would be superfluous for him to support it.

12 But there are many terms whose scope is by no means fixed, so that any successful employment of them requires a certain amount of explicit definition. One has to define them because one knows that their correct definitions are not perceived. A good example of this type of term is "liberty" in John Stuart Mill's famous essay of that name. Mill proposes to argue certain propositions about liberty and the individual, but before he can do this, he must go through a long process of defining. Only after that is completed, can he use "liberty" as a genus by which to approve or disapprove of certain actions. Anyone today predicating an argument upon "democracy" must do the same thing. "Democracy" is surrounded by so much nebulosity that one cannot, until this labor is performed, expect much similarity of conception. That is to say, it is not in the public mind now a clear genus.

13 The process of argument is, of course, the same in both instances, the difference being that in the first the genus is ready-made; in the second it has to be made. It is well to take notice of this because many arguments will be encountered by the students in their reading which devote most of their space to setting up the genera. Not until these are fixed is the writer prepared to make propositions with reference to special occurrences.

Consequence

14 In a consequence argument, one presents the casual relationships among experiences. As with arguments from genus and definition, these arguments may employ self-evident and widely accepted causal linkings, or the writer may seek to establish linkings which are less well recognized. Such arguments most frequently move directly from cause to effect or from effect to cause. The simple cause-to-effect argument is well illustrated in Burke's *Speech on American Taxation,* where the movement of the argument is from the cause (unjust treatment of the American Colonies) to the effect (discontent, disorder, disobedience). The classic argument from effect to cause is the proof of the existence of God from the existence of order in the universe. The argument here consists of observing the effect and then postulating a cause which will explain this effect.

15 A more complex argument is sometimes called the "argument from sign." Many causes have a multiplicity of effects. A cold snap not only will produce ice on ponds but will cause people to dress warmly. When one observes some of the effects and argues from them to the cause and thence to another effect, he is arguing from sign. The ice and the wearing of warm clothing are effects of the cause, coldness. By observing one effect, we can reason to the cause and thence to another effect, which, in this example, is a course of action.

16 All these arguments are in constant use in our civilization. The politician argues that, if he is elected (cause), there will be better government (effect); he argues that the present corruption in government (effect) must have been produced by a corrupt administration (cause); and that his happy home, successful career, and firm church and civic affiliations are clear signs that he will administer the office he seeks wisely and honestly.

Likeness and Difference

17 Likeness and difference are really two separate topics. But their structure as arguments is sufficiently similar to warrant their being grouped together. There is no significant difference between likeness and what we are more familiar with as analogy. Similarly, difference corresponds to what some logicans call "negative analogy." An important thing to remember in both is that they rest, as arguments, on two instances; that is, in using likeness or difference, we argue from one case to another, unlike the practice in induction, where we argue from a large number of particular cases to a general rule or law.

18 A distinction is sometimes drawn between two uses of likeness, or analogy. The rhetorician Whately, for example, suggests that it may be used, not only "to *prove* the proposition in question, but to make it more *clearly under-stood."* We must not mistake for argument, he goes on to tell us, what is used for clarification. When we reflect that "analogy" is sometimes used synonymously with "metaphor," we can see that the situation can become still further complicated. For our purposes, however, we can disregard such distinctions. Actually, it could be plausibly asserted that all comparisons are used, in varying degrees, for argument. Hence we will not go far wrong if we treat them as arguments.

Testimony and Authority

19 In that it seldom stands alone as the primary source of an extensive argument, testimony and authority differs from the other topics. It is an "external" source of argument, because its force is derived not from the immediate subject matter of the discourse but from consideration of the competence and integrity of the witness: if good and wise men believe this, it must be so. This topic may be directed toward the confirmation of either a general proposition or a specific circumstance. Testimony and authority involves also the writer's attempt to establish his own credibility as a witness or probity as a judge and, conversely, in some instances an effort to show that his opponent is careless with facts and unsound in judgment. Finally, style itself, through the use of terminology or even syntax associated with revered persons, ideas, or institutions, may constitute a subtle appeal to authority.

III

20 It may be objected that, although this approach to the teaching of argument has theoretical attractiveness, its relevance to the workaday job of writing a composition is somewhat tenuous. Some may feel, as some of us did during preliminary discussions of the idea, that, however plausible the introduction of the topics might appear when reflected upon in the teacher's study, it would only create confusion in the classroom by setting up another barrier of terminology between the student's thought and his written argument. However, on the basis of experience, we are now convinced that the topics can be intimately related to the student's problems in writing arguments, that they help the student to clarify the ideas which he wishes to set down on paper, and that, above all, they fulfill their primary purpose—the stimulation of the student's powers to discover relevant and effective arguments.

21 Perhaps the nature of this interplay between theory and practice may be suggested by a brief account of the way in which we familiarize our students with topical analysis. First, in order to make clear what a topic is and to exemplify the four topics chosen, we present a series of brief argumentative passages, classified according to the topic primarily employed in each. Thus, under genus, we show Tom Paine using a definition of a "true" constitution to support his argument that the British government is fundamentally lawless. As soon as the students show some ability to understand and recognize particular topics, they are asked to write a series of brief arguments in which they experiment with the appropriateness of various topical approaches. It should be noted that the students are *not* told to create an argument illustrating a particular topic but, instead, are instructed to write arguments supporting or attacking certain propositions which are chosen for their simplicity, closeness to students' interests, and capacity to stir controversy.

22   Obviously, in any reasonably complex argument, a skillful writer will draw upon a variety of topics, moving easily from one to another as he develops the full significance of his thought. Consequently, after introducing the topics through brief, categorized excerpts, we turn our attention to the examination of several substantial arguments—among them *The Federalist,* No. 10; Lincoln's First Inaugural Address; Thoreau's "Civil Disobedience"; Swift's "A Modest Proposal"; Bertrand Russell's "A Free Man's Worship"; Newman's "Knowledge Its Own End"—in which various topical approaches can be observed in the less artificial context of full, rich, and actual disputation. Accompanying the study of these texts is the writing of two or three fairly long arguments in which the student has an opportunity to practice not merely his ability to recognize relevant topics but also his skill in incorporating various topical arguments into a systematic and persuasive whole.

23   The most significant result traceable, we believe, to experimentation with the program outlined above has been a striking increase in the richness of students' arguments. With the topics providing a guide line, our writers show much less timidity about thrusting themselves into the heart of argumentative situations, instead of coyly and cautiously skirting the edges, as they have often done in the past. This fact has done much to strengthen our conviction that instruction in argumentation has a primary role in the composition course. In so far as familiarity with the rhetorical topics improves the young writer's ability to look for and recognize rational arguments which are appropriate to the line of thought or action he is advocating, the approach we have described makes it possible to deal seriously with argumentation. Placed in the posture of argument, students who know how to employ the topics are not so likely either to freeze or to foam. They have demonstrated that, given a technique to assist them in locating and evaluating arguments, they have something to say about controversial subjects.

Richard L. Larson: A Plan for Teaching Rhetorical Invention

One of the problems with the topics as a generating device for composition, especially when they are set forth, as they are earlier in this chapter and in the previous article, as categories or headings, like definition, similarity, difference, *is that they tend to just "sit there," inert and unprovocative of ideas. Consequently, students are at a loss as to how to get the topics to turn up ideas for them on some subject or thesis. When the topics are posed in the form of questions, however, they seem to work better for students as generating devices, perhaps because a question, by its very nature, stimulates a response. The formula of one-word questions often taught in journalism schools as a guide to what must be included in the lead of a news story— who? what? when? where? how?—is a topical device of this kind. In the following selection, Richard L. Larson, Director of Freshman English at the University of Hawaii, sets down a series of topical questions that can be productive of ideas when students are asked to write on subjects or propositions. In the first part of the article from which this list of questions was taken, Professor Larson says, "I propose, therefore, that in our teaching of 'invention' we make a persistent effort to force students to become as familiar as possible with the facts, and possible relationships among the facts, about experiences on which they might write, and also that we force them to examine the facts underlying concepts they consider important and the content of propositions on which they may want to write. . . . I propose that students come to this thorough knowledge of their experiences, concepts, and propositions through a process of systematic questioning—questioning which students engage in mostly by themselves, rather than questioning conducted for them by the teacher. . . . Not all the questions, of course, will produce useful answers for every subject, and the student should learn which questions provide valuable ideas on which subjects and which ones are comparatively fruitless on those subjects" (pp. 128-9).*

I. "Topics" That Invite Comment
   A. *Writing about Single Items (in present existence)*
      What are its precise physical characteristics (shape, dimensions, composition, etc.)?

From "Discovery Through Questioning: A Plan for Teaching Rhetorical Invention," *College English*, XXX (November 1968), 126-34. Reprinted by permission of the National Council of Teachers of English and Richard L. Larson.

How does it differ from things that resemble it?

What is its "range of variation" (how much can we change it and still identify it as the thing we started with)?

Does it call to mind other objects we have observed earlier in our lives? why? in what respects?

From what points of view can it be examined?

What sort of structure does it have?

How do the parts of it work together?

How are the parts put together?

How are the parts proportioned in relation to each other?

To what structure (class or sequence of items) does it belong?

Who or what produced it in this form? Why?

Who needs it?

Who uses it? for what?

What purposes might it serve?

How can it be evaluated, for these purposes?

B. *Writing about Single Completed Events, or Parts of an Ongoing Process (These questions can apply to scenes and pictures, as well as to works of fiction and drama.)*

Exactly what happened? (Tell the precise sequence: who? what? when? how? why? Who did what to whom? why? What did what to what? how?)

What were the circumstances in which the event occurred? What did they contribute to its happening?

How was the event like or unlike similar events?

What were its causes?

What were its consequences?

What does its occurrence imply? What action (if any) is called for?

What was affected (indirectly) by it?

What, if anything, does it reveal or emphasize about some general condition?

To what group or class might it be assigned?

Is it (in general) good or bad? by what standard? How do we arrive at the standard?

How do we know about it? What is the authority for our information? How reliable is the authority? How do we know it to be reliable? (or unreliable?)

How might the event have been changed or avoided?

To what other events was it connected? how?

To what kinds of structure (if any) can it be assigned? On what basis?

C. *Writing about Abstract Concepts* (*e.g., "religion," "socialism"*)

To what specific items, groups of items, events, or groups of events, does the word or words connect, in your experience or imagination?

What characteristics must an item or event have before the name of the concept can apply to it?

How do the referents of that concept differ from the things we name with similar concepts (e.g., "democracy" and "socialism")?

How has the term been used by writers whom you have read? How have they implicitly defined it?

Does the word have "persuasive" value? Does the use of it in connection with another concept seem to praise or condemn the other concept?

Are you favorably disposed to all things included in the concept? Why or why not?

D. *Writing about Collections of Items* (*in present existence*) [These questions are in addition to the questions about single items, which can presumably be asked of each item in the group.]

What, exactly, do the items have in common?

If they have features in common, how do they differ?

How are the items related to each other, if not by common characteristics? What is revealed about them by the possibility of grouping them in this way?

How may the group be divided? What bases for division can be found?

What correlations, if any, may be found among the various possible sub-groups? Is anything disclosed by the study of these correlations?

Into what class, if any, can the group as a whole be put?

E. *Writing about Groups of Completed Events, Including Processes* [These questions are in addition to questions about single completed events; such questions are applicable to each event in the group. These questions also apply to literary works, principally fiction and drama.]

What have the events in common?

If they have features in common, how do they differ?

How are the events related to each other (if they are not part of a chronological sequence)? What is revealed by the possibility of grouping them in this way (these ways)?

What is revealed by the events when taken as a group?

How can the group be divided? On what bases?

What possible correlations can be found among the several sub-groups?

Into what class, if any, can the events taken as a group fit?

Does the group belong to any other structures than simply a larger group of similar events? (Is it part of a more inclusive chronological sequence? one more piece of evidence that may point toward a conclusion about history? and so on)

To what antecedents does the group of events look back? Where can they be found?

What implications, if any, does the group of events have? Does the group point to a need for some sort of action?

II. "Topics" with "Comments" Already Attached

A. *Writing about Propositions (statements set forth to be proved or disproved)*

What must be established for the reader before he will believe it?

Into what sub-propositions, if any, can it be broken down? (What smaller assertions does it contain?)

What are the meanings of key words in it?

To what line of reasoning is it apparently a conclusion?

How can we contrast it with other, similar, propositions? (How can we change it, if at all, and still have roughly the same proposition?)

To what class (or classes) of propositions does it belong?

How inclusive (or how limited) is it?

What is at issue, if one tries to prove the proposition?

How can it be illustrated?

How can it be proven (by what kinds of evidence)?

What will or can be said in opposition to it?

Is it true or false? How do we know? (direct observation, authority, deduction, statistics, other sources?)

Why might someone disbelieve it?

What does it assume? (What other propositions does it take for granted?)

What does it imply? (What follows from it?) Does it follow from the proposition that action of some sort must be taken?

What does it reveal (signify, if true)?

If it is a prediction, how probable is it? On what observations of past experience is it based?

If it is a call to action, what are the possibilities that action can be taken? (Is what is called for feasible?) What are the probabilities that the action, if taken, will do what it is supposed to do? (Will the action called for work?)

B. *Writing about Questions (interrogative sentences)*

Does the question refer to past, present, or future time?

What does the question assume (take for granted)?

In what data might answers be sought?

Why does the question arise?

What, fundamentally, is in doubt? How can it be tested? evaluated?
What propositions might be advanced in answer to it?
  Is each proposition true?
  If it is true:
    What will happen in the future? What follows from it?
    Which of these predictions are possible? probable?
    What action should be taken (avoided) in consequence?
    [Most of the other questions listed under "Propositions" also
    apply.]

External Aids to Invention

We have been considering the *topics,* those "places" to which the writer can
resort for help in inventing or discovering arguments. The topics might be
termed the "artistic means of persuasion" (*technoi pisteis*), because they are
the means taught by the art of rhetoric. In addition to these, Aristotle spoke
of the "non-artistic means of persuasion" (*atechnoi pisteis*)—"non-artistic"
in the sense that these resources did not belong specifically to the art of
rhetoric; the information came from "outside."

If reference books had been abundant in fifth-century Athens, Aristotle
would certainly have encouraged his students to consult them as external
aids to invention. Because of the need for a plentiful stock of special knowledge, Cicero and Quintilian maintained that a broad liberal education was
the best background for an orator. While acquiring this broad background,
students can compensate for their deficiencies by knowing about and resorting to the standard reference books. Although most college libraries are well
stocked with reference works, many students do not know that they exist,
or do not know what kind of information is contained in them, or do not
know how to use them to find the information they contain.

Since encyclopedias are the reference works that students are most familiar
with, the more prominent ones will be merely mentioned here. Most students
have at one time or other consulted either the *Encyclopedia Americana* (New
York: Encyclopedia Americana Corporation, 1949, 30 volumes) or the *Encyclopaedia Britannica* (Chicago: Encyclopaedia Britannica, 1949, 24 volumes),
but they should be reminded to make more use of the Index (the last volume
in each set) and the yearbooks, and they should not neglect the long scholarly
articles written by noted British authors in the ninth and eleventh editions
of the *Britannica.* The articles in *Collier's Encyclopedia* (New York: P. F.
Collier & Son Corporation, 1950, 20 volumes) are written on a level between

that of the juvenile encyclopedias students may have used at home and that of the adult encyclopedias just mentioned. Students should become familiar with the new edition of the famous *Chambers's Encyclopaedia* (London and New York: Oxford University Press, 1950, 15 volumes), the most respected of the general reference works published in England. Of more specialized interest are the *Encyclopedia of the Social Sciences* (New York: Macmillan Company, 1930-35, 15 volumes), the *Jewish Encyclopedia* (New York: Funk and Wagnalls Company, 1901-06, 12 volumes) or the more up-to-date *Universal Jewish Encyclopedia* (New York: Universal Jewish Encyclopedia, Inc., 1939-44, 10 volumes), and the *Catholic Encyclopedia* (New York: Catholic Encyclopedia, 1907-14, 16 volumes), which will soon be superseded by a new edition.*

But if students are to mature intellectually, they must learn that encyclopedias, valuable as they are, are not their first and last resource. Accordingly, the following section will discuss a number of reference works, readily available in public or college libraries, that students can consult to find material on whatever subject they are writing about. The exposition will point out the kind of information that can be found in these works and then explain the organization and use of the work. For information about reference works not covered in this section, students can consult guides like the following:

Isadore Mudge, *A Guide to Reference Books,* 6th ed. (Chicago: American Library Association, 1936).

Constance M. Winchell, *Guide to Reference Books,* 7th ed. (Chicago: American Library Association, 1951). Supplements in 1954, 1956, 1960, 1963.

Arthur J. Walford, *Guide to Reference Materials* (New York: R. R. Bowker Co., 1959). Supplement, 1963.

Biography

> **Dictionary of National Biography,** ed. Leslie Stephen and Sidney Lee. Originally published in 63 volumes by Smith, Elder & Co., 1885-1900; reissued in 21 volumes by Macmillan, 1908-09.

A cyclopedia of British biography on the plan and scope of some of the other European biographical collections (the French, 40 volumes, 1843-63; the Dutch, 24 volumes, 1852-78; the Austrian, 60 volumes, 1856-91; the German, 55 volumes, 1875-1900). On January 1, 1885, the first volume appeared, containing 505 biographies written by 87 contributors. Within fifteen years, this monumental 63-volume work, containing 29,120 biographies, was completed. In the autumn of 1901, three supplementary volumes were published, con-

---

* *New Catholic Encyclopedia* (New York: McGraw-Hill, 1967, 15 volumes).

taining about 800 biographical sketches of noteworthy Englishmen who had died while the work was in progress and about 200 memoirs of prominent people who had been overlooked in the original master-list. (This became Volume XXII of the Macmillan re-issue.) In 1912 Macmillan issued three more volumes to cover the years 1901–11. The Oxford University Press has been publishing the supplementary volumes, each covering a decade.

According to the original prospectus, the *Dictionary of National Biography* (*DNB*) was designed to provide "full, accurate, and concise biographies of all noteworthy inhabitants of the British Islands and the Colonies (exclusive of living persons) from the earliest historical period to the present time." The lives are arranged alphabetically according to surnames. If the student seeks the biography of a British subject who died in the twentieth century, he should consult the appropriate supplementary volume.

The value of the *DNB* is that it is often the only source of biographical information about British men and women who were prominent enough to have merited mention in newspapers and histories but not prominent enough to have merited a full-length biography or even a biographical sketch in an encyclopedia. The *DNB* is also helpful to someone seeking relatively brief but authoritative biographies of prominent statesmen, generals, clergymen, scientists, writers, painters, etc. The longest biography in the *DNB* is the 49-page memoir that Sidney Lee wrote on Shakespeare. Although many of the biographees are given less than a page, most of the prominent ones receive an extended but compact treatment. Additional sources of biographical information, whenever available, are listed in the bibliography at the end of each article.

> **Dictionary of American Biography,** ed. Allen Johnson and others (New York, Charles Scribner's Sons, 1928–36), 20 vols.; Volume XXI, Supplement One; Volume XXII, Supplement Two.

This collection of American biographies, initiated by the American Council of Learned Societies in 1922, was patterned on the *Dictionary of National Biography*. The editorial committee set down these negative restrictions: (1) no living persons; (2) no persons who had not lived in the territory known as the United States; (3) no British officers serving in America after the colonies had declared their independence. The positive qualification for inclusion was stated in rather general terms: "those who have made some significant contribution to American life." These criteria permitted the admission into the *DAB* of people who are not, strictly speaking, Americans: Lafayette, for instance.

The original twenty volumes contained 13,633 biographical articles. Supplement One (to December 31, 1935), published in 1944, added 652 memoirs. Supplement Two (to December 31, 1940), published in 1958, added 585 biographies.

Like the *DNB,* the *DAB* is often the only source of biographical information about deceased, relatively obscure Americans; but the *DAB* also provides compact biographical sketches of prominent Americans. The memoir of Benjamin Franklin, for instance, occupies twenty-five full columns in Volume VI. James Franklin (1696/7–1735), his half-brother, rates only a column and a half in the same volume. The biographies are based on reliable, original sources of information, many of which are listed in the carefully selected bibliographies at the end of each article. The biographies are arranged alphabetically according to the last name of the subject.

Who's Who in America: A Biographical Dictionary of Notable Living Men and Women (Chicago: A. N. Marquis Co., 1899–   ).

This is a valuable source of biographical data about prominent *living* Americans. Begun in 1899, this work is revised and re-issued every two years. The introduction to Volume XXX gives the criteria for inclusion:

> The standards of admission divide the eligible into two classes: (1) those selected on account of special prominence in creditable lives of effort, making them the subjects of extensive interest, inquiry, or discussion; (2) those included arbitrarily on account of position—civil, military, religious, educational, corporate, or organizational.

Among those in the second category are all members of congress and the cabinet, federal judges, governors of states, heads of the larger universities, military officers above the rank of brigadier general, members of the National Academy, bishops and chief ecclesiastics of the larger religious denominations. Insisting that its biographees lead "creditable lives," the Marquis Company automatically drops from later volumes any biographee who has been convicted of a major crime or felony.

Most of the biographees supply their own biographical information. Although the *kinds* of information sought are fixed by the editors, the *amount* of information supplied is left largely up to the biographee. In Volume XXX, for instance, President Eisenhower has only 19 lines; his brother Milton, the president of Johns Hopkins University, has 52 lines.

The student should remember that this is a reference source for *living Americans* only. When a person dies, he may then be relegated to another Marquis publication, *Who Was Who in America.* The three volumes of this work now available draw from the entire span of *Who's Who in America* Volumes I-XXXI. In order to find information on his subject, the student must remember to consult those volumes covering the years when the subject was in the public eye.

The Marquis Company also publishes periodically four regional biographical works: *Who's Who in the East; Who's Who in the Midwest; Who's Who in the West; Who's Who in the South and Southwest.* Whereas only three out of 10,000 Americans merit inclusion in the national *Who's Who in America,* an additional twelve out of 10,000 living Americans are included in the regional volumes. So if a student does not find an entry in the national volume, he should consult the appropriate regional volume.

Who's Who (London: Adam and Charles Black; New York: Macmillan, 1848–   ).

Who's Who, the older British work, first published in 1848, served as the pattern for the American biographical dictionary. It supplies biographical information about noteworthy living British subjects, and its criteria of eligibility are much the same as those in the American dictionary.

Each volume of *Who's Who* begins with an obituary of the prominent people who have died since the last volume appeared. Once deceased, these people appear in a later volume of a companion work called *Who Was Who.* Five volumes of *Who Was Who* have now been published, covering the period 1897–1960.

The term "Who's Who" has become as much of a household word as "Webster's," and people often use the term indiscriminately to refer to both the American and the British works.

International Who's Who (London: Europe Publications, 1935–   ).

The biographies in this annual compilation are very brief, but a great many notable people throughout the world are covered. Many of the people covered in this work are included in the various national biographical dictionaries, but this is a convenient reference work for those who cannot afford to buy several of the national dictionaries. Another valuable feature of the work is that notable people from smaller countries whose biographies are not available in the usual sources are included.

Current Biography (New York: H. W. Wilson Company, 1940–   ).

Current Biography, published annually, is another valuable source of biographical information about prominent contemporary people. It is different in many ways from *Who's Who in America* and *Who's Who:* the 1941 volume of *Current Biography,* for instance, contains only 991 biographical sketches, but it is world wide in its scope. The biographical sketches in *Current Biography* are composed by members of the editorial staff, not supplied by the biographees.

Here is the typical organization of a volume of *Current Biography:*

1. The biographical section, arranged alphabetically according to last names. This section comprises full biographies (usually two or three pages) of the prominent living persons selected for that particular year and short obituary notices of some prominent persons who have died that year.
2. A necrology—a list of *all* the prominent people who have died that year.
3. Index to biographies (in that particular volume) by profession.
4. A cumulative index of biographees. If the student does not find in this volume a biography of the subject he is seeking, this section will refer him to any earlier volume in which this subject is included.

Now that more than twenty volumes have appeared, *Current Biography* has become a valuable source of biographical information about world figures. Although each volume has an index of previously published biographies, the student will save time in finding the volume and pages if he will consult the two volumes that carry the cumulative indexes for the entire twenty-year span of this reference work. The 1950 volume provides a cumulative index for 1940–1950; the 1960 volume, the cumulative index for 1951–1960.

Contemporary Authors (Detroit: Gale Research, 1962–   ).

Unlike the other biographical reference works mentioned so far, this one concentrates on the members of a single profession—active, living authors. Novelists, short-story writers, poets, playwrights, authors of juvenile books, non-fiction writers, authors of textbooks are all eligible for inclusion. An Analysis made of the listings in *Contemporary Authors* revealed that over 75 per cent of the authors were not covered in any other biographical source. During its first year, *CA* was issued in quarterly volumes, but since 1963 two semi-annual volumes have been published every year, each containing about 2000 biographical sketches.

The biographical information in these sketches is presented in clearly marked-off sections, which follow this pattern: Personal (details about birth, education, marriage, children, religion, address); Career (positions held, honors and prizes won); Writings (a complete bibliography of all published books and occasionally of substantial monographs); Work in Progress; Sidelights (hobbies, avocations, comments about achievements and personality by others and sometimes by the author himself); Biographical and Critical Sources (if any have been published on this author). The second volume published each year carries a cumulative index of all authors covered from 1962 to date.

Chamber's Biographical Dictionary, ed. J. O. Thorne, new ed. (New York: St. Martin's Press, 1961).

Webster's Biographical Dictionary (Springfield, Mass.: G. & C. Merriam Co., 1943)

Dictionary of Catholic Biography, ed. John J. Delaney and James Edwin Tobin (New York: Doubleday, 1961).

The most famous of these one-volume reference works is *Chambers's Biographical Dictionary*. First published in 1897, it has recently appeared in a new edition of 1,432 double-column pages containing some 15,000 biographical articles. It treats of the famous men and women of all periods, all countries, and all occupations and professions. The amount of coverage varies with the prominence of the biographee. The present editor has adopted this standard sequence of basic information: (1) surname, (2) Christian names and titles, (3) pronunciation (of difficult or unusual names), (4) date of birth and death, (5) nationality and main occupation, (6) birthplace (if known). At the end of the articles on the major figures there is a list of works where additional information may be found. A unique feature of this work is the subject index of some 6,000 items through which biographees may be traced through titles of works, events, places, campaigns, nicknames, etc.

Webster's Biographical Dictionary presents about 40,000 brief biographies of historical and contemporary figures in 1,732 pages. Published in 1943, this work is not as up-to-date on living men and women as the new edition of *Chambers's*. It is, however, a handy, surprisingly comprehensive source of biographical information about a large number of world figures.

As its title indicates, *The Dictionary of Catholic Biography* is a reference work of more limited scope. It does not cover living men and women, but the biographies of the 3,000 Catholics that it does supply in its 1,260 double-column pages are usually more extensive than those in the other two one-volume biographical dictionaries. In the appendix there is a list of patron saints and a 14-page chart correlating the reigns of popes and world rulers.

Biography Index: A Cumulative Index to Biographical Material in Books and Magazines (New York: H. W. Wilson Company, 1946–).

The *Biography Index* is a helpful guide to biographical material in currently published, English-language books and pamphlets, in over 1,500 periodicals, in some legal and medical journals, and in the obituary notices of the New York *Times*. All types of biographical material are indexed: "pure biography, critical material of biographical significance, autobiography, letters, diaries, memoirs, journals, genealogies, fiction, drama, poetry, bibliographies, obituaries, pictorial works, and juvenile literature."

The *Biography Index* has two main parts: (1) the subject index, arranged alphabetically by last name; (2) the index to professions and occupations (large categories, like Authors, are listed by nationality—American, Australian, British, etc.). The value of the latter section is that it can direct the inquirer to all the biographical material written, in some specific year, about men associated with some profession. A student assigned to do a paper on, say, atomic physicists since World War II could collect a bibliography in short order by consulting this section.

As evidence of the amazing comprehensiveness of this work, the first bound volume of *Biography Index* (January 1946 to July 1949) contains the names of over 40,000 biographees, classified into some 1,000 categories in the index to professions and occupations. Paperbound supplements are published quarterly and are bound in a separate volume, with a cumulative index, each year. Subsequently, a three-year cumulation is published and bound in a separate volume.

Concordances and Books of Quotations

> **Bartlett's Familiar Quotations:** A Collection of Passages, Phrases, and Proverbs Traced to Their Sources in Ancient and Modern Literature by John Bartlett, 12th ed., rev. and enl. by Christopher Morley and Louella D. Everett (Boston: Little, Brown and Company, 1948); 13th ed. (Centennial), 1955; 14th ed., 1968.

Bartlett's Familiar Quotations is the best known and perhaps the most frequently used reference guide to quotations. John Bartlett, a New England publisher, compiled his first book of quotations in 1855, and continued to edit it through its ninth edition in 1891. In 1914 Nathan Haskell Dole edited the tenth edition. Christopher Morley and Louella D. Everett edited the book in its eleventh (1937) and twelfth (1948) editions; the thirteenth (1955) and fourteenth (1968) editions were compiled by the staff of Little, Brown under the direction of Emily Morison Beck.

All of us, at some time or another, have needed an apt quotation to illustrate, enhance, or substantiate something we have written, or the exact wording of a quotation, or the author of the quotation, or the name of the work in which the quotation first appeared, or the exact place in a work (e.g. the specific line-number in a poem) where the quotation appeared. If we can remember any key-word in the quotation, it is likely that we can find the answer to such questions in a reference work like *Bartlett's Familiar Quotations*.

Let us suppose that we want to discover the source of the quotation, "Hope springs eternal in the human breast." Since quotations are not indexed under prepositions, pronouns, conjunctions, articles, and common words, like *is* and *was*, we can find this quotation indexed under any one of five key-words: *Hope, springs, eternal, human, breast*. The number of entries in *Bartlett's* listed under each of the five key-words is as follows: *Hope*, 156; *springs*, 20; *eternal*, 70; *human*, 190; *breast*, 59. The student who looked for this quotation under *springs* would probably have found the quotation sooner than the student who looked under the word *human*. Looking at the word *springs* in the Index of the Thirteenth Edition of *Bartlett's*, he would have found, four entries down in the list, this reference: "hope, eternal, 316a." Turning to the front half of *Bartlett's*, to the a-column (the left-hand column of the two-column page) on page 316, he would have discovered that "Hope springs eternal in the human breast" is the 95th line of Alexander Pope's *Essay on Man*, Epistle I.

The Fourteen Edition of *Bartlett's* is a book of more than 1750 pages, carrying more than 20,000 quotations from 2250 authors; the Index has some 117,000 entries. Except for the quotations from anonymous sources and from such collective works as the Book of Common Prayer and the Bible, which are placed at the end of the text portion of the book, the quotations in *Bartlett's* are arranged chronologically according to the time in which the authors wrote. Occasionally, there are footnotes that explain, amplify, or correlate the quotations.

When *Bartlett's* fails us, we can sometimes trace the elusive quotation by consulting one of the other concordances to quotations:

> **Hoyt's New Cyclopedia of Practical Quotations,** ed. Jehiel Keeler Hoyt, new ed. (New York: Somerset Books, 1947).

> **Home Book of Quotations, Classical and Modern,** ed. Burton Egbert Stevenson, 5th ed. (New York: Dodd, Mead, 1947).

> **A New Dictionary of Quotations on Historical Principles from Ancient and Modern Sources,** ed. H. L. Mencken (New York: Knopf, 1942).

> **The Oxford Dictionary of Quotations,** ed. Bernard Darwin, 2d ed. (London: Oxford University Press, 1953).

> **Dictionary of Quotations,** ed. Bergen Evans (New York: Delacorte Press, 1968).

H. L. Mencken's concordance contains many humorous, iconoclastic, or off-beat quotations that are not found in other concordances. A distinctive feature of *The Oxford Dictionary of Quotations* is that it carries quotations from Greek, Latin, French, German, and Italian authors in the original language (with English translations appended). The 791 pages of quotations in Bergen Evans's book are spiced with over 2000 witty historical and explanatory comments by the editor. Because the quotations in this concordance are arranged alphabetically according to topic or idea, it is easier to find an apt quotation for a certain subject in Evans's book than in the others mentioned.

> John Bartlett, **New and Complete Concordance or Verbal Index to Words, Phrases, and Passages in the Dramatic Works of Shakespeare with a Supplementary Concordance to the Poems** (London: Macmillan, 1894).

> Martin Spevack, **A Complete and Systematic Concordance to the Works of Shakespeare,** 6 volumes (Hildesheim: Georg Olms, 1969–).

In English, a concordance is available for all the major poets—Chaucer, Spenser, Milton, Pope, Wordsworth, Byron, Keats, Browning, Tennyson, and many other "greats." Among the concordances available for the lesser poets are those for Thomas Wyatt, Robert Herrick, Thomas Gray, Oliver Goldsmith, Robert Burns, and A. E. Housman. Although handbooks are frequently prepared as a helpful guide for the reading of prose writers, concordances to prose works are a rarity. Occasionally, however, as in the case of James Joyce, concordances are published for individual prose works.

As might be expected, many concordances have been prepared for Shakespeare's works. The best and the most comprehensive of these is the one compiled by the same John Bartlett who published *Familiar Quotations.*

This concordance works in the same way as the others we have considered. All of the lines in Shakespeare's poems and plays are indexed under all of the significant words in the line. Bartlett uses the act, scene, and line numbering as given in the 1891 Globe Edition of Shakespeare, and he always prints the entire line in his index, not just a portion of it.

Some people use a concordance like this as the basis for a stylistic study of an author or, more specifically, for a study of his diction. Did Shakespeare ever use such-and-such a word? How many times did he use a particular word? What about the range and variety of his vocabulary? A study of Shakespeare's imagery could also be worked out with the aid of a concordance.

The Martin Spevack concordance was done with the aid of an IBM 7094 computer, using the text of the new *Riverside Shakespeare* edited by

G. Blakemore Evans. In 1969 the first three of the projected six volumes were published: Vol. I: Drama and Character Concordances to the Folio Comedies, 1,333 pp.; Vol. II: Drama and Character Concordances to the Folio Histories, Concordances to the Non-Dramatic Works, 1,387 pp; Vol. III: Drama and Character Concordances to the Folio Tragedies and *Pericles, The Two Noble Kinsmen,* and *Sir Thomas More,* 1,609 pp. When this project is finished it will provide valuable data for all kinds of linguistic studies, because one of the features of this concordance is that it records the frequency of each word and the relative frequency (expressed in percentage) of each word in the play and in the speeches of each character.

Biblical Concordances

> James Strong, **The Exhaustive Concordance of the Bible** (the Authorized and Revised versions of the King James text) (Nashville: Abingdon, 1894, 1947).

> Newton Wayland Thompson and Raymond Stock, **Complete Concordance to the Bible** (Douay Version) (St. Louis: Herder, 1942, rev. ed., 1945).

> **Nelson's Complete Concordance of the Revised Standard Version of the Bible,** Compiled by Univac Under the Supervision of John W. Ellison (New York: Thomas Nelson, 1957).

Only three of the many biblical concordances are listed above—one for the King James or Authorized Version of the Bible; one for the Douay or Roman Catholic version; and one for the Revised Standard Version completed in 1952. Every college library of any size is sure to have one or more of the biblical concordances on its reference shelves. It took James Strong some thirty years to compile his concordance; it took Remington Rand's Univac only about 1000 hours to index more than 350,000 biblical contexts from the RSVB. When the Cambridge and Oxford University Presses complete their publication of the *New English Bible,* someone will undoubtedly prepare a concordance, probably with the aid of an electronic computing machine, for this latest English translation.

The index system of a biblical concordance works in much the same way as it does in *Bartlett's Familiar Quotations,* but whereas *Bartlett's* reproduces the quotations it indexes, the biblical concordances do not include the text of the Bible.

A complete concordance indexes *all* passages from the Bible, not just the familiar quotations from it. If one can remember any key word in a quotation (quotations are not indexed under articles, pronouns, prepositions, conjunctions, or auxiliary or linking verbs), he can find what he is looking for.

There are other uses for a concordance too. One could use the concordance to find out, for instance, whether the word *sacrament* ever occurred in the Old or New Testaments. One could find out when such a word as *bishop* became a part of ecclesiastical terminology, whether the Old Testament prophets ever used the word, whether Christ ever used the word in the Gospels, or whether it is found only in the Acts of the Apostles or in the Epistles. The concordance can serve too as a kind of *harmony*—that is, as a reference guide to various passages in the Bible where parallel or identical ideas or wordings occur.

Indexes to Periodicals

The Readers' Guide to Periodical Literature (New York: H. W. Wilson Company, 1900–   ).

Of all the periodical indexes, the *Readers' Guide* is the one the student has most likely used during his high-school years. It is an extremely useful reference guide to articles, stories, poems, and plays published in more than one hundred American magazines during the twentieth century. Since March, 1935, it has been appearing twice a month. The indexing is cumulated, first in annual volumes and then in two-year volumes which contain in one alphabetical listing all entries for the period covered.

The Readers' Guide is primarily a subject and author index, but short stories, poems, plays, and motion pictures are listed by title as well as under the author's name. When entries appear under a person's name in two different listings, the first group of articles refers to articles *by* that person as an author; the second group of articles refers to articles *about* that person as a subject. Here are examples, first of an author entry, then of a subject entry:

WALKER, John S.
Thermonuclear reactions: can they be used for man's benefit?
For Affairs 33:605-14 Jl '55

The first thing that appears under the author's name is the title of his article (usually only the first word is capitalized). Then appears the name of the magazine, in abbreviated form (at the front of each volume a key to abbreviations is given). This article appeared in *Foreign Affairs*. Following the title of the magazine is a series of numbers specifying the issue of the magazine in which this article appeared. The number before the colon is the volume number of the periodical (the bound volume of the periodical in the library usually carries this same volume number). After the colon are the page numbers of the article. A + sign after a page number indicates that the article is continued on other pages toward the back of the magazine. Then the date of the issue is given in abbreviated form. If the magazine is a monthly, as in this case, only the month (July) and the year (1955) are given; if the magazine is a weekly (see below), the month (March), day (12), and year (1955) are given. If the student is compiling a list of articles for later investigation, he should be careful to record the exact volume number and date of the magazine, because the librarian will need this information on the call-slip that the student submits.

> CENSORSHIP
> Art of censorship. H. Smith. Sat R 38:24 Mr 12 '55
> Light in San Diego. Nation 180:389 My 7 '55
> Minnesota menaced by vigilante censors. Christian Cent 72:468-9
> Ap 20 '55

The second item is a subject heading (Censorship). All the articles published on that subject during the period covered by this particular volume will be listed, and often there will be "see also" references to other subject headings. In the subject entries, the titles of articles are given first. Then the name of the author is given (in subject entries the author's first name is represented by the initial capital only). The absence of a name after the title of the article indicates an anonymous or unsigned article.

International Index (New York: H. W. Wilson Company, 1907–1965); since 1965 entitled **Social Sciences and Humanities Index.**

The *International Index* is a useful supplementary index to periodical literature. During the first fifty years of its coverage, the *International Index* covered foreign-language periodicals as well as English-language periodicals. With the volume for 1955–57, the title of this reference work was changed from *International Index to Periodicals* to *International Index, A Guide to Periodical Literature in Social Sciences and Humanities;* with Vol. XIX (April 1965—March 1966) the title was again changed, to *Social Sciences and Humanities Index.* With these changes of title, the coverage of scientific and foreign-language periodicals was curtailed in favor of concentration on the more scholarly English-language journals throughout the world which deal with the social sciences and the humanities. At present this reference work indexes about 175 journals. Published quarterly in paperback editions, it eventually appears as a bound volume with a two-year cumulation. A subject and author index, it uses the same style of notation as the *Readers' Guide.* Students seeking a full bibliography of magazine articles on some subject should consult the *International Index (Social Sciences and Humani-*

ties Index) in addition to the *Readers' Guide*. For certain subjects (e.g. topics of more scholarly interest), it is a more useful reference guide to periodicals than is the *Readers' Guide*.

> **The 19th Century Readers' Guide,** 1890–99, 2 vols. (New York: H. W. Wilson Co., 1944).

The *Readers' Guide* and the *International Index* cover the periodical litera-ture of the twentieth century; the *19th Century Guide* covers the last decade of the nineteenth century. Published in two volumes, this periodical guide indexes material in fifty-one English and American magazines that were being published late in the last century. In some cases, the indexing has been extended beyond the limits specified by the title. *The National Geographic Magazine,* for instance, is indexed from 1888, the year it began publication, to December 1908, when it begins to be indexed by the *Readers' Guide*. The British *Cornhill Magazine,* a periodical that published contributions from such distinguished writers as Thackeray, Ruskin, Arnold, and Trollope, is indexed from January 1890, to December 1922, when it was picked up by the *International Index*. The *19th Century Guide* adopts the standard list of subject headings and cross references used by the other periodical guides, has author entries, and gives title indexes to short stories, novels, plays, and poems.

> **Poole's Index to Periodical Literature,** ed. William Frederick Poole and William I. Fletcher, 6 vols. (New York: Houghton Mifflin, 1882–1907).

Poole's Index is the only index to English-language periodicals of the nine-teenth century up to 1890. It was initiated by William F. Poole, librarian at the Mercantile Library of Boston, the public libraries in Cincinnati and Chicago, and, at the time of his death in 1894, the famous Newberry Library in Chicago. His colleague William Fletcher had a hand in the preparation of all the volumes and after Poole's death was assisted by Franklin O. Poole and Mary Poole. *Poole's Index* with its five supplements covered 479 different periodicals and included more than 590,000 references.

  Poole's Index is a subject index only. Writers are entered only when they are treated as subjects. Thus Thomas Babington Macaulay's contributions to the *Edinburgh Review* are entered not under Macaulay's name but under the subjects he wrote about—Milton, church and state, Clive, Machiavelli, etc. Critical articles on poetry, the drama, and prose fiction appear under the name of the author whose work is being criticized. Hence a critical article on *Dombey and Son* would appear under "Charles Dickens."

Poole did not supply the date of the magazine in his references. A typical reference following the title of an article looks like this: Fortn 29:816. The Table of Abbreviations in the front of the volume shows that "Fortn" is the abbreviation for *Fortnightly Review*. The number before the colon is the volume number; the number after the colon is the first page of the article. By consulting the chronological conspectus at the front of the volume, the student would discover that volume 29 of the *Fortnightly Review* appeared in 1878. The chronological conspectus also indicates the volume numbers of the same date in other periodicals, so that from this table the student could trace the discussion of a subject in several contemporary periodicals.

A paperbound volume, *Poole's Index: Date and Volume Key*, by Marion V. Bell and Jean C. Bacon (Chicago: Association of College and Reference Libraries, 1957), usually found on the shelves alongside *Poole's Index*, arranges the 479 periodical titles in a single alphabetical listing, with the year supplied for each volume of each periodical.

Other Indexes

Here is a list, with brief descriptions, of some other periodical indexes, which can usually be found on the reference shelves of public and college libraries. (All of them, except the *Catholic Periodical Index*, are published by the H. W. Wilson Company of New York):

Agricultural Index (1916–to date)—Published monthly. Later published in bound volumes in annual and two-year cumulations. A subject index to anything connected with agriculture in periodicals, pamphlets, and bulletins and in documents published by federal and state agricultural agencies.

The Art Index (1929–to date)—Published quarterly. Later cumulated in annual and two-year volumes. A subject and author index to periodicals and museum bulletins in the fields of archaeology, architecture, ceramics, ornament, engraving, graphic arts, landscaping, painting, sculpture.

The Education Index (1929–to date)—Published monthly, except in June and August, with annual and two-year cumulations. A subject and author index to periodicals, books, monographs, bulletins, and reports on anything connected with education.

Industrial Arts Index (1913–1957)—Published monthly. Later cumulated in annual bound volumes. This is a subject index only to periodical literature on business, finance, applied science, and technology. In 1958, this reference guide was divided into two separate publications: *The Applied Science and Technology Index* (covering aeronautics, automation, chemistry, construction, electrical communication, engineering, geology, metallurgy, physics, and transportation) and the *Business Periodicals Index* (covering accounting, insurance, public administration, taxation, and other allied subjects).

Catholic Periodical Index (1930–to date)—Published quarterly by the Catholic Library Association of Washington, D.C., this periodical guide eventually appears in a bound volume with a two-year cumulation. It indexes about 200 Catholic periodicals published in various parts of the world, many of which are not included in the *Readers' Guide* or the *International Index*.

Essay and General Literature Index (New York: H. W. Wilson Co., 1934–).

This is an author and subject index (with title entries where needed) to collections of essays, articles, and miscellaneous works of some reference value. The first five cumulative volumes cover the period from 1900 through 1959. Supplements appear semi-annually and annually, and eventually the cumulations appear in a bound volume that covers about a five-year period.

The special value of the *Essay and General Literature Index* is that this reference work can guide the student to collections that print essays, articles, stories, poems, etc. which have been long out of print or which are not readily available in earlier editions or in bound periodicals. Sometimes the student knows of or discovers through the periodical guides an essay or article that would be extremely useful for a paper he is writing, but in checking the library he learns to his dismay that this library does not have the book or the bound periodical in which this piece originally appeared. He should not, however, abandon all hope of getting a copy of this piece. The *Essay and General Literature Index* may indicate that it has been printed in a collection or anthology, of which the library has a copy. At the back of each bound volume is a list of all the books indexed in that volume, and many librarians put a check mark opposite the titles that the library has in the stacks. The essays and articles reprinted in the "readers" that the student may have bought for some of his college courses are, or will be, indexed in this reference work.

New York Times Index (New York: New York Times Index, 1913–).

Times Official Index (London: Times Office, 1906–).

Some public and university libraries keep a file of the local newspapers and provide some kind of index to these newspapers. They are more likely, however, to maintain files of some of the great newspapers, like the London *Times* and the *New York Times,* both of which publish annual indexes to their copy.

Formerly, libraries and newspaper "morgues" retained copies of the newspapers, but these stacks were awkward to store, difficult to handle, and susceptible to slow decay. Now, thanks to the microfilming process, an entire year's issue of a newspaper can be included on a few rolls of film. Using a microfilm reader, the researcher can quickly turn to the particular issue and feature he is interested in and can take notes from the enlarged reproduction of the newspaper type.

Obviously, an index to a newspaper can save the researcher hours of time. The London *Times* is indexed from 1906 to the present in quarterly accumulations. The *New York Times Index* has been appearing since 1913 in quarterly, monthly, or fortnightly issues. But each year these separate issues are cumulated and bound into a single volume that libraries retain on their reference shelves.

The *New York Times Index* is a subject index only. Articles and features are not entered by the titles or headlines they had in the newspaper. Instead, the compilers supply a phrase or sentence which concisely describes the substance of the piece. For each entry under the subject heading, the date, page number, and column are given (for Sunday issues the section-number of the paper is also supplied)—e.g. Je 8, III, 3:4 (June 8—the year is supplied by the particular annual volume being used—section 3, page 3, column 4).

If the student is tracing a news item that was covered over several days, he can, by turning the microfilm reader to earlier or later issues, find additional material. The *New York Times Index* can also serve as an informal index to other newspapers, for major news events will most likely be covered in local newspapers on the same date as they were covered in the *New York Times.*

Handbooks

World Almanac and Book of Facts (New York: New York World-Telegram and Sun Corporation, 1868–to date).

Information Please Almanac (1947–to date; various publishers, currently Simon and Schuster, New York).

These almanacs are such rich storehouses of miscellaneous information that every student should buy one or the other. A large portion of each edition of the almanacs is reprinted every year without any changes, because certain kinds of data, like the names of the presidents and vice-presidents of the United States or the capitals of each state of the Union, are not subject to change. For that kind of information, a 1940 almanac is just as useful to the student as a 1962 almanac. Other kinds of information, however, do change from year to year. If the student is seeking statistics on the federal tax revenue for 1960, he must consult the almanac covering that year. The student should browse through one of these volumes in a bookstore to get an adequate notion of the great variety of useful information supplied.

The *Information Please Almanac* contains more signed articles than does the *World Almanac,* and its coverage of foreign countries is more extensive. Because of the miscellaneous nature of the information, neither almanac arranges its material in alphabetical order. Instead, extremely detailed indexes to the material in each volume are provided. Frequent cross-references point to additional material.

English Literature

The Oxford Companion to English Literature, ed. Sir Paul Harvey, 4th ed. revised by Dorothy Eagle (Oxford Clarendon Press, 1967).

The New Century Handbook of English Literature, ed. Clarence L. Barnhart (New York: Appleton-Century-Crofts, 1956).

American Literature

The Oxford Companion to American Literature, ed. James D. Hart, 4th ed. (New York: Oxford University Press, 1965).

The Reader's Encyclopedia of American Literature, ed. Max J. Herzberg (New York: Thomas Y. Crowell Co., 1962).

American Authors and Books, ed. W. J. Burke and Will D. Howe, aug. and rev. by Irving Weiss (New York: Crown, 1962).

World Drama

The Oxford Companion to the Theatre, ed. Phyllis Hartnoll, 3d ed. (New York: Oxford University Press, 1967).

The Reader's Encyclopedia of World Drama, ed. John Gassner and Edward Quinn (New York: Thomas Y. Crowell Co., 1969).

All of these handbooks supply the same kind of information about literature and the arts. Their scope is defined by their titles. Here is the kind of information that can be found in these alphabetically arranged handbooks:

1. Short biographical sketches of poets, novelists, short-story writers, playwrights, essayists, artists, musicians.
2. Short biographical sketches of statesmen, scientists, philosophers, historians, actors, military men—especially those who have some relation to literature.
3. Plot summaries of novels, plays, operas, and long narrative poems.
4. Résumés of major lyric, didactic, and satirical poems.
5. Identification of major characters in novels, plays, operas, and narrative poems.
6. Explanations of Biblical, classical, and mythological allusions.
7. Definitions of literary terms—e.g. heroic couplet, Shakespearean sonnet, pathetic fallacy.
8. Short essays on literary trends and movements—realism, existentialism, New Criticism.
9. Explanations of historical and geographical references which have some pertinence to literature and the arts—e.g. Gunpowder Plot, Fleet Street, Waterloo.
10. Short essays on famous musical compositions and works of art which have had some influence on literature—e.g. Elgin Marbles, Mona Lisa, Mozart's *Don Giovanni*.

Some of this information will be found in any one of the seven handbooks listed at the head of this article. But the student seeking information about an American author or an American novel would probably find the most complete information in one of the handbooks devoted exclusively to American literature. For anything connected with the theater, the articles in the *Oxford Companion to the Theatre* are likely to be fuller and more satisfactory than those in the other handbooks. The student should understand, however, that all of these handbooks supply only the essential facts; for studies in depth he will have to turn to other sources.

Cassell's Encyclopedia of World Literature, ed. S. H. Steinberg, 2 vols. (New York: Funk and Wagnalls Co., 1954).

The Reader's Encyclopedia, ed. William Rose Benét, 2d ed. (New York: Thomas Y. Crowell Co., 1965).

Whereas the previously mentioned handbooks dealt with the literature and art of particular countries or a special art form, these two handbooks provide the same kinds of information about world literature and art. William Rose Benét's handbook covers the major world literatures—English, French, German, Italian, Russian, Greek, and Latin. *Cassell's* covers these literatures and, in addition, such minor ones as Armenian, Basque, Breton, Eskimo, Polynesian, Yiddish—cultures usually neglected by English-language reference works. In its two volumes of 2086 double-column pages, *Cassell's* treats of some eighty literatures. The articles in *Cassell's* are arranged alphabetically in three different sections:

Part I   Histories of the Literatures of the World and General Literary Subjects, pp. 1-574.

Part II   Biographies of Authors Who Died Before 1 August 1914.

Part III   Biographies of Authors Who Were Living on 1 August 1914 or Who Were Born after That Date.

Part I contains about 550 articles ranging in length from two lines to the 10,000 words it devotes to the Bible. In addition to long articles on such subjects as printing and publishing (35 columns), biography (12 columns), English literature (26 columns), and Russian literature (12 columns), there are shorter articles on such topics as epigrams, rhetoric, alliterative verse, commedia dell'arte. Major articles and biographies are followed by brief bibliographies.

While William Rose Benét's *Reader's Encyclopedia* is not as comprehensive and expansive as *Cassell's*, it is a handy one-volume source of essential information about world literature and the arts.

The Oxford Companion to Classical Literature, ed. Sir Paul Harvey (Oxford: Clarendon Press, 1955).

The New Century Classical Handbook, ed. Catherine B. Avery (New York: Appleton-Century-Crofts, 1962).

Crowell's Handbook of Classical Literature, ed. Lillian Feder (New York: Thomas Y. Crowell Co., 1964).

These three handbooks are rich mines of classical lore. They (1) identify the figures of myth and legend; (2) provide biographies of dramatists, poets, sculptors, painters, philosophers, generals, and statesmen; (3) give résumés of such epics as the *Iliad, Odyssey,* and *Aeneid* and of the dramas of Aeschylus, Sophocles, Euripides, Aristophanes; (4) supply information about places of mythological, historical, and archaeological interest; (5) have articles on rivers, mountains, shrines, ancient works of art, ruins, and monuments; (6) define classical terms. *The New Century Classical Handbook* has a great many illustrations and photographs and spells out phonetically Anglicized pronunciations of classical proper names—an especially helpful feature. Some information about classical subjects can be found in the handbooks of English, American, and world literature, but since these handbooks concentrate on classical lore, their coverage is more extensive and expansive.

Granger's Index to Poetry, 5th ed. (New York: Columbia University Press, 1962).

This famous reference guide to poetry has been in existence now for over half a century. This latest edition has four kinds of indexes to poems collected in over 500 of the most important anthologies published through June 30, 1960: (1) title index; (2) author index; (3) first-line index; (4) subject index. If the student can remember anything about the poem that he is trying to recover, he should be able to trace it with the aid of this reference guide. The subject index can also be used to find several poems dealing with a particular topic. The student will have to resort to an index of quotations, like *Bartlett's,* if all he can remember of a poem is a line other than the first line.

Grove's Dictionary of Music and Musicians, 4th ed. by H. C. Colles, 6 vols.; 5th ed. by Eric Blom, 10 vols. (New York: St. Martin's Press, 1940, 1954, 1961).

The Oxford Companion to Music, ed. Percy A. Scholes, 10th ed. revised and edited by John Owen Ward (New York: Oxford University Press, 1970).

Sir George Grove published the first edition of this famous reference work in 1879, contributing to it major articles on Beethoven, Mendelssohn, and Schubert, which were not dropped until the fifth edition. Grove arbitrarily set the beginning date of his coverage at A.D. 1450, but with the recent growth of knowledge about ancient music, especially about medieval plain-song, later editors included articles about the music of much earlier eras. An American Supplement, first added in the third edition, has been retained and amplified in the fourth and fifth. Approximately a half of the total contents of the fifth edition, some four million words, is new. Hundreds of expert contributors have written articles on such subjects as these: (1) definitions of musical terms; (2) explanations of the forms and methods of musical composition; (3) studies of the origin, development, and structure of musical instruments; (4) histories of various musical societies; (5) notices of composition, production, and contents of important works; (6) lists of the principal published collections of music; (7) biographies of composers, singers, players, patrons, etc.

The Oxford Companion to Music makes no pretense of rivaling *Grove's Dictionary,* but the 1133 double-column pages in the 1955 edition provide a wealth of information about music and musicians. Throughout the text there are over 1100 portraits and pictures, and at the back of the book there is a pronouncing glossary of some 7000 terms and names that appear in the articles.

> **An Encyclopedia of World History: Ancient, Medieval, and Modern, Chronologically Arranged,** ed. William L. Langer, 4th ed. (Cambridge, Mass.: Houghton Mifflin Co., 1968).
>
> **Encyclopedia of American History,** ed. Richard B. Morris, rev. ed. (New York: Harper & Row, 1961).

The Langer book is a reworking of the *Epitome of History* that the German professor Dr. Karl Ploetz prepared and that William H. Tillinghast translated into English in 1883. In this revised edition, the coverage of this rich storehouse of historical facts has been brought down to the end of World War II in 1945. If the student has trouble locating the information he is seeking by following the geographical and chronological indicators at the top of each page, he can consult the highly detailed index. The historical narrative is interspersed with many black-and-white maps and almost a hundred genealogical tables of the major ruling families, and the Appendix provides lists of the Roman and Byzantine emperors, the popes, and the British, French, and Italian ministries.

The Morris book is a comparable handbook for American history. It has three main divisions: Part I, chronologically arranged, which presents major political and military events of the nation from the pre-Columbian era to the inauguration of President John F. Kennedy in January 1961; Part II, topically organized, which presents such non-political aspects of American history as constitutional developments, westward expansion, and economic, scientific, and cultural trends; Part III, alphabetically arranged, which presents brief biographical sketches of some 400 notable Americans. Scattered throughout the more than 800 double-column pages of the text are charts, tables, and historical maps. An extremely detailed Index serves as a key to the wealth of information in this handbook.

Dictionaries, Atlases, and Gazetteers

A good desk dictionary, like *Webster's Seventh New Collegiate Dictionary,* the *New World Dictionary,* the *American College Dictionary,* Funk and Wagnalls' *Standard College Dictionary,* the *Random House Dictionary* (College Edition), or the *American Heritage Dictionary* will supply the routine information that a student seeks about the spelling, syllabification, pronunciation, and meaning of words, as well as providing some brief information about many proper names. Occasionally, however, a student may have to consult unabridged and other special dictionaries, and therefore he should become familiar with the special dictionaries that are usually available on the reference shelves of libraries.

The Oxford English Dictionary on Historical Principles, ed. James A. H. Murray, Henry Bradley, William A. Craigie, and C. T. Onions, 10 vols. and supplement (Oxford: Clarendon Press, 1884–1928). Supplement, 1933.

The greatest dictionary of the English language—in fact, the greatest dictionary ever compelled for any language—is the *New English Dictionary* (*NED*) or, as it has been referred to since about 1895, the *Oxford English Dictionary* (*OED*). The idea for this comprehensive dictionary originated in a suggestion that Richard Chevenix Trench, then Dean of Westminster, made to the Philological Society of England in 1857. It was decided right from the start that this dictionary would provide a historical study of the language, and several hundred readers were engaged to select and transcribe quotations which would be the basis of the historical conspectus. Some 1300 additional readers, most of them non-professional students of the language, culled three and a half million quotation slips from more than 5000 authors of all periods.

The first volume of the *OED* was published in 1884; the tenth volume was published in 1928—forty-four years after the first volume appeared and seventy years after the Philological Society passed the resolution to publish the dictionary. In 1933 a 336-page supplement was published to cover the recent additions to the language (either new words or new senses) and some words that had been overlooked in the main dictionary. The ten volumes of "the Principal Dictionary" have a total of 15,487 pages with 1,827,306 illustrative quotations.

In the preface to the first volume, the editors stated, "The aim of this Dictionary is to furnish an adequate account of the meaning, origin, and history of English words now in general use, or known to have been in use at any time during the last seven hundred years." In accordance with this objective, the *OED* supplies (1) the variant spellings a word has had down through the years; (2) the etymology of the word, established by the methods of modern philological science; (3) the pronunciation of the word (usually the pronunciation that prevailed at the time that particular volume was published); (4) the various meanings a word has had; (5) quotations illustrating the spellings and meanings, ranging from the first known occurrence of the word in printed works to the recent occurrences of the word in modern texts. Each illustrative quotation is preceded by the date of the occurrence, the name of the author, a short-title reference to the source, and the page number in the source. It should be emphasized that the earliest date supplied is not necessarily the date when the word was first used; this date indicates the earliest discovered written record of the use of the word.

A Dictionary of American English on Historical Principles, ed. Sir William A. Craigie and James R. Hulbert, 4 vols. (Chicago: University of Chicago Press, 1938–44).

A Dictionary of Americanisms on Historical Principles, ed. Mitford M. Mathews, 2 vols. (Chicago: University of Chicago Press, 1951).

William A. Craigie, one of the editors of the *OED*, worked with Professor James R. Hulbert of the University of Chicago to produce a historical dictionary of American English. As the editors said in their preface, this dictionary would include "not only words and phrases which are clearly or apparently of American origin or have greater currency here than elsewhere, but also every word denoting something which has a real connection with the development of the country and the history of its people." Using the historical principle that informed the *OED* and supplying the same kind of information, Craigie and Hulbert aimed to show how American English was distinguished from the languages of England and other English-speaking countries. The short-title references used in the citations are expanded in the 23-page bibliography. The end of the nineteenth century was arbitrarily chosen as the cut-off point for the admission of words to the lexicon, but many of the illustrative quotations are taken from works published during the first twenty-five years of the twentieth century.

In January of 1944, the year in which the last volume of the *DAE* was published, Mitford M. Mathews and his staff began preparation for *A Dictionary of Americanisms* (abbreviated *DA*). The *DA* would seem to be superfluous, but Professor Mathews felt that the *DAE* had marked as Americanisms many terms which he had reasons to reject and that the *DAE* had omitted some terms that were clearly Americanisms. The narrower scope of the *DA* is due to Mathew's definition of "Americanism": "a word or expression that originated in the United States." This criterion admitted into the word-list "outright coinages," as *appendicitis, hydrant, tularemia;* such words as *adobe, campus, gorilla,* which first became English in the United States; and terms such as *faculty, fraternity, refrigerator,* when used in senses first given them in American usage." A 33-page bibliography gives the full titles of works cited in the illustrative quotations.

For many kinds of historical, cultural, and linguistic information about Americanisms, the student should consult one of these two dictionaries.

The Century Dictionary and Cyclopedia, ed. William Dwight Whitney and Benjamin E. Smith, 12 vols. (New York: The Century Company, 1889–1914).

The Century Dictionary is generally regarded as the best multi-volume unabridged dictionary ever produced by a commercial publisher in America. Under the general editorship of William Dwight Whitney, the first edition appeared between 1889 and 1891. A cyclopedia of names appeared in 1894, an atlas in 1897, and two supplementary volumes in 1909. The final edition in 1914 was produced in a 12-volume set. The total number of words and names in the completed work was more than 500,000. Since about 1920, this great dictionary, which typographically is the most attractive and readable dictionary ever produced, has been out of print. Most college libraries, however, have a set on the reference shelves, and occasionally one can find a set in a secondhand bookstore.

This dictionary was designed to be as complete a record of *literary* English as possible. One of its values for the student of literature is the generous coverage given to obsolete words and forms, such as the Middle English of Chaucer's time. Moreover, the words and idioms of sixteenth- and seventeenth-century literature are more adequately covered than in any other American dictionary. The *Century Dictionary* gives illustrative quotations, presents full and accurate etymological information, lists synonyms for about 7000 words, and for many of the words adds a short informative essay.

The sub-title of the *Cyclopedia of Names* reveals the scope of this volume: *A Pronouncing and Etymological Dictionary of Names in Geography, Biography, Mythology, History, Ethnology, Art, Archaeology, Fiction, Etc.* This valuable dictionary of proper names has been made available in a separate publication: *The New Century Cyclopedia of Names,* in 3 vols. (New York: Appleton-Century-Crofts, 1954).

Among the 305 highly detailed colored maps in the world atlas are forty historical maps. There is an index, containing 170,000 names of towns, villages, cities, mountains, rivers, etc., with indications of where to locate them on the maps printed in the atlas.

Other Atlases and Gazetteers

Goode's World Atlas, 11th ed. (Chicago: Rand McNally & Co., 1960).

The Times's Atlas of the World, 5 vols. (London: The Times Office, 1955–60).

Hammond's Ambassador World Atlas, 2d ed. (Maplewood, N.J.: C. S. Hammond & Co., 1961).

Prentice-Hall's World Atlas (Englewood Cliffs, N.J.: Prentice-Hall, 1958).

Historical Atlas, ed. William R. Shepherd, 8th ed. (New York: Barnes and Noble, 1956).

Atlas of World History, ed. R. R. Palmer (Chicago: Rand McNally & Co., 1957).

Columbia Lippincott Gazetteer of the World, ed. Leon E. Seltzer (New York: Columbia University Press, 1952).

Webster's Geographical Dictionary: A Dictionary of Names of Places with Geographical and Historical Information and Pronunciations (Springfield, Mass.: G. & C. Merriam Co., 1955).

Webster's Third New International Dictionary, ed. Philip B. Gove (Springfield, Mass.: Merriam-Webster Company, 1961).

Most college students at one time or another have consulted the second edition of this unabridged dictionary, which was published in 1934. From now on, they will be consulting the third edition. The second was advertised as containing 600,000 entries, including the proper names in its biographical and gazetteer sections. The third edition is advertised as containing among its 450,000 entries 100,000 new words or meanings. Although the third edition has dropped the biographical and gazetteer sections, the Merriam-Webster Company publishes them as separate, portable dictionaries.

Webster's Third New International Dictionary is the most complete, up-to-date record of American English now in existence.* It covers the thousands of technical terms that have inundated the language in the last twenty-five years as well as the slang and colloquial idioms that have been added to the language. Most of the entries are illustrated by quotations, many of them from contemporary prose.

Origins: A Short Etymological Dictionary of Modern English, ed. Eric Partridge (New York: Macmillan, 1958).

Among the useful dictionaries compiled by Eric Partridge are *A Dictionary of Slang and Unconventional English* (now in its fifth edition), *A Dictionary of the Underworld, British and American,* and *Shakespeare's Bawdy: A Study and a Glossary*. For anyone who delights in the study of words, *Origins* is the most fascinating of Partridge's dictionaries.

* The Unabridged Edition of *The Random House Dictionary of the English Language,* published in 1966, is actually the latest of the larger dictionaries, but with only 260,000 entries it is not the most complete.

Unlike the other dictionaries that we have looked at in this section, *Origins* does not give the pronunciation or meanings of words. It confines itself to the etymology of some 12,000 of the commonest words in modern English. But the 15-page section on prefixes, the 22-page section on suffixes, and the 100-page section on compound-forming elements will help the student with thousands of learned and technical words in the language. The medical student, for instance, who detects some form of the element *glosso-* (from the Greek word meaning "tongue") can guess at the meaning of words like *glossograph, glossology, glossotomy, glottiscope, glottogenic.*

Although a number of abbreviations are used, the etymologies are traced in discursive prose that can be readily understood by the ordinary layman. A valuable feature of this dictionary is that all cognates are gathered under one heading and their etymologies traced in that section. Under the word *light,* for instance, more than fifty cognates are grouped—words like *leven, enlighten, Lucy, lucid, lucubration, luminary, lunatic, sublunary, luster, luxury, elucidate, illuminate, illustrate, leukemia.* The bonus for the student from such an arrangement is that while looking up the etymology of the word *light* he is made aware of many related and derivative words.

Any of the dictionaries mentioned in this section will supply etymological information about words, but for more extensive information about the history of words, the student should turn to *Origins* or to one of the following:

> **The Oxford Dictionary of English Etymology,** ed. C. T. Onions with the assistance of W. W. S. Friedrichsen and R. W. Burchfield (Oxford: Clarendon Press, 1966).

> **An Etymological Dictionary of the English Language,** ed. Walter W. Skeat, rev. ed. (Oxford: Clarendon Press, 1956).

> **A Concise Etymological Dictionary of Modern English,** ed. Ernest Weekley, rev. ed. (London: Secker & Warburg, 1952).

Other Specialized Dictionaries

The titles of the following dictionaries indicate the nature and scope of their coverage:

> **A Dictionary of Slang and Unconventional English,** ed. Eric Partridge, 7th ed. (London: Macmillan, 1970).

> **Dictionary of American Slang,** ed. Harold Wentworth and Stuart Berg Flexner (New York: Thomas Y. Crowell, 1960).

> **The American Thesaurus of Slang,** ed. Lester V. Berrey and M .Van den Bark, 2d ed. (New York: Thomas Y. Crowell, 1953).

A Dictionary of the Underworld, British and American, ed. Eric Partridge (New York and London: Macmillan, 1950).

Dictionary of American Underworld Lingo, ed. Hyman E. Goldin, Frank O'Leary, and Morris Lipsius (New York: Twayne Publishers, 1950).

English Dialect Dictionary, ed. Joseph Wright, 6 vols. (London: H. Frowde; New York: G. P. Putnam, 1898–1905).

A Pronouncing Dictionary of American English, ed. John S. Kenyon and Thomas A. Knott (Springfield, Mass.: G. & C. Merriam Co., 1944).

Bibliographies

A bibliography is a list of books and articles on a certain subject or author. A bibliography of an author lists works *by* that author and/or works *about* him. Each field of study has standard reference works directing the student to the published material in that discipline, and as the student progresses in his field of specialization, he will become familiar with the standard bibliographical guides in his specialized study. Here we will treat of two general guides to bibliographies in all fields and then of the principal bibliographical guides for English and American literature.

A World Bibliography of Bibliographies, ed. Theodore Besterman, 4th ed., 5 vols. Geneva, 1965).

This reference work, which was first published privately by its editor in 1939–40, is the most notable of the English-language bibliographies of bibliographies. The phrase "bibliography of bibliographies" may sound like double talk, but it is simply the term for a reference work that provides all the publication information about printed bibliographies on a variety of subjects. Someone assigned to do a term paper on witchcraft might want to discover whether a bibliography has ever been compiled on this subject. Besterman's work would not list the titles of works on witchcraft; it would simply give the titles of any *bibliographies* that had been compiled of such works. If the library had copies of those bibliographies, then the student would be able to assemble a list of books and articles pertinent to the subject he has been assigned to write on. Besterman's work would be a logical starting place for anyone launching upon a major piece of research.

As the title suggests, Besterman's work is international in its scope. It covers bibliographies in the humanities, the sciences, and technology, but it is limited to separately published bibliographies—that is, to books, monographs, or pamphlets which are devoted exclusively or primarily to bibliography. Hence the bibliographies given at the end of chapters or at the back of a book would not be listed in Besterman.

The bibliographies are arranged alphabetically according to subjects. An author index refers the student to the volume and pages of this work where a particular author's bibliography is listed. Since the searcher for a bibliography does not usually know the name of the compiler, he will probably have to consult the subject index. Frequent cross-references direct the student to bibliographies on allied subjects.

The Cumulative Book Index (New York: H. W. Wilson, 1933– to date).

Published every month except August, the *Cumulative Book Index* is an author, title, and subject catalogue of new books published in English in all countries of the world. These monthly issues are cumulated (at irregular intervals) and published in huge bound volumes, which are usually kept in the librarian's workroom but are available to the student for consultation.

Every published book is catalogued at least three times in a single alphabetical listing: once under the author's last name; once under the first significant word in the title; and at least once under a subject heading (there are frequent cross-references to other subject headings). The author entry supplies the fullest information about a book: (1) full name of the author (including pseudonym, if any); (2) complete title of the book; (3) name of publisher (or source from which the book may be obtained); (4) date of publication; (5) paging; (6) price of the book; (7) the Library of Congress catalogue card number.

The student can use the *Cumulative Book Index* as a bibliographical aid by consulting the subject headings. If he were doing a paper, for instance, on "Linguistics in the Curriculum," he could, by consulting the subject heading "Linguistics" or some sub-division of that heading in all the published volumes of the *Cumulative Book Index,* collect a complete bibliography of all the English-language books published on linguistics since 1928. From that complete list, he would then have to select the books that had a special pertinence to the subject of his paper.

The Cambridge Bibliography of English Literature, ed. F. W. Bateson, 5 vols. (Cambridge University Press, 1941). Vol. V, Supplement, 1957); The New Cambridge Bibliography of English Literature, ed. George Watson (Cambridge University Press, 1969–).*

* Volume 3: 1800–1900, comprising 1,956 pages, of the updated edition was published in 1969.

The *CBEL* is commonly acknowledged to be the standard bibliography of English language and literature. It is a descendant of the 15-volume *Cambridge History of English Literature,* ed. A. W. Ward and A. R. Waller, 1907–16, which included a selected bibliography at the end of each chapter. The province of the *CBEL* is all writings (whether in English or in Latin) of literary interest by natives of what is now the British Commonwealth up to the year 1900. Although no English writer who achieved prominence after 1900 is included, critical articles published as late as 1940 are admitted. Volume V, the supplement, records the more scholarly publications that appeared between 1940 and the beginning of 1955.

The *CBEL* is arranged chronologically rather than alphabetically. The quickest way for a student to locate the bibliography for an author or subject is to consult Volume IV, the index. Consulting the index under "Boswell," the student would find this kind of entry:

Boswell, James (1740–1795), II, 55, 92, **650f**, 903.

Printed in bold type, the **650f** indicates the main bibliographical entry in Volume II for the biographer of Samuel Johnson. The other numbers direct the student to pages in Volume II where other scholarly works pertinent to Boswell are listed. The general introduction in Volume I includes bibliographies on a number of subjects that could not be conveniently distributed among the various periods—e.g. bibliographies, histories, prosody, anthologies.

In the author entries, the works *by* an author are listed first, then the works *about* an author. The former listing follows this arrangement: (1) bibliographies and concordances (if any) published about the author; (2) the works of the author, published separately or in collections during his lifetime; (3) the modern editions of the author's works. Under the works *about* an author are listed biographical and critical studies of the author beginning with his contemporaries.

English majors may want to buy the one-volume condensation of the *CBEL* for their private reference library: *The Concise Cambridge Bibliography of English Literature, 600-1950,* ed. George Watson (1958).

Literary History of the United States, ed. Robert E. Spiller, Willard Thorp, Thomas H. Johnson, Henry Seidel Canby, Richard M. Ludwig, 3 vols. (New York: Macmillan, 1948); 3d ed., 2 vols. (1963).

The first two volumes of the first edition of the *LHUS* (the first volume of the 3d ed.) present a fairly complete history of the literature of the United

States. Volume III (Vol. II of the 3d. ed.) is devoted exclusively to a bibliography of American literature, divided into four main sections:

I. Guide to Resources (e.g. Bibliographical Centers, Published Catalogs and Directories, Union Lists and Collections, etc.)
II. Bibliographies: Literature and Cultures (the subdivisions of this section are arranged according to periods and types of literature)
III. Bibliographies: Movements and Influences
IV. Bibliographies: Individual Authors

Whereas the bibliographies in the *CBEL* are disposed chronologically, the 207 American authors covered in the bibliography volume of the *LHUS* are arranged alphabetically. Because of this arrangement, the student does not have to consult the index at the back of the volume in order to locate the bibliographies of individual authors, but he can consult the index for page numbers in the history volume(s) where the author is discussed and for page numbers for bibliographies and studies of subjects. The 1000-page bibliography in the Third Edition is divided into two parts: Part I lists works published through 1946; Part II lists works published through 1957. The author entries include notices of bibliographies, concordances, separate and collected works, edited texts and reprints, biography and criticism, and location of important manuscript copies.

Annual Bibliographies

Any bibliography begins to date as soon as it is published. It continues to be useful, of course, as a record of the books and articles published during the period that it covers, but the record necessarily stops shortly before the date of publication. Several of the literary journals keep the scholar informed about all the important work that has been done on language and literature during the previous year. The most comprehensive annual bibliography of literature is that published every spring in a special supplement of *PMLA*. This bibliography covers all periods of the major Western languages—English, French, German, Spanish, Italian, Portuguese, Scandinavian, Dutch, and about ten East European languages. Some of the other literary journals publish annual bibliographies of a specific period: Medieval Period—*Speculum;* Renaissance—*Studies in Philology;* Restoration and Eighteenth Century—*Philological Quarterly* (July issue); Romantic Period—*Philological Quarterly* (April issue); Victorian Period—*Victorian Studies;* Modern Period —*Twentieth-Century Literature;* American Literature (all periods)—*American Literature.*

Syntopicon

> **The Great Ideas:** A Syntopicon of Great Books of the Western World, ed. Mortimer J. Adler and William Gorman, 2 vols. (Chicago: Encyclopaedia Britannica, Inc., 1952).

The Syntopicon, Volumes 2 and 3 of the 54-volume set of *The Great Books of the Western World,* is such a unique and valuable reference work that it merits a fuller exposition than we gave the other reference works. The term *syntopicon* is a coinage signifying "collection of topics." As a collection of topics, the Syntopicon is a reference resource that the ancient rhetoricians might have wished were available in their time as a guide to the relatively more specialized knowledge that a speaker or writer needs when he has to develop a particular subject. Mortimer J. Adler said of this mammoth index that it is "the exact reverse of the giant comptometers which are fed data and do the thinking for the people; the Syntopicon feeds people the data—the issues and the various positions taken on them—and lets the human mind do its own thinking."

Some 443 works of seventy-four authors are printed in Volumes 4 to 54 of the Great Books, and Professor Adler had to decide on a basic list of great ideas which would serve as a detailed index to the topics discussed in the selected "great books" and in the Bible, the text of which is not presented in the set. Professor Adler pared his list of great ideas down to a manageable one hundred and two, including such topics as aristocracy, beauty, democracy, evolution, fate, good and evil, love, nature, pleasure and pain, rhetoric, sign and symbol, time, wealth. A staff of indexers launched upon a series of readings of the Great Books to gather references to discussions of these ideas by the great authors. Eventually, the basic ideas were subdivided into 3000 topics.

Each of the 102 chapters of the Syntopicon consists of five parts:

I. Introduction. This is an essay summarizing the history of the discussion of the idea treated in that chapter. The various interpretations of the idea are reviewed, and the problems and controversies raised by the continual "conversation" about the idea are discussed.

II. Outline of the Topics. This section sets forth in outline form the major themes of the discussion about the idea. Although there is an average of thirty topics to each chapter, the actual number varies from as few as six topics in a chapter to as many as seventy-six.

III. References. This section, arranged topically, is the heart of the Syntopicon. Under each topic the exact location is indicated of all passages in the Great Books set related to that topic. Here is a typical entry:

35 Locke *Human Understanding* Bk. II, ch. xxi, 178a-200d

The inquirer is here referred to Volume 35 of the Great Books set, where John Locke's *Essay on Human Understanding* is reprinted in its entirety. The "Bk. II, ch. xxi" is a reference to the author's division of his treatise, which also enables the inquirer to find the relevant passage in some other edition of the author's work. The "178a-200d" cites the first and last page, together with page section, of the relevant passage in Volume 35. The order in which the references are arranged enables the inquirer to pursue the discussion of some theme in a historical sequence or in a select group of authors or in a particular period. References to the Bible, if any, are always listed first.

IV. Cross-References. This section directs the inquirer to other chapters in the Syntopicon where similar or related topics are treated. In addition to directing the inquirer to allied material, the cross-references make him aware of the interrelationships among the great ideas.

V. Additional Readings. This section refers the reader to other works not reprinted in the Great Books set. These bibliographies are divided into two sections: (1) works written by authors represented in Volumes 4-54 of *Great Books of the Western World;* (2) works by authors not included in the Great Books set. In this section, the additional readings are listed only by author and title, but in the Bibliography of Additional Readings at the back of the second volume of the Syntopicon, the full bibliographical information about each work is supplied.

Another valuable reference feature of the Syntopicon is the inventory of terms. This section serves as a kind of table of contents for the Syntopicon. Mortimer Adler remarks about this section in his introduction: "The person who wishes to use the Syntopicon as a reference book, in order to learn what the great books have to say on a particular subject, must be able to find that subject among the 3000 topics. The primary function of the Inventory of Terms is to enable him to find the topic or topics which either clearly express or approximately represent the subject of his inquiry."

For example, one of the terms that is likely to be involved in a discussion of Rhetoric is *persuasion*. Consulting the term *persuasion* in the inventory of terms, the inquirer would find this notation:

Persuasion: see RHETORIC, 1-5/b see also DIALECTIC 5; EMOTION 5d; INDUCTION 4b; LANGUAGE 8; OPINION 2c; PLEASURE AND PAIN 10b; REASONING 5d.

The terms printed in block-capitals refer the inquirer to one of the 102 alphabetically arranged chapters in the Syntopicon; the numbers and lowercase letters refer the inquirer to the particular sub-division of the references section of that chapter. This section will in turn direct the inquirer to the passages in the Great Books where the term *persuasion* is a major term of the discussion.

No exposition can adequately convey an idea of the wealth of information to be found in the pages of this unique reference work or make entirely clear how it works. The student should browse through it to discover for himself the nature, scope, and method of this valuable guide to the wisdom of the ages.

Exercise

Since no amount of lecturing will do as much to acquaint students with reference works as will consulting the works to find answers to specific questions, this exercise is designed to get students to use the reference works discussed in the section on external aids to invention.

The answers to a few of the following questions could be found in one of the standard encyclopedias, the card catalogue in the library, or a desk dictionary. In every case, the student should consult the reference work where he is *most likely* to find the information. For instance, if the student wanted the date of publication of the novel *Vanity Fair,* he might find this information in a handbook of world literature, like William Rose Benét's *The Reader's Encyclopedia;* but since William Makepeace Thackeray, the author of *Vanity Fair,* is an English novelist, it is *more likely* that the student will find this information in a handbook devoted exclusively to English literature, like the *Oxford Companion to English Literature* or *The New Century Handbook of English Literature.*

In doing this exercise, the student should (1) write out the problem as it is stated below; (2) write out the answer to the problem (sometimes this will involve copying the answer as it appears in the reference work; in this case it should be copied exactly and put in quotation marks); (3) designate the source of the information—title of the reference work (underlined), edition of the work (if the work consulted is an edition later than the first—e.g. revised, second, etc.), the volume number (only in the case of a multivolume reference work), the exact page number on which the answer was found. The following is a format that the student might observe in doing this exercise:

Problem: Who established the American string quartet known as the Flonzaley Quartet?

Answer: Edward J. De Coppet of New York City established the Flonzaley
               Quartet.
Source: *Grove's Dictionary of Music and Musicians,* 3d ed., II, 254.

You Want to Find:

1. When Sir Robert Peel, the man responsible for the repeal of the Corn
   Laws in 1842, became Lord Rector of the University of Glasgow.
2. In which of Frank Norris's novels the character Curtis Jadwin appeared.
3. Whether the *Dictionary of American English* and *The Dictionary of
   Americanisms* agree on the *date* when "O.K." or "okay" was first used
   as a verb in the sense of "to approve." (Give date and source of first
   occurrence as given in each dictionary.)
4. When and where Sir Harold Nicolson, the noted contemporary biographer, was born.
5. Whether the term *bishop* ever occurs in the New Testament (if so, cite
   the passages where the term occurs).
6. Some magazine articles on the subject of censorship of moving pictures
   that appeared in English-language publications published outside the
   United States during the years 1955–1958.
7. When and where Arkady A. Sobalev, chief of the Soviet Union's permanent delegation at the United Nations, was born and in what field he
   took his university degree.
8. In what year John Hancock was elected to be the first governor of the
   state of Massachusetts.
9. During what years Ignazio Raimondi, the Neapolitan violinist and com-
   poser, served as director of concerts at Amsterdam.
10. At least six articles that appeared in American magazines in 1958 on the
    subject of foreign students in the United States.
11. Whether there is any collected edition of the works of Thomas Babing-
    ton Macaulay.
12. Why Juan Luis Vives, the Spanish humanist and teacher of rhetoric,
    was imprisoned by Henry VIII.
13. A copy of Eileen Duggan's poem "Victory."
14. The meaning of the allusion, in a book about the Greeks, "battle of
    Leuctra."
15. Whether Frederick Jackson Turner's essay "The Frontier in American
    History" was reprinted in any collection or anthology published between
    1948 and 1954.
16. In what novel by Dostoyevsky the character Nikolay Vsyevolodovich
    Stavrogin appeared.

17. At least three book-length biographical studies of the poet Emily Dickinson.

18. The earliest recorded use of the word *knight* as a designation of an order or rank and then the earliest recorded use of the word, in the same sense, spelled as we spell the word today.

19. The names of some contemporary puppeteers (like Burr Tillstrom) and then some biographical articles on these puppeteers in periodicals and newspapers between 1949 and 1952.

20. The source of the quotation, "There is no grievance that is a fit object of redress by mob law."

21. How many years Walter Paul Paepcke served as president of the Container Corporation of America.

22. What title Juan Bautista Diamante, the seventeenth-century Spanish dramatist, gave to his adaptation of Corneille's play *Le Cid*.

23. Whether the *Oxford English Dictionary* and the *Century Dictionary* agree that the word *romp,* as a noun meaning "a merry, lively girl who indulges in boisterous play," first came into use during the early years of the eighteenth century.

24. At least six articles on the Corn Laws that appeared at any time during the first seventy-five years of the nineteenth century.

25. Whether a bibliography has ever been compiled on the subject of witchcraft (if so, list two or three).

26. What the literary term "Spenserian stanza" means.

27. Whether Shakespeare ever used the word *rhetoric* in his plays (and if so, where).

28. The meaning of the term *astronaut*.

29. Six magazine articles that appeared in 1893 on the subject of the World's Columbian Exposition in Chicago.

30. When Pierre Lambert Goossens, Catholic archbishop of Mechlin in Belgium, was made a cardinal.

Readings

The following readings have been provided to serve as texts for the study of the principles of logic and rhetoric that have been discussed in this chapter. Theory exemplifies and proves itself in these readings. Many of the authors represented here were aware of, if they were not thoroughly schooled in, rhetorical principles. Those authors who were not conscious of the rhetorical tradition confirm, by their practice, the soundness and workability of the principles that the rhetoricians had arrived at inductively.

While the readings can be used for the study of many of the things discussed in this chapter—inductive and deductive reasoning, the ethical appeal, the emotional appeal, the external aids to invention—they are designed primarily as working texts for the analysis of the common topics and the special topics. In the process of composition, the topics serve as the initiators of a line of development; in analyzing these texts for evidence of the operation of the topics, the student is working backward from the finished text to what was, consciously or unconsciously, the beginning of the process. The student may realize two benefits from this exercise: he will see that the topics are indeed aids to the discovery of "the available means of persuasion in any given case"; and he will develop another technique for the close reading of texts. Once a reader begins to approach a text from the point of view of the topics, it is surprising how soon he develops an "eye" for the topics in any expository or argumentative prose that he reads.

The first three readings, taken from Greek literature, are examples of, respectively, deliberative discourse, judicial discourse, and ceremonial discourse. Extended analyses of these three readings have been provided to serve as models for the student's analyses of the other readings. The student should begin his analysis by classifying the text according to type, since such a classification will alert him to the special topics that will be operating in the text. The student will also find it useful to make an outline of the major divisions of the text he is analyzing.

In addition to the student's own analyses of the readings, another exercise can be worked off the selections. The sample analyses have made little or no attempt to assess the validity of the arguments and the effectiveness of the rhetoric. Taking up where these analyses leave off, the student can evaluate these readings and the others that follow.

To facilitate reference to the parts of the texts, numbers have been appended to each paragraph.

Xenophon Talks to the Soldiers

Xenophon, the author of the military memoirs from which the following speech is taken, was born in Athens about 430 B.C. From association with Socrates, he later wrote Memorabilia, Apology, *and* Symposium, *three works that present the only contemporary portraits we have of Socrates aside from Plato's* Dialogues. *In his late twenties, Xenophon joined the expedition of Cyrus the Younger to drive Cyrus's brother Artaxerxes from the throne of Persia. When Cyrus was killed in the battle of Cunaxa in 401 B.C. and*

Xenophon, *The Persian Expedition* [*Anabasis*], trans. Rex Warner, The Penguin Classics (Harmondsworth, Eng.: Penguin Books, 1949), Bk. III, Ch. 2, pp. 105-12. Reprinted by permission of the publishers.

several of the Greek leaders had been treacherously slain by the Persian general Tissaphernes, Xenophon was elected one of the new generals. As we saw in the Embassy Scene from Homer's Iliad *in Chapter I, Greek military leaders prided themselves as much on their skill with words as on their skill with arms. In the instance of deliberative discourse that follows, Xenophon displays the rhetorical skill with which he induces his fellow-soldiers to adopt his plan of retreat. Subsequently, he safely led his troops from hostile Cunaxa through Armenia to the Black Sea, an accomplishment that has often been compared with the successful evacuation of the beleaguered British troops at Dunkirk during World War II.*

1   Dawn was just breaking when the new officers were chosen, and they came to the centre of the camp and decided to post sentries and call the soldiers to a meeting. When the rest of the army was assembled, Chirisophus stood up first and spoke as follows: "Soldiers, our position is undoubtedly difficult. We have lost some very able generals and captains and soldiers, and in addition to that even Ariaeus's men, who used to be on our side, have turned traitor to us. All the same what we have to do is to surmount our difficulties like brave men, not to give in, but to try, if we can, to win honour and safety by victory. And if that is beyond us, then at least let us die with honour, and never, so long as we live, come into the power of our enemies. For if we do, we shall have to suffer, I imagine, the sort of fate which I pray the gods will bring upon our opponents."

2   Next Cleanor of Orchomenus stood up and spoke as follows: "You can see with your own eyes, soldiers, how perjured and godless the King is. You can see the treachery of Tissaphernes. He it was who said that he was a neighbour of Greece, and that he would attach the greatest importance to saving our lives. On this understanding he swore an oath to us in person, he in person gave us his right hand, and in person he deceived our generals and made prisoners of them, showing so little respect for Zeus, the guardian of hospitality, that he actually shared a meal with Clearchus and then used this very fact to entrap and destroy our officers. Then there is Ariaeus, whom we were prepared to make King, and with whom we exchanged guarantees that neither would betray the other: he too, showing no fear of the gods or respect for the memory of the dead Cyrus, though he was treated with the utmost distinction by Cyrus when he was alive, has now left us and joined Cyrus's bitterest enemies, with whom he is attempting to injure us, who were Cyrus's friends. Well, I pray that the gods will give these men what they deserve. As for us, who see all this, we must never again be deceived by them, but must fight as hard as we can, and bear whatever is the will of heaven."

3   After him Xenophon stood up. He had put on the best-looking uniform

that he could, thinking that, if the gods granted victory, victory deserved the best-looking armour, or if he was to die, then it was right for him to put on his best clothes and be wearing them when he met his death. He began his speech as follows: "Cleanor has spoken of the natives' perjury and treachery, and I feel sure that you agree with what he has said. If, then, we want to make friends with them again, we shall have to be very downhearted indeed, when we consider what happened to our generals, who, because they trusted in their good faith, put themselves into their hands. But if our purpose is to take our arms in our hands and to make them pay for what they have done and for the future to fight total war against them, then, with the help of heaven, we have many glorious hopes of safety."

4 Just as he was saying this, someone sneezed, and, when the soldiers heard it, they all with one accord fell on their knees and worshipped the god who had given this sign. Xenophon went on: "I think, soldiers, that, since an omen from Zeus the Saviour appeared just when we were speaking about safety, we ought to make a vow that we will give thank-offerings to the god for our safety in the place where we first reach friendly soil, and we should also vow to offer sacrifices to the other gods to the best of our ability. Whoever agrees with this, put up his hand."

5 Then they all raised their hands, and afterwards they made their vows and sang the paean.

5 The claims of religion having been thus satisfied, Xenophon started again and spoke as follows: "I was just saying that we had many glorious hopes of safety. First of all, we have kept our oaths to the gods, while our enemies have broken theirs, and in addition to this perjured themselves in transgressing the truce. This being so, it is reasonable to suppose that the gods will be against our enemies, but will fight on our side; and they are capable of quickly making even the strong weak, and of saving the weak easily, when such is their will, even if they are in the midst of danger. And next I shall remind you of the dangers which our fathers also have been through, so that you may realise that it is right for you to be brave men and that, with the help of the gods, the brave find safety even from the worst of difficulties. Remember how the Persians and their friends came with an enormous army, thinking that they would wipe Athens off the face of the earth; but the Athenians had the courage to stand up to them by themselves, and they defeated them. On that occasion they had made a vow to Artemis that they would sacrifice to her a goat for every one of their enemies whom they killed, but, since they could not get hold of enough goats, they decided to sacrifice five hundred every year, and they are still sacrificing them today. Then, when Xerxes later on collected his innumerable army and came against Greece, there was another occasion when your fathers defeated the fathers of these people both on land and on sea. You can find proof of all this in

the trophies we have, but the greatest piece of evidence of all is the freedom of the cities in which you have been born and brought up. For you worship no man as a master, but only the gods. These were the men whose sons you are; and I shall certainly not say that you dishonour your fathers. Not many days ago you were in battle order against the children of our old enemies, and, though they were many times your number, you, with the help of the gods, defeated them. And on that occasion you showed yourselves brave men in order to get Cyrus a kingdom; but now the fight is on for your own safety, and therefore I am sure it is right to expect from you much greater courage and a much greater will to victory. Then, too, you ought to feel much greater confidence against the enemy. On the last occasion you had no experience of them and you could see their prodigious numbers, but all the same in the spirit of your fathers you had the courage to set about them. Now, however, when you know from experience that, even if they are many times your number, they are not anxious to face you, what reason have you to be afraid of them any longer? Do not imagine that we are any the worse off because the native troops who were previously in our ranks have now left us. They are even greater cowards than the natives whom we have beaten, and they made this clear by deserting us and fleeing to the other side. It is far better to see people who want to be the first to run away standing in one's enemy's army than in one's own ranks.

7 "If any of you feel disheartened because of the fact that we have no cavalry, while the enemy have great numbers of them, you must remember that ten thousand cavalry only amount to ten thousand men. No one has ever died in battle through being bitten or kicked by a horse; it is men who do whatever gets done in battle. And then we are on a much more solid foundation than cavalrymen, who are up in the air on horseback, and afraid not only of us but of falling off their horses: we, on the other hand, with our feet planted on the earth, can give much harder blows to those who attack us and are much more likely to hit what we aim at. There is only one way in which cavalry have an advantage over us, and that is that it is safer for them to run away than it is for us.

8 "You may, of course, be quite confident about the fighting, but upset by the fact that Tissaphernes will no longer show you the way, nor will the King provide opportunities of buying food. If this is so, then consider whether it is better to have Tissaphernes to guide us, a man who is quite clearly working against us, or to have prisoners whom we shall order to show us the way and who will know that, if they make any mistakes which affect us, they will be mistakes that will also affect their own persons and their own lives. And on the question of supplies, is it better to buy in the markets which they provide, where we have to pay a lot to buy a little (and we have no longer even got the money), or is it better to beat them in battle and

then take our supplies for ourselves, each man taking the quantity he feels like having?

9 "You may realise that these alternatives are the better ones, but still think that the rivers are an insuperable obstacle and regard yourselves as having been led properly into a trap by crossing them. If so, then I will ask you to consider whether the natives have not done here a very stupid thing. For all rivers, however impassable they may be at a distance from their springs, can be forded, and without so much as getting one's knees wet, if one follows them up towards their sources. And even if we cannot get across the rivers, even if no one comes forward to show us the way, even then we have no reason to get downhearted. We would not call the Mysians better men than we are, yet we know that they hold many large and prosperous cities in the King's country and against the King's will. We know that the same is true of the Pisidians, and we saw with our own eyes how the Lycaonians have seized the fortified positions in the plains and enjoy the profit of the land that belongs to these natives. Now in our case I should say that we ought not to make it obvious that we are setting off home, but we should make our dispositions as though we had the idea of settling here. I am certain that the King would offer the Mysians all the guides they wanted, and would give them numbers of hostages to guarantee his good faith in sending them out of the country, and would actually build roads for them, even though they wanted to go away in four-horse chariots. And I am certain that he would be three times as pleased to do all this for us, if he saw that we were planning to stay here. No, what I am really afraid of is that, if we once learn to live a life of ease and luxury, enjoying the company of these fine great women, the wives and daughters of the Medes and Persians, we might be like the Lotus-eaters and forget about our road home. So I think that it is right and reasonable for us to make it our first endeavour to reach our own folk in Greece and to demonstrate to the Greeks that their poverty is of their own choosing, since they might see people who have a wretched life in their own countries grow rich by coming out here. Soldiers, I need not elaborate the point. It is obvious that all these good things come to the conquerors.

10 "I must, however, deal with these questions—how we can make our march as free from danger as possible, and how, if we have to fight, we can fight to the best advantage. The first suggestion I shall make to you is to set fire to all the waggons we have, so that we may not be led by our animals but may be able to march wherever the interest of the army dictates. Then we should set fire to our tents as well: they too cause difficulties in transport, and are no use either for fighting or for getting provisions. Then let us get rid of all inessentials in the rest of our equipment, only keeping what we have for the purpose of fighting and eating or drinking, so that as many

of us as possible may carry arms and as few as possible carry baggage. When people are defeated, as you know, all their property changes hands; and if we win, we must look upon our enemies as if they were carrying baggage for us.

11 "It remains for me to mention what I think is the most important point of all. You can see what our enemies thought about it. They did not dare to make war on us until they had made prisoners of our generals, and this was because they thought that, so long as we had commanders and we were obedient to them, we were capable of coming out on top in the fighting; but once they had seized our commanders they thought that we would collapse through lack of control and lack of discipline. It is therefore necessary that the generals we have now should take much greater care than those we had before, and that those in the ranks should be much better disciplined and much more ready to obey their officers now than they were before. In cases of disobedience, we ought to vote that whichever of you happens to be on the spot should join with the officers in enforcing punishment. That would be the bitterest disappointment to our enemies; for, on the day that this is voted, they will see not one Clearchus but ten thousand, each one intolerant of any unsoldierly action.

12 "But it is time for me to make an end. It may be that the enemy will be upon us at once. If you agree with the suggestions I have made, then let us have them passed officially as soon as possible, so that they may be put into practice. If anyone knows a better way of going about things than the one I have outlined, then let him have the courage to tell us of it, even if he is only a common soldier. The safety which we are looking for is everyone's concern."

13 Afterwards Chirisophus spoke. "If we want," he said, "to pass any other measure in addition to those which Xenophon suggests, we can do so in a moment or two. I propose that, with no delay, we should vote that what he has just suggested is the best course to pursue. Will those who agree put up their hands?"

14 They all put their hands up, and Xenophon got up again and spoke as follows: "Soldiers, listen to the additional proposals which I have to make. Obviously we must march somewhere where we can get provisions, and I gather that there are some fine villages not more than two miles away from here. But I should not be surprised if the enemy, like cowardly dogs that run after and try to bite anyone who goes past them, but run away from anyone who chases them,—I should not be surprised if they too follow in our tracks as we go away. Perhaps then it would be safer for us to march with the hoplites forming a hollow square, so that the baggage and the general crowd may be more secure inside. If, then, we were told now who should be in the front of the square and organise the leading detachments,

and who should be on the two flanks, and who should be responsible for the rear, we should not have to plan all this when the enemy are approaching us, but could immediately make use of those who have been specially detailed for the job. If anyone has a better suggestion to make, let us adopt it. If not, then I propose that Chirisophus should lead the square: he has the additional advantage of being a Spartan. Two generals, the oldest ones, should look after the two flanks; and the youngest of us, that is Timasion and myself, should be responsible for the rear. I suggest this as a temporary measure. Later on we shall have tried out this order of march, and we can decide on what seems best as different circumstances arise. If anyone has a better suggestion to make, I should like him to put it forward."

15 Then, as nobody raised any objections, Xenophon said, "Will those who agree with this put up their hands?" And the proposal was carried.

16 "Now then," he continued, "we must leave the meeting and put into operation what we have decided. Whoever wants to see his own people again must remember to be a brave soldier: that is the only way of doing it. Whoever wants to keep alive must aim at victory. It is the winners who do the killing and the losers who get killed. And those who want money must try to win battles. The winners can not only keep what they have themselves, but can take what belongs to the losers."

Analysis of the Topics
in "Xenophon Talks to the Soldiers"

Xenophon's address to the Greek army is clearly an example of deliberative oratory. Xenophon is concerned with convincing the soldiers to adopt a certain course of action. That the decision about the course of action is not made by the officers and imposed on the soldiers is evidenced by the fact that at the end of Xenophon's speech the question is put to the vote of the entire army. Moreover, the question is debatable, since there are alternatives to the course of action that Xenophon proposes.

The Greeks are in desperate straits at this point. Hired by Cyrus to overthrow his brother King Artaxerxes, the Greeks had clashed with the Persian forces at Cunaxa, near the site of ancient Babylon. Although the Greeks won this battle, Cyrus was killed by a stray javelin, and subsequently his native troops deserted, leaving the Greeks without any supporting cavalry. During a truce that followed the battle, Tissaphernes invited the Greek commanders to a conference and then treacherously slew them. Not only are the Greeks at this point without their experienced generals and without cavalry troops, but they are surrounded by hostile people, deprived of native guides, and cut off from their homeland, a thousand miles away, by seemingly impassable rivers. The 10,000 men with their cumbersome baggage trains have a crucial decision to make. What do they do now? Having disclosed his plan of action to the officers in the preceding chapter, Xenophon now assembles the soldiers and talks to them.

This passage, which constitutes the whole of the second chapter of Book III of the *Anabasis*, falls into five main parts:

1. Introduction, in which the men are put into the proper mood by two brief speeches and by a religious omen (paragraphs 1-5).
2. Xenophon's arguments to convince the men that they have a chance to win their way to safety (paragraph 6).
3. Xenophon's answers to the counter-arguments that might be proposed (paragraphs 7-9).
4. Xenophon's practical proposals for effectuating his plan (paragraphs 10-11).
5. Conclusion, in which the matter is put to a vote and Xenophon makes some additional proposals and a final plea for his cause (paragraphs 12-16).

The narrative framework can be regarded as providing the Introduction and Conclusion of Xenophon's speech; the speech itself has only three parts: the argument, the refutation, and the plan of action.

The brief speeches of Chirisophus (paragraph 1) and Cleanor (paragraph 2) and the omen of the sneeze which interrupts Xenophon's opening remarks (paragraphs 3-5) can be said to put the men into the proper emotional disposition for Xenophon's address. By reminding the soldiers of the gravity of the situation, Chirisophus is playing on the emotion of fear and indirectly stirring up their sense of honor. By reminding the soldiers of the treachery of the Persians, Cleanor is arousing their resentment and anger against the enemy. The sneeze comes fortuitously, but Xenophon shrewdly takes advantage of the accident to lend a religious sanction to the Greek cause. The Greeks are in a favorable mood now, but they still have to be persuaded.

The deliberative orator commonly exploits the special topics of the *worthy* (the good) and/or the *advantageous*. In other words, when the deliberative orator is seeking to persuade someone, he must show that what he proposes is worthy of pursuit for its own sake or is conducive to the well-being or happiness of the audience. In developing these special topics, the orator will have recourse to many of the common topics. Let us see what use Xenophon makes of the topics in his speech.

In paragraph 6, Xenophon advances a number of arguments to stir up the soldier's will and courage to fight their way through to safety. The first argument that he advances is designed to show that fighting (the alternative is surrendering) is a worthy course of action. The argument takes the form of an enthymeme: since we have kept our oaths, while the enemy have broken theirs, it is reasonable to suppose that the gods will support us against our enemies. The full syllogistic argument, which in this case leads to a probable conclusion, might run something like this:

> The gods will support those who keep their oaths.
> We have kept our oaths.
> The gods will support us.

The orator is arguing a future fact here and using an antecedent-consequent topic to develop his argument: being faithful to our oaths (antecedent) will lead to the support of the gods (consequent).

The second argument that Xenophon advances in this paragraph is also calculated to convince the men of the worthiness of bravery. In support of this contention, Xenophon makes use of the common topic of precedent, reminding the men of how bravely their forefathers fought against Persian invasions of the homeland. As signs that such brave fighting was a good, he cites the many trophies the Greeks gained and the present freedom of their cities.

In the next argument, Xenophon makes use of the common topic of comparison to advance the topic of the possible. He compares the situation at the battle of Cunaxa with the situation now. At Cunaxa, the men proved that they could fight as bravely and effectively as their fathers once fought. But at Cunaxa, the men were fighting for Cyrus, a foreigner; now they are fighting for their own safety. By using an *a fortiori* argument, Xenophon is trying to convince them of what is possible now. If they fought so effectively for a foreigner, how much more effectively they should be able to fight when they are fighting for themselves. In other words, if the more difficult task is possible, the less difficult is even more possible.

As another argument in support of what is feasible now, Xenophon reminds the soldiers that they are more experienced troops now than they were at the battle of Cunaxa. The consequence of more experience is greater confidence and therefore greater chance of success.

Xenophon next assures the Greeks that the loss of Cyrus's mercenaries is really a gain, for cowards can never be an asset to one's side. Implicit in this enthymeme is the suggestion that the defection of the cowardly mercenaries will prove to be an advantage to the Greeks. What was possible for the Greeks to accomplish when their forces were filled out with cowardly, unreliable troops will be even more possible when the army is made up exclusively of troops motivated by a cohesive loyalty.

Having advanced arguments to support his contention that fighting, rather than surrendering, is the more worthy and advantageous course of action, Xenophon in the next three paragraphs (7, 8, 9) anticipates and answers some of the counter-arguments.

First of all, he allays the soldiers' apprehensions about the enemy's cavalry by minimizing the effectiveness of cavalry in battle. Resorting to the common topic of comparison, Xenophon recognizes that there is a difference between fighting on foot and fighting on horses, but he argues that the difference gives the Greeks an advantage. It is men, after all, rather than horses that deal the death blow; and as far as men go, we can match them man for man. Then too a soldier can deal a more effective blow when his feet are planted on solid ground than when he is on a precarious perch in the saddle. There is, however, one advantage to fighting on horses: men on horseback can run away faster. The humorous irony of this last gibe was calculated to inspirit the men.

In paragraph 8, Xenophon attempts to allay the soldiers' misgivings about losing Tissaphernes as a guide through this hostile, unknown country and about losing the opportunity to buy food from the natives. In resorting again to the common topic of comparison, this time to contrast the situation then with the situation now, Xenophon makes effective use of the sub-topic of degree (more and less). Tissaphernes was a good guide through this country, but a captured guide will be even better. Since, as we now know, Tissaphernes was secretly working against us, he could not really be relied on as a guide; but a native guide that we capture will prove to be more reliable because he knows that we will kill him if he dares to mislead us. Likewise, we have an advantage now in the procurement of supplies. Until now we have had to purchase our supplies in the market place. Now that a breach has developed in our pact with the Persians, we no longer have to live up to this gentleman's agreement; we can take by force what we no longer have the obligation or the money to buy. In both cases, then, we are better off now than we were before.

In paragraph 9, Xenophon allays the soldiers' anxieties about being trapped in a hostile country. In reply to the argument that the rivers are impassable, Xenophon resorts to the topic of contradiction. He seems to be arguing in this way: rivers are either passable or not passable (a contradictory disjunctive proposition); but these rivers are passable (if we cannot ford them at their deepest part, we can always ford them near their sources, where they are shallow); so it is false to propose that these rivers are impassable. But suppose, he then suggests, that we grant the impossibility of fording the rivers. What then? Xenophon assures the soldiers that they need not feel downhearted at this prospect. Resorting to an *a fortiori* argument again, he points out to them that if the Mysians, Pisidians, and Lycaonians, who are decidedly lesser men than the Greeks, can seize and hold large, prosperous cities in this kingdom against the will of the Persians, surely the Greeks can do the same thing.

Xenophon then resorts to the topic of future fact, to suggest the more likely eventuality. If we made it appear that we intended to settle down in this country the king would do everything in his power to facilitate our departure from his kingdom. To support this argument from future fact, Xenophon is using the principle that where the desire or the opportunity to do something exists, the thing will be done. The clinching argument now in Xenophon's refutation takes a subtle turn. His principal fear, he tells the soldiers, is that they will become so enamored of the life of luxury that it is possible to enjoy in this country that they, like Homer's Lotus Eaters, will not want to go home. He is holding out to them the prospect of the *goods* that can be theirs if they decide to stay, or are forced to stay, in this country —"a life of ease and luxury," "the company of these fine great women." As Xenophon says at the end of this paragraph, "All these good things come to the conquerors." The subtlety of this argument resides in the suggestion that even if they cannot fight their way out of this country the prospect of a forced sojourn here is far from bleak. So in any case it is better to fight than to lay down their arms. By fighting, they either win their way to the safety of their homeland or win for themselves a life of ease and luxury.

Having argued that fighting bravely is both a worthy and an advantageous course of action and having refuted the counter-arguments, Xenophon now lays down some practical suggestions for the campaign ahead (paragraph 10-11). It is not enough that he convince the men that this is the course of action to follow; he must show them how it can be pursued successfully. In the first sentence of paragraph 10, Xenophon discloses the purpose of what he is now about to do: "I must, however, deal with these questions—how we can make our march as free from danger as possible, and how, if we have to fight, we can fight to the best advantage." As Aristotle said in Book I, Chapter 7, of the *Rhetoric,* "Things are 'practicable' in two senses: (1) it is possible to do them, (2) it is easy to do them." By proposing some practical suggestions for the march that lies ahead of the men, Xenophon can show them that it is possible or easy to implement the ideal of fighting bravely. Accordingly, he makes two practical suggestions: (1) they must jettison non-essential baggage so that they will have greater mobility; (2) they must tighten up the discipline of the army.

In the final paragraph (16), Xenophon suggests that the soldiers may have one or more of the following *ends* in view: (1) to see their people again; (2) to stay alive; (3) to make money. Then he reminds them that these three ends can be effected only by fighting bravely. He has posed an either/or situation for them: either you fight, or you fail to realize whatever end you have in view. A close examination of this disjunctive proposition would reveal a logical flaw, but at this point, the soldiers are in no mood to take a close look at the logic. By using some clever rhetorical strategies, Xenophon has persuaded them that their situation, which before had seemed so desperate, is hopeful. Future events proved Xenophon to be right (the famed 10,000 fought and marched their way over 1500 foot-weary miles to the coast of the Black Sea), but, of course, the eventuality cannot be used to assess the effectiveness of this deliberative speech. The speech must be assessed on its immediate persuasiveness.

Socrates' Apology

Born in 469 B.C., Socrates was one of that remarkable group of poets, dramatists, philosophers, orators, statesmen, and generals who were responsible for Athens attaining its Golden Age in the fifth century B.C. He himself bequeathed no writing to posterity. His life, his philosophy, and his dialectical method are known to us only through the works of Plato and Xenophon. In 399 B.C., at the age of seventy, he was brought to trial in Athens, ostensibly on the charge that he was corrupting the youth and advocating the worship of new gods but really because he had become a troublesome citizen with his questioning of the policies and values of the Athenian Establishment. In the following instance of judicial rhetoric, we see him defending himself (the primary meaning of apology) against the charges leveled against him. Although Socrates speaks in the monologue form in the early part of the Apology, *his more usual method of conducting a discourse is illustrated in the question-and-answer dialogue with Meletus that begins with paragraph 13.*

1   How you, O Athenians, have been affected by my accusers, I cannot tell; but I know that they almost made me forget who I was—so persuasively did they speak; and yet they have hardly uttered a word of truth. But of the many falsehoods told by them, there was one which quite amazed me;—I mean when they said that you should be upon your guard and not allow yourselves to be deceived by the force of my eloquence. To say this, when they were certain to be detected as soon as I opened my lips and proved myself to be anything but a great speaker, did indeed appear to me most shameless—unless by the force of eloquence they mean the force of truth; for if such is their meaning, I admit that I am eloquent. But in how different a way from theirs! Well, as I was saying, they have scarcely spoken the truth at all; from me you shall hear the whole truth, but not delivered after their manner in a set oration duly ornamented with fine words and phrases. No, by heaven! I shall use the words and arguments which occur to me at the

From *The Dialogues of Plato,* trans. Benjamin Jowett, 4th ed. (Oxford: At the Clarendon Press, 1953), Vol. I, pp. 341-53. Reprinted by permission of the publishers.

moment, for I am confident in the justice of my cause;[1] at my time of life I ought not to be appearing before you, O men of Athens, in the character of a boy inventing falsehoods—let no one expect it of me. And I must particularly beg of you to grant me this favour:—If I defend myself in my accustomed manner, and you hear me using the words which many of you have heard me using habitually in the agora, at the tables of the money-changers, and elsewhere, I would ask you not to be surprised, and not to interrupt me on this account. For I am more than seventy years of age, and appearing now for the first time before a court of law, I am quite a stranger to the language of the place; and therefore I would have you regard me as if I were really a stranger, whom you would excuse if he spoke in his native tongue, and after the fashion of his country:—Am I making an unfair request of you? Never mind the manner, which may or may not be good; but think only of the truth of my words, and give heed to that: let the speaker speak truly and the judge decide justly.

2   And first, I have to reply to the older charges and to my first accusers, and then I will go on to the later ones. For of old I have had many accusers, who have accused me falsely to you during many years; and I am more afraid of them than of Anytus and his associates, who are dangerous, too, in their own way. But far more dangerous are the others, who began when most of you were children, and took possession of your minds with their falsehoods, telling of one Socrates, a wise man, who speculated about the heaven above, and searched into the earth beneath, and made the worse appear the better cause. The men who have besmeared me with this tale are the accusers whom I dread; for their hearers are apt to fancy that such inquirers do not believe in the existence of the gods. And they are many, and their charges against me are of ancient date, and they were made by them in the days when some of you were more impressible than you are now—in childhood, or it may have been in youth—and the cause went by default, for there was none to answer. And hardest of all, I do not know and cannot tell the names of my accusers; unless in the chance case of a comic poet. All who from envy and malice have persuaded you—some of them having first convinced themselves—all this class of men are most difficult to deal with; for I cannot have them up here, and cross-examine them, and therefore I must simply fight with shadows in my own defence, and argue when there is no one who answers. I will ask you then to take it from me that my opponents are of two kinds; one recent, the other ancient: and I hope that you will see the propriety of my answering the latter first, for these accusations you heard long before the others, and much oftener.

3   Well, then, I must make my defence, and endeavour to remove from

---

[1] Or, I am certain that I am right in taking this course.

your minds in a short time, a slander which you have had a long time to take in. May I succeed, if to succeed be for my good and yours, or likely to avail me in my cause! The task is not an easy one; I quite understand the nature of it. And so leaving the event with God, in obedience to the law I will now make my defence.

4 I will begin at the beginning, and ask what is the accusation which has given rise to the slander of me, and in fact has encouraged Meletus to prefer this charge against me. Well, what do the slanderers say? They shall be my prosecutors, and this is the information they swear against me: 'Socrates is an evil-doer; a meddler who searches into things under the earth and in heaven, and makes the worse appear the better cause, and teaches the aforesaid practices to others.' Such is the nature of the accusation: it is just what you have yourselves seen in the comedy of Aristophanes,[1] who has introduced a man whom he calls Socrates, swinging about and saying that he walks on air, and talking a deal of nonsense concerning matters of which I do not pretend to know either much or little—not that I mean to speak disparagingly of anyone who is a student of natural philosophy. May Meletus never bring so many charges against me as to make me do that! But the simple truth is, O Athenians, that I have nothing to do with physical speculations. Most of those here present are witnesses to the truth of this, and to them I appeal. Speak then, you who have heard me, and tell your neighbours whether any of you have ever known me hold forth in few words or in many upon such matters. . . . You hear their answer. And from what they say of this part of the charge you will be able to judge of the truth of the rest.

5 As little foundation is there for the report that I am a teacher, and take money; this accusation has no more truth in it than the other. Although, if a man were really able to instruct mankind, this too would, in my opinion, be an honour to him. There is Gorgias of Leontium, and Prodicus of Ceos, and Hippias of Elis, who go the round of the cities, and are able to persuade the young men to leave their own citizens by whom they might be taught for nothing, and come to them whom they not only pay, but are thankful if they may be allowed to pay them. There is at this time a Parian philosopher residing in Athens, of whom I have heard; and I came to hear of him in this way:—I came across a man who has spent more money on the sophists than the rest of the world put together, Callias, the son of Hipponicus, and knowing that he had sons, I asked him: 'Callias,' I said, 'if your two sons were foals or calves, there would be no difficulty in finding someone to put over them; we should hire a trainer of horses, or a farmer probably, who would improve and perfect them in the appropriate virtue and excellence; but as they are human beings, whom are you thinking of placing over them?

[1] Aristoph. *Clouds*, 225 foll.

Is there anyone who understands human and civic virtue? You must have thought about the matter, for you have sons; is there anyone?' 'There is,' he said. 'Who is he?' said I; 'and of what country? and what does he charge?' 'Evenus the Parian,' he replied; 'he is the man, and his charge is five minas.' Happy is Evenus, I said to myself, if he really has this wisdom, and teaches at such a moderate charge. Had I the same, I should have been very proud and conceited; but the truth is that I have no knowledge of the kind.

6 I dare say, Athenians, that someone among you will reply, 'Yes, Socrates, but what *is* your occupation? What is the origin of these accusations which are brought against you; there must have been something strange which you have been doing? All these rumours and this talk about you would never have arisen if you had been like other men: tell us, then, what is the cause of them, for we should be sorry to judge hastily of you.' Now I regard this as a fair challenge, and I will endeavour to explain to you the reason why I am called wise and have such an evil fame. Please to attend then. And although some of you may think I am joking, I declare that I will tell you the entire truth. Men of Athens, this reputation of mine has come of a certain sort of wisdom which I possess. If you ask me what kind of wisdom, I reply, wisdom such as may perhaps be attained by man, for to that extent I am inclined to believe that I am wise; whereas the persons of whom I was speaking have a kind of superhuman wisdom, which I know not how to describe, because I have it not myself; and he who says that I have, speaks falsely, and is taking away my character. And here, O men of Athens, I must beg you not to interrupt me, even if I seem to say something extravagant. For the word which I will speak is not mine. I will refer you to a witness who is worthy of credit; that witness shall be the god of Delphi—he will tell you about my wisdom, if I have any, and of what sort it is. You must have known Chaerephon; he was early a friend of mine, and also a friend of yours, for he shared in the recent exile of the people, and returned with you. Well, Chaerephon, as you know, was very impetuous in all his doings, and he went to Delphi and boldly asked the oracle to tell him whether—as I was saying, I must beg you not to interrupt—he actually asked the oracle to tell him whether anyone was wiser than I was, and the Pythian prophetess answered that there was no man wiser. Chaerephon is dead himself; but his brother, who is in court, will confirm the truth of what I am saying.

7 Why do I mention this? Because I am going to explain to you why I have such an evil name. When I heard the answer, I said to myself, What can the god mean? and what is the interpretation of his riddle? for I know that I have no wisdom, small or great. What then can he mean when he says that I am the wisest of men? And yet he is a god, and cannot lie; that would be against his nature. After long perplexity, I thought of a method of trying the question. I reflected that if I could only find a man wiser than myself,

then I might go to the god with a refutation in my hand. I should say to him, 'Here is a man who is wiser than I am; but you said that I was the wisest.' Accordingly I went to one who had the reputation of wisdom, and observed him—his name I need not mention, he was a politician; and in the process of examining him and talking with him, this, men of Athens, was what I found. I could not help thinking that he was not really wise, although he was thought wise by many, and still wiser by himself; and thereupon I tried to explain to him that he thought himself wise, but was not really wise; and the consequence was that he hated me, and his enmity was shared by several who were present and heard me. So I left him, saying to myself as I went away: Well, although I do not suppose that either of us knows anything really worth knowing, I am at least wiser than this fellow—for he knows nothing, and thinks that he knows; I neither know nor think that I know. In this one little point, then, I seem to have the advantage of him. Then I went to another who had still higher pretensions to wisdom, and my conclusion was exactly the same. Whereupon I made another enemy of him, and of many others besides him.

8   Then I went to one man after another, being not unconscious of the enmity which I provoked, and I lamented and feared this: but necessity was laid upon me,—the word of God, I thought, ought to be considered first. And I said to myself, Go I must to all who appear to know, and find out the meaning of the oracle. And I swear to you, Athenians,—for I must tell you the truth—the result of my mission was just this: I found that the men most in repute were nearly the most foolish; and that others less esteemed were really closer to wisdom. I will tell you the tale of my wanderings and of the 'Herculean' labours, as I may call them, which I endured only to find at last the oracle irrefutable. After the politicians, I went to the poets; tragic, dithyrambic, and all sorts. And there, I said to myself, you will be instantly detected; now you will find out that you are more ignorant than they are. Accordingly, I took them some of the most elaborate passages in their own writings, and asked what was the meaning of them—thinking that they would teach me something. Will you believe me? I am ashamed to confess the truth, but I must say that there is hardly a person present who would not have talked better about their poetry than they did themselves. So I learnt that not by wisdom do poets write poetry, but by a sort of genius and inspiration; they are like diviners or soothsayers who also say many fine things, but do not understand the meaning of them. The poets appeared to me to be much in the same case; and I further observed that upon the strength of their poetry they believed themselves to be the wisest of men in other things in which they were not wise. So I departed, conceiving myself to be superior to them for the same reason that I was superior to the politicians.

9   At last I went to the artisans, for I was conscious that I knew nothing at

all, as I may say, and I was sure that they knew many fine things; and here I was not mistaken, for they did know many things of which I was ignorant, and in this they certainly were wiser than I was. But I observed that even the good artisans fell into the same error as the poets;—because they were good workmen they thought that they also knew all sorts of high matters, and this defect in them overshadowed their wisdom; and therefore I asked myself on behalf of the oracle, whether I would like to be as I was, neither having their knowledge nor their ignorance, or like them in both; and I made answer to myself and to the oracle that I was better off as I was.

10   This inquisition has led to my having many enemies of the worst and most dangerous kind, and has given rise also to many imputations, including the name of 'wise'; for my hearers always imagine that I myself possess the wisdom which I find wanting in others. But the truth is, O men of Athens, that God only is wise; and by his answer he intends to show that the wisdom of men is worth little or nothing; although speaking of Socrates, he is only using my name by way of illustration, as if he said, He, O men, is the wisest, who, like Socrates, knows that his wisdom is in truth worth nothing. And so I go about the world, obedient to the god, and search and make inquiry into the wisdom of anyone, whether citizen or stranger, who appears to be wise; and if he is not wise, then in vindication of the oracle I show him that he is not wise; and my occupation quite absorbs me, and I have had no time to do anything useful either in public affairs or in any concern of my own, but I am in utter poverty by reason of my devotion to the god.

11   There is another thing:—young men of the richer classes, who have not much to do, come about me of their own accord; they like to hear people examined, and they often imitate me, and proceed to do some examining themselves; there are plenty of persons, as they quickly discover, who think that they know something, but really know little or nothing; and then those who are examined by them instead of being angry with themselves are angry with me: This confounded Socrates, they say; this villainous misleader of youth!—and then if somebody asks them, Why, what evil does he practise or teach? they do not know, and cannot tell; but in order that they may not appear to be at a loss, they repeat the ready-made charges which are used against all philosophers about teaching things up in the clouds and under the earth, and having no gods, and making the worse appear the better cause; for they do not like to confess that their pretence of knowledge has been detected—which is the truth; and as they are numerous and ambitious and energetic, and speak vehemently with persuasive tongues, they have filled your ears with their loud and inveterate calumnies. And this is the reason why my three accusers, Meletus and Anytus and Lycon, have set upon me; Meletus, who has a quarrel with me on behalf of the poets; Anytus, on behalf of the craftsmen and politicians; Lycon, on behalf of the rhetoricians:

and as I said at the beginning, I cannot expect to get rid of such a mass of calumny all in a moment. And this, O men of Athens, is the truth and the whole truth; I have concealed nothing, I have dissembled nothing. And yet, I feel sure that my plainness of speech is fanning their hatred of me, and what is their hatred but a proof that I am speaking the truth?—Hence has arisen the prejudice against me; and this is the reason of it, as you will find out either in this or in any future inquiry.

12 I have said enough in my defence against the first class of my accusers; I turn to the second class. They are headed by Meletus, that good man and true lover of his country, as he calls himself. Against these, too, I must try to make a defence:—Let their affidavit be read: it contains something of this kind: It says that Socrates is a doer of evil, inasmuch as he corrupts the youth, and does not receive the gods whom the state receives, but has a new religion of his own. Such is the charge; and now let us examine the particular counts. He says that I am a doer of evil, and corrupt the youth; but I say, O men of Athens, that Meletus is a doer of evil, in that he is playing a solemn farce, recklessly bringing men to trial from a pretended zeal and interest about matters in which he really never had the smallest interest. And the truth of this I will endeavour to prove to you.

13 Come hither, Meletus, and let me ask a question of you. You attach great importance to the improvement of youth?

14 Yes, I do.

15 Tell the judges, then, who is their improver; for you must know, as you take such interest in the subject, and have discovered their corrupter, and are citing and accusing me in this court. Speak, then, and tell the judges who is the improver of youth:—Observe, Meletus, that you are silent, and have nothing to say. But is this not rather disgraceful, and a very considerable proof of what I was saying, that you have no interest in the matter? Speak up, friend, and tell us who their improver is.

16 The laws.

17 But that, my good sir, is not my question: Can you not name some person—whose first qualification will be that he knows the laws?

18 The judges, Socrates who are present in court.

19 What, do you mean to say, Meletus, that they are able to instruct and improve youth?

20 Certainly they are.

21 What, all of them, or some only and not others?

22 All of them.

23 Truly, that is good news! There are plenty of improvers, then. And what do you say of the audience,—do they improve them?

24 Yes, they do.

25 And the senators?

26 Yes, the senators improve them.

27 But perhaps the members of the assembly corrupt them?—or do they too improve them?

28 They improve them.

29 Then every Athenian improves and elevates them; all with the exception of myself; and I alone am their corrupter? Is that what you affirm?

30 That is what I stoutly affirm.

31 I am very unfortunate if you are right. But suppose I ask you a question: Is it the same with horses? Does one man do them harm and all the world good? Is not the exact opposite the truth? One man is able to do them good, or at least very few;—the trainer of horses, that is to say, does them good, but the ordinary man does them harm if he has to do with them? Is not that true, Meletus, of horses, or of any other animals? Most assuredly it is; whether you and Anytus say yes or no. Happy indeed would be the condition of youth if they had one corrupter only, and all the rest of the world were their benefactors. But you, Meletus, have sufficiently shown that you never had a thought about the young: your carelessness is plainly seen in your not caring about the very things which you bring against me.

32 And now, Meletus, I adjure you to answer me another question: Which is better, to live among bad citizens, or among good ones? Answer, friend, I say; the question is one which may be easily answered. Do not the good do their neighbours good, and the bad do them evil?

33 Certainly.

34 And is there anyone who would rather be injured than benefited by those who live with him? Answer, my good friend, the law requires you to answer—does anyone like to be injured?

35 Certainly not.

36 And when you accuse me of corrupting and deteriorating the youth, do you allege that I corrupt them intentionally or unintentionally?

37 Intentionally, I say.

38 But you have just admitted that the good do their neighbours good, and the evil do them evil. Now, is that a truth which your superior wisdom has recognized thus early in life, and am I, at my age, in such darkness and ignorance as not to know that if a man with whom I have to live is corrupted by me, I am very likely to be harmed by him; and yet I corrupt him, and intentionally, too—so you say, although neither I nor any other human being is ever likely to be convinced by you. But either I do not corrupt them, or I corrupt them unintentionally; and on either view of the case you lie. If my offence is unintentional, the law has no cognizance of unintentional offences: you ought to have taken me privately, and warned and admonished me; for if I had had instruction, I should have left off doing what I only did unintentionally—beyond doubt I should; but you would have nothing to say to me and refused to teach me. And now you bring me up in this court, which is a place not of instruction, but of punishment.

39 It will be very clear to you, Athenians, as I was saying, that Meletus has never had any care, great or small, about the matter. But still I should like to know, Meletus, in what I am affirmed to corrupt the young. I suppose you mean, as I infer from your indictment, that I teach them not to acknowledge the gods which the state acknowledges, but some other new divinities or spiritual agencies in their stead. These are the lessons by which I corrupt the youth, as you say.

40 Yes, that I say emphatically.

41 Then, by the gods, Meletus, of whom we are speaking, tell me and the court, in somewhat plainer terms, what you mean! for I do not as yet understand whether you affirm that I teach other men to acknowledge some gods, and therefore that I do believe in gods, and am not an entire atheist—this you do not lay to my charge,—but only you say that they are not the same gods which the city recognizes—the charge is that they are different gods. Or, do you mean that I am an atheist simply, and a teacher of atheism?

42 I mean the latter—that you are a complete atheist.

43 What an extraordinary statement! Why do you think so, Meletus? Do you mean that I do not believe in the god-head of the sun or moon, like the rest of mankind?

44 I assure you, judges, that he does: for he says that the sun is stone, and the moon earth.

45 Friend Meletus, do you think that you are accusing Anaxagoras? Have you such a low opinion of the judges, that you fancy them so illiterate as not to know that these doctrines are found in the books of Anaxagoras the Clazomenian, which are full of them? And so, forsooth, the youth are said to be taught them by Socrates, when they can be bought in the book-market for one drachma at most; and they might pay their money, and laugh at Socrates if he pretends to father these extraordinary views. And so, Meletus, you really think that I do not believe in any god?

46 I swear by Zeus that you verily believe in none at all.

47 Nobody will believe you, Meletus, and I am pretty sure that you do not believe yourself. I cannot help thinking, men of Athens, that Meletus is reckless and impudent, and that he has brought this indictment in a spirit of mere wantonness and youthful bravado. Has he not compounded a riddle, thinking to try me? He said to himself:—I shall see whether the wise Socrates will discover my facetious self-contradiction, or whether I shall be able to deceive him and the rest of them. For he certainly does appear to me to contradict himself in the indictment as much as if he said that Socrates is guilty of not believing in the gods, and yet of believing in them—but this is not like a person who is in earnest.

48 I should like you, O men of Athens, to join me in examining what I conceive to be his inconsistency; and do you, Meletus, answer. And I must remind the audience of my request that they would not make a disturbance if I speak in my accustomed manner:

49 Did ever man, Meletus, believe in the existence of human things, and not of human beings? ... I wish, men of Athens, that he would answer, and not be always trying to get up an interruption. Did ever any man believe in horsemanship, and not in horses? or in flute-playing, and not in flute-players? My friend, no man ever did; I answer to you and to the court, as you refuse to answer for yourself. But now please to answer the next question: Can a man believe in the existence of things spiritual and divine, and not in spirits or demigods?

50 He cannot.

51 How lucky I am to have extracted that answer, by the assistance of the court! But then you swear in the indictment that I teach and believe in divine or spiritual things (new or old, no matter for that); at any rate, I believe in spiritual things,—so you say and swear in the affidavit; and yet if I believe in them, how can I help believing in spirits or demigods;—must I not? To be sure I must; your silence gives consent. Now what are spirits or demigods? are they not either gods or the sons of gods?

52 Certainly they are.

53 But this is what I call the facetious riddle invented by you: the demigods or spirits are gods, and you say first that I do not believe in gods, and then again that I do believe in gods; that is, if I believe in demigods. For if the demigods are the illegitimate sons of gods, whether by nymphs, or by other mothers, as some are said to be—what human being will ever believe that there are no gods when there are sons of gods? You might as well affirm the existence of mules, and deny that of horses and asses. Such nonsense, Meletus, could only have been intended by you to make trial of me. You have put this into the indictment because you could think of nothing real of which to accuse me. But no one who has a particle of understanding will ever be convinced by you that a man can believe in the existence of things divine and superhuman, and the same man refuse to believe in gods and demigods and heroes.

54 I have said enough in answer to the charge of Meletus: any elaborate defence is unnecessary. You know well the truth of my statement that I have incurred many violent enmities; and this is what will be my destruction if I am destroyed;—not Meletus, nor yet Anytus, but the envy and detraction of the world, which has been the death of many good men, and will probably be the death of many more; there is no danger of my being the last of them.

Analysis of the Topics in "Socrates' Apology"

Although only about half of Socrates' *Apology* is reproduced here, there is a fair enough sample for analysis of this classic example of judicial rhetoric. Judicial rhetoric is exercised most frequently in the courtroom, but this kind of persuasive discourse comprehends as well all extra-courtroom defenses of actions and character. If we understand the term *apologize* in its Greek sense of "to defend" and the term *categorize* in its Greek sense of "to accuse," we have two terms which most aptly describe the basic functions of judicial discourse. This term can comprehend works as various as Newman's *Apologia Pro Vita Sua*, Zola's *J'accuse*, Pope's *Epistle to Dr. Arbuthnot*, and the catalogue of charges against the king of England in the *Declaration of Independence*. If we are haled into court today we would probably entrust our defense to a lawyer. But there may be many occasions in life when we will be called upon to justify our conduct outside the courtroom.

Socrates' defense is a serious affair, for Socrates is liable to the death sentence if the jury returns a verdict of guilty. As every schoolboy knows, Socrates lost his case and was made to drink the fatal "cup of hemlock." Almost everyone today who reads the *Apology* feels that Socrates had successfully answered the charges against him. The jury that heard Socrates' eloquent plea in the Athenian assembly was not more obtuse than modern readers; it happened that a number of extra-legal considerations played a part in their verdict. We will ignore here these extra-legal considerations that prejudiced the decision and concentrate on the speech itself.

As we have seen, the special topics that figure in judicial discourse are justice and injustice (or right and wrong, understood in their legal sense). In pursuing these special topics, the judicial speaker or writer is concerned primarily with one of these three questions: (1) whether the charge is so (*an sit*); (2) what the nature of the charge is (*quid sit*); (3) how serious the charge is (*quale sit*). In the course of a trial, the court may consider all three of these questions, but ultimately it must decide which one of these questions is at issue in a particular case. If *an sit* is the point at issue, evidence will be the main special topic; if *quid sit*, definition; if *quale sit*, motives or causes of action. In pursuit of the issue, the judicial pleader will pursue several of the common topics too. Let us see how the various topics operate in the *Apology*.

First of all, let us look at a general outline of the portion of the *Apology* that is reproduced here:

1. Socrates' introductory remarks to the assembly (paragraph 1).
2. *Narratio*—the statement of the charges (paragraph 2).

3. Refutation of the old charges (paragraphs 4-12).
4. Refutation of the recent charges—Socrates' cross-examination of Meletus (paragraphs 13-53).
5. Concluding remarks (paragraph 54).

In the opening paragraph, Socrates is setting the tone of the ethical appeal that he hopes his entire speech will exert. With typical ironic modesty, Socrates praises the eloquence of his accusers and depreciates his own skill as an orator. Lacking rhetorical skill, he will place his confidence in the justice of his cause, trusting that the recital of the truth and the whole truth will exonerate him. The reminder that he is seventy years old might be viewed as an emotional appeal for the sympathy or mercy of the court, but since Socrates nowhere else in the speech sounds this note, he seems to be reluctant to entrust his vindication to the emotional response of his hearers. Strategically, this avoidance of emotional appeal may have been a mistake, but distrust of emotion was typical of Socrates.

Resorting to the common topic of division in the second paragraph, Socrates divides the charges into two general classes, the ancient and the recent, and announces that he will answer the two groups of charges in turn. He does not specify the charges under these two general heads, being content here to indicate the general organization of his defense.

In paragraph 4 (after the transitional third paragraph) Socrates specifies the ancient charges. According to the "affidavit," he is charged with (1) being a student of natural philosophy; (2) making the worse appear the better cause; (3) being a teacher of these doctrines and taking money for his teaching. Pursuing the question of whether the first charge is true (*an sit*), Socrates denies the charge, maintaining that he has never engaged in speculations about physical matters. For confirmation of his claim, he calls for the testimony of those present. "Speak then," he says, "you who have heard me, and tell your neighbours whether any of you have ever known me hold forth in few words or in many upon such matters." This invitation meets with a stony silence from the audience. The implication of this silence is that there is no evidence to substantiate this ancient charge. It is simply not true. Since it is not true, Socrates does not have to go on to consider the nature of the offense and the seriousness of the offense.

Nor is there any evidence to substantiate the charge that he is a teacher and accepts money for his services. One wonders why no one in the assembly challenged Socrates' denial that he was a teacher. Socrates is certainly known to us, as he must have been to his contemporaries, as a teacher. Probably what is involved here is a matter of definition. What Socrates may be implying here—and he seems to be arguing this point in the next paragraph where he pursues the question of whether he is a wise man—is that technically he does not and cannot qualify as a teacher. After denying the charge, Socrates touches for a moment on the *quale sit* of the charge. Even if he were a qualified teacher who took money for his services, as do the sophists Gorgias and Prodicus and Hippias and Evenus, he would not consider this a crime. Resorting to analogy, Socrates reminds his audience that just as we would not consider it a crime if a trainer took a fee for improving foals or calves, so we should not consider it a crime if a teacher takes money for improving the minds of young people.

Socrates does not confront the charge that he makes the worse appear the better cause, but a denial of this charge seems to be implicit in his denial of the other two charges, and this charge is refuted really by some of the later arguments.

In paragraph 6, Socrates moves on to consider the reason why these false charges were levelled against him. Surely there must be some grounds for these charges. Their origin, Socrates thinks, lies in the pronouncement by the Delphic Oracle, "Socrates is the wisest man." When this Delphic pronouncement was reported to Socrates, he reasoned in the form of an enthymeme: "The god must be right, because a god cannot lie." But in what sense can the god be right in claiming that Socrates is the wisest of men?

In seeking an answer to this question, Socrates turns, in paragraph 7, to the common topic of definition. He recounts (in paragraphs 7, 8, 9) his experiences with politicians, poets, and artisans. He visited these men because they were supposedly wise and he wanted to find out why they were wise. But these so-called wise men disillusioned him. They were not really wise at all, and what was worse, they did not acknowledge or even recognize that they were ignorant. As a result of these inquiries, Socrates discovered the sense in which it could be said that he was the wisest of men: he alone knew that he did not know.

It is this rather paradoxical superiority that accounts for the animosity against Socrates. Moreover, the young people, who by nature relish the exposure of pretenders, began to imitate Socrates by examining charlatans. The pretenders to knowledge, disgruntled by their exposure, resorted to the standard but unproven charges made against all philosophers—that they teach things up in the clouds, that they have no gods, and that they make the worse appear the better cause. Prejudice, then, has motivated the wild, indiscriminate charges. Prejudice has prompted not only the old accusers but the recent accusers as well. Meletus is responding on behalf of the poets; Anytus, on behalf of the craftsmen and politicians; Lycon, on behalf of rhetoricians. Socrates concludes this part of his defense with an appeal to some rather dubious logic: "and what is their hatred but a proof that I am speaking the truth?" Socrates regards *hatred* as a sign. By the rules of strict logic, this sign cannot lead to an infallible conclusion. But the student may remember that Aristotle also recognized the effectiveness, for rhetorical purposes, of signs which lead only to probable conclusions. This kind of sign, as in the case of all probabilities, can produce only belief, not conviction.

In paragraph 12, Socrates specifies the charges made by the second group of accusers: (1) that I am a doer of evil; (2) that I corrupt the youth; (3) that I do not believe in the gods of the state; (4) that I set up other gods. Socrates reverses the first charge on Meletus; he will endeavor to show that it is *Meletus* who is the doer of evil, because he is not really serious about these matters. This reversing of the charge is a device recommended by all the classical rhetoricians. It puts the accuser on the defensive, and if the counter-charge can be substantiated, it takes the pressure off the defender.

In paragraphs 13-53, as we saw in the outline, Socrates cross-examines Meletus. Socrates shifts here from the discursive method of the early part of his defense to the question-and-answer style of dialectic. But although he has shifted his method, he does not abandon recourse to the special and common topics.

In paragraphs 18-38 of this section, Socrates examines the justice of the charge that he is a corrupter of the youth. At the outset of this cross-examination, Socrates resorts to the common topic of contraries. He says, in effect, "If I am a corrupter of youth, there must be some people whom Meletus regards as being improvers of youth." Who are these improvers of youth? Socrates gets Meletus to affirm that the judges, the audience, the senators, the members of the assembly—in fact, all Athenians except Socrates —improve the youth. Socrates proceeds to reduce this claim to absurdity by resorting to an analogy (the topic of similarity). Just as horses are improved, not by everyone but by the one man who is an excellent horse-trainer, so youth are improved not by the many but by the one. So Meletus' claim that Socrates alone corrupts the youth and that all other men improve the youth is manifestly absurd. (Note that there is an implied *a fortiori* argument in Socrates' application of the analogy.)

In paragraphs 32-8, Socrates approaches the same charge from another tack. First of all, he prompts Meletus to agree to the truth of three propositions: (1) the good do good to their neighbors; the evil do evil; (2) everyone would rather be benefited than injured by another; (3) I corrupt the youth either intentionally or unintentionally. Having secured agreement on these three propositions, Socrates uses the third of them as the starting point of his refutation. As we saw in the exposition of contradiction under the common topic of comparison, contradictory propositions are incompatible—that is, they cannot both be true. And we saw also that if one proposition is proved to be false, the other is automatically true. Socrates' strategy is to show that the proposition "Socrates corrupts the youth intentionally" is false. Note how cleverly he makes use of the other two propositions that Meletus has agreed to:

> But how could I corrupt the youth intentionally? If I corrupt them, they become evil. Once they become evil, they are liable to harm me (because, as we agreed, the evil do evil). But since I—like everyone else—would rather be benefited than injured by my neighbor, it is not likely that I would intentionally produce the kind of person who would injure me. So we can dismiss the charge that I corrupt the youth intentionally.

The argument has been reduced now to two possibilities (and we can regard these as contraries): either I do not corrupt the youth, or I corrupt them *un*intentionally. Socrates now deals with these contraries in this fashion:

> Let's arbitrarily rule out the first possibility, since you have formally accused me of corrupting the youth. That leaves us with the possibility that I corrupt the youth unintentionally. But if I corrupt the youth *un*intentionally, I am not subject to the law, and I should not be in this courtroom at all.

By demonstrating the absurdity of Meletus' charge, Socrates has been indirectly proving what he said he would prove: that Meletus could not have made these charges seriously and that therefore he is the real doer of evil.

In paragraphs 39-53, Socrates demonstrates the inconsistency of the charge that he is an atheist. He detects in items 3 and 4 of this indictment a flagrant contradiction: item 3 claims that he does not believe in the gods; item 4 implies that he does believe in the gods. To prove that item 3 is untrue, Socrates makes use of the common topics of similarity and genus and species. He gets Meletus to admit that one cannot believe in humanity without believing in human beings, in horsemanship without believing in horses, in flute-playing without believing in flute-players; in other words, one cannot believe in the genus without believing in the species. Similarly, one cannot believe in divine agencies (as item 4 claims) without believing in spirits and demi-gods. So the charge that Socrates does not believe in the gods is utterly false. By the principle of contradiction, if one proposition in a contradictory opposition is false, the other proposition is true. Therefore Socrates *does* believe in the gods.

In paragraph 54, the last paragraph in the selection reproduced here, Socrates points out that he has successfully answered the charges levelled by Meletus and Anytus. He recognizes, however, that during his lifetime he has incurred the enmity of many people and that it is this enmity, rather than the indictments, that will eventually prove to be his undoing. Throughout this half of the *Apology,* Socrates has employed a negative strategy—the strategy of refutation—but from this point on Socrates will be advancing positive arguments for his innocence.

It might be pointed out finally that a great part of Socrates' strategy throughout this section was an effort to minimize Meletus' ethical appeal. At the same time that he is refuting Meletus' charges he is showing indirectly that Meletus is not a man of good sense, good character, and good will. Meletus' ethical appeal is further diminished by his frequent reluctance to answer Socrates' pointed questions. The crowning touch was the incremental irony of Socrates' repeated reference to Meletus as "my friend"—an irony that becomes as damaging as Mark Antony's use of the epithet "honorable men" in the famous "Friends, Romans, countrymen" speech in Shakespeare's *Julius Caesar*.

Pericles' Funeral Oration

Pericles was an Athenian statesman, who ruled from 461 to 429 B.C. The following oration has come to be regarded as the classic prototype of the kind of epideictic or ceremonial rhetoric that is exemplified, in our own country, by Abraham Lincoln's Gettysburg Address. It was delivered in 430 B.C. to honor the soldiers who fought and died in the first campaign of the Peloponnesian War against Sparta and her allies. The only record we have of this famous eulogy is the reconstruction of it from Thucydides' historical account of the Peloponnesian War. Thucydides (460–400 B.C.) confesses in the introductory chapter of his work that he has not reproduced the exact words of this and the other speeches reported in his history but that he has faithfully preserved the substance and the spirit of those speeches. Pericles dwells not so much on the courage and sacrifice of the dead soldiers as on the merits of the Athenian style of democracy which produced these heroes.

1 In the same winter the Athenians, following their annual custom, gave a public funeral for those who had been the first to die in the war. These funerals are held in the following way: two days before the ceremony the bones of the fallen are brought and put in a tent which has been erected, and people make whatever offerings they wish to their own dead. Then there is a funeral procession in which coffins of cypress wood are carried on

Thucydides, *The Peloponnesian War*, trans. Rex Warner (Harmondsworth, Eng.: Penguin Books, 1954), Bk. II, Ch. 4, pp. 115-23. Reprinted by permission of the Bodley Head.

wagons. There is one coffin for each tribe, which contains the bones of members of that tribe. One empty bier is decorated and carried in the procession: this is for the missing, whose bodies could not be recovered. Everyone who wishes to, both citizens and foreigners, can join in the procession, and the women who are related to the dead are there to make their laments at the tomb. The bones are laid in the public burial-place, which is in the most beautiful quarter outside the city walls. Here the Athenians always bury those who have fallen in war. The only exception is those who died at Marathon, who, because their achievement was considered absolutely outstanding, were buried on the battlefield itself.

2 When the bones have been laid in the earth, a man chosen by the city for his intellectual gifts and for his general reputation makes an appropriate speech in praise of the dead, and after the speech all depart. This is the procedure at these burials, and all through the war, when the time came to do so, the Athenians followed this ancient custom. Now, at the burial of those who were the first to fall in the war Pericles, the son of Xanthippus, was chosen to make the speech. When the moment arrived, he came forward from the tomb and, standing on a high platform, so that he might be heard by as many people as possible in the crowd, he spoke as follows:

3 "Many of those who have spoken here in the past have praised the institution of this speech at the close of our ceremony. It seemed to them a mark of honour to our soldiers who have fallen in war that a speech should be made over them. I do not agree. These men have shown themselves valiant in action, and it would be enough, I think, for their glories to be proclaimed in action, as you have just seen it done at this funeral organized by the state. Our belief in the courage and manliness of so many should not be hazarded on the goodness or badness of one man's speech. Then it is not easy to speak with a proper sense of balance, when a man's listeners find it difficult to believe in the truth of what one is saying. The man who knows the facts and loves the dead may well think that an oration tells less than what he knows and what he would like to hear: others who do not know so much may feel envy for the dead, and think the orator over-praises them, when he speaks of exploits that are beyond their own capacities. Praise of other people is tolerable only up to a certain point, the point where one believes that one could do oneself some of the things one is hearing about. Once you get beyond this point, you will find people becoming jealous and incredulous. However, the fact is that this institution was set up and approved by our forefathers, and it is my duty to follow the tradition and do my best to meet the wishes and the expectations of every one of you.

4 "I shall begin by speaking about our ancestors, since it is only right and proper on such an occasion to pay them the honour of recalling what they did. In this land of ours there have always been the same people living from

generation to generation up till now, and they, by their courage and their virtues, have handed it on to us, a free country. They certainly deserve our praise. Even more so do our fathers deserve it. For to the inheritance they had received they added all the empire we have now, and it was not without blood and toil that they handed it down to us of the present generation. And then we ourselves, assembled here today, who are mostly in the prime of life, have, in most directions, added to the power of our empire and have organized our State in such a way that it is perfectly well able to look after itself both in peace and in war.

5 "I have no wish to make a long speech on subjects familiar to you all: so I shall say nothing about the warlike deeds by which we acquired our power or the battles in which we or our fathers gallantly resisted our enemies, Greek or foreign. What I want to do is, in the first place, to discuss the spirit in which we faced our trials and also our constitution and the way of life which has made us great. After that I shall speak in praise of the dead, believing that this kind of speech is not inappropriate to the present occasion, and that this whole assembly, of citizens and foreigners, may listen to it with advantage.

6 "Let me say that our system of government does not copy the institutions of our neighbours. It is more the case of our being a model to others, than of our imitating anyone else. Our constitution is called a democracy because power is in the hands not of a minority but of the whole people. When it is a question of settling private disputes, everyone is equal before the law; when it is a question of putting one person before another in positions of public responsibility, what counts is not membership of a particular class, but the actual ability which the man possesses. No one, so long as he has it in him to be of service to the state, is kept in political obscurity because of poverty. And, just as our political life is free and open, so is our day-to-day life in our relations with each other. We do not get into a state with our next-door neighbour if he enjoys himself in his own way, nor do we give him the kind of black looks which, though they do no real harm, still do hurt people's feelings. We are free and tolerant in our private lives; but in public affairs we keep to the law. This is because it commands our deep respect.

7 "We give our obedience to those whom we put in positions of authority, and we obey the laws themselves, especially those which are for the protection of the oppressed, and those unwritten laws which it is an acknowledged shame to break.

8 "And here is another point. When our work is over, we are in a position to enjoy all kinds of recreation for our spirits. There are various kinds of contests and sacrifices regularly throughout the year; in our own homes we find a beauty and a good taste which delight us every day and which drive

away our cares. Then the greatness of our city brings it about that all the good things from all the world flow in to us, so that to us it seems just as natural to enjoy foreign goods as our own local products.

9 "Then there is a great difference between us and our opponents in our attitude towards military security. Here are some examples: Our city is open to the world, and we have no periodical deportations in order to prevent people observing or finding out secrets which might be of military advantage to the enemy. This is because we rely, not on secret weapons, but on our own real courage and loyalty. There is a difference, too, in our educational systems. The Spartans, from their earliest boyhood, are submitted to the most laborious training in courage; we pass our lives without all these restrictions, and yet are just as ready to face the same dangers as they are. Here is proof of this: When the Spartans invade our land, they do not come by themselves, but bring all their allies with them; whereas we, when we launch an attack abroad, do the job ourselves, and, though fighting on foreign soil, do not often fail to defeat opponents who are fighting for their own hearths and homes. As a matter of fact, none of our enemies has ever yet been confronted with our total strength, because we have to divide our attention between our navy and the many missions on which our troops are sent on land. Yet, if our enemies engage a detachment of our forces and defeat it, they give themselves credit for having thrown back our entire army; or, if they lose, they claim that they were beaten by us in full strength. There are certain advantages, I think, in our way of meeting danger voluntarily, with an easy mind, instead of with a laborious training, with natural rather than with state-induced courage. We do not have to spend our time practising to meet sufferings which are still in the future; and when they are actually upon us show ourselves just as brave as these others who are always in strict training. This is one point in which, I think, our city deserves to be admired. There are also others:

10 "Our love of what is beautiful does not lead to extravagance; our love of the things of the mind does not make us soft. We regard wealth as something to be properly used, rather than as something to boast about. As for poverty, no one need be ashamed to admit it: the real shame is in not taking practical measures to escape from it. Here each individual is interested not only in his own affairs but in the affairs of the state as well: even those who are mostly occupied with their own business are extremely well-informed on general politics—this is a peculiarity of ours: we do not say that a man who takes no interest in politics is a man who minds his own business; we say that he has no business here at all. We Athenians, in our own persons, take our decisions on policy or submit them to proper discussions: for we do not think that there is an incompatibility between words and deeds; the worst thing is to rush into action before the consequences have been properly

debated. And this is another point where we differ from other people. We are capable at the same time of taking risks and of estimating them beforehand. Others are brave out of ignorance; and, when they stop to think, they begin to fear. But the man who can most truly be accounted brave is he who knows the meaning of what is sweet in life and of what is terrible, and then goes out undeterred to meet what is to come.

11 "Again, in questions of general good feeling there is a great contrast between us and most other people. We make friends by doing good to others, not by receiving good from them. This makes our friendship all the more reliable, since we want to keep alive the gratitude of those who are in our debt by showing continued goodwill to them: whereas the feelings of one who owes us something lack the same enthusiasm, since he knows that, when he repays our kindness, it will be more like paying back a debt than giving something spontaneously. We are unique in this. When we do kindnesses to others, we do not do them out of any calculations of profit or loss: we do them without afterthought, relying on our free liberality. Taking everything together then, I declare that our city is an education to Greece, and I declare that in my opinion each single one of our citizens, in all the manifold aspects of life, is able to show himself the rightful lord and owner of his own person, and do this, moreover, with exceptional grace and exceptional versatility. And to show that this is no empty boasting for the present occasion, but real tangible fact, you have only to consider the power which our city possesses and which has been won by those very qualities which I have mentioned. Athens, alone of the states we know, comes to her testing time in a greatness that surpasses what was imagined of her. In her case, and in her case alone, no invading enemy is ashamed at being defeated, and no subject can complain of being governed by people unfit for their responsibilities. Mighty indeed are the marks and monuments of our empire which we have left. Future ages will wonder at us, as the present age wonders at us now. We do not need the praises of a Homer, or of anyone else whose words may delight us for the moment, but whose estimation of facts will fall short of what is really true. For our adventurous spirit has forced an entry into every sea and into every land; and everywhere we have left behind us everlasting memorials of good done to our friends or suffering inflicted on our enemies.

12 "This, then, is the kind of city for which these men, who could not bear the thought of losing her, nobly fought and nobly died. It is only natural that every one of us who survive them should be willing to undergo hardships in her service. And it was for this reason that I have spoken at such length about our city, because I wanted to make it clear that for us there is more at stake than there is for others who lack our advantages; also I wanted my words of praise for the dead to be set in the bright light of

evidence. And now the most important of these words has been spoken. I have sung the praises of our city; but it was the courage and gallantry of these men, and of people like them, which made her splendid. Nor would you find it true in the case of many of the Greeks, as it is true of them, that no words can do more than justice to their deeds.

13 "To me it seems that the consummation which has overtaken these men shows us the meaning of manliness in its first revelation and in its final proof. Some of them, no doubt, had their faults; but what we ought to remember first is their gallant conduct against the enemy in defence of their native land. They have blotted out evil with good, and done more service to the commonwealth than they ever did harm in their private lives. No one of these men weakened because he wanted to go on enjoying his wealth: no one put off the awful day in the hope that he might live to escape his poverty and grow rich. More to be desired than such things, they chose to check the enemy's pride. This, to them, was a risk most glorious, and they accepted it, willing to strike down the enemy and relinquish everything else. As for success or failure, they left that in the doubtful hands of Hope, and when the reality of battle was before their faces, they put their trust in their own selves. In the fighting, they thought it more honourable to stand their ground and suffer death than to give in and save their lives. So they fled from the reproaches of men, abiding with life and limb the brunt of battle; and, in a small moment of time, the climax of their lives, a culmination of glory, not of fear, were swept away from us.

14 "So and such they were, these men—worthy of their city. We who remain behind may hope to be spared their fate, but must resolve to keep the same daring spirit against the foe. It is not simply a question of estimating the advantages in theory. I could tell you a long story (and you know it as well as I do) about what is to be gained by beating the enemy back. What I would prefer is that you should fix your eyes every day on the greatness of Athens as she really is, and should fall in love with her. When you realize her greatness, then reflect that what made her great was men with a spirit of adventure, men who knew their duty, men who were ashamed to fall below a certain standard. If they ever failed in an enterprise, they made up their minds that at any rate the city should not find their courage lacking to her, and they gave to her the best contribution that they could. They gave her their lives, to her and to all of us, and for their own selves they won praises that never grow old, the most splendid of sepulchres—not the sepulchre in which their bodies are laid, but where their glory remains eternal in men's minds, always there on the right occasion to stir others to speech or to action. For famous men have the whole earth as their memorial: it is not only the inscriptions on their graves in their own country that mark them out; no, in foreign lands also, not in any visible form but in people's hearts, their memory abides and grows. It is for you to try to be like them. Make up your minds that happiness depends on being free, and freedom depends on being courageous. Let there be no relaxation in face of the perils of the war. The people who have most excuse for despising death are not the wretched and unfortunate, who have no hope of doing well for themselves, but those who run the risk of a complete reversal in their lives, and who would feel the difference most intensely, if things went wrong for them. Any intelligent man would find a humiliation caused by his own slackness more painful to bear than death, when death comes to him unperceived, in battle, and in the confidence of his patriotism.

15 "For these reasons I shall not commiserate with those parents of the dead, who are present here. Instead I shall try to comfort them. They are well aware that they have grown up in a world where there are many changes and chances. But this is good fortune—for men to end their lives with honour, as these have done, and for you honourably to lament them: their life was set to a measure where death and happiness went hand in hand. I know that it is difficult to convince you of this. When you see other people happy you will often be reminded of what used to make you happy too. One does not feel sad at not having some good thing which is outside one's experience: real grief is felt at the loss of something which one is used to. All the same, those of you who are of the right age must bear up and take comfort in the thought of having more children. In your own homes these new children will prevent you from brooding over those who are no more, and they will be a help to the city, too, both in filling the empty places, and in assuring her security. For it is impossible for a man to put forward fair and honest views about our affairs if he has not, like everyone else, children whose lives may be at stake. As for those of you who are now too old to have children, I would ask you to count as gain the greater part of your life, in which you have been happy, and remember that what remains is not long, and let your hearts be lifted up at the thought of the fair fame of the dead. One's sense of honour is the only thing that does not grow old, and the last pleasure, when one is worn out with age, is not, as the poet said, making money, but having the respect of one's fellow men.

16 "As for those of you here who are sons or brothers of the dead, I can see a hard struggle in front of you. Everyone always speaks well of the dead, and, even if you rise to the greatest heights of heroism, it will be a hard thing for you to get the reputation of having come near, let alone equalled, their standard. When one is alive, one is always liable to the jealousy of one's competitors, but when one is out of the way, the honour one receives is sincere and unchallenged.

17 "Perhaps I should say a word or two on the duties of women to those among you who are now widowed. I can say all I have to say in a short word of advice. Your great glory is not to be inferior to what God has made you, and the greatest glory of a woman is to be least talked about by men, whether they are praising you or criticizing you. I have now, as the law demanded, said what I had to say. For the time being our offerings to the dead have been made, and for the future their children will be supported at the public expense by the city, until they come of age. This is the crown and prize which she offers, both to the dead and to their children, for the ordeals they have faced. Where the rewards of valour are the greatest, there you will find also the best and bravest spirits among the people. And now, when you have mourned for your dear ones, you must depart."

Analysis of the Topics in "Pericles' Funeral Oration"

Pericles' noble utterance is the prototype of all memorial addresses. The death of loved ones or of heroes invariably calls forth generous tributes, heartfelt sentiments, and noble resolutions. This most emotional of all human events usually manages to escape the blight of sentimentality, probably because we the survivors feel that no expression of sentiment, however extravagant, can be in excess of the occasion that prompts it. There is danger, of course, that when time removes us from emotional involvement with the occasion and the deceased, elegies will strike us as being maudlin. It is the perspective of time that separates the deathless prose from the perishable. Lincoln's *Gettysburg Address* and Pericles' *Funeral Oration* are two of the epideictic utterances that impress us as being as eloquent and genuine now as they were the day they were delivered from the podium.

In the first two paragraphs of the selection, Thucydides gives us the background for Pericles' speech. The statement that the city fathers expected "an appropriate speech in praise of the dead" indicates that the speech is to be of the epideictic variety—or, as we have chosen to call it, *ceremonial*. This is to be a speech of display in which a man or group of men is to be praised or censured. The audience does not have to be persuaded, as in the case of deliberative and forensic discourse, to make a decision; the audience has merely to be convinced—or at least to be confirmed in its belief—that a man or group of men is deserving of praise or censure. There is, of course, a certain indirect deliberative purpose to such a speech; if the audience can be convinced that the men are deserving of praise it may be induced to go and be likewise.

We may divide Pericles' oration into four parts:

1. Introduction (paragraphs 3-5).
2. Praise of the Athenian people (paragraphs 6-12).
3. Praise of the dead heroes (paragraphs 13-16).
4. Conclusion (paragraph 17).

It might strike the student as odd that Pericles should devote more of his speech to the praise of the Athenian people, past and present, than to the praise of the war heroes. Pericles accounts for this proportion in paragraph 12, where he says, "And it was for this reason that I have spoken at such length about our city, because I wanted to make it clear that for us there is more at stake than there is for others who lack our advantages; also I wanted my words of praise for the dead to be set in the bright light of evidence." In other words, praise of the Athenian people reflects praise on the men who died in their cause, who sacrificed their own enjoyment of this way of life so that others could enjoy it. "The people who have the most excuse for despising death," Pericles says (paragraph 14), "are not the wretched and unfortunate, who have no hope of doing well for themselves, but those who run the risk of a complete reversal in their lives, and who feel the difference most intensely, if things went wrong for them." (Note how the common topic of more and less is operating here.)

The special topics for ceremonial discourse are the virtues, physical attributes, actions and achievements, and sayings of the men being praised; another resort is the testimony of others. Throughout the speech, Pericles touches on several of the virtues that characterize the Athenian people and the dead heroes. In reference to the former he mentions the following virtues:

1. *Justice* (respect for the natural and legal rights of men).
   In our democratic government, we allow for and encourage the free exercise of the rights of citizenship (paragraph 6). In private disputes, everyone is equal before the law (paragraph 6). Our day-to-day relations with one another are free and equal (paragraph 6). We obey those we have invested with authority, and we respect both written and unwritten law (paragraph 7).

2. *Wisdom* (an intellectual virtue).
   We cultivate beauty and the things of the mind (paragraphs 8 and 10). We have an enlightened attitude toward wealth and poverty (paragraph 10). We believe that all citizens should be well-informed about political affairs (paragraph 10).

3. *Prudence* (another intellectual virtue).
   We have a superior policy on military security and training (paragraph 9). We have a penchant for deliberation before rushing into action (paragraph 10). We are capable not only of taking risks but of estimating them beforehand (paragraph 10).

4. *Magnanimity* and *Liberality*.
   We are fond of doing good to others (paragraph 11). And we do good to others, not out of any calculation of profit and loss to us

but out of a generous disposition (paragraph 11). We make friends by doing good to others, not by receiving good from them (paragraph 11).

As might be expected, the virtue that Pericles stresses as belonging to the soldiers in paragraphs 13-16 is courage. He also touches on their honorableness (gallantry), loyalty, and unselfishness. But as Pericles indicated in paragraph 3, he is more disposed to entrust the glorification of the soldiers to the record of their actions and achievements than to the qualities of the speeches made over them. As he says, "Our belief in the courage and manliness of so many should not be hazarded on the goodness or badness of one man's speech." All references in these paragraphs to the soldiers' actions and achievements are variations on the double theme that they fought gallantly and that they made the supreme sacrifice, their lives. There is no recital of the physical attributes of the men (with the possible exception of the mention of their manliness) or of their sayings. And the only recourse to the testimony of others is Pericles' reminder that these men have established their memorial in people's hearts.

Ceremonial discourse offers more opportunity for the use of the topics of amplification and depreciation than the other two kinds of discourse. Frequently throughout the speech Pericles attempts to magnify the deeds and virtues of the Athenians by mentioning that the deeds and virtues were *unique* or were *better* or were more *frequent* or were produced under more *adverse circumstances*. The common topic of comparison is frequently resorted to in the speech. The most pronounced example of this topic is found in paragraph 9, where Pericles contrasts the military policies of Athens with those of other countries (Pericles is thinking mainly of Sparta). This comparison reveals marked differences, and in arguing where the advantage lies in these differences, Pericles resorts to some of the criteria that help one decide questions of more and less (the topic of degree). In the words addressed to the parents, the wives, the sons and brothers, of the dead men, he makes great use of the common topics of future fact. He seems to be suggesting that if the survivors do *this* and *this, this* will come to pass (future fact, in other words, is being argued with the topic of antecedent-consequent). The past facts are all confirmed by the prosperity, stature, and esteem presently enjoyed by the Athenian people.

Pericles' oration is a classic example of how one proceeds when one seeks to praise someone, whether that praise be in a formal address like this, in a toastmaster's introductory remarks about a featured speaker, in a letter of reference, in a citation, in an obituary, in a memoir. One expatiates on those virtues, attributes, deeds, achievements, testimonies which reflect credit on the man being extolled. The same basic strategy is used when one seeks to discredit someone. In ceremonial discourse, perhaps more than in the other two kinds, the nature of the subject will be the major factor determining what can be said, for the success of this kind of discourse depends mainly on the truth or credibility of what is said. In paragraph 3, Pericles adverted to the difficulty in executing this kind of discourse successfully:

> Then it is not easy to speak with a proper sense of balance, when a man's listeners find it difficult to believe in the truth of what one is saying. The man who knows the facts and loves the dead may well think that an oration tells less than what he knows and what he would like to hear; others who do not know so much may feel envy for the dead, and think the orator over-praises them, when he speaks of exploits that are beyond their own capacities. Praise of other people is tolerable only up to a certain point, the point where one believes that one could do oneself some of the things one is hearing about. Once you get beyond this point, you will find people becoming jealous and incredulous.

The student might well take these judicious words—and the example of the speech itself—as his guide in the preparation of any discourse designed to praise or censure his fellow man.

James Madison: The Federalist, No. 10

On September 17, 1787, the Constitution of the United States was finally drafted and signed by the fifty-some members of the Constitutional Convention in Philadelphia. The newly drafted Constitution, however, still had to be ratified by the state conventions of at least nine of the original thirteen colonies. We who take our Constitution so much for granted find it difficult to believe that this incomparable document had to be "sold" to the people of the new confederacy of states. But the anti-Federalists soon marshalled their forces to defeat the ratification of the Constitution. They argued that the strong central government established by the Constitution was a threat to the autonomy of the states, that the Constitution gave too much power to the Chief Executive, that it instituted a dangerous system of federal courts, and that it opened the way to oppressive taxation. Five of the small states, however, quickly ratified the Constitution—Delaware, Maryland, New Jersey, Connecticut, and South Carolina. The most formidable opposition came from Pennsylvania, Massachusetts, Virginia, and New York. Because New York was a key state in the opposition, Alexander Hamilton, only thirty years old at the time, conceived the idea of publishing a series of articles refuting the objections to the Constitution and extolling its virtues, and he enlisted the help of James Madison of Virginia and John Jay of New York. In a series of eighty-five articles, published in various New York newspapers from October 1787 to April 1788, Publius—the pseudonym adopted for all the papers —exercised all the rhetorical skill at his command to persuade the New York convention to adopt the Constitution. James Madison, who wrote only about a third of the Federalist Papers (Jay wrote only five), was the author of No. 10, which appeared in the New York Packet *on Friday, November 23, 1787. It epitomizes the clear, eloquent style and the compelling logic with which Hamilton, Madison, and Jay argued their case. New York's eventual ratification by a narrow margin was inconsequential, because by that time the necessary nine states had adopted the Constitution. In the article that immediately follows "Federalist, No. 10," Mark Ashin provides a thoroughgoing topical analysis of Madison's argument.*

1   Among the numerous advantages promised by a well-constructed Union, none deserves to be more accurately developed than its tendency to break and control the violence of faction. The friend of popular governments never finds himself so much alarmed for their character and fate, as when he contemplates their propensity to this dangerous vice. He will not fail, therefore, to set a due value on any plan which, without violating the principles to which he is attached, provides a proper cure for it. The instability, injustice, and confusion introduced into the public councils, have, in truth, been the mortal diseases under which popular governments have everywhere perished; as they continue to be the favorite and fruitful topics from which the adversaries to liberty derive their most specious declamations. The valuable improvements made by the constitutions on the popular models, both ancient and modern, cannot certainly be too much admired; but it would be an unwarrantable partiality to contend that they have as effectually obviated the danger on this side, as was wished and expected. Complaints are everywhere heard from our most considerate and virtuous citizens, equally the friends of public and private faith, and of public and personal liberty, that our governments are too unstable, that the public good is disregarded in the conflicts of rival parties, and that measures are too often decided, not according to the rules of justice and the rights of the minor party, but by the superior force of an interested and overbearing majority. However anxiously we may wish that these complaints had no foundation, the evidence of known facts will not permit us to deny that they are in some degree true. It will be found, indeed, on a candid review of our situation, that some of the distresses under which we labor have been erroneously charged on the operations of our governments; but it will be found, at the same time, that other causes will not alone account for many of our heaviest misfortunes; and, particularly, for that prevailing and increasing distrust of public engagements and alarm for

private rights, which are echoed from one end of the continent to the other. These must be chiefly, if not wholly, effects of the unsteadiness and injustice with which a factious spirit has tainted our public administrations.

2   By a faction, I understand a number of citizens, whether amounting to a majority or minority of the whole, who are united and actuated by some common impulse of passion, or of interest, adverse to the rights of other citizens or to the permanent and aggregate interests of the community.

3   There are two methods of curing the mischiefs of faction: the one, by removing its causes; the other, by controlling its effects.

4   There are again two methods of removing the causes of faction: the one, by destroying the liberty which is essential to its existence; the other, by giving to every citizen the same opinions, the same passions, and the same interests.

5   It could never be more truly said than of the first remedy, that it was worse than the disease. Liberty is to faction what air is to fire, an aliment without which it instantly expires. But it could not be less folly to abolish liberty, which is essential to political life, because it nourishes faction, than it would be to wish the annihilation of air, which is essential to animal life, because it imparts to fire its destructive agency.

6   The second expedient is as impracticable as the first would be unwise. As long as the reason of man continues fallible, and he is at liberty to exercise it, different opinions will be formed. As long as the connection subsists between his reason and his self-love, his opinions and his passions will have a reciprocal influence on each other; and the former will be objects to which the latter will attach themselves. The diversity in the faculties of men, from which the rights of property originate, is not less an insuperable obstacle to a uniformity of interests. The protection of these faculties is the first object of government. From the protection of different and unequal faculties of acquiring property, the possession of different degrees and kinds of property immediately results; and from the influence of these on the sentiments and views of the respective proprietors, ensues a division of the society into different interests and parties.

7   The latent causes of faction are thus sown in the nature of man; and we see them everywhere brought into different degrees of activity, according to the different circumstances of civil society. A zeal for different opinions concerning religion, concerning government, and many other points, as well of speculation as of practice; an attachment to different leaders ambitiously contending for pre-eminence and power; or to persons of other descriptions whose fortunes have been interesting to the human passions, have, in turn, divided mankind into parties, inflamed them with mutual animosity, and rendered them much more disposed to vex and oppress each other than to cooperate for their own common good. So strong is this propensity of man-

kind to fall into mutual animosities, that where no substantial occasion presents itself, the most frivolous and fanciful distinctions have been sufficient to kindle their unfriendly passions and excite their most violent conflicts. But the most common and durable source of factions has been the various and unequal distribution of property. Those who hold and those who are without property have ever formed distinct interests in society. Those who are creditors and those who are debtors fall under a like discrimination. A landed interest, a manufacturing interest, a mercantile interest, a moneyed interest, with many lesser interests, grow up of necessity in civilized nations, and divide them into different classes, actuated by different sentiments and views. The regulation of these various and interfering interests forms the principal task of modern legislation and involves the spirit of party and faction in the necessary and ordinary operations of the government.

8   No man is allowed to be a judge in his own cause, because his interest would certainly bias his judgment, and, not improbably, corrupt his integrity. With equal, nay with greater reason, a body of men are unfit to be both judges and parties at the same time; yet what are many of the most important acts of legislation, but so many judicial determinations, not indeed concerning the rights of single persons, but concerning the rights of large bodies of citizens? And what are the different classes of legislators but advocates and parties to the causes which they determine? Is a law proposed concerning private debts? It is a question to which the creditors are parties on one side and the debtors on the other. Justice ought to hold the balance between them. Yet the parties are, and must be, themselves the judges; and the most numerous party, or, in other words, the most powerful faction must be expected to prevail. Shall domestic manufactures be encouraged, and in what degree, by restrictions on foreign manufactures? are questions which would be differently decided by the landed and the manufacturing classes, and probably by neither with a sole regard to justice and the public good. The apportionment of taxes on the various descriptions of property is an act which seems to require the most exact impartiality; yet there is, perhaps, no legislative act in which greater opportunity and temptation are given to a predominant party to trample on the rules of justice. Every shilling with which they overburden the inferior number, is a shilling saved to their own pockets.

9   It is in vain to say that enlightened statesmen will be able to adjust these clashing interests and render them all subservient to the public good. Enlightened statesmen will not always be at the helm. Nor, in many cases, can such an adjustment be made at all without taking into view indirect and remote considerations, which will rarely prevail over the immediate interest which one party may find in disregarding the rights of another or the good of the whole.

10   The inference to which we are brought is that the *causes* of faction cannot be removed and that relief is only to be sought in the means of controlling its *effects*.

11   If a faction consists of less than a majority, relief is supplied by the republican principle, which enables the majority to defeat its sinister views by regular vote. It may clog the administration, it may convulse the society; but it will be unable to execute and mask its violence under the forms of the Constitution. When a majority is included in a faction, the form of popular government, on the other hand, enables it to sacrifice to its ruling passion or interest both the public good and the rights of other citizens. To secure the public good and private rights against the danger of such a faction, and at the same time to preserve the spirit and the form of popular government, is then the great object to which our inquiries are directed. Let me add that it is the great desideratum by which this form of government can be rescued from the opprobrium under which it has so long labored, and be recommended to the esteem and adoption of mankind.

12   By what means is this object attainable? Evidently by one of two only. Either the existence of the same passion or interest in a majority at the same time must be prevented, or the majority, having such coexistent passion or interest, must be rendered, by their number and local situation, unable to concert and carry into effect schemes of oppression. If the impulse and the opportunity be suffered to coincide, we well know that neither moral nor religious motives can be relied on as an adequate control. They are not found to be such on the injustice and violence of individuals, and lose their efficacy in proportion to the number combined together, that is, in proportion as their efficacy becomes needful.

13   From this view of the subject it may be concluded that a pure democracy, by which I mean a society consisting of a small number of citizens, who assemble and administer the government in person, can admit of no cure for the mischiefs of faction. A common passion or interest will, in almost every case, be felt by a majority of the whole; a communication and concert result from the form of government itself; and there is nothing to check the inducements to sacrifice the weaker party or an obnoxious individual. Hence it is that such democracies have ever been spectacles of turbulence and contention; have ever been found incompatible with personal security or the rights of property; and have in general been as short in their lives as they have been violent in their deaths. Theoretic politicians, who have patronized this species of government, have erroneously supposed that by reducing mankind to a perfect equality in their political rights, they would, at the same time, be perfectly equalized and assimilated in their possessions, their opinions, and their passions.

14   A republic, by which I mean a government in which the scheme of representation takes place, opens a different prospect and promises the cure for which we are seeking. Let us examine the points in which it varies from pure democracy, and we shall comprehend both the nature of the cure and the efficacy which it must derive from the Union.

15 The two great points of difference between a democracy and a republic are: first, the delegation of the government, in the latter, to a small number of citizens elected by the rest; secondly, the greater number of citizens, and greater sphere of country, over which the latter may be extended.

16 The effect of the first difference is, on the one hand, to refine and enlarge the public views, by passing them through the medium of a chosen body of citizens, whose wisdom may best discern the true interest of their country, and whose patriotism and love of justice will be least likely to sacrifice it to temporary or partial considerations. Under such a regulation, it may well happen that the public voice, pronounced by the representatives of the people, will be more consonant to the public good than if pronounced by the people themselves, convened for the purpose. On the other hand, the effect may be inverted. Men of factious tempers, of local prejudices, or of sinister designs, may, by intrigue, by corruption, or by other means, first obtain the suffrages, and then betray the interests, of the people. The question resulting is, whether small or extensive republics are more favorable to the election of proper guardians of the public weal; and it is clearly decided in favor of the latter by two obvious considerations:

17 In the first place, it is to be remarked that, however large it may be, they must be limited to a certain number, in order to guard against the confusion of a multitude. Hence, the number of representatives in the two cases not being in proportion to that of the two constituents and being proportionally greater in the small republic, it follows that, if the proportion of fit characters be not less in the large than in the small republic, the former will present a greater option, and consequently a greater probability of a fit choice.

18 In the next place, as each representative will be chosen by a greater number of citizens in the large than in the small republic, it will be more difficult for unworthy candidates to practice with success the vicious arts by which elections are too often carried; and the suffrages of the people being more free, will be more likely to center in men who possess the most attractive merit and the most diffusive and established characters.

19 It must be confessed that in this, as in most other cases, there is a mean, on both sides of which inconveniences will be found to lie. By enlarging too much the number of electors, you render the representative too little acquainted with all their local circumstances and lesser interests; as by reducing it too much, you render him unduly attached to these and too little fit to comprehend and pursue great national objects. The federal Constitution forms a happy combination in this respect; the great and aggregate interests being referred to the national, the local and particular to the State legislatures.

20   The other point of difference is the greater number of citizens and extent of territory which may be brought within the compass of republican than of democratic government; and it is this circumstance principally which renders factious combinations less to be dreaded in the former than in the latter. The smaller the society, the fewer probably will be the distinct parties and interests composing it; the fewer the distinct parties and interests, the more frequently will a majority be found of the same party; and the smaller the number of individuals composing a majority, and the smaller the compass within which they are placed, the more easily will they concert and execute their plans of oppression. Extend the sphere, and you take in a greater variety of parties and interests; you make it less probable that a majority of the whole will have a common motive to invade the rights of other citizens; or if such a common motive exists, it will be more difficult for all who feel it to discover their own strength and to act in unison with each other. Besides other impediments, it may be remarked that, where there is a consciousness of unjust or dishonorable purposes, communication is always checked by distrust in proportion to the number whose concurrence is necessary.

21   Hence, it clearly appears, that the same advantage which a republic has over a democracy in controlling the effects of faction is enjoyed by a large over a small republic—is enjoyed by the Union over the States composing it. Does the advantage consist in the substitution of representatives whose enlightened views and virtuous sentiments render them superior to local prejudices and to schemes of injustice? It will not be denied that the representation of the Union will be most likely to possess these requisite endowments. Does it consist in the greater security afforded by a greater variety of parties, against the event of any one party being able to outnumber and oppress the rest? In an equal degree does the increased variety of parties comprised within the Union increase this security. Does it, in fine, consist in the greater obstacles opposed to the concert and accomplishment of the secret wishes of an unjust and interested majority? Here, again, the extent of the Union gives it the most palpable advantage.

22   The influence of factious leaders may kindle a flame within their particular States, but will be unable to spread a general conflagration through the other States. A religious sect may degenerate into a political faction in a part of the Confederacy; but the variety of sects dispersed over the entire face of it must secure the national councils against any danger from that source. A rage for paper money, for an abolition of debts, for an equal division of property, or for any other improper or wicked project, will be less

apt to pervade the whole body of the Union than a particular member of it; in the same proportion as such a malady is more likely to taint a particular country or district than an entire State.

23   In the extent and proper structure of the Union, therefore, we behold a republican remedy for the diseases most incident to republican government. And according to the degree of pleasure and pride we feel in being republicans, ought to be our zeal in cherishing the spirit and supporting the character of Federalists.

PUBLIUS (1787)

Mark Ashin: The Argument of Madison's "Federalist," No. 10"

In the January issue of *College English,* some members of the English staff at the College of the University of Chicago questioned the value of trying to teach argument in a writing course by concentrating exclusively on the technique of formal logic. Their contention was that, while training in the inductive and deductive forms of logic would enable a student to judge the validity of arguments already constructed, such training does little or nothing to supply the young student's greatest need, some technique for discovering the material which makes up an argument. After an analysis of this problem, they recommended the introduction into courses in argument of an up-to-date system of rhetoric based upon what the classical rhetoricians called "the Topics," a term which can be translated as "the sources from which arguments are drawn." The four sources of argument which they described in detail and which the English staff at the College has tested in practice are the ideas of Genus or Definition, Consequence, Likeness and Difference, and Authority. Readers interested in the theory underlying this point of view are referred to the article in question.[1] However, even those who may be convinced that this new attack on the problem of teaching argument sounds promising in the abstract will certainly have many questions about how this rhetorical approach operates in the classroom. It is the aim of the present article to satisfy this curiosity, at least in part, by applying "topical" considerations to the analysis and interpretation of a classroom text, a recognized masterpiece of polemics, Madison's *Federalist,* No. 10.

This particular *Federalist* paper, on the control of faction in popular governments, has long since achieved political immortality as a classic defense of the theory of republicanism. Its usefulness as an instrument in teaching

[1] Bilsky, Hazlett, Streeter, and Weaver, "Looking for an Argument," *College English,* XIV (January, 1953), 210-16.

From *College English,* XV (October 1953), 37-45. Reprinted by permission of the National Council of Teachers of English and Professor Ashin.

has been equally well demonstrated. It has been a required reading in civics and social science courses to give students an understanding of the theoretical bases of our Constitution. It has served the teacher of logic and argument as a cogent example of the controlling power of syllogistic reasoning. Practically every text in the social and intellectual history of the United States singles it out to illustrate the Federalist position during the political controversy surrounding the adoption of the Constitution. Even Vernon L. Parrington, whose great book is a crusade against Federalist conservatism, paid tribute to it as a worthy enemy by calling it "the remarkable tenth number, which compresses within a few pages pretty much the whole Federalist theory of political science." There is no denying that much can be and has been done with conventional modes of logical analysis to reveal the effectiveness of Madison's reasoning, since the essay is practically made-to-order as a sample of the syllogism in operation. However, I believe that to supplement a formal analysis with a consideration of the main sources from which the author draws the material for his arguments can immeasurably enrich the English teacher's handling of deduction, since it can present, on a level understandable to all, the characteristic operation of Madison's mind as he proceeds with his demonstrations.

As will be seen, the major sources of argument for Madison are *definitions* and *consequences*. In any considered statement of political theory, careful definitions of key terms, used both as starting points (see the definition of "faction" in paragraph 2) and as stages in the argument (see the implied definition of "man" in paragraph 6), are required to clarify a position. In addition, to induce an audience to accept a recommended course of action, no more compelling motive can be invented than one which argues for the good consequences which will necessarily follow the adoption of your proposal and the evil consequences which will follow the adoption of any other.

The problem with which Madison was concerned and the direction of his reasoning are indicated in his opening sentences:

> Among the numerous advantages promised by a well constructed Union, none deserves to be more accurately developed than its tendency to break and control the violence of faction. The friend of popular governments never finds himself so much alarmed for their character and fate, as when he contemplates their propensity to this dangerous vice. He will not fail, therefore, to set a due value on any plan which, without violating the principles to which he is attached, provides a proper cure for it.

However, the explicit statement of his aim is reserved for paragraph 11, after he has disposed of the visionary thesis that the causes of faction can be removed, and has turned to the practical task of describing how to control its effects. First indicating that a majority rather than a minority faction is the main danger in popular government, he states:

> To secure the public good and private rights against the danger of such a faction, and at the same time to preserve the spirit and the form of popular government, is then the great object to which our inquiries are directed.

Madison thus sets himself the task of arguing for a particular design of government which will provide a "republican remedy" for the factional disturbances fostered by popular government, while, at the same time, preserving the spirit and the form of popular government. From a point high on the ladder of abstraction, this aim seems an impossible one, since it appears to call for the elimination of an effect while preserving the cause which leads to that effect. The very nature of this aim demands the careful discrimination of causes and effects which is characteristic of Madison's argument.

The formal pattern of Madison's logic is a series of "either-or" syllogisms, which, by eliminating the rejected alternatives, progressively narrow the inquiry down to the particular conclusion that a federal republic, such as that outlined in the proposed Constitution, can best control the effects of faction. In his first paragraph he presents a convincing rhetorical justification for his concern with the dangers of faction. From what general field of consideration of source of argument could he best derive the details which would make his readers equally concerned? The experiences of six years of government under the Articles of Confederation—experiences shared intimately and grievously by most of his audience—could be generalized into a statement of the *consequences*[2] which result from the operation of factions in an environment of freedom. So the indictment begins. Popular governments reveal a propensity to "this dangerous vice," factions. Once in existence, factions lead directly to instability, injustice, and confusion in the public councils. These, in turn, lead ultimately to the death of popular governments, "as they continue to be the favorite and fruitful topics[3] from which the adversaries to liberty derive their most specious declamation." Even though the various state constitutions of America are an improvement over popular models of the ancient and modern world, they have neither prevented the rise, nor effectively controlled the spread, of factional conflicts in the form of rival parties.

---

[2] The terms "definition," "consequences," "likeness-difference," and "testimony-authority" have been italicized to call attention to Madison's uses of the sources of argument.
[3] Madison's use of the term "topics" in this quotation is in the same classical tradition which motivates the present article. "Instability," "injustice," and "confusion" are simply particularized *consequences* of faction in popular governments.

It is important to note that, in his introductory paragraph, Madison sets up the basic dichotomy which operates throughout his entire argument. The opposing terms are "justice," "the public good," and "minority rights," on the one hand, and, on the other, "majority faction."

> Complaints are everywhere heard from our most considerate and virtuous citizens, equally the friends of public and private faith, and of public and personal liberty, that our governments are too unstable, that the public good is disregarded in the conflicts of rival parties, and that measures are too often decided, not according to the rules of justice and the rights of the minor party, but by the superior force of an interested and overbearing majority.

The same dichotomy underlies the controlling *definition* of faction in paragraph 2:

> By a faction, I understand a number of citizens, whether amounting to a majority or minority of the whole, who are united and actuated by some common impulse of passion, or of interest, adverse to the rights of other citizens, or to the permanent and aggregate interests of the community.

Having demonstrated the disastrous consequences of faction in popular government and having defined his key term, Madison can proceed, in paragraph 3, to the logical development of his argument. The alternative syllogism set up there controls the movement of thought in the rest of the essay. "There are two methods of curing the mischiefs of faction: the one, by removing its causes; the other, by controlling its effects." This gives us a syllogism with the following form:

> Either A [*we can remove causes*] or B [*we can control effects*].

The minor premise, which is developed in the first half of Madison's argument [paragraphs 3–10], is that we cannot remove the causes of faction, since they are grounded in the nature of man:

> Not A [*we cannot remove causes*].

It follows that we must devote our efforts to controlling the effects:

> Therefore, B [*we can control effects*].

An analysis of the argument for the minor premise reveals that A, the attempt to remove the causes of faction, is composed of two alternatives:

> There are again two methods of removing the causes of faction: the one, by destroying the liberty which is essential to its existence; the other, by giving to every citizen the same opinions, the same passions, and the same interests.

These alternatives can be formally symbolized as A_1 and A_2.

A_1 [*destroying liberty*] is dismissed easily and speedily by means of an analogy or, in other words, by an argument based on *likenesses and differences:*

> Liberty is to faction what air is to fire, an aliment without which it instantly expires. But it could not be less folly to abolish liberty, which is essential to political life, because it nourishes faction, than it would be to wish the annihilation of air, which is essential to animal life, because it imparts to fire its destructive agency.

The first analogical proportion [Liberty:Faction:: Air:Fire], which would logically lead to the inference that we ought to destroy liberty, since it causes faction, is immediately modified by changing the second and fourth terms in the proportion [Liberty:Political Life:: Air:Animal Life]. The folly of abolishing liberty as a cure for faction is self-evident. Madison does not need to devote time to this argument, since part of his fundamental aim was to preserve the spirit and form of popular government. Any measure which would cure faction by abolishing liberty is, as he says, a remedy worse than the disease.[4]

The argument against A_2 [*making all citizens alike in their passions, opinions, and interests*] is much more intricate and worthier of intensive study. Madison concludes that this alternative is impracticable, and his reasons for so deciding depend upon his view of human nature or, in other words, upon propositions drawn from the source of *definition*. In paragraphs 6–10, Madison uses the principles of Lockean psychology to prove that man, by nature, possesses faculties which operate to make factional conflicts inevitable. Men have a fallible reason which, in an environment of liberty, will lead to the formation of different opinions. There is a connection between reason and self-love which will direct the passions created by the latter to the support of the opinions resulting from the former. In addition to the fundamental characteristics—reason and self-love—men possess a diversity of other faculties which are the origin of different aptitudes for accumulating property. Since it is the first object of government to protect these diverse faculties and thus to protect the ensuing differences in degrees and kinds of property and since diverse property interests will inevitably influence the opinions and passions of the respective proprietors, society must always be divided into different interests and parties. As a result, "the latent causes of faction are thus sown in the nature of man."

In paragraph 7, Madison develops the *consequences* of the definition which

---

[4] This analogy, simple as it seems, can open the way to a devastating refutation of the argument that the totalitarian or one-party state is better than a free government because it can eliminate factions.

he has established. Anything sown in the nature of man will spring up in everything he does. These latent causes reveal themselves in all aspects of civil society. Factions can result from a zeal for different opinions in religion, in government, and, indeed, in all the speculative and practical affairs of mankind; from an emotional attachment to ambitious leaders; or from conflicts over even frivolous and fanciful distinctions. However, "the most common and durable source of factions has been the various and unequal distribution of property." And here Madison expresses simply and directly a view of the economic basis of political government which derives from a tradition much older than that of Marx:

> Those who hold and those who are without property have ever formed distinct interests in society. Those who are creditors, and those who are debtors, fall under a like discrimination. A landed interest, a manufacturing interest, a mercantile interest, a moneyed interest, with many lesser interests, grow up of necessity in civilized nations, and divide them into different classes, actuated by different sentiments and views. The regulation of these various and interfering interests forms the principal task of modern legislation, and involves the spirit of party and faction in the necessary and ordinary operations of the government.

The last proposition—that the spirit of faction is involved in the ordinary operations of government—requires an extension to another sphere of the *definition* of man previously presented. It is required in order to refute a possible objection. The counterargument might be raised that, since men's natures divide them into conflicting parties, it is the task of government somehow to stand above the conflicts and reconcile them in the interests of justice and the common good. This thesis would imply that legislators are superior to ordinary men in not being influenced by their own interests. To disprove this possible point of view, Madison continues in paragraph 8 with a *definition* of the two main factors in government—acts of legislation and legislators. Acts of legislation, such as laws concerning private debts, tariffs, and property taxes, are defined by Madison as judicial determinations concerning the rights of large bodies of citizens; and legislators are defined as advocates and parties to the causes which they determine. The self-love of the lawmakers will inevitably result in decisions which represent, not the principles of abstract justice, but their own party interests. Madison thinks it vain to depend upon the influence of "enlightened statesmen" to adjust the clash of diverse interests in the light of justice and the public good. Not only will such statesmen not always be at the helm, but in many cases the legislative questions will be so complex and pressing that it will be almost impossible for statesmen to act in an enlightened fashion.

Thus the first half of the paper, consisting of two powerful arguments based upon *definitions* of man and government, has led to the conclusion that all citizens cannot be made alike in their passions, opinions, and interests. As a result, "the inference to which we are brought is, that the *causes* of faction cannot be removed, and that relief is only to be sought in the means of controlling its *effects.*" If we glance again at the controlling alternative syllogism:

> Either A [*we can remove causes*] or B [*we can control effects*],
> Not A,
> Therefore, B,

we see that the argument from *likeness and difference* (directed against A_1) and the argument from *definition* (directed against A_2) have provided support for the minor premise: we cannot remove the causes of faction. The remainder of Madison's essay is devoted to substantiating the conclusion: therefore, we can control its effects.

The argument for B is much more complex than the argument against A. It is indicative of Madison's practical orientation as a political theorist that his main concern is with the control of effects rather than with the removal of causes. Removing the causes of something is a drastic but superficially simple alternative, whereas controlling effects usually involves a range of contingent methods whose varying degrees of success depend upon a multitude of factors which require careful analysis.

Before attacking the problem of the proper means for controlling the effects of faction, Madison further clarifies his problem by distinguishing between the dangers resulting from a minority and a majority faction. This key distinction, as we have seen, was set forth in the initial definition of "faction" in paragraph 2, "a number of citizens, whether amounting to a majority or minority of the whole. . . ." In paragraph 11, Madison uses another argument from *definition* to dismiss the dangers of a minority faction:

> If a faction consists of less than a majority, relief is supplied by the republican principle, which enables the majority to defeat its sinister views by regular vote.

Should this seem too cavalier a dismissal of a serious problem, one with which every state is plagued, Madison continues by revealing both his awareness of what a fanatical minority can do in a free society and the reason for his relative lack of concern. "It may clog the administration, it may convulse the society; but it will be unable to execute and mask its violence under the forms of the Constitution." The danger from a minority faction however serious, lies in the realm of practical administration and can, at the worst, be eliminated by the police power of the state. On the other hand, when a majority of the people coalesce into a faction, the very form of popular government enables such a faction to trample on the rights of other citizens and sacrifice the public good to its ruling passion. Here, exactly, was the concern of the Federalist theoreticians. How could the majority, operating in a mood of sudden and concerted aggression, be restrained from violating the rights of minorities and the over-all interests of the community?

The crucial importance of this question for Madison is indicated by the fact that, immediately after the distinction between minority and majority faction in paragraph 11, he makes explicit the aim of his essay:

> To secure the public good and private rights against the danger of such a faction [majority], and at the same time to preserve the spirit and form of popular government, is then the great object to which our inquiries are directed.

The argument in the second half of the essay involves the answer to two questions: (1) What, in theory, are the best means of controlling the effects of majority faction? and (2) Which form of popular government is best able to put these means into effect?

In form, the second main argument resembles the first, since it also starts with a division of alternatives. There are two means for controlling the effects of majority faction:

> Either the existence of the same passion or interest in a majority at the same time must be prevented, or the majority, having such coexistent passion or interest, must be rendered, by their number and local situation, unable to concert and carry into effect schemes of oppression.

These alternatives may be symbolized as B_1 and B_2. For a true picture of Madison's logical procedure, it is important to note that in the first argument both A_1 and A_2 were rejected, thus giving us a negative minor premise. However, the conclusion is a positive one. This means that both B_1 and B_2 are acceptable means of preventing majority oppression, with B_2 acting as an auxiliary method in case it is impossible to achieve B_1. Using these two methods as standards of judgment, Madison can turn his attention to the analysis of the two main forms of popular government—the pure democracy and the republic—to see which, by nature, can best control the effects of majority faction.

Again using the source of *definition,* Madison concludes that a pure democracy, "by which I mean a society consisting of a small number of citizens, who assemble and administer the government in person, can admit of no cure for the mischiefs of faction." Such a government, because its form permits both the creation and the immediate assertion of a majority passion or interest, will be able at will to sacrifice the rights of minorities or even of individuals obnoxious to the majority. Madison might have been thinking of the condemnation of Socrates by a majority of the Athenian citizens, since he supports his theoretical analysis at this point by a reference to history:

> Hence it is that such democracies have ever been spectacles of turbulence and contention; have ever been found incompatible with personal security or the rights of property; and have in general been as short in their lives as they have been violent in their deaths.

The general effect of this argument is similar to that in the first half of the essay, since pure democracy fails because it believes that, by making all men politically equal, it can equalize their possessions, their opinions, and their passions. Madison has already disposed of such a visionary hope.

By *definition,* a republic differs from a pure democracy in two important respects: in its form and in the magnitude of its possible operation. It is a form of popular government in which power is delegated to representatives elected by the people, and it can therefore be extended over a greater number of citizens and over a greater area than can a pure democracy. The definitions of these two forms of popular government prepare the way for the rather involved reasoning which starts at paragraph 16 and continues to the end. These paragraphs can be related to the rest of the argument by seeing them as detailed statements of the *consequences* resulting from the two main points of difference between a democracy and a republic. Paragraphs 16–19 deal with the effects of the difference in form, paragraph 20 with the difference in magnitude.

The formal difference—the principle of delegative power—does not by itself provide a guaranty that majority factions will be controlled. Acting as a cause, it may lead to opposite effects. When the opinions of the people are sifted through a body of representatives who may be influenced by patriotism and the love of justice, the process might result in refining and enlarging the public views and, probably, lead to decisions advancing the public good. However, the effect may as easily be inverted. As Madison puts it:

> Men of factious tempers, of local prejudices, or of sinister designs, may, by intrigue, by corruption, or by other means, first obtain the suffrages, and then betray the interests, of the people.

Since the delegative form of government alone provides no certainty that majority factions can be controlled, Madison then proceeds to the corollary question of whether small or large republics are best able to elect good legislators. Paragraphs 17 and 18 present two considerations which decide the question in favor of the large republic. Fundamentally, these two paragraphs present the probable *consequences* of the smaller ratio between representatives and constituents which characterizes the large republic by contrast with the small one. A hypothetical example will clarify the rather close reasoning of these paragraphs. Madison starts with the assumption that, regardless of the size of the republic, the representatives must be numerous enough to guard against the cabals of a few, and limited enough to avoid the confusion of a multitude. Let us suppose that the range for an efficient legislative body is from 100 to 500 representatives. If the smaller number, 100, is selected by the constituents of a small republic, say 10,000 voters, the ratio is 1 : 100. If the larger number, 500, is selected by 5,000,000 voters, the ratio is 1 : 10,000. Therefore, if it be granted that the proportion of good men is the same in both states, the large republic will present a much wider choice and, consequently, the greater probability of a fit choice. The second consideration in favor of a large republic is that, since each representative will be chosen by many more voters, there will be less chance for the voters to be fooled by unworthy candidates using the tricks of the demagogue. The argument in paragraph 17 depends for its force solely on numerical ratios. There will be more good men in a large republic from which to make a wise choice. Paragraph 18 adds the consideration that it will be harder to fool the many than to fool the few.

Madison then goes back to the second main difference between a democracy and a republic—the greater number of citizens and larger extent of territory which can be brought within the compass of the republican form. And here he sums up the *consequences* of his definitions in such a way as to re-emphasize the superiority of a republic over a democracy, on the one hand, and of a large republic over a small one, on the other:

> The smaller the society, the fewer probably will be the distinct parties and interests composing it; the fewer the distinct parties and interests, the more frequently will a majority be found of the same party; and the smaller the number of individuals composing a majority, and the smaller the compass within which they are placed, the more easily will they concert and execute their plans of oppression. Extend the sphere and you take in a greater variety of parties and interests; you make it less probable that a majority of the whole will have a common motive to invade the rights of other citizens; or if such a common motive exists, it will be more difficult for all who feel it to discover their own strength, and to act in unison with each other.

Thus a large republic can control the effects of faction better than any other form of popular government and "in the extent and proper structure of the Union, therefore, we behold a republican remedy for the diseases most incident to republican government." Madison concludes by identifying true republicanism with the Federalist advocacy of the proposed Constitution.

Madison's powerful plea for a federal republic can be felt most strongly when the sources of his argument are brought to light and his particular propositions are seen operating in the deductive form which moves relentlessly from assumptions and premises to conclusions. Many English teachers will be content to clarify the argumentative methods from which *The Federalist,* No. 10, derives its logical power. But others, perhaps those with an interest in political theory, will want to have their students examine the assumptions and challenge the conclusions of Madison's argument. Although possible refutations are beyond the scope of this article, an understanding of the sources can help in outlining some promising lines of attack. For instance, the fundamental dichotomy set up by Madison is that between the "public good," on the one hand, and "majority faction," on the other. Madison is careful to define what he opposes; but the term "the public good" remains an undefined ideal which controls his judgments but which is never pinned down. For those of us who, almost without thinking, identify the public good with the majority will, Madison's analysis seems shockingly undemocratic. The question could be asked: How can the public good be achieved or, for that matter, even known with certainty if majority faction is considered the main danger in a republic? Another point of possible refutation rests in Madison's cynical definition of man in paragraphs 6 and 7. Would a Jeffersonian or perhaps even a Christian definition of man lead to different conclusions? Finally, some question could be raised about whether large republics actually do produce a higher quality of legislators than small ones. Madison was arguing that national representatives would, in all probability, be better than those in a state legislature. However, we might ask whether our Congress today can compare in quality with the much smaller Constitutional Convention or, if that is unfair, even with the Congress of Madison's own day.

These questions, and others, would be directed toward awakening the student's interest not only in the vital subject matter of Madison's article but also in the intellectually exciting rigors of logical procedure. Through the step-by-step reconstruction of Madison's argument, the student can be led to see how a commanding piece of rhetoric came into being. By studying Madison's sources of argument and seeing how the forms of syllogistic reasoning are filled with material drawn from the realms of theory and experience, the student writer, faced with the challenge of supporting a proposition, can learn to use these directing ideas, the sources, to make his own arguments richer, more controlled, and, ultimately, more convincing.

Martin Luther King, Jr.: Letter from Birmingham Jail *

During the second half of the 1950's and most of the 1960's, the most charis-
matic figure in the civil-rights movement, especially in the passive-resistance,
non-violent phase of it, was certainly the Rev. Martin Luther King, Jr. Born
in Atlanta, Georgia, January 15, 1929, he received his B.A. degree at Morehouse
College in Atlanta and his Ph.D. degree at Boston University in 1955. He
first came into public prominence when he led the successful bus boycott in
Montgomery, Alabama, following the arrest of Mrs. Rosa Parks, a Negro
seamstress, on December 1, 1955, when she refused to give up her seat in
the front of a bus on her way home from work. In 1957, he was elected
president of the Southern Christian Leadership Conference (SCLC), an
organization that sought to touch the conscience of the nation and to effect
the passage of social legislation by the strategies of civil-disobedience in-
herited from Mahatma Gandhi and ultimately from Henry David Thoreau.
In 1964, Dr. King was awarded the Nobel Peace Prize, the youngest man
ever to win that prize. On April 4, 1968, he was killed by an assassin's bullet
in Memphis, Tennessee. Dr. King exercised his influence mainly through his
eloquent oratory and through his participation in such physical demonstra-
tions as marches and sit-ins. In the following selection, however, we find
him exerting his rhetorical talents in the written medium, largely of course
because at the time he was locked up in a Birmingham jail. ("Never before,"
he tells us in the letter itself, "have I written so long a letter.") The letter was
prompted by a public statement made on April 12, 1963, by the eight clergy-
men named in the author's footnote—a statement deploring the use of street
demonstrations and urging the white and Negro citizens of Alabama "to
observe the principles of law and order and common sense." This piece of

---

* AUTHOR'S NOTE: This response to a published statement by eight fellow clergymen
from Alabama (Bishop C. C. J. Carpenter, Bishop Joseph A. Durick, Rabbi Hilton L.
Grafman, Bishop Paul Hardin, Bishop Holan B. Harmon, the Reverend George M.
Murray, the Reverend Edward V. Ramage and the Reverend Earl Stallings) was composed under somewhat constricting circumstances. Begun on the margins of the newspaper in which the statement appeared while I was in jail, the letter was continued
on scraps of writing paper supplied by a friendly Negro trusty, and concluded on a
pad my attorneys were eventually permitted to leave me. Although the text remains in
substance unaltered, I have indulged in the author's prerogative of polishing it for
publication.

judicial rhetoric, cast in the form of an "open letter," has a double audience —immediately the eight clergymen who signed the public statement but ultimately the people of the nation and even the world.

April 16, 1963

My Dear Fellow Clergymen:

1   While confined here in the Birmingham city jail, I came across your recent statement calling my present activities "unwise and untimely." Seldom do I pause to answer criticism of my work and ideas. If I sought to answer all the criticisms that cross my desk, my secretaries would have little time for anything other than such correspondence in the course of the day, and I would have no time for constructive work. But since I feel that you are men of genuine good will and that your criticisms are sincerely set forth, I want to try to answer your statement in what I hope will be patient and reasonable terms.

2   I think I should indicate why I am here in Birmingham, since you have been influenced by the view which argues against "outsiders coming in." I have the honor of serving as president of the Southern Christian Leadership Conference, an organization operating in every southern state, with headquarters in Atlanta, Georgia. We have some eighty-five affiliated organizations across the South, and one of them is the Alabama Christian Movement for Human Rights. Frequently we share staff, educational and financial resources with our affiliates. Several months ago the affiliate here in Birmingham asked us to be on call to engage in a nonviolent direct-action program if such were deemed necessary. We readily consented, and when the hour came we lived up to our promise. So I, along with several members of my staff, am here because I was invited here. I am here because I have organizational ties here.

3   But more basically, I am in Birmingham because injustice is here. Just as the prophets of the eighth century B.C. left their villages and carried their "thus saith the Lord" far beyond the boundaries of their home towns, and just as the Apostle Paul left his village of Tarsus and carried the gospel of Jesus Christ to the far corners of the Greco-Roman world, so am I compelled to carry the gospel of freedom beyond by own home town. Like Paul, I must constantly respond to the Macedonian call for aid.

4   Moreover, I am cognizant of the interrelatedness of all communities and states. I cannot sit idly by in Atlanta and not be concerned about what happens in Birmingham. Injustice anywhere is a threat to justice everywhere. We are caught in an inescapable network of mutuality, tied in a single garment of destiny. Whatever affects one directly, affects all indirectly. Never again can we afford to live with the narrow, provincial "outside

agitator" idea. Anyone who lives inside the United States can never be considered an outsider anywhere within its bounds.

5 You deplore the demonstrations taking place in Birmingham. But your statement, I am sorry to say, fails to express a similar concern for the conditions that brought about the demonstrations. I am sure that none of you would want to rest content with the superficial kind of social analysis that deals merely with effects and does not grapple with underlying causes. It is unfortunate that demonstrations are taking place in Birmingham, but it is even more unfortunate that the city's white power structure left the Negro community with no alternative.

6 In any nonviolent campaign there are four basic steps: collection of the facts to determine whether injustices exist; negotiation; self-purification; and direct action. We have gone through all these steps in Birmingham. There can be no gainsaying the fact that racial injustice engulfs this community. Birmingham is probably the most thoroughly segregated city in the United States. Its ugly record of brutality is widely known. Negroes have experienced grossly unjust treatment in the courts. There have been more unsolved bombings of Negro homes and churches in Birmingham than in any other city in the nation. These are the hard, brutal facts of the case. On the basis of these conditions, Negro leaders sought to negotiate with the city fathers. But the latter consistently refused to engage in good-faith negotiation.

7 Then, last September, came the opportunity to talk with leaders of Birmingham's economic community. In the course of the negotiations, certain promises were made by the merchants—for example, to remove the stores' humiliating racial signs. On the basis of these promises, the Reverend Fred Shuttlesworth and the leaders of the Alabama Christian Movement for Human Rights agreed to a moratorium on all demonstrations. As the weeks and months went by, we realized that we were the victims of a broken promise. A few signs, briefly removed, returned; the others remained.

8 As in so many past experiences, our hopes had been blasted, and the shadow of deep disappointment settled upon us. We had no alternative except to prepare for direct action, whereby we would present our very bodies as a means of laying our case before the conscience of the local and the national community. Mindful of the difficulties involved, we decided to undertake a process of self-purification. We began a series of workshops on nonviolence, and we repeatedly asked ourselves: "Are you able to accept blows without retaliating?" "Are you able to endure the ordeal of jail?" We decided to schedule our direct-action program for the Easter season, realizing that except for Christmas, this is the main shopping period of the year. Knowing that a strong economic-withdrawal program would be the by-product of direct action, we felt that this would be the best time to bring pressure to bear on the merchants for the needed change.

9   Then it occurred to us that Birmingham's mayoralty election was coming up in March, and we speedily decided to postpone action until after election day. When we discovered that the Commissioner of Public Safety, Eugene "Bull" Connor, had piled up enough votes to be in the run-off, we decided again to postpone action until the day after the run-off so that the demonstrations could not be used to cloud the issues. Like many others, we waited to see Mr. Connor defeated, and to this end we endured postponement after postponement. Having aided in this community need, we felt that our direct-action program could be delayed no longer.

10   You may well ask: "Why direct action? Why sit-ins, marches and so forth? Isn't negotiation a better path?" You are quite right in calling for negotiation. Indeed, this is the very purpose of direct action. Nonviolent direct action seeks to create such a crisis and foster such a tension that a community which has constantly refused to negotiate is forced to confront the issue. It seeks so to dramatize the issue that it can no longer be ignored. My citing the creation of tension as part of the work of the nonviolent-resister may sound rather shocking. But I must confess that I am not afraid of the word "tension." I have earnestly opposed violent tension, but there is a type of constructive, nonviolent tension which is necessary for growth. Just as Socrates felt that it was necessary to create a tension in the mind so that individuals could rise from the bondage of myths and half-truths to the unfettered realm of creative analysis and objective appraisal, so must we see the need for nonviolent gadflies to create the kind of tension in society that will help men rise from the dark depths of prejudice and racism to the majestic heights of understanding and brotherhood.

11   The purpose of our direct-action program is to create a situation so crisis-packed that it will inevitably open the door to negotiation. I therefore concur with you in your call for negotiation. Too long has our beloved Southland been bogged down in a tragic effort to live in monologue rather than dialogue.

12   One of the basic points in your statement is that the action that I and my associates have taken in Birmingham is untimely. Some have asked: "Why didn't you give the new city administration time to act?" The only answer that I can give to this query is that the new Birmingham administration must be prodded about as much as the outgoing one, before it will act. We are sadly mistaken if we feel that the election of Albert Boutwell as mayor will bring the millennium to Birmingham. While Mr. Boutwell is a much more gentle person than Mr. Connor, they are both segregationists, dedicated to maintenance of the status quo. I have hope that Mr. Boutwell will be reasonable enough to see the futility of massive resistance to desegregation. But he will not see this without pressure from devotees of civil rights.

My friends, I must say to you that we have not made a single gain in civil rights without determined legal and nonviolent pressure. Lamentably, it is an historical fact that privileged groups seldom give up their privileges voluntarily. Individuals may see the moral light and voluntarily give up their unjust posture; but, as Reinhold Niebuhr has reminded us, groups tend to be more immoral than individuals.

13 We know through painful experience that freedom is never voluntarily given by the oppressor; it must be demanded by the oppressed. Frankly, I have yet to engage in a direct-action campaign that was "well timed" in the view of those who have not suffered unduly from the disease of segregation. For years now I have heard the word "Wait!" It rings in the ear of every Negro with piercing familiarity. This "Wait" has almost always meant "Never." We must come to see, with one of our distinguished jurists, that "justice too long delayed is justice denied."

14 We have waited for more than 340 years for our constitutional and God-given rights. The nations of Asia and Africa are moving with jetlike speed toward gaining political independence, but we still creep at horse-and-buggy pace toward gaining a cup of coffee at a lunch counter. Perhaps it is easy for those who have never felt the stinging darts of segregation to say, "Wait." But when you have seen vicious mobs lynch your mothers and fathers at will and drown your sisters and brothers at whim; when you have seen hate-filled policemen curse, kick and even kill your black brothers and sisters; when you see the vast majority of your twenty million Negro brothers smothering in an airtight cage of poverty in the midst of an affluent society; when you suddenly find your tongue twisted and your speech stammering as you seek to explain to your six-year-old daughter why she can't go to the public amusement park that has just been advertised on television, and see tears welling up in her eyes when she is told that Funtown is closed to colored children, and see ominous clouds of inferiority beginning to form in her little mental sky, and see her beginning to distort her personality by developing an unconscious bitterness toward white people; when you have to concoct an answer for a five-year-old son who is asking: "Daddy, why do white people treat colored people so mean?"; when you take a cross-country drive and find it necessary to sleep night after night in the uncomfortable corners of your automobile because no motel will accept you; when you are humiliated day in and day out by nagging signs reading "white" and "colored"; when your first name becomes "nigger," your middle name becomes "boy" (however old you are) and your last name becomes "John," and your wife and mother are never given the respected title "Mrs."; when you are harried by day and haunted by night by the fact that you are a Negro, living constantly at tiptoe stance, never quite knowing what to expect next,

and are plagued with inner fears and outer resentments; when you are forever fighting a degenerating sense of "nobodiness"—then you will understand why we find it difficult to wait. There comes a time when the cup
of endurance runs over, and men are no longer willing to be plunged into
the abyss of despair. I hope, sirs, you can understand our legitimate and
unavoidable impatience.

15   You express a great deal of anxiety over our willingness to break laws.
This is certainly a legitimate concern. Since we so diligently urge people to
obey the Supreme Court's decision of 1954 outlawing segregation in the
public schools, at first glance it may seem rather paradoxical for us consciously to break laws. One may well ask: "How can you advocate breaking
some laws and obeying others?" The answer lies in the fact that there are
two types of laws: just and unjust. I would be the first to advocate obeying
just laws. One has not only a legal but a moral responsibility to obey just
laws. Conversely, one has a moral responsibility to disobey unjust laws. I
would agree with St. Augustine that "an unjust law is no law at all."

16   Now, what is the difference between the two? How does one determine
whether a law is just or unjust? A just law is a man-made code that squares
with the moral law or the law of God. An unjust law is a code that is out of
harmony with the moral law. To put it in the terms of St. Thomas Aquinas:
An unjust law is a human law that is not rooted in eternal law and natural
law. Any law that uplifts human personality is just. Any law that degrades
human personality is unjust. All segregation statutes are unjust because
segregation distorts the soul and damages the personality. It gives the segre-
gator a false sense of superiority and the segregated a false sense of inferiority. Segregation, to use the terminology of the Jewish philosopher
Martin Buber, substitutes an "I-it" relationship for an "I-thou" relationship
and ends up relegating persons to the status of things. Hence segregation is
not only politically, economically and sociologically unsound, it is morally
wrong and sinful. Paul Tillich has said that sin is separation. Is not segregation an existential expression of man's tragic separation, his awful estrange-
ment, his terrible sinfulness? Thus it is that I can urge men to obey the 1954
decision of the Supreme Court, for it is morally right; and I can urge them
to disobey segregation ordinances, for they are morally wrong.

17   Let us consider a more concrete example of just and unjust laws. An
unjust law is a code that a numerical or power majority group compels a
minority group to obey but does not make binding on itself. This is *difference* made legal. By the same token, a just law is a code that a majority
compels a minority to follow and that it is willing to follow itself. This is
sameness made legal.

18   Let me give another explanation. A law is unjust if it inflicted on a
minority that, as a result of being denied the right to vote, had no part in

enacting or devising the law. Who can say that the legislature of Alabama which set up that state's segregation laws was democratically elected? Throughout Alabama all sorts of devious methods are used to prevent Negroes from becoming registered voters, and there are some counties in which, even though Negroes constitute a majority of the population, not a single Negro is registered. Can any law enacted under such circumstances be considered democratically structured?

19 Sometimes a law is just on its face and unjust in its application. For instance, I have been arrested on a charge of parading without a permit. Now, there is nothing wrong in having an ordinance which requires a permit for a parade. But such an ordinance becomes unjust when it is used to maintain segregation and to deny citizens the First-Amendment privilege of peaceful assembly and protest.

20 I hope you are able to see the distinction I am trying to point out. In no sense do I advocate evading or defying the law, as would the rabid segregationist. That would lead to anarchy. One who breaks an unjust law must do so openly, lovingly, and with a willingness to accept the penalty. I submit that an individual who breaks a law that conscience tells him is unjust, and who willingly accepts the penalty of imprisonment in order to arouse the conscience of the community over its injustice, is in reality expressing the highest respect for law.

21 Of course, there is nothing new about this kind of civil disobedience. It was evidenced sublimely in the refusal of Shadrach, Meshach and Abednego to obey the laws of Nebuchadnezzar, on the ground that a higher moral law was at stake. It was practiced superbly by the early Christians, who were willing to face hungry lions and the excruciating pain of chopping blocks rather than submit to certain unjust laws of the Roman Empire. To a degree, academic freedom is a reality today because Socrates practiced civil disobedience. In our own nation, the Boston Tea Party represented a massive act of civil disobedience.

22 We should never forget that everything Adolf Hitler did in Germany was "legal" and everything the Hungarian freedom fighters did in Hungary was "illegal." It was "illegal" to aid and comfort a Jew in Hitler's Germany. Even so, I am sure that, had I lived in Germany at the time, I would have aided and comforted my Jewish brothers. If today I lived in a Communist country where certain principles dear to the Christian faith are suppressed, I would openly advocate disobeying that country's antireligious laws.

23 I must make two honest confessions to you, my Christian and Jewish brothers. First, I must confess that over the past few years I have been gravely disappointed with the white moderate. I have almost reached the regrettable conclusion that the Negro's great stumbling block in his stride toward freedom is not the White Citizen's Counciler or the Ku Klux Klanner, but the white moderate, who is more devoted to "order" than to justice; who prefers a negative peace which is the absence of tension to a positive peace which is the presence of justice; who constantly says: "I agree with you in the goal you seek, but I cannot agree with your methods of direct action"; who paternalistically believes he can set the timetable for another man's freedom; who lives by a mythical concept of time and who constantly advises the Negro to wait for a "more convenient season." Shallow understanding from people of good will is more frustrating than absolute misunderstanding from people of ill will. Lukewarm acceptance is much more bewildering than outright rejection.

24   I had hoped that the white moderate would understand that law and order exist for the purpose of establishing justice and that when they fail in this purpose they become the dangerously structured dams that block the flow of social progress. I had hoped that the white moderate would understand that the present tension in the South is a necessary phase of the transition from an obnoxious negative peace, in which the Negro passively accepted his unjust plight, to a substantive and positive peace, in which all men will respect the dignity and worth of human personality. Actually, we who engage in nonviolent direct action are not the creators of tension. We merely bring to the surface the hidden tension that is already alive. We bring it out in the open, where it can be seen and dealt with. Like a boil that can never be cured so long as it is covered up but must be opened with all its ugliness to the natural medicines of air and light, injustice must be exposed, with all the tension its exposure creates, to the light of human conscience and the air of national opinion before it can be cured.

25   In your statement you assert that our actions, even though peaceful, must be condemned because they precipitate violence. But is this a logical assertion? Isn't this like condemning a robbed man because his possession of money precipitated the evil act of robbery? Isn't this like condemning Socrates because his unswerving commitment to truth and his philosophical inquiries precipitated the act by the misguided populace in which they made him drink hemlock? Isn't this like condemning Jesus because his unique God-consciousness and never-ceasing devotion to God's will precipitated the evil act of crucifixion? We must come to see that, as the federal courts have consistently affirmed, it is wrong to urge an individual to cease his efforts to gain his basic constitutional rights because the quest may precipitate violence. Society must protect the robbed and punish the robber.

26   I had also hoped that the white moderate would reject the myth concerning time in relation to the struggle for freedom. I have just received a letter from a white brother in Texas. He writes: "All Christians know that the colored people will receive equal rights eventually, but it is possible that you are in too great a religious hurry. It has taken Christianity almost two

thousand years to accomplish what it has. The teachings of Christ take time to come to earth." Such an attitude stems from a tragic misconception of time, from the strangely irrational notion that there is something in the very flow of time that will inevitably cure all ills. Actually, time itself is neutral; it can be used either destructively or constructively. More and more I feel that the people of ill will have used time much more effectively that have the people of good will. We will have to repent in this generation not merely for the hateful words and actions of the bad people but for the appalling silence of the good people. Human progress never rolls in on wheels of inevitability; it comes through the tireless efforts of men willing to be co-workers with God, and without this hard work, time itself becomes an ally of the forces of social stagnation. We must use time creatively, in the knowledge that the time is always ripe to do right. Now is the time to make real the promise of democracy and transform our pending national elegy into a creative psalm of brotherhood. Now is the time to lift our national policy from the quicksand of racial injustice to the solid rock of human dignity.

27 You speak of our activity in Birmingham as extreme. At first I was rather disappointed that fellow clergymen would see my nonviolent efforts as those of an extremist. I began thinking about the fact that I stand in the middle of two opposing forces in the Negro community. One is a force of complacency, made up in part of Negroes who, as a result of long years of oppression, are so drained of self-respect and a sense of "somebodiness" that they have adjusted to segregation; and in part of a few middle-class Negroes who, because of a degree of academic and economic security and because in some ways they profit by segregation, have become insensitive to the problems of the masses. The other force is one of bitterness and hatred, and it comes perilously close to advocating violence. It is expressed in the various black nationalist groups that are springing up across the nation, the largest and best-known being Elijah Muhammad's Muslim movement. Nourished by the Negro's frustration over the continued existence of racial discrimination, this movement is made up of people who have lost faith in America, who have absolutely repudiated Christianity, and who have concluded that the white man is an incorrigible "devil."

28 I have tried to stand between these two forces, saying that we need emulate neither the "do-nothingism" of the complacent nor the hatred and despair of the black nationalist. For there is the more excellent way of love and nonviolent protest. I am grateful to God that, through the influence of the Negro church, the way of nonviolence became an integral part of our struggle.

29 If this philosophy had not emerged, by now many streets of the South would, I am convinced, be flowing with blood. And I am further convinced

that if our white brothers dismiss as "rabble-rousers" and "outside agitators" those of us who employ nonviolent direct action, and if they refuse to support our nonviolent efforts, millions of Negroes will, out of frustration and despair, seek solace and security in black-nationalist ideologies—a development that would inevitably lead to a frightening racial nightmare.

30 Oppressed people cannot remain oppressed forever. The yearning for freedom eventually manifests itself, and that is what has happened to the American Negro. Something within has reminded him of his birthright of freedom, and something without has reminded him that it can be gained. Consciously or unconsciously, he has been caught up by the *Zeitgeist,* and with his black brothers of Africa and his brown and yellow brothers of Asia, South America and the Caribbean, the United States Negro is moving with a sense of great urgency toward the promised land of racial justice. If one recognizes this vital urge that has engulfed the Negro community, one should readily understand why public demonstrations are taking place. The Negro has many pent-up resentments and latent frustrations, and he must release them. So let him march; let him make prayer pilgrimages to the city hall; let him go on freedom rides—and try to understand why he must do so. If his repressed emotions are not released in nonviolent ways, they will seek expression through violence; this is not a threat but a fact of history. So I have not said to my people: "Get rid of your discontent." Rather, I have the creative outlet of nonviolent direct action. And now this approach is tried to say that this normal and healthy discontent can be channeled into being termed extremist.

31 But though I was initially disappointed at being categorized as an extremist, as I continued to think about the matter I gradually gained a measure of satisfaction from the label. Was not Jesus an extremist for love: "Love your enemies, bless them that curse you, do good to them that hate you, and pray for them which despitefully use you, and persecute you." Was not Amos an extremist for justice: "Let justice roll down like waters and righteousness like an ever-flowing stream." Was not Paul an extremist for the Christian gospel: "I bear in my body the marks of the Lord Jesus." Was not Martin Luther an extremist: "Here I stand; I cannot do otherwise, so help me God." And John Bunyan: "I will stay in jail to the end of my days before I make a butchery of my conscience." And Abraham Lincoln: "This nation cannot survive half slave and half free." And Thomas Jefferson: "We hold these truths to be self-evident, that all men are created equal . . ." So the question is not whether we will be extremists, but what kind of extremists we will be. Will we be extremists for hate or for love? Will we be extremists for the preservation of injustice or for the extension of justice? In that dramatic scene on Calvary's hill three men were crucified. We must never forget that all three were crucified for the same crime—the crime of extremism. Two were extremists for immorality, and thus fell below their environment. The other, Jesus Christ, was an extremist for love, truth and goodness, and thereby rose above his environment. Perhaps the South, the nation and the world are in dire need of creative extremists.

32 I had hoped that the white moderate would see this need. Perhaps I was too optimistic; perhaps I expected too much. I suppose I should have realized that few members of the oppressor race can understand the deep groans and passionate yearnings of the oppressed race, and still fewer have the vision to see that injustice must be rooted out by strong, persistent and determined action. I am thankful, however, that some of our white brothers in the South have grasped the meaning of this social revolution and committed themselves to it. They are still all too few in quantity, but they are big in quality. Some—such as Ralph McGill, Lillian Smith, Harry Golden, James McBride Dabbs, Ann Braden and Sarah Patton Boyle—have written about our struggle in eloquent and prophetic terms. Others have marched with us down nameless streets of the South. They have languished in filthy, roach-infested jails, suffering the abuse and brutality of policemen who view them as "dirty nigger-lovers." Unlike so many of their moderate brothers and sisters, they have recognized the urgency of the moment and sensed the need for powerful "action" antidotes to combat the disease of segregation.

33 Let me take note of my other major disappointment. I have been so greatly disappointed with the white church and its leadership. Of course, there are some notable exceptions. I am not unmindful of the fact that each of you has taken some significant stands on this issue. I commend you, Reverend Stallings, for your Christian stand on this past Sunday, in welcoming Negroes to your worship service on a nonsegregated basis. I commend the Catholic leaders of this state for integrating Spring Hill College several years ago.

34 But despite these notable exceptions, I must honestly reiterate that I have been disappointed with the Church. I do not say this as one of those negative critics who can always find something wrong with the church. I say this as a minister of the gospel, who loves the church; who was nurtured in its bosom; who has been sustained by its spiritual blessings and who will remain true to it as long as the cord of life shall lengthen.

35 When I was suddenly catapulted into the leadership of the bus protest in Montgomery, Alabama, a few years ago, I felt we would be supported by the white church. I felt that the white ministers, priests and rabbis of the South would be among our strongest allies. Instead, some have been outright opponents, refusing to understand the freedom movement and misrepresenting its leaders; all too many others have been more cautious than courageous and have remained silent behind the anesthetizing security of stained-glass windows.

36 In spite of my shattered dreams, I came to Birmingham with the hope that the white religious leadership of this community would see the justice of our cause and, with deep moral concern, would serve as the channel through which our just grievances could reach the power structure. I had hoped that each of you would understand. But again I have been disappointed.

37 I have heard numerous southern religious leaders admonish their worshipers to comply with a desegregation decision because it is the law, but I have longed to hear white ministers declare: "Follow this decree because integration is morally right and because the Negro is your brother." In the midst of blatant injustices inflicted upon the Negro, I have watched white churchmen stand on the sideline and mouth pious irrelevancies and sanctimonious trivialities. In the midst of a mighty struggle to rid our nation of racial and economic injustice, I have heard many ministers say: "Those are social issues, with which the gospel has no real concern." And I have watched many churches commit themselves to a completely other-worldly religion which makes a strange, un-Biblical distinction between body and soul, between the sacred and the secular.

38 I have traveled the length and breadth of Alabama, Mississippi and all the other southern states. On sweltering summer days and crisp autumn mornings I have looked at the South's beautiful churches with their lofty spires pointing heavenward. I have beheld the impressive outlines of her massive religious-education buildings. Over and over I have found myself saying: "What kind of people worship here? Who is their God? Where were their voices when the lips of Governor Barnett dripped with words of interposition and nullification? Where were they when Governor Wallace gave a clarion call for defiance and hatred? Where were their voices of support when bruised and weary Negro men and women decided to rise from the dark dungeons of complacency to the bright hills of creative protest?"

39 Yes, these questions are still in my mind. In deep disappointment I have wept over the laxity of the church. But be assured that my tears have been tears of love. There can be no deep disappointment where there is not deep love. Yes, I love the church. How could I do otherwise? I am in the rather unique position of being the son, the grandson and the great-grandson of preachers. Yes, I see the church as the body of Christ. But, oh! How we have blemished and scarred that body through social neglect and through fear of being nonconformists.

40 There was a time when the church was very powerful—in the time when the early Christians rejoiced at being deemed worthy to suffer for what they believed. In those days the church was not merely a thermometer that recorded the ideas and principles of popular opinion; it was a thermostat that transformed the mores of society. Whenever the early Christians entered a town, the people in power became disturbed and immediately sought to convict the Christians for being "disturbers of the peace" and "outside agitators." But the Christians pressed on, in the conviction that they were "a colony of heaven," called to obey God rather than man. Small in number, they were big in commitment. They were too God-intoxicated to be "astronomically intimidated." By their effort and example they brought an end to such ancient evils as infanticide and gladiatorial contests.

41 Things are different now. So often the contemporary church is a weak, ineffectual voice with an uncertain sound. So often it is an archdefender of the status quo. Far from being disturbed by the presence of the church, the power structure of the average community is consoled by the church's silent —and often even vocal—sanction of things as they are.

42 But the judgment of God is upon the church as never before. If today's church does not recapture the sacrificial spirit of the early church, it will lose its authenticity, forfeit the loyalty of millions, and be dismissed as an irrelevant social club with no meaning for the twentieth century. Every day I meet young people whose disappointment with the church has turned into outright disgust.

43 Perhaps I have once again been too optimistic. Is organized religion too inextricably bound to the status quo to save our nation and the world? Perhaps I must turn my faith to the inner spiritual church, the church within the church, as the true *ekklesia* and the hope of the world. But again I am thankful to God that some noble souls from the ranks of organized religion have broken loose from the paralyzing chains of conformity and joined us as active partners in the struggle for freedom. They have left their secure congregations and walked the streets of Albany, Georgia, with us. They have gone down the highways of the South on tortuous rides for freedom. Yes, they have gone to jail with us. Some have been dismissed from their churches, have lost the support of their bishops and fellow ministers. But they have acted in the faith that right defeated is stronger than evil triumphant. Their witness has been the spiritual salt that has preserved the true meaning of the gospel in these troubled times. They have carved a tunnel of hope through the dark mountain of disappointment.

44 I hope the church as a whole will meet the challenge of this decisive hour. But even if the church does not come to the aid of justice, I have no despair about the future. I have no fear about the outcome of our struggle in Birmingham, even if our motives are at present misunderstood. We will reach the goal of freedom in Birmingham and all over the nation, because the goal of America is freedom. Abused and scorned though we may be, our destiny is tied up with America's destiny. Before the pilgrims landed at Plymouth, we were here. Before the pen of Jefferson etched the majestic words of the Declaration of Independence across the pages of history, we were here. For more than two centuries our forebears labored in this country without wages; they made cotton king; they built the homes of their masters while suffering gross injustice and shameful humiliation—and yet out of a bottomless vitality they continued to thrive and develop. If the inexpressible cruelties of slavery could not stop us, the opposition we now face will surely fail. We will win our freedom because the sacred heritage of our nation and the eternal will of God are embodied in our echoing demands.

45 Before closing I feel impelled to mention one other point in your statement that has troubled me profoundly. You warmly commended the Birmingham police force for keeping "order" and "preventing violence." I doubt that you would have so warmly commended the police force if you had seen its dogs sinking their teeth into unarmed, nonviolent Negroes. I doubt that you would so quickly commend the policemen if you were to observe their ugly and inhumane treatment of Negroes here in the city jail; if you were to watch them push and curse old Negro women and young Negro girls; if you were to see them slap and kick old Negro men and young boys; if you were to observe them, as they did on two occasions, refuse to give us food because we wanted to sing our grace together. I cannot join you in your praise of the Birmingham police department.

46 It is true that the police have exercised a degree of discipline in handling the demonstrators. In this sense they have conducted themselves rather "nonviolently" in public. But for what purpose? To preserve the evil system of segregation. Over the past few years I have consistently preached that nonviolence demands that the means we use must be as pure as the ends we seek. I have tried to make clear that it is wrong to use immoral means to attain moral ends. But now I must affirm that it is just as wrong, or perhaps even more so, to use moral means to preserve immoral ends. Perhaps Mr. Connor and his policemen have been rather nonviolent in public, as was Chief Pritchett in Albany, Georgia, but they have used the moral means of nonviolence to maintain the immoral end of racial injustice. As T. S. Eliot has said: "The last temptation is the greatest treason: To do the right deed for the wrong reason."

47 I wish you had commended the Negro sit-inners and demonstrators of Birmingham for their sublime courage, their willingness to suffer and their amazing discipline in the midst of great provocation. One day the South will recognize its real heroes. They will be the James Merediths, with the noble sense of purpose that enables them to face jeering and hostile mobs, and with the agonizing loneliness that characterizes the life of the pioneer. They will be old, oppressed, battered Negro women, symbolized in a seventy-two-year-old woman in Montgomery, Alabama, who rose up with a sense of dignity and with her people decided not to ride segregated buses, and who responded with ungrammatical profundity to one who inquired about her weariness: "My feets is tired, but my soul is at rest." They will be the young high school and college students, the young ministers of the gospel and a host of their elders, courageously and nonviolently sitting in at lunch counters and willingly going to jail for conscience' sake. One day the South will know that when these disinherited children of God sat down at lunch counters, they were in reality standing up for what is best in the American dream and for the most sacred values in our Judaeo-Christian heritage, thereby bringing our nation back to those great wells of democracy which were dug deep by the founding fathers in their formulation of the Constitution and the Declaration of Independence.

48 Never before have I written so long a letter. I'm afraid it is much too long to take your precious time. I can assure you that it would have been much shorter if I had been writing from a comfortable desk, but what else can one do when he is alone in a narrow jail cell, other than write long letters, think long thoughts and pray long prayers?

49 If I have said anything in this letter that overstates the truth and indicates an unreasonable impatience, I beg you to forgive me. If I have said anything that understates the truth and indicates my having a patience that allows me to settle for anything less than brotherhood, I beg God to forgive me.

50 I hope this letter finds you strong in the faith. I also hope that circumstances will soon make it possible for me to meet each of you, not as an integrationist or a civil-rights leader but as a fellow clergyman and a Christian brother. Let us all hope that the dark clouds of racial prejudice will soon pass away and the deep fog of misunderstanding will be lifted from our fear-drenched communities, and in some not too distant tomorrow the radiant stars of love and brotherhood will shine over our great nation with all their scintillating beauty.

Yours for the cause of Peace and Brotherhood,

Martin Luther King, Jr.

Edmund Burke: Letter to a Noble Lord

In 1794, after the trial of Warren Hastings, in which he had been one of the relentless prosecutors, Edmund Burke (1729–1797) retired from the House of Commons, where he had served for almost thirty years, and his son Richard was nominated to take his place. As a reward for his long service in the government, Burke was proposed for the peerage, with the title of Lord Beaconsfield, but upon the death of his son Richard in August of 1794, Burke lost all interest in any titular honors. King George III then bestowed a pen-

sion on Burke but failed to go through the formality of submitting the award to Parliament for approval. Francis Russell (1762–1802), the fifth Duke of Bedford, raised an objection to the pension in the House of Lords. As did Martin Luther King in his "Letter from Birmingham Jail," Burke attempted to vindicate himself in the form of an "open letter," which John Morley, the nineteenth-century critic, called "the most splendid repartee in the English language." Only about a third of the 1796 Letter is reproduced here; about twenty paragraphs have been omitted from the beginning of the Letter and about the same number of paragraphs from the end. In the paragraph immediately preceding the first paragraph printed here, Burke said, "The awful state of the time, and not myself or my own justification, is my true object in what I now write, or in what I shall ever write or say."

1   The Duke of Bedford conceives that he is obliged to call the attention of the House of Peers to his Majesty's grant to me, which he considers excessive and out of all bounds.

2   I know not how it has happened, but it really seems that, whilst his Grace was meditating his well-considered censure upon me, he fell into a sort of sleep. Homer nods; and the Duke of Bedford may dream; and as dreams (even his golden dreams) are apt to be ill-pieced and incongruously put together, his Grace preserved his idea of reproach to *me*, but took the subject-matter from the Crown grants *to his own family.* This is "the stuff of which his dreams are made." In that way of putting things together his Grace is perfectly in the right. The grants to the house of Russell were so enormous, as not only to outrage economy, but even to stagger credulity. The Duke of Bedford is the leviathan among all the creatures of the Crown. He tumbles about his unwieldy bulk; he plays and frolics in the ocean of the royal bounty. Huge as he is, and whilst "he lies floating many a rood," he is still a creature. His ribs, his fins, his whalebone, his blubber, the very spiracles through which he spouts a torrent of brine against his origin and covers me all over with the spray—everything of him and about him is from the throne. Is it for *him* to question the dispensation of the royal favour?

3   I really am at a loss to draw any sort of parallel between the public merits of his Grace, by which he justifies the grants he holds, and these services of mine, on the favourable construction of which I have obtained what his Grace so much disapproves. In private life, I have not at all the honour of acquaintance with the noble Duke. But I ought to presume, and it costs me nothing to do so, that he abundantly deserves the esteem and love of all who live with him. But as to public service, why truly it would not be more ridiculous for me to compare myself in rank, in fortune, in splendid descent, in youth, strength, or figure, with the Duke of Bedford, than to make a parallel between his services and my attempts to be useful to my country. It would

not be gross adulation, but uncivil irony, to say that he has any public merit of his own to keep alive the idea of the services by which his vast landed pensions were obtained. My merits, whatever they are, are original and personal; his are derivative. It is his ancestor, the original pensioner, that has laid up this inexhaustible fund of merit, which makes his Grace so very delicate and exceptious about the merit of all other grantees of the Crown. Had he permitted me to remain in quiet, I should have said, 'tis his estate; that's enough. It is his by law; what have I to do with it or its history? He would naturally have said on his side, 'tis this man's fortune.—He is as good now as my ancestor was two hundred and fifty years ago. I am a young man with very old pensions; he is an old man with very young pensions,— that's all.

4 Why will his Grace, by attacking me, force me reluctantly to compare my little merit with that which obtained from the Crown those prodigies of profuse donation, by which he tramples on the mediocrity of humble and laborious individuals? I would willingly leave him to the herald's college, which the philosophy of the *sans culottes* (prouder by far than all the Garters, and Norroys, and Clarencieux, and Rouge Dragons, that ever pranced in a procession of what his friends call aristocrats and despots) will abolish with contumely and scorn. These historians, recorders, and blazoners of virtues and arms, differ wholly from that other description of historians, who never assign any act of politicians to a good motive. These gentle historians, on the contrary, dip their pens in nothing but the milk of human kindness. They seek no further for merit than the preamble of a patent or the inscription on a tomb. With them every man created a peer is first a hero ready made. They judge of every man's capacity for office by the offices he has filled; and the more offices the more ability. Every general officer with them is a Marlborough; every statesman a Burleigh; every judge a Murray or a Yorke. They who, alive, were laughed at or pitied by all their acquaintance, make as good a figure as the best of them in the pages of Guillim, Edmondson, and Collins.

5 To these recorders, so full of good nature to the great and prosperous, I would willingly leave the first Baron Russell, and Earl of Bedford, and the merits of his grants. But the aulnager, the weigher, the meter of grants, will not suffer us to acquiesce in the judgment of the prince reigning at the time when they were made. They are never good to those who earn them. Well then; since the new grantees have war made on them by the old, and that the word of the sovereign is not to be taken, let us turn our eyes to history, in which great men have always a pleasure in contemplating the heroic origin of their house.

6 The first peer of the name, the first purchaser of the grants, was a Mr. Russell, a person of an ancient gentleman's family raised by being a minion

of Henry the Eighth. As there generally is some resemblance of character to create these relations, the favourite was in all likelihood much such another as his master. The first of those immoderate grants was not taken from the ancient demesne of the Crown, but from the recent confiscation of the ancient nobility of the land. The lion having sucked the blood of his prey, threw the offal carcass to the jackal in waiting. Having tasted once the food of confiscation, the favourites became fierce and ravenous. This worthy favourite's first grant was from the lay nobility. The second, infinitely improving on the enormity of the first, was from the plunder of the church. In truth his Grace is somewhat excusable for his dislike to a grant like mine, not only in its quantity, but in its kind so different from his own.

7 Mine was from a mild and benevolent sovereign; his from Henry the Eighth.

8 Mine had not its fund in the murder of any innocent person of illustrious rank or in the pillage of any body of unoffending men. His grants were from the aggregate and consolidated funds of judgments iniquitously legal and from possessions voluntarily surrendered by the lawful proprietors, with the gibbet at their door.

9 The merit of the grantee whom he derives from was that of being a prompt and greedy instrument of a *levelling* tyrant, who oppressed all descriptions of his people, but who fell with particular fury on everything that was *great and noble*. Mine has been, in endeavouring to screen every man, in every class, from oppression, and particularly in defending the high and eminent, who in the bad times of confiscating princes, confiscating chief governors, or confiscating demagogues, are the most exposed to jealousy, avarice, and envy.

10 The merit of the original grantee of his Grace's pensions was in giving his hand to the work and partaking the spoil with a prince, who plundered a part of the national church of his time and country. Mine was in defending the whole of the national church of my own time and my own country, and the whole of the national churches of all countries, from the principles and the examples which lead to ecclesiastical pillage, thence to a contempt of *all* prescriptive titles, thence to the pillage of *all* property, and thence to universal desolation.

11 The merit of the origin of his Grace's fortune was in being a favourite and chief adviser to a prince, who left no liberty to their native country. My endeavour was to obtain liberty for the municipal country in which I was born and for all descriptions and denominations in it. Mine was to support with unrelaxing vigilance every right, every privilege, every franchise, in this my adopted, my dearer, and more comprehensive country; and not only to preserve those rights in this chief seat of empire, but in every nation, in every land, in every climate, language, and religion, in the vast domain that

is still under the protection, and the larger that was once under the protection, of the British Crown.

12 His founder's merits were, by arts in which he served his master and made his fortune, to bring poverty, wretchedness, and depopulation on his country. Mine were, under a benevolent prince, in promoting the commerce, manufacture, and agriculture of his kingdom; in which his Majesty shows an eminent example, who even in his amusements is a patriot, and in hours of leisure an improver of his native soil.

13 His founder's merit was the merit of a gentleman raised by the arts of a court, and the protection of a Wolsey, to the eminence of a great and potent lord. His merit in that eminence was, by instigating a tyrant to injustice, to provoke a people to rebellion. My merit was, to awaken the sober part of the country, that they might put themselves on their guard against any one potent lord, or any greater number of potent lords, or any combination of great leading men of any sort, if ever they should attempt to proceed in the same courses, but in the reverse order; that is, by instigating a corrupted populace to rebellion and, through that rebellion, introducing a tyranny yet worse than the tyranny which his Grace's ancestor supported and of which he profited in the manner we behold in the despotism of Henry the Eighth.

14 The political merit of the first pensioner of his Grace's house was that of being concerned as a counsellor of state in advising, and in his person executing, the conditions of a dishonourable peace with France; the surrendering the fortress of Boulogne, then our out-guard on the Continent. By that surrender, Calais, the key of France and the bridle in the mouth of that power, was, not many years afterwards, finally lost. My merit has been in resisting the power and pride of France, under any form of its rule; but in opposing it with the greatest zeal and earnestness, when that rule appeared in the worst form it could assume; the worst indeed which the prime cause and principle of all evil could possibly give it. It was my endeavour by every means to excite a spirit in the House where I had the honour of a seat, for carrying on, with early vigour and decision, the most clearly just and necessary war, that this or any nation ever carried on; in order to save my country from the iron yoke of its power and from the more dreadful contagion of its principles; to preserve, while they can be preserved, pure and untainted, the ancient, inbred integrity, piety, good nature, and good humour of the people of England, from the dreadful pestilence, which, beginning in France, threatens to lay waste the whole moral, and in a great degree the whole physical, world, having done both in the focus of its most intense malignity.

15 The labours of his Grace's founder merited the curses, not loud but deep, of the Commons of England, on whom *he* and his master had effected a *complete parliamentary reform,* by making them, in their slavery and humiliation, the true and adequate representatives of a debased, degraded,

and undone people. My merits were, in having had an active, though not always an ostentatious, share, in every one act, without exception, of undisputed constitutional utility in my time, and in having supported, on all occasions, the authority, the efficiency, and the privileges of the Commons of Great Britain. I ended my services by a recorded and fully reasoned assertion on their own journals of their constitutional rights and a vindication of their constitutional conduct. I laboured in all things to merit their inward approbation, and (along with the assistance of the largest, the greatest, and best of my endeavours) I received their free, unbiased, public, and solemn thanks.

16   Thus stands the account of the comparative merits of the Crown grants which compose the Duke of Bedford's fortune as balanced against mine. In the name of common sense, why should the Duke of Bedford think that none but of the House of Russell are entitled to the favour of the Crown? Why should he imagine that no king of England has been capable of judging of merit but King Henry the Eighth? Indeed, he will pardon me; he is a little mistaken; all virtue did not end in the first Earl of Bedford. All discernment did not lose its vision when his Creator closed his eyes. Let him remit his rigour on the disproportion between merit and reward in others, and they will make no inquiry into the origin of his fortune. They will regard with much more satisfaction, as he will contemplate with infinitely more advantage, whatever in his pedigree has been dulcified by an exposure to the influence of heaven in a long flow of generations, from the hard, acidulous, metallic tincture of the spring. It is little to be doubted that several of his forefathers in that long series have degenerated into honour and virtue. Let the Duke of Bedford (I am sure he will) reject with scorn and horror the counsels of the lecturers, those wicked panders to avarice and ambition, who would tempt him, in the troubles of his country, to seek another enormous fortune from the forfeitures of another nobility and the plunder of another church. Let him (and I trust that yet he will) employ all the energy of his youth and all the resources of his wealth to crush rebellious principles which have no foundation in morals and rebellious movements that have no provocation in tyranny.

17   Then will be forgot the rebellions, which, by a doubtful priority in crime, his ancestor had provoked and extinguished. On such a conduct in the noble Duke, many of his countrymen might, and with some excuse might, give way to the enthusiasm of their gratitude and, in the dashing style of some of the old declaimers, cry out that if the fates had found no other way in which they could give a Duke of Bedford and his opulence as props to a tottering world, then the butchery of the Duke of Buckingham might be tolerated; it might be regarded even with complacency, whilst in the heir of confiscation they saw the sympathizing comforter of the martyrs who suffered under the cruel confiscation of this day; whilst they behold with admiration his zealous protection of the virtuous and loyal nobility of France and his manly support to his brethren, the yet standing nobility and gentry of his native land. Then his Grace's merit would be pure, and new, and sharp, as fresh from the mint of honour. As he pleased he might reflect honour on his predecessors or throw it forward on those who were to succeed him. He might be the propagator of the stock of honour, or the root of it, as he thought proper.

18 Had it pleased God to continue to me the hopes of succession, I should have been, according to my mediocrity and the mediocrity of the age I live in, a sort of founder of a family; I should have left a son, who, in all the points in which personal merit can be viewed, in science, in erudition, in genius, in taste, in honour, in generosity, in humanity, in every liberal sentiment and every liberal accomplishment, would not have shown himself inferior to the Duke of Bedford or to any of those whom he traces in his line. His Grace very soon would have wanted all plausibility in his attack upon that provision which belonged more to mine than to me. He would soon have supplied every deficiency and symmetrized every disproportion. It would not have been for that successor to resort to any stagnant wasting reservoir of merit in me or in any ancestry. He had in himself a salient, living spring of generous and manly action. Every day he lived he would have re-purchased the bounty of the Crown and ten times more, if ten times more he had received. He was made a public creature; and had no enjoyment whatever but in the performance of some duty. At this exigent moment, the loss of a finished man is not easily supplied.

19 But a Disposer whose power we are little able to resist and whose wisdom it behooves us not at all to dispute, has ordained it in another manner and (whatever my querulous weakness might suggest) a far better. The storm has gone over me; and I lie like one of those old oaks which the late hurricane has scattered about me. I am stripped of all my honours, I am torn up by the roots and lie prostrate on the earth! There, and prostrate there, I most unfeignedly recognize the Divine justice and in some degree submit to it. But whilst I humble myself before God, I do not know that it is forbidden to repel the attacks of unjust and inconsiderate men. The patience of Job is proverbial. After some of the convulsive struggles of our irritable nature, he submitted himself and repented in dust and ashes. But even so, I do not find him blamed for reprehending, and with a considerable degree of verbal asperity, those ill-natured neighbours of his, who visited his dunghill to read moral, political, and economical lectures on his misery. I am alone. I have none to meet my enemies in the gate. Indeed, my Lord, I greatly deceive myself, if in this hard season I would give a peck of refuse wheat for all that is called fame and honour in the world. This is the appetite but of a few. It is a luxury, it is a privilege, it is an indulgence for those who are at their ease. But we are all of us made to shun disgrace, as we are made to shrink from pain and poverty and disease. It is an instinct; and under the direction of reason, instinct is always in the right. I live in an inverted order. They who ought to have succeeded me are gone before me. They who should have been to me as posterity are in the place of ancestors. I owe to the dearest relation (which ever must subsist in memory) that act of piety, which he would have performed to me; I owe it to him to show that he was not descended, as the Duke of Bedford would have it, from an unworthy parent.

20   The Crown has considered me after long service; the Crown has paid the Duke of Bedford by advance. He has had a long credit for any services which he may perform hereafter. He is secure, and long may he be secure, in his advance, whether he performs any services or not. But let him take care how he endangers the safety of that constitution which secures his own utility or his own insignificance; or how he discourages those who take up, even puny arms, to defend an order of things which, like the sun of heaven, shines alike on the useful and the worthless. His grants are ingrafted on the public law of Europe, covered with the awful hoar of innumerable ages. They are guarded by the sacred rules of prescription, found in that full treasury of jurisprudence from which the jejuneness and penury of our municipal law has, by degrees, been enriched and strengthened. This prescription I had my share (a very full share) in bringing to its perfection. The Duke of Bedford will stand as long as prescriptive law endures; as long as the great stable laws of property, common to us with all civilized nations, are kept in their integrity and without the smallest intermixture of laws, maxims, principles, or precedents of the grand Revolution. They are secure against all changes but one. The whole revolutionary system, institutes, digest, code, novels, text, gloss, comment, are not only the same but they are the very reverse, and the reverse fundamentals, of all the laws on which civil life has hitherto been upheld in all the governments of the world. The learned professors of the rights of man regard prescription, not as a title to bar all claim, set up against all possession—but they look on prescription as itself a bar against the possessor and proprietor. They hold an immemorial possession to be no more than a long-continued and therefore an aggravated injustice.

21   Such are *their* ideas; such *their* religion, and such *their* law. But as to *our* country and *our* race, as long as the well-compacted structure of our church and state, the sanctuary, the holy of holies of that ancient law, defended by reverence, defended by power, a fortress at once and a temple, shall stand inviolate on the brow of the British Sion—as long as the British monarchy, not more limited than fenced by the orders of the state, shall, like the proud Keep of Windsor, rising in the majesty of proportion and girt with the double belt of its kindred and coeval towers, as long as this awful structure

shall oversee and guard the subjected land—so long the mounds and dykes of the low, fat Bedford level will have nothing to fear from all the pickaxes of all the levellers of France. As long as our sovereign lord the king and his faithful subjects, the Lords and Commons of this realm—the triple cord which no man can break; the solemn, sworn, constitutional frank-pledge of this nation; the firm guarantees of each other's beings and each other's rights; the joint and several securities, each in its place and order, for every kind and every quality of property and of dignity; as long as these endure, so long the Duke of Bedford is safe: and we are all safe together—the high from the blights of envy and the spoliations of rapacity; the low from the iron hand of oppression and the insolent spurn of contempt....

Thomas Henry Huxley: Science and Culture

In the two selections that follow, we observe Thomas Henry Huxley (1825–95) and Matthew Arnold (1822–88) engaged in a vigorous debate on the relative merits of what C. P. Snow in our own time has called the "Two Cultures," the sciences and the humanities. Huxley was the most eloquent of the nineteenth-century spokesmen for the sciences. Having studied medicine as a young man, he became widely known for his research in comparative anatomy and embryology, for his courageous defense of Charles Darwin's theories of evolution, for his advocacy of higher education for women and Negroes, for his lectures at several working-men's colleges, and for his contributions to sociology and ethics. His "Science and Culture" was delivered as an address at the opening of Sir Josiah Mason's Science College in Birmingham, England, on October 1, 1880. His essay is presented here in an abbreviated version, fifteen paragraphs having been omitted from the beginning and four paragraphs at the end.

Along with John Henry Newman, Matthew Arnold stands as one of the dauntless nineteenth-century champions of liberal education. A son of the famous Dr. Thomas Arnold of Rugby, Arnold took only a second-class honors degree at Balliol College, Oxford, in 1844, but the following year he won a fellowship at Oriel College, Oxford. A distinguished poet, critic, and essayist in his own right, he was twice elected to the Chair of Poetry at Oxford. For thirty-five years of his life, he served as an Inspector of Schools in England, a job in which he exerted his influence to bring about compulsory education for young people of all social strata. His "Literature and Science" was first delivered as the Rede Lecture at Cambridge University and was subsequently published in the August, 1882 issue of Nineteenth Century. In a slightly revised version, it was again delivered during his

American lecture tour of 1883-4. It too is reproduced here in an abbreviated version, but the section printed here is essentially the same lecture that he delivered at Cambridge and in America. It is instructive to observe these two formidable polemicists locking horns over a matter which both of them took very seriously.

1 I hold very strongly by two convictions:—The first is that neither the discipline nor the subject-matter of classical education is of such direct value to the student of physical science as to justify the expenditure of valuable time upon either; and the second is that for the purpose of attaining real culture, an exclusively scientific education is at least as effectual as an exclusively literary education.

2 I need hardly point out to you that these opinions, especially the latter, are diametrically opposed to those of the great majority of educated Englishmen, influenced as they are by school and university traditions. In their belief, culture is obtainable only by a liberal education; and a liberal education is synonymous, not merely with education and instruction in literature, but in one particular form of literature, namely, that of Greek and Roman antiquity. They hold that the man who has learned Latin and Greek, however little, is educated; while he who is versed in other branches of knowledge, however deeply, is a more or less respectable specialist, not admissible into the cultured caste. The stamp of the educated man, the University degree, is not for him.

3 I am too well acquainted with the generous catholicity of spirit, the true sympathy with scientific thought, which pervades the writings of our chief apostle of culture, to identify him with these opinions; and yet one may cull from one and another of those epistles to the Philistines, which so much delight all who do not answer to that name, sentences which lend them some support.

4 Mr. Arnold tells us that the meaning of culture is "to know the best that has been thought and said in the world." It is the criticism of life contained in literature. That criticism regards "Europe as being, for intellectual and spiritual purposes, one great confederation, bound to a joint action and working to a common result; and whose members have, for their common outfit, a knowledge of Greek, Roman, and Eastern antiquity, and of one another. Special, local, and temporary advantages being put out of account, that modern nation will in the intellectual and spiritual sphere make most progress, which most thoroughly carries out this programme. And what is that but saying that we too, all of us, as individuals, the more thoroughly we carry it out, shall make the more progress?"

5 We have here to deal with two distinct propositions. The first, that a

criticism of life is the essence of culture; the second, that literature contains the materials which suffice for the construction of such a criticism.

6 I think that we must all assent to the first proposition. For culture certainly means something quite different from learning or technical skill. It implies the possession of an ideal and the habit of critically estimating the value of things by comparison with a theoretic standard. Perfect culture should supply a complete theory of life, based upon a clear knowledge alike of its possibilities and of its limitations.

7 But we may agree to all this and yet strongly dissent from the assumption that literature alone is competent to supply this knowledge. After having learnt all that Greek, Roman, and Eastern antiquity have thought and said and all that modern literatures have to tell us, it is not self-evident that we have laid a sufficiently broad and deep foundation for that criticism of life which constitutes culture.

8 Indeed, to any one acquainted with the scope of physical science, it is not at all evident. Considering progress only in the "intellectual and spiritual sphere," I find myself wholly unable to admit that either nations or individuals will really advance, if their common outfit draws nothing from the stores of physical science. I should say that an army, without weapons of precision and with no particular base of operations, might more hopefully enter upon a campaign on the Rhine, than a man, devoid of a knowledge of what physical science has done in the last century, upon a criticism of life.

9 When a biologist meets with an anomaly, he instinctively turns to the study of development to clear it up. The rationale of contradictory opinions may with equal confidence be sought in history.

10 It is, happily, no new thing that Englishmen should employ their wealth in building and endowing institutions for educational purposes. But five or six hundred years ago, deeds of foundation expressed or implied conditions as nearly as possible contrary to those which have been thought expedient by Sir Josiah Mason. That is to say, physical science was practically ignored, while a certain literary training was enjoined as a means to the acquirement of knowledge which was essentially theological.

11 The reason of this singular contradiction between the actions of men alike animated by a strong and disinterested desire to promote the welfare of their fellows is easily discovered.

12 At that time, in fact, if any one desired knowledge beyond such as could be obtained by his own observation or by common conversation, his first necessity was to learn the Latin language, inasmuch as all the higher knowledge of the western world was contained in works written in that language. Hence, Latin grammar, with logic and rhetoric, studied through Latin, were the fundamentals of education. With respect to the substance of the knowl-

edge imparted through this channel, the Jewish and Christian Scriptures, as interpreted and supplemented by the Romish Church, were held to contain a complete and infallibly true body of information.

13 Theological dicta were, to the thinkers of those days, that which the axioms and definitions of Euclid are to the geometers of these. The business of the philosophers of the middle ages was to deduce, from the data furnished by the theologians, conclusions in accordance with ecclesiastical degrees. They were allowed the high privilege of showing, by logical process, how and why that which the Church said was true, must be true. And if their demonstrations fell short of or exceeded this limit, the Church was maternally ready to check their aberrations,—if need were, by the help of the secular arm.

14 Between the two, our ancestors were furnished with a compact and complete criticism of life. They were told how the world began and how it would end; they learned that all material existence was but a base and insignificant blot upon the fair face of the spiritual world and that nature was, to all intents and purposes, the playground of the devil; they learned that the earth is the centre of the visible universe and that man is the cynosure of things terrestrial; and more especially was it inculcated that the course of nature had no fixed order, but that it could be, and constantly was, altered by the agency of innumerable spiritual beings, good and bad, according as they were moved by the deeds and prayers of men. The sum and substance of the whole doctrine was to produce the conviction that the only thing really worth knowing in this world was how to secure that place in a better, which, under certain conditions, the Church promised.

15 Our ancestors had a living belief in this theory of life and acted upon it in their dealings with education, as in all other matters. Culture meant saintliness—after the fashion of the saints of those days; the education that led to it was, of necessity, theological; and the way to theology lay through Latin.

16 That the study of nature—further than was requisite for the satisfaction of everyday wants—should have any bearing on human life was far from the thoughts of men thus trained. Indeed, as nature had been cursed for man's sake, it was an obvious conclusion that those who meddled with nature were likely to come into pretty close contact with Satan. And if any born scientific investigator followed his instincts, he might safely reckon upon earning the reputation, and probably upon suffering the fate, of a sorcerer.

17 Had the western world been left to itself in Chinese isolation, there is no saying how long this state of things might have endured. But happily it was not left to itself. Even earlier than the thirteenth century, the development of Moorish civilization in Spain and the great movement of the

Crusades had introduced the leaven which, from that day to this, has never ceased to work. At first, through the intermediation of Arabic translations, afterwards by the study of the originals, the western nations of Europe became acquainted with the writings of the ancient philosophers and poets and, in time, with the whole of the vast literature of antiquity.

18 Whatever there was of high intellectual aspiration or dominant capacity in Italy, France, Germany, and England, spent itself for centuries in taking possession of the rich inheritance left by the dead civilizations of Greece and Rome. Marvelously aided by the invention of printing, classical learning spread and flourished. Those who possessed it prided themselves on having attained the highest culture then within the reach of mankind.

19 And justly. For, saving Dante on his solitary pinnacle, there was no figure in modern literature, at the time of the Renascence, to compare with the men of antiquity; there was no art to compete with their sculpture; there was no physical science but that which Greece had created. Above all, there was no other example of perfect intellectual freedom—of the unhesitating acceptance of reason as the sole guide to truth and the supreme arbiter of conduct.

20 The new learning necessarily soon exerted a profound influence upon education. The language of the monks and schoolmen seemed little better than gibberish to scholars fresh from Vergil and Cicero, and the study of Latin was placed upon a new foundation. Moreover, Latin itself ceased to afford the sole key to knowledge. The student who sought the highest thought of antiquity found only a second-hand reflection of it in Roman literature and turned his face to the full light of the Greeks. And after a battle, not altogether dissimilar to that which is at present being fought over the teaching of physical science, the study of Greek was recognized as an essential element of all higher education.

21 Thus the Humanists, as they were called, won the day; and the great reform which they effected was of incalculable service to mankind. But the Nemesis of all reformers is finality; and the reformers of education, like those of religion, fell into the profound, however common, error of mistaking the beginning for the end of the work of reformation.

22 The representatives of the Humanists, in the nineteenth century, take their stand upon classical education as the sole avenue to culture, as firmly as if we were still in the age of Renascence. Yet, surely, the present intellectual relations of the modern and the ancient worlds are profoundly different from those which obtained three centuries ago. Leaving aside the existence of a great and characteristically modern literature, of modern painting, and, especially, of modern music, there is one feature of the present state of the civilized world which separates it more widely from the Renascence than the Renascence was separated from the middle ages.

23 This distinctive character of our own times lies in the vast and constantly increasing part which is played by natural knowledge. Not only is our daily life shaped by it, not only does the prosperity of millions of men depend upon it, but our whole theory of life has long been influenced, consciously or unconsciously, by the general conceptions of the universe which have been forced upon us by physical science.

24 In fact, the most elementary acquaintance with the results of scientific investigation shows us that they offer a broad and striking contradiction to the opinion so implicitly credited and taught in the middle ages.

25 The notions of the beginning and the end of the world entertained by our forefathers are no longer credible. It is very certain that the earth is not the chief body in the universe and that the world is not subordinated to man's use. It is even more certain that nature is the expression of a definite order with which nothing interferes and that the chief business of mankind is to learn that order and govern themselves accordingly. Moreover, this scientific "criticism of life" presents itself to us with different credentials from any other. It appeals not to authority, nor to what anybody may have thought or said, but to nature. It admits that all our interpretations of natural fact are more or less imperfect and symbolic, and bids the learner seek for truth not among words but among things. It warns us that the assertion which outstrips evidence is not only a blunder but a crime.

26 The purely classical education advocated by the representatives of the Humanists in our day gives no inkling of all this. A man may be a better scholar than Erasmus and know no more of the chief causes of the present intellectual fermentation than Erasmus did. Scholarly and pious persons, worthy of all respect, favour us with allocutions upon the sadness of the antagonism of science to their mediaeval way of thinking, which betray an ignorance of the first principles of scientific investigation, an incapacity for understanding what a man of science means by veracity and an unconsciousness of the weight of established scientific truths, which is almost comical.

27 There is no great force in the *tu quoque* argument, or else the advocates of scientific education might fairly enough retort upon the modern Humanists that they may be learned specialists, but that they possess no such sound foundation for a criticism of life as deserves the name of culture. And, indeed, if we were disposed to be cruel, we might urge that the Humanists have brought this reproach upon themselves, not because they are too full of the spirit of the ancient Greek, but because they lack it.

28 The period of the Renascence is commonly called that of the "Revival of Letters," as if the influences then brought to bear upon the mind of Western Europe had been wholly exhausted in the field of literature. I think it is very commonly forgotten that the revival of science, effected by the same agency, although less conspicuous, was not less momentous.

College, seeing that its inclusion would probably lead to the introduction of the ordinary smattering of Latin and Greek.

33 Nevertheless, I am the last person to question the importance of genuine literary education or to suppose that intellectual culture can be complete without it. An exclusively scientific training will bring about a mental twist as surely as an exclusively literary training. The value of the cargo does not

29 In fact, the few and scattered students of nature of that day picked up the clue to her secrets exactly as it fell from the hands of the Greeks a thousand years before. The foundations of mathematics were so well laid by them that our children learn their geometry from a book written for the schools of Alexandria two thousand years ago. Modern astronomy is the natural continuation and development of the work of Hipparchus and of Ptolemy; modern physics of that of Democritus and of Archimedes; it was long before modern biological science outgrew the knowledge bequeathed to us by Aristotle, by Theophrastus, and by Galen.

30 We cannot know all the best thoughts and sayings of the Greeks unless we know what they thought about natural phenomena. We cannot fully apprehend their criticism of life unless we understand the extent to which that criticism was affected by scientific conceptions. We falsely pretend to be the inheritors of their culture, unless we are penetrated, as the best minds among them were, with an unhesitating faith that the free employment of reason, in accordance with scientific method, is the sole method of reaching truth.

31 Thus I venture to think that the pretensions of our modern Humanists to the possession of the monopoly of culture and to the exclusive inheritance of the spirit of antiquity must be abated, if not abandoned. But I should be very sorry that anything I have said should be taken to imply a desire on my part to depreciate the value of a classical education, as it might be and as it sometimes is. The native capacities of mankind vary no less than their opportunities; and while culture is one, the road by which one man may best reach it is widely different from that which is most advantageous to another. Again, while scientific education is yet inchoate and tentative, classical education is thoroughly well organized upon the practical experience of generations of teachers. So that, given ample time for learning and destination for ordinary life or for a literary career, I do not think that a young Englishman in search of culture can do better than follow the course usually marked out for him, supplementing its deficiencies by his own efforts.

32 But for those who mean to make science their serious occupation or who intend to follow the profession of medicine or who have to enter early upon the business of life,—for all these, in my opinion, classical education is a mistake; and it is for this reason that I am glad to see "mere literary education and instruction" shut out from the curriculum of Sir Josiah Mason's compensate for a ship's being out of trim; and I should be very sorry to think that the Scientific College would turn out none but lopsided men.

34 There is no need, however, that such a catastrophe should happen. Instruction in English, French, and German is provided, and thus the three greatest literatures of the modern world are made accessible to the student. French and German, and especially the latter language, are absolutely indispensable to those who desire full knowledge in any department of science. But even supposing that the knowledge of these languages acquired is not more than sufficient for purely scientific purposes, every Englishman has, in his native tongue, an almost perfect instrument of literary expression· and, in his own literature, models of every kind of literary excellence. If an Englishman cannot get literary culture out of his Bible, his Shakespeare, his Milton, neither, in my belief, will the profoundest study of Homer and Sophocles, Vergil and Horace, give it to him.

35 Thus, since the constitution of the College makes sufficient provision for literary as well as for scientific education and since artistic instruction is also contemplated, it seems to me that a fairly complete culture is offered to all who are willing to take advantage of it.

36 But I am not sure that at this point the "practical" man, scotched but not slain, may ask what all this talk about culture has to do with an Institution, the object of which is defined to be "to promote the prosperity of the manufactures and the industry of the country." He may suggest that what is wanted for this end is not culture, not even a purely scientific discipline, but simply a knowledge of applied science.

37 I often wish that this phrase, "applied science," had never been invented. For it suggests that there is a sort of scientific knowledge of direct practical use, which can be studied apart from another sort of scientific knowledge, which is of no practical utility and which is termed "pure science." But there is no more complete fallacy than this. What people call applied science is nothing but the application of pure science to particular classes of problems. It consists of deductions from those general principles, established by reasoning and observation, which constitute pure science. No one can safely make these deductions until he has a firm grasp of the principles; and he can obtain that grasp only by personal experience of the operations of observation and of reasoning on which they are founded.

38 Almost all the processes employed in the arts and manufactures fall within the range either of physics or of chemistry. In order to improve them,

one must thoroughly understand them; and no one has a chance of really understanding them unless he has obtained that mastery of principles and that habit of dealing with facts, which is given by long-continued and well-directed purely scientific training in the physical and the chemical laboratory. So that there really is no question as to the necessity of purely scientific discipline, even if the work of the College were limited by the narrowest interpretation of its stated aims.

39 And as to the desirableness of a wider culture than that yielded by science alone, it is to be recollected that the improvement of manufacturing processes is only one of the conditions which contribute to the prosperity of industry. Industry is a means and not an end; and mankind work only to get something which they want. What that something is depends partly on their innate, and partly on their acquired, desires.

40 If the wealth resulting from prosperous industry is to be spent upon the gratification of unworthy desires, if the increasing perfection of manufacturing processes is to be accompanied by an increasing debasement of those who carry them on, I do not see the good of industry and prosperity.

41 Now it is perfectly true that men's views of what is desirable depend upon their characters and that the innate proclivities to which we give that name are not touched by any amount of instruction. But it does not follow that even mere intellectual education may not, to an indefinite extent, modify the practical manifestation of the characters of men in their actions, by supplying them with motives unknown to the ignorant. A pleasure-loving character will have pleasure of some sort; but, if you give him the choice, he may prefer pleasures which do not degrade him to those which do. And this choice is offered to every man who possesses in literary or artistic culture a never-failing source of pleasures, which are neither withered by age, nor staled by custom, nor embittered in the recollection by the pangs of self-reproach.

Matthew Arnold: Literature and Science

1 I am going to ask whether the present movement for ousting letters from their old predominance in education and for transferring the predominance in education to the natural sciences—whether this brisk and flourishing movement ought to prevail and whether it is likely that in the end it really will prevail. An objection may be raised which I will anticipate. My own studies have been almost wholly in letters, and my visits to the field of the natural sciences have been slight and inadequate, although those sciences have always strongly moved my curiosity. A man of letters, it will perhaps be said, is not

competent to discuss the comparative merits of letters and natural science as means of education. To this objection I reply, first of all, that his incompetence, if he attempts the discussion but is really incompetent for it, will be abundantly visible; nobody will be taken in; he will have plenty of sharp observers and critics to save mankind from that danger. But the line I am going to follow is, as you will soon discover, so extremely simple, that perhaps it may be followed without failure even by one who for a more ambitious line of discussion would be quite incompetent.

2 Some of you may possibly remember a phrase of mine which has been the object of a good deal of comment; an observation to the effect that in our culture, the aim being *to know ourselves and the world,* we have, as the means to this end, *to know the best which has been thought and said in the world.* A man of science, who is also an excellent writer and the very prince of debaters, Professor Huxley, in a discourse at the opening of Sir Josiah Mason's college at Birmingham, laying hold of this phrase, expanded it by quoting some more words of mine, which are these: "The civilized world is to be regarded as now being, for intellectual and spiritual purposes, one great confederation, bound to a joint action and working to a common result; and whose members have for their proper outfit a knowledge of Greek, Roman, and Eastern antiquity, and of one another. Special local and temporary advantages being put out of account, that modern nation will in the intellectual and spiritual sphere make most progress which most thoroughly carries out this programme."

3 Now on my phrase, thus enlarged, Professor Huxley remarks that when I speak of the above-mentioned knowledge as enabling us to know ourselves and the world, I assert *literature* to contain the materials which suffice for thus making us know ourselves and the world. But it is not by any means clear, says he, that after having learnt all which ancient and modern literatures have to tell us, we have laid a sufficiently broad and deep foundation for the criticism of life, that knowledge of ourselves and the world, which constitutes culture. On the contrary, Professor Huxley declares that he finds himself "wholly unable to admit that either nations or individuals will really advance, if their outfit draws nothing from the stores of physical science. An army without weapons of precision, and with no particular base of operations, might more hopefully enter upon a campaign on the Rhine, than a man, devoid of a knowledge of what physical science has done in the last century, upon a criticism of life."

4 This shows how needful it is for those who are to discuss any matters together, to have a common understanding as to the sense of the terms they employ—how needful and how difficult. What Professor Huxley says, implies just the reproach which is so often brought against the study of *belles lettres,* as they are called: that the study is an elegant one, but slight and

ineffectual; a smattering of Greek and Latin and other ornamental things, of little use for any one whose object is to get at truth and to be a practical man. So, too, M. Renan talks of the "superficial humanism" of a school-course which treats us as if we were all going to be poets, writers, preachers, orators, and he opposes this humanism to positive science or the critical search after truth. And there is always a tendency in those who are remonstrating against the predominance of letters in education to understand by letters *belles lettres* and by *belles lettres* a superficial humanism, the opposite of science or true knowledge.

5 But when we talk of knowing Greek and Roman antiquity, for instance, which is the knowledge people have called the humanities, I for my part mean a knowledge which is something more than a superficial humanism, mainly decorative. "I call all teaching *scientific*," says Wolf, the critic of Homer, "which is systematically laid out and followed up to its original sources. For example: a knowledge of classical antiquity is scientific when the remains of classical antiquity are correctly studied in the original languages." There can be no doubt that Wolf is perfectly right; that all learning is scientific which is systematically laid out and followed up to its original sources and that a genuine humanism is scientific.

6 When I speak of knowing Greek and Roman antiquity, therefore, as a help to knowing ourselves and the world, I mean more than a knowledge of so much vocabulary, so much grammar, so many portions of authors in the Greek and Latin languages—I mean knowing the Greeks and Romans, and their life and genius, and what they were and did in the world; what we get from them and what is its value. That, at least, is the ideal; and when we talk of endeavouring to know Greek and Roman antiquity, as a help to knowing ourselves and the world, we mean endeavouring so to know them as to satisfy this ideal, however much we may still fall short of it.

7 The same also as to knowing our own and other modern nations, with the like aim of getting to understand ourselves and the world. To know the best that has been thought and said by the modern nations is to know, says Professor Huxley, "only what modern *literatures* have to tell us; it is the criticism of life contained in modern literature." And yet "the distinctive character of our times," he urges, "lies in the vast and constantly increasing part which is played by natural knowledge." And how, therefore, can a man, devoid of knowledge of what physical science has done in the last century, enter hopefully upon a criticism of modern life?

8 Let us, I say, be agreed about the meaning of the terms we are using. I talk of knowing the best which has been thought and uttered in the world; Professor Huxley says this means knowing *literature*. Literature is a large word; it may mean everything written with letters or printed in a book. Euclid's *Elements* and Newton's *Principia* are thus literature. All knowledge

290 DISCOVERY OF ARGUMENTS

that reaches us through books is literature. But by literature Professor Huxley means *belles lettres*. He means to make me say, that knowing the best which has been thought and said by the modern nations is knowing their *belles lettres* and no more. And this is no sufficient equipment, he argues, for a criticism of modern life. But as I do not mean, by knowing ancient Rome, knowing merely more or less of Latin *belles lettres* and taking no account of Rome's military and political and legal and administrative work in the world; and as, by knowing ancient Greece, I understand knowing her as the giver of Greek art and the guide to a free and right use of reason and to scientific method, and the founder of our mathematics and physics and astronomy and biology—I understand knowing her as all this and not merely knowing certain Greek poems and histories and treatises and speeches—so as to the knowledge of modern nations also. By knowing modern nations, I mean not merely knowing their *belles lettres,* but knowing also what has been done by such men as Copernicus, Galileo, Newton, Darwin. "Our ancestors learned," says Professor Huxley, "that the earth is the centre of the visible universe and that man is the cynosure of things terrestrial; and more especially was it inculcated that the course of nature had no fixed order, but that it could be, and constantly was, altered." But for us now, continues Professor Huxley, "the notions of the beginning and the end of the world entertained by our forefathers are no longer credible. It is very certain that the earth is not the chief body in the material universe and that the world is not subordinated to man's use. It is even more certain that nature is the expression of a definite order, with which nothing interferes." "And yet," he cries, "the purely classical education advocated by the representatives of the humanists in our day gives no inkling of all this!"

9 In due place and time I will just touch upon that vexed question of classical education; but at present the question is as to what is meant by knowing the best which modern nations have thought and said. It is not knowing their *belles lettres* merely which is meant. To know Italian *belles lettres* is not to know Italy, and to know English *belles lettres* is not to know England. Into knowing Italy and England there comes a great deal more, Galileo and Newton amongst it. The reproach of being a superficial humanism, a tincture of *belles lettres,* may attach rightly enough to some other disciplines; but to the particular discipline recommended when I proposed knowing the best that has been thought and said in the world, it does not apply. In that best I certainly include what in modern times has been thought and said by the great observers and knowers of nature.

10 There is, therefore, really no question between Professor Huxley and me as to whether knowing the great results of the modern scientific study of nature is not required as a part of our culture, as well as knowing the products of literature and art. But to follow the processes by which those results

are reached, ought, say the friends of physical science, to be made the staple of education for the bulk of mankind. And here there does arise a question between those whom Professor Huxley calls with playful sarcasm "the Levites of culture," and those whom the poor humanist is sometimes apt to regard as its Nebuchadnezzars.

11 The great results of the scientific investigation of nature we are agreed upon knowing, but how much of our study are we bound to give to the processes by which those results are reached? The results have their visible bearing on human life. But all the processes, too, all the items of fact, by which those results are reached and established, are interesting. All knowledge is interesting to a wise man, and the knowledge of nature is interesting to all men. It is very interesting to know that from the albuminous white of the egg the chick in the egg gets the materials for its flesh, bones, blood, and feathers, while from the fatty yolk of the egg it gets the heat and energy which enable it at length to break its shell and begin the world. It is less interesting, perhaps, but still it is interesting, to know that when a taper burns, the wax is converted into carbonic acid and water. Moreover, it is quite true that the habit of dealing with facts, which is given by the study of nature, is, as the friends of physical science praise it for being, an excellent discipline. The appeal, in the study of nature, is constantly to observation and experiment; not only is it said that the thing is so, but we can be made to see that it is so. Not only does a man tell us that when a taper burns the wax is converted into carbonic acid and water, as a man may tell us, if he likes, that Charon is punting his ferry-boat on the river Styx, or that Victor Hugo is a sublime poet, or Mr. Gladstone the most admirable of statesmen; but we are made to see that the conversion into carbonic acid and water does actually happen. This reality of natural knowledge it is which makes the friends of physical science contrast it, as a knowledge of things, with the humanist's knowledge, which is, say they, a knowledge of words. And hence Professor Huxley is moved to lay it down that "for the purpose of attaining real culture, an exclusively scientific education is at least as effectual as an exclusively literary education." And a certain President of the Section for Mechanical Science in the British Association is, in Scripture phrase, "very bold," and declares that if a man, in his mental training, "has substituted literature and history for natural science, he has chosen the less useful alternative." But whether we go these lengths or not, we must admit that in natural science the habit gained of dealing with facts is a most valuable discipline and that everyone should have some experience of it.

12 More than this, however, is demanded by the reformers. It is proposed to make the training in natural science the main part of education, for the great majority of mankind at any rate. And here, I confess, I part company with the friends of physical science, with whom up to this point I have been

agreeing. In differing from them, however, I wish to proceed with the utmost caution and diffidence. The smallness of my own acquaintance with the disciplines of natural science is ever before my mind, and I am fearful of doing these disciplines an injustice. The ability and pugnacity of the partisans of natural science make them formidable persons to contradict. The tone of tentative inquiry, which befits a being of dim faculties and bounded knowledge, is the tone I would wish to take and not to depart from. At present it seems to me that those who are for giving to natural knowledge, as they call it, the chief place in the education of the majority of mankind, leave one important thing out of their account: the constitution of human nature. But I put this forward on the strength of some facts not at all recondite, very far from it; facts capable of being stated in the simplest possible fashion, and to which, if I so state them, the man of science will, I am sure, be willing to allow their due weight.

13 Deny the facts altogether, I think, he hardly can. He can hardly deny that when we set ourselves to enumerate the powers which go to the building up of human life, and say that they are the power of conduct, the power of intellect and knowledge, the power of beauty, and the power of social life and manners—he can hardly deny that this scheme, though drawn in rough and plain lines enough, and not pretending to scientific exactness, does yet give a fairly true representation of the matter. Human nature is built up by these powers; we have the need for them all. When we have rightly met and adjusted the claims of them all, we shall then be in a fair way for getting soberness and righteousness with wisdom. This is evident enough, and the friends of physical science would admit it.

14 But perhaps they may not have sufficiently observed another thing: namely, that the several powers just mentioned are not isolated, but there is, in the generality of mankind, a perpetual tendency to relate them one to another in divers ways. With one such way of relating them I am particularly concerned now. Following our instinct for intellect and knowledge, we acquire pieces of knowledge; and presently, in the generality of men, there arises the desire to relate these pieces of knowledge to our sense for conduct, to our sense for beauty—and there is weariness and dissatisfaction if the desire is balked. Now in this desire lies, I think, the strength of that hold which letters have upon us.

15 All knowledge is, as I said just now, interesting; and even items of knowledge which from the nature of the case cannot well be related, but must stand isolated in our thoughts, have their interest. Even lists of exceptions have their interest. If we are studying Greek accents, it is interesting to know that *pais* and *pas,* and some other monosyllables of the same form of declension, do not take the circumflex upon the last syllable of the genitive plural, but vary, in this respect, from the common rule. If we are studying

physiology, it is interesting to know that the pulmonary artery carries dark blood and the pulmonary vein carries bright blood, departing in this respect from the common rule for the division of labour between the veins and the arteries. But every one knows how we seek naturally to combine the pieces of our knowledge together, to bring them under general rules, to relate them to principles; and how unsatisfactory and tiresome it would be to go on forever learning lists of exceptions or accumulating items of fact which must stand isolated.

16 Well, that same need of relating our knowledge, which operates here within the sphere of our knowledge itself, we shall find operating also outside that sphere. We experience, as we go on learning and knowing—the vast majority of us experience—the need of relating what we have learnt and known to the sense which we have in us for conduct, to the sense which we have in us for beauty.

17 A certain Greek prophetess of Mantineia in Arcadia, Diotima by name, once explained to the philosopher Socrates that love and impulse and bent of all kinds is, in fact, nothing else but the desire in men that good should forever be present to them. This desire for good, Diotima assured Socrates, is our fundamental desire, of which fundamental desire every impulse in us is only one particular form. And therefore this fundamental desire it is, I suppose—this desire in men that good should be forever present to them— which acts in us when we feel the impulse for relating our knowledge to our sense for conduct and to our sense for beauty. At any rate, with men in general the instinct exists. Such is human nature. And the instinct, it will be admitted, is innocent, and human nature is preserved by our following the lead of its innocent instincts. Therefore, in seeking to gratify this instinct in question, we are following the instinct of self-preservation in humanity.

18 But, no doubt, some kinds of knowledge cannot be made to directly serve the instinct in question, cannot be directly related to the sense of beauty, to the sense for conduct. These are instrument-knowledges; they lead on to other knowledges which can. A man who passes his life in instrument-knowledges is a specialist. They may be invaluable as instruments to do something beyond, for those who have the gift thus to employ them; and they may be disciplines in themselves wherein it is useful for everyone to have some schooling. But it is inconceivable that the generality of men should pass all their mental life with Greek accents or with formal logic. My friend Professor Sylvester, who is one of the first mathematicians in the world, holds transcendental doctrines as to the virtue of mathematics, but those doctrines are not for common men. In the very Senate House and heart of our English Cambridge I once ventured, though not without an apology for my profaneness, to hazard the opinion that for the majority of mankind a little of mathematics, even, goes a long way. Of course this is quite consistent with their being of immense importance as an instrument to something else; but it is the few who have the aptitude for using them, not the bulk mankind. **19** The natural sciences do not, however, stand on the same footing with these instrument-knowledges. Experience shows us that the generality of men will find more interest in learning that, when a taper burns, the wax is converted into carbonic acid and water, or in learning the explanation of the phenomenon of dew, or in learning how the circulation of the blood is carried on, than they find in learning that the genitive plural of *pais* and *pas* does not take the circumflex on the termination. And one piece of natural knowledge is added to another, and others are added to that, and at last we come to propositions so interesting as Mr. Darwin's famous proposition that "our ancestor was a hairy quadruped furnished with a tail and pointed ears, probably arboreal in his habits." Or we come to propositions of such reach and magnitude as those which Professor Huxley delivers, when he says that the notions of our forefathers about the beginning and the end of the world were all wrong and that nature is the expression of a definite order with which nothing interferes.

20 Interesting indeed, these results of science are, important they are, and we should all of us be acquainted with them. But what I now wish you to mark is that we are still, when they are propounded to us and we receive them, we are still in the sphere of intellect and knowledge. And for the generality of men there will be found, I say, to arise, when they have duly taken in the proposition that their ancestor was "a hairy quadruped furnished with a tail and pointed ears, probably arboreal in his habits," there will be found to arise an invincible desire to relate this proposition to the sense in us for conduct and to the sense in us for beauty. But this the men of science will not do for us and will hardly even profess to do. They will give us other pieces of knowledge, other facts, about other animals and their ancestors, or about plants, or about stones, or about stars; and they may finally bring us to those great "general conceptions of the universe, which are forced upon us all," says Professor Huxley, "by the progress of physical science." But still it will be *knowledge* only which they give us; knowledge not put for us into relation with our sense for conduct, our sense for beauty, and touched with emotion by being so put; not thus put for us, and therefore, to the majority of mankind, after a certain while, unsatisfying, wearying.

21 Not to the born naturalist, I admit. But what do we mean by a born naturalist? We mean a man in whom the zeal for observing nature is so uncommonly strong and eminent that it marks him off from the bulk of mankind. Such a man will pass his life happily in collecting natural knowledge and reasoning upon it, and will ask for nothing, or hardly anything, more. I have heard it said that the sagacious and admirable naturalist whom we lost not very long ago, Mr. Darwin, once owned to a friend that for his part he did not experience the necessity for two things which most men find so necessary to them—religion and poetry; science and the domestic affections, he thought, were enough. To a born naturalist, I can well understand that this should seem so. So absorbing is his occupation with nature, so strong his love for his occupation, that he goes on acquiring natural knowledge and reasoning upon it, and has little time or inclination for thinking about getting it related to the desire in man for conduct, the desire in man for beauty. He relates it to them for himself as he goes along, so far as he feels the need; and he draws from the domestic affections all the additional solace necessary. But then Darwins are extremely rare. Another great and admirable master of natural knowledge, Faraday, was a Sandemanian. That is to say, he related his knowledge to his instinct for conduct and to his instinct for beauty by the aid of that respectable Scottish sectary, Robert Sandeman. And so strong, in general, is the demand of religion and poetry to have their share in a man, to associate themselves with his knowing, and to relieve and rejoice it, that, probably, for one man amongst us with the disposition to do as Darwin did in this respect, there are at least fifty with the disposition to do as Faraday.

22   Education lays hold upon us, in fact, by satisfying this demand. Professor Huxley holds up to scorn mediaeval education with its neglect of the knowledge of nature, its poverty even of literary studies, its formal logic devoted to "showing how and why that which the Church said was true must be true." But the great mediaeval Universities were not brought into being, we may be sure, by the zeal for giving a jejune and contemptible education. Kings have been their nursing fathers, and queens have been their nursing mothers, but not for this. The mediaeval Universities came into being because the supposed knowledge, delivered by Scripture and the Church, so deeply engaged men's hearts, by so simply, easily, and powerfully relating itself to their desire for conduct, their desire for beauty. All other knowledge was dominated by this supposed knowledge and was subordinated to it, because of the surpassing strength of the hold which it gained upon the affections of men, by allying itself profoundly with their sense for conduct, their sense for beauty.

23   But now, says Professor Huxley, conceptions of the universe fatal to the notions held by our forefathers have been forced upon us by physical science. Grant to him that they are thus fatal, that the new conceptions must and will soon become current everywhere, and that every one will finally perceive them to be fatal to the beliefs of our forefathers. The need of humane letters, as they are truly called, because they serve the paramount desire in men that good should be forever present to them—the need of humane letters, to establish a relation between the new conceptions and our instinct for beauty, our instinct for conduct, is only the more visible. The Middle Age could do without humane letters, as it could do without the study of nature, because

its supposed knowledge was made to engage its emotions so powerfully. Grant that the supposed knowledge disappears, its power of being made to engage the emotions will of course disappear along with it—but the emotions themselves, and their claim to be engaged and satisfied, will remain. Now if we find by experience that humane letters have an undeniable power of engaging the emotions, the importance of humane letters in a man's training becomes not less, but greater, in proportion to the success of modern science in extirpating what it calls "mediaeval thinking."

24   Have humane letters, then, have poetry and eloquence, the power here attributed to them of engaging the emotions, and do they exercise it? And if they have it and exercise it, *how* do they exercise it, so as to exert an influence upon man's sense for conduct, his sense for beauty? Finally, even if they both can and do exert an influence upon the senses in question, how are they to relate to them the results—the modern results—of natural science? All these questions may be asked. First, have poetry and eloquence the power of calling out the emotions? The appeal is to experience. Experience shows that for the vast majority of men, for mankind in general, they have the power. Next, do they exercise it? They do. But then, *how* do they exercise it so as to affect man's sense for conduct, his sense for beauty? And this is perhaps a case for applying the Preacher's words: "Though a man labour to seek it out, yet he shall not find it; yea, farther, though a wise man think to know it, yet shall he not be able to find it." Why should it be one thing, in its effect upon the emotions, to say, "Patience is a virtue," and quite another thing, in its effect upon the emotions, to say with Homer, ιλητὸν γὰρ Μοῖραι θυμὸν θέσαν ἀνθρώποισιν—"for an enduring heart have the destinies appointed to the children of men"? Why should it be one thing, in its effect upon the emotions, to say with the philosopher Spinoza, *Felicitas in ea consistit quod homo suum esse conservare potest*—"Man's happiness consists in his being able to preserve his own essence," and quite another thing, in its effect upon the emotions, to say with the Gospel, "What is a man advantaged, if he gain the whole world, and lose himself, forfeit himself?" How does this difference of effect arise? I cannot tell, and I am not much concerned to know; the important thing is that it does arise and that we can profit by it. But how, finally, are poetry and eloquence to exercise the power of relating the modern results of natural science to man's instinct for conduct, his instinct for beauty? And here again I answer that I do not know *how* they will exercise it, but that they can and will exercise it I am sure. But I do not mean that modern philosophical poets and modern philosophical moralists are to come and relate for us, in express terms, the results of modern scientific research to our instinct for conduct, our instinct for beauty. But I mean that we shall find, as a matter of experience, if we know the best that has been thought and uttered in the world—we shall find that the art and poetry and

eloquence of men who lived, perhaps long ago, who had the most limited natural knowledge, who had the most erroneous conceptions about many important matters—we shall find that this art, and poetry, and eloquence, have in fact not only the power of refreshing and delighting us; they have also the power—such is the strength and worth, in essentials, of their authors' criticism of life—they have a fortifying, and elevating, and quickening, and suggestive power, capable of wonderfully helping us to relate the results of modern science to our need for conduct, our need for beauty. Homer's conceptions of the physical universe were, I imagine, grotesque; but really, under the shock of hearing from modern science that "the world is not subordinated to man's use and that man is not the cynosure of things terrestrial," I could, for my own part, desire no better comfort than Homer's line which I quoted just now, τλητὸν γὰρ Μοῖραι θυμὸν θέσαν ἀνθρώποισιν—"for an enduring heart have the destinies appointed to the children of men"!

25   And the more that men's minds are cleared, the more that the results of science are frankly accepted, the more that poetry and eloquence come to be received and studied as what in truth they really are—the criticism of life by gifted men, alive and active with extraordinary power at an unusual number of points—so much the more will the value of humane letters, and of art also, which is an utterance having a like kind of power with theirs, be felt and acknowledged, and their place in education be secured.

26   Let us, therefore, all of us, avoid indeed as much as possible any invidious comparison between the merits of humane letters, as means of education, and the merits of the natural sciences. But when some President of a Section for Mechanical Science insists on making the comparison and tells us that "he who in his training has substituted literature and history for natural science has chosen the less useful alternative," let us make answer to him that the student of humane letters only, will, at least, know also the great conceptions brought in by modern physical science, for science, as Professor Huxley says, forces them upon us all. But the student of the natural sciences only, will, by our very hypothesis, know nothing of humane letters; not to mention that in setting himself to be perpetually accumulating natural knowledge, he sets himself to do what only specialists have in general the gift for doing genially. And so he will probably be unsatisfied, or at any rate incomplete, and even more incomplete than the student of humane letters only.

27   I once mentioned in a school-report how a young man in one of our English training colleges having to paraphrase the passage in *Macbeth* beginning,

> Can'st thou not minister to a mind diseased?

turned this line into, "Can you not wait upon the lunatic?" And I remarked what a curious state of things it would be if every pupil of our national schools knew, let us say, that the moon is two thousand one hundred and sixty miles in diameter, and thought at the same time that a good paraphrase for

> Can'st thou not minister to a mind diseased?

was, "Can you not wait upon the lunatic?" If one is driven to choose, I think I would rather have a young person ignorant about the moon's diameter, but aware that "Can you not wait upon the lunatic?" is bad, than a young person whose education had been such as to manage things the other way.

28 Or to go higher than the pupils of our national schools. I have in my mind's eye a member of our British Parliament who comes to travel here in America, who afterwards relates his travels and who shows a really masterly knowledge of the geology of this great country and of its mining capabilities, but who ends by gravely suggesting that the United States should borrow a prince from our Royal Family, and should make him their king, and should create a House of Lords of great landed proprietors after the pattern of ours; and then America, he thinks, would have her future happily and perfectly secured. Surely, in this case, the President of the Section for Mechanical Science would himself hardly say that our member of Parliament, by concentrating himself upon geology and mineralogy and so on, and not attending to literature and history, had "chosen the more useful alternative."

29 If then there is to be separation and option between humane letters on the one hand and the natural sciences on the other, the great majority of mankind, all who have not exceptional over-powering aptitudes for the study of nature, would do well, I cannot but think, to choose to be educated in humane letters rather than in the natural sciences. Letters will call out their being at more points, will make them live more.

Once the student has discovered, through the process of invention, or discovery of material, something to say on a given subject, he is faced with the problem of selecting and marshalling the available material in order to effect his purpose. Since usually he cannot, and should not, use all the material available to him, he has to select what is most pertinent and cogent. This selected material must then be put in some order, for without order the force of even the best material, though chosen with the keenest of discretion, will be weakened. The classical rhetoricians dealt with the problems of selection and arrangement under that part of rhetoric that the Greeks called *taxis* and the Latins called *dispositio;* we will use the term *arrangement.*

If we are to profit from the classical precepts about *dispositio,* we must come to a clear understanding of what *dispositio* meant for the ancients. For many people, disposition means simply the study of the several parts of a discourse: (1) the *exordium* or introduction; (2) the *narratio* or statement of facts or circumstances that need to be known about the subject of our discourse; (3) the *confirmatio* or proof of our case; (4) the *refutatio* or discrediting of the opposing views; (5) the *peroratio* or conclusion. Classical rhetoric did deal with those parts and in that sequence; but it was concerned with something more. It was concerned also with the strategic planning of the whole composition.

Quintilian hints at the more important concern of disposition when he says that it is to oratory what generalship is to war. It would be folly to hold a general to a fixed, predetermined disposition of his forces. He must be left free to distribute his troops in the order and proportion best suited to cope with the situation in which he may find himself at any particular moment. So he will mass some of his troops at one point on the battle line, thin them out at other points, keep other troops in reserve, and perhaps concentrate his crack troops at the most crucial area. Guided by judgment and imagination, the general stands ready to make whatever adjustments in strategy eventualities may dictate.

Cicero made explicit the twofold aspect of disposition when he said that the orator "ought first to find out what he should say; next to dispose and arrange his matter, not only in a certain order, but according to the weight of the matter and the judgment of the speaker" (*De Oratore*, I, 31). The person bent on persuasion will be guided in his decisions about the appropriate disposition of his resources by a number of considerations:

1. The kind of discourse in which he is engaged—whether deliberative, judicial, or ceremonial.
2. The nature of his subject—a consideration which in turn will determine the quantity and quality of the matter available to him.
3. His own *ēthos*—his personality, his moral and philosophical bias, his limitations and capabilities.
4. The nature of his audience—their age, their social, political, economic, and educational level, their mood at the moment.

What all of this suggests is that disposition is what Aristotle meant by *techne:* an art by which one adapts means to an end.

What the classical rhetoricians seemed to be striving for under *dispositio* was that "subsuming form" which Ronald S. Crane spoke of when he described his own experience in composing an essay. The passage deserves to be quoted in full:

The process of literary composition has often been rather crudely divided, especially by authors of textbooks on English writing, into two stages: a stage of preparatory reading, thinking, planning, incubation, and a stage of putting the materials thus assembled into words; and what happens in the second stage has usually been represented as a direct transference to paper of the ideas or imaginations which the writer has come into possession of in the first stage—as a simple matter, that is, of giving to an acquired content an appropriate verbal form. I have myself taught this easy doctrine to students; but never, I believe, since I began to meditate on the disturbing fact that all too frequently, when I have attempted to write an essay after a long and interested concentration on the subject, and the noting of many exciting ideas and patterns of key terms, and the construction of what looked like a perfect outline, I have found myself unable to compose the first sentence, or even to know what it ought to be about, or, having forced myself to go on, to bring the thing to a satisfying conclusion, whereas, on other occasions, with no more complete preparation, no greater desire to write, and no better state of nerves, I have discovered, to my delight, that nearly everything fell speedily into place, the right words came (or at any rate words which I couldn't change later on), and the sentences and paragraphs followed one another with scarcely a hitch and in an order that still seemed to me the inevitable one when I came to reread the essay in cold blood.

I have had so many more experiences of the first sort than of the second that I have tried to isolate the reason for the difference. And the best way I can explain it is to say that what I failed to attain in the former cases and did somehow, at one moment or another of the total process, in the latter was a kind of intuitive glimpse of a possible subsuming form for the materials, or at least those I attached most importance to, which I had assembled in my mind and notes—a form sufficiently coherent and intelligible, as a form in my mind, so that I could know at once what I must or could do, and what I need not or ought not to do, in what order and with what emphasis in the various parts, in developing my arguments and putting them into words. I have never been able to write anything which seemed to me, in retrospect, to possess any quality of organic wholeness, however uninteresting or thin, except in response to such a synthesizing idea. It is more than a general intention, more than a "theme," and more than an outline in the usual sense of that word; it is, as I have said, a shaping or directing cause, involving at the same time, and in some sort of correlation, the particular conceptual form my subject is to take in my essay, the particular mode of argument or of rhetoric I am to use in discussing it, and the particular end my discussion is to serve: I must know, in some fashion, at least these three things before I can proceed with any ease or success.

From Ronald S. Crane, *The Languages of Criticism and the Structure of Poetry,* The Alexander Lectures, 1951-52. Reprinted by permission of the University of Toronto Press.

If Professor Crane's analysis of the writing process is accurate, composition would seem to exact from the writer a number of preliminary, as well as current, judgments and decisions. In Book VII, Chapter X of his *Institutio Oratoria,* Quintilian pointed out that disposition was concerned with judgments and decisions about questions like these:

1. When is an introduction necessary and when can it be omitted or abbreviated?
2. When should we make our statement of facts continuous and when should we break it up and insert it *passim?*
3. Under what circumstances can we omit the statement of facts altogether?

4. When should we begin by dealing with the arguments advanced by our opponents and when should we begin by proposing our own arguments?

5. When is it advisable to present our strongest arguments first and when is it best to begin with our weakest arguments and work up to our strongest?

6. Which of our arguments will our audience readily accept and which of them must they be induced to accept?

7. Should we attempt to refute our opponents' arguments as a whole or deal with them in detail?

8. How much ethical appeal must we exert in order to conciliate the audience?

9. Should we reserve our emotional appeals for the conclusion or distribute them throughout the discourse?

10. What evidence or documents should we make use of and where in the discourse will this kind of argument be most effective?

These and many other questions will confront the student when he sits down to plan his composition and will call forth all his powers of discretion to decide. The student's native good sense and intuition will be indispensable when he has to make crucial decisions about appropriate strategies, but rhetoric can lay down certain general principles to guide him at this stage. It remains for the student, however, to discern where and how these principles are applicable to a particular situation.

It must be emphasized at this point that the disposition of one's material is not an indifferent matter. The importance of proper arrangement is pointed up by the incident in which the two great Athenian orators, Aeschines and Demosthenes, were engaged in an oratorical contest concerning Ctesiphon's proposal that Demosthenes be rewarded for his services with a golden crown. On that occasion, Aeschines proposed to the judges that Demosthenes be constrained to observe the same order of argument as he had followed in presenting his. But Demosthenes was quick to see that Aeschines' order would be disadvantageous to his own presentation. Accordingly, he pleaded with the judges to allow him to follow whatever order he saw fit. Demosthenes perceived that the arrangement of his arguments could be the decisive factor in the contest. The best of arguments could be weakened or nullified if inserted in the wrong place or if presented with inappropriate emphasis or proportion.

The Parts of a Discourse

Most rhetoricians recognized five parts for the usual argumentative discourse: *exordium, narratio, confirmatio* or *probatio, refutatio,* and *peroratio.* These terms were explained briefly in the introductory chapter of this book. In this text we will deal with four parts, using these labels: introduction, statement of fact, confirmation, and conclusion. This kind of partitioning of the discourse differs from the outlining system that the student may have learned. The outline is usually organized topically; this system of partitioning is determined by the *functions* of the various parts of a discourse.

We will use these four parts as the organizing principle of this chapter, but in accordance with the classical view of *dispositio,* we will be constantly pointing out the adjustments that one may have to make in sequence, proportion, emphasis, and coloring to fit a particular subject, occasion, purpose, or audience.

Introduction

Etymologically, *introduction* means "a leading into." The Greek and Latin rhetorical terms for this part carried the same suggestion. The Greek term *proemium* meant "before the song"; the Latin term *exordium* meant "beginning a web"—by mounting a woof or laying a warp. The basic function then of the introduction is to lead the audience into the discourse. Instinctively we feel that an abrupt, immediate entry into the body of our discourse would unsettle and confuse the audience. We sense that in most instances an audience must, as it were, be "eased into" the subject of the discourse.

Generally this preparation of the audience has a twofold aspect: (1) it informs the audience of the end or object of our discourse, and (2) it disposes the audience to be receptive to what we say. Conceivably, an audience could be well enough informed about a subject and sufficiently predisposed in our favor that the introduction could be made very brief or might be dispensed with entirely. Even under those conditions, however, most of us would feel that some kind of prelude was necessary—if nothing else a joke, an apt quotation, an entertaining anecdote, an ingratiating gesture toward the audience. Aristotle remarked that the introduction to some speeches was comparable to the preliminary flourishes that flute players made before their performance—an overture in which the musicians merely displayed what they could play best in order to gain the favor and attention of the audience for the main performance. Without this kind of "ornamental" introduction, the discourse would have an abrupt, negligent, unfinished air about it. So it is a rare discourse that plunges immediately into "the heart of the matter."

Informing the Audience

Granting then that most compositions require some kind of prelude, let us consider the first of the two main functions of the introduction—informing the audience of the end or subject of our discourse. In doing this, we are seeking to orient the audience, but, even more importantly, we are seeking to convince the audience that the subject of our discourse is worthy of their attention. We can render our subject attractive to the audience by showing that it is important, or momentous, or relevant to the interests of the audience, or startling, or pleasant. The nature of the subject that we have to deal with will determine, of course, which of these topics we will exploit. A subject that is trifling cannot, by any exercise of ingenuity, be made to appear important or momentous. But a trifling subject could be made to appear agreeable or exotic enough to warrant our attention.

Richard Whately in his *Elements of Rhetoric* invented a number of terms to designate the various kinds of introduction designed to arouse interest in our subject:

> 1. *Introduction Inquisitive*—to show that our subject is important, curious, or interesting.

In this example of the "introduction inquisitive," Arnold J. Toynbee asks a provocative question and then seeks to sustain the interest of the reader by suggesting the importance to the modern world of the answer to that question:

> Does history repeat itself? In our Western world in the eighteenth and nineteenth centuries, this question used to be debated as an academic exercise. The spell of well-being which our civilization was enjoying at the time had dazzled our grandfathers into the quaint pharisaical notion that they were "not as other men are"; they had come to believe that our Western society was exempt from the possibility of falling into those mistakes and mishaps that have been the ruin of certain other civilizations whose history, from beginning to end, is an open book. To us, in our generation, the old question has rather suddenly taken on a new and very practical significance. We have awakened to the truth (how, one wonders, could we ever have been blind to it?) that Western man and his works are no more invulnerable than the now extinct civilizations of the Aztecs and the Incas, the Sumerians and the Hittites. So to-day, with some anxiety, we are searching the scriptures of the past to find out whether they contain a lesson that we can decipher. Does history give us

any information about our own prospects? And, if it does, what is the burden of it? Does it spell out for us an inexorable doom, which we can merely await with folded hands—resigning ourselves, as best we may, to a fate that we cannot avert or even modify by our own efforts? Or does it inform us, not of certainties, but of probabilities, or bare possibilities, in our own future? The practical difference is vast, for, on this second alternative, so far from being stunned into passivity, we should be roused to action. On this second alternative, the lesson of history would not be like an astrologer's horoscope; it would be like a navigator's chart, which affords the seafarer who has the intelligence to use it a much greater hope of avoiding shipwreck than when he was sailing blind, because it gives him the means, if he has the skill and courage to use them, of steering a course between charted rocks and reefs.

From *Civilization on Trial,* 1948. Reprinted by permission of Oxford University Press, Inc.

2. *Introduction Paradoxical*—to show that although the points we are trying to establish seem improbable, they must after all be admitted.

Here, from the pen of the British drama critic Kenneth Tynan, is an example of the "introduction paradoxical":

The most characteristic English play on the subject of physical love is Shakespeare's *Antony and Cleopatra.* It is characteristic because it has no love scenes. The English, as their drama represents them, are a nation endlessly communicative about love without ever enjoying it. Full-blooded physical relationships engaged in with mutual delight are theatrically tabu. Thwarted love is preferred, the kind Mr. Coward wrote about in *Brief Encounter,* where two married people (married, of course, to two other people) form a sad and meagre attachment without being able to follow it through. At the end of a play on some quite different subject—religion, perhaps, or politics—it is customary for the hero to say, as he does in *Robert's Wife:* "I was deeply in love with a fine woman," and for the wife to reply: "My dear, dear husband"; but there should be no hint elsewhere in the text that they have as much as brushed lips.

From *Curtains.* Copyright © 1961 by Kenneth Tynan. Reprinted by permission of Atheneum Publishers.

3. *Introduction Corrective*—to show that our subject has been neglected, misunderstood, or misrepresented.

In the first paragraph of the following "introduction corrective," George Orwell states that there is general agreement about the problem but that there is widespread misunderstanding about the cause and the significance of the problem; then in the second paragraph Orwell suggests the "corrective" line that his essay will take:

> Most people who bother with the matter at all would admit that the English language is in a bad way, but it is generally assumed that we cannot by conscious action do anything about it. Our civilization is decadent and our language—so the argument runs—must inevitably share in the general collapse. It follows that any struggle against the abuse of language is a sentimental archaism, like preferring candles to electric light or hansom cabs to aeroplanes. Underneath this lies the half-conscious belief that language is a natural growth and not an instrument which we shape for our own purposes.
>
> Now, it is clear that the decline of a language must ultimately have political and economic causes: it is not due simply to the bad influence of this or that individual writer. But an effect can become a cause, reinforcing the original cause and producing the same effect in an intensified form, and so on indefinitely. A man may take to drink because he feels himself to be a failure, and then fail all the more completely because he drinks. It is rather the same thing that is happening to the English language. It becomes ugly and inaccurate because our thoughts are foolish, but the slovenliness of our language makes it easier for us to have foolish thoughts. The point is that the process is reversible. Modern English, especially written English, is full of bad habits which spread by imitation and which can be avoided if one is willing to take the necessary trouble. If one gets rid of these habits one can think more clearly, and to think clearly is a necessary first step toward political regeneration: so that the fight against bad English is not frivolous and is not the exclusive concern of professional writers. I will come back to this presently, and I hope that by that time the meaning of what I have said here will have become clearer. Meanwhile, here are five specimens of the English language as it is now habitually written.

> From George Orwell, "Politics and the English Language," *Shooting an Elephant and Other Essays*. Reprinted by permission of Harcourt Brace Jovanovich, Miss Sonia Brownell, and Secker & Warburg, Ltd.

4. *Introduction Preparatory*—to explain an unusual mode of developing our subject; or to forestall some misconception of our purpose; or to apologize for some deficiencies.

Here, in the first paragraph of Rachel Carson's *The Sea Around Us,* is an example of the "introduction preparatory," an introduction in which Miss Carson explains how she will proceed, lacking eye-witness accounts of the event, in tracing the history of the beginning of the ocean:

Beginnings are apt to be shadowy, and so it is with the beginnings of that great mother of life, the sea. Many people have debated how and when the earth got its ocean, and it is not surprising that their explanations do not always agree. For the plain and inescapable truth is that no one was there to see, and in the absence of eye-witness accounts there is bound to be a certain amount of disagreement. So if I tell here the story of how the young planet Earth acquired an ocean, it must be a story pieced together from many sources and containing many whole chapters the details of which we can only imagine. The story is founded on the testimony of the earth's most ancient rocks, which were young when the earth was young; on other evidence written on the face of the earth's satellite, the moon; and on hints contained in the history of the sun and the whole universe of star-filled space. For although no man was there to witness this cosmic birth, the stars and the moon and the rocks were there, and, indeed, had much to do with the fact that there is an ocean.

From *The Sea Around Us,* 1951. Reprinted by permission of Oxford University Press, Inc.

5. *Introduction Narrative*—to rouse interest in our subject by adopting the anecdotal lead-in.

The anecdotal opening is one of the oldest and most effective gambits for seizing the attention of the reader. Here, from an article in *The Nation* about the mysterious murder of eight-year-old Melvin Dean Nimer's mother and father, is an example of the "introduction narrative":

A light flashed on the central switchboard of the New York Telephone Company office in Forest Avenue, West Brighton, S. I., at precisely 2:04 A.M., September 2, 1958. Mrs. Catherine B. Thompson, one of the operators on duty, plugged in on the line. She heard the sound of heavy breathing. "Hello," she said, "hello." There was no answer, just that heavy, breathing sound. Mrs. Thompson turned to another operator, Mrs. Florence Parkin, and asked her to trace the call. Mrs. Parkin quickly found that it was coming from a house at 242 Vanderbilt Avenue. Then she cut in on the line, holding it open, while Mrs. Thompson notified police that something appeared to be wrong.

Even as Mrs. Thompson was speaking to the desk sergeant at the St. George police station, Mrs. Parkin heard the labored breathing on the line turn into a voice. A woman gasped: "I've been stabbed."

The operator immediately cut the police in on the conversation, and both she and the desk officer heard the woman repeat: "I've been stabbed. I've been attacked with a knife." A second later, the voice added: "My husband has been stabbed, too."

Then there was silence. It lasted only a second. Then a new voice, a little boy's voice, came on the wire.

"My mother is bleeding," the voice said.

Mrs. Thompson told the boy police already were on the way.

"I'll wait for the police outside," he said.

"No," she told him, "you better stay with your mother."

Such was the beginning of a drama that was to shock the nation.

From Fred J. Cook and Gene Gleason, "He Never Had a Chance," *A View of The Nation: An Anthology, 1955-1959,* ed. H. M. Christman, pp. 152-3. Reprinted by permission of THE NATION, 333 Sixth Avenue, New York.

These are the common ways in which authors rouse interest in their subject at the same time that they are informing their readers of the object of their discourse. Obviously, there will be times when we do not have to rouse interest in the subject. The subject may be sufficiently interesting in itself (did Dr. Kinsey have to generate interest in his report about the sexual behavior of men and women?). Or the particular circumstances may make the subject interesting (did Winston Churchill have to fan interest in his subject when he got up in the House of Commons to deliver his "Blood, Toil, Tears, and Sweat" speech?). Or a subject will have its own interest for a particular kind of audience (did the speaker at a convention of geneticists have to whip up an interest in his report on DNA, the element that may hold the key to the creation of human life in a test tube?). Considerations of this sort will determine whether the speaker or writer will have to spend any time in his introduction rousing interest in his subject.

Ingratiating Oneself with the Audience

Even when we do not have to rouse interest in our subject, we may have to spend some time in the introduction establishing our credit with the audience. This function of the introduction, which the Latin rhetoricians called *insinuatio,* is closely tied up with the *ethical appeal* that a discourse must exert. Sometimes an author has to convince an audience that he is qualified to speak on some subject. At other times, he must counteract prejudices or misconceptions either about himself or about the subject of his discourse. Or he must rouse hostility toward those whose point of view he is going to oppose in his discourse.

As the term *insinuation* suggests, the author must, in establishing his authority or counteracting prejudices, proceed with the utmost subtlety. To blatantly lay out his intellectual and moral qualifications—"to flaunt his clippings," as it were—could impress his audience as mere boasting and thereby nullify the intended effect of his recital. Good sense and good taste must guide the writer in presenting his credentials. An audience will usually accept a man's display of his qualifying credentials if he recites the facts with due restraint and a becoming humility. The man who says, "I have spent fifteen years studying the problems of juvenile delinquency in such cities as New York, Chicago, and Los Angeles," will do more to establish his qualifications than the man who says, "My thoroughgoing studies of the problems of juvenile delinquency in many parts of the country have completely discredited the half-baked notions of those who have investigated the problems with more zeal than wisdom." The man who jingles his Phi Beta Kappa key usually stirs up more resentment than confidence.

In the following example, we observe C. P. Snow modestly presenting his qualifications to write about "the two cultures," the sciences and the humanities.

> It is about three years since I made a sketch in print of a problem which had been on my mind for some time. It was a problem I could not avoid just because of the circumstances of my life. The only credentials I had to ruminate on the subject at all came through those circumstances, through nothing more than a set of chances. Anyone with similar experience would have seen much the same things and I think made very much the same comments about them. It just happened to be an unusual experience. By training I was a scientist; by vocation I was a writer. That was all. It was a piece of luck, if you like, that arose through coming from a poor home.
>
> But my personal history isn't the point now. All that I need say is that I came to Cambridge and did a bit of research here at a time of major scientific activity. I was privileged to have a ringside view of one of the most wonderful creative periods in all physics. And it happened through the flukes of war—including meeting W. L. Bragg in the buffet on Kettering station on a very cold morning in 1939, which had a determining influence on my practical life—that I was able, and indeed morally forced, to keep that ringside view ever since. So for thirty years I have had to be in touch with scientists not only out of curiosity, but as a part of a working existence. During the same thirty years I was trying to shape the books I wanted to write, which in due course took me among writers.
>
> From *The Two Cultures: and a Second Look*, 1965. Reprinted by permission of Cambridge University Press.

The man who has to minimize prejudices against him must be equally discreet, but he can usually be more open-handed than the man who has to establish his qualifications. No one resents the man who openly strives to clear himself of charges and misconceptions. An audience's natural sense of fair play stands ready to hear "the other side of the story."

In seeking to remove prejudices, the speaker or writer has a number of courses open to him. He can

1. deny the charges that have created the prejudices against him.
2. admit the charges but deny their alleged magnitude.
3. cite a compensating virtue or action.
4. attribute the discrediting action to an honest mistake on his part or to an accident or to an inescapable compulsion.
5. cite others who were guilty of the same thing but were not so charged.
6. substitute a different motive or cause for the one alleged.
7. inveigh against calumny and malicious insinuation in general.
8. cite the testimony of those who take a different view of the matter.

Here is a short example of a man seeking to remove a prejudice against him. Because of his sympathetic writings about the American colonists, Edmund Burke, the great British Parliamentarian, was suspected of pro-American tendencies and of grounding his sympathies not so much on abstract principles as on considerations of expediency. Note how he meets these charges:

> I am charged with being an American. If warm affection towards those over whom I claim any share of authority be a crime, I am guilty of this charge. But I do assure you (and they who know me publicly and privately will bear witness to me) that if ever one man lived more zealous than another for the supremacy of Parliament and the rights of this imperial crown, it was myself. Many others indeed might be more knowing in the extent or the foundation of these rights. I do not pretend to be an antiquary, a lawyer, or qualified for the chair of professor in metaphysics. I never ventured to put your solid interests upon speculative grounds. My having constantly declined to do so has been attributed to my incapacity for such disquisitions; and I am inclined to believe it is partly the cause. I never shall be ashamed to confess that where I am ignorant I am diffident. I am indeed not very solicitous to clear myself of this imputed incapacity, because men even less conversant than I am in this kind of subtleties and placed in stations to which I ought not to aspire, have, by the mere force of civil discretion, often conducted the affairs of great nations with distinguished felicity and glory.
>
> From *A Letter to John Farr and John Harris, Esqurs., Sheriffs of the City of Bristol, on the Affairs of America,* 1777.

Arousing hostility against one's opponent is usually more effective in the conclusion than in the introduction, for it is easier to discredit a man's *ethos* after one has demolished his arguments. But sometimes it is more expedient to stir up animosity in the introduction. If circumstances make it difficult or impossible to clear oneself of prejudices or suspicion, one might be able to gain a hearing by showing that one's opponent is a fool or a knave. And this is best done in the introduction. We saw how Socrates early in the *Apology* sought to raise suspicions about Meletus's integrity. Socrates thereby "softened up" the audience for his subsequent refutation of Meletus's charges.

In these opening paragraphs of *The Rights of Man* (1791–92), Thomas Paine is seeking to prejudice the audience against Edmund Burke, the man whose political and social views Paine is going to attack in the main body of his book:

> Among the incivilities by which nations or individuals provoke and irritate each other, Mr. Burke's pamphlet on the French Revolution [Burke's *Reflections on the Revolution in France* (1790)] is an extraordinary instance. Neither the people of France nor the National Assembly were troubling themselves about the affairs of England or the English Parliament; and that Mr. Burke should commence an unprovoked attack upon them, both in Parliament and in public, is a conduct that cannot be pardoned on the score of manners, nor justified on that of policy.
>
> There is scarcely an epithet of abuse to be found in the English language with which Mr. Burke has not loaded the French nation and the National Assembly. Everything which rancor, prejudice, ignorance, or knowledge could suggest is poured forth in the copious fury of near four hundred pages. In the strain and on the plan Mr. Burke was writing, he might have written on to as many thousands. When the tongue or the pen is let loose in a frenzy of passion, it is the man, and not the subject, that becomes exhausted.
>
> Hitherto Mr. Burke has been mistaken and disappointed in the opinions he had formed of the affairs of France, but such is the ingenuity of his hope, or the malignancy of his despair, that it furnishes him with new pretenses to go on. There was a time when it was impossible to make Mr. Burke believe there would be any revolution in France. His opinion then was that the French had neither spirit to undertake it nor fortitude to support it; and now that there is one, he seeks an escape by condemning it.

What we have been saying about the content and strategy of the introduction adds up to this: the introduction seeks to render the audience *attentive, benevolent*—that is, well-disposed toward the writer and his cause, and *docile*—that is, ready to be instructed or persuaded. In order to determine what must be done in the introduction to effect these ends, we must consider (1) what we have to say, (2) before whom, (3) under what circumstances, (4) what the prepossessions of the audience are likely to be, (5) how much time or space has been allotted to us. An honest confrontation of those considerations will tell us, not only what we must do in the introduction but how long it has to be. If we see that there is no need to render our audience attentive, benevolent, and docile, our introduction can be very brief—a few ingratiating flourishes and a brief statement of the thesis. But if the occasion demands that the audience be "conditioned," then our introduction may have to be more elaborate.

One caution needs to be stressed here: introductions tend to be disproportionately long. At some time or other, the student has probably heard the classic advice, "Throw away the first page of your rough draft and begin your final draft at the top of page two." Obviously we cannot follow this advice in any mechanical fashion, but the principle here is fundamentally sound. Our first draft is often encumbered with excess fat. One of the reasons why a long "warming up" is so common is that there is a natural inertia to be overcome before we can get under way. Often it is the student with little to say on an assigned topic who produces the top-heavy introduction. He has 800 words to write. If he can spend 400 of these words on preliminaries, he can put off that formidable moment when he has to get down to the subject...and then there are only 400 words to go! If the discipline of the topics can fill up the "dry wells," perhaps we can prevent this tendency to pad the introduction.

Allotted wordage is becoming more and more a major consideration in the determination of the length of introductions. Since space is at such a premium in modern newspapers and magazines, editors are insisting on strict observance of specified word limits. It may be that the nature of our subject or of our audience calls for a fairly elaborate introduction, but we have been asked to develop our thesis in 1200 words. So we shall have to ignore the exigency and get into the body of our discourse as soon as possible. One's writing can profit from the discipline of observing word-limits: nothing serves better to trim the fat from one's prose. Anyone who has been required to write book reviews in 300 to 350 words soon learns many salutary lessons about economy of means.

No mention has been made so far of the kind of opening that immediately captures the reader's interest. In books on the technique of fiction or the feature story, this kind of opening is often called "the hook." A provocative question, a startling hyperbole, an intriguing paradox—these are some of the devices we are advised to use in order to buttonhole our reader. Norman Cousins uses the provocative question effectively in the opening paragraphs of his article "Don't Resign from the Human Race":

> Have you ever wondered what you would say if you were suddenly called upon to defend the human race?
> Suppose you were invited to participate in a great debate or, better still, a mock court trial called for the purpose of deciding whether the human species had justified its right to survive—whether, on the basis

of its virtues and weaknesses, it was actually entitled to the gift of life. Suppose your job was that of attorney for the defense. How would you go about collecting your evidence? What witnesses would you call? What arguments would you use?

From *Saturday Review,* August 7, 1948. Reprinted by permission of the SATURDAY REVIEW, 25 West 45th Street, New York.

There are a number of reasons why such an opening is an attention-getter. First, although the initial question is a *rhetorical question*—a type that does not require a direct and immediate answer from the audience or reader—it does challenge the audience, make them more alert. Another reason for the effectiveness of this particular question is that it is both an unusual question —imagine suggesting that the human race has to justify its right to existence! —and an important one—it may concern our very existence. So the elements of surprise and importance are contributing to the effectiveness of the gambit. The second paragraph further challenges us by posing a hypothetical situation: suppose you were called upon to be the defense attorney for the human race. The final three questions suggest some of the problems that would face us in that capacity. So these opening paragraphs both alert us and disconcert us. Challenged by the importance of the question asked and perhaps somewhat chagrined that we do not have a ready answer for this important question, we are now "set up" to listen to this man's answer.

The student must exercise good taste and judgment when he searches for the opening calculated to arrest attention. The overtly and excessively clever opening can repel readers rather than engage them. (The *New Yorker,* in one of its regular filler features, has a label for such brashly clever openings— Letters We Never Finished Reading.) As usual, the most reliable guide in regard to attractive openings is the nature and temper of the audience.

The closing lines of the introduction should be so managed that they lead easily and naturally into the next division of the discourse. The problem of transition is basically one of coherence. We want the parts of our discourse to "hang together," and while we would like the sutures to be as unobtrusive as possible, we nevertheless want our readers to be aware that they are passing over into another division of the discourse. Aristotle himself, that great master of exposition, is not at all hesitant about marking his transitions explicitly. For instance, at the end of Chapter 1 in Book I of the *Rhetoric* he says, "Let us now try to give some account of the systematic principles of rhetoric itself—of the right method and means of succeeding in the object set before us. We must make as it were a fresh start, and before going further define what rhetoric is." Throughout the *Rhetoric*—in fact, through-out most of his treatises—Aristotle carefully plants these transitional markers —often at the end of a chapter, sometimes at the beginning of a new chapter, occasionally at divisions of an especially long and involved exposition. Sometimes, just the logical development of our thought allows us to glide into the next division without our having to use "pointers." No rule-of-thumb can be laid down to tell us when it is best to mark our transitions explicitly and when we can rely on the logic of our thought development to carry the reader over into the next division. In this respect—as we have seen so often in the discussion of rhetorical strategies—the particular situation will dictate its own exigencies.

One final point about introductions. The things we strive to do in the introduction—to render the audience attentive, benevolent, and docile—have sometimes to be done at various points in the discourse, especially in long discourses. As some of the rhetoricians observed, it is sometimes more necessary to make a play for the attention of the audience at a later stage in the discourse than it is in the introduction. In fact, we can usually rely on a certain natural attentiveness in our audience at the beginning of our discourse, which may flag as we continue. In that case, we may have to pull our audience up again. Likewise, when we are about to launch forth into a particularly delicate argument, we may have to make another play for the good will of our audience.

Statement of Fact

We have used the term *statement of fact* to designate the second division of a discourse for want of a better term to translate the Latin *narratio. Narration* has taken on meanings for us that it did not have for the Romans. *Statement of fact* has its own ambiguities for us, but the term suggests more accurately than does *narration* what it is that we do in this part of expository and argumentative prose.

Statement of fact figured principally in forensic oratory. In this division of a forensic speech, the advocate set forth the essential facts of the case under consideration. "On the night of March 15," we can imagine him saying, "Gaius Maximus was murdered in a back alley off the Forum. It has been alleged that my client, who was seen in the Forum that evening and who was known to be a political enemy of the deceased, was the murderer. Suspicion about my client has not been dispelled by the revelation that at the time of the murder my client was seen. . . ." If the prosecuting lawyer had previously set forth these facts, the defending lawyer might use this part in his speech to add pertinent facts or to correct details in the prosecution's statement. In a court trial, what often initiates this part of the trial is the reading of the formal indictment against the defendant—in other words, the defining of the issue in the case. For example, here was the indictment read by Attorney General A. T. Stewart on the second day of the "Monkey Trial" in July

1925—a trial that became a *cause célèbre* partly because of the conflict that developed in the courtroom between William Jennings Bryan and Clarence Darrow:

> That John Thomas Scopes, heretofore on the 24th of April, 1925, in the county aforesaid, then and there, unlawfully did wilfully teach in the public schools of Rhea County, Tennessee, which said public schools are supported in part and in whole by the public school fund of the state, a certain theory and theories that deny the story of the divine creation of man as taught in the Bible, and did teach instead thereof that man has descended from a lower order of animals, he, the said John Thomas Scopes, being at the time, and prior thereto, a teacher in the public schools of Rhea County, Tennessee, aforesaid, against the peace and dignity of the State.
>
> From the official transcript of the trial *State of Tennessee vs. John Thomas Scopes,* Nos. 5231 and 5232, in the Circuit Court of Rhea County, Tennessee,
> p. 123.

Anyone familiar with the trial or with *Inherit the Wind,* the play based on the trial, knows that the argument frequently drifted far from the charge specified in that indictment. But despite all the pyrotechnic oratory about the larger issues involved in this case, the jury did eventually return a verdict of "guilty as charged."

Since the province of forensic discourse is the past, there is usually a set of facts or details to be recited for the benefit of the judge and jury. Ordinarily these "facts" have to be stated before they can be proved or refuted, and so *narratio* became a regular part of the oratory of the courtroom. Deliberative oratory, on the other hand, deals with the future, and consequently there are, strictly speaking, no "facts" to be recited. Because deliberative oratory argues about things that must be done, rather than things that have been done, *narratio* was regarded as an unnecessary, certainly as a dispensable, part of this kind of speech.

But the deliberative orator—and the ceremonial orator too—often felt the need to recite past events as a basis for his recommendations about the future. As a result, *narratio* began to figure in deliberative and ceremonial oratory as well as in forensic. Whether or not statement of fact is a necessary part of deliberative or ceremonial discourse is debatable; but the fact of the matter is that most discourses, of whatever kind, *do* devote a section—the one immediately following the introduction—to a statement of fact. Recognizing that a *statement of fact* can often be dispensed with, let us go on to consider what is done and in what manner in this part of a discourse.

The statement of fact is fundamentally *expository*. In this section we are informing our readers of the circumstances that need to be known about our subject. If the readers are sufficiently informed about the subject under consideration, we can dispense with this part altogether. But most of the time, even well-informed readers will appreciate, even if they do not require, some recital of the circumstances, the details, the state of the question.

It is customary for authors of scholarly articles to summarize briefly the history of the idea they are going to discuss in their article. Here is an example of that kind of statement of fact from an article entitled "Charles Lamb's Contribution to the Theory of Dramatic Illusion." The final sentence of the author's introduction provides a transition to the statement of fact: "Before discussing Lamb's view, which was the product of numerous visits to the playhouse, it would be well to keep in mind the broad outlines of the main theories advanced before the Romantic period." The article continues:

> Neo-classical theory was committed, or thought it was committed, to advocating the dramatic unities of time, place, and action because it insisted upon the necessity of literal delusion. As might be expected, the late seventeenth century emphasized the rational aspect of the unities: it is unreasonable, the argument ran, to think that a spectator is able to pretend that the events of two days can be crowded into a few hours, or to demand that the audience, having transported itself to Asia, should be required to leap to Africa a few moments later. To make such demands is unfair, and to think that an audience can comply with them is, this view maintains, unreasonable. But in the eighteenth century a reply was evolved which gained increasing acceptance with audiences and with literary critics. Reasonable or not, this counterargument said, the mind can transport itself as easily to Africa from Asia as it can journey to Asia in the first place. The problem is not one of "reason" or "reasonableness," but of what, in fact (not in theory), the imagination is capable of doing. Dr. Johnson is somewhat in this second tradition, but he goes further than merely saying that the mind can hop about from place to place and condense time and space at its will. He insists that the playwright should not encumber himself with the unities (which at best might prevent a man from being a bad playwright, but could never make him a good one), but he denied that the spectator is literally deluded (by imagination or by reason) into believing he is watching a reality and not a play. Such is Johnson's broad theoretical generalization. We should perhaps keep in mind his practice—his reluctance, for example, to read *King Lear,* because Cordelia's death caused him such pain.
>
> From Sylvan Barnet, "Charles Lamb's Contribution to the Theory of Dramatic Illusion," *PMLA*, LXIX (Dec. 1954), 1150-59. Reprinted by permission of the Modern Language Association of America.

Because of the audience for which this article was written—mainly teachers of English on the university level—this summary of previous doctrines can be more abbreviated than it could be if the article were directed to a lay audience. This summary does not so much *inform* the audience as *remind* it.

As in this example from a scholarly article, we often will have occasion to present a summary of what others have thought or said on the theme we are going to develop in our composition. Closely allied to this kind of summary of relevant views advanced by others is the summary of views that we are going to support or refute in our essay. In the following example, Norman Podhoretz summarizes the main theses from Hannah Arendt's book *Eichmann in Jerusalem* that he is going to take issue with in his article. The final sentence of Mr. Podhoretz's introduction, which provides a transition to this statement of fact, read, "The point to begin with, then, is Miss Arendt's thesis, and the problem to settle is whether it justifies the distortions of perspective it creates and the cavalier treatment of evidence it impels." Then—

> According to Miss Arendt, the Nazis, in order to carry out their genocidal plan against the Jews, needed Jewish cooperation and in fact received it "to a truly extraordinary degree." This cooperation took the form of "administrative and police work," and it was extended by "the highly assimilated Jewish communities of Central and Western Europe" no less abundantly than by "the Yiddish-speaking masses of the East." In Amsterdam as in Warsaw, in Berlin as in Budapest, Miss Arendt writes,
>
> > Jewish officials could be trusted to compile the lists of persons and of their property, to secure money from the deportees to defray the expenses of their deportation and extermination, to keep track of vacated apartments, to supply police forces to help seize Jews and get them on trains, until, as a last gesture, they handed over the assets of the Jewish community in good order for final confiscation.
>
> All this has long been known. What is new is Miss Arendt's assertion that if the Jews (or rather, their leaders) had not cooperated in this fashion, "there would have been chaos and plenty of misery but the total number of victims would hardly have been between four and a half to six million people."
>
> So much for the Jews. As for the Nazis, carrying out the policy of genocide required neither that they be monsters nor pathological Jew-haters. On the contrary: since the murder of Jews was dictated by the law of the state, and since selfless loyalty to the law was regarded by the Germans under Hitler as the highest of virtues, it even called for a certain idealism to do what Eichmann and his cohorts did. Miss Arendt in this connection quotes the famous remark attributed to Himmler: "To have stuck it out and, apart from exceptions caused by human weakness, to have remained decent, that is what has made us hard." Eichmann, then, was telling the truth when he denied having been an anti-Semite: he did his duty to the best of his ability, and he would have performed with equal zeal even if he had loved the Jews. Thus, also, the Israeli

prosecutor Gideon Hausner was absurdly off the point in portraying Eichmann as a brute and a sadist and a fiend: Eichmann was in actual fact a banal personality, a nonentity whose evil deeds flowed not from anything in his own character, but rather from his position in the Nazi system.

This system is, of course, known as totalitarianism, and it is totalitarianism that brings the two halves of Miss Arendt's thesis together. Long ago, David Rousset, Bruno Bettelheim, and Miss Arendt herself taught us that securing the complicity of the victim is one of the distinguishing ambitions of totalitarian states, and her tale of Jewish complicity here is offered (at least on the surface) as yet another illustration of this point. Long ago, too, she and her colleagues taught us that totalitarian states aim at the destruction of common-sense reality and the creation of a new reality moulded to the lineaments of the official ideology, and her conception of Eichmann as an ordinary man whose conscience was made to function "the other way around" is similarly set forth in illustration of the more general point. Obviously, though, this ordinary man could not have been turned into so great and devoted a perpetrator of evil if the system had not been so tightly closed—if, that is to say, there had been voices to protest or gestures of resistance. Such voices as existed, however, were in Miss Arendt's judgment pathetically small and thin, and such gestures of resistance as were displayed she finds relatively insignificant. Not only did "good society everywhere" accept the Final Solution with "zeal and eagerness," but the Jews themselves acquiesced and even cooperated—as we have seen—"to a truly extraordinary degree." Here, then, is the finishing touch to Miss Arendt's reading of the Final Solution, and the explanation she gives for dwelling on Jewish complicity: this chapter of the story, she says, "offers the most striking insight into the totality of the moral collapse the Nazis caused in respectable European society—not only in Germany but in almost all countries, not only among the persecutors but also among the victims."

From Norman Podhoretz, "Hannah Arendt on Eichmann: A Study in the Perversity of Brilliance," *Commentary*, XXXVI (Sept. 1963), 201-8. Copyright 1963 by the American Jewish Committee and reprinted by their permission.

The passage just quoted may strike the student as being an inordinately long statement of fact. But it is not really long when viewed in relation to the entire article, which covers eight double-column pages in the magazine. We quoted a fairly long passage to show what proportion a statement of fact might take in an extended discourse. In a shorter article, of course, the statement of fact, if one was needed, would have to be considerably condensed. As always, the importance and complexity of the subject matter and the depth of treatment we choose to give it will also dictate the proper length of the statement of fact. If Mr. Podhoretz had been writing a mere review of Miss Arendt's book he could not have given as much space as he does here to the *narratio.*

Quintilian advises that the instruction of the audience in the statement of fact be *lucid, brief,* and *plausible.* These three qualities are, of course, relative to the speech situation. An exposition that is lucid and plausible for one audience might not be either for another. Therefore, as in our discussion of the strategies of the introduction, we can lay down no hard-and-fast rules about the management of the statement of fact. We must adapt our means to the *ad hoc* situation. All we can do here is point to some of the ways that might be used to achieve the qualities that Quintilian mentions, and trust to the student to choose those ways which will best fit the situation in which he finds himself.

Lucidity is largely a matter of style, a matter of so selecting and arranging words that we easily communicate our meaning to our audience. We will delay our discussion of this means of securing lucidity until the next chapter, on style. Lucidity, of course, should characterize all parts of the discourse. Here we will mention only those means of securing lucidity peculiar to the statement of fact. We will be clear if, first of all, we develop our exposition sufficiently to set forth all the facts that need to be known. A severe abridgement of the exposition could result in obscurity. On the other hand, an excessive elaboration could so clutter up the exposition that the main points are obscured. An *orderly* presentation of the facts will also aid lucidity. Sometimes *chronological order* will be the organizing principle of our exposition—first this happened, then this, then this, etc. At other times we will employ an order that moves *from the general to the particular* or *from the more familiar to the less familiar.*

Another aid to lucidity is the device that the Greeks called *enargeia* and that we may translate as *palpability* or *vividness. Enargeia* will be especially useful when our statement of fact lends itself more to a narrative treatment than to an expository treatment—as, for instance, in a recital of past events. Here if we can paint a word-picture of the scene instead of merely telling what happened we can produce that vividness—not to mention the emotional impact—which will etch the "facts" in the imaginations of our readers. One can imagine a prosecuting lawyer describing Raskolnikov's crime in words like these:

> He pulled the axe quite out, swung it with both arms, scarcely conscious of himself, and almost without effort, almost mechanically, brought the blunt side down on her head.... The old woman was as always bareheaded. Her thin, light hair, streaked with grey, thickly smeared with grease, was plaited in a rat's tail and fastened by a broken horn comb which stood out on the nape of her neck. As she was so short, the blow fell on the very top of her skull. She cried out, but very faintly, and suddenly sank all of a heap on the floor, raising her hands to her head.
>
> From Fyodor Dostoyevsky, *Crime and Punishment,* Part I, Chapter 7, translated by Constance Garnett.

In Dostoyevsky's novel, this vivid narrative is not part of a prosecuting law-yer's representation in a courtroom, but such a description could be, and often has been, the manner in which a lawyer manages the statement of fact in a case. There is no doubt about the clarity and effectiveness of such a presenta-tion. And while *enargeia* can be employed in other parts of a discourse, it most often finds its opportunity in the statement of fact.

Before we leave the subject of lucidity, we should make the point that clarity of statement does not always serve our purpose. There may be occa-sions when it is expedient for us deliberately to obfuscate the exposition. If the facts tell against us, it might be best at this point to omit the statement of fact altogether or to render our exposition ambiguous. It might be that a frank, lucid recital of the facts would so alienate our audience that they would become indisposed to listen to our proofs later on. The particular situ-ation will dictate when it is prudent to adopt the strategy of omission or obfuscation.

Brevity of statement, as we remarked in our comments on the passage quoted from Norman Podhoretz's article, will also be determined by the particular situation. Aristotle scoffed at the prescription that the statement of fact be brief. He asked why the statement of fact had to be short or long. Why couldn't it be just right? In this characteristic insistence on the *via media,* Aristotle is calling for the length that is appropriate to the needs of the moment. The principle of "just enough" is the only general prescript that has validity here. We will achieve this due brevity if (1) we start our recital at a point where it begins to concern our readers (comparable to Horace's precept that we begin a story *in medias res* instead of *ab ovo*); (2) we ex-clude all irrelevancies; (3) we excise anything, however relevant, which contributes little or nothing to our readers' understanding of our case or to their friendly disposition toward our cause.

The plausibility of the statement of fact will result partly from the ethical tone of the discourse itself or from the ethical image of the writer. Readers will believe that the situation is as it has been described if they trust the authority or the character of the writer. The ethical appeal, of course, is im-portant in all parts of the discourse, but we must not minimize its importance in this part of the discourse, which is concerned with a bare recital of the facts.

We can further enhance the credibility of our statement of fact by being careful not to say anything contrary to nature or to historical fact, by assign-ing believable causes or reasons for events, by trusting more to understate-ment than to hyperbole. An audience is amazingly quick to detect that a writer "doth protest too much." If we alienate the credence of our readers at this state of the discourse, we jeopardize our chances of holding them when we come to the all-important stage of proof.

Confirmation

The use of the term *confirmation* to label this part may suggest that this division figures only in persuasive discourse. But if we regard *confirmation* or *proof* as the designation of that part where we get down to the main business of our discourse, this term can be extended to cover expository as well as argumentative prose. The previously discussed parts, the introduction and the statement of fact, certainly figure in both expository and argumentative discourse. If these two parts are regarded as the preliminaries, confirmation then may be regarded as the core, the central part, the main body, of our discourse—the part in which we do what we set out to do, whether that be to explain or to persuade. A good deal of what we say about confirmation is, of course, applicable only to argumentative discourse, but many of the precepts concerning this part of the discourse are equally applicable to expository prose. When we are talking about confirmation in the narrow sense of demonstrating or refuting an argument, this will be readily apparent to the student.

Because of the difficulty of illustrating the disposition of arguments by quoting short passages, such as we used in illustrating the previous two parts, we shall postpone exemplifying the points made until we come to consider whole essays in the readings at the end of this chapter.

It is in this part of the discourse principally that we use the material we have gathered in the process of invention. We must select and dispose this material for maximum effectiveness. The processes of invention and disposition are not really as independent of one another as we may have suggested by giving them separate treatments. In reading, the activity of evaluation can take place almost simultaneously with the activity of comprehension. Likewise, in composing, we are often engaged with the problems of selecting and arranging our material even while we are engaged in discovering our material. We have discussed invention and disposition separately partly because there is a sense in which we must *discover* before we can *arrange* and partly because there is a pedagogical convenience to a separate discussion of these two processes.

One of the main problems we face in this part of the discourse is the problem of sequence. What point do we take up first? Once we have dealt with that point, then what point do we take up? In expository discourse, we can sometimes organize our material according to a chronological scheme—as, for instance, in an explanation of a relatively simple process, like changing a tire. In the exposition of a more complicated subject, we may have to move from the general to the particular or from the familiar to the unknown.

Usually the nature of the thing to be explained will suggest the appropriate procedure.

In argumentative discourse, however, these organizing principles cannot always be relied on, for we are faced with questions like these: should I begin with my weakest arguments and build up to my strongest arguments? should I refute the opposing arguments first and then present my arguments, or should I establish my case first and then refute the opposition? As usual, the particular situation will dictate the appropriate strategy, and perhaps all that can be done here is to lay down some guidelines for the student.

As a general rule, in presenting our own arguments we should not descend from our strongest arguments to our weakest. More often than not, such an anticlimactic order will considerably weaken the effectiveness of our suasive efforts. We want to leave our strongest argument ringing in the memory of our audience; hence we usually place it in the emphatic final position. If we present our strongest arguments first and then add a series of weaker arguments, we will diminish the effectiveness of the strong ones. The audience may get the impression that our case, solid at first sight, is beginning to unravel. The weaker arguments will strike the audience as being so many "after-thoughts." This suggests that the writer does not really have confidence in the cogency of his strong arguments, that he feels the need for adding some props. If he thus betrays a lack of confidence, he will dispel the confidence of his readers.

If we have available a number of arguments of co-ordinate value, we can arrange these arguments in almost any order. But even here we might be guided by certain principles. Where our arguments are of relatively equal strength, it might be best to present first those arguments that are likely to have suggested themselves to our readers. If we gain concurrence for the familiar arguments, we condition our readers to receive the unfamiliar. We have confirmed what they suspected and then have added what they did not know before.

If we have available to us a number of relatively strong and weak arguments, we might find it best to start out with a strong argument, then slip in some of the weaker arguments, and then end up with the strongest argument. The initial strong argument conditions the audience to receive the weaker arguments; but then, just when the weaker arguments threaten to diminish the effectiveness of our opening argument, we come in with our strongest argument. The surprise that attends the introduction of a strong argument just when it seemed that we had "shot our bolt" will enhance the cogency of the final argument.

Refutation

So far we have been dealing only with the strategic sequence of arguments when we have merely to confirm our own case. Some additional problems present themselves when we have also to refute opposing views. In a public debate, involving an alternation of speakers, opposing views are actually voiced, and we have to decide which of the opposing arguments must be dealt with and whether we should refute the arguments first and then present our own arguments or present our own first and then refute the opposition. When we sit down to write an argumentative piece, there is no opponent whom we must confront and answer. Nevertheless, there usually is implicit in the issue we are discussing an opposing view that we must meet and dispose of. In such cases, it is not enough to establish our own case. However cogent our arguments may be, doubts will remain in the minds of our readers if we do not anticipate the objections to our thesis and answer those objections.

If the opposing views have been well received by the audience, it is usually advisable that we refute those views before we attempt to present our own arguments. People who are favorably disposed to the opposite point of view will not readily open their minds to our arguments, however valid and cogent they may be. The ground must be cleared, as it were, before we can parade our support.

It can never be an inflexible rule, however, that we must first refute the opposing arguments before we present our own. Where the opposing arguments are relatively weak, we can afford to delay answering them until after we have established our own case. In such instances, the cogency of our arguments will further dispose the audience to recognize the weakness of the opposing arguments. And even when the opposing arguments are strong and are favorably received by the audience, it will sometimes be expedient to delay refuting them. When an audience, for instance, is inordinately hostile to our view, the wisest strategy may be to keep the opposing arguments out of sight as long as possible. By reminding a hostile audience of opposing arguments at the outset, we could so confirm the audience in their prejudices that they would not lend an ear to our refutation of those arguments. Under those circumstances, presenting our own arguments first might dispose an audience at least to listen to our refutation.

As has been constantly emphasized so far in this chapter, no inflexible rules can be laid down dictating what must be done and in what sequence. The writer must be prepared to adapt his means to his end and to adjust his strategies to fit the particular situation. He must "feel" his way through any given situation. Because some writers have a natural sense, or develop a sense, for what are the "right" means in any given situation, they often succeed where others fail. Unfortunately, rhetoric cannot give rules-of-thumb that will cover every situation, but we can briefly review some of the available means of refuting opposing views.

Refutation by Appeal to Reason

There are two general ways in which we can refute a proposition: we can prove the contradictory of that proposition; we can demolish the arguments by which the proposition is supported. As we saw in the previous chapter, if we prove that one of a pair of contradictory propositions is true, we automatically prove that the other proposition is false. Proving a contradictory proposition can be the most compelling kind of refutation, since all men, because of their rational nature, readily recognize the principle that a thing cannot at the same time *be* and *not be*.

We are not always presented, however, with the convenience of contradictorily opposed arguments. More often we are faced with the challenge of refuting *contrary* propositions. One side maintains that a certain course of action is wise, and the other side maintains that it is foolish. In that case, we must knock out the props supporting the contrary assertion. We can do this (1) by denying the truth of one of the premises on which the argument rests and proving, perhaps through evidence or testimony, that the premise is false, or (2) by objecting to the inferences drawn from the premises. In rejecting the inferences, we say such things as, "I admit the principle, but I deny that it leads to such a consequence" or "I admit the principle but I deny that it applies in this case" or "Your assertion is true, but it has no force as an argument to support your conclusion."

These are ways of refuting arguments logically, but sometimes we have to deal with probabilities, which cannot be demolished by means of strict logic. In that case, we must draw on those enthymemes and examples which, if they do not refute the opposition conclusively, do have persuasive value. The emotional and ethical appeals, which we discussed in the previous chapter, will play their part in refutation too.

Refutation by Emotional Appeals

Knowledge of one's audience is perhaps nowhere more important than when one is using emotional appeals. A miscalculation about the temper of one's audience could destroy or reverse the intended effect. The wrong emotional appeal or an emotional appeal applied at an inappropriate place in the discourse or a disproportionate emotional appeal could not only render our refutation ineffectual but also diminish confidence in our previously established proof.

It should be obvious that emotional appeals will succeed better with some audiences than with others. One's problems with emotional appeals will increase in proportion to the heterogeneity of the audience. One can appreciate Senator Richard Nixon's dilemma in 1952 when he had to make decisions about the kind and degree of emotional appeal to employ in his address to a nationwide television audience in defense of his handling of campaign funds. Judging from the response to his speech, one would have to conclude that Mr. Nixon calculated wisely. His references to "the cloth coat" and to the "little dog Checkers" totally alienated one segment of the television audience. But for the majority of the audience, those references were the emotional touches which capped his apologia.

It would seem that when addressing a large, heterogeneous audience, one must estimate which emotional appeals are likely to succeed with the major portion of the audience. In other words, we may have to sacrifice the concurrence of one part of our audience in order to gain the assent of the major portion. The author who writes a piece for the *New Republic* or *Commonweal* or *The National Review* has, in many ways, an easier task than the author who writes an argumentative piece for *Life* or *Look,* because the writer for magazines of limited circulation can presume more political, philosophical, or religious homogeneity in his audience than can the writer for the mass-circulation magazines.

Refutation by Ethical Appeal

The ethical appeal must pervade all parts of the discourse, but it is nowhere more important than in this part where we are seeking to prove our case or refute the opposition. So important is the ethical appeal in effecting persuasion that Aristotle said "it is more fitting for a good man to display himself as an honest fellow than as a subtle reasoner" (*Rhetoric,* III, 17). Sometimes when our case is weak, the ethical appeal, exerted either by the image of the writer or by the tone of the discourse, will carry the day. The effectiveness of the ethical appeal where one's case is weak was particularly evident in the speech that General Douglas MacArthur delivered before Congress in 1951 when he returned to this country after being relieved of his command in Korea. Old soldiers *do* die, but they sometimes achieve a kind of immortality in the minds of the people they have served.

Refutation by Wit

The Earl of Shaftesbury once claimed that "ridicule is the test of truth." Shaftesbury was suggesting that if what was alleged to be the truth could survive the onslaught of ridicule it must really be the truth. If Shaftesbury's claim can be accepted at all it must be accepted with reservations. A genuine truth might very well be reduced to absurdity by a witty rhetorician, but it would remain the truth despite its having been discredited in the minds of the audience.

Jests, sarcasm, and irony can be effective tools for refutation, but they must be used with the utmost discretion. The Greek rhetorician Gorgias advised that we should "kill our opponent's seriousness with our ridicule and his ridicule with our seriousness." Gorgias was shrewd enough to see that many times we cannot counteract the opposition by employing similar tactics. And since it is often difficult to "top" a display of wit, we might do well to avoid matching humorous sallies with our opponent and to adopt a becoming seriousness. On the other hand, we can sometimes destroy the effectiveness of a soberly presented argument by wittily reducing the argument to absurdity. The student must be cautioned however; he risks the dissipation of his ethical appeal if his wit is merely a cloak for weak or specious arguments. Witty but empty retorts can fool some of the people some of the time, but the man who is scrupulous about his tactics will not sacrifice integrity for success.

A joke can be used simply to disarm an audience or to dispose an audience favorably. When a joke is employed for these purposes, it is most often found in the introduction, the most obvious place for those devices which are calculated to ingratiate the speaker or writer with his audience. But the disarming kind of joke can sometimes be used in the confirmation also—as, for instance, when we are about to launch into an argument that we suspect will not readily gain acceptance.

But the joke can also be used for purposes of refutation if it provides some kind of analogy to the point we are seeking to discredit. The analogous joke can induce an audience to take an objective view of the point being discussed. If we can get an audience laughing at a situation somewhat removed from the point being attacked, we will find it easier to make the audience perceive the absurdity when we make an application of the analogy.

With certain audiences, the more sophisticated varieties of humor will succeed best. One of the most effective kinds of sophisticated humor, especially for the purpose of disarming an audience, is the good-humored bantering in which the speaker or writer makes depreciatory remarks about himself. Almost everyone responds favorably to the man who takes himself down a peg or two, mainly because everyone likes to feel that a man, however exalted, is human after all and that he does not exaggerate his own importance or achievements. Although depreciation of others may sometimes backfire on us, belittling of ourselves will never arouse anyone's resentment and rarely undercut anyone's confidence in us.

The light touch resulting from an urbane finesse with words is another brand of humor that wears well with certain audiences, especially with the educated. As will be seen in the next chapter on style, many of the figures of speech can be used for this kind of beguiling verbal humor. Puns, for instance, have come to be regarded as a low form of humor, but most of the great writers, from Shakespeare to James Thurber, indulged in plays on words (the rhetoricians called it *paronomasia*) and felt no need to apologize for their verbal acrobatics. Irony is a subtle form of verbal ingenuity, and while irony comes naturally to most people ("My dear, it's a *beautiful* hat!"), we must exercise great care in using this trope. Because of its subtlety, irony can easily be misunderstood. There are college students even today who misread Swift's ironical *Modest Proposal*.

Sarcasm is another mode of humor that requires a master hand, for it can easily go wrong. Sarcasm seems to succeed best when it is directed at an individual; it is risky when it is directed at nationalities, classes, ranks, or vocations. That this should be so is rather curious, for of all modes of satirical wit, sarcasm is the one that most closely borders on uncharitableness. One might think that since the caustic gibe at an individual comes closer to violating the virtue of charity than the gibe at a group of people, personal sarcasm would be most likely to elicit unfavorable reactions in the audience. But human nature is so constituted that it will tolerate, even enjoy, the vituperation of an individual. The same London society that chuckled over Alexander Pope's vitriolic portrait of Lord John Hervey under the guise of "Sporus" would have been angered if his portrait had been directed at the class of aristocratic courtiers that Lord Hervey represented. The psychology behind this perverse pleasure is pointed up by La Rochefoucauld's famous maxim, "In the misfortune of our best friends, we often find something that pleases us."

The rhetoricians are unanimous in their condemnation of ribald jests in formal discourse. The "dirty story" may provoke laughter when told in small, intimate groups, but in a public discourse, it almost invariably offends and alienates a larger audience. Likewise, we usually react unfavorably to a ribald joke when we see it in print. It is difficult to imagine any situation when a ribald jest will serve our purpose. For rhetorical reasons, then, as well as for moral reasons, we should avoid the use of obscenity and a *double-entendre* in our discourses.

The type of literature that makes most use, for rhetorical purposes, of the varieties of humor that we have discussed—and of some that we have not discussed, like parody and burlesque—is satire. And it is notable that some of the greatest English satirists, like Ben Jonson, John Dryden, Alexander Pope, and Jonathan Swift, were thoroughly schooled in classical rhetoric. The student will learn his best lessons about the skillful uses of humor for rhetorical purposes from reading the great satirists. And the student will acquire another method of reading and analyzing satiric literature if he will approach such literature as a manifestation of the kind of rhetoric we have been studying in this book.

Quintilian once said (*Instit. Orat.,* VI, iii, 26) that "there are no jests so insipid as those which parade the fact that they are intended to be witty." We might very well take these words as a general caution about the use of humor for rhetorical purposes. Humor that merely calls attention to our desire to be "funny" or to be "one of the boys" will alienate more people than it will win. Humor is an extremely difficult art, and if the student does not have a natural gift or an acquired skill for humor, he would do best to avoid the use of this available means of persuasion. And he must also remember that there are many occasions when humor of any kind is wholly inappropriate. We round back finally to that cardinal principle of rhetoric: the subject, the occasion, the audience, and the personality of the speaker or writer will dictate the means we should employ to effect our purpose.

Conclusion

A look at the terms that the classical rhetoricians used to designate the conclusion will give us a hint of what the rhetoricians conceived the function of this part of a discourse to be. The most common Greek term was *epilogos,* from the verb *epilegein,* meaning "to say in addition." An even more instructive Greek term for this part was *anakephalaiōsis,* which is the equivalent of the Latin *recapitulatio,* from which we have the English "recapitulation." The common Latin term for this part was *peroratio,* a word which in the prefix *per-* suggested "a finishing off" of one's plea. What the Latins meant by "finishing off" is suggested by the two heads under which Quintilian treated of the peroration—*enumeratio* (an enumeration or summing-up) and *affectus* (producing the appropriate emotion in the audience).

While it is obvious that some discourses, because of the nature of the subject or situation or because of the limitations of time or allotted wordage, can dispense with an elaborate conclusion, the natural tendency for us, when we speak or write formally, is to "round off" what we have been molding in the earlier parts of the discourse. Without a conclusion, the discourse strikes us as merely *stopping* rather than *ending.* We are conscious too that because the conclusion stands in the final position in the discourse it is the part that is "left with" the audience, the part that lingers longest in the memory. Accordingly, this is the part where we feel the urge to pull out all the stops, where we tend to display the most conspicuous stylistic eloquence and emotional intensity. Because of this natural urge to sound the full diapason of our stylistic and emotional resources, we sometimes overdo these effects and thereby detract from the solid achievements of the earlier parts of the discourse. Discretion must be as alive here as it was in the earlier parts.

Aristotle taught that generally we strive to do four things in the conclusion:

1. to inspire the audience with a favorable opinion of ourselves and an unfavorable opinion of our opponents;
2. to amplify the force of the points we have made in the previous section and to extenuate the force of the points made by the opposition;
3. to rouse the appropriate emotions in the audience;
4. to restate in a summary way our facts and arguments.

Aristotle is suggesting that these are the things that we *may* do in the conclusion, not that we *must* do all of them in every discourse. Limitations of space may prevent our spinning out an elaborate conclusion. The nature of our subject or of our audience may make it inadvisable to attempt any kind of emotional appeal. When our arguments have been direct and uncomplicated, there may be no necessity to recapitulate or amplify them. The student will note, for instance, how short the conclusion is to Macaulay's speech reproduced among the readings at the end of this chapter. The advice here, as in other parts of the discourse, is that we should do what needs to be done, not what convention says must be done.

Of the four things that Aristotle designates, *recapitulation* is the one that will most often figure in the conclusion. Normally when we come to the end of a discourse, we all feel the need to restate in general terms the points we have set forth in detail in the body of the discourse. This inclination is prompted perhaps by our feeling that we must refresh the memory of our audience. Then too there is the awareness that facts and arguments the force of which was blunted by details will gain in effect when set forth in capsule form at the end of the discourse.

Sometimes an author will explicitly signal that he is about to recapitulate the points he has made in the body of the essay. Here is an example of a formally announced recapitulation, together with the author's declaration of his reasons for the recapitulation, from the concluding paragraphs of an article, the thesis of which was set forth in the first sentence of the article: "I maintain that democratic manners—typified by the practice of calling the boss by his first name—have reached the point in our country where they conduce not to the preservation of personal dignity but to the abject submission of one man to another."

I have nearly finished. But I know that some fool—most likely, one with a Ph.D.—will read this article and forever after assert as a well-known fact that I yearn for a restoration of Tsardom, for a reinvigoration of the Hindu caste system and for a truly Chinese subjugation of women and children. So let me recapitulate, in the course of which I shall add one or two points that I forgot to mention earlier.

A sensible system of manners, sensibly formal, performs various services. Besides acting as a constant reminder of some important facts of life, it affords human beings the distinctly human satisfaction of symbolic expression. Besides making collective living possible, it provides a person, thanks to its formalities, with protective armor against collective pressures. For these formalities allow the individual to acquiesce in the social order while reserving his final judgment of it. They enable him to pledge his loyalty to men in authority without making those fine adjustments whose long-term results are the same as those of brainwashing.

Democratic manners in America are eating the heart out of American democracy. With no impressive way of saluting the system, and the position which a given official occupies in it, one must prostrate himself before the man. There is a country where such prostration is even more prostrate than in America. There the humblest citizen calls his mighty ruler *comrade.*

I suggest a prudent reform in American manners, not a revolution. If the only alternative to egalitarian manners is a nerveless society exhausted by protocol and ceremony, then this discussion is futile. But that is not the only alternative, except in the minds of latter-day Jacobins for whom the stratifications of the *ancien régime* are more real than the proletarianizations of their own time. There are in-between solutions, attuned to reality, however they resist simple and consistent formulation, as the English know, and as America, in her own fashion, can discover. Pedantic democrats presume to speak for wisdom, creative ability and service, as against mere money in the bank. But without a rectification of manners most men would rather achieve a Cadillac than such virtues, for these virtues, unacknowledged in any regular way, do not show on a man, at least not conspicuously, whereas a Cadillac shows on anyone, conspicuously.

From Morton J. Cronin, "The Tyranny of Democratic Manners," *The New Republic,* January 20, 1958. Reprinted by permission of the author and The New Republic, 1244 Nineteenth St., Washington, D.C.

To realize the value of such a recapitulation, the student would have to study this passage in conjunction with the body of the article, where the author developed his points at some length. And whereas the author here explicitly informs his readers that he is going to recapitulate the points he has made in the article and tells them why he feels the need to do so, most of the time, writers slip into recapitulation without explicitly alerting the reader. Most of the time it is fairly obvious that the author is summarizing his points.

How important recapitulation can be is nowhere more dramatically demonstrated than in a court trial. The jury has spent days, sometimes weeks, listening to highly detailed testimony and cross-examination. Surely at the end of this period, the jury has all the material it needs to render a verdict. But, as anyone knows who has witnessed a real or a fictional trial, both the prosecuting and defending attorneys present a summary of their cases before the jury is sent out to deliberate its verdict. The prosecutor and defender spend most of their time in this summary reminding the jury of the main points established during the course of the trial. Not only are the issues and arguments sharpened by these summaries, but coming one upon the other in rapid succession, they gain a cumulative force.

Let us view a fictional example of such a summary. Because this summary is tightly controlled by the novelist, it is probably less rambling than the summaries lawyers present in actual trials. In this scene from the novel *To Kill a Mockingbird*, Atticus, the lawyer defending a Negro falsely accused of raping a white girl, is making his final plea to the jury:

> "Gentlemen," he was saying, "I shall be brief, but I would like to use my remaining time with you to remind you that this case is not a difficult one, it requires no minute sifting of complicated facts, but it does require you to be sure beyond all reasonable doubt as to the guilt of the defendant. To begin with, this case should never have come to trial. This case is as simple as black and white.
>
> "The state has not produced one iota of medical evidence to the effect that the crime Tom Robinson is charged with ever took place. It has relied instead upon the testimony of two witnesses whose evidence has not only been called into serious question on cross-examination, but has been flatly contradicted by the defendant. The defendant is not guilty, but somebody in this courtroom is.
>
> "I have nothing but pity in my heart for the chief witness for the state, but my pity does not extend so far as to her putting a man's life at stake, which she has done in an effort to get rid of her own guilt.
>
> "I say guilt, gentlemen, because it was guilt that motivated her. She has committed no crime, she has merely broken a rigid and time-honored code of our society, a code so severe that whoever breaks it is hounded from our midst as unfit to live with. She is the victim of cruel poverty and ignorance, but I cannot pity her: she is white. She knew full well the enormity of her offense, but because her desires were stronger than the code she was breaking, she persisted in breaking it. She persisted, and her subsequent reaction is something that all of us have known at one time or another. She did something every child has done—she tried to put the evidence of her offense away from her. But in this case she was

no child hiding stolen contraband: she struck out at her victim—of necessity she must put him away from her—he must be removed from her presence, from this world. She must destroy the evidence of her offense.

"What was the evidence of her offense? Tom Robinson, a human being. She must put Tom Robinson away from her. Tom Robinson was her daily reminder of what she did. What did she do? She tempted a Negro.

"She was white, and she tempted a Negro. She did something that in our society is unspeakable: she kissed a black man. Not an old Uncle, but a strong young Negro man. No code mattered to her before she broke it, but it came crashing down on her afterwards.

"Her father saw it, and the defendant has testified as to his remarks. What did her father do? We don't know, but there is circumstantial evidence to indicate that Mayella Ewell was beaten savagely by someone who led almost exclusively with his left. We do know in part what Mr. Ewell did: he did what any God-fearing, persevering, respectable white man would do under the circumstances—he swore out a warrant, no doubt signing it with his left hand, and Tom Robinson now sits before you, having taken the oath with the only good hand he possesses—his right hand.

"And so a quiet, respectable, humble Negro who had the unmitigated temerity to 'feel sorry' for a white woman has had to put his word against two white people's. I need not remind you of their appearance and conduct on the stand—you saw them for yourselves. The witnesses for the state, with the exception of the sheriff of Maycomb County, have presented themselves to you gentlemen, to this court, in the cynical confidence that their testimony would not be doubted, confident that you gentlemen would go along with them on the assumption—the evil assumption—that *all* Negroes lie, that *all* Negroes are basically immoral beings, that *all* Negro men are not to be trusted around our women, an assumption one associates with minds of their caliber.

"Which, gentlemen, we know is in itself a lie as black as Tom Robinson's skin, a lie I do not have to point out to you. You know the truth, and the truth is this: some Negroes lie, some Negroes are immoral, some Negro men are not to be trusted around women—black or white. But this is a truth that applies to the human race and to no particular race of men. There is not a person in this courtroom who has never told a lie, who has never done an immoral thing, and there is no man living who has never looked upon a woman without desire."

From Harper Lee, *To Kill a Mockingbird,* Chapter 20. Copyright © 1960 by Harper Lee. Reprinted by permission of J. B. Lippincott Co.

Atticus goes on for three more paragraphs, appealing to the theme of equal justice for all in the courts. Anyone who has read *To Kill a Mockingbird* or has seen the movie based on the novel remembers how skillfully Atticus Finch had argued the points he is summarizing here and how necessary it was for him, considering the kind of jurymen he had to deal with, to remind the jury of the arguments in the case and to put the trial in its proper perspective. A summation like this does more, however, than merely remind the audience of the salient points; it continues and reinforces the persuasion which is the main object of the speech. So while Atticus's recapitulation is largely expository, it is argumentative, right down to the final period.

Closely allied to the kind of conclusion that recapitulates or summarizes, is the one that *generalizes*. This is the kind of conclusion that broadens and extends the view of the problem or issue that we have been considering in the body of the discourse, that considers the ultimate consequences of the views we have been arguing or refuting, that recommends an attitude to adopt or a course of action to follow. To put it another way, this is the kind of conclusion that presents the general conclusions we have arrived at as a result of considering our subject.

At the 1959 convention of the National Council of Teachers of English, Professor Warner G. Rice argued for the abolition of the Freshman English course in college. In rebuttal, Professor Albert R. Kitzhaber argued for a revision of the present English course. Here, in the concluding paragraph of his speech, Professor Kitzhaber generalizes on the points he had argued in the body of his speech:

> I can sum up very briefly my position with regard to the question we are discussing. I am dissatisfied with the present Freshman English course in its typical form; but I am convinced that any radical amelioration must wait on, not precede, changes in the English curriculum in high school. Attempted coercion of high school English teachers would get us nowhere. They would like to do a better job of teaching writing quite as much as we would like to have them do it; but we must help them, working with them as equals on a problem neither they nor we have so far been able to solve properly. If our combined efforts lead to the results we want, the need for this present Freshman course would disappear—but not the need for a new Freshman course that would take advantage of and build upon the revised high school courses. I would argue that such a course ought to be of at least as much value to the freshman as any other course he might take in that year—valuable because it would concentrate on trying to raise the level of his writing skill from competence to distinction, and valuable also because it would contribute significantly to his liberal education through the continued study of literature and language. Both of these are rightful concerns of an English department.
>
> Indeed, I think they are obligations.

From "Death—or Transfiguration?" *College English,* XXI (April, 1960), 367-73. Reprinted by permission of the author and the National Council of Teachers of English.

It is in the summarizing kind of conclusion that we have the best opportunity to engage in what the rhetoricians called *amplification* and *extenuation*. Amplification is the process by which we highlight, by which we make as "big as possible," the points we have made; amplification is a way of reminding audiences of the importance or cogency or superiority of our points. Extenuation does just the opposite: it insists that the points made by the opposition are insignificant, weak, or inferior. The common topics that we most resort to when we are seeking to amplify our own points or to minimize our opponent's points are the topic of size and the topic of degree. In other words, we try to emphasize or de-emphasize either the absolute or the relative magnitude of the points we have made. Of course we try to do this when we are presenting our arguments, but it can be helpful to our cause to engage in some amplifying and extenuating in a summary way in the conclusion.

One final caution about the recapitulation; let it be as brief as possible. Otherwise the conclusion will take on the proportions of a second discourse, and it will serve only to weary and alienate the audience. Nothing so exasperates an audience as the speaker or writer who goes "on and on" after he has announced that he is about to conclude. A disproportionate conclusion is usually more damaging to the effect of an essay than a disproportionate introduction. A fresh audience may be disposed to forgive a treadmill introduction, but a weary audience will invariably resent the interminable conclusion.

Emotional appeals, as we have seen, are appropriate in any part of the discourse. Traditionally, however, the conclusion has been the part in which emotional appeals have figured most prominently. Present-day students have not been exposed very much to the Chautauqua style of oratory that was very popular in the early years of this century, but a look at the speeches of a flamboyant orator like William Jennings Bryan would show them how speakers once indulged the natural urge to pull out all the emotional stops in the peroration. Probably more familiar to modern students, Sir Winston Churchill was an orator in the grand old tradition. An example of the rousing kind of emotional appeal is found in the peroration of Sir Winston Churchill's famous speech to the House of Commons on May 13, 1940:

> I say to the House as I said to Ministers who have joined this government, I have nothing to offer but blood, toil, tears, and sweat. We have before us an ordeal of the most grievous kind. We have before us many, many months of struggle and suffering.
>
> You ask, what is our policy? I say it is to wage war by land, sea, and air. War with all our might and with all the strength God has given us, and to wage war against a monstrous tyranny never surpassed in the dark and lamentable catalogue of human crime. That is our policy.

> You ask, what is our aim? I can answer in one word. It is victory. Victory at all costs—victory in spite of all terrors—victory, however long and hard the road may be, for without victory there is no survival.
>
> Let that be realized. No survival for the British Empire, no survival for all that the British Empire has stood for, no survival for the urge, the impulse of the ages, that mankind shall move forward toward his goal.
>
> I take up my task in buoyancy and hope. I feel sure that our cause will not be suffered to fail among men.
>
> I feel entitled at this juncture, at this time, to claim the aid of all and to say, "Come then, let us go forward together with our united strength."

Even today most of us have a nostalgic fondness for this kind of oratory, and occasionally, such as at a nominating convention, we are treated to a display of this rousing brand of oratory. Generally, however, we profess to be suspicious of grandiloquent exploitations of our emotions. And while we have probably misjudged our susceptibility to emotional appeals, it is true that bombastic displays of emotion have largely passed out of fashion.

Today we are more likely to regard as fitting the temperate kind of emotional appeal that Abraham Lincoln exerted in his "Second Inaugural Address." In this example, a good deal of the emotional appeal is produced by the choice of diction and by the rhythm and structure of the sentences:

> The Almighty has His own purposes. "Woe unto the world because of offenses! for it must needs be that offenses come; but woe to that man by whom the offense cometh." If we shall suppose that American slavery is one of those offenses which, in the providence of God, must needs come, but which, having continued through His appointed time, He now wills to remove, and that He gives to both North and South this terrible war, as the woe due to those by whom the offense came, shall we discern therein any departure from those divine attributes which the believers in a living God always ascribe to Him? Fondly do we hope, fervently do we pray, that this mighty scourge of war may speedily pass away. Yet, if God wills that it continue until all the wealth piled by the bond-man's two hundred and fifty years of unrequited toil shall be sunk, and until every drop of blood drawn with the lash shall be paid by another drawn with a sword, as was said three thousand years ago, so still it must be said, "The judgments of the Lord are true and righteous altogether."
>
> With malice towards none, with charity for all, with firmness in the right, as God gives us to see the right, let us strive on to finish the work we are in—to bind up the nation's wounds—to care for him who shall have borne the battle, and for his widow and his orphan—to do all which may achieve and cherish a just and lasting peace among ourselves and with all nations.

To note the passing of the bombastic style is not to admit that we have ceased to be responsive to emotional appeals or that we have ceased to employ emotional appeals. What has happened is that emotional appeals, especially as they appear in conclusions, tend to be more subtle and more restrained than they were in this country even fifty years ago. We seem to be relying less on direct emotional appeals and more on such indirect means as the graces of style. The rhythms of our sentences, for instance, exert an influence on the emotions that is no less real for being all but unnoticeable. We shall consider these emotional effects at greater length in the chapter on style.

Whether we need to resort to emotional appeals in the conclusion and how hard we should come down on the emotional appeals will depend largely on the nature of our audience. It is extremely important that the speaker or writer gauge, as accurately as possible, the temper of the known or probable audience for his discourse. Some audiences will be less susceptible to emotional appeals than others. A professional group, for instance, inclined by temperament or training to accept or reject a proposal on its proven merits, may be impervious, even hostile, to any appeal to their emotions on matters of professional interest. An audience's susceptibility to emotional appeals could vary, of course, with the subject being discussed. A group of doctors, for instance, could be offended by any emotional appeal when they were being urged to adopt some new drug or technique; but on a subject like government sponsorship of medical insurance, this same group could be wide open to emotional appeals. Then too when the available means of logical persuasion on a given subject are weak—or at least weaker than those of the opposition—we may find it expedient to resort to emotional persuasion. Quintilian saw the effectiveness of emotional appeal in such a situation: "Proofs, it is true, may induce the judges to regard our case as superior to that of our opponent, but the appeal to the emotions will do more, for it will make them wish our case to be better. And what they wish, they will also believe."—*Instit. Orat.* VI, ii, 5. Quintilian went so far as to claim that "it is in its power over the emotions that the life and soul of oratory is to be found" (VI, ii, 7). The great Latin rhetorician may seem to be encouraging the use of any kind of unethical means to accomplish our purpose. But anyone who recalls Quintilian's view that the ideal orator is "the good man speaking" must reject this imputation. Quintilian is merely giving frank recognition to the fact that, men being what they are, emotional appeal will in some circumstances be the most effective of the available means of persuasion. This recognition is not the same as sanctioning any and all exploitations of emotion, for the classical rhetoricians did not regard emotional appeals as illegitimate *per se*. Men sometimes abused this means of persuasion, but the fact that some men abused this power did not invalidate all uses of this resource.

The fourth thing we may do, and sometimes feel compelled to do, in the conclusion is to dispose the audience favorably toward ourselves. If we have not exerted an *ethical appeal* in the earlier parts of our discourse, it is probably too late to try to exert it in the conclusion. We have seen that as early as the introduction, we may have to ingratiate ourselves with a hostile audience or post our credentials with a skeptical audience, and in later parts of the discourse, we may frequently have to bolster the credit we have established with our audience. To delay establishing a favorable image of ourselves until the conclusion would usually jeopardize our chances of persuading an audience. So when we make an effort in the conclusion to dispose an audience favorably toward ourselves, we should be merely renewing and reinforcing the ethical appeal that has been working in earlier parts of the discourse.

The kinds of ethical appeal that seem to be most appropriate in the conclusion are the frank confession of our shortcomings, honest acknowledgment of the strength of the opposing case, and magnanimous gestures toward vindictive opponents. It is well to leave our audience with the impression that we have no illusions about ourselves or our position, that we have a respect for truth wherever we find it, and that we are capable of returning charity for malice. The audience gets the impression that the man capable of making frank confessions and generous concessions is not only a good man but a man so confident of the strength of his position that he can afford to concede points to the opposition.

We observed in the section on the introduction that if we feel it necessary to arouse hostility against our opponent, it is usually better to do this in the conclusion rather than in the introduction. It is easier, for one thing, to arouse hostility against an opponent *after* we have demolished his arguments. Circumstances, however, might dictate that it would be better to arouse this hostility early in the discourse. In the reading from the *Apology* in the previous chapter, we saw that Socrates deemed it necessary to stir up animosity against Meletus quite early in his speech of defense.

Concluding Remarks on Arrangement

In this chapter, we have been reviewing the usual parts of an extensive discourse, noting what is normally done in each of these parts and remarking the adjustments that frequently have to be made to fit the particular situation. Almost no rule about arrangement is inflexible. Anything "bends" to the exigencies of the moment—to the demands, in other words, of the subject, or the kind of discourse, or the personality or ability of the writer, or the temper of the audience. Where so many adjustments may have to be made to the *ad hoc* situation, very few hard-and-fast precepts can be laid down. Some students succeed better than others in making these strategic adjustments because they have been endowed with sound instincts for what is effective in any given situation. But other students, not so gifted, can through experience and practice and guidance acquire a measure of this skill. Experience and practice the student must gain on his own; this text attempts to supply the general guidance that a student may need.

All that rhetoric can do is point out that given this subject or this purpose or this audience, this is what the student may have to do in some part of the discourse, and this is how he might do what he has to do. Disposition then becomes something more than the conventional system for organizing a discourse, something more than just a system of outlining the composition; it becomes a discipline that trains the student in the judicious selection and use of available means to the desired end.

Since so many decisions about arrangement depend upon the given situation, it would be well for the student now to study some readings in order to see how some authors have managed arrangement in their given situation.

Readings

Thomas Babington Macaulay: Education

The advantage in starting our study of arrangement with a fairly long piece of connected discourse, is that the long piece has more parts, and it is easier to discern how important it is to arrange these many parts in such a way as to achieve maximum unity, coherence, and effectiveness. For our first example, then, we have chosen Thomas Babington Macaulay's speech on the advantages of a state-supported educational system, delivered in the House of Commons on April 19, 1847.

A bill was up before the House of Commons in the spring of 1847, asking for an appropriation of one hundred thousand pounds to help finance a school system for those people who could not afford to send their children to private schools. When Lord John Russell moved that the bill be put to a vote of the House, Thomas Duncombe, the Member for Finsbury, proposed the following amendment:

> *That previous to any grant of public money being assented to by this House for the purpose of carrying out the scheme of national education, as developed in the Minutes of the Committee of Council on Education*

in August and December last, which minutes have been presented to both Houses of Parliament by command of Her Majesty, a select Committee be appointed to inquire into the justice and expediency of such a scheme and its probable annual cost; also to inquire whether the regulations attached thereto do not unduly increase the influence of the crown, invade the constitutional functions of Parliament, and interfere with the religious convictions and civil rights of Her Majesty's subjects.

As a result of Macaulay's speech in opposition to that proposed amendment and of the subsequent debate in the House, the amendment was soundly defeated. Somewhat ironically, however, Macaulay was defeated the following July when he stood for re-election for Edinburgh.

Americans, with their flourishing network of public schools, may find it difficult to sympathize with the opposition offered by the Member for Finsbury to a system of subsidized schools, but there are a number of issues raised in Macaulay's speech which are still being vigorously debated in America today—principally the issue of federal vs. state support and control.

1   You will not wonder, Sir, that I am desirous to catch your eye this evening. The first duty which I performed, as a Member of the Committee of Council which is charged with the superintendence of public instruction, was to give my hearty assent to the plan which the honourable Member for Finsbury calls on the House to condemn. I am one of those who have been accused in every part of the kingdom, and who are now accused in Parliament, of aiming, under specious pretences, a blow at the civil and religious liberties of the people. It is natural therefore that I should seize the earliest opportunity of vindicating myself from so grave a charge.

2   The honourable Member for Finsbury must excuse me if, in the remarks which I have to offer to the House, I should not follow very closely the order of his speech. The truth is that a mere answer to his speech would be no defence of myself or of my colleagues. I am surprised, I own, that a man of his acuteness and ability should, on such an occasion, have made such a speech. The country is excited from one end to the other by a great question of principle. On that question the Government has taken one side. The honourable Member stands forth as the chosen and trusted champion of a great party which takes the other side. We expected to hear from him a full exposition of the views of those in whose name he speaks. But, to our astonishment, he has scarcely even alluded to the controversy which has divided the whole nation. He has entertained us with sarcasms and personal anecdotes: he has talked much about matters of mere detail: but I must say that, after listening with close attention to all that he has said, I am quite unable to discover whether, on the only important point which is in issue,

he agrees with us or with that large and active body of Nonconformists which is diametrically opposed to us. He has sat down without dropping one word from which it is possible to discover whether he thinks that education is or that it is not a matter with which the State ought to interfere. Yet that is the question about which the whole nation has, during several weeks, been writing, reading, speaking, hearing, thinking, petitioning, and on which it is now the duty of Parliament to pronounce a decision. That question once settled, there will be, I believe, very little room for dispute. If it be not competent to the State to interfere with the education of the people, the mode of interference recommended by the Committee of Council must of course be condemned. If it be the right and the duty of the State to make provision for the education of the people, the objections made to our plan will, in a very few words, be shown to be frivolous.

3 I shall take a course very different from that which has been taken by the honourable gentleman. I shall in the clearest manner profess my opinion on that great question of principle which he has studiously evaded; and for my opinion I shall give what seem to me to be unanswerable reasons.

4 I believe, Sir, that it is the right and the duty of the State to provide means of education for the common people. This proposition seems to me to be implied in every definition that has ever yet been given of the functions of a government. About the extent of those functions there has been much difference of opinion among ingenious men. There are some who hold that it is the business of a government to meddle with every part of the system of human life, to regulate trade by bounties and prohibitions, to regulate expenditure by sumptuary laws, to regulate literature by a censorship, to regulate religion by an inquisition. Others go to the opposite extreme, and assign to Government a very narrow sphere of action. But the very narrowest sphere that ever was assigned to governments by any school of political philosophy is quite wide enough for my purpose. On one point all the disputants are agreed. They unanimously acknowledge that it is the duty of every government to take order for giving security to the persons and property of the members of the community.

5 This being admitted, can it be denied that the education of the common people is a most effectual means of securing our persons and our property? Let Adam Smith answer that question for me. His authority, always high, is, on this subject, entitled to peculiar respect, because he extremely disliked busy, prying, interfering governments. He was for leaving literature, arts, sciences, to take care of themselves. He was of opinion that the State ought not to meddle with the education of the rich. But he has expressly told us that a distinction is to be made, particularly in a commercial and highly civilised society, between the education of the rich and the education of the poor. The education of the poor, he says, is a matter which deeply concerns

the commonwealth. Just as the magistrate ought to interfere for the purpose of preventing the leprosy from spreading among the people, he ought to interfere for the purpose of stopping the progress of the moral distempers which are inseparable from ignorance. Nor can this duty be neglected without danger to the public peace. If you leave the multitude uninstructed, there is serious risk that religious animosities may produce the most dreadful disorders. The most dreadful disorders! Those are Adam Smith's own words; and prophetic words they were. Scarcely had he given this warning to our rulers when his prediction was fulfilled in a manner never to be forgotten. I speak of the No Popery riots of 1780. I do not know that I could find in all history a stronger proof of the proposition that the ignorance of the common people makes the property, the limbs, the lives of all classes insecure. Without the shadow of a grievance, at the summons of a madman, a hundred thousand people rise in insurrection. During a whole week, there is anarchy in the greatest and wealthiest of European cities. The parliament is besieged. Your predecessor sits trembling in his chair and expects every moment to see the door beaten in by the ruffians whose roar he hears all round the house. The peers are pulled out of their coaches. The bishops in their lawn are forced to fly over the tiles. The chapels of foreign ambassadors, buildings made sacred by the law of nations, are destroyed. The house of the Chief Justice is demolished. The little children of the Prime Minister are taken out of their beds and laid in their night clothes on the table of the Horse Guards, the only safe asylum from the fury of the rabble. The prisons are opened. Highwaymen, housebreakers, murderers, come forth to swell the mob by which they have been set free. Thirty-six fires are blazing at once in London. Then comes the retribution. Count up all the wretches who were shot, who were hanged, who were crushed, who drank themselves to death at the rivers of gin which ran down Holborn Hill; and you will find that battles have been lost and won with a smaller sacrifice of life. And what was the cause of this calamity, a calamity which, in the history of London ranks with the great plague and the great fire? The cause was the ignorance of a population which had been suffered, in the neighbourhood of palaces, theatres, temples, to grow up as rude and stupid as any tribe of tattooed cannibals in New Zealand, I might say as any drove of beasts in Smithfield Market.

6   The instance is striking; but it is not solitary. To the same cause are to be ascribed the riots of Nottingham, the sack of Bristol, all the outrages of Ludd, and Swing, and Rebecca, beautiful and costly machinery broken to pieces in Yorkshire, barns and haystacks blazing in Kent, fences and buildings pulled down in Wales. Could such things have been done in a country in which the mind of the labourer had been opened by education, in which he had been taught to find pleasure in the exercise of his intellect, taught to revere his Maker, taught to respect legitimate authority, and taught at the

same time to seek the redress of real wrongs by peaceful and constitutional means?

7 This then is my argument. It is the duty of Government to protect our persons and property from danger. The gross ignorance of the common people is a principal cause of danger to our persons and property. Therefore. it is the duty of the Government to take care that the common people shall not be grossly ignorant.

8 And what is the alternative? It is universally allowed that, by some means, Government must protect our persons and property. If you take away education, what means do you leave? You leave means such as only necessity can justify, means which inflict a fearful amount of pain, not only on the guilty, but on the innocent who are connected with the guilty. You leave guns and bayonets, stocks and whipping-posts, treadmills, solitary cells, penal colonies, gibbets. See then how the case stands. Here is an end which, as we all agree, governments are bound to attain. There are only two ways of attaining it. One of those ways is by making men better, and wiser, and happier. The other way is by making them infamous and miserable. Can it be doubted which way we ought to prefer? Is it not strange, is it not almost incredible, that pious and benevolent men should gravely propound the doctrine that the magistrate is bound to punish and at the same time bound not to teach? To me it seems quite clear that whoever has a right .to hang has a right to educate. Can we think without shame and remorse that more than half of those wretches who have been tied up at Newgate in our time might have been living happily, that more than half of those who are now in our gaols might have been enjoying liberty and using that liberty well, that such a hell on earth as Norfolk Island need never have existed, if we had expended in training honest men but a small part of what we have expended in hunting and torturing rogues.

9 I would earnestly entreat every gentleman to look at a report which is contained in the Appendix to the First Volume of the Minutes of the Committee of Council. I speak of the report made by Mr. Seymour Tremenheare on the state of that part of Monmouthshire which is inhabited by a population chiefly employed in mining. He found that, in this district, towards the close of 1839, out of eleven thousand children who were of an age to attend school, eight thousand never went to any school at all, and that most of the remaining three thousand might almost as well have gone to no school as to the squalid hovels in which men who ought themselves to have been learners pretended to teach. In general these men had only one qualification for their employment; and that was their utter unfitness for every other employment. They were disabled miners or broken hucksters. In their schools all was stench and noise and confusion. Now and then the clamour of the boys was silenced for two minutes by the furious menaces of the master; but

it soon broke out again. The instruction given was of the lowest kind. Not one school in ten was provided with a single map. This is the way in which you suffered the minds of a great population to be formed. And now for the effects of your negligence. The barbarian inhabitants of this region rise in an insane rebellion against the Government. They come pouring down their valleys to Newport. They fire on the Queen's troops. They wound a magistrate. The soldiers fire in return; and too many of these wretched men pay with their lives the penalty of their crime. But is the crime theirs alone? Is it strange that they should listen to the only teaching that they had? How can you, who took no pains to instruct them, blame them for giving ear to the demagogue who took pains to delude them? We put them down, of course. We punished them. We had no choice. Order must be maintained; property must be protected; and, since we had omitted to take the best way of keeping these people quiet, we were under the necessity of keeping them quiet by the dread of the sword and the halter. But could any necessity be more cruel? And which of us would run the risk of being placed under such necessity a second time?

10   I say, therefore, that the education of the people is not only a means, but the best means, of attaining that which all allow to be a chief end of government; and, if this be so, it passes my faculties to understand how any man can gravely contend that Government has nothing to do with the education of the people.

11   My confidence in my opinion is strengthened when I recollect that I hold that opinion in common with all the greatest lawgivers, statesmen, and political philosophers of all nations and ages, with all the most illustrious champions of civil and spiritual freedom, and especially with those men whose names were once held in the highest veneration by the Protestant Dissenters of England. I might cite many of the most venerable names of the old world; but I would rather cite the example of that country which the supporters of the Voluntary system here are always recommending to us as a pattern. Go back to the days when the little society which has expanded into the opulent and enlightened commonwealth of Massachusetts began to exist. Our modern Dissenters will scarcely, I think, venture to speak contumeliously of those Puritans whose spirit Laud and his High Commission Court could not subdue, of those Puritans who were willing to leave home and kindred, and all the comforts and refinements of civilised life, to cross the ocean, to fix their abode in forests among wild beasts and wild men, rather than commit the sin of performing, in the House of God, one gesture which they believed to be displeasing to Him. Did those brave exiles think it inconsistent with civil or religious freedom that the State should take charge of the education of the people? No, sir; one of the earliest laws enacted by the Puritan colonists was that every township, as soon as the Lord had in-

creased it to the number of fifty houses, should appoint one to teach all children to write and read, and that every township of a hundred houses should set up a grammar school. Nor have the descendants of those who made this law ever ceased to hold that the public authorities were bound to provide the means of public instruction. Nor is this doctrine confined to New England. "Educate the people" was the first admonition addressed by Penn to the colony which he founded. "Educate the people" was the legacy of Washington to the nation which he had saved. "Educate the people" was the unceasing exhortation of Jefferson; and I quote Jefferson with peculiar pleasure, because, of all the eminent men that have ever lived, Adam Smith himself not excepted, Jefferson was the one who most abhorred everything like meddling on the part of governments. Yet the chief business of his later years was to establish a good system of State education in Virginia.

12 And, against such authority as this, what have you who take the other side to show? Can you mention a single great philosopher, a single man distinguished by his zeal for liberty, humanity, and truth, who, from the beginning of the world down to the time of this present Parliament, ever held your doctrines? You can oppose to the unanimous voice of all the wise and good, of all ages, and of both hemispheres, nothing but a clamour which was first heard a few months ago, a clamour in which you cannot join without condemning, not only all whose memory you profess to hold in reverence, but even your former selves.

13 This new theory of politics has at least the merit of originality. It may be fairly stated thus. All men have hitherto been utterly in the wrong as to the nature and objects of civil government. The great truth, hidden from every preceding generation, and at length revealed, in the year 1846, to some highly respectable ministers and elders of dissenting congregations, is this. Government is simply a great hangman. Government ought to do nothing except by harsh and degrading means. The one business of Government is to handcuff, and lock up, and scourge, and shoot, and stab, and strangle. It is odious tyranny in a government to attempt to prevent crime by informing the understanding and elevating the moral feeling of a people. A statesman may see hamlets turned, in the course of one generation, into great seaport towns and manufacturing towns. He may know that on the character of the vast population which is collected in those wonderful towns depends the prosperity, the peace, the very existence of society. But he must not think of forming that character. He is an enemy of public liberty if he attempts to prevent those hundreds of thousands of his countrymen from becoming mere Yahoos. He may, indeed, build barrack after barrack to overawe them. If they break out into insurrection, he may send cavalry to sabre them; he may mow them down with grape shot; he may hang them, draw them, quarter them, anything but teach them. He may see, and may shudder as

he sees, throughout large rural districts, millions of infants growing up from infancy to manhood as ignorant, as mere slaves of sensual appetite, as the beasts that perish. No matter. He is a traitor to the cause of civil and religious freedom if he does not look on with folded arms, while absurd hopes and evil passions ripen in that rank soil. He must wait for the day of his harvest. He must wait till the Jaquerie comes, till farm houses are burning, till threshing machines are broken in pieces; and then begins his business, which is simply to send one poor ignorant savage to the county gaol, and another to the antipodes, and a third to the gallows.

14   Such, Sir, is the new theory of government which was first propounded in the year 1846, by some men of high note among the Nonconformists of England. It is difficult to understand how men of excellent abilities and excellent intentions—and there are, I readily admit, such men among those who hold this theory—can have fallen into so absurd and pernicious an error. One explanation only occurs to me. This is, I am inclined to believe, an instance of the operation of the great law of reaction. We have just come victorious out of a long and fierce contest for the liberty of trade. While that contest was undecided, much was said and written about the advantages of free competition and about the danger of suffering the State to regulate matters which should be left to individuals. There has consequently arisen in the minds of persons who are led by words and who are little in the habit of making distinctions a disposition to apply to political questions and moral questions principles which are sound only when applied to commercial questions. These people, not content with having forced the Government to surrender a province wrongfully usurped, now wish to wrest from the Government a domain held by a right which was never before questioned and which cannot be questioned with the smallest show of reason. "If," they say, "free competition is a good thing in trade, it must surely be a good thing in education. The supply of other commodities, of sugar, for example, is left to adjust itself to the demand; and the consequence is that we are better supplied with sugar than if the Government undertook to supply us. Why then should we doubt that the supply of instruction will, without the intervention of the Government, be found equal to the demand?"

15   Never was there a more false analogy. Whether a man is well supplied with sugar is a matter which concerns himself alone. But whether he is well supplied with instruction is a matter which concerns his neighbours and the State. If he cannot afford to pay for sugar, he must go without sugar. But it is by no means fit that, because he cannot afford to pay for education, he should go without education. Between the rich and their instructors there may, as Adam Smith says, be free trade. The supply of music masters and Italian masters may be left to adjust itself to the demand. But what is to become of the millions who are too poor to procure without assistance the

services of a decent schoolmaster? We have indeed heard it said that even these millions will be supplied with teachers by the free competition of benevolent individuals who will vie with each other in rendering this service to mankind. No doubt there are many benevolent individuals who spend their time and money most laudably in setting up and supporting schools; and you may say, if you please, that there is, among these respectable persons, a competition to do good. But do not be imposed upon by words. Do not believe that this competition resembles the competition which is produced by the desire of wealth and by the fear of ruin. There is a great difference, be assured, between the rivalry of philanthropists and the rivalry of grocers. The grocer knows that if his wares are worse than those of other grocers, he shall soon go before the Bankrupt Court, and his wife and children will have no refuge but the workhouse; he knows that if his shop obtains an honourable celebrity, he shall be able to set up a carriage and buy a villa; and this knowledge impels him to exertions compared with which the exertions of even very charitable people to serve the poor are but languid. It would be strange infatuation indeed to legislate on the supposition that a man cares for his fellow creatures as much as he cares for himself.

16 Unless, Sir, I greatly deceive myself, those arguments, which show that the Government ought not to leave to private people the task of providing for the national defence, will equally show that the Government ought not to leave to private people the task of providing for national education. On this subject, Mr. Hume has laid down the general law with admirable good sense and perspicuity. I mean David Hume, not the Member for Montrose, though that honourable gentleman will, I am confident, assent to the doctrine propounded by his illustrious namesake. David Hume, Sir, justly says that most of the arts and trades which exist in the world produce so much advantage and pleasure to individuals that the magistrate may safely leave it to individuals to encourage those arts and trades. But he adds that there are callings which, though they are highly useful, nay, absolutely necessary to society, yet do not administer to the peculiar pleasure or profit of any individual. The military calling is an instance. Here, says Hume, the government must interfere. It must take on itself to regulate these callings and to stimulate the industry of the persons who follow these callings by pecuniary and honourary rewards.

17 Now, Sir, it seems to me that, on the same principle on which Government ought to superintend and to reward the soldier, Government ought to superintend and to reward the schoolmaster. I mean, of course, the schoolmaster of the common people. That his calling is useful, that his calling is necessary, will hardly be denied. Yet it is clear that his services will not be adequately remunerated if he is left to be remunerated by those whom he teaches or by the voluntary contributions of the charitable. Is this disputed?

Look at the facts. You tell us that schools will multiply and flourish exceedingly, if the Government will only abstain from interfering with them. Has not the Government long abstained from interfering with them? Has not everything been left, through many years, to individual exertion? If it were true that education, like trade, thrives most where the magistrate meddles least, the common people of England would now be the best educated in the world. Our schools would be model schools. Everyone would have a well chosen little library, excellent maps, a small but neat apparatus for experiments in natural philosophy. A grown person unable to read and write would be pointed at like Giant O'Brien or the Polish Count. Our schoolmasters would be as eminently expert in all that relates to teaching as our cutlers, our cottonspinners, our engineers are allowed to be in their respective callings. They would, as a class, be held in high consideration; and their gains would be such that it would be easy to find men of respectable character and attainments to fill up vacancies.

18 Now, is this the case? Look at the charges of the judges, at the resolutions of the grand juries, at the reports of public officers, at the reports of voluntary associations. All tell the same sad and ignominious story. Take the reports of the Inspectors of Prisons. In the House of Correction at Hertford, of seven hundred prisoners one half could not read at all; only eight could read and write well. Of eight thousand prisoners who had passed through Maidstone Prison, the proportion that could read and write well seems to have been still smaller. Turn from the registers of prisoners to the registers of marriages. You will find that about a hundred and thirty thousand couples were married in the year 1844. More than forty thousand of the bridegrooms and more than sixty thousand of the brides did not sign their names, but made their marks. Nearly one third of the men and nearly one half of the women, who are in the prime of life, who are to be the parents of the Englishmen of the next generation, who are to bear a chief part in forming the minds of the Englishmen of the next generation, cannot write their own names. Remember, too, that though people who cannot write their own names must be grossly ignorant, people may write their own names and yet have very little knowledge. Tens of thousands who were able to write their names had in all probability received only the wretched education of a common day school. We know what such a school too often is: a room crusted with filth, without light, without air, with a heap of fuel in one corner and a brood of chickens in another; the only machinery of instruction a dog-eared spelling-book and a broken slate; the masters the refuse of all other callings, discarded footmen, ruined pedlars, men who cannot work a sum in the rule of three, men who cannot write a common letter without blunders, men who do not know whether the earth is a sphere or a cube, men who do not know whether Jerusalem is in Asia or America. And to

such men, men to whom none of us would entrust the key of his cellar, we have entrusted the mind of the rising generation, and, with the mind of the rising generation, the freedom, the happiness, the glory of our country.

19 Do you question the accuracy of this description? I will produce evidence to which I am sure that you will not venture to take an exception. Every gentleman here knows, I suppose, how important a place the Congregational Union holds among the Nonconformists and how prominent a part Mr. Edward Baines has taken in opposition to State education. A Committee of the Congregational Union drew up last year a report on the subject of education. That report was received by the Union; and the person who moved that it should be received was Mr. Edward Baines. That report contains the following passage:

> If it were necessary to disclose facts to such an assembly as this, as to the ignorance and debasement of the neglected portions of our population in towns and rural districts, both adults and juvenile, it could easily be done. Private information communicated to the Board, personal observation and investigation of the various localities, with the published documents of the Registrar General, and the reports of the state of prisons in England and Wales, published by order of the House of Commons, would furnish enough to make us modest in speaking of what has been done for the humbler classes and make us ashamed that the sons of the soil of England should have been so long neglected and should present to the enlightened traveller from other shores such a sad spectacle of neglected cultivation, lost mental power, and spiritual degradation.

Nothing can be more just. All the information which I have been able to obtain bears out the statements of the Congregational Union. I do believe that the ignorance and degradation of a large part of the community to which we belong ought to make us ashamed of ourselves. I do believe that an enlightened traveller from New York, from Geneva, or from Berlin, would be shocked to see so much barbarism in the close neighbourhood of so much wealth and civilisation. But is it not strange that the very gentlemen who tell us in such emphatic language that the people are shamefully ill-educated should yet persist in telling us that under a system of free competition the people are certain to be excellently educated? Only this morning the opponents of our plan circulated a paper in which they confidently predict that free competition will do all that is necessary, if we will only wait with patience. Wait with patience! Why, we have been waiting ever since the Heptarchy. How much longer are we to wait! Till the year 2847? Or till the year 3847? That the experiment has as yet failed you do not deny. And why should it have failed? Has it been tried in unfavourable circumstances? Not so; it has been tried in the richest, and in the freest, and in the most charitable country in all Europe. Has it been tried on too small a scale? Not so; millions have been subjected to it. Has it been tried during too short a time? Not so; it has been going on during ages. The cause of the failure then is plain. Our whole system has been unsound. We have applied the principle of free competition to a case to which that principle is not applicable.

20   But, Sir, if the state of the southern part of our island has furnished me with one strong argument, the state of the northern part furnishes me with another argument, which is, if possible, still more decisive. A hundred and fifty years ago England was one of the best governed and most prosperous countries in the world; Scotland was perhaps the rudest and poorest country that could lay any claim to civilisation. The name of Scotchman was then uttered in this part of the island with contempt. The ablest Scotch statesmen contemplated the degraded state of their poorer countrymen with a feeling approaching to despair. It is well known that Fletcher of Saltoun, a brave and accomplished man, a man who had drawn his sword for liberty, who had suffered proscription and exile for liberty, was so much digusted and dismayed by the misery, the ignorance, the idleness, the lawlessness of the common people, that he proposed to make many thousands of them slaves. Nothing, he thought, but the discipline which kept order and enforced exertion among the negroes of a sugar colony, nothing but the lash and the stocks, could reclaim the vagabonds who infested every part of Scotland from their indolent and predatory habits, and compel them to support themselves by steady labour. He therefore, soon after the Revolution, published a pamphlet, in which he earnestly and, as I believe, from the mere impulse of humanity and patriotism, recommended to the Estates of the Realm this sharp remedy, which alone, as he conceived, could remove the evil. Within a few months after the publication of that pamphlet a very different remedy was applied. The Parliament which sat at Edinburgh passed an act for the establishment of parochial schools. What followed? An improvement such as the world had never seen took place in the moral and intellectual character of the people. Soon, in spite of the rigour of the climate, in spite of the sterility of the earth, Scotland became a country which had no reason to envy the fairest portions of the globe. Wherever the Scotchman went—and there were few parts of the world to which he did not go—he carried his superiority with him. If he was admitted into a public office, he worked his way up to the highest post. If he got employment in a brewery or a factory, he was soon the foreman. If he took a shop, his trade was the best in the street. If he enlisted in the army, he became a colour-serjeant. If he went to a colony, he was the most thriving planter there. The Scotchman of the seventeenth century had been spoken of in London as we speak of the Esquimaux. The Scotchman of the eighteenth century was an object, not of

scorn, but of envy. The cry was that, wherever he came, he got more than his share; that, mixed with Englishmen or mixed with Irishmen, he rose to the top as surely as oil rises to the top of water. And what had produced this great revolution? The Scotch air was still as cold, the Scotch rocks were still as bare as ever. All the natural qualities of the Scotchman were still what they had been when learned and benevolent men advised that he should be flogged, like a beast of burden, to his daily task. But the State had given him an education. That education was not, it is true, in all respects what it should have been. But, such as it was, it had done more for the bleak and dreary shores of the Forth and the Clyde than the richest of soils and the most genial of climates had done for Capua and Tarentum. Is there one member of this House, however strongly he may hold the doctrine that the Government ought not to interfere with the education of the people, who will stand up and say that, in his opinion, the Scotch would now have been a happier and a more enlightened people if they had been left, during the last five generations, to find instruction for themselves?

21 I say then, Sir, that if the science of Government be an experimental science this question is decided. We are in a condition to perform the inductive process according to the rules laid down in the Novum Organum. We have two nations closely connected, inhabiting the same island, sprung from the same blood, speaking the same language, governed by the same Sovereign and the same Legislature, holding essentially the same religious faith, having the same allies and the same enemies. Of these two nations one was, a hundred and fifty years ago, as respects opulence and civilisation, in the highest rank among European communities; the other in the lowest rank. The opulent and highly civilised nation leaves the education of the people to free competition. In the poor and half barbarous nation the education of the people is undertaken by the State. The result is that the first are last and the last first. The common people of Scotland—it is vain to disguise the truth—have passed the common people of England. Free competition, tried with every advantage, has produced effects of which, as the Congregational Union tell us, we ought to be ashamed and which must lower us in the opinion of every intelligent foreigner. State education, tried under every disadvantage, has produced an improvement to which it would be difficult to find a parallel in any age or country. Such an experiment as this would be regarded as conclusive in surgery or chemistry, and ought, I think, to be regarded as equally conclusive in politics.

22 These, Sir, are the reasons which have satisfied me that it is the duty of the State to educate the people. Being firmly convinced of that truth, I shall not shrink from proclaiming it here and elsewhere, in defiance of the loudest clamour that agitators can raise. The remainder of my task is easy. For if the great principle for which I have been contending is admitted,

the objections which have been made to the details of our plan will vanish fast. I will deal with those objections in the order in which they stand in the amendment moved by the honourable Member for Finsbury.

23 First among his objections he places the cost. Surely, Sir, no person who admits that it is our duty to train the minds of the rising generation can think a hundred thousand pounds too large a sum for that purpose. If we look at the matter in the lowest point of view, if we consider human beings merely as producers of wealth, the difference between an intelligent and a stupid population, estimated in pounds, shillings, and pence, exceeds a hundredfold the proposed outlay. Nor is this all. For every pound that you have saved in education, you will spend five in prosecution, in prisons, in penal settlements. I cannot believe that the House, having never grudged anything that was asked for the purpose of maintaining order and protecting property by means of pain and fear, will begin to be niggardly as soon as it is proposed to effect the same objects by making the people wiser and better.

24 The next objection made by the honourable Member to our plan is that it will increase the influence of the Crown. This sum of a hundred thousand pounds may, he apprehends, be employed in corruption and jobbing. Those schoolmasters who vote for ministerial candidates will obtain a share of the grant; those schoolmasters who vote for opponents of the ministry will apply for assistance in vain. Sir, the honourable Member never would have made this objection if he had taken the trouble to understand the minutes which he has condemned. We propose to place this part of the public expenditure under checks which must make such abuses as the honourable Member anticipates morally impossible. Not only will there be those ordinary checks which are thought sufficient to prevent the misapplication of the many millions annually granted for the army, the navy, the ordnance, the civil government; not only must the Ministers of the Crown come every year to this House for a vote and be prepared to render an account of the manner in which they have laid out what had been voted in the preceding year; but when they have satisfied the House, when they have got their vote, they will still be unable to distribute the money at their discretion. Whatever they may do for any schoolmaster must be done in concert with those persons who, in the district where the schoolmaster lives, take an interest in education and contribute out of their private means to the expense of education. When the honourable gentleman is afraid that we shall corrupt the schoolmasters, he forgets, first, that we do not appoint the schoolmasters; secondly, that we cannot dismiss the schoolmasters; thirdly, that managers who are altogether independent of us can, without our consent, dismiss the schoolmasters; and fourthly, that without the recommendation of those managers we can give nothing to the schoolmasters. Observe, too, that such a recommendation will not be one of those recommendations

which goodnatured easy people are too apt to give to everybody who asks; nor will it at all resemble those recommendations which the Secretary of the Treasury is in the habit of receiving. For every pound which we pay on the recommendation of the managers, the managers themselves must pay two pounds. They must also provide the schoolmaster with a house out of their own funds before they can obtain for him a grant from the public funds. What chance of jobbing is there here? It is common enough, no doubt, for a Member of Parliament who votes with Government to ask that one of those who zealously supported him at the last election may have a place in the Excise or the Customs. But such a member would soon cease to solicit if the answer were, "Your friend shall have a place of fifty pounds a year, if you will give him a house and settle on him an income of a hundred a year." What chance then, I again ask, is there of jobbing? What, say some of the dissenters of Leeds, is to prevent a Tory Government, a High Church Government, from using this parliamentary grant to corrupt the schoolmasters of our borough and to induce them to use all their influence in favour of a Tory and High Church candidate? Why, Sir, the dissenters of Leeds themselves have the power to prevent it. Let them subscribe to the schools; let them take a share in the management of the schools; let them refuse to recommend to the Committee of Council any schoolmaster whom they suspect of having voted at any election from corrupt motives; and the thing is done. Our plan, in truth, is made up of checks. My only doubt is whether the checks may not be found too numerous and too stringent. On our general conduct there is the ordinary check, the parliamentary check. And, as respects those minute details which it is impossible that this House can investigate, we shall be checked, in every town and in every rural district, by boards consisting of independent men zealous in the cause of education.

25 The truth is, Sir, that those who clamour most loudly against our plan have never thought of ascertaining what it is. I see that a gentleman, who ought to have known better, has not been ashamed publicly to tell the world that our plan will cost the nation two millions a year and will paralyse all the exertions of individuals to educate the people. These two assertions are uttered in one breath. And yet, if he who made them had read our minutes before he railed at them, he would have seen that his predictions are contradictory; that they cannot both be fulfilled; that, if individuals do not exert themselves, the country will have to pay nothing; and that, if the country has to pay two millions, it will be because individuals have exerted themselves with such wonderful, such incredible, vigour as to raise four millions by voluntary contributions.

26 The next objection made by the honourable Member for Finsbury is that we have acted unconstitutionally and have encroached on the functions of

Parliament. The Committee of Council he seems to consider as an unlawful assembly. He calls it sometimes a self-elected body and sometimes a self-appointed body. Sir, these are words without meaning. The Committee is no more a self-elected body than the Board of Trade. It is a body appointed by the Queen; and in appointing it, Her Majesty has exercised, under the advice of her responsible Ministers, a prerogative as old as the monarchy. But, says the honourable Member, the constitutional course would have been to apply for an Act of Parliament. On what ground? Nothing but an Act of Parliament can legalise that which is illegal. But whoever heard of an Act of Parliament to legalise what was already beyond all dispute legal? Of course, if we wished to send aliens out of the country or to detail disaffected persons in custody without bringing them to trial, we must obtain an Act of Parliament empowering us to do so. But why should we ask for an Act of Parliament to empower us to do what anybody may do, what the honourable Member for Finsbury may do? Is there any doubt that he or anybody else may subscribe to a school, give a stipend to a monitor, or settle a retiring pension on a preceptor who has done good service? What any of the Queen's subjects may do the Queen may do. Suppose that her privy purse were so large that she could afford to employ a hundred thousand pounds in this beneficent manner; would an Act of Parliament be necessary to enable her to do so? Every part of our plan may lawfully be carried into execution by any person, Sovereign or subject, who has the inclination and the money. We have not the money; and for the money we come, in a strictly constitutional manner, to the House of Commons. The course which we have taken is in conformity with all precedent, as well as with all principle. There are military schools. No Act of Parliament was necessary to authorise the establishing of such schools. All that was necessary was a grant of money to defray the charge. When I was Secretary at War it was my duty to bring under Her Majesty's notice the situation of the female children of her soldiers. Many such children accompanied every regiment, and their education was grievously neglected. Her Majesty was graciously pleased to sign a warrant by which a girls' school was attached to each corps. No act of Parliament was necessary. For to set up a school where girls might be taught to read and write and sew and cook was perfectly legal already. I might have set it up myself, if I had been rich enough. All that I had to ask from Parliament was the money. But I ought to beg pardon for arguing a point so clear.

27 The next objection to our plans is that they interfere with the religious convictions of Her Majesty's subjects. It has been sometimes insinuated, but it has never been proved, that the Committee of Council has shown undue favour to the Established Church. Sir, I have carefully read and considered the minutes; and I wish that every man who has exerted his eloquence

against them had done the same. I say that I have carefully read and considered them and that they seem to me to have been drawn up with exemplary impartiality. The benefits which we offer we offer to people of all religious persuasions alike. The dissenting managers of schools will have equal authority with the managers who belong to the Church. A boy who goes to meeting will be just as eligible to be a monitor and will receive just as large a stipend, as if he went to the cathedral. The schoolmaster who is a nonconformist and the schoolmaster who is a conformist will enjoy the same emoluments and will, after the same term of service, obtain, on the same conditions, the same retiring pension. I wish that some gentleman would, instead of using vague phrases about religious liberty and the rights of conscience, answer this plain question. Suppose that in one of our large towns there are four schools, a school connected with the Church, a school connected with the Independents, a Baptist school, and a Wesleyan school; what encouragement, pecuniary or honorary, will, by our plan, be given to the school connected with the Church, and withheld from any of the other three schools? Is it not indeed plain that, if by neglect or maladministration the Church school should get into a bad state, while the dissenting schools flourish, the dissenting schools will receive public money and the Church school will receive none?

28 It is true, I admit, that in rural districts which are too poor to support more than one school the religious community to which the majority belongs will have an advantage over other religious communities. But this is not our fault. If we are as impartial as it is possible to be, you surely do not expect more. If there should be a parish containing nine hundred churchmen and a hundred dissenters, if there should, in that parish, be a school connected with the Church, if the dissenters in that parish should be too poor to set up another school, undoubtedly the school connected with the Church will, in that parish, get all that we give; and the dissenters will get nothing. But observe that there is no partiality to the Church, as the Church, in this arrangement. The churchmen get public money, not because they are churchmen, but because they are the majority. The dissenters get nothing, not because they are dissenters but because they are a small minority. There are districts where the case will be reversed, where there will be dissenting schools, and no Church schools. In such cases, the dissenters will get what we have to give, and the churchmen will get nothing.

29 But, Sir, I ought not to say that a churchman gets nothing by a system which gives a good education to dissenters, or that a dissenter gets nothing by a system which gives a good education to churchmen. We are not, I hope, so much conformists, or so much nonconformists, as to forget that we are Englishmen and Christians. We all, Churchmen, Presbyterians, Independ-

ents, Baptists, Methodists, have an interest in this, that the great body of the people should be rescued from ignorance and barbarism. I mentioned Lord George Gordon's mob. That mob began, it is true, with the Roman Catholics; but long before the tumults were over, there was not a respectable Protestant in London who was not in fear for his house, for his limbs, for his life, for the lives of those who were dearest to him. The honourable Member for Finsbury says that we call on men to pay for an education from which they derive no benefit. I deny that there is one honest and industrious man in the country who derives no benefit from living among honest and industrious neighbours rather than among rioters and vagabonds. This matter is as much a matter of common concern as the defence of our coast. Suppose that I were to say, "Why do you tax me to fortify Portsmouth? If the people of Portsmouth think that they cannot be safe without bastions and ravelins, let the people of Portsmouth pay the engineers and masons. Why am I to bear the charge of works from which I derive no advantage?" You would answer, and most justly, that there is no man in the island who does not derive advantage from these works, whether he resides within them or not. And, as every man, in whatever part of the island he may live, is bound to contribute to the support of those arsenals which are necessary for our common security, so is every man, to whatever sect he may belong, bound to contribute to the support of those schools on which, not less than on our arsenals, our common security depends.

30   I now come to the last words of the amendment. The honourable Member for Finsbury is apprehensive that our plan may interfere with the civil rights of Her Majesty's subjects. How a man's civil rights can be prejudiced by his learning to read and write, to multiply and divide, or even by his obtaining some knowledge of history and geography, I do not very well apprehend. One thing is clear, that persons sunk in that ignorance in which, as we are assured by the Congregational Union, great numbers of our countrymen are sunk, can be free only in name. It is hardly necessary for us to appoint a Select Committee for the purpose of inquiring whether knowledge be the ally or the enemy of liberty. He is, I must say, but a shortsighted friend of the common people who is eager to bestow on them a franchise which would make them all-powerful, and yet would withhold from them that instruction without which their power must be a curse to themselves and to the State.

31   This, Sir, is my defence. From the clamour of our accusers I appeal with confidence to the country to which we must, in no long time, render an account of our stewardship. I appeal with still more confidence to future generations, which while enjoying all the blessings of an impartial and efficient system of public instruction, will find it difficult to believe that the

authors of that system should have had to struggle with a vehement and pertinacious opposition, and still more difficult to believe that such an opposition was offered in the name of civil and religious freedom.

Analysis of Macaulay's Speech with Special Emphasis on Its Arrangement

Macaulay's speech is a fruitful document for the study of the topics of argument, and students might well spend time analyzing the operation of the topics in this piece of deliberative discourse. But although we will frequently refer to the arguments in the speech, the chief emphasis in this analysis will be upon the arrangement and function of the various parts.

Several contemporaries have testified that Macaulay's delivery was quite unprepossessing. He spoke rapidly, with very little modulation and inflection of the voice and with few gestures. But for all that, he was a remarkably effective parliamentary orator. His speeches on the First Reform Bill, on Copyright, and on the Ten Hours Bill are regarded as classics of English oratory. It was the substance and style of his speeches which proved so effective with his audiences. As Lord Lytton, one of his political opponents, said of him: "It was certainly, however, the brilliant art with which his speeches were composed upon oratorical principles, both as to arrangement of argument and liveliness of phraseology, that gave them that prodigious effect which they (at least the earlier ones) produced upon a mixed audience, and entitles this eminent personage to the fame of a very considerable orator." Let us analyze Macaulay's strategy in selecting and disposing his arguments in order to win over the opponents of the proposed bill.

Throughout this chapter on arrangement we have repeatedly observed that it is impossible, in the abstract, to lay down any hard and fast precepts about the proper disposition of the material one has gathered in the process of invention. Considerations of the occasion, the subject matter, the personality of the speaker or writer, the temper of the audience will dictate what the speaker or writer will have to do. Now we have a specific instance, and we can at least speculate about the decisions this particular orator made on this particular occasion.

First of all, let us look at the over-all organization of the speech:

> Introduction (paragraphs 1-3).
> Proof (paragraphs 4-30)
>   A. Confirmation of his own views (paragraphs 4-22)
>   B. Refutation of objections (paragraphs 23-30)
> Conclusion (paragraph 31)

A number of things are immediately apparent from this overview of the speech. First of all, it is notable how small a proportion of this long speech (about 9500 words) is devoted to the introduction and the conclusion. Secondly, one notes that there is no statement of fact. (We shall try to account for this proportion and this omission when we study the parts in detail.) Thirdly, one observes that Macaulay devotes the major portion of his speech (eighteen paragraphs) to the *positive* arguments in support of his stand.

Now let us study the strategy of the several parts. As we observed earlier in this chapter, the introduction does one or both of two things—it informs and/or disposes an audience. In the first paragraph of this introduction, Macaulay explains why he feels obliged to challenge the Member for Finsbury: he must vindicate himself from the implied charge that he has promoted this education bill out of base motives. He is hinting here that if he can prove his case, he will, indirectly, remove the taint on his *ethos*. This is primarily a deliberative discourse, but because of the subsidiary purpose— exonerating himself—it has overtones of judicial discourse. So the first paragraph was intended principally to dispose the audience favorably by exerting an ethical appeal.

In the second paragraph of the introduction, Macaulay is doing two things: he explains why he cannot follow the order of his opponent's speech, and he is prejudicing the audience against his opponent. It would be a strategic mistake, Macaulay explains, to follow the order of his opponent's speech, because his opponent has avoided any discussion of the central issue in this matter: whether the State has any right or duty to interfere in the education of its citizens. If he were to avoid discussing this issue he could not exonerate himself or help the cause of his colleagues. By pointing out his opponent's avoidance of this central issue, Macaulay raises grave doubts in the minds of his hearers about the good sense and good will of his opponent. How could a man, seriously bent on forestalling the passage of the bill now before the House, avoid discussing the principle that is at the heart of the matter?

The third paragraph of the introduction is a transitional paragraph in which Macaulay informs his audience of how he will proceed in the argumentative part of his discourse. He will set forth, unequivocally, how he himself stands on the basic issue and then give the reasons for the stand he takes. In other words, Macaulay has decided that the better strategy in this case is to present his case first and then proceed to refute the objections. As was observed earlier in this chapter, when one has confidence in the strength of one's case, it is usually better to present that case first. Once the audience has been exposed to the cogency of one's case, the audience will be inclined to recognize more readily the weakness of the opposing case when one proceeds to the refutation.

Paragraph 4 marks Macaulay's entry into the argumentative part of the discourse. As we observed, this speech lacks the statement of fact, because in this instance there is no need to rehearse the state of the case. The members of the House know the facts; they have been discussing the matter for several days already. Macaulay is not going to risk boring his audience by laboring the obvious. He realizes that he must spend most of his time on the podium trying to sway any doubtful colleagues to his point of view.

The first sentence of paragraph 4—"it is the right and the duty of the State to provide means of education for the common people"—is the conclusion that Macaulay hopes to establish in his speech. The major premise upon which this conclusion is based is stated at the end of this paragraph—"it is the duty of every government to take order for giving security to the persons and property of the members of the community." Since there is universal agreement about this function of government, Macaulay does not have to spend time proving the truth of this proposition. What he has to prove is the truth of his minor premise.

This minor premise is presented in the first sentence of the next paragraph —"the education of the common people is a most effectual means of securing our persons and our property." The rest of the *confirmation* portion of the speech is devoted to a series of arguments—arguments from example, from testimony, from analogy—to prove that educating the common people is the best means of "securing our persons and our property."

We see then what great care Macaulay has taken to orient his audience at the outset of his speech. He exposes his ground-plan and makes it very clear what he is seeking to do. The human mind naturally delights in the perception of order of any kind, and when it is alerted at the outset to a plan, it is prepared to follow the working out of that plan. There will be times— especially when our case is weak or when an audience is unusually hostile— when it is better to conceal our plan until we are well launched into our argument. But since Macaulay has confidence in the strength of his case and since he knows that most of the members of the House concur with him, he decides to take advantage of what can be gained by "ordering" his discourse at the outset and thereby revealing his strategy.

The first argument that Macaulay presents in paragraph 5 is an argument from testimony. And it is notable that the *first* authority he cites in support of his minor premise is Adam Smith. Adam Smith was a judicious choice, because after the publication of his *Wealth of Nations* (1776) he was generally regarded as the foremost champion of the free-enterprise system in political economy. Macaulay realizes that the people he has to convince are those who are fearful of government interference in the political, economic, and social affairs of men. What an advantage it will be to him if he can enlist in support of his contention the man who represents, for the unconvinced, the chief spokesman of the laissez-faire philosophy. Fortunately for his cause, Macaulay finds Adam Smith to be "an available means of persuasion" in this case, for Adam Smith had once contended that the education of the poor *was* the proper business of the Commonwealth.

To demonstrate how wise Adam Smith's contention was, Macaulay cites examples, in the rest of paragraph 5 and in paragraph 6, of what happens when the Commonwealth does not take care for the education of the poor. There were No Popery riots led by Lord George Gordon in 1780, four years after Adam Smith made his unheeded recommendation, and there were subsequent riots in the industrial counties of the North.

In paragraphs 4-7 Macaulay has set forth, briefly and cogently, his main argument, summarizing it in the form of a syllogism in paragraph 7. And as we have seen, it is strategically advisable to advance positive arguments and a strong argument first, *when our case is strong*. But if Macaulay now leaves unanswered the major objection to his main argument, there will linger in the minds of the opposing faction the suspicion that he has avoided the opposing argument because it is stronger than his own argument. So he must meet this opposing argument head on, and this he does in paragraphs 8-10.

"And what is the alternative?" Macaulay asks at the beginning of paragraph 8. In meeting the opposing argument, he sets up an either-or situation. A government, he says, can protect persons and property either by educating the people or by putting people in prison. We can ignore the question of whether these are the *only* alternatives. Macaulay is merely taking advantage of the fact that the opposition has proposed punitive measures as the alternative to educating the people. In other words, since the opposition has not suggested other ways in which the government can fulfill its acknowledged duty to protect the lives and property of its citizens, Macaulay can deal exclusively with the alternative that the opposition *has* proposed.

In paragraph 9, Macaulay cites the example of what happened in Monmouthshire to show that punitive measures are ineffectual in protecting the lives and property of the people. In the short paragraph 10, Macaulay generalizes from this single example: education of the people is not only *a* means but the *best* means of attaining the chief end of a government.

In paragraph 11, Macaulay attempts to reinforce his generalization by presenting another example—the example of the Protestant Dissenters in Massachusetts. By citing this example, Macaulay again displays his great rhetorical skill. Most of the opposition to state-supported schools in England was coming from Dissenting groups—sects like the Puritans, Baptists, Independents, and Methodists. Macaulay realizes how impressive it will be if he cites the example of what the Puritans who emigrated to the New World did when they established their commonwealths. They immediately made provisions for the establishment of public schools in every township. Macaulay then cites the testimony of men like William Penn, George Washington, and Thomas Jefferson—men who were wary of government interference—in support of his contention that it is prudent to educate the common people.

In paragraphs 12-15, Macaulay returns to the opposing argument in a further attempt to refute it. His main efforts here are devoted to a highly emotional appeal, in paragraph 13, calculated to reduce to absurdity the view that "Government is simply a great hangman," and to his refutation, in paragraphs 14 and 15, of the analogical argument that if free competition is a good thing in business affairs, it must be a good thing in education.

In paragraphs 16-19, Macaulay counters the argument he has just refuted, with an analogical argument of his own: just as government ought to provide for the national defense, so it ought to provide for the education of the people. He supports his own argument with an argument of David Hume—another Dissenter—who maintained that some vocations are necessary for the well-being of society but will not be undertaken unless there is adequate compensation offered. Since teaching is one of those vital vocations that private enterprise is not likely to compensate adequately, the government should assume the responsibility of rewarding the schoolmaster. Up to this point, however, the government has not supported public education, and the result has been mass illiteracy, a condition that is confirmed by statistics from various sources, which, Macaulay shrewdly reminds his audience, is the Congregational Union, a Nonconformist agency.

Macaulay saves his most impressive example until last—the example of what state-supported education has accomplished in Scotland (paragraphs 20-21). The reminder about the educational system in Scotland must have been particularly impressive to the Dissenters in Macaulay's audience, because Scotland, with its national religion of Presbyterianism, was a stronghold of the Nonconformist spirit. The example of Scotland was impressive for another reason too. By showing how Scotland, with far fewer physical and economic advantages, had outstripped England in the matter of elementary education, Macaulay must have piqued the patriotic pride of Englishmen.

Paragraph 22 is a transitional paragraph, signaling the end of his argument for the principle enunciated at the beginning of paragraph 4 and preparing the audience for the next section of the speech—the refutation of the specific objections made by the Member for Finsbury. If there was any doubt about Macaulay's choosing to delay answering the objections until this point in the speech, the doubt would be cleared up by Macaulay's own statement in this paragraph. "For if the great principle for which I have been contending is admitted," Macaulay says here, "the objections which have been made to the details of our plan will vanish fast." Macaulay also reveals something about the arrangement of the following section: he will deal with the objections in the order in which they were proposed in the amendment of the Member for Finsbury. Also, the audience can more easily check that he has answered *all* of the objections. He might have adopted another order—for instance, dealing with the most serious objection first, then going on to the next most serious—but by choosing to follow his opponent's order, he subtly discloses his confidence that he can easily demolish the objections—in whatever order they come.

In paragraphs 23-30, Macaulay states and refutes in turn each of the five objections leveled against the proposed bill:

1. Objection to the cost of the bill (paragraph 23)
2. Objection to the increased influence of the Crown (paragraphs 24-25)
3. Objection to the unconstitutionality of the proposed bill (paragraph 26)
4. Objection to the interference with the religious convictions of the people (paragraphs 27-29)
5. Objection to the interference with the civil rights of the people (paragraph 30)

By the time Macaulay comes to his conclusion in paragraph 31, he has been haranguing his colleagues for at least an hour. He could now launch into a peroration that would briefly recapitulate his arguments, reinforce his ethical appeal, and rouse his audience to the proper emotional pitch. Instead, he concludes his speech with three sentences (99 words) of successively greater length.

Macaulay must have sensed that nothing more was to be gained, *with this particular audience,* by prolonging his speech. By this time, the audience has been subjected to so much debate on this matter that they will be grateful to the orator who sits down when he has made his point. These members of the House of Commons, who are being asked to appropriate a large sum of money, are hardheaded, practical men answerable to their constituents. Under the circumstances, they are not likely to be susceptible to emotional appeal. They are going to be impressed by arguments which prove, or at least persuade them, that this measure is worthy, advantageous, or feasible. So Macaulay contents himself in the conclusion with a brief appeal: a reminder that the members of the House are accountable (1) to all the citizens of the country, and (2) to future generations. That reminder will prompt his audience to weigh the moral importance of their forthcoming vote.

Robert M. Hutchins: Morals, Religion, and Higher Education

Robert Maynard Hutchins was once a "disturber" of American higher education much in the way that young people today are "disturbers"—although he was calling for reforms in the structure and content of the curriculum somewhat different from the reforms that students today are demanding. Born in Brooklyn, New York, in 1899, he became dean of the Yale Law School while still in his twenties, and then in 1929, at the age of thirty, he became president of the University of Chicago. During his term as president and later as chancellor (1945–51), he was a persistently controversial figure on the educational scene. He abandoned intercollegiate football at Chicago, instituted the system whereby gifted students could start college after their second year of high school and could further accelerate their graduation by passing examinations for exemptions from courses, was a promoter, along with his colleague Mortimer Adler, of the Great Books course, and was a frequent defender of himself and the University of Chicago against the charge of being "Communist inspired." The titles of some of his books give some indication of the battles he was fighting: Education for Freedom *(1943),* The Conflict in Education *(1953),* What's a College For? *(1960).* He is now the Chairman of the Fund for the Republic, which supports, among other things, the Center for the Study of Democratic Institutions in Santa Barbara, California. Hutchins originally delivered the following discourse as the Bedell Lecture at Kenyon College in October 1948, but later adapted the speech for inclusion in a collection of his essays entitled* Freedom, Education, and the Fund: Essays and Addresses, 1946–1956 *(New York: Meridian Books, 1956), pp. 81–100. Reprinted by permission of the author.*

1   This essay is an inquiry into problems that are among the hardest in education. I cannot pretend that I have solved any of them. The inquiry will take us through some of the solutions that have been offered. If in the process it appears that these solutions are inadequate, I beg the reader not to despair; for it may be possible to discover solutions that may be workable and sound. I believe that higher education can make a unique contribution to morals and religion. I do not believe that it can make some of the contributions expected of it, and I think that these expectations obscure the real purposes and achievements of higher education. The object of this essay must therefore be rather more to clear the ground than to erect a building. I can regard the building attempted here as at best a very modest structure, which will accomplish more than I am entitled to hope for it if it serves as temporary shelter to those who may design the ultimate edifice.

2   The essay uses the words "morals," "religion," and "higher education" in a definite sense. The sense may be wrong, but it is consistently employed. By morals I mean good habits. Good habits are those which are good for the organism in question. To know what is good for an organism, you have to know the nature of that organism. If man is an animal like any other, then there is no reason why we should expect him to have habits any different from the other animals. For by good habits we do not mean obedience to conventions. That lies in the sphere of etiquette, rather than morals, and we are concerned here with morals.

3   For example, the Kinsey Report has no moral significance. The Report seems to proceed on the assumption that, since man is an animal like any other, and since morals are purely conventional, a moral revolution may be effected by showing that we do not live according to the conventions we profess. To show that men do not live according to the conventions they profess merely shows that they do not live according to the conventions they profess. It shows nothing at all about what is good for man or what is bad for him. The fact that a great many men may be doing what is bad for them is neither new nor relevant. A man may change a convention by getting the leaders of society to join him in breaking it. A man cannot change bad to good even if he gets all his fellow-men to conspire with him.

4   By religion I mean belief in and obedience to God. This may not require adherence to a church or creed; but it demands religious faith. Faith is not reason, but it is something more than a vague, sentimental desire to do good and be good. The problem of faith and reason has agitated mankind for centuries, and I could not deal with it here, even if I knew how. But the kind of religion I am talking about is one that is sustained by both reason and faith. We see in St. Augustine's *Confessions* the way in which a man may come to the sort of religious conviction that has meaning. St. Augustine's conversion followed after tremendous wrestling with the intellectual difficulties of Christianity and was prepared by the conquest of those difficulties.

5   By higher education I mean that education which takes place in institutions beyond the secondary level as secondary education is usually defined. I mean the education that is given by the colleges and universities of this country. I do not believe that these institutions are properly organized. The college should occupy the area now uneasily filled by the last two years of high school and the first two years of college, and the university should begin its work at the beginning of the conventional junior year in college. But for the purposes of this essay I am willing to regard all the colleges of the United States as offering higher education. I am willing to include all universities, too, even though I believe that a university is a place where all professors and all students are engaged in independent study, and in this view a true university has not yet arisen in our country.

6 We are concerned, then, with what goes on or with what should go on in certain institutions, in institutions of a certain kind. And it is important to notice that what goes on or should go on in these institutions is severely limited to what can go on in them. What can go on in them is in part determined by the age of the students with whom they have to deal and by the length of time that they spend in the institutions. At any university, if an alumnus "succeeds" in later life, it is customary for the university to take the credit for it; if he goes to the penitentiary, it is said that he was bad material and should never have been admitted. President Truman's Commission on Higher Education sees the student going to college in the moral and intellectual state of the newborn babe and graduating four, or even two, years later as a mature and autonomous member of society. The Commission, like most people who know far less about education, places on the educational institution a responsibility for the total development of the individual by starting and ending with the wrong assumptions.

7 The assumption that a college freshman has no habits is in obvious contradiction to the facts of life. The assumption that if he has no habits, or, if his habits are all bad, he can acquire in four years a set of good habits that will last all his life is certainly naive. My guess is that eighteen is a greater age than we who are past it are willing to admit. It is flattering to us, and it makes our work easier, to feel that our students are children who can do nothing and learn little without our help and supervision; but to suppose that a boy or girl of eighteen has been unaffected by his home and by society is not merely factually inaccurate; it gives higher education a false conception of its task and its possibilities; and it must contribute to that prolongation of adolescence which is so distressing a feature of American life.

8. We are concerned here, then, with what certain institutions can do in a certain period of time with certain people of a certain age.[1] And in each institution there will be a certain number of these young people, and usually a number larger than one per instructor. Rousseau's *Émile* contains some interesting educational suggestions, but it can help us in the solution of few of the practical problems that affect an educational system: Émile had a tutor and never went to school.[2] We are discussing what can be done in scholastic institutions at a certain level.

---

[1] "We must remember that the whole problem of intellectual education is controlled by lack of time. If Methuselah was not an educated man, it was his own fault or that of his teachers" (A. N. Whitehead, *The Aims of Education*, p. 96).

[2] Cf.: "All Souls College, Oxford, planned better than it knew when it limited the number of its undergraduates to four; four is exactly the right number for any college which is really intent on getting results" (Albert Jay Nock, *Memoirs of a Superfluous Man*, Vol. III, chap. 3).

9 John Stuart Mill faced this question in his inaugural address at St. Andrew's. He said: "No one can dispense with an education directed expressly to the moral as well as the intellectual part of his being. Such education, so far as it is direct, is either moral or religious; and these may either be treated as distinct or as different aspects of the same thing. The subject we are now considering is not education as a whole, but scholastic education, and we must keep in view the inevitable limitations of what schools and universities can do. It is beyond their power to educate morally or religiously. Moral and religious education consist in training the feelings and the daily habits; and these are, in the main, beyond the sphere and inaccessible to the control of public education. It is the home, the family, which gives us the moral or religious education we really receive; and this is completed, and modified, sometimes for the better, often for the worse, by society and the opinions and feelings with which we are there surrounded."

10 So Cardinal Newman insisted over and over again that the purpose of a university was intellectual and not moral. The utilitarian philosopher and the Catholic theologian came to the same conclusion, though perhaps for different reasons. To the role of the family Newman adds that of the church, which, characteristically, Mill does not mention in his discussion of moral and religious education. They both hold that it is beyond the power of higher education to educate morally and religiously. Both Newman and Mill view the world about them as containing various agencies and institutions, each with a purpose of its own. The sphere of the family or the church is not the sphere of educational institutions; the sphere of educational institutions is not that of the family or the church.

11 Mill and Newman were writing in the nineteenth century, when both church and family were more effective in their spheres than they are today. Would their conclusion be any different now, when, we are told, the family is disintegrating and the church is dying? I think not. Even if they assumed that the family was going to pieces and the church on the way to extinction, Newman and Mill would hardly suppose that the way to revive these institutions was to turn over their functions to another agency. This could only guarantee the destruction of the family and the church. And, if the attempt were made to turn their functions over to the educational system, it would guarantee the increasing confusion of that agency. If we can find out what the proper function of the education system is, we shall discover at the same time, I am sure, that the performance of that function will require all the attention and intelligence that the educational system can command.

12 Mill emphasizes another point: some phases of human development are determined by the impact of society in adult life. In our time the impact of society, particularly as it makes itself felt through what are called the media of mass communication, of which Mill and Newman were fortunately ig-

norant, is, I think, the most important factor in moral and cultural development. I do not see how any educational system can be expected to cope with the comic book, the radio, the motion picture, the slick-paper magazine, television, and the sensational press. The tremendous skill and the enormous resources available to these moral and cultural agencies make them more influential in molding the lives of our people than the whole educational system. And even if the educational system had more money and more skill, as it certainly should have, there appears to be a kind of Gresham's law of culture, under which bad stuff drives out good. Probably because of original sin, human beings seem to prefer demoralization to improvement.

13   The usual answer to this is that we shall educate human beings to be better and to prefer to be better than worse. This seems to me to overlook the limited time that the educational system has at its disposal and the limited influence that it can therefore have upon the lives of those who, even while they are temporarily committed to its care, are soaking up through every pore poisons transmitted by every device that the triumphs of science and technology now make it possible to subject them to.

14   An officer of the General Electric Company has lately commented on cultural benefits conferred upon us by television. He said that the principal market for television sets was saloons and that therefore the contribution of this triumph of science and technology to the advance of civilization was more booze, less fresh air, and the same old ball game.

15   In *A Study of History* Mr. Toynbee deals at length with the stumbling blocks that have prevented universal free education from ushering in a new era of happiness and well-being for Western society. The dangerous consequence of the introduction of universal free education in Great Britain in 1870, Toynbee argues, was the triumph of yellow journalism—and later the movies—which succeeded in creating an intellectual tyranny more deadening than the illiteracy from which free schooling had rescued the masses.[3] The only remedy to this situation, Toynbee continues, is to raise the level of mass cultivation.[4]

16   We must heartily agree with Mr. Toynbee that it is desirable to raise the level of mass cultivation. From the point of view of Mr. Toynbee's aims, universal liberal education, rather than universal schooling, is indicated. But to hope that even the best training in criticism can cope with the constant storm of triviality and propaganda that now beats upon the citizen seems

---

[3] (London, 1939), IV, 193-94; also *ibid.*, p. 196.

[4] *Ibid.*, pp. 196-7; cf. Aldous Huxley, *Science, Liberty, and Peace* (New York, 1946), p. 9: "But in actual historical fact the spread of free compulsory education, and, along with it, the cheapening and acceleration of the older methods of printing, have almost everywhere been followed by an increase in the power of ruling oligarchies at the expense of the masses."

to me to expect too much of any educational system. Such training should certainly be given, and given to everybody. But an educational system cannot reform a society, and Mr. Toynbee is calling for nothing less.

17 I can pursue this subject no further, for that way madness lies. I can only assume that the educational system will continue to do its best in the hope that some day a sort of mass conversion will overtake our people, and they will want to be better. If they do not want to be better, the educational system cannot make them so. And the educational system cannot make them want to be so. All it can do is to offer an opportunity and, perhaps, an example of which those who wish to swim against the tide can avail themselves. It is, of course, imperative that this opportunity and this example should constantly be held before our people.

18 Let us return to Newman and Mill. They do not say that moral and religious education is unimportant. On the contrary, they both feel that moral and religious education is more important than intellectual education. So do I. The question is not whether moral and religious education is important, but what colleges and universities can do about it. No one would favor a nation of highly intelligent and well-trained robbers, murderers, thieves, arsonists, and forgers. And no one would contend that knowledge of the arts and sciences automatically leads to the development of good moral habits.

19 Aristotle said that it is impossible to be wise without being good, and impossible to be good without being wise. But this cannot be taken to mean that it is impossible to be good without qualifying for the Ph.D. degree. We all know good scholars who are bad men; and I have known some illiterates who seemed good to me. Aristotle meant that it is impossible to be good without being prudent, or practically wise, because the imprudent man does not know how to adjust means to ends; and it is impossible to be prudent, or practically wise, without being good, because the bad man is seeking the wrong ends. Though prudence is a habit of the mind, it seems to me that habit of the mind which higher education is least qualified and least likely to teach. The development of prudence requires long experience and reflection. Aristotle said that young men should not listen to lectures on moral philosophy, because they have had no experience; they would have only the vaguest and most abstract notions of what was under discussion. As I indicated earlier, college and university students are likely to be more mature than we think they are. They are not blank tablets upon which the teacher can write anything he pleases. They have habits, and many, if not most, of them have learned something of religion. But by saying that they are more mature than we think they are I do not mean to say they are mature. They are not experienced adults. It is hard to disagree with Aristotle's principle that subjects that require experience do not convey their full meaning to the inexperienced.

20   For this reason we may lament the low estate of the education of adults in this country. Moral and political philosophy, history, and literature yield up their full lessons only to those who have had the experience to comprehend them. If they are taught to the inexperienced and never taught again, they are never comprehended. A boy will read a few plays of Shakespeare in high school and never look at them for the rest of his life. Shakespeare remains for him a quaint ancient writer who did not know how to spell very well, but who has managed to leave us a large number of quotations for funeral orations and Fourth of July addresses. This does not mean that Shakespeare should not be taught in high school. It means that if he is read only in high school, we never get more than a fraction of what he has to give us. My favorite illustration is *Macbeth*. When I taught *Macbeth* to students in a preparatory school, it was a blood-and-thunder story. It was a good blood-and-thunder story, and one well worth teaching; but it was a blood-and-thunder story still. *Macbeth* can mean to us what it meant to Shakespeare only if we have had enough experience, vicarious or otherwise, of marriage and ambition to understand the issues and their implications.

21   These considerations suggest that the curriculum in our schools and colleges is upside down. It is assumed that children are primarily interested in the life about them and that subjects dealing with the life about them command their attention and enlist their understanding; hence the increasing prominence of the social studies in the schools. Nothing in my experience suggests that children are more interested in American history than in arithmetic and the stories of ancient Greece. Those subjects which are commonly supposed to be too abstract for the young, like mathematics, grammar, logic, astronomy, and music, are the best subjects for the young precisely because they are abstract. Their comprehension requires no experience or maturity. I see no escape from the proposition that subjects that require experience and maturity cannot be profitably taught to the inexperienced and immature.

22   At any rate it seems to me that higher education probably cannot teach prudence or practical wisdom, that habit of the mind by which we select the right means to the end. Nor can it, I believe, teach good habits of action. It cannot teach morals.

23   The moral virtues are habits, and habits are formed by acts. We can have no assurance that courses in elementary, intermediate, and advanced goodness will be followed by good acts. In fact, such courses seem likely to induce precisely the opposite behavior. The boarding school in the country, and to some extent the college in a small town, may be able to prevent its students from the habitual performance of acts so bad that they violate the law or outrage the conventions. But even this opportunity is denied the metropolitan university, half the students of which live at home, far from

the benevolent influence of the dean of men and the dean of women. In any event this kind of control must be of the most superficial and negative order. It will not do to say that higher education should try to prevent crime. What we are seeking to discover is the means by which higher education can promote the formation of good habits; it can hardly hope to do so by courses in how to be good.

24 Nor can it hope to do so by means of extra-curricular activities, at least on that industrial or "big-time" scale with which we in America are familiar. Under this system a few highly trained but somewhat underpaid experts go through the discipline and sometimes suffer the fate of the gladiators of old while the rest of the college observes their conduct on Saturday afternoons in the spirit of a Roman holiday. I confess I am unable to see what this has to do with morals, religion, or higher education, except as to the experts referred to. They indeed may develop some habits, and some of the habits may be good. The four cardinal virtues are traditionally supposed to be courage, temperance, justice, and prudence; and the athlete may be compelled, in so far as he is an athlete, to give some appearance of them all.

25 The courage that is required to meet the shock of a 225-pound steel-worker imported from Gary, and the temperance required at the training table, and the justice required to obey the rules, and the prudence required to select the right means to the end of victory doubtless bear some relation to the courage, temperance, justice, and prudence that moralists had in mind when they isolated and described the cardinal virtues. But the effect of the activities of the experts on the moral character of the rest of the college must be slight at best. My class never saw Yale win a big game, and it was said of the coach of that time that he had conferred one inestimable moral benefit upon the student body: he had taught them not to bet—or at least not to bet on Yale. I do not depreciate this contribution; for temperance and prudence would seem to forbid gambling. But this contribution, important as it is, seems to me negligible in contrast to the enormous expenditure of time, money, effort, and interest that went into the acquisition of it.

26 Even if extra-curricular activities had the decisively beneficial influence on character that their devotees claim for them, that would hardly help us to answer the question of the special role of higher education in the formation of character; for extra-curricular activities could be conducted more effectively if there were no curriculum at all. They could be and are conducted in YMCA's or Boy Scout encampments, at country clubs and among the Campfire Girls. Extra-curricular activities are not the peculiar property of educational institutions, nor do they serve to clarify the peculiar part that educational institutions can play in the formation of character.

27 Higher education cannot hope to make students good by compulsory religious exercises. If a college or university has decided to be secular, in the

sense that it requires no religious tests of its students or faculty, if it wants to appeal to those of no faith, of little faith, and many faiths, it cannot compel worship. It may compel attendance; my classmates came to morning chapel with overcoats over their pajamas and coughed the speaker down.[5] After five years of coughing, compulsory chapel was abolished. There was moaning among some of the trustees, alumni, and faculty; but a college cannot have it both ways. It cannot hold itself out as secular and then demand that its members go through religious ceremonies as a condition of being allowed to continue as members.

28   The great majority of the endowed colleges and universities of this country have long since passed from under the control of the religious groups that founded them; and public institutions seem required by the Constitution to be secular. Yet it must be admitted that religion is of the greatest moral importance. If the whole world practiced Aristotle's *Ethics,* the whole world would be much better off than it is today. But I doubt if any single man, to say nothing of the whole world, can practice Aristotle's *Ethics* without the support and inspiration of religious faith. This Aristotle himself seemed to recognize; for the ideal man whom he holds up to our admiration is one who is almost divine. The modern critic is inclined to scoff at the Aristotelian dictum that men are rational animals. It is no longer fashionable to refer to the rationality of man. But Aristotle was saying not merely that men are rational but also that they are animal.[6] Because men are animal, because the flesh is weak and life is hard, the moral virtues cannot be consistently practiced without divine aid.

29   Metaphysics and what is called natural theology deal with the ultimate questions. But intellectual history reveals nothing so clearly as their inadequacy for the task. The existence and nature of God, the character and destiny of the human soul, and the salvation of man are problems that remain obscure in the light of natural reason. Or consider human life without religion and history without providence. A perfect theory of democracy can be made out of the metaphysical and ethical writings of Aristotle. But as he himself did not have the fortitude to follow his premises to their conclusions and admit all men to participation in their own government, so it is improbable that the practice of democracy now or in the future can be achieved merely by the demonstration of its reasonableness. Men, simply because they

---

[5] There is some reason to believe that this is the group Milton had in mind when he referred to
>"...Eli's sons, who fill'd
>With lust and violence the house of God."
>   (*Paradise Lost,* Bk. I, line 495).

[6] "Of new biological standpoints which last century gave us one most fruitful has been that of man as one of the animals. The thought is after all merely a return to the common-sense of Aristotle" (Sherrington, *Man on His Nature,* New York, 1939).

are men, are unlikely to find within themselves the power that can bring the good life and the good state to pass. As Reinhold Niebuhr pointed out in his Gifford lectures, all anthropocentric ethical doctrines fail at this point: they overlook the fallen nature of man and assume that without grace he can reach a terrestrial end to which, almost by definition, no being with such a nature can ever attain.

30 No one could have been more conscious of the dependence of morals upon religion than Cardinal Newman, and it was he who said that the purpose of a university was intellectual, not moral. Our question is not whether the educational system can give us everything that is indispensable to the good life. If a college cannot make its students religious, it cannot, to that extent, make them good.

31 Why cannot higher education make its students religious? Why can it not exact a religious commitment from all entering students and apply religious tests determining or affecting their progress through, and graduation from, the institution? Why can it not insist that all members of the faculty shall be members in good standing of Christian churches and shall perform their religious duties with the same regularity and obligation as they now perform their teaching duties?

32 Perhaps a college could do these things, but it would be unfortunate if it did. Faith is one of the theological virtues; it may be deserved, but it is not earned. It is a gift of God. Those who have been denied this gift should not be denied educational opportunities.

33 As to the professors, let us imagine that the college or university has a choice between a man who is a third-rate historian or physicist but an ardent believer and one who is a first-rate historian or physicist and an atheist? Which should it choose? I approach this question with some diffidence, for I am not at all sure of the answer. John Stuart Mill had an answer. He said: "The moral or religious influence which an university can exercise consists less in any express teaching than in the pervading tone of the place. Whatever it teaches, it should teach as penetrated by a sense of duty; it should present all knowledge as chiefly a means to worthiness of life, given for the double purpose of making each of us practically useful to his fellow-creatures and of elevating the character of the species itself; exalting and dignifying our nature."

34 Mill says that the moral and religious influence of a university consists in its pervading tone. If the pervading tone is moral and religious, moral and religious influence will follow. But how is the pervading tone set? The pervading tone of higher education must be set by those who guide its destinies and teach its students. If they are moral and religious, the tone may be that which Mill would like to hear. If they are not, the tone may be something else altogether.

35 Since we are agreed that it is more important to be good than to be intellectual and that it is hard, if not impossible, to be good without being religious, and since we want higher education to exert a moral and religious influence through its pervading tone, it would seem to follow that men should not be appointed to the faculties of colleges and universities unless they are moral and religious men. Yet we know that every day men are appointed to faculties after a most painstaking investigation of their intellectual attainments but without any inquiry into their moral habits or their religious beliefs. I do it every day myself. We do not ask whether the prospective appointee is afflicted with scientism, skepticism, or secularism. We do not request him to state whether he believes in God or whether or not he thinks morals are indistinguishable from the mores and are relative, like the mores, to time and place. We ask what his training has been, what his record was, what his publications are, and what are the prospects of his publishing any more. We ask, in short, whether he has discovered any truths in his specialty and whether he can be expected to seek for and, perhaps, discover additional truths. It would be regarded as an impertinence in a secular institution to ask a prospective faculty member about anything outside his specialty, unless, of course, rumors of flagrant immorality likely to embarrass the college had reached the president's ears. These would have to be inquired into and all fears on this score set at rest. But everybody would be shocked at the suggestion that it is proper to investigate a man's beliefs or to ask what, if anything, he stands for.

36 It is perfectly fair for higher education to say that its aim is the pursuit and transmission of truth. For this purpose the institution is divided into departments, sub-departments, and sub-sections of sub-departments. The assumption is that nobody can discover the whole truth but that by a collective effort on the part of specialists in many fields the institution as such may get closer to the whole truth than any single individual.

37 The reason it is perfectly fair for a college or university to say that its aim is the pursuit and transmission of truth is that in our society only these institutions have this aim. So Mill said of morals and religion: "What is special to an university on these subjects belongs chiefly, like the rest of its work, to the intellectual department. An university exists for the purpose of laying open to each succeeding generation, as far as the conditions of the case admit, the accumulated treasure of the thoughts of mankind."

38 In this view a college or university is a place where people think. And the test of all its work, the test of the work of professors and students, the test of every course and every research project is: how much thought does it require? But can this be all? Does this mean that as long as there is thought it makes no difference what is thought about, or are some things more important to think about than others?

39 The practices of higher education in America do not conform to the views of Mill, to say nothing of meeting the further question I have raised concerning the relative importance of things to be thought about. The three types of curriculum current in this country may be called the life-activities centered curriculum, the student-interest centered curriculum, and the professor-interest centered curriculum. The life-activities centered curriculum is exemplified by the course of study of a women's college, which is based on a job analysis of the diaries of several hundred mature women. The categories of the activities of these women constitute the structure of the college curriculum, although women, perhaps, ought to do and may even be doing things that these mature women did not do. The student-interest centered curriculum, apparently on the theory that it is hopeless to try to understand education or to figure out what an education should be, simply takes the expression of interest on the part of the student as revealing what he should study, for who knows what he should study, anyway? The professor-interest centered curriculum is the more usual variety. Each professor and each department want the whole time of the student so that he can be thoroughly trained in the professor's or the department's specialty. Since it is obviously impossible for the student's whole time to be spent in this way, the curriculum is determined by a process of pulling, hauling, and log-rolling; and finally emerges as a sort of checkerboard across which the bewildered student moves, absorbing from each square, it is hoped, a little of something that each professor or each department has to offer him.

40 None of these courses of study has any necessary connection with thinking. The activities of mature women may have had little to do with thinking. Some students may not be interested in thought. And I have heard of professors and departments who believed that their function was to cram their students with information. It is hard to contemplate such courses of study without agreeing with Henry Adams, who said, "The chief wonder of education is that it does not ruin everybody concerned in it, teachers and taught."

41 If we insist that colleges and universities should be devoted to thinking and if we insist that they should, if possible, think about important things, we may perhaps find the way in which higher education may make its unique contribution to morals and religion. Most of our educational institutions are and will probably remain secular, in the sense that they are not controlled by any church and are open to everybody regardless of his religious faith or lack of it. But there is another kind of secularism that besets the higher learning in America, and that is secularism in the sense in which we say that religion is insignificant, it is outmoded, it is equivalent to superstition. This kind of secularism higher education can and should repel. If a college or university is going to think and to think about important things, then it must think about religion. It is perhaps not necessary that all the faculty should be religious; it would be desirable that most of them, at least, should take religion seriously.

42   The same is true of morals. If a college or university is to think and think about important things, then it must think about morals, for we have admitted throughout that morals are most important. It may not be necessary that all the faculty be good; it would be desirable that most of them, at least, take goodness seriously.

43   If we grant that the purpose of higher education is to think and to think about important things for the purpose of learning as much of the truth as possible about these things and transmitting it to each succeeding generation, we see immediately that certain moral and religious consequences follow. In the first place, higher education then supplies the intellectual foundations of morals and religion. This is a contribution of the first importance, and it is, I believe, a contribution to morals and religion that only higher education can make.

44   As to religion, I need only refer again to St. Augustine to make the point that the resolution of intellectual difficulties seems to me, if not necessary, at least highly desirable as a prelude to or concomitant of religious faith. As to morals, habits are so much a function of the circumstances under which they were formed that we can have little assurance of their continuance in other circumstances unless the person who has the habits knows why he should retain them. As habits are formed by acts, they are broken by the cessation of these acts or by the continued performance of conflicting acts. The child carefully nurtured in good habits that he practices without comprehending the reasons for doing so is likely to fall from grace when he casts off the parental apron strings. The serious consideration of the intellectual foundations of good habits should supply him with the conviction he needs in order to keep up in adult life the good work begun in childhood.

45   The curriculum, then, should include the knowledge and understanding of the principles of morality. It should include both natural and sacred theology; for how can a man call himself educated who does not grasp the leading ideas that since the dawn of history have animated mankind? The institution must be committed to taking morality and religion seriously. This commitment involves a third: if the object of higher education is the truth, then, in order to take morality and religion seriously, the institution must believe that there is some truth and some discoverable truth about morality and religion. According to the dogmas of scientism, skepticism, and secularism there is no such truth. If there is truth at all, it is truth discoverable in the laboratory, by what is called the scientific method. I recently heard a minister of a Protestant church state at a public meeting

that no man could tell whether a given act was right or wrong. I replied that he was a moral relativist, thinking that he would be so stung by this reproach that he might reconsider his position. Instead he proudly answered, "Of course I am a moral relativist," as though to say that anybody who is not a moral relativist is an unenlightened, unscientific, medieval reactionary.

46 We should all admit, I suppose, that a moral act is one performed in the right way under the right circumstances; but the notion that under some circumstances it could be right, for example, for one man to kill another with malice aforethought must mean that there is no difference between good and bad, between right and wrong, that there is no moral law and there are no moral principles that higher education can take seriously. It must mean that there are no morals; there are only the mores; and there is no religion; there is only superstition. If higher education is to take morality and religion seriously, it must repudiate these dogmas; for the truths of morality and religion never have been and never can be discovered by experiment or by any allegedly "scientific" means. Morality and religion cannot be taken seriously unless the possibility of attaining truth by philosophical inquiry and by revelation is admitted. It is necessary to believe that philosophy is something more than words and that it is possible to be rational and religious at the same time.[7]

47 By the commitments to which I have referred, higher education may directly contribute to the formation of character. The indirect contributions it may make are, perhaps, almost as important. These are the moral by-products of its intellectual work. The life of learning requires the support of the moral virtues; and an arduous academic career must tend to develop those virtues. Without courage or fortitude no one can long stick at the painful task of thinking and studying. Without temperance no one can resist the momentary pleasures and distractions that interfere with study. Without at least some rudimentary sort of prudence no one can allocate his time and plan his work so as to make the most of his academic opportunities. Without justice, which involves a right relation to one's teachers and fellow-students, no one can conduct himself in the academic community in a way that respects the rights of the mind. I might add that as the student owes a debt of justice to his teachers, so his teachers owe a debt of justice to him, which they do not discharge by regaling him with last year's lecture notes.

48 The first obligation of an intellectual institution is to set high intellectual standards and to insist on good intellectual work. There is something in

[7] Cf. the report of O. H. Malik, vice-chancellor of the University of the Punjab to the Preparatory Conference of University Representatives, published by UNESCO (Paris, 1948), pp. 132-3.

Woodrow Wilson's remark that character is a by-product—a by-product of hard work well done.[8] The indirect contribution of higher education to morals cannot be made if educational institutions confer academic recognition on those who have done little more for four years than sit out their time. Habits of industry, habits of initiative, habits of tolerance, and habits of independent judgment can all be promoted by the course of study itself and by the methods by which the educational process is carried on.

49 If the bulk of the instruction is given by lectures, if the duty of the student is to take notes on lectures and to read textbooks, memorizing material to be regurgitated on the examinations given by the teacher who has taught the course, he may develop the habit of memory and the habit of studying the prejudices or curves of those whose favor he hopes to win. The first of these is a good and important habit, though perhaps not the best or most important of the intellectual virtues. The second is a habit valuable to salesmen, advertising men, college presidents, and others who spend their lives trying to get something from other people. But it is a habit into which most Americans seem to fall naturally; they do not need to go to college to get it. The value of the discussion method of instruction, of demanding a great deal of independent work from the student, and of a system of external examinations that requires study of the subject rather than the teacher, is that the habits of action, as well as the habits of thought and knowledge, formed by these means are closely analogous to, if they are not identical with, the four cardinal virtues.

50 I should add that there is a certain moral failure on the part of an educational institution that does not try to make its work something other than the accumulation of miscellaneous credits; for it seems unjust to expect the student to work hard on trivial, irrelevant, incoherent, and meaningless material. The vice of the adding-machine method of education is that it has a way of making even important subject matter seem trivial, irrelevant, incoherent, and meaningless.

51 There is a certain moral failure, too, on the part of an educational institution that does not allow the student to make his own the treasure of the accumulated thoughts of the race. So the failure of the elective system was a moral failure. The official historian of Harvard said of President Eliot that he had defrauded the Harvard students of their cultural heritage. The failure of vocational education is of the same variety: in the name of a

8 "I hear a great deal about character being the object of education. I take leave to believe that a man who cultivates his character consciously will cultivate nothing except what will make him intolerable to his fellow-men....Character...is a by-product. It comes, whether you will or not, as a consequence of a life devoted to the nearest duty, and the place in which character would be cultivated, if it be a place of study, is a place where study is the object and character the result" (address before the Phi Beta Kappa Society, Yale University, 1908).

specious commercial or industrial dexterity it cheats the student out of his place in the stream of human history.

52   An educational institution should be a community. A community must have a common aim, and the common aim of the educational community is the truth. It is not necessary that the members of the educational community agree with one another. It is necessary that they communicate with one another, for the basis of community is communication. In order to communicate with one another, the members of the community must understand one another, and this means that they must have a common language and a common stock of ideas. Any system of education that is based on the training of individual differences is fraudulent in this sense. The primary object of education should be to bring out our common humanity. For though men are different, they are also the same, and their common humanity, rather than their individual differences, requires development today as at no earlier era in history.

53   How, then, can higher education escape dogmatism, narrowness, the invasion of academic freedom, and failure in its proper intellectual task and still do its duty by morals and religion? A possible answer lies in the Great Conversation. The Great Conversation began with the Greeks, the Hebrews, the Hindus, and the Chinese and has continued to the present day. It is a conversation that deals, perhaps more extensively than it deals with anything else, with morals and religion. The questions of the nature and existence of God, the nature and destiny of man, and the organization and purpose of human society are the recurring themes of the Great Conversation.

54   There may be many ways in which a college or university can continue the Great Conversation, but it would seem off-hand that one of the best ways is through the reading and discussion by all the students of the books in which the Great Conversation has been carried on by the greatest men who have taken part in it. I emphasize discussion because of the contributions that this method makes to the moral and intellectual habits we desire; and I emphasize reading and discussion by all the students and faculty because in this way the formation of a community can be advanced. To continue and enrich the Great Conversation is the object of higher education.

55   The Civilization of the Dialogue is the only civilization worth having and the only civilization in which the whole world can unite. It is, therefore, the only civilization we can hope for, because the world must unite or be blown to bits. The Civilization of the Dialogue requires communication. It requires a common language and a common stock of ideas. It assumes that every man has reason and that every man can use it. It preserves to every man his independent judgment and, since it does so, it deprives any man or any group of men of the privilege of forcing their judgment upon any

other man or group of men. The Civilization of the Dialogue is the negation of force. We have reached the point, in any event, when force cannot unite the world; it can merely destroy it. Through continuing and enriching the Great Conversation higher education not only does its duty by morals and religion; it not only performs its proper intellectual task: it also supports and symbolizes the highest hopes and the highest aspirations of mankind.

Analysis of Hutchins's Essay with Emphasis on Its Arrangement

Robert M. Hutchins's deliberative discourse runs to about the same length as Macaulay's deliberative speech on education. It should be instructive to compare the strategies of arrangement in these two discourses. What we soon discover when we look closely at the two discourses is that the differences in subject matter, purpose, and audience call for basically different strategies of organization. Both men are talking about problems of education; but Macaulay is concerned with the way to finance a system of universal education, while Hutchins is concerned with the content of the curriculum of the colleges. This difference of subject matter does not, of itself, call for a different arrangement of parts, but when this difference is combined with the difference in purpose and kind of audience, we begin to see why the two men developed their discourses in different ways. Macaulay's purpose is to persuade his audience of legislators to take some action—in this case, to vote in favor of a bill which will appropriate money. Hutchins's purpose is to persuade his audience, made up largely of people involved in, or at least interested in, higher education to adopt his point of view about the place of morals and religion in the university curriculum. Macaulay has to swing the votes of a hostile opposition; Hutchins has to influence the views of a generally sympathetic but largely uncommitted audience. Macaulay's audience, because of the lengthy debate that had already taken place in the House of Commons, was already well informed about the issues; Hutchins's audience is interested in the problems of education but has not as yet formed firm convictions about the particular problem being discussed in this discourse.

As we have seen, Macaulay decided that the best strategy in his situation was to argue his case first and then refute the opposing arguments. Hutchins adopts a different tactic. He refutes the opposing arguments first and then advances his own proposal and the arguments supporting that proposal. Macaulay had so much confidence in the strength of his arguments that he felt he could more easily demolish the opposition by presenting his case first. Hutchins, on the other hand, felt that he could best "sell" his view by first clearing away the erroneous notions about the role of morals and religion in the college curriculum.

By withholding his proposal until the end, Hutchins also adds suspense to his discourse. As he knocks down, one by one, the prevailing views about the place of morals and religion in the curriculum, the audience becomes increasingly curious about what *he* thinks the proper role of morals and religion is. And Hutchins has cleverly laid the groundwork for this suspense by announcing in the very first paragraph that "higher education can make a unique contribution to morals and religion." One can almost feel the growing curiosity of the audience as Hutchins proceeds: if these are *not* the contributions that higher education can make, what *is* the "unique contribution" that it can make?

Because this is a fairly long essay, the student might appreciate at the outset an overview of the organization. The outline of the main divisions of the essay runs something like this:

> Introduction (paragraphs 1-5)
> I. Refutation of the prevailing views about the place of morals and religion in higher education (paragraphs 6-35)
> II. Proposal and justification of his own view of the unique contribution that higher education can make to morals and religion (paragraphs 36-52)
> Conclusion (paragraphs 53-5)

From this outline, one can see that Hutchins devotes thirty paragraphs to demolishing the commonly proposed "solutions," while devoting only seventeen paragraphs to justifying his own proposal. But this proportion is not as top-heavy as it may at first appear. We must remember that Hutchins has to refute *several* proposals; he has to justify only *one* proposal. And when we consider that he devoted about half as many paragraphs to the support of that one proposal, we are made aware that Hutchins had to do a considerable amount of "selling" of his proposal. He did not take it for granted that once he had refuted the other proposals his audience would immediately "buy" his proposal. Having cleared the ground, he still had to exert a great deal of rhetorical skill to get his audience to accept the "building" he wanted to erect on the cleared ground. As he said at the end of his first paragraph, "I can regard the building attempted here as at best a very modest structure, which will accomplish more than I am entitled to hope for it if it serves as temporary shelter to those who may design the ultimate edifice."

Let us take a closer look at the parts now to see what Hutchins is doing in each of them and to speculate about their functions.

We saw from the outline that the first five paragraphs of the essay constitute the introduction. What does Hutchins do in this introduction? In the first paragraph, he informs the audience, in a general way, of the theme of the essay:

> I believe that higher education can make a unique contribution to morals and religion. I do not believe that it can make some of the contributions expected of it, and I think that these expectations obscure the real purpose and achievements of higher education.

Note that the theme is stated in general terms. Hutchins does not tell us here what the "unique contribution" is. We have already indicated why he does not tell his audience what this contribution is: he wants to arouse their curiosity.

Hutchins also exerts a subtle ethical appeal in this first paragraph. Note the modesty and diffidence of his claims in this first paragraph—"I cannot pretend that I have solved any of them"; "it may be possible"; "I believe"; "I do not believe"; "I think"; "at best a very modest structure"; "more than I am entitled to hope for it." Hutchins comes to his audience—the original audience for the speech when it was first delivered at Kenyon College and the later readers of the printed essay—with a certain antecedent reputation. He is a well-known and esteemed spokesman on education. Very soon after he had become Chancellor of the University of Chicago, he acquired the reputation of being "the gadfly of American education." But here we see this renowned educator announcing his subject and his purpose with an ingratiating modesty.

In the next four paragraphs of the introduction, Hutchins defines three of the key terms of the essay—"morals," "religion," and "higher education." Whenever we have any doubts that our audience will understand some of the important terms of our discourse, we do well to define those terms—and as early as possible in the discourse. Note that Hutchins does not claim that his definitions are the *only* definitions. He is merely telling his audience what *he* means by these terms. Logicians sometimes call such definitions "stipulative definitions." Whenever we cannot establish final, precise definitions of terms, we can, in the interests of getting on with a discussion, stipulate the meaning we attach to the terms. In some cases, of course, we could prejudice the discussion in our favor—we could "beg the question"—by the definitions we propose. But in this instance, Hutchins is not "stacking the cards" in his favor; he is merely preparing his audience to understand the subsequent discussion.

After this relatively short introduction of five paragraphs, Hutchins launches into his refutation of the claims commonly advanced about the contributions that higher education can make to morals and religion. The topic that serves as the organizing principle of most of his counterarguments is the topic of the possible: can this proposal do what its advocates say it can do for the development of moral and religious habits? In refuting the various claims, he relies a great deal on the testimony of prominent and respected men who have written on the problems of education (e.g. Mill, Newman, Aristotle, Toynbee); on definitions (e.g. the nature of man and his learning processes, the nature of education); on examples, from his own and others' experience; on analogies (e.g. how he taught *Macbeth* to inexperienced preparatory-school students).

Although there is a discernible order to the progress of Hutchins's refutation, one would have a difficult time demonstrating that at every step Hutchins has observed an *inevitable* order. For instance, is there any reason why Hutchins had to consider the contributions that athletics can make to the formation of good habits before he considered the contribution that compulsory religious exercises can make? If we thought enough about it, we might be able to propose *a* reason, but it probably would not be a compelling reason. To say that the order of the arguments at some point is a rather arbitrary one is not to say that the essay is disorderly. Hutchins does ramble at times; he could tighten up the essay at several points; he could help his readers if he used transitional devices and connecting links more often. But all in all, Hutchins is too much of a disciplined thinker to write a chaotic discourse. The fact that no mature reader would get "lost" in this long essay is evidence that there is order here—order that one does not have to search very hard to find. Throughout the essay, one part leads naturally, if not always inevitably, into the next part.

It would be tedious to trace out, step by step, the course of the argument through the forty-seven paragraphs of the body of the essay, but perhaps we can learn something about arrangement of parts by hitting just the high points. The main proposition that Hutchins is intent on refuting is this: higher education can make students moral and religious. His arguments attack this proposition from various angles. He starts out by questioning whether the moral and religious education of students falls within the province of the schools at all. To support his own views on this matter, he brings to bear the pronouncements of two noted nineteenth-century writers who, one might expect, would have contrary opinions about the place of morals and religion in higher education. John Stuart Mill is associated in the minds of educated people—and Hutchins's audience is made up largely of educated people—with the rationalism of the nineteenth century, and as a "liberal," he represented, at least for the members of the Oxford Movement, a threat to the religious spirit of the Victorian Age. Hutchins finds that Mill once made the same point that he himself is making—that scholastic education cannot make students moral or religious. Cardinal Newman is another famous spokesman on education, his *Idea of a University* being generally regarded as the classic statement about the function and end of a liberal education. Moreover, Newman is a Catholic and an opponent of the rationalist, utilitarian movement that Mill represented. But surprisingly—and conveniently for Hutchins's purpose—Newman holds the same view on this matter as Mill does. Neither Newman nor Mill denies that religious and moral training is important; as a matter of fact they agree that such training is pre-eminently important. What they are both saying is that the chief, if not the exclusive, function of a university is to train students intellectually; it is the function of the church and the family to train young men and women morally and religiously.

Although Hutchins's first argument addresses itself to the question of whether a university should educate its students morally and religiously rather than to the question of whether it can so educate them, it was a good argument to start out with because it concerns itself with the principle involved here rather than with the more debatable practicality of the matter.

From this point on, however, Hutchins deals with what a university *can* do to educate its students morally and religiously. He presents and expatiates on a number of reasons why the university cannot contribute substantially to the moral and religious development of the students:

1. The student's extra-mural environment—the home, his companions, mass media—has more of an impact on his religious and moral habits than the school does.
2. The schools have only a limited time to exert an influence on the student.
3. Good habits (Hutchins's synonym for "morals") are formed by acts, and mere instruction in good habits does not necessarily lead to acts.
4. Nor can the schools form good habits by the extra-curricular activities they offer—sports, for instance, or compulsory religious activities.
5. Nor can the schools make students religious, for a religious disposition depends on faith, and faith, we are told, is a gift that God grants to some and denies to others. (Can we deny educational opportunities to those who have been denied the gift of faith?)
6. The solidest base for good moral habits is a strong religious faith, but since, as we have just said, the schools cannot give their students this religious faith, they cannot hope to make much of a contribution to the moral development of the students.

The last question in this sequence that Hutchins addresses himself to—the hiring of professors—seems to be rather gratuitously added to the discussion. At least it is not as germane to the main argument as the other points are. When he makes the point, for instance, that schools do not usually inquire into the religious and moral disposition of the teachers they hire, he is talking, not about what schools should do or can do but about what, in actual practice, they do do. Hutchins might have left out this last part without loss to his argument—especially since he confesses that he has not entirely made up his own mind about what policies schools should adopt in hiring teachers.

If the student inspects the six arguments outlined above, he will see, as we suggested earlier, that there is no *necessary* order to the arrangement. The arguments do not always grow one out of the other, nor do they build climactically. They are just six pertinent, cogent arguments set down one after the other. Of the five most common principles of organization—the logical, the chronological, the spatial, the climactic, the associative—we might say that the associative order prevails here: Hutchins is setting down his arguments in the order in which they occur to him. The students might consider whether some other order could have been more effective.

In paragraph 36, Hutchins makes the transition to the positive part of his discourse. Up to this point he has been refuting, rejecting. Now he must propose and justify the "unique contribution" that he claimed education could make to morals and religion. We have already commented on the suspense value of delaying his proposal until now. But he has gained something more than the interest that can be generated by suspense; he has conditioned his audience to be more receptive to his proposal. Once the counterproposals have been dealt with, his audience is less likely to be indifferent to his proposal than it would have been if he had made his proposal at the beginning. The mood of Hutchins's audience at this point must be something like this: All right, you have rejected the claims that others have made. What is there left to say? Does the study of morals and religion deserve *any* place in the college curriculum? If so, show us.

Hutchins's method of argument in this section is basically deductive. The main stages of his argument could be set forth in the form of a syllogism:

> The proper function of a university is to lead its students to think about important matters.
>
> The study of the intellectual foundations of morals and religion would lead students to think about important matters.
>
> Therefore, the study of the intellectual foundations of morals and religion would be the proper function of a university.

This constitutes the skeleton of his argument. But he devotes seventeen paragraphs to putting some meat on these bare bones. What accounts for most of the expansion is that Hutchins has to set up his premises and convince his audience of the truth of the premises.

He establishes his first premise, for instance, mainly by definition. He asserts that the proper object of a university is the pursuit and transmission of truth. Among all the institutions in our society, only a university has this aim. And he quotes Mill again to corroborate his view. It is not quite clear, however, just how Hutchins gets from the proposition that the object of a university is to pursue and transmit truth to the proposition which serves as the major premise of his syllogism. In the first sentence of paragraph 43 he *hints* at how he got from one proposition to the other—"If we grant that the purpose of higher education is to think and to think about important things *for the purpose of learning as much of the truth as possible* about these things and transmitting it to each succeeding generation, . . ." (italics added) —but he does not carry us, by a series of carefully reasoned steps, from one proposition to the other.

Hutchins takes most of paragraphs 36-52 to establish the truth of his minor premise—"The study of the intellectual foundations of morals and religion would lead students to think about important matters." In doing this, he brings most of his arguments to bear on two points: (1) the importance of morals and religion and (2) the intellectual and practical benefits to be realized from the study of morals and religion. Just as he used quotations from prominent spokesmen on education to refute arguments in the first part of his discourse, so he uses here the authority of noted spokesmen to support his contention—Henry Adams, Woodrow Wilson, St. Augustine. We must remember that Hutchins's choice of authorities throughout the discourse has been dictated by the nature of his audience. Several of these authorities might have been unimpressive—because unfamiliar—to another kind of audience.

Hutchins decided that there was no need to recapitulate and reinforce his arguments in the conclusion of his discourse (paragraphs 53-5). Instead, he chose to enlarge on the subject of the proper intellectual function of the university. This permits him to expatiate on one of his favorite topics—the Great Conversation. This plea for the Great Conversation may seem to be extraneous to the main subject of the discourse, but when one recalls that Hutchins began both the refutation and confirmation parts of his discourse with the claim that the cultivation of the intellect should be the primary concern of the university, the conclusion seems not as irrelevant as it first appeared. And in the last sentence of the essay, Hutchins unites and extends the themes of this long discourse: "Through continuing and enriching the Great Conversation higher education not only does its duty by morals and religion; it not only performs its proper intellectual task; it also supports and symbolizes the highest hopes and highest aspirations of mankind."

So we have seen how one man organized his arguments on the role of morals and religion in higher education. If we were writing an essay on the same subject, we might, without any great loss in effectiveness, have arranged some of the parts differently, but given the same body of arguments, the same general purpose, and the same audience, we would probably find ourselves adopting the same basic strategy of arrangement that Hutchins employed.

Henry David Thoreau: Civil Disobedience

The ultimate inspiration for the many manifestations of "body rhetoric"—marches, sit-ins, lie-ins, confrontations—which became so much a part of the world scene in the 1960's is generally acknowledged to be Henry David Thoreau's essay "Civil Disobedience." Mahatma Gandhi confessed that as a young man he took the name and the tactics of his passive-resistance movement from Thoreau's essay. The term civil disobedience, *he said, was the most suitable English equivalent of the Indian word* Satyagraha. *First delivered as a lecture, under the title "Resistance to Civil Government," the text was subsequently published in 1849 in* Aesthetic Papers. *Fresh from his famous sojourn at Walden Pond (1845–47), where he had gone, he tells us, "to front only the essential facts of life," Thoreau felt compelled to write this piece in order to arouse his fellow-citizens against the evils of the current Mexican War and the imminent Fugitive Slave Law. Thoreau had studied rhetoric at Harvard under Edward T. Channing, the third Boylston Professor of Rhetoric and Oratory. He once said, "The one great rule of composition—and if I were a professor of rhetoric I should insist on this—is to speak the truth." But there is more than just "speaking the truth" to Thoreau's effectiveness as a persuader. For one thing, he is noted for his vigorous, aphoristic, paradoxical style. The "ethical appeal" of the man himself also exercises a strong influence. And despite the apparently associational sequence of his prose there is a discernible order to the disposition of his arguments.*

1 I heartily accept the motto,—"That government is best which governs least"; and I should like to see it acted up to more rapidly and systematically. Carried out it finally amounts to this, which also I believe,—"That government is best which governs not at all"; and when men are prepared for it, that will be the kind of government which they will have. Government is at best but an expedient; but most governments are usually, and all governments are sometimes, inexpedient. The objections which have been brought

against a standing army, and they are many and weighty, and deserve to prevail, may also at last be brought against a standing government. The standing army is only an arm of the standing government. The government itself, which is only the mode which the people have chosen to execute their will, is equally liable to be abused and perverted before the people can act through it. Witness the present Mexican war, the work of comparatively a few individuals using the standing government as their tool; for, in the outset, the people would not have consented to this measure.

2   This American government,—what is it but a tradition, though a recent one, endeavoring to transmit itself unimpaired to posterity, but each instant losing some of its integrity? It has not the vitality and force of a single living man; for a single man can bend it to his will. It is a sort of wooden gun to the people themselves. But it is not the less necessary for this; for the people must have some complicated machinery or other, and hear its din, to satisfy that idea of government which they have. Governments show thus how successfully men can be imposed on, even impose on themselves, for their own advantage. It is excellent, we must all allow. Yet this government never of itself furthered any enterprise, but by the alacrity with which it got out of its way. *It* does not keep the country free. *It* does not settle the West. *It* does not educate. The character inherent in the American people has done all that has been accomplished; and it would have done somewhat more, if the government had not sometimes got in its way. For government is an expedient by which men would fain succeed in letting one another alone; and, as has been said, when it is most expedient, the governed are most let alone by it. Trade and commerce, if they were not made of India-rubber, would never manage to bounce over the obstacles which legislators are continually putting in their way; and, if one were to judge these men wholly by the effects of their actions and not partly by their intentions, they would deserve to be classed and punished with those mischievous persons who put obstructions on the railroads.

3   But, to speak practically and as a citizen, unlike those who call themselves no-government men, I ask for, not at once no government, but *at once* a better government. Let every man make known what kind of government would command his respect, and that will be one step toward obtaining it.

4   After all, the practical reason why, when the power is once in the hands of the people, a majority are permitted, and for a long period continue, to rule is not because they are most likely to be in the right, nor because this seems fairest to the minority, but because they are physically the strongest. But a government in which the majority rule in all cases cannot be based on justice, even as far as men understand it. Can there not be a government in which majorities do not virtually decide right and wrong, but conscience?

—in which majorities decide only those questions to which the rule of expediency is applicable? Must the citizen ever for a moment, or in the least degree, resign his conscience to the legislator? Why has every man a conscience, then? I think that we should be men first, and subjects afterward. It is not desirable to cultivate a respect for the law, so much as for the right. The only obligation which I have a right to assume is to do at any time what I think right. It is truly enough said, that a corporation has no conscience; but a corporation of conscientious men is a corporation *with* a conscience. Law never made men a whit more just; and, by means of their respect for it, even the well-disposed are daily made the agents of injustice. A common and natural result of an undue respect for law is, that you may see a file of soldiers, colonel, captain, corporal, privates, powder-monkeys, and all, marching in admirable order over hill and dale to the wars, against their wills, ay, against their common sense and consciences, which makes it very steep marching indeed, and produces a palpitation of the heart. They have no doubt that it is a damnable business in which they are concerned; they are all peaceably inclined. Now, what are they? Men at all? or small movable forts and magazines, at the service of some unscrupulous man in power? Visit the Navy-Yard, and behold a marine, such a man as an American government can make, or such as it can make a man with its black arts,—a mere shadow and reminiscence of humanity, a man laid out alive and standing, and already, as one may say, buried under arms with funeral accompaniments, though it may be,—

> "Not a drum was heard, not a funeral note,
>   As his corse to the rampart we hurried;
> Not a soldier discharged his farewell shot
>   O'er the grave where our hero we buried."

5   The mass of men serve the state thus, not as men mainly, but as machines, with their bodies. They are the standing army, and the militia, jailors, constables, posse comitatus, etc. In most cases there is no free exercise whatever of the judgment or of the moral sense; but they put themselves on a level with wood and earth and stones; and wooden men can perhaps be manufactured that will serve the purpose as well. Such command no more respect than men of straw or a lump of dirt. They have the same sort of worth only as horses and dogs. Yet such as these even are commonly esteemed good citizens. Others—as most legislators, politicians, lawyers, ministers, and office-holders—serve the state chiefly with their heads; and, as they rarely make any moral distinctions, they are as likely to serve the Devil, without *intending* it, as God. A very few, as heroes, patriots, martyrs, reformers in the great sense, and *men,* serve the state with their consciences also, and so necessarily resist it for the most part; and they are commonly

treated as enemies by it. A wise man will only be useful as a man, and will not submit to be "clay," and "stop a hole to keep the wind away," but leave that office to his dust at least :—

> "I am too high-born to be propertied,
> To be a secondary at control,
> Or useful serving-man and instrument
> To any sovereign state throughout the world."

6   He who gives himself entirely to his fellow-men appears to them useless and selfish; but he who gives himself partially to them is pronounced a benefactor and philanthropist.

7   How does it become a man to behave toward this American government to-day? I answer, that he cannot without disgrace be associated with it. I cannot for an instant recognize that political organization as *my* government which is the *slave's* government also.

8   All men recognize the right of revolution; that is, the right to refuse allegiance to, and to resist, the government, when its tyranny or its inefficiency are great and unendurable. But almost all say that such is not the case now. But such was the case, they think, in the Revolution of '75. If one were to tell me that this was a bad government because it taxed certain foreign commodities brought to its ports, it is most probable that I should not make an ado about it, for I can do without them. All machines have their friction; and possibly this does enough good to counterbalance the evil. At any rate, it is a great evil to make a stir about it. But when the friction comes to have its machine, and oppression and robbery are organized, I say, let us not have such a machine any longer. In other words, when a sixth of the population of a nation which has undertaken to be the refuge of liberty are slaves, and a whole country is unjustly overrun and conquered by a foreign army, and subjected to military law, I think that it is not too soon for honest men to rebel and revolutionize. What makes this duty the more urgent is the fact that the country so overrun is not our own, but ours is the invading army.

9   Paley, a common authority with many on moral questions, in his chapter on the "Duty of Submission to Civil Government," resolves all civil obligation into expediency; and he proceeds to say, "that so long as the interest of the whole society requires it, that is, so long as the established government cannot be resisted or changed without public inconveniency, it is the will of God that the established government be obeyed, and no longer. . . . This principle being admitted, the justice of every particular case of resistance is reduced to a computation of the quantity of the danger and grievance on the one side, and of the probability and expense of redressing it on the other." Of this, he says, every man shall judge for himself. But Paley appears

never to have contemplated those cases to which the rule of expediency does not apply, in which a people, as well as an individual, must do justice, cost what it may. If I have unjustly wrested a plank from a drowning man, I must restore it to him though I drown myself. This, according to Paley, would be inconvenient. But he that would save his life, in such a case, shall lose it. This people must cease to hold slaves, and to make war on Mexico, though it cost them their existence as a people.

10 In their practice, nations agree with Paley; but does any one think that Massachusetts does exactly what is right at the present crisis?

> "A drab of state, a cloth-o'-silver slut,
>   To have her train borne up, and her soul trail in the dirt."

Practically speaking, the opponents to a reform in Massachusetts are not a hundred thousand politicians at the South, but a hundred thousand merchants and farmers here, who are more interested in commerce and agriculture than they are in humanity, and are not prepared to do justice to the slave and to Mexico, *cost what it may*. I quarrel not with far-off foes, but with those who, near at home, coöperate with, and do the bidding of, those far away, and without whom the latter would be harmless. We are accustomed to say, that the mass of men are unprepared; but improvement is slow, because the few are not materially wiser or better than the many. It is not so important that many should be as good as you, as that there be some absolute goodness somewhere; for that will leaven the whole lump. There are thousands who are *in opinion* opposed to slavery and to the war, who yet in effect do nothing to put an end to them; who, esteeming themselves children of Washington and Franklin, sit down with their hands in their pockets, and say that they know not what to do, and do nothing; who even postpone the question of freedom to the question of free-trade, and quietly read the prices-current along with the latest advices from Mexico, after dinner, and, it may be, fall asleep over them both. What is the price-current of an honest man and patriot to-day? They hesitate, and they regret, and sometimes they petition; but they do nothing in earnest and with effect. They will wait, well disposed, for others to remedy the evil, that they may no longer have it to regret. At most, they give only a cheap vote, and a feeble countenance and God-speed, to the right, as it goes by them. There are nine hundred and ninety-nine patrons of virtue to one virtuous man. But it is easier to deal with the real professor of a thing than with the temporary guardian of it.

11 All voting is a sort of gaming, like checkers or backgammon, with a slight moral tinge to it, a playing with right and wrong, with moral questions; and betting naturally accompanies it. The character of the voters is not staked. I cast my vote, perchance, as I think right; but I am not vitally

concerned that that right should prevail. I am willing to leave it to the majority. Its obligation, therefore, never exceeds that of expediency. Even voting *for the right* is *doing* nothing for it. It is only expressing to men feebly your desire that it should prevail. A wise man will not leave the right to the mercy of chance, nor wish it to prevail through the power of the majority. There is but little virtue in the action of masses of men. When the majority shall at length vote for the abolition of slavery, it will be because they are indifferent to slavery, or because there is but little slavery left to be abolished by their vote. *They* will then be the only slaves. Only *his* vote can hasten the abolition of slavery who asserts his own freedom by his vote.

12   I hear of a convention to be held at Baltimore, or elsewhere, for the selection of a candidate for the Presidency, made up chiefly of editors, and men who are politicians by profession; but I think, what is it to any independent, intelligent, and respectable man what decision they may come to? Shall we not have the advantage of his wisdom and honesty, nevertheless? Can we not count upon some independent votes? Are there not many individuals in the country who do not attend conventions? But no: I find that the respectable man, so called, has immediately drifted from his position, and despairs of his country, when his country has more reason to despair of him. He forthwith adopts one of the candidates thus selected as the only *available* one, thus proving that he is himself *available* for any purposes of the demagogue. His vote is of no more worth than that of any unprincipled foreigner or hireling native, who may have been bought. O for a man who is a *man,* and, as my neighbor says, has a bone in his back which you cannot pass your hand through! Our statistics are at fault: the population has been returned too large. How many *men* are there to a square thousand miles in this country? Hardly one. Does not America offer any inducement for men to settle here? The American has dwindled into an Odd Fellow,—one who may be known by the development of his organ of gregariousness, and a manifest lack of intellect and cheerful self-reliance; whose first and chief concern, on coming into the world, is to see that the Almshouses are in good repair; and, before yet he has lawfully donned the virile garb, to collect a fund for the support of the widows and orphans that may be; who, in short, ventures to live only by the aid of the Mutual Insurance company, which has promised to bury him decently.

13   It is not a man's duty, as a matter of course, to devote himself to the eradication of any, even the most enormous wrong; he may still properly have other concerns to engage him; but it is his duty, at least, to wash his hands of it, and, if he gives it no thought longer, not to give it practically his support. If I devote myself to other pursuits and contemplations, I must first see, at least, that I do not pursue them sitting upon another man's

shoulders. I must get off him first, that he may pursue his contemplations too. See what gross inconsistency is tolerated. I have heard some of my townsmen say, "I should like to have them order me out to help put down an insurrection of the slaves, or to march to Mexico;—see if I would go"; and yet these very men have each, directly by their allegiance, and so indirectly, at least, by their money, furnished a substitute. The soldier is applauded who refuses to serve in an unjust war by those who do not refuse to sustain the unjust government which makes the war; is applauded by those whose own act and authority he disregards and sets at naught; as if the state were penitent to that degree that it hired one to scourge it while it sinned, but not to that degree that it left off sinning for a moment. Thus, under the name of Order and Civil Government, we are all made at last to pay homage to and support our own meanness. After the first blush of sin comes its indifference; and from immoral it becomes, as it were, *un*-moral, and not quite unnecessary to that life which we have made.

14 The broadest and most prevalent error requires the most disinterested virtue to sustain it. The slight reproach to which the virtue of patriotism is commonly liable, the noble are most likely to incur. Those who, while they disapprove of the character and measures of a government, yield to it their allegiance and support are undoubtedly its most conscientious supporters, and so frequently the most serious obstacles to reform. Some are petitioning the state to dissolve the Union, to disregard the requisitions of the President. Why do they not dissolve it themselves,—the union between themselves and the state,—and refuse to pay their quota into its treasury? Do not they stand in the same relation to the state that the state does to the Union? And have not the same reasons prevented the state from resisting the Union which have prevented them from resisting the state?

15 How can a man be satisfied to entertain an opinion merely, and enjoy *it*? Is there any enjoyment in it, if his opinion is that he is aggrieved? If you are cheated out of a single dollar by your neighbor, you do not rest satisfied with knowing that you are cheated, or with saying that you are cheated, or even with petitioning him to pay you your due; but you take effectual steps at once to obtain the full amount, and see that you are never cheated again. Action from principle, the perception and the performance of right, changes things and relations; it is essentially revolutionary, and does not consist wholly with anything which was. It not only divides states and churches, it divides families; ay, it divides the *individual,* separating the diabolical in him from the divine.

16 Unjust laws exist: shall we be content to obey them, or shall we endeavor to amend them, and obey them until we have succeeded, or shall we transgress them at once? Men generally, under such a government as this, think that they ought to wait until they have persuaded the majority to

alter them. They think that, if they should resist, the remedy would be worse than the evil. But it is the fault of the government itself that the remedy *is* worse than the evil. *It* makes it worse. Why is it not more apt to anticipate and provide for reform? Why does it not cherish its wise minority? Why does it cry and resist before it is hurt? Why does it not encourage its citizens to be on the alert to point out its faults, and *do* better than *it* would have them? Why does it always crucify Christ, and excommunicate Copernicus and Luther, and pronounce Washington and Franklin rebels?

17 One would think, that a deliberate and practical denial of its authority was the only offense never contemplated by government; else, why has it not assigned its definite, its suitable and proportionate penalty? If a man who has no property refuses but once to earn nine shillings for the state, he is put in prison for a period unlimited by any law that I know, and determined only by the discretion of those who placed him there; but if he should steal ninety times nine shillings from the state, he is soon permitted to go at large again.

18 If the injustice is part of the necessary friction of the machine of government, let it go, let it go: perchance it will wear smooth,—certainly the machine will wear out. If the injustice has a spring, or a pulley, or a rope, or a crank, exclusively for itself, then perhaps you may consider whether the remedy will not be worse than the evil; but if it is of such a nature that it requires you to be the agent of injustice to another, then, I say, break the law. Let your life be a counter friction to stop the machine. What I have to do is to see, at any rate, that I do not lend myself to the wrong which I condemn.

19 As for adopting the ways which the state has provided for remedying the evil, I know not of such ways. They take too much time, and a man's life will be gone. I have other affairs to attend to. I came into this world, not chiefly to make this a good place to live in, but to live in it, be it good or bad. A man has not everything to do, but something; and because he cannot do *everything,* it is not necessary that he should do *something* wrong. It is not my business to be petitioning the Governor or the Legislature any more than it is theirs to petition me; and if they should not hear my petition, what should I do then? But in this case the state has provided no way: its very Constitution is the evil. This may seem to be harsh and stubborn and unconciliatory; but it is to treat with the utmost kindness and consideration the only spirit that can appreciate or deserve it. So is all change for the better, like birth and death, which convulse the body.

20 I do not hesitate to say, that those who call themselves Abolitionists should at once effectually withdraw their support, both in person and property, from the government of Massachusetts and not wait till they constitute a majority of one, before they suffer the right to prevail through them. I think that it is enough if they have God on their side, without waiting for that other one. Moreover, any man more right than his neighbors constitutes a majority of one already.

21 I meet this American government, or its representative, the state government, directly, and face to face, once a year—no more—in the person of its tax-gatherer; this is the only mode in which a man situated as I am necessarily meets it; and it then says distinctly, Recognize me; and the simplest, most effectual, and, in the present posture of affairs, the indispensablest mode of treating with it on this head, of expressing your little satisfaction with and love for it, is to deny it then. My civil neighbor, the taxgatherer, is the very man I have to deal with,—for it is, after all, with men and not with parchment that I quarrel,—and he has voluntarily chosen to be an agent of the government. How shall he ever know well what he is and does as an officer of the government, or as a man, until he is obliged to consider whether he shall treat me, his neighbor, for whom he has respect, as a neighbor and well-disposed man, or as a maniac and disturber of the peace, and see if he can get over this obstruction to his neighborliness without a ruder and more impetuous thought or speech corresponding with his action. I know this well, that if one thousand, if one hundred, if ten men whom I could name,—if ten *honest* men only,—if *one* HONEST man, in this State of Massachusetts, *ceasing to hold slaves,* were actually to withdraw from this copartnership, and be locked up in the county jail therefor, it would be the abolition of slavery in America. For it matters not how small the beginning may seem to be: what is once well done is done forever. But we love better to talk about it: that we say is our mission. Reform keeps many scores of newspapers in its service, but not one man. If my esteemed neighbor, the State's ambassador, who will devote his days to the settlement of the question of human rights in the Council Chamber, instead of being threatened with the prisons of Carolina, were to sit down the prisoner of Massachusetts, that State which is so anxious to foist the sin of slavery upon her sister,—though at present she can discover only an act of inhospitality to be the ground of a quarrel with her,—the Legislature would not wholly waive the subject the following winter.

22 Under a government which imprisons any unjustly, the true place for a just man is also a prison. The proper place to-day, the only place which Massachusetts has provided for her freer and less desponding spirits, is in her prisons, to be put out and locked out of the State by her own act, as they have already put themselves out by their principles. It is there that the fugitive slave, and the Mexican prisoner on parole, and the Indian come to plead the wrongs of his race should find them; on that separate, but more free and honorable ground, where the State places those who are not *with*

her, but *against* her,—the only house in a slave State in which a free man can abide with honor. If any think that their influence would be lost there, and their voices no longer afflict the ear of the State, that they would not be as an enemy within its walls, they do not know by how much truth is stronger than error, nor how much more eloquently and effectively he can combat injustice who has experienced a little in his own person. Cast your whole vote, not a strip of paper merely, but your whole influence. A minority is powerless while it conforms to the majority; it is not even a minority then; but it is irresistible when it clogs by its whole weight. If the alternative is to keep all just men in prison, or give up war and slavery, the State will not hesitate which to choose. If a thousand men were not to pay their tax-bills this year, that would not be a violent and bloody measure, as it would be to pay them, and enable the State to commit violence and shed innocent blood. This is, in fact, the definition of a peaceable revolution, if any such is possible. If the tax-gatherer, or any other public officer, asks me, as one has done, "But what shall I do?" my answer is, "If you really wish to do anything, resign your office." When the subject has refused allegiance, and the officer has resigned his office, then the revolution is accomplished. But even suppose blood should flow. Is there not a sort of blood shed when the conscience is wounded? Through this wound a man's real manhood and immortality flow out, and he bleeds to an everlasting death. I see this blood flowing now.

23 I have contemplated the imprisonment of the offender, rather than the seizure of his goods,—though both will serve the same purpose,—because they who assert the purest right, and consequently are most dangerous to a corrupt State, commonly have not spent much time in accumulating property. To such the State renders comparatively small service, and a slight tax is wont to appear exorbitant, particularly if they are obliged to earn it by special labor with their hands. If there were one who lived wholly without the use of money, the State itself would hesitate to demand it of him. But the rich man—not to make any invidious comparison—is always sold to the institution which makes him rich. Absolutely speaking, the more money, the less virtue; for money comes between a man and his objects, and obtains them for him; and it was certainly no great virtue to obtain it. It puts to rest many questions which he would otherwise be taxed to answer; while the only new question which it puts is the hard but superfluous one, how to spend it. Thus his moral ground is taken from under his feet. The opportunities of living are diminished in proportion as what are called the "means" are increased. The best thing a man can do for his culture when he is rich is to endeavor to carry out those schemes which he entertained when he was poor. Christ answered the Herodians according to their condition. "Show me the tribute-money," said he;—and one took a penny out of his pocket;—

if you use the money which has the image of Cæsar on it and which he has made current and valuable, that is, *if you are men of the State,* and gladly enjoy the advantages of Cæsar's government, then pay him back some of his own when he demands it. "Render therefore to Cæsar that which is Cæsar's, and to God those things which are God's,"—leaving them no wiser than before as to which was which; for they did not wish to know.

24   When I converse with the freest of my neighbors, I perceive that, whatever they may say about the magnitude and seriousness of the question, and their regard for the public tranquility, the long and the short of the matter is, that they cannot spare the protection of the existing government, and they dread the consequences to their property and families of disobedience to it. For my own part, I should not like to think that I ever rely on the protection of the State. But, if I deny the authority of the State when it presents its tax-bill, it will soon take and waste all my property, and so harass me and my children without end. This is hard. This makes it impossible for a man to live honestly, and at the same time comfortably, in outward respects. It will not be worth the while to accumulate property; that would be sure to go again. You must hire or squat somewhere, and raise but a small crop, and eat that soon. You must live within yourself, and depend upon yourself always tucked up and ready for a start, and not have many affairs. A man may grow rich in Turkey even, if he will be in all respects a good subject of the Turkish government. Confucius said: "If a state is governed by the principles of reason, poverty and misery are subjects of shame; if a state is not governed by the principles of reason, riches and honors are the subjects of shame." No: until I want the protection of Massachusetts to be extended to me in some distant Southern port, where my liberty is endangered, or until I am bent solely on building up an estate at home by peaceful enterprise, I can afford to refuse allegiance to Massachusetts, and her right to my property and life. It costs me less in every sense to incur the penalty of disobedience to the State than it would to obey. I should feel as if I were worth less in that case.

25   Some years ago, the State met me in behalf of the Church, and commanded me to pay a certain sum toward the support of a clergyman whose preaching my father attended, but never I myself. "Pay," it said, "or be locked up in the jail." I declined to pay. But, unfortunately, another man saw fit to pay it. I did not see why the schoolmaster should be taxed to support the priest, and not the priest the schoolmaster; for I was not the State's schoolmaster, but I supported myself by voluntary subscription. I did not see why the lyceum should not present its tax-bill, and have the State to back its demand, as well as the Church. However, at the request of the selectmen, I condescended to make some such statement as this in writing: —"Know all men by these presents, that I, Henry Thoreau, do not wish

to be regarded as a member of any incorporated society which I have not joined." This I gave to the town clerk; and he has it. The State, having thus learned that I did not wish to be regarded as a member of that church, has never made a like demand on me since; though it said that it must adhere to its original presumption that time. If I had known how to name them, I should then have signed off in detail from all the societies which I never signed on to; but I did not know where to find a complete list.

26 I have paid no poll-tax for six years. I was put into a jail once on this account, for one night; and, as I stood considering the walls of solid stone, two or three feet thick, the door of wood and iron, a foot thick, and the iron grating which strained the light, I could not help being struck with the foolishness of that institution which treated me as if I were mere flesh and blood and bones, to be locked up. I wondered that it should have concluded at length that this was the best use it could put me to, and had never thought to avail itself of my services in some way. I saw that, if there was a wall of stone between me and my townsmen, there was a still more difficult one to climb or break through before they could get to be as free as I was. I did not for a moment feel confined, and the walls seemed a great waste of stone and mortar. I felt as if I alone of all my townsmen had paid my tax. They plainly did not know how to treat me, but behaved like persons who are underbred. In every threat and in every compliment there was a blunder; for they thought that my chief desire was to stand the other side of that stone wall. I could not but smile to see how industriously they locked the door on my meditations, which followed them out again without let or hindrance, and *they* were really all that was dangerous. As they could not reach me, they had resolved to punish my body; just as boys, if they cannot come at some person against whom they have a spite, will abuse his dog. I saw that the State was half-witted, that it was timid as a lone woman with her silver spoons, and that it did not know its friends from its foes, and I lost all my remaining respect for it, and pitied it.

27 Thus the State never intentionally confronts a man's sense, intellectual or moral, but only his body, his senses. It is not armed with superior wit or honesty, but with superior physical strength. I was not born to be forced. I will breathe after my own fashion. Let us see who is the strongest. What force has a multitude? They only can force me who obey a higher law than I. They force me to become like themselves. I do not hear of *men* being *forced* to live this way or that by masses of men. What sort of life were that to live? When I meet a government which says to me, "Your money or your life," why should I be in haste to give it my money? It may be in a great strait, and not know what to do: I cannot help that. It must help itself; do as I do. It is not worth the while to snivel about it. I am not responsible for the successful working of the machinery of society. I am not the son of the

engineer. I perceive that, when an acorn and a chestnut fall side by side, the one does not remain inert to make way for the other, but both obey their own laws, and spring and grow and flourish as best they can, till one, perchance, overshadows and destroys the other. If a plant cannot live according to its nature, it dies; and so a man.

28 The night in prison was novel and interesting enough. The prisoners in their shirt-sleeves were enjoying a chat and the evening air in the doorway, when I entered. But the jailer said, "Come, boys, it is time to lock up"; and so they dispersed, and I heard the sound of their steps returning into the hollow apartments. My roommate was introduced to me by the jailer as "a first-rate fellow and a clever man." When the door was locked, he showed me where to hang my hat, and how he managed matters there. The rooms were whitewashed once a month; and this one, at least, was the whitest, most simply furnished, and probably the neatest apartment in the town. He naturally wanted to know where I came from, and what brought me there; and, when I had told him, I asked him in my turn how he came there, presuming him to be an honest man, of course; and, as the world goes, I believe he was. "Why," said he, "they accuse me of burning a barn; but I never did it." As near as I could discover, he had probably gone to bed in a barn when drunk, and smoked his pipe there; and so a barn was burnt. He had the reputation of being a clever man, had been there some three months waiting for his trial to come on, and would have to wait as much longer; but he was quite domesticated and contented, since he got his board for nothing, and thought that he was well treated.

29 He occupied one window, and I the other; and I saw that if one stayed there long, his principal business would be to look out the window. I had soon read all the tracts that were left there, and examined where former prisoners had broken out, and where a grate had been sawed off, and heard the history of the various occupants of that room; for I found that even here there was a history and a gossip which never circulated beyond the walls of the jail. Probably this is the only house in the town where verses are composed, which are afterward printed in a circular form, but not published. I was shown quite a long list of verses which were composed by some young men who had been detected in an attempt to escape, who avenged themselves by singing them.

30 I pumped my fellow-prisoner as dry as I could, for fear I should never see him again; but at length he showed me which was my bed, and left me to blow out the lamp.

31 It was like traveling into a far country, such as I had never expected to behold, to lie there for one night. It seemed to me that I never had heard the town-clock strike before, nor the evening sounds of the village; for we slept with the windows open, which were inside the grating. It was to see my native village in the light of the Middle Ages, and our Concord was turned into a Rhine stream, and visions of knights and castles passed before me. They were the voices of old burghers that I heard in the streets. I was an involuntary spectator and auditor of whatever was done and said in the kitchen of the adjacent village-inn,—a wholly new and rare experience to me. It was a closer view of my native town. I was fairly inside of it. I never had seen its institutions before. This is one of its peculiar institutions; for it is a shire town. I began to comprehend what its inhabitants were about.

32   In the morning, our breakfasts were put through the hole in the door, in small oblong-square tin pans, made to fit, and holding a pint of chocolate, with brown bread, and an iron spoon. When they called for the vessels again, I was green enough to return what bread I had left; but my comrade seized it, and said that I should lay that up for lunch or dinner. Soon after he was let out to work at haying in a neighboring field, whither he went every day, and would not be back till noon; so he bade me good-day, saying that he doubted if he should see me again.

33   When I came out of prison,—for some one interfered, and paid that tax, —I did not perceive that great changes had taken place on the common, such as he observed who went in a youth and emerged a tottering and gray-headed man; and yet a change had to my eyes come over the scene,—the town, and State, and country,—greater than any that mere time could effect. I saw yet more distinctly the State in which I lived. I saw to what extent the people among whom I lived could be trusted as good neighbors and friends; that their friendship was for summer weather only; that they did not greatly propose to do right; that they were a distinct race from me by their prejudices and superstitions, as the Chinamen and Malays are; that in their sacrifices to humanity they ran no risks, not even to their property; that after all they were not so noble but they treated the thief as he had treated them, and hoped, by a certain outward observance and a few prayers, and by walking in a particular straight though useless path from time to time, to save their souls. This may be to judge my neighbors harshly; for I believe that many of them are not aware that they have such an institution as the jail in their village.

34   It was formerly the custom in our village, when a poor debtor came out of jail, for his acquaintances to salute him, looking through their fingers, which were crossed to represent the grating of a jail window, "How do ye do?" My neighbors did not thus salute me, but first looked at me, and then at one another, as if I had returned from a long journey. I was put into jail as I was going to the shoemaker's to get a shoe which was mended. When I was let out the next morning, I proceeded to finish my errand, and, having put on my mended shoe, joined a huckleberry party, who were impatient to put themselves under by conduct; and in half an hour,—for the horse

was soon tackled,—was in the midst of a huckleberry field, on one of our highest hills, two miles off, and then the State was nowhere to be seen.

35 This is the whole history of "My Prisons."

36 I have never declined paying the highway tax, because I am as desirous of being a good neighbor as I am of being a bad subject; and as for supporting schools, I am doing my part to educate my fellow-countrymen now. It is for no particular item in the tax-bill that I refuse to pay it. I simply wish to refuse allegiance to the State, to withdraw and stand aloof from it effectually. I do not care to trace the course of my dollar, if I could, till it buys a man or a musket to shoot with,—the dollar is innocent,—but I am concerned to trace the effects of my allegiance. In fact, I quietly declare war with the State, after my fashion, though I will still make what use and get what advantage of her I can, as is usual in such cases.

37 If others pay the tax which is demanded of me, from a sympathy with the state, they do but what they have already done in their own case, or rather they abet injustice to a greater extent than the State requires. If they pay the tax from a mistaken interest in the individual taxed, to save his property, or prevent his going to jail, it is because they have not considered wisely how far they let their private feelings interfere with the public good.

38 This, then, is my position at present. But one cannot be too much on his guard in such a case, lest his action be biased by obstinacy or an undue regard for the opinions of men. Let him see that he does only what belongs to himself and to the hour.

39 I think sometimes, Why, this people mean well, they are only ignorant; they would do better if they knew how: why give your neighbors this pain to treat you as they are not inclined to? But I think again, This is no reason why I should do as they do, or permit others to suffer much greater pain of a different kind. Again, I sometimes say to myself, When may millions of men, without heat, without ill will, without personal feeling of any kind, demand of you a few shillings only, without the possibility, such is their constitution, of retracting or altering their present demand, and without the possibility, on your side, of appeal to any other millions, why expose yourself to this overwhelming brute force? You do not resist cold and hunger, the winds and the waves, thus obstinately; you quietly submit to a thousand similar necessities. You do not put your head into the fire. But just in proportion as I regard this as not wholly a brute force, but partly a human force, and consider that I have relations to those millions as to so many millions of men, and not of mere brute or inanimate things, I see that appeal is possible, first and instantaneously, from them to the Maker of them, and, secondly, from them to themselves. But if I put my head deliberately into the fire, there is no appeal to fire or to the Maker of fire, and I have only myself to

blame. If I could convince myself that I have any right to be satisfied with men as they are, and to treat them accordingly, and not according, in some respects, to my requisitions and expectations of what they and I ought to be, then, like a good Mussulman and fatalist, I should endeavor to be satisfied with things as they are, and say it is the will of God. And, above all, there is this difference between resisting this and a purely brute or natural force, that I can resist this with some effect; but I cannot expect, like Orpheus, to change the nature of the rocks and trees and beasts.

40 I do not wish to quarrel with any man or nation. I do not wish to split hairs, to make fine distinctions, or set myself up as better than my neighbors. I seek rather, I may say, even an excuse for conforming to the laws of the land. I am but too ready to conform to them. Indeed, I have reason to suspect myself on this head; and each year, as the tax-gatherer comes round, I find myself disposed to review the acts and position of the general and State governments, and the spirit of the people, to discover a pretext for conformity.

> "We must affect our country as our parents,
> And if at any time we alienate
> Our love or industry from doing it honor,
> We must respect effects and teach the soul
> Matter of conscience and religion,
> And not desire of rule or benefit."

I believe that the State will soon be able to take all my work of this sort out of my hands, and then I shall be no better a patriot than my fellow-countrymen. Seen from a lower point of view, the Constitution, with all its faults, is very good; the law and the courts are very respectable; even this State and this American government are, in many respects, very admirable, and rare things, to be thankful for, such as a great many have described them; but seen from a point of view a little higher, they are what I have described them; seen from a higher still, and the highest, who shall say what they are, or that they are worth looking at or thinking of at all?

41 However, the government does not concern me much, and I shall bestow the fewest possible thoughts on it. It is not many moments that I live under a government, even in this world. If a man is thought-free, fancy-free, imagination-free, that which *is not* never for a long time appearing *to be* to him, unwise rulers or reformers cannot fatally interrupt him.

42 I know that most men think differently from myself; but those whose lives are by profession devoted to the study of these or kindred subjects content me as little as any. Statesmen and legislators, standing so completely within the institution, never distinctly and nakedly behold it. They speak of moving society, but have no resting-place without it. They may be men of a certain experience and discrimination, and have no doubt invented ingenious

and even useful systems, for which we sincerely thank them; but all their wit and usefulness lie within certain not very wide limits. They are wont to forget that the world is not governed by policy and expediency. Webster never goes behind government, and so cannot speak with authority about it. His words are wisdom to those legislators who contemplate no essential reform in the existing government; but for thinkers, and those who legislate for all time, he never once glances at the subject. I know of those whose serene and wise speculations on this theme would soon reveal the limits of his mind's range and hospitality. Yet, compared with the cheap professions of most reformers, and the still cheaper wisdom and eloquence of politicians in general, his are almost the only sensible and valuable words, and we thank Heaven for him. Comparatively, he is always strong, original, and, above all, practical. Still, his quality is not wisdom, but prudence. The lawyer's truth is not Truth, but consistency or a consistent expediency. Truth is always in harmony with herself, and is not concerned chiefly to reveal the justice that may consist with wrong-doing. He well deserves to be called, as he has been called, the Defender of the Constitution. There are really no blows to be given by him but defensive ones. He is not a leader, but a follower. His leaders are the men of '87. "I have never made an effort," he says, "and never propose to make an effort; I have never countenanced an effort, and never mean to countenance an effort, to disturb the arrangement as originally made, by which the various States came into the Union." Still thinking of the sanction which the Constitution gives to slavery, he says, "Because it was a part of the original compact,—let it stand." Notwithstanding his special acuteness and ability, he is unable to take a fact out of its merely political relations, and behold it as it lies absolutely to be disposed of by the intellect, —what, for instance, it behooves a man to do here in America to-day with regard to slavery,—but ventures, or is driven to make some such desperate answer as the following, while professing to speak absolutely, and as a private man,—from which what new and singular code of social duties might be inferred? "The manner," says he, "in which the governments of those States where slavery exists are to regulate it is for their own consideration, under their responsibility to their constituents, to the general laws of propriety, humanity, and justice, and to God. Associations formed elsewhere, springing from a feeling of humanity, or other cause, have nothing whatever to do with it. They have never received any encouragement from me, and they never will."

43 They who know of no purer sources of truth, who have traced up its stream no higher, stand, and wisely stand, by the Bible and the Constitution, and drink at it there with reverence and humility; but they who behold where it comes trickling into this lake or that pool, gird up their loins once more, and continue their pilgrimage toward its fountain-head.

44 No man with a genius for legislation has appeared in America. They

are rare in the history of the world. There are orators, politicians, and eloquent men, by the thousand; but the speaker has not yet opened his mouth to speak who is capable of settling the much-vexed questions of the day. We love eloquence for its own sake, and not for any truth which it may utter, or any heroism it may inspire. Our legislators have not yet learned the comparative value of free-trade and of freedom, of union, and of rectitude, to a nation. They have no genius or talent for comparatively humble questions of taxation and finance, commerce and manufacturers and agriculture. If we were left solely to the wordy wit of legislators in Congress for our guidance, uncorrected by the seasonable experience and the effectual complaints of the people, America would not long retain her rank among the nations. For eighteen hundred years, though perchance I have no right to say it, the New Testament has been written; yet where is the legislator who has wisdom and practical talent enough to avail himself of the light which it sheds on the science of legislation?

45 The authority of government, even such as I am willing to submit to,— for I will cheerfully obey those who know and can do better than I, and in many things even those who neither know nor can do so well,—is still an impure one: to be strictly just, it must have the sanction and consent of the governed. It can have no pure right over my person and property but what I concede to it. The progress from an absolute to a limited monarchy, from a limited monarchy to a democracy, is a progress toward a true respect for the individual. Even the Chinese philosopher was wise enough to regard the individual as the basis of the empire. Is a democracy, such as we know it, the last improvement possible in government? Is it not possible to take a step further towards recognizing and organizing the rights of man? There will never be a really free and enlightened State until the State comes to recognize the individual as a higher and independent power, from which all its own power and authority are derived, and treats him accordingly. I please myself with imagining a State at last which can afford to be just to all men, and to treat the individual with respect as a neighbor; which even would not think it inconsistent with its own repose if a few were to live aloof from it, not meddling with it, nor embraced by it, who fulfilled all the duties of neighbors and fellowmen. A State which bore this kind of fruit, and suffered it to drop off as fast as it ripened, would prepare the way for a still more perfect and glorious State, which also I have imagined, but not yet anywhere seen.

George Wald: A Generation in Search of a Future

On March 4, 1969, George Wald, professor of biology at Harvard and the 1967 winner of the Nobel Prize in physiology and medicine, delivered this speech to a crowd of 1200 students and faculty gathered in the Kresge Auditorium on the campus of M.I.T. as part of the "March 4 movement" to protest the misuse of science by the military-industrial complex. By the time that Dr. Wald rose to speak early in the afternoon, the crowd had been rendered restless and disgruntled by the succession of speeches that had begun at 9:00 that morning. But before long, George Wald, speaking from notes, had electrified his audience, and when he finished he was acclaimed by a prolonged standing ovation. One explanation for the immediate impact and the subsequent fame of "The Speech," as it has come to be referred to, is that Dr. Wald managed to articulate, perhaps better than young people have been able to do themselves, the reasons for the present discontent and rebellion among those under thirty years of age. It should be instructive to analyze not only the substance of Wald's arguments but the order in which he has marshalled them.

1 All of you know that in the last couple of years there has been student unrest breaking at times into violence in many parts of the world: in England, Germany, Italy, Spain, Mexico and needless to say, in many parts of this country. There has been a great deal of discussion as to what it all means. Perfectly clearly it means something different in Mexico from what it does in France, and something different in France from what it does in Tokyo, and something different in Tokyo from what it does in this country. Yet unless we are to assume that students have gone crazy all over the world, or that they have just decided that it's the thing to do, there must be some common meaning.

2 I don't need to go so far afield to look for that meaning. I am a teacher, and at Harvard, I have a class of about 350 students—men and women—most of them freshmen and sophomores. Over these past few years I have felt increasingly that something is terribly wrong—and this year ever so much more than last. Something has gone sour, in teaching and in learning. It's almost as though there were a widespread feeling that education has become irrelevant.

From the text as printed, from a tape-recording, in the *Boston Globe,* March 8, 1969. Substantial excerpts from the speech were also reproduced in the Talk of the Town section of the *New Yorker,* XLV (March 22, 1969), 29-31. Reprinted by permission of the author.

3 A lecture is much more of a dialogue than many of you probably appreciate. As you lecture, you keep watching the faces; and information keeps coming back to you all the time. I began to feel, particularly this year, that I was missing much of what was coming back. I tried asking the students, but they didn't or couldn't help me very much.

4 But I think I know what's the matter, even a little better than they do. I think that this whole generation of students is beset with a profound uneasiness. I don't think that they have yet quite defined its source. I think I understand the reasons for their uneasiness even better than they do. What is more, I share their uneasiness.

5 What's bothering those students? Some of them tell you it's the Vietnam War. I think the Vietnam War is the most shameful episode in the whole of American history. The concept of War Crimes is an American invention. We've committed many War Crimes in Vietnam; but I'll tell you something interesting about that. We were committing War Crimes in World War II, even before the Nuremburg trials were held and the principle of war crimes stated. The staturation bombing of German cities was a War Crime. Dropping atom bombs on Hiroshima and Nagasaki was a War Crime. If we had lost the war, some of our leaders might have had to answer for those actions.

6 I've gone through all of that history lately, and I find that there's a gimmick in it. It isn't written out, but I think we established it by precedent. That gimmick is that if one can allege that one is repelling or retaliating for an *aggression*—after that everything goes. And you see we are living in a world in which all wars are wars of defense. All War Departments are now Defense Departments. This is all part of the double talk of our time. The aggressor is always on the other side. And I suppose this is why our ex-Secretary of State, Dean Rusk—a man in whom repetition takes the place of reason, and stubbornness takes the place of character—went to such pains to insist, as he still insists, that in Vietnam we are repelling an aggression. And if that's what we are doing—so runs the doctrine—anything goes. If the concept of war crimes is ever to mean anything, they will have to be defined as categories of acts, regardless of alleged provocation. But that isn't so now.

7 I think we've lost that war, as a lot of other people think, too. The Vietnamese have a secret weapon. It's their willingness to die, beyond our willingness to kill. In effect they've been saying, you can kill us, but you'll have to kill a lot of us, you may have to kill all of us. And thank heavens, we are not yet ready to do that.

8 Yet we have come a long way—far enough to sicken many Americans, far enough even to sicken our fighting men. Far enough so that our national symbols have gone sour. How many of you can sing about "the rockets'

red glare, bombs bursting in air" without thinking those are *our* bombs and *our* rockets bursting over South Vietnamese villages? When those words were written, we were a people struggling for freedom against oppression. Now we are supporting real or thinly disguised military dictatorships all over the world, helping them to control and repress peoples struggling for their freedom.

9 But that Vietnam War, shameful and terrible as it is, seems to me only an immediate incident in a much larger and more stubborn situation.

10 Part of my trouble with students is that almost all the students I teach were born since World War II. Just after World War II, a series of new and abnormal procedures came into American life. We regarded them at the time as temporary aberrations. We thought we would get back to normal American life some day. But those procedures have stayed with us now for more than 20 years, and those students of mine have never known anything else. They think those things are normal. Students think we've always had a Pentagon, that we have always had a big army, and that we always had a draft. But those are all new things in American life; and I think that they are incompatible with what America meant before.

11 How many of you realize that just before World War II the entire American army including the Air Force numbered 139,000 men? Then World War II started, but we weren't yet in it; and seeing that there was great trouble in the world, we doubled this army to 268,000 men. Then in World War II it got to be 8 million. And then World War II came to an end, and we prepared to go back to a peacetime army somewhat as the American army had always been before. And indeed in 1950—you think about 1950, our international commitments, the Cold War, the Truman Doctrine, and all the rest of it—in 1950 we got down to 600,000 men.

12 Now we have 3.5 million men under arms: about 600,000 in Vietnam, about 300,000 more in "support areas" elsewhere in the Pacific, about 250,000 in Germany. And there are a lot at home. Some months ago we were told that 300,000 National Guardsmen and 200,000 reservists—so half a million men—had been specially trained for riot duty in the cities.

13 I say the Vietnam War is just an immediate incident, because so long as we keep that big an army, it will always find things to do. If the Vietnam War stopped tomorrow, with that big a military establishment, the chances are that we would be in another such adventure abroad or at home before you knew it.

14 As for the draft: Don't reform the draft—get rid of it.

15 A peacetime draft is the most un-American thing I know. All the time I was growing up I was told about oppressive Central European countries and Russia, where young men were forced into the army; and I was told

what they did about it. They chopped off a finger, or shot off a couple of toes; or better still, if they could manage it, they came to this country. And we understood that, and sympathized, and were glad to welcome them.

16 Now by present estimates four to six thousand Americans of draft age have left this country for Canada, another two or three thousand have gone to Europe, and it looks as though many more are preparing to emigrate.

17 A few months ago I received a letter from the Harvard Alumni Bulletin posing a series of questions that students might ask a professor involving what to do about the draft. I was asked to write what I would tell those students. All I had to say to those students was this: If any of them had decided to evade the draft and asked my help, I would help him in any way I could. I would feel as I suppose members of the underground railway felt in pre-Civil War days, helping runaway slaves to get to Canada. It wasn't altogether a popular position then; but what do you think of it now?

18 A bill to stop the draft was recently introduced in the Senate (S. 503), sponsored by a group of senators that ran the gamut from McGovern and Hatfield to Barry Goldwater. I hope it goes through; but any time I find that Barry Goldwater and I are in agreement, that makes me take another look.

19 And indeed there are choices in getting rid of the draft. I think that when we get rid of the draft, we must also cut back the size of the armed forces. It seems to me that in peacetime a total of one million men is surely enough. If there is an argument for American military forces of more than one million men in peacetime, I should like to hear that argument debated.

20 There is another thing being said closely connected with this: that to keep an adequate volunteer army, one would have to raise the pay considerably. That's said so positively and often that people believe it. I don't think it is true.

21 The great bulk of our present armed forces are genuine volunteers. Among first-term enlistments, 49 percent are true volunteers. Another 30 percent are so-called "reluctant volunteers," persons who volunteer under pressure of the draft. Only 21 percent are draftees. All re-enlistments, of course, are true volunteers.

22 So the great majority of our present armed forces are true volunteers. Whole services are composed entirely of volunteers: the Air Force for example, the Navy, almost all the Marines. That seems like proof to me that present pay rates are adequate. One must add that an Act of Congress in 1967 raised the base pay throughout the services in three installments, the third installment still to come, on April 1, 1969. So it is hard to understand why we are being told that to maintain adequate armed services on a volunteer basis will require large increases in pay; that they will cost an extra $17 billion per year. It seems plain to me that we can get all the armed forces we need as volunteers, and at present rates of pay.

23 But there is something ever so much bigger and more important than the draft. That bigger thing, of course, is the militarization of our country. Ex-President Eisenhower warned us of what he called the military-industrial complex. I am sad to say that we must begin to think of it now as the military-industrial-labor union complex. What happened under the plea of the Cold War was not alone that we built up the first big peace time army in our history, but we institutionalized it. We built, I suppose, the biggest government building in our history to run it, and we institutionalized it.

24 I don't think we can live with the present military establishment and its $80 billion a year budget, and keep America anything like we have known it in the past. It is corrupting the life of the whole country. It is buying up everything in sight: industries, banks, investors, universities; and lately it seems also to have bought up the labor unions.

25 The Defense Department is always broke; but some of the things they do with that $80 billion a year would make Buck Rogers envious. For example: the Rocky Mountain Arsenal on the outskirts of Denver was manufacturing a deadly nerve poison on such a scale that there was a problem of waste disposal. Nothing daunted, they dug a tunnel two miles deep under Denver, into which they have injected so much poisoned water that beginning a couple of years ago Denver began to experience a series of earth tremors of increasing severity. Now there is a grave fear of a major earthquake. An interesting debate is in progress as to whether Denver will be safer if that lake of poisoned water is removed or left in place. (N.Y. *Times,* July 4, 1968; *Science,* Sept. 27, 1968).

26 Perhaps you have read also of those 6000 sheep that suddenly died in Skull Valley, Utah, killed by another nerve poison—a strange and, I believe, still unexplained accident, since the nearest testing seems to have been 30 miles away.

27 As for Vietnam, the expenditure of fire power has been frightening. Some of you may still remember Khe Sanh, a hamlet just south of the Demilitarized Zone, where a force of U.S. Marines was beleaguered for a time. During that period we dropped on the perimeter of Khe Sanh more explosives than fell on Japan throughout World War II, and more than fell on the whole of Europe during the years 1942 and 1943.

28 One of the officers there was quoted as having said afterward, "It looks like the world caught smallpox and died." (N.Y. *Times,* Mar. 28, 1968.)

29 The only point of government is to safeguard and foster life. Our government has become preoccupied with death, with the business of killing and being killed. So-called Defense now absorbs 60 percent of the national budget, and about 12 percent of the Gross National Product.

30 A lively debate is beginning again on whether or not we should deploy antiballistic missiles, the ABM. I don't have to talk about them, everyone else here is doing that. But I should like to mention a curious circumstance. In September, 1967, or about 1½ years ago, we had a meeting of M.I.T. and Harvard people, including experts on these matters, to talk about whether anything could be done to block the Sentinel system, the deployment of ABM's. Everyone present thought them undesirable; but a few of the most knowledgeable persons took what seemed to be the practical view, "Why fight about a dead issue? It has been decided, the funds have been appropriated. Let's go on from there."

31 Well, fortunately, it's not a dead issue.

32 An ABM is a nuclear weapon. It takes a nuclear weapon to stop a nuclear weapon. And our concern must be with the whole issue of nuclear weapons.

33 There is an entire semantics ready to deal with the sort of thing I am about to say. It involves such phrases as "those are the facts of life." No—they are the facts of death. I don't accept them, and I advise you not to accept them. We are under repeated pressure to accept things that are presented to us as settled—decisions that have been made. Always there is the thought: let's go on from there! But this time we don't see how to go on. We will have to stick with those issues.

34 We are told that the United States and Russia between them have by now stockpiled in nuclear weapons approximately the explosive power of 15 tons of TNT for every man, woman and child on earth. And now it is suggested that we must make more. All very regrettable, of course; but those are "the facts of life." We really would like to disarm; but our new Secretary of Defense has made the ingenious proposal that now is the time to greatly increase our nuclear armaments so that we can disarm from a position of strength.

35 I think all of you know there is no adequate defense against massive nuclear attack. It is both easier and cheaper to circumvent any known nuclear defense system than to provide it. It's all pretty crazy. At the very moment we talk of deploying ABM's, we are also building the MIRV, the weapon to circumvent ABM's.

36 So far as I know, the most conservative estimates of Americans killed in a major nuclear attack, with everything working as well as can be hoped and all foreseeable precautions taken, run to about 50 millions. We have become callous to gruesome statistics, and this seems at first to be only another gruesome statistic. You think, Bang!—and next morning, if you're still there, you read in the newspapers that 50 million people were killed.

37 But that isn't the way it happens. When we killed close to 200,000 people with those first little, old-fashioned uranium bombs that we dropped on

Hiroshima and Nagasaki, about the same number of persons was maimed, blinded, burned, poisoned and otherwise doomed. A lot of them took a long time to die.

38 That's the way it would be. Not a bang, and a certain number of corpses to bury; but a nation filled with millions of helpless, maimed, tortured and doomed persons, and the survivors of a nuclear holocaust will be huddled with their families in shelters, with guns ready to fight off their neighbors, trying to get some uncontaminated food and water.

39 A few months ago Sen. Richard Russell of Georgia ended a speech in the Senate with the words: "If we have to start over again with another Adam and Eve, I want them to be Americans; and I want them on this continent and not in Europe." That was a United States senator holding a patriotic speech. Well, here is a Nobel Laureate who thinks that those words are criminally insane. (Prolonged applause.)

40 How real is the threat of full-scale nuclear war? I have my own very inexpert idea, but realizing how little I know and fearful that I may be a little paranoid on this subject, I take every opportunity to ask reputed experts. I asked that question of a very distinguished professor of government at Harvard about a month ago. I asked him what sort of odds he would lay on the possibility of full-scale nuclear war within the foreseeable future. "Oh," he said comfortably, "I think I can give you a pretty good answer to that question. I estimate the probability of full-scale nuclear war, provided that the situation remains about as it is now, at 2 percent per year." Anybody can do the simple calculation that shows that 2 percent per year means that the chance of having that full-scale nuclear war by 1990 is about one in three, and by 2000 it is about 50-50.

41 I think I know what is bothering the students. I think that what we are up against is a generation that is by no means sure that it has a future.

42 I am growing old, and my future, so to speak, is already behind me. But there are those students of mine who are in my mind always; and there are my children, two of them now 7 and 9, whose future is infinitely more precious to me than my own. So it isn't just their generation; it's mine too. We're all in it together.

43 Are we to have a chance to live? We don't ask for prosperity, or security; only for a reasonable chance to live, to work out our destiny in peace and decency. Not to go down in history as the apocalyptic generation.

44 And it isn't only nuclear war. Another overwhelming threat is the population explosion. That has not yet even begun to come under control. There is every indication that the world population will double before the year 2000; and there is a widespread expectation of famine on an unprecedented scale in many parts of the world. The experts tend to differ only in the estimates of when those famines will begin. Some think by 1980, others think

they can be staved off until 1990, very few expect that they will not occur by the year 2000.

45   That is the problem. Unless we can be surer than we now are that this generation has a future, nothing else matters. It's not good enough to give it tender loving care, to supply it with breakfast foods, to buy it expensive educations. Those things don't mean anything unless this generation has a future. And we're not sure that it does.

46   I don't think that there are problems of youth, or student problems. All the real problems I know are grown-up problems.

47   Perhaps you will think me altogether absurd, or "academic," or hopelessly innocent—that is, until you think of the alternatives—if I say as I do to you now: we have to get rid of those nuclear weapons. There is nothing worth having that can be obtained by nuclear war: nothing material or ideological, no tradition that it can defend. It is utterly self-defeating. Those atom bombs represent an unusable weapon. The only use for an atom bomb is to keep somebody else from using one. It can give us no protection, but only the doubtful satisfaction of retaliation. Nuclear weapons offer us nothing but a balance of terror; and a balance of terror is still terror.

48   We have to get rid of those atomic weapons, here and everywhere. We cannot live with them.

49   I think we've reached a point of great decision, not just for our nation, not only for all humanity, but for life upon the Earth. I tell my students, with a feeling of pride that I hope they will share, that the carbon, nitrogen and oxygen that make up 99 percent of our living substance, were cooked in the deep interiors of earlier generations of dying stars. Gathered up from the ends of the universe, over billions of years, eventually they came to form in part the substance of our sun, its planets and ourselves. Three billion years ago life arose upon the Earth. It seems to be the only life in the solar system. Many a star has since been born and died.

50   About two million years ago, man appeared. He has become the dominant species on the Earth. All other living things, animal and plant, live by his sufferance. He is the custodian of life on Earth. It's a big responsibility.

51   The thought that we're in competition with Russians or with Chinese is all a mistake, and trivial. Only mutual destruction lies that way. We are one species, with a world to win. There's life all over this universe, but in all the universe we are the only men.

52   Our business is with life, not death. Our challenge is to give what account we can of what becomes of life in the solar system, this corner of the universe that is our home and, most of all, what becomes of men—all men of all nations, colors, and creeds. It has become one world, a world for all men. It is only such a world that now can offer us light and the chance to go on.

Leopold Tyrmand: Children of the Century and Heroes of Our Time

Just as George Wald in the previous selection seeks to probe the sources of the anxieties and disillusionments of young people today, so Leopold Tyrmand in this selection seeks to provide an historical perspective on the current revolutionary temper by comparing the young militants today with the Romantic rebels of the nineteenth century. By doing so, Mr. Tyrmand convinces us that the rebellion of the young today is not as unique as we may have thought. In a later section of his book, Mr. Tyrmand, who is an emigrant from Eastern Europe, tells us that he "decided to defend America against itself," because although he regards the criticism of America that has traditionally come from the intellectual elite as "a priceless element of renewal and progress," he believes that America's traditional defender, the simple man in the street, needs to have his faith in his country bolstered. It may be easier for the student to see the organization of the parts in this six-paragraph selection than in the much longer, more complex discourses by Henry David Thoreau and George Wald. Because of the shorter compass, the student can easily trace out how the author moves from the repetitive statements of the thesis in the first paragraph, to an exposure in paragraphs 2 and 3 of the similarities between contemporary militants and nineteenth-century rebels, to a warning in paragraph 4 about the dangers of such rebellions, to an observation in paragraph 5 about some other, more productive heroes of the nineteenth century, and finally in paragraph 6 to an exposure of the differences between contemporary militants and nineteenth-century rebels.

1 The adolescent American revolutionary of today is a repetition. His predecessor was the Romantic rebel of the first quarter of the nineteenth century. Their ideals and ways of thought are similar. Their behavior patterns are all but identical. The textures of their lives tend to have much in common. Even their concepts of outward accessories and symbols have some striking resemblances.

2 The Romantic rebel turned against the insensitiveness that was, in his eyes, embodied in his contemporaries, against the post-feudal system of society, against political tyranny, and against the blight he perceived in oncoming industrialization. He derived pride from his lofty "loneliness,"

From *Notebooks of a Dilettante* (Macmillan, 1970). Copyright © 1969, 1970 by Leopold Tyrmand. Originally published in the *New Yorker*, XLV (August 16, 1969). Reprinted by permission of The Macmillan Company.

which was then the fashionable word for alienation. He felt contempt for conventions, for order, and for all bonds except the natural ones. He yearned for individual distinction, strove to prove himself, and valued flights of ambitions, fresh impulses of the heart, intensity of emotion and action. He had his passionate chroniclers, some of them the literary geniuses of his epoch; Goethe, Byron, Pushkin, Alfred de Vigny perpetuated his memorable traits. By the force of their art, they monumentalized both his virtues and his ridiculous aspects. They made the gap between him and his environment appear wider than it really was, and that was a great publicity hat trick —one that has also been skillfully performed by the American press of late —because nothing attracts more surely than the cumulative, much advertised partisanship of the attractive or than mythology disguised as reporting. Alfred de Musset coined for the Romantic rebel a proud and tender epithet: "L'Enfant du Siècle." Mikhail Lermontov called him, more forcefully, "Geroy Nashego Vremeni," or "A Hero of Our Time." They made of him the Style of the Era—a notion encompassing everything from *Weltanschauung* to hairdo. He was a paradigm to be followed by those who craved glossy prescribed and codified ideals for instant use.

3   The Romantic rebel was persecuted by those he combatted, but the persecution was not really severe. The feudal and monarchic structures were antique, and therefore were in transition. Those who embodied them felt old and tired, and grew skeptical about the set of values they were supposed to protect. They revelled in political machinations, malicious wisdom, and irony. A rebel had to have perpetrated a serious misdeed to be seriously chastised. The monarchs and their governments bestowed upon revolutionaries all kinds of compromises and courtesies—passports, with exit visas when needed, and mild punishments that made heroes out of them for a song. The monarchs flirted with the revolutionaries, praised their audacity, invited them to court, encouraged their effronteries, bantered with them, and perversely helped to build up their publicity.

4   History has proved that the Romantic rebellion was reactionary rather than progressive. Its followers consistently turned against civilization and finally despaired of progress. In the more distant future, their decadent anti-rationalism strengthened the ideological premises of Fascism and Nazism. Before that, however, the crumbling monarchic orders became constitutional, were transformed into cradles of modern liberalism, positivism, and scientific advancement, developed industry and humanitarianism, and nurtured the best traditions of tolerance, restraint, and social forbearance.

5   There were other heroes at the time, but they were less conspicuous, being more modest. Nevertheless, they were often accused of opportunism. These were the men busy extracting the secrets of life from nature and

contributing significantly to various branches of science, conquering disease and extending human life. They thereby helped insure that the next edition of the Heroes of Our Time, when they appeared on the world scene, would be mass-produced and thus infinitely more numerous.

6 The distinction between the Romantic and the Hero of *Our* Time lies in their different sense of pride. The former wanted to fight, and welcomed all the consequences of the struggle. He considered feudalism an evil, scorned it, didn't want anything from it, and recognized its right to fight back in self-defense. Being chiefly aristocratic in origin, the Romantic rebel cared for dignity and knew that only a readiness to pay the full price would give it to him. He welcomed persecution, for it gave his fight moral legitimacy. The Hero of *Our* Time demands all possible privileges from the order he tries to shatter. He claims the right to ruin without responsibility; in fact, he asks for the right to annihilate from those he desires to annihilate. Their resistance he calls oppression. Their arguments in defense of themselves and their values he brands as conformism. What do you call it when someone who has been beaten up for some abusive attack, which he proclaims a virtue, vilifies his chastiser, forgetting to mention that he himself attacked in order to bite off the other's ear? A Romantic rebel would have called it undignified, and perhaps would have added the word "squalid."

IV / STYLE

The third part of classical rhetoric was concerned with style. Once arguments had been discovered, selected, and arranged, they had to be put into words. Words—either the sound symbols or the graphic symbols—serve as the medium of communication between the speaker or writer and his audience. *Elocutio,* the Latin word for style, carried this notion of "speaking out." *Lexis,* the usual Greek word for style, carried the triple notion of "thought" and "word" (both of these notions contained in the Greek word *logos*) and "speaking" (*legein*). The threefold implication of *lexis* indicates that the Greek rhetoricians conceived of style as that part of rhetoric in which we take the *thoughts* collected by invention and put them into *words* for the *speaking out* in delivery. Cardinal Newman's definition of style carried much the same idea: "Style is a thinking out into language."

It is this "thinking out into language" that presents the most formidable problem in composition for many students. The sight of a blank sheet of paper paralyzes them. It may be some comfort to such students to know that the transcription of words on a sheet of paper can be difficult even for professional writers. Writing never becomes easy; it just becomes easier. Alfred North Whitehead once said, "Style, in its finest sense, is the last acquirement of the educated mind; it is also the most useful." The difficulty that everyone has, in varying degrees, in putting thoughts into language stems partly from the inertia that must be overcome at the beginning of any task, partly from the lack of something to say, partly from indecisiveness about what to say first, and partly from the variety of possible ways to say something.

Inertia is a problem that can be overcome only by will power. One must

414

simply sit down and resolve to write something on a piece of paper. Lack of things to say may be solved by the procedures discussed in the chapter on discovery of arguments. Indecisiveness about the order of the parts may be resolved by attention to the suggestions presented in the chapter on arrangement. The problems posed by the fact that thoughts and feelings can be worded in a variety of ways will be the principal concern of this chapter.

One notion about style that needs to be erased at the outset is that style is simply "the dress of thought." It is difficult to determine just which school of rhetoric gave currency to the notion that style was ornament or embellishment, like the tinsel draped over the bare branches of a Christmas tree, but it is certain that none of the prominent classical rhetoricians—Isocrates, Aristotle, Demetrius, Longinus, Cicero, Quintilian—ever preached such a doctrine. All of these taught that there is an integral and reciprocal relationship between matter and form. "Thought and speech are inseparable from each other"—those words of John Henry Newman express the view of style that all the best rhetoricians held. According to this view, matter must be fitted to the form, and form to the matter.

This notion of the integral relationship between matter and form is the basis for any true understanding of the rhetorical function of style. It precludes the view that style is merely the ornament of thought or that style is merely the vehicle for the expression of thought. Style does provide a vehicle for thought, and style can be ornamental; but style is something more than that. It is another of the "available means of persuasion," another of the means of arousing the appropriate emotional response in the audience, and another of the means of establishing the proper ethical image.

If the student adopts this functional notion of style, he will have gone part of the way toward solving some of his writing problems. He will begin to regard style in the way that Stendhal conceived of it: *Le style est ceci: Ajouter à une pensée donnée toutes les circonstances propres à produire tout l'effet que doit produire cette pensée* ("Style is this: to add to a given thought all the circumstances fitted to produce the whole effect which the thought is intended to produce"). The student will be guided in his choice of "the circumstances fitted to produce the whole effect" by a consideration of his subject matter, the occasion, his purpose, his own personality, and his audience. Jonathan Swift's definition of style as "proper words in proper places" is not much help to the student until he has some criteria for deciding what is proper. The determination of what is proper can be arrived at only in relation to the above-named considerations.

Since *proper* is a relative term, there cannot be such a thing as an absolute "best style." A writer must be in command of a variety of styles, in order to draw on that style which is most appropriate to the situation. This is not to say that his several styles will differ radically from one another. Just as there is a common strain in the range of dialects that he commands in his speech, so in his writing there will be a certain tenor that persists as he ranges from the most formal prose to the most relaxed prose. Each man, in other words, has his idiom—an idiom that is recognizable in all his dialects and styles. His various styles will result from the variations that he works on this common tenor.

How does the student acquire the variety of styles needed for the variety of subject matter, occasion, and audience that he is bound to confront? The classical rhetoricians taught that a man acquired versatility of style in three ways: (1) through a study of precepts or principles (*ars*), (2) through practice in writing (*exercitatio*), (3) through imitation of the practice of others (*imitatio*). Rhetoric textbooks are concerned mainly with laying down the principles that will guide the student in acquiring effective styles. Practice and imitation are exercises that the student usually performs outside the classroom. For his homework, he is required to write themes; or he may be asked to read "good writers," or to write a stylistic analysis of some writer, or to imitate passages of good writing.

Although this chapter will deal mainly with the precepts of effective writing, specimens of prose will be presented later for observation, analysis, and imitation. Practice in writing will have to come from the writing assignments set by the instructor, but at this point it is important to remind the student that practice in writing is the most beneficial of the three means. Precepts and imitation can *teach* the student how to write, but it is only by writing that the student will *learn* how to write. *One learns to write by writing.* Once is enough to enunciate that truism; but its truth cannot be recalled often enough.

With these few general remarks about style, we are ready to consider some of the precepts about style.

Grammatical Competence

In the study of style, we should be clear about the provinces of grammar and rhetoric. Just as the confusion between *grammar* and *usage* produced a great deal of needless controversy, so the confusion between *grammar* and *rhetoric* could hamper an intelligent discussion of the effective use of language. There are times, of course, when considerations of grammar will shade over into considerations of rhetoric. But while it is generally true that we must possess grammatical competence before we can develop an effective style, "good grammar" does not invariably produce "good rhetoric." Nor does "bad grammar" invariably produce "bad rhetoric." In April 1927, while awaiting execution in prison, Bartolomeo Vanzetti made this statement to a reporter:

> If it had not been for these thing, I might have live out my life, talking at street corners to scorning men. I might have die, unmarked, unknown, a failure. Now we are not a failure. This is our career and our triumph. Never in our full life can we hope to do such work for tolerance, for justice, for man's understanding of man, as now we do by an accident.

There are a number of errors in grammar and idiom in this utterance, but the passage has such a moving eloquence about it that it has become the most memorable statement to issue from the famous Sacco-Vanzetti case. Translated into flawless English, the utterance loses a great deal of its rhetorical effectiveness.

The smallest unit that falls within the province of rhetoric is the word. Unlike grammar, rhetoric is not concerned with *parts* of words, such as *morphemes* (the smallest segments that have meaning) and *phonemes* (those contrasting sound segments which enable a native speaker of the language to "hear" different words). It might be well at this point to set side by side the provinces of grammar and rhetoric:

GRAMMAR: phoneme—syllable—word—phrase—clause
RHETORIC: word—phrase—clause—paragraph—division—whole composition

It is clear from this schema that grammar and rhetoric overlap in the areas of the word, the phrase, and the clause. But although grammar and rhetoric deal with these common elements, their concern with these elements is not, strictly speaking, the same. Commonly we think of grammar as being concerned with "correctness" and of rhetoric as being concerned with "effectiveness." What we mean—or what we should mean—when we say that grammar is concerned with "correctness" is that grammar is preoccupied with how a particular language works—how words are formed and how words can be put together in phrases and clauses. What we mean when we say that rhetoric is concerned with "effectiveness" is that rhetoric deals with the choice of the "best" from a number of *possible* expressions in a language.

We can illustrate the difference by looking at an English sentence:

> He already has forgive them for leaving, before the curtain fell, the theater.

What the grammarian would pounce on here would be the word *forgive*. He would point out that modern English forms the perfect tense of the third-person singular verb with the auxiliary verb *has* and the past participle of the main verb. Once the grammarian had changed the verb in this sentence to *has forgiven,* he would have no more grammatical errors to correct in the sentence—that is, he would have to make no further changes in word order, inflections, or function words. But if the grammarian were to assume the additional role of the rhetorician, he would probably recommend further changes in the sentence. Although it is grammatically possible to place the word *already* and the clause *before the curtain fell* in the positions they now occupy in the sentence, it would be rhetorically advisable to alter the word order. The rhetorician would recommend that, in normal circumstances, the sentence read this way:

> He has already forgiven them for leaving the theater before the curtain fell.

He would probably justify the changes in word order on the grounds that the sentence reads more naturally, more euphoniously, that way. There might be a rhetorical situation which would justify placing the adverb clause where it was in the original sentence, but it is difficult to imagine what that situation would be. On the other hand, it is easy to imagine a situation that would justify putting *already* at the head of the sentence. If, for instance, we wanted to emphasize the time element, we might say, "Already he has forgiven them..."

Grammar would be concerned with the disposition of a word or clause only if the placement were impossible in English or would change the intended meaning of the sentence. English grammar would not permit this arrangement of words, for instance: *He has forgiven already them.* And if we were to say, "He had forgiven them before the curtain fell for leaving," the grammarian might ignore the awkward placement of the adverb clause, but he would have to point out that by such placement we have changed the meaning of the sentence: the adverb clause now modifies *had forgiven;* in the original sentence the adverb clause modified the gerund *leaving.*

Rhetoric and grammar are concerned, of course, with something more than just the placement of words, phrases, and clauses in a sentence, but this discussion of placement does illustrate the difference in the interest that grammar and rhetoric take in words.

Choice of Diction

An Adequate Vocabulary

Classical rhetoricians commonly considered style under two main heads: choice of diction, and composition of words in sentences. We will consider first the choice of diction.

In order to develop a good style, the student must have, in addition to grammatical competence, an ample vocabulary. How does he acquire the rich vocabulary he needs to develop a good style? There is no magic formula, certainly; the best advice that one can give the student is to urge him to read at every opportunity. There is no doubt that persistent reading will add immeasurably to his vocabulary resources. Every English teacher is willing to testify that the best writing is usually done by those students who have been omnivorous readers. Not only do such students have more to say on any given subject, but they seem to have at their command the words they need to express what they have to say. We more easily remember the words that we encounter repeatedly in our reading. How we remember and recall words at the appropriate time is not known. But we do know that a man cannot give what he does not have. The man who reads a great deal is more likely to encounter new words than the man who merely keeps his ears open to the speech that is constantly swirling about him. The reason for this is that the vocabulary for impromptu talk and conversation is considerably more limited than the vocabulary for written prose.

The writer who has words ready when he needs them is in a happy condition indeed. When apt words come readily, he knows that he has gained command over words. He must feel something of the assurance displayed by the centurion in the New Testament: "I say to one, 'Go,' and he goes, and to another, 'Come,' and he comes." What is especially fortunate about such a verbal facility is that words which present themselves readily are likely to be the "proper words in proper places." When we have to strain for the *mot juste,* there is always the danger that the word finally chosen will be slightly awry.

So the student who wants to acquire an adequate vocabulary should heed the advice to read, read, read. But let him not trust solely to unconscious acquisition. Although he will absorb many new words merely by meeting them frequently, he will accelerate the assimilation of new words if he will take the trouble to look up the meaning of unfamiliar words as he meets them. As Henry James said, "Try to be one of the people on whom nothing is lost!" The student will be amazed at how quickly and solidly his vocabulary grows if he takes the trouble to consult his dictionary every time he meets a new word.

Consulting the meaning of new words as one meets them is the best of the *conscious* methods of increasing one's vocabulary. It is best because it is functional: the student is pursuing the meanings of words that he needs to know in order to understand what he reads.

There are other conscious ways to accelerate the acquisition of a rich vocabulary. One of these is to study lists of "new," "unusual," or "useful" words. We can add rapidly to our stock of words by such a systematic study of word-lists, and the student who feels himself to be notably deficient in vocabulary can expedite the catching-up process by learning and constantly reviewing a recommended list of words. There are many vocabulary studies available, which the student who wants to add quickly to his knowledge of words would be well advised to consult.

The student should be warned, however, that this is the least satisfactory of the methods of vocabulary study. For one thing, he is studying words in isolation, not in a context. Studying words out of context can have a number of unfortunate consequences. First of all, knowledge of words tends to become an end in itself instead of a means. For another thing, the meanings of words studied out of context tend not to "stick" with the student as readily as they do when words are seen in the context of the reading that the student does. Any teacher who has subjected his students to the study of selected word-lists knows how often he has been disappointed by seeing few of these words appear in the writing his students submit to him. The third consequence of studying words out of context is that students often use these words ineptly or unidiomatically. The student who writes, "George ate his chicken with hedonistic gusto," reveals his awareness that *hedonistic* has some connection with sensuous pleasure, but he reveals also that he has not yet acquired the fine sense of knowing when words "fit." Nor does it help much to insist that the student should compose a sentence using the word he has just looked up, because if he has not seen or heard the word used aptly he has no guide to its use. The student should not be discouraged, of course, from investigating the meanings of words that he finds in some recommended list, because there is always some profit in such a pursuit, but the student should be aware of the limitations of such an approach to words.

If writers have any reference tools on their desks, they are most likely to have a dictionary and a thesaurus. Writers often resort to their dictionary for spelling, for syllabication of words, for meanings of words. They do not resort to a thesaurus as often as they do to a dictionary, but it is the rare writer who has not sometime felt the need to consult a thesaurus. A thesaurus is indeed a valuable vocabulary-aid when the exact word that we need does not come to us readily.

The most famous thesaurus—the one which has become as much associated with synonymy as Webster is with lexicography and Bulfinch with mythology—is *Roget's Thesaurus of English Words and Phrases,* compiled originally by an English physician, Peter Mark Roget, and first published in London in 1852. Roget arranged his "treasury of words" under topical headings. Subsequent editors have revised the original *Thesaurus,* adding new words and removing some that had become obsolete, and the most recent editors have arranged the entries in alphabetical order to facilitate use. There are many inexpensive editions of *Roget's* available today, as well as other thesauruses prepared by modern editors. The student will find enough use for a thesaurus to warrant his buying a copy.

A thesaurus merely lists synonyms (and some antonyms) for the entry word, with cross-references to other entries. Since synonyms seldom if ever are identical in meaning, a student needs considerable knowledge of words and a fine discrimination to use a thesaurus intelligently. Suppose that the student is composing a paragraph describing the people who attended the opening of an opera season. In one of the sentences, he wants to convey the idea that the women who attended this event displayed a lack of taste and moderation in the way they dressed. He has written the sentence this way:

> The ladies ostentatiously showed off their silks and satins and diamonds.

But he is not satisfied with the sentence. For one thing, he does not like the awkwardness of *showed off*. For another thing, he senses that there is something repetitious about *ostentatiously showed off* (doesn't *ostentation* mean "a show"?) Well, he will have to reword, perhaps recast, the sentence. If the new words or new phrases do not come to him immediately, he may find help in a thesaurus. But where does he start in the thesaurus?

Part of the difficulty in using a thesaurus is knowing just which entry one should consult. If one merely wants a substitute for a word, he has only to consult the entry for that word in the thesaurus. But sometimes one has an idea that he wants to convey, but no word for that idea suggests itself. In that case, one must conjure up some word or some concept (and it was here that Roget's original topical categories were helpful) that is close to the notion he wants to convey. Even a remote word will give him a starting point in the thesaurus. Synonyms for that word and cross-references to other words will move him closer to the exact word.

The student in our instance is not sure, however, whether he needs just a substitute word or whether he needs an entirely new way of phrasing what he means to say. But since "showing off" is the general idea that he wants to convey with this sentence, he decides to start by consulting the entry *ostentation*. In *Roget's* he finds, as he will in most thesauruses, that the synonyms are grouped under part-of-speech headings—noun, verb, adjective, adverb. Looking at the list of synonyms under each part-of-speech heading may suggest to the student how to reword or revise his unsatisfactory sentence. He would like to keep, if he can, the "silks and satins and diamonds" of his present sentence because these words are concrete and sensory. (Perhaps without knowing it, the student has produced the figure of synecdoche—the material here standing for the thing made from it.) From the nouns listed under *ostentation*, he experiments with various combinations:

> The ladies made a *display* (or *show, flourish, parade*) of their silks and satins and diamonds.

Perhaps adding the adjective *vulgar* (or *garish, gaudy, glittering*) would reveal his value judgment on the scene—would, in other words, reveal his attitude toward the scene:

> The ladies made a vulgar display of their silks and satins and diamonds.

Then he experiments with some verb combinations suggested by the synonyms listed under *ostentation: to exhibit, to display, to parade, to flaunt, to prink, to primp*. He finally settles on the verb *flaunt*—

> The ladies flaunted their silks and satins and diamonds.

—because *flaunt* combines all the notions and attitudes that he tried to convey in his original sentence; and *flaunt,* being concrete and picturesque, fits well with the figure of speech that follows it.

A thesaurus can be a valuable aid when "the proper word in the proper place" does not immediately present itself. But the student should be on his guard against the temptations offered by such a treasury. Those who have gone through a period of serious effort to improve their style may recall how difficult it was at times to resist the temptation to replace all the drab, ordinary words with some of the resplendent, polysyllabic words discovered in a thesaurus. A student, for instance, might compose a sentence like this:

> After the fire had been put out, the police roped off the street and prevented all sightseers from strolling past the charred ruins.

But that is too lackluster, he tells himself. So mining his lexicographical lode for some sesquipedalian nuggets, he bedizens his humdrum sentence in this fashion:

> After the conflagration had been extinguished, the police obstructed the thoroughfare and forefended all inquisitive spectators from perambulating before the incinerated residue of the pyrogenic catastrophe.

Fortunately, the student who persists in his efforts to improve his style eventually outgrows his penchant for such polysyllabic anfractuosities. Perhaps the price that one has to pay for an enriched vocabulary is a period of addiction to "big" words. The ordeal will inflict no permanent damage if the student can "kick the habit" in its early stages.

Purity, Propriety, and Precision of Diction

So far in our discussion of diction we have touched on two qualifications that the student must have if he is to improve his style: he must know the grammar of his language, and he must have an adequate vocabulary. Our concern from this point on will be mainly with the *rhetorical* competence that a student must have in order to make wise choices among words. George Campbell pointed up the distinction between grammatical and rhetorical competence in this way: "the grammatical art bears much the same relation to the rhetorical which the art of the mason bears to that of the architect."

The prime quality of prose style is *clarity*—or, to use the sonorous Latinate term, *perspicuity*. Since the object of rhetorical prose is persuasion, it follows that such prose must communicate with those who are to be persuaded. And if rhetorical prose must communicate, it follows that it must, above all, be clear. As one might expect from the man who viewed rhetoric as an activity that always involved an audience, Aristotle held that "language which does not convey a clear meaning fails to perform the very function of language." Lord Macaulay, one of the masters of the limpid prose style, put it this way: "The first rule of all writing—that rule to which every other is subordinate —is that the words used by the writer shall be such as most fully and precisely convey his meaning to the great body of his readers."

Clarity comes from selecting words carefully and arranging them well. Leaving aside the problem of arrangement for now, how can a writer learn to select the proper words? He will be helped in making his selection by keeping three criteria in mind—purity, propriety, and precision. While some judgments about whether language is pure, appropriate, and precise can be made only when the writer sees words in a sentence and when he views them in relation to his subject, purpose, and audience, it is still possible to say something about the purity, propriety, and precision of isolated words.

The discussion of *purity of diction* involves us, willy-nilly, in a consideration of those much-maligned criteria that George Campbell set forth in the eighteenth century to determine "good usage." In order to merit the stamp of approval, words must be, according to Campbell, in *reputable* use, in *national* use, and in *present* use. Despite the relativity of these criteria, there would seem to be little practical difficulty in using at least two of the criteria —national use and present use—to help us determine whether our diction is "pure" and therefore clear. If we are to communicate with a contemporary audience, it stands to reason that we must use current words and idioms— that is, words and idioms, however "old" they may be, that are understood by people today. Likewise, we must use the words which have a national currency. This criterion demands that we avoid dialectical words, technical words, coinages, and foreign words. But this second criterion immediately calls for some qualification. If we view words in relation to an audience, for instance, we see that there are some situations which call for localisms, technical jargon, neologisms, and even foreign words.

When we try the third criterion, reputable use, we run into more difficulty. Campbell proposed this standard for judging reputable locutions: "whatever modes of speech are authorized as good by the writings of a great number, if not the majority, of celebrated authors." But is it conceivable that in a modern pluralistic society we could ever arrive at any consensus about who our "celebrated authors" are? Moreover, if two "celebrated authors" are in conflict on a matter of usage, which author do we follow?—the one who is *more* celebrated? And is it possible for the ordinary educated person to determine in every case, or even in many cases, whether a certain locution is sanctioned by a "great number" or "the majority" of celebrated authors?

These practical difficulties lead many people to rely on some arbiter of usage. The best source of such guidance is a reference work that boldly claims to be an arbiter. Fortunately, there are a few esteemed dictionaries of usage available. These dictionaries offer reliable guidance because the men or women who prepared them had good taste in language to start with and refined their taste with a close study of actual usage.

The most famous of these reference words is H. W. Fowler's *A Dictionary of Modern English Usage,* first published in 1926 but many times reprinted. This book has become a bible of usage for many famous writers and editors. Fowler was himself a lexicographer, having compiled, with the help of his brother Francis George Fowler, *The Concise Oxford Dictionary.* To his sound knowledge of the English language, Fowler added a discriminating taste, and he wrote with such grace and wit that he was himself an exemplar of the "good English" that he advocated. It was Fowler who assured us, once and for all, that it was permissible at times, even advisable, to split an infinitive or to end a sentence with a preposition. And he made household words of some of the headings in his alphabetically arranged dictionary—tags like Battered Ornaments, Cannibalism, Elegant Variation, Out of the Frying Pan, Sturdy Indefensibles.

The student will have to consult *A Dictionary of Modern English Usage* to discover for himself the value and flavor of this admirable reference work. But here is a taste of Fowler's wit and judgment, taken from his article on the subject we have just been discussing—purity of diction:

> PURISM. Now & then a person may be heard to 'confess', in the pride that apes humility, to being 'a bit of a purist'; but *purist* & *purism* are for the most part missile words, which we all of us fling at anyone who insults us by finding not good enough for him some manner of speech that is good enough for us. It is in that disparaging sense that the words are used in this book; by *purism* is to be understood a needless & irritat-

ing insistence on purity or correctness of speech. Pure English, however, even apart from the great numbers of elements (vocabulary, grammar, idiom, pronunciation, & so forth) that go to make it up, is so relative a term that almost every man is potentially a purist & a sloven at once to persons looking at him from a lower & a higher position in the scale than his own. The words have therefore not been very freely used; that they should be renounced altogether would be too much to expect considering the subject of the book. But readers who find a usage stigmatized as purism have a right to know the stigmatizer's place in the purist scale, if his stigma is not to be valueless. Accordingly, under headings of various matters with which purism is concerned, a few articles are now mentioned illustrating the kind of view that may be expected in other articles of a similar nature: ...

Dictionary of Modern English Usage, Oxford University Press, pp. 474-5. Reprinted by permission of the Clarendon Press, Oxford.

With the passage of time, Fowler's dictionary was bound to become outdated—at least on some matters of usage. And as the gap between British English and American English widened, American writers began to see that Fowler was not relevant to some of the locutions that had developed in the United States.

In order to fill the need for an up-to-date dictionary of usage that would pay special attention to American English, the Oxford University Press in 1957 published Margaret Nicholson's *A Dictionary of American-English Usage.* In her Preface, Miss Nicholson announces that her book is an adaptation of, not a replacement for, Fowler's *MEU.* She has retained many of Fowler's long articles, has abridged others, and has added a number of her own entries on modern Americanisms.

In 1957 Bergen Evans and Cornelia Evans published a completely new dictionary of American usage, *A Dictionary of Contemporary American Usage* (Random House). Writers who are loyal to Fowler will continue to use *due to* only in adjectival structures (*His absence was due to sickness,* but not, *The government failed due to widespread discontent with its policies*). But those writers who have come to trust the painstaking study that the Evanses have made of actual usage will probably be guided by this statement about the present status of *due to:*

> *due to* may be used to qualify a noun, as in *a mistake due to carelessness.* This use of *due to* was listed by Dr. Johnson as "proper, but not usual." Since then it has become a familiar form of speech and no one thinks of objecting to it. But the words are also used today to qualify a verb, as in *he failed, due to carelessness.* This construction is relatively new and is condemned by some grammarians.
>
> In both cases the words *due to* are being used as *owing to* might be used. It is claimed that *due to* is acceptable in the first case but not in the

second, and that only the form *owing to* may be used with a verb. This distinction cannot be defended on theoretical grounds, since *due to* and *owing to* are grammatically alike. The critics usually content themselves with saying that *"due to* cannot be used to qualify a verb." But it is used to qualify a verb, millions of times every day. And it is used in this way in very respectable places. A tablet in front of the Old State House in Philadelphia reads: *Here the Continental Congress sat from the date it convened, May 10, 1775, until the close of the Revolution, except when, in 1776-77, it sat in Baltimore, and in 1777-78, in Lancaster and York, due to the temporary occupation of Philadelphia by the British army.* (See also *owe.*)

From *A Dictionary of Contemporary American Usage* by Bergen Evans and
Cornelia Evans. Copyright © 1957 by Bergen Evans and Cornelia Evans.
Reprinted by permission of Random House, Inc.

Any of the three dictionaries of usage we have discussed would be a valuable addition to the student's library. If the student's dictionary does not settle his doubts about the "purity" of a certain expression, a dictionary of usage can be of real help to him. He should be cautioned, however, not to develop a neurotic concern about usage. If American schools had been as much concerned with grammar, logic, and rhetoric, as they have been with "good usage," the quality of student writing today might better than it generally is.

The principal point to be emphasized about purity of diction is that one's language must be intelligible and acceptable to an audience. There will always be a certain level of diction below which a speaker or writer will never slip, however crude and unlettered his audience may be. There is a large stock of words, a reservoir of "basic English," that will always be intelligible and acceptable to any audience. Deviations from this basic stock of ordinary words will be governed mainly by the nature of the audience addressed.

Propriety or appropriateness is the quality of diction that can least be judged in isolation; it always implies a judgment made in relation to something else. Conceivably, we could look at isolated words and make some judgment about whether they were current or national or reputable, but it is impossible to judge the appropriateness of isolated words.

Diction is appropriate when it suits our subject matter, our purpose, the occasion, and the audience. Unfortunately, there are no handbooks that can help the student make judgments about the appropriateness of his diction. Everyone seems to be endowed with a certain minimal sense of appropriateness—a sense absorbed from the experience of living in a society. Instinctively, we "tone up" our everyday language when we shift from a situation in which we are addressing our peers and intimates to a situation in which we are addressing, say, the dean of the college. We make similar adjustments in our diction as our subject matter, occasion, and purpose change.

The refinements of this minimal sense of appropriateness will come naturally, as our experience deepens and our education advances, and will develop in proportion to our native intelligence and our conscious efforts to improve this sense. Just as certain people seem to inherit and develop a superior ability to get along with their fellow men, so some of them develop a keener sense than others for the appropriateness of their language.

Involved in this matter of appropriateness are the connotations of words. When we are concerned with the purity or precision of diction, we are concerned mainly with the denotations of words—with the dictionary meanings of verbal symbols. But in our choice of appropriate diction we must also take into consideration the connotations of words—those emotional and tonal qualities that come to be associated with words. We cannot control the connotations that cluster around a word; we can only be aware of those connotations and take advantage of them. It makes a great difference whether we call a man a "politician" or a "statesman." Because of the connotations that attend these words, the first word will tend, with most audiences, to dishonor the man, while the second word will tend to honor him.

The connotations of words have great rhetorical value—for example, in promoting the emotional appeal of a discourse. Robert H. Thouless has ably demonstrated the emotional value of connotations in his analysis of the diction in two verses by John Keats:

> In *The Eve of St. Agnes*, Keats has written:
>> Full on this casement shone the wintry moon,
>> And threw warm gules on Madeline's fair breast.
>
> These are beautiful lines. Let us notice how much of their beauty follows from the proper choice of emotionally colored words and how completely it is lost if these words are replaced by neutral ones. The words with strikingly emotional meanings are *casement, gules, Madeline, fair,* and *breast. Casement* means simply a kind of window with emotional and romantic associations. *Gules* is the heraldic name for red, with the suggestion of romance which accompanies all heraldry. *Madeline* is simply a girl's name, but one calling out favorable emotions absent from a relatively plain and straightforward name. *Fair* simply means, in objective fact, that her skin was white or uncolored—a necessary condition for the colors of the window to show—but also fair implies warm emotional preference for an uncolored skin rather than one which is yellow, purple, black, or any of the other colors which skin might be. *Breast* has also similar emotional meanings, and the aim of scientific description might have been equally well attained if it had been replaced by such a neutral word as *chest.*

Let us now try the experiment of keeping these two lines in a metrical form, but replacing all the emotionally colored words by neutral ones, while making as few other changes as possible. We may write:

Full on this window shone the wintry moon
Making red marks on Jane's uncolored chest.

No one will doubt that all of its poetic value has been knocked out of the passage by these changes. Yet the lines still mean the same in external fact; they still have the same objective meaning. It is only the emotional meaning which has been destroyed.

From Robert H. Thouless, *How To Think Straight*. Copyright 1932 by Robert H. Thouless. Reprinted by permission of Simon and Schuster, New York.

The student is probably well aware by now that poets exploit the emotional values of words, but he is not always alert to the subtle emotional effects exerted by connotation in a prose text. Faced with the evidence of H. L. Mencken's scholarly three-volume study of American English, we have to concede that he had a profound knowledge of his native language, but perhaps we are not sufficiently aware of how he manipulated the connotations of words to effect his rhetorical purpose. Consider this example, in which Mencken is seeking to influence our attitude toward a certain kind of teacher:

Such idiots, despite the rise of "scientific" pedagogy, have not died out in the world. I believe that our schools are full of them, both in pantaloons and in skirts. There are fanatics who love and venerate spelling as a tom-cat loves and venerates catnip. There are grammatomaniacs; schoolmarms who would rather parse than eat; specialists in an objective case that doesn't exist in English; strange beings, otherwise sane and even intelligent and comely, who suffer under a split infinitive as you or I would suffer under gastro-enteritis. There are geography cranks, able to bound Mesopotamia and Baluchistan. There are zealots for long division, experts in the multiplication table, lunatic worshipers of the binomial theorem. But the system has them in its grip. It combats their natural enthusiasm diligently and mercilessly. It tries to convert them into mere technicians, clumsy machines.

From H. L. Mencken, "Pedagogy," *A Mencken Chrestomathy*, New York: Alfred A. Knopf, 1949, p. 305. Reprinted by permission of the publisher.

We cannot examine all the techniques that Mencken uses in his satirical writings, but we can note here the subtle way in which he influences our reactions simply by his choice of words. A good deal of the effect of this passage is produced by Mencken's "name-calling." The "names" that Mencken used here are heavily freighted with emotional overtones—*idiots, fanatics, schoolmarms* (one of Mencken's favorite derogatory epithets), *cranks, zealots, lunatic worshipers*. All of these words carry the discrediting connotation of extreme, irrational commitment to a cause—the taint of "enthusiasm" that many critics ascribed to the evangelical sects in eighteenth- and nineteenth-century England. Where Mencken fails to find an emotional epithet to suit his purpose, he invents one—*grammatomaniacs*. Most readers do not know what *gastro-enteritis* means; but they do not have to know—the word just *sounds* awful. Notice how Mencken, in the second sentence of this passage, indicates that he is talking about both men and women teachers—"in pantaloons and in skirts." *Pantaloons* was an especially clever choice. *Pants* would have been the word that most of us would have chosen as the counterpart of *skirts*. But Mencken detected the extra connotative value of the wor*d pantaloons,* suggesting to a modern audience something archaic, slightly feminine. Note too how Mencken uses a simile in the third sentence to depreciate the object of his satire, comparing devotees of correct spelling to the lowly, back-alley *tom-cat*. One of the deadliest words in the English language is the word *mere*. Mencken uses this word with devastating effectiveness at the end of this passage, where he begins to shift his ground of attack, warning us that these "enthusiastic" pedagogues are now in danger of being turned into dis-passionate machines as a result of their exposure to "teachers' college" bunkum. What is more chilling than to be called a "mere technician"?

We see then that the connotations of words must be considered in any judgment about the appropriateness of diction. Sensitivity to the connotations of words cannot be taught; it must be learned. What is even harder for the student to acquire is a fine sense for knowing how far to go in exploiting the emotional force of connotations. Mencken perhaps goes too far in the passage we have just considered. In most of his satirical writings, he relied too heavily on the shock technique that derived from the use of hyperbolic, simplistic diction. Many people are alienated rather than persuaded by his intemperate language. A clever writer can sometimes be too clever for his own good. It does not take a sledge-hammer to drive a nail.

Playing a New Game: Changed Meanings

Most of you know what the words listed below mean now. Find out what those words meant before the 1960's. A dictionary will help you discover the denotations of the words. For the connotations of many of the words you may have to consult your parents or some other adults over thirty.

Americans have never been willing to leave the English language alone, and the 1960s' bequest of new words to the '70's is a fairly large one. But the

From *Life*, LXVIII (January 23, 1970), p. 28. Reprinted by permission of Time, Inc. © 1970 Time Inc.

most striking linguistic phenomenon of the '60s is old words that have acquired vivid new meanings. Herewith our own 1970 Abridged Dictionary of current words and phrases that meant something quite different to most people a decade ago:

acid	grass	rap
AFL	hangup	rock
Apollo	hawk	salt
bag	head	silo
black	joint	soul
blitz	Sen. McCarthy	split
bread	mace	Dr. Spock
brother	militant	stoned
busing	Minuteman	straight
bust	moratorium	topless
Camelot	pad	transplant
camp	panther	trip
demonstration	pig	tune in
dove	pill	turn on
drop out	pot	Wallace
freak	Pueblo	weatherman

We turn now to the third quality, precision. The word *precision* has its roots in the Latin verb *praecidere*, "to cut off." A precise word is a word shorn of all superfluous and irrelevant notions, a word that signifies neither more nor less than we intend to say. Words may be dubbed "imprecise" (1) when they do not express exactly what we intended to say; (2) when they express the idea but not quite fully; (3) when they express the idea but with something more than we intended.

The student who writes, "I was pleased by his fulsome praise," has not said what he intended to say. If he consults the dictionary meaning of *fulsome* ("disgusting or offensive, mainly because of its excessiveness or insincerity"), he will see how wide of the mark he has come. If he writes, "I thought it was a tremendous performance," he conveys the general idea that he approved of the performance, but he conveys no exact notion of the particular way in which this performance was "tremendous." When he writes, "As a result of examining the basic flaws in the situation, he came up with a radical solution to the problem," he chooses an apt word in *radical* (a solution that gets at the *root* of the problem), but unwittingly he suggests an additional meaning that he did not intend (a solution that is *wild* or *subversive*). A word then will be inexact if it expresses *too little* or *too much* or if it is *too general*.

It is perhaps better to discuss faulty idiom here than under the head of pure diction, because, like the diction cited in the previous paragraph, faulty idiom "misses the mark." The reason why lapses in idiom constitute one of the commonest faults in student writing is that idiom, like connotation, is one of the tricky aspects of language. Dictionaries and handbooks of usage will more often be helpful to the student in matters of idiom than in matters of connotation, but the most reliable guide to correct idiom is the student's own awareness of how his native language is spoken. The student who has not read very much or who has not kept his ears open to the turns of phrase is the one most likely to violate the idiom of the language.

The "turns of phrase" in the previous sentence suggests an important observation about idiom. No single word, considered in isolation, can be declared unidiomatic. If we say of a certain word, "Native speakers of the language do not use that word," we are saying simply that such a word does not exist in the English language. A word can be classified as unidiomatic only in relation to some other word or words. No one could say of the word *for* that it is unidiomatic; either it is an English word or it is not. *For* can become unidiomatic only when it is used in conjunction with another word, as with the word *unequal,* in the sentence, "The judge proved to be unequal for the task." Then we can point out that native speakers of the language do not use the preposition *for* with *unequal;* they say "unequal *to* the task."

What complicates the difficulty is that grammar is of no help to the student in deciding matters of idiom. There is nothing ungrammatical in the locution "unequal for the task." Idiom is a matter of usage rather than of grammar: native speakers just do not say "unequal for." Neither is logic of much help to the student in regard to idiom. When we say, for instance, "He *looked up* the word in the dictionary," we are, in a sense, violating logic, because when we consult a word in the dictionary, we are more likely to *look down* the page to find the word than to *look up* the page. But "look up a word" is the correct idiom simply because that is the way people say it.

Sometimes the prefixes of words will provide a clue to the idiomatic preposition that goes with those words. So we say, "he *de*parted *from* the scene," "the crowd *e*merged *from* the stadium," "he *is ad*verse *to* the proposal," "they *com*pared it *with* the first version," "the station-wagon *col*lided *with* the motorcycle," "he *abs*tained *from* all alcoholic beverages." But the lexical meaning of these Latin prefixes is not always a clue to the proper preposition, for we also say, "in *con*trast *to*" (as well as "in *con*trast *with*"), "he *de*parted *for* the station," "she *com*pared him *to* an overgrown bear."

Since neither grammar nor logic is a reliable guide to proper idiom, we must develop our own awareness of the peculiar way in which native speakers of the language say certain things. Perhaps the last proficiency we acquire in learning a foreign language is a sense for the idioms of the language. It is a commonplace that the best way to attune our ear to the idioms of a foreign language is to live for a time in a community where that language is spoken exclusively. So in learning the idioms of our own language, we must *listen* to the speech that is all about us, and we must carefully observe the turns of phrase in the contemporary prose we read. Teachers can point out lapses in idiom and can correct the idiom in the student's writing, but in the absence of any "rules" about idiom, the student must develop his own sense for the idiosyncrasies of expression. He must become aware not only of the proper idiom but of the subtle changes of meaning and tone affected by idiom. In an article on the idiomatic preposition, John Nist has illustrated some of the vagaries of idiom:

> Doting grandparents may indulge in loving pride and make *over* a favorite one-toothed blue-eyed darling. But a pouting lover had better make *up with* his sweetheart first; his chances of making *out* are otherwise very slim. An imbiber can conceivably be sleeping *in* while sleeping *out* for the sole sake of sleeping it *off*. How many a long-suffering son-in-law has had a run *in* with her whose kiss is colder than a mackerel because he intended to *run out* on his wife by running *off with* the understanding secretary? One of the favorite maxims of chilly age for flaming youth goes like this: Be careful how you live it *up;* you may never live it *down!* A philosopher chews *upon* a difficult thought; an able prosecutor chews *up* the defense attorney's arguments; a catcher chews *over* the signals with his pitcher; a diner chews *around* the bone; and an angry man chews *out* his offensive neighbor. A cut*up* at the party may cut *out* from the stag line and cut *in* on the belle of the ball. And he who goes all *out* in tracking down the tricky idiomatic preposition will undoubtedly find himself all *in*.

> From John Nist, "The Idiomatic Preposition," *Word Study*, XXXIX (Dec. 1963), 1-4. By permission of the author and publisher. From *Word Study*, copyright 1963 by G. & C. Merriam Co., Publishers of the Merriam-Webster Dictionaries.

Many other observations might be made about diction, such as that diction should be "natural," "vigorous," "concrete," "graceful," "harmonious," but these epithets merely represent alternate ways of saying that diction should be *pure, appropriate,* and *precise*. Besides, our judgments about the naturalness, vigor, concreteness, gracefulness, and harmony of diction—or, to use our own terms, the purity, propriety, and precision of diction—can best be made when we view diction in the context of a sentence and in relation to our rhetorical purpose. There will be times, for instance, when it might suit our purpose to make our diction awkward or insipid or abstract or ugly or unmusical.

In summary: Since words are the building-blocks of our sentences, it is obvious that we must have an adequate supply of words to erect the kind of edifice we have planned. When our supply of words is low, we will have to make some effort to add to our stock. Our working vocabulary will naturally expand as our experience and education expand, but we can accelerate the expansion by reading a great deal and by consulting dictionaries and thesauruses. Since we seek to communicate with others, it stands to reason that our diction must first of all be intelligible—intelligible, that is, to a particular audience. It will be mainly the audience that will determine whether we can use learned words or technical terms or foreign words or slang. The audience, the subject matter, the occasion, and our purpose constitute the criteria for judging the appropriateness of our diction. In addition to choosing intelligible and appropriate diction, we must choose diction that is as precise as the situation permits and demands. Dictionaries and handbooks of usage will help solve some of the student's problems with usage, idiom, and connotation, but the student will have to depend mainly on the development of his own sensitivity to these aspects of language.

Composition of the Sentence

Words are symbols of ideas, but they do not begin to "say" anything until we put them together. Sentences, which are syntactical units composed of words, "say" something, partly because of the *lexical content* (the meaning) of the words and partly because of the *grammatical forms* that govern words put together in patterns. Up to this point, we have been speaking mainly about the lexical aspect of words. As we move now to a discussion of the composition of the sentence, we must begin to be concerned with syntax. Eventually, we will be led into a discussion of another aspect of language: how the *rhetorical forms* of sentences, the schemes, constitute a third carrier of meaning.

As we pointed out in the previous section on choice of diction, no one can begin to develop a style until he has a basic competence in the grammar of the language. We presume that the student has this basic competence and is thus ready to develop the rhetorical competence he needs in order to compose effective sentences.

Rhetorical competence plays its part in the writing process when there are choices to be made from among two or more grammatical possibilities. Stylistic variations in the syntax of the sentence cannot ignore the grammar of the language. Any changes we make for rhetorical effect must respect the grammatical possibilities of the language.

As a starting point for our discussion of the rhetoric of the sentence, let us take this minimal sentence:

The boy loves the girl.

Native speakers of the language recognize this as a pattern of words that make a statement. They know the meanings of the words, and they are familiar with the grammar of the sentence: the function word *the,* the inflectional concordance between the subject and predicate, and the word order. Anyone who wanted to make a statement, in the English language, about a young male of the human species having a certain emotional attitude toward a young female of the human species would be limited in the words he could choose to express this idea and even more severely limited in the way he could put these words together to say what he wanted to say. As far as *rhetoric* goes, there is very little he could do with this sentence. He might make some different choice of words—proper nouns to replace the *boy* and *girl* or a synonymous verb to replace *loves*—to make the sentence rhetorically more effective. But there is almost nothing he could do to alter the grammar of the sentence. He cannot say "Boy love girl" or "Loves the boy the girl." No, he must dispose whatever words he chooses in the usual pattern for a statement—subject-verb-complement (S-V-C)—and use the proper inflectional forms.

It is when we begin to expand this minimal sentence pattern that rhetoric has a bearing. There are a number of ways in which we can expand this sentence, and within each of the various ways there are often alternatives. Once there are alternatives, there are choices to be made; and once choices are to be made, rhetoric comes into the picture.

One of the ways in which we can expand our minimal sentence is by adding single-word, phrasal, or clausal modifiers to the *head word* in the S or V or C. For instance:

The tall, handsome boy sincerely loves the short, homely girl.

Can we alter the order of any of these modifiers? Yes, we can make *some* changes—changes that are grammatically and idiomatically possible but not always stylistically advisable. For example, we could make these changes:

The boy, tall and handsome, loves sincerely the short, homely girl.

Rarely does one see adjectival single-word modifiers placed *after* the head word in the complement:... *sincerely loves the girl, short and homely.* The following order is also possible in English:

Tall and handsome, the boy loves the short, homely girl sincerely.

We might choose this order, for instance, if we wanted to emphasize the boy's tallness and handsomeness and the sincerity of his love for the girl.

Another way to expand the minimal sentence is to use prepositional phrases as modifiers of any one or all of the head words in the S-V-C pattern:

> The boy from Montana loves, with uncommon fervor, the girl from Missouri.

Prepositional phrases used as adjectival modifiers are almost always placed *after* the noun or pronoun they modify. There are some instances, however, when the prepositional phrase used adjectivally will be placed *before* the noun that it modifies. For example,

> About this development, he had been given no advance warning.

(Here the phrase *about this development* modifies *warning*.)

Prepositional phrases used adverbially have more freedom of movement than do prepositional phrases used adjectivally. There are three other places where the phrase *with uncommon fervor* could be placed in our sentence:

> With uncommon fervor, the boy from Montana loves the girl from Missouri.
> The boy from Montana loves the girl from Missouri with uncommon fervor.
> The boy from Montana with uncommon fervor loves the girl from Missouri.

There are a number of other ways in which we could expand our minimal sentence:

1. compounding the head words in the S-V-C pattern;
2. juxtaposing appositives to the head words in the S-V-C pattern;
3. using verbals or verbal phrases (participles, gerunds, and infinitives) in the S-V-C pattern;
4. using noun clauses to serve as the S or the C in the S-V-C pattern;
5. using adjective clauses to modify the S or C head word in the S-V-C pattern;
6. using adverb clauses to modify the V in the S-V-C pattern.

We could go on to illustrate these methods of expanding the sentence and to investigate the alternatives (if any) in word order of each of these methods, but the student can pursue these matters in the structural and transformational grammars now available. This brief excursion into the syntax of the English sentence serves to give a general idea of what we mean by the rhetoric of the sentence.

When we are presented with a number of syntactical choices, all of them grammatically and idiomatically possible, we will elect the possibility that best serves our purpose at the moment. If, for instance, one of the possibilities allows us to put a word or phrase in an emphatic position and if emphasis of that word or phrase is what we want at that point, then we should take advantage of that possibility. There are times when we want to de-emphasize a word or phrase, and in that case we should elect that possibility which would bury the word or phrase somewhere in the interior of the sentence. We might elect another grammatical possibility on the grounds that this disposition of words improved the rhythm of the sentence. Sometimes we might reject a grammatical possibility because it lends itself to ambiguity. (Such a case would be the "squinting modifier" in the sentence "The bandmaster strutted along *gaily* twirling his baton.") And of course we sometimes elect a grammatical possibility for no other reason than that we want to avoid monotony of sentence structure.

There is another point to be made here about the rhetoric of the sentence. Style, like grammar, is part of the expressive system of a language. Just as grammatical devices, like word order and inflections, are carriers of meaning, so the forms of sentence—the *schemes,* as the Renaissance rhetoricians called them—are expressive of meaning too. For example, let us consider the rhetorical device of parallelism. When we have to express a series of similar or equivalent "meanings," we usually resort to the grammatical device of compounding, and we reinforce the co-ordinate value of the compounded elements with the rhetorical device of parallelism.

We can illustrate how parallelism can be expressive of meaning by looking at a sentence in which it is a pronounced feature:

> He [the president of a large, complex university] is expected to be a friend of the students, a colleague of the faculty, a good fellow with the alumni, a sound administrator with the trustees, a good speaker with the public, an astute bargainer with the foundations and the federal agencies, a politician with the state legislatures, a friend of industry, labor, and agriculture, a persuasive diplomat with donors, a champion of education generally, a supporter of the professions (particularly law and medicine), a spokesman to the press, a scholar in his own right, a public servant at the state and national levels, a devotee of opera and football equally, a decent human being, a good husband and father, an active member of a church.

From Clark Kerr, *The Uses of the University,* Harvard University Press, 1963. Reprinted by permission of the publishers.

This is an unusually long sentence, but it is so well articulated that it conveys its meaning clearly. The expansion, all of which takes place in the complement part of the sentence, is managed with a series of parallel structures. The student could learn the whole art of parallelism from a close study of this remarkable sentence. An analysis of the sentence reveals several levels of parallelism and enough variation in the basic pattern to break an otherwise monotonous rhythm. The basic pattern is this:

indefinite article	noun	prepositional phrase
a	friend	of the students
a	colleague	of the faculty

Dr. Kerr varies the rhythm of this basic pattern in several ways: (1) by introducing an adjective before the noun ("a good fellow with the alumni"); (2) by throwing in an adverb ("a champion generally"); (3) by inserting a parenthesis ("particularly law and medicine"); (4) by compounding the objects of the preposition ("a friend of industry, labor, and agriculture") or by compounding the adjectives modifying the object of the preposition ("a public servant at the state and national levels").

The main point that we want to make about this sentence, however, is that the rhetorical form is one of the carriers of meaning. The theme of Dr. Kerr's essay is that the modern university has become so huge and complex that it can no longer be regarded as a *uni*-versity but must be regarded now as a *multi*-versity. The point he is making in the section of the essay from which the above sentence was taken is that the president of such a multiversity must wear many hats, must be many things to many people. In this sentence he is enumerating some of the capacities in which the president is expected to serve, using a series of phrases. This compounding (without conjunctions, for the most part) is one of the expressive devices for indicating the variety of roles the president must play. But because Dr. Kerr also wants to indicate that the president is expected to play each of these roles equally well he uses the device of parallelism, which serves to reinforce the co-ordinate value of these several capacities. Dr. Kerr does not expect his reader to remember all these roles; he wants only to convey the general impression of the heavy burden that the president carries. Incidentally, the *length* of the sentence has a rhetorical function too: the long cataloguing is weighty and exhausting to the reader, as the job is to the president.

In the next sentence but one, Dr. Kerr makes use of antithesis, another rhetorical device, to convey the notion of the contrary qualities that the president must combine in his personality. Here is that sentence of 114 words:

> He should be firm, yet gentle; sensitive to others, insensitive to himself; look to the past and the future, yet be firmly planted in the present; both visionary and sound; affable, yet reflective; know the value of a dollar and realize that ideas cannot be bought; inspiring in his visions yet cautious in what he does; a man of principle yet able to make a deal;

a man with broad perspective who will follow the details conscientiously; a good American but ready to criticize the status quo fearlessly; a seeker of truth where the truth may not hurt too much; a source of public pronouncements when they do not reflect on his own institution.

From Clark Kerr, *The Uses of the University*, Harvard University Press, 1963. Reprinted by permission of the publishers.

The various levels of parallelism and antithesis in this sentence look like this when laid out schematically:

```
He   should be   firm  /  yet gentle
                 sensitive      /        insensitive
                      to others              to himself
       look                         /  yet be firmly planted
          to the past and the future                      in the present
                  both visionary / and sound
                  affable / yet reflective
       know the value of a dollar / and realize the ideas cannot be bought
                  inspiring         /   yet cautious
                      in his visions        in what he does

              a man           /  yet able
                 of principle         to make a deal
```

(antithesis persists, but parallelism is violated: a noun, *man,* yoked with an adjective, *able; man* modified by prepositional phrase but *able* modified by infinitive phrase)

a man
   with broad perspective
   who will follow the details conscientiously

(again the antithesis is in the words—*broad perspective* / *details*—rather than in the structure)

a good American / but ready
                      to criticize the status quo fearlessly

(departure from parallelism again)

a seeker
   of truth
      where the truth may not hurt too much

a source
   of public pronouncements
      when they do not reflect on his own institution

As we shall make clear when we come to discuss the figures of speech, the rhetoricians commonly associated the various schemes and tropes with the topics of *logos, pathos,* and *ēthos.* Antithesis, for instance, was tied up with the topic of dissimilarity or with the topic of contraries. In the third book of his *Rhetoric,* Aristotle pointed out the value of antithesis in discourse: "Such a form of speech is satisfying, because of the significance of contrasted ideas is easily felt, especially when they are thus put side by side." Whether Dr. Kerr was aware of the theory of antithesis is immaterial. What is important is that by putting his "contrasted ideas" in juxtaposition, he has assisted the communication of his meaning.

Up to this point we have been concentrating on only a few stylistic features —word order, methods of expansion, parallelism, antithesis. It is time now to consider a broader range of stylistic features, not only so that we can get to know what these various features are and how they function but so that we can derive the maximum benefit from the exercises in imitation later on in the chapter and can incorporate some of these features into our own style.

Study of Style

Before the student can benefit from a close observation of stylistic features, he must have some technique for analyzing prose style. Because the modern student has spent so little time analyzing prose style, he may be ignorant of what to look for in sentences and paragraphs. He has undoubtedly been impressed by the style of certain prose writers, but he is almost tongue-tied when asked to point out what it is he particularly admires about their style. The best he can do is to characterize various styles with such general, subjective epithets as "clear," "crisp," "urbane," "orotund," "whimsical," "heavy," "flowing," "staccato." The New Criticism has given the student a technique and a terminology for analyzing poetry, but most students do not know where to begin if they are asked to analyze the style of a piece of prose.

First, let us set down, in outline form a list of features that one can look for when analyzing prose style.

A. Kind of diction
   1. general or specific
   2. abstract or concrete
   3. formal or informal
   4. Latinate (usually polysyllabic) or Anglo-Saxon (usually monosyllabic)
   5. common words or jargon
   6. referential (denotative) or emotive (connotative)

    B. Length of sentences (measured in number of words)
    C. Kinds of sentences
       1. grammatical: simple, compound, complex, compound-complex
       2. rhetorical: loose, periodic, balanced, antithetical
       3. functional: statement, question, command, exclamation
    D. Variety of sentence patterns
       1. inversions
       2. sentence openers
       3. method and location of expansion
    F. Means of articulating sentences (coherence devices)
    G. Use of figures of speech
    H. Paragraphing
       1. length (measured in number of words and number of sentences)
       2. kind of movement or development in paragraphs
       3. use of transitional devices

Most of the items in this outline represent features that lend themselves to objective study. Some of the either/or combinations under "Kind of diction" are relative, and opinions about them could vary. But most of the features lend themselves to objective study in the same way that grammatical features (word order, inflections, function words) do. There are a number of incalculable features of style about which we might never be able to secure general agreement, but if we are to develop any system for analyzing prose style we must start with those features that are objectively observable.

Kind of Diction

The kind of diction that a writer habitually uses can tell us a great deal about the quality of his mind and the quality of his style. We made the point earlier that a writer must be in command of several styles, so that he can accommodate his manner to various subject matters, occasions, purposes, and audiences. But even within this range of styles, there will be a certain persistent level of style associated with that author. Dr. Johnson and Oliver Goldsmith displayed their versatility by trying their hands at several literary genres, but whether they were writing poems or plays or novels or familiar essays or critical essays, they maintained a certain note that identified the style as their own and no one else's. That peculiar note was achieved partly by the kind of diction they used: Johnson's philosophical, polysyllabic, Latinate diction; Goldsmith's concrete, familiar, colloquial diction. The "weight" of a man's style can be measured partly by the syllabic composition of his words. The "tone" of his style can be measured partly by the texture of his words—their phonic values, their relative abstractness or concreteness, their level of usage. Judgments about the formality or informality of a man's style are made largely on the basis of the level of diction used.

Length of Sentences

The average length of sentences also can lead to some valid generalizations about a man's style. Modern prose style is characterized by sentences which are generally shorter than those of earlier centuries. (The narrow columns into which journalistic prose is fitted undoubtedly had some influence on the shortening of the sentence.) But we still discover remarkable variations in sentence-length in modern writers. We can arrive at a tenable generalization about a writer's characteristic sentence-length by counting the words in, say, five hundred consecutive sentences and then dividing the total number of words by the number of sentences. Having determined this average sentence-length, we would have to pursue the more important consideration: what relation does this characteristic sentence-length have to the rhetorical situation?

Kinds of Sentences

Some very interesting observations can be made about a man's style and his habits of thought by studying the kinds of sentences he used and the proportions in which he used the various kinds. W. K. Wimsatt, for instance, in his valuable study *The Prose Style of Samuel Johnson,* saw in Dr. Johnson's persistent use of parallel and antithetical clauses a reflection of the bent of his mind: "Johnson's prose style is a formal exaggeration—in places a caricature—of a certain pair of complementary drives, the drive to assimilate ideas, and the drive to distinguish them—to collect and to separate." And so Dr. Johnson disposed his collection of ideas in parallel structures; he reinforced the distinctions in ideas by juxtaposing them in antithetical structures.

The history of the prose style of most Western languages reveals a gradual evolution from a paratactic syntax—stringing together a series of co-ordinate structures without conjunctions—to the most sophisticated of sentence patterns, subordination. In Anglo-Saxon, for instance—the earliest extant record of the English language—we note the lack of the relative pronoun and the subordinating conjunction, two of the grammatical devices by which Modern English renders clauses dependent. When we catalogue the kinds of grammatical sentences found in modern professional prose, we find surprisingly few compound sentences. Modern writers expand their sentences more by subordination and apposition than by compounding. Observation of the grammatical kinds of sentences can tell us a great deal about someone's prose style and can point up significant deficiencies in our own prose style.

Variety of Sentence Patterns

A study of variety in sentence patterns also has some valuable lessons to teach us about style. For one thing, such a study can dispel many of the myths about prose style. It is true that professional writers command a greater variety of lexical and syntactical resources than unpracticed writers do, but they do not make a fetish of variety for its own sake. Professor Francis Christensen made a study, for instance, of sentence-openers in the first two hundred sentences of some narrative and expository works written by modern American writers. Here are the results of his findings in the expository pieces:

Expository	Sentence Openers	Adverbial	Verbal	Inverted	Co-ord. Conj.
Carson, *Sea Around Us*	79	74	4	1	29
M. Chute, *Shakespeare of London*	64	63	0	1	4
De Voto, *Easy Chair*	51	50	1	0	16
Edman, *Arts and the Man*	37	33	2	2	14
Highet, *Art of Teaching*	47	45	2	0	22
Mencken, *Vintage Mencken*	72	67	5	0	9
Lloyd & Warfel, *American English*	77	72	4	1	4
Trilling, *Liberal Imagination* (pp. 216-34)	60	57	3	0	34
Van Doren, *Shakespeare: Four Tragedies*	32	32	0	0	29
Wilson, *Literary Chronicle: 1920-1950* (pp. 9-29, 422-27)	56	51	3	2	14
TOTAL	575	544	24	7	175
PERCENTAGE	28.75	27.20	1.15	0.40	8.75

From Francis Christensen, "Notes Toward a New Rhetoric: I. Sentence Openers," *College English*, XXV (October, 1963), 9. Reprinted by permission of the National Council of Teachers of English and Francis Christensen. Cf. William K. Riley, "Sentence Openers in Freshman Writing," *College English*, XXVI (December, 1964), 228-30.

The numbers in the first column indicate the number of sentences, among the two hundred studied in each piece, that had sentence openers (words, phrases, or clauses which are not part of the subject cluster); the numbers under the next four columns mark the various kinds of sentence openers. Rachel Carson had the highest percentage of sentence openers (39.5 per cent); Mark Van Doren had the lowest percentage (16 per cent). But the combined percentages show that almost three-quarters of the sentences written by these authors started out with the subject cluster rather than the sentence openers and that almost 95 per cent of the 575 sentence openers were of the adverbial type.

These figures would seem to indicate that some of our esteemed modern writers do not, contrary to common opinion and to the advice given in some writing texts, strive for a notable variety in the ways they begin their sentences. And the figures also invalidate the prescription about not beginning a sentence with a co-ordinating conjunction. Descriptive studies of other aspects of prose as it is actually written would probably destroy some additional illusions about how professional writers create their effects.

Sentence Euphony

Prose rhythm is one of the most difficult aspects of style to analyze. Perhaps the closest thing we have to the elaborate prosody that the Greeks and Romans devised for their quantitative languages is the system for scanning the English sentence that George Saintsbury worked out in his *A History of English Prose Rhythm* (Edinburgh, 1912). The euphony and rhythm of sentences undoubtedly play a part in the communicative and persuasive process—especially in producing emotional effects—but students would be ill advised to spend a great deal of time learning a system for scanning prose sentences. Euphony and rhythm are largely a matter for the ear, and students would do just as well to read their prose aloud in order to catch awkward rhythms, clashing vowel and consonant combinations (as in this five-word phrase), and distracting jingles. If, for instance, the student who wrote the following sentence had read it aloud, he might have caught the distracting repetition of the *ect* sound: "I will show how the testimony affected some people indirectly connected with the selection of the jurors." It is probably more important to apply this test when one is preparing a discourse for oral delivery, but most good writers apply this test also to prose that they know will be read silently. The sentence which is difficult to enunciate is often a grammatically or rhetorically defective sentence.

But if the student is not content with relying on his ear for testing the rhythm of his sentences, he can resort to the fairly simple method of marking the stresses in series of words. With a little more ingenuity, he might be able to group the stressed and unstressed syllables into feet. In scanning poetry, we can get by with knowing the five most common feet in classical prosody: iambic ($\smile$ —), trochaic (— $\smile$), anapaestic ($\smile$ $\smile$ --), dactylic

($-\;\smile\;\smile$), and spondaic ($-\;-$). To scan prose, however, we need a great many more combinations. In her book, *The Anatomy of Prose,* Marjorie Boulton defines twenty-three different combinations, which constitute, she says, "all the possible feet used in English prose." (Students who want to pursue these technicalities can consult pp. 55-7 of her book.) To illustrate this system of scansion, here is the way that Miss Boulton scanned the first nine verses of Psalm 90 in the Authorized Version of the Bible:

Lord, thou/ has been/ our dwelling place/ in all generations./

Before/ the mountains/ were brought forth,/ or ever/ thou hadst formed/ the earth/ and the world,/ even/ from everlasting/ to everlasting,/ thou art God./

Thou turnest man/ to destruction;/ and sayest,/ Return,/ ye children/ of men./

For a thousand/ years in/ thy sight/ are but/ as yesterday/ when it is past,/ and as a watch/ in the night./

Thou carriest/ them away/ as with a flood;/ they are as a sleep:/ in the morning/ they are like grass/ which groweth up./

In the morning/ it flourisheth,/ and groweth up;/ in the evening/ it is cut down,/ and withereth./

For we are consumed/ by thine anger,/ and by thy wrath/ are we troubled./

Thou hast set/ our iniquities/ before thee,/ our secret sins/ in the light/ of thy countenance./

For all/ our days/ are passed/ away/ in thy wrath;/ we spend/ our years/ as a tale/ that is told./

From Marjorie Boulton, *The Anatomy of Prose,* London: Routledge and Kegan Paul, 1954, p. 58. Reprinted by permission of the publishers.

Miss Boulton goes on to say about this passage: "My stresses will not, I think, be disputed much, though even on this point some ears might object; many readers will probably disagree with the division into feet at some point. However, we can now see the contrast of stressed, monosyllabic endings and lighter endings, with the finality of the stress at the end on a heavy monosyllable. We see how the important words are also placed where, with their own strong stresses, they are surrounded by weak stresses to make them stronger by contrast. We may also notice, if we are beginners, that the four-syllable and five-syllable feet are needed to describe prose accurately."

Articulation of Sentences

An investigation of the ways in which a writer articulates his sentences can be one of the most fruitful exercises for the student who wants to improve the quality of his own prose. Coherence is a troublesome problem for most students. They usually develop a sense for unity and emphasis long before they master coherence. Cultivating the habit of thinking in an orderly, logical fashion is the best way to insure that one will express his thoughts coherently. But practiced writers use a number of linguistic devices to assist the coherent display of their thoughts. Let us see how an accomplished writer like Matthew Arnold makes his prose "hang together." Some of the verbal devices he uses to promote coherence are italicized; others will be pointed out in the commentary afterward.

> The critical power is of lower rank than the creative. *True;* but in assenting to *this proposition, one or two things* are to be kept in mind. It is undeniable that the exercise of a *creative* power, that a free *creative* activity, is the highest function of man; *it* is *so* by man's finding in it his true happiness. *But* it is undeniable, *also,* that men may have the sense of exercising *this free creative activity* in *other* ways than in producing great works of literature or art; if it were not *so,* all but a very few men would be shut out from the *true happiness* of all men. *They may have it* in well-doing, *they may have it* in learning, *they may have it* even in criticising. *This* is *one thing* to be kept in mind. *Another* is that the exercise of the *creative* power in the production of *great works of literature or art,* however high *this* exercise of *it* may rank, is not at all epochs and under all conditions possible; *and* that *therefore* labour may be vainly spent in attempting *it, which* might with more fruit be used in preparing for *it,* in rendering *it* possible. *This creative power* works with elements, with materials; what if *it* has not *those materials,* those *elements,* ready for *its* use? *In that case, it* must surely wait till *they* are ready.
>
> From Matthew Arnold, "The Function of Criticism at the Present Time," *Essays in Criticism,* First Series, 1865.

Most coherence devices (pronouns, demonstrative adjectives, repeated words and phrases, and some of the conjunctions) point backwards to what has just been said, thus connecting what has been said with what is about to be said. One of the commonest devices in Matthew Arnold's prose—so common, in fact, that it has become a distinctive mark of his style—is the frequent repetition of key words and phrases. Arnold was a great phrase-maker, and once he had coined a phrase that carried the theme of an essay, he repeated that phrase time and time again in the essay. So conspicuous was this mannerism in his prose that one is inclined to believe that the cardinal principle of his expository technique was the famous pedagogical maxim, "Repetition is the mother of studies." The most obtrusive repetition in this selection is the word *creative*—the key word of this paragraph and one of the two key words in the entire essay. The repetition then of substantive words is one of the linguistic means of stitching our sentences together.

Arnold also frequently uses demonstrative pronouns and demonstrative adjectives (*this, that; these, those*) and personal pronouns. The original meaning of the word *demonstrate* is "to show, to point." Demonstrative pronouns and adjectives usually point backwards, tying what follows to what has gone before. By their very nature, all pronouns (except indefinite pronouns, like *anyone* and *someone*) point to a referent. Because of the close relationship between the pronoun and its referent, it is extremely important to be sure the referent is clear. When it is vague or, worse yet, when the referent is not there at all, the coherence of our writing is bound to suffer.

Good writers also make liberal use of conjunctions and conjunctive adverbs for stitching sentences together. The chief grammatical function of co-ordinating conjunctions is to splice together words, phrases, and clauses. But when co-ordinating conjunctions are placed at the beginning of the sentence (and Professor Christensen's chart reveals how often modern writers do this), these conjunctions assume the rhetorical function of providing a logical bridge between sentences. Conjunctive adverbs—words like *however, nevertheless, moreover, also, indeed, therefore*—are even more common devices for aiding coherence. One can point up the logical relationship between sentences simply by inserting the appropriate conjunctive word.

We will note only two additional devices that Arnold uses to connect his sentences. Fragmentary sentences can sometimes strengthen coherence. We have an instance of this in the second sentence of Arnold's paragraph. The single word *True* constitutes an elliptical sentence. Filled out, the ellipsis would read something like this: "That proposition is true." The single word here conveys a meaning only because of its juxtaposition to the previous sentence; since it has to look backward to the previous sentence in order to become meaningful, it is "tied" to that sentence. This same principle of "dependent meaning" prevails in conversation, where we often talk in fragmentary sentences ("Where are you going tonight?" "The movies." "With whom?" "Charlotte.").

Another device that Arnold uses in this paragraph is parallelism, which is reinforced by the figure of anaphora (repetition of identical words at the beginning of successive phrases). Three independent clauses are set down, one after the other ("They may have it in well-doing, they may have it in learning, they may have it even in criticising"). Although there are no conjunctions (asyndeton) to tie the clauses together grammatically, the clauses are connected by parallel structure and identical words. In addition to the functions that we noted in the analysis of Clark Kerr's two sentences, parallelism can also be used for coherence.

The passage quoted from Matthew Arnold exemplifies most of the verbal devices that good writers use to articulate their sentences. Good writers use such devices so unobtrusively that the sutures hardly show. A study of how an author uses them will help to account for the clarity of one man's prose and the fuzziness of another's.

Figures of Speech

Since we are going to devote a long section of this chapter to a discussion of figures of speech, this is not the place to discuss them in detail. Suffice it to say here that they constitute one of the most revealing features of a man's prose style. If they are apt and fresh, they can contribute greatly to the clarity, liveliness, and interest of a man's style. But they must not be cultivated for their own sake. The excessive, strained use of figures proved to be detrimental to the "gracefulness" for which the Euphuistic writers of the sixteenth century were striving in their prose. On the other hand, the absence or scarcity of figurative language can have a deadening effect on style. Although it is not true that Jonathan Swift excluded all figurative language from his prose, it is true that he used figurative language sparingly. That rarity of metaphorical language may have been what Dr. Johnson had in mind when he made his famous comment on Swift's style: "For purposes merely didactic, when something is to be told that was not known before, [his style] is in the highest degree proper, but against that inattention by which known truths are suffered to lie neglected, it makes no provision; it instructs, but does not persuade."

Paragraphing

There is a style of paragraphing as well as a style of sentence structure. Paragraphing, like punctuation, is a feature only of the written language. As a matter of fact, we can regard paragraphing as a typographical device for punctuating units of thought larger than the thought conveyed by a single sentence. The student is so accustomed to seeing, in the print he reads, indentations of segments of thought that he comes to take paragraphing as much for granted as he does the left-to-right movement of printed words.

And because the indentations are always there on the printed page, the student does not realize how much the marking off of thought-units facilitates his reading. Perhaps the best way to show the student how typographical devices contribute to the readability of printed prose is to reproduce a passage of prose with no punctuation, capitalization, or paragraphing:

> it seems to me that it was far from right for the professor of english in yale the professor of english literature in columbia and wilkie collins to deliver opinions on cooper's literature without having read some of it it would have been much more decorous to keep silent and let persons talk who have read cooper cooper's art has some defects in one place in deerslayer and in the restricted space of two thirds of a page cooper has scored 114 offenses against literary art out of a possible 115 it breaks the record there are nineteen rules governing literary art in the domain of romantic fiction some say twenty two in deerslayer cooper violated eighteen of them these eighteen require that a tale shall accomplish something and arrive somewhere but the deerslayer tale accomplishes nothing and arrives in the air they require that the episodes of a tale shall be necessary parts of the tale and shall help to develop it but as the deerslayer tale is not a tale and accomplishes nothing and arrives nowhere the episodes have no rightful place in the work since there was nothing for them to develop they require that the personages in a tale shall be alive except in the case of corpses and that always the reader shall be able to tell the corpses from the others but this detail has often been overlooked in the deerslayer tale

If the student has difficulty making sense out of this river of words, he should be grateful to those printers and grammarians who invented typographical devices to mark off meaningful segments of thought. After trying out various combinations, the student might eventually be able to make sense of this passage, especially in those sections where there are enough grammatical signals to tell him what words are related. He will probably make faster progress in deciphering the passage if he reads it aloud, because the voice will add another grammatical element, intonation, which is the vocal equivalent of the graphic marks of punctuation. But there will be spots in this passage which will remain ambiguous, because grammar will allow in those places two or more combinations of words, each of which would make sense.

Now let us reproduce the passage as Mark Twain wrote it, restoring his punctuation, capitalization, and paragraphing:

> It seems to me that it was far from right for the Professor of English in Yale, the Professor of English Literature in Columbia, and Wilkie Collins to deliver opinions on Cooper's literature without having read

some of it. It would have been much more decorous to keep silent and let persons talk who have read Cooper.

Cooper's art has some defects. In one place in *Deerslayer,* and in the restricted space of two-thirds of a page, Cooper has scored 114 offenses against literary art out of a possible 115. It breaks the record.

There are nineteen rules governing literary art in the domain of romantic fiction—some say twenty-two. In *Deerslayer* Cooper violated eighteen of them. These eighteen require:

1. That a tale shall accomplish something and arrive somewhere. But the *Deerslayer* tale accomplishes nothing and arrives in the air.

2. They require that the episodes of a tale shall be necessary parts of the tale and shall help to develop it. But as the *Deerslayer* tale is not a tale, and accomplishes nothing and arrives nowhere, the episodes have no rightful place in the work, since there was nothing for them to develop.

3. They require that the personages in a tale shall be alive, except in the case of corpses, and that always the reader shall be able to tell the corpses from the others. But this detail has often been overlooked in the *Deerslayer* tale.... [Twain goes on to designate, in a series of short, numbered paragraphs, the remaining fifteen "rules."]

From Mark Twain, "Fenimore Cooper's Literary Offenses," 1895.

The typographical device which contributes most, of course, to clarifying the syntax of a succession of words is the device for marking off sentences—an initial capital letter and end-punctuation (period, question mark, exclamation point). We underestimate, perhaps, how much of a contribution to clarity is made by other typographical devices—such simple things as commas, capital letters, italics, hyphens, quotation marks. Nor should we overlook the contribution that indentation of paragraphs makes to ease of reading. The value of paragraphing is evident in the Mark Twain passage. Indentation marks the shifts in the development of thought and indicates the relationship of the parts. Simply by setting off the violated rules in separate paragraphs and further marking them with numbers, Mark Twain makes it clear that he is specifying a series of parts.

A study of the density of an author's paragraphs tells us a great deal about the "weight" of his style. Many considerations, of course, dictate whether paragraphs will be long or short—the subject matter, the occasion, the audience. Narrative, for instance, especially when it is dealing with rapid action, often moves along in a series of short paragraphs. In dialogue, too, each shift of speaker is indicated by a new paragraph. For purposes of transition or emphasis, an author will insert a one- or two-sentence paragraph. And when one is writing copy for the narrow columns of a newspaper, he will rather arbitrarily chop up his prose into very short paragraphs.

But when all allowances have been made for such conventions and for various rhetorical situations, it remains true that professional writers generally write longer paragraphs than unpracticed writers do. Many of the one- and two-sentence paragraphs that students write have no rhetorical justification whatever. Such short paragraphs simply reveal that the students have not developed their thoughts adequately. They have nothing more to say, or think they have nothing more to say, on the idea presented in that paragraph. Perhaps by resorting to the topics to find something to say, the student will be able to put some meat on the bare bones of his paragraph.

A Student Report on a Study of Style

We have devoted several pages to a discussion of the objectively observable features of style because it is by this kind of close analysis that one learns why the style of an author produces its effects and learns also how to go about improving his own style. To illustrate the profit to be derived from such a close study, we will present the results of a student project.*

Two sections of an Honors Freshman class were set the task of making a comparative analysis of the length of sentences and paragraphs in a specified number of paragraphs in F. L. Lucas's essay "What Is Style?" and in all the paragraphs of one of their expository themes. For the purposes of this study, a sentence was defined as "a group of words beginning with a capital letter and ending with some mark of end-punctuation." The students were told that in choosing eight paragraphs from the Lucas essay they should avoid short transitional paragraphs and any paragraphs containing two or more sentences of quoted material. The students were presented with a mimeographed sheet containing the following items to be filled in:

EVALUATION	PROFESSIONAL	STUDENT
A. Total number of words in the piece studied	_____	_____
B. Total number of sentences in the piece studied	_____	_____
C. Longest sentence (in no. of words)	_____	_____
D. Shortest sentence (in no. of words)	_____	_____
E. Average sentence (in no. of words)	_____	_____
F. Number of sentences that contain more than 10 words *over* the average sentence	_____	_____
G. Percentage of sentences that contain more than 10 words over the average	_____	_____

* For an account of similar projects devised for an Advanced Composition course at the University of Nebraska, see Margaret E. Ashida and Leslie T. Whipp, "A Slide-Rule Composition Course," *College English*, XXV (October, 1963), 18-22.

EVALUATION	PROFESSIONAL	STUDENT
H. Number of sentences that contain 5 words or more *below* the average	————	————
I. Percentage of sentences that contain 5 words or more below the average	————	————
J. Paragraph length		
longest paragraph (in no. of sentences)	————	————
shortest paragraph (in no. of sentences)	————	————
average paragraph (in no. of sentences)	————	————

The numbers that the students entered in the first column differed according to the paragraphs they chose to study, but we can give some mean figures for four of the items in the list:

1. The average length of Lucas's sentences was 20.8 words.
2. About 17 per cent of Lucas's sentences were ten words or more over the average.
3. About 40 per cent of Lucas's sentences were five words or more below the average.
4. Lucas averaged 7.6 sentences per paragraph—a fairly well-developed paragraph.

Most of the students found that their average sentence matched the length of Lucas's average sentence. Many of the students were surprised to learn, however, that they had a higher percentage of above-average sentences and a strikingly lower percentage of below-average sentences. Perhaps the most dramatic difference that the students noted was in paragraph development. At least half of the students found that they were averaging between three and four sentences in their paragraphs.

In addition to filling out the mimeographed sheet, the students submitted an essay in which they commented on what they had learned about style from this exercise. Excerpts from their essays are reproduced below.

First of all, here are some of the students' comments about sentence length and sentence variety:

> I found that the percentage of sentences in Lucas's essay that contained more than ten words over the average sentence was 17%, while mine was a mere 3%. But the percentage of his sentences that contained five words or more below the average was 39% compared to my 16%. I see now that I must strive for greater variety of sentence structure and length in my themes in order for the pieces to be more effective.

· · · · ·

My average sentence length is very close to that of Mr. Lucas. I think this is misleading, however, since in my high school newspaper work I acquired the habit of gathering more than one thought in a single sentence. My sentence length is good, but my sentence content could be improved. Another factor that was evident is that I tend to use fewer short sentences than professional writers do. I think I can explain this lack of short sentences by considering the subject matter of the themes I write. I have noticed that in the past I would use longer, more involved (and less clear) sentences to write about things I didn't feel completely at ease in writing about. I use short sentences to present ideas that are very lucid to me.

· · · · ·

One thing I found is that good prose doesn't necessarily imply long verbose sentences and polysyllabic words.

· · · · ·

There is not quite enough variety in length or pattern in my sentences. Even my longer sentences tend to be of the compound variety rather than the complex or compound-complex type.

Now for some excerpts from students' comments on paragraphing:

This paragraph analysis revealed some drastic differences in style. My paragraphs, surprisingly, are considerably longer than Lucas's. The average number of sentences per paragraph in my work is twelve, whereas Mr. Lucas's average is about eight. My longest paragraph has sixteen sentences, twice the professional's average. This could indicate poor paragraph planning and division on my part. My extended paragraphs seem much like run-on sentences and probably have a tiring effect on my reader.

· · · · ·

My longest paragraph is 17 sentences, almost 10 sentences over my average paragraph length; Lucas's longest paragraph has 10 sentences, less than 3 sentences over his average paragraph length. Also, in this long paragraph the average length of sentences is 14 words, which is 7 words per sentence below the average for the whole theme. And in this same paragraph of mine there are 12 out of the total 17 sentences which contain 5 words or more below the average sentence. The reason for this paragraph being strikingly different from my average paragraph is that I used a different style of writing in this paragraph. I tried to make an emotional appeal to back up my arguments, using short questions and terse statements. In trying to give the effect of an impassioned speech, I departed from my usual prose style; thus this paragraph is not representative of my usual style of paragraphing.

· · · · ·

In Lucas's piece there is an average of 126 words per paragraph, while I have an average of only 70 words per paragraph. I probably should use more words to develop my ideas, not for the sake of wordiness but for the sake of being more fully understood. I leave out examples and explanations which may be vital to the clarity of the theme.

. . . . .

In the paragraphs I chose to study, Mr. Lucas used a total of fifty-six sentences. I used a total of fifty-four sentences in my theme. This averages to approximately seven sentences per paragraph in both essays. However, this similarity is slightly invalid. In choosing the Lucas paragraphs, I was careful to choose only those which were of an "average" length; I purposely skipped those paragraphs which seemed short. One of the paragraphs in my theme contained only three sentences, but I had to count it. This tended to lower my average number of sentences per paragraph, whereas Mr. Lucas's average was slightly inflated because only "average" paragraphs were studied.

. . . . .

Another thing that I realized when doing this stylistic study is that in the professional writers' work the paragraphs fit together like the pieces in a jigsaw puzzle. Each paragraph develops a separate thought but becomes an integral part of the whole. I have trouble tying my ideas together. Although all my ideas relate to the theme topic, often I find that they do not follow in a logical pattern.

In addition to commenting on sentences and paragraphs, several students commented on other features of style that they had noted in doing this study. Here are some excerpts from those comments:

I see now that enlarging my vocabulary is necessary to improve my style. I don't mean necessarily that I must start using bigger words; I mean rather that I must learn when certain words should be used. I must learn to use big words only when they fall naturally into place and when they can be fully understood by the intended audience. Professional writers do not always use big words, but their knowledge of words enables them to use the proper word at the proper time.

. . . . .

One characteristic of Lucas's style which I don't like and which I think I avoided in my writing is the excessive use of parentheses and dashes. I certainly feel that a parenthesis or a dash is appropriate at times, and, in fact, I used a dash four times in my writing. But I believe that Mr. Lucas overworked parentheses and dashes. I feel that the reader's train of thought is broken when the writing contains many dashes or parentheses.

. . . . .

Lucas brings his writing to life by the use of figures of speech. When he says, "Men are often taken, like rabbits, by the ears," his writing becomes vivid and distinctive. Another of Mr. Lucas's figures of speech, "There are blustering signatures that swish across the page like cornstalks bowed before a tempest," shows that he avoids the trite, overworked figures. He searches for new and fresh expressions. I noticed that in my piece of writing there wasn't a single simile, metaphor, or personification.

. . . . .

Although Lucas's longest sentence is twice as long as my longest sentence, my sentence is harder to follow. This difference in readability can be attributed partly to the number of syllables. Although syllable-count was not included on the study sheet, it has a great bearing on the clarity of one's prose. The majority of words in Lucas's sentences are monosyllabic. Because of the monosyllabic diction, the interest of the reader is not bogged down by heavy words.

. . . . .

This study also confirmed something I was already suspicious of—I don't write really long sentences. This, I believe, is due to the fact that I am afraid of the punctuation a long sentence may require. It is much simpler to write two short sentences correctly than to write one long sentence correctly. Since we were graded in high school more on correctness than on style, I formed the habit of writing two shorter sentences rather than one long one. I guess I'll have to start worrying about style as well as correctness if I want to become a good writer.

. . . . .

I noticed how well the parts of Mr. Lucas's essay were proportioned and how mine seemed rather top-heavy. A closer look showed me that I overdevelop the beginnings of my essays, often leaving the middle thinly developed.

. . . . .

I have noticed that sometimes my sentences sound artificial and stiff because I place adverb clauses and verbal phrases where they do not fit naturally. . . . Good professional writers have mastered the art of appropriateness. I have found that most professional writers' long sentences are surprisingly easy to follow, while my long sentences are frequently too involved to be understood.

. . . . .

Here are a few excerpts from the students' comments on the general value of a close study like this. What is particularly notable is that the students retained their sense of perspective. They saw no merit in cultivating any feature of style for its own sake; a stylistic device became a virtue only when it contributed to the effectiveness of the passage in which it occurred:

> I know that this study of sentence and paragraph length has been beneficial to me, but I would like to consider the choice and arrangement of words used by professional authors. I may be wrong, but to me an author's word choice and word arrangement is more important than the length of his sentences and paragraphs.

. . . . .

> I believe, however, that this comparison between my prose and Lucas's reveals simply a difference in style and that no definite decisions can be made about what I should do with my prose style. In order to make such a decision, I would have to compare my vocabulary and sentence structure with Mr. Lucas's when both of us were writing on the same subject-matter.

. . . . .

> In general, style depends on a person's individuality and his basic knowledge of English grammar. It doesn't depend on how long the sentences are or how short they are. Mr. Lucas has successfully combined English grammar with his own personal touch to produce a good piece of prose. My own style suffers from the fact that my knowledge of English grammar has not yet developed enough to aid my individuality of expression.

. . . . .

> Although this study cannot definitely determine whether my style is good or bad (since there is no entirely good or bad style), it can show the major similarities and differences between my style and a typical modern style.

. . . . .

> The style of a professional—in this case, F. L. Lucas—shouldn't be slavishly copied, for it is only by evolving his own style that a student gains enough command over the language to become an effective writer.

. . . . .

Here are three additional charts for the tabulation of other stylistic features. Students may devise their own charts for the quantitative study of objectively observable stylistic features not included here.

Stylistic Study—II
(Grammatical Types of Sentence)

A *simple* sentence is a sentence beginning with a capital letter, containing one independent clause, and ending with terminal punctuation.

A *compound* sentence is a sentence beginning with a capital letter, containing two or more independent clauses, and ending with terminal punctuation.

A *complex* sentence is a sentence beginning with a capital letter, containing one independent clause and one or more dependent clauses, and ending with terminal punctuation.

A *compound-complex* sentence is a sentence beginning with a capital letter, containing two or more independent clauses and one or more dependent clauses, and ending with terminal punctuation.

Title of professional essay_____
Author_____

	PROFESSIONAL	STUDENT
A. Total number of sentences in essay	———	———
B. Total number of simple sentences	———	———
C. Percentage of simple sentences	———	———
D. Total number of compound sentences	———	———
E. Percentage of compound sentences	———	———
F. Total number of complex sentences	———	———
G. Percentage of complex sentences	———	———
H. Total number of compound-complex sentences	———	———
I. Percentage of compound-complex sentences	———	———

Sequence of Grammatical Types

Set down the sequence of grammatical types in paragraphs ——— and ———, using these abbreviations: S, Cp, Cx, Cp-Cx.
In ——— paragraph:_____
In ——— paragraph:_____

Stylistic Study—III

(Sentence Openers)

Title of professional essay_____
Author_____

For this study, use only *declarative* sentences. No interrogative or imperative sentences.

Total number of declarative sentences: Professional——   Student——

SENTENCES BEGINNING WITH	PROFESSIONAL		STUDENT	
	No.	%	No.	%
A. Subject (e.g. *John* broke the window. *The high cost* of living will offset . . .)	——	——	——	——
B. Expletive (e.g. *It* is plain that . . . *There* are ten Indians. Exclamations: *Alas, Oh*)	——	——	——	——
C. Coordinating conjunction (e.g. *and, but, or, nor, for, yet, so*)	——	——	——	——
D. Adverb word (e.g. *first, thus, moreover, nevertheless, namely*)	——	——	——	——
E. Conjunctive phrase (e.g. *on the other hand, as a consequence*)	——	——	——	——
F. Prepositional phrase (e.g. *after the game, in the morning*)	——	——	——	——
G. Verbal phrase (e.g. participial, gerundive, or infinitive phrase)	——	——	——	——
H. Adjective phrase (e.g. *Tired but happy,* we —— . . .)	——	——	——	——
I. Absolute phrase (e.g. *The ship having arrived safely,* we . . .)	——	——	——	——
J. Adverb clause (e.g. *When the ship arrived safely,* we . . .)	——	——	——	——
K. Front-Shift (e.g. inverted word order: The expense we could not bear. Gone was the wind. Happy were they to be alive.)	——	——	——	——

Stylistic Study—IV

(Diction)

Title of professional essay———————————————————
Author———————————————————————————

For this investigation, confine yourself to this range of paragraphs: paragraph —— through ——. For the investigation of your own prose, confine yourself to a comparable number of paragraphs.

In A, B, and C, below, count only *substantive words*—nouns, pronouns, verbs, verbals, adjectives, and adverbs.

	PROFESSIONAL	STUDENT
A. Total number of substantive words in the passage	————	————
B. Total number of monosyllabic substantive words	————	————
C. Percentage of monosyllabic substantive words	————	————
D. Total number of nouns and pronouns in the passage	————	————
E. Total number of *concrete* nouns and pronouns	————	————
F. Percentage of concrete nouns and pronouns	————	————
G. Total number of *finite verbs* in all dependent and independent clauses in the passage	————	————
H. What percentage does G represent of A?	————	————
I. Total number of linking verbs	————	————
J. Percentage of linking verbs (using A)	————	————
K. Total number of active verbs (do not count linking verbs)	————	————
L. Percentage of active verbs (using A)	————	————
M. Total number of passive verbs (do not count linking verbs)	————	————
N. Percentage of passive verbs (using A)	————	————
O. Total number of adjectives in the passage (do not count participles or articles)	————	————
P. Average number of adjectives per sentence (divide by the total number of sentences in the passage)	————	————

So much for this discussion of what to look for when one analyzes prose style. The student will be further aided in developing his own style and in developing a technique for analyzing style by practicing some of the imitation exercises recommended in a later section of this chapter. The student is also urged to read the stylistic analyses of Addison's *Spectator* essay and of President Kennedy's Inaugural Address at the end of this chapter.

Figures of Speech

We come now to a consideration of figures of speech. It is fair enough to regard figures of speech as the "graces of language," as the "dressing of thought," as "embellishments," for indeed they do "decorate" our prose and give it "style," in the couturier's sense. But it would be a mistake to regard embellishment as the chief or sole function of figures. The classical rhetoricians certainly did not look upon them as decorative devices primarily. Metaphor, according to Aristotle, did give "charm and distinction" to our expression; but even more than that, metaphor was another way to *give* "clearness" and "liveliness" to the expression of our thoughts. Figures, in his view, provided one of the best ways to strike that happy balance between "the obvious and the obscure," so that our audience could grasp our ideas promptly and thereby be disposed to accept our arguments.

"What, then, can oratorical imagery effect?" Longinus asked. He was even more explicit than Aristotle in pointing out the rhetorical function of figures: "Well, it is able in many ways to infuse vehemence and passion into spoken words, while more particularly when it is combined with the argumentative passages it not only persuades the hearer but actually makes him its slave." —*On the Sublime,* XV, 9.

It was Quintilian who most explicitly related the figures to the *logos, pathos,* and *ēthos* of argument. Quintilian looked upon the figures as another means of lending "credibility to our arguments," of "exciting the emotions," and of winning "approval for our characters as pleaders" (*Instit. Orat.,* IX, i). This view of the function of figures of speech is perhaps the most reliable attitude to adopt toward these devices of style. Because figures can render our thoughts vividly concrete, they help us to communicate with our audience clearly and effectively; because they stir emotional responses, they can carry truth, in Wordsworth's phrase, "alive into the heart by passion"; and because they elicit admiration for the eloquence of the speaker or writer, they can exert a powerful ethical appeal.

Sister Miriam Joseph in her book *Shakespeare's Use of the Arts of Language* reclassified the more than two hundred figures distinguished by the Tudor rhetoricians according to the four categories: grammar, logos, pathos, and ethos. In doing this, she was able to demonstrate, quite convincingly, that the three "schools" of rhetoric during the Renaissance (the Ramists, the traditionalists, and the figurists) saw the figures as being intimately connected with the topics of invention. Metaphor, for instance, involving comparison of like things, is tied up with the topic of similarity; antithesis, involving the juxtaposition of opposites, is tied up with the topic of dissimilarity or of contraries. Then there were figures, like apostrophe, that were calculated to work directly on the emotions, and figures, like comprobatio, that were calculated to establish the ethical image of the speaker or writer. In our exposition we shall frequently point out the relationship of the figures either with grammar or with the three modes of persuasive appeal.

The mention of two hundred figures of speech in the previous paragraph may have appalled the student. If pressed, most students could name—even if they could not define or illustrate—a half dozen figures of speech. But where did those *other* figures come from? and what are they? In their passion for anatomizing and categorizing knowledge, the Humanists of the Renaissance delighted in classifying and sub-classifying the figures. Admittedly, they were being overly subtle in distinguishing such a multitude of figures. The most widely used classical handbook in the Renaissance schools, *Rhetorica ad Herennium,* required the students to learn only 65 figures. Susenbrotus, in his popular *Epitome troporum ac schematum* (1540), distinguished 132 figures. But Henry Peacham, in his 1577 edition of *The Garden of Eloquence,* pushed the number up to 184. Pity the poor Tudor schoolboy who was expected to define and illustrate and to use in his own compositions a goodly number of these figures.

We are not going to plague the student with a long catalogue of figures, but we are going to introduce more figures than he has met with in his previous study of style. If nothing else, the student should become aware, through this exposure, that his language has more figurative resources than he was conscious of. And he may discover that he has been using many of the figures of speech all his life. For men did not begin to use figures of speech only after academicians had classified and defined them; rather, the figures were classified and defined after men had been using them for centuries. Like the principles of grammar, poetics, and rhetoric, the doctrine of the figures was arrived at inductively. Rhetoricians merely gave "names" to the verbal practices of their fellow men.

What do we mean by the term "figures of speech"? We mean the same thing that Quintilian meant when he used the term *figura:* "any deviation, either in thought or expression, from the ordinary and simple method of speaking, a change analogous to the different positions our bodies assume when we sit down, lie down, or look back.... Let the definition of a figure, therefore, be *a form of speech artfully varied from common usage* (Ergo figura sit arte aliqua novata forma dicendi)"—*Instit. Orat.,* IX, i, 11.

We will use "figures of speech" as the generic term for any artful deviations from the ordinary mode of speaking or writing. But we will divide the figures of speech into two main groups—the *schemes* and the *tropes.* A scheme (Greek *schēma,* form, shape) involves a deviation from the ordinary pattern or arrangement of words. A trope (Greek *tropein,* to turn) involves a deviation from the ordinary and principal signification of a word.

Both types of figures involve a *transference* of some kind: a trope, a transference of meaning; a scheme, a transference of order. When Shakespeare's Mark Antony said, "Brutus is an honorable man," he was using the trope called irony, because he was "transferring" the ordinary meaning of the word *honorable* to convey a different meaning to his audience. If Mark Antony had said, "Honorable is the man who gives his life for his country," he would have been using a species of the scheme hyperbaton, because he would be "transferring" the usual order of words. In a sense, of course, both schemes and tropes involve a change of "meaning," since both result in effects that are different from the ordinary mode of expression. But for all practical purposes, our distinction is clear enough to enable the student to distinguish between a scheme and a trope.

The terms used to label the various figures appear formidable—strange, polysyllabic words, most of them merely transliterated from the Greek. But technical terms, in any discipline, are always difficult at first sight; they are difficult, however, mainly because they are unfamiliar. Whenever we study a new discipline we have to learn the "names" of things peculiar to that discipline. Inevitably these specialized terms will be puzzling, but they will remain puzzling only until we learn to connect the *sign* with the concept or thing for which it stands. The word *tree* is difficult for the child only until he learns to associate the sound or the graphic mark of this word with the thing that it designates. The term *prosopopeia* will frighten the student at first, but once he gets to the point where he can immediately associate the term with its significance, *prosopopeia* will be no more frightening to the student than the familiar terms *metaphor* and *simile*. We could, as the Renaissance rhetorician George Puttenham tried to do, invent English terms for the various figures, but since they would have to be coined terms, they would not necessarily be any easier to learn than the classical terms. However, wherever a familiar Anglicized term exists for a figure, we will use that term instead of the classical one.

In any case, we must not look upon terminology as an end in itself. Just as we can speak and write our native language without knowing the names of the parts of speech, so we can use and respond to figurative language without knowing the names of the figures. Nomenclature, in any study, is a convenience for purposes of classification and discussion. But an awareness of the various figures of speech can increase our verbal resources, and if we make a conscious effort to learn the figures of speech, it is likely that we will resort to them more often.

The Schemes

Schemes of Words

We shall not dwell very long on schemes of words because while they occur frequently in poetry—especially in the poetry of earlier centuries—they rarely occur in prose. The schemes of words (sometimes called *orthographical schemes,* because they involve changes in the spelling or sound of words) are formed (1) by adding or subtracting a letter or a syllable at the beginning, middle, or end of a word, or (2) by exchanging sounds. Terms like the following are of more concern to the grammarian and the prosodist than to the rhetorician:

> *prosthesis*—adding a syllable in front of word—e.g. *beloved* for *loved*
>
> *epenthesis*—adding a syllable in the middle of word—e.g. *visitating* for *visiting*
>
> *proparalepsis*—adding a syllable at the end of word—e.g. *climature* for *climate*
>
> *aphaeresis*—subtracting a syllable from the beginning of word—e.g. *'neath* for *beneath*
>
> *syncope*—subtracting a syllable from the middle of word—e.g. *prosprous* for *prosperous*
>
> *apocope*—subtracting a syllable from the end of word—e.g. *even* for *evening*
>
> *metathesis*—transposition of letters in a word—e.g. *clapse* for *clasp*
>
> *antisthecon*—change of sound—e.g. *wrang* for *wrong*

One can easily see that all of these involve a change in the shape or configuration of words. Poets used to employ such schemes to accommodate the rhyme or the rhythm of a line of verse. And because such changes are associated primarily with poetry, it is customary to regard such altered words as "poetic diction." Perhaps the situation in modern prose where we are most likely to use schemes of words would be the dialogue in a story. If a character in a story habitually clipped syllables from his words or mispronounced certain words, we might try to indicate those speech habits with spelling changes. Readers of *Finnegan's Wake* could supply numerous examples of other uses that James Joyce made of orthographical schemes in his remarkably ingenious prose.

Schemes of Construction

1. *Schemes of Balance*
Parallelism—similarity of structure in a pair or series of related words, phrases, or clauses.

Examples: He tried to make the law clear, precise, and equitable.

> . . . for the support of this declaration, with a firm reliance on the protection of Divine Protection, we mutually pledge to each other our Lives, our Fortunes, and our sacred Honor.—The Declaration of Independence

> We must now hope that Mr. Moynahan will devote his next decade to those four or five more novels which will banish his vacillations and uncertainties, purge his unneeded influences, and perfect his native gifts for language, landscape, and portraiture.—L. E. Sissman, *The New Yorker,* September 20, 1969

> It is certain that if you were to behold the whole woman, there is that dignity in her aspect, that composure in her motion, that complacency in her manner, that if her form makes you hope, her merit makes you fear.—Richard Steele, *Spectator,* No. 113

> I am a simple citizen who wants to live in peace and not be taxed out of existence or poisoned out of oxygen or sonically boomed out of my sanity and my home by all the things you do to help me, to defend me, to better provide me speed, electricity, national prestige, and freedom from bugs.—Talk of the Town, *The New Yorker,* November 26, 1966

> It is rather for us to be here dedicated to the great task remaining before us—that from those honored dead we take increased devotion to that cause for which they gave the last full measure of devotion; that we here highly resolve that these dead shall not have died in vain; that this nation, under God, shall have a new birth of freedom; and that government of the people, by the people, for the people, shall not perish from the earth.—Abraham Lincoln

Parallelism is one of the basic principles of grammar and rhetoric. The principle demands that equivalent things be set forth in co-ordinate grammatical structures. So nouns must be yoked with nouns, prepositional phrases with prepositional phrases, adverb clauses with adverb clauses. When this principle is ignored, not only is the grammar of co-ordination violated, but the rhetoric of coherence is wrenched. Students must be made to realize that violations of parallelism are serious, not only because they impair communication but because they reflect disorderly thinking. Whenever the student sees a co-ordinating conjunction in one of his sentences, he should check to make sure that the elements joined by the conjunction are of the same grammatical kind. Such a check would prevent him from writing sentences like these, all taken from student papers:

> Teenagers who dance the frug or the jerk are either wild or juvenile delinquents or both.

> Other common complaints are the failure of *Webster's Third* to include encyclopedic matter and for its technique of definition.

> Was this act rational and premeditated, or was it irrational and a spur-of-the-moment?

> He sounds like a nobleman threatened with revolution and who fears liberation of the masses.

> This situation not only is a problem for the fan, but it also affects the athletes. (A common violation of parallelism when correlative conjunctions are used.)

When the parallel elements are similar not only in structure but in length (that is, the same number of words, even the same number of syllables), the scheme is called *isocolon*. For example: His purpose was *to impress the ignorant, to perplex the dubious,* and *to confound the scrupulous.* The addition of symmetry of length to similarity of structure contributes greatly to the rhythm of sentences. Obviously, the student should not strive for isocolon every time he produces parallel structure. Such regularity of rhythm would approach the recurrent beat of verse.

Since parallelism is a device that we resort to when we are specifying or enumerating pairs or series of like things, it is easy to see the intimate relationship between this device of form and the topic of similarity. See the analysis of the rhetorical effect of parallelism in Clark Kerr's sentence in the previous section.

Antithesis—the juxtaposition of contrasting ideas, often in parallel structure.

Examples: Though studious, he was popular; though argumentative, he was modest; though inflexible, he was candid; and though metaphysical, yet orthodox.—Dr. Samuel Johnson on the character of the Reverend Zacariah Mudge, in the *London Chronicle,* May 2, 1769

Essex thought him wanting in zeal as a friend; Elizabeth thought him wanting in duty as a subject.—Thomas Babington Macaulay, "Francis Bacon" (1837)

Our knowledge separates as well as it unites; our orders disintegrate as well as bind; our art brings us together and sets us apart.—J. Robert Oppenheimer, *The Open Mind* (1955)

Those who have been left out, we will try to bring in. Those left behind, we will help to catch up.—Richard M. Nixon, Inaugural Address, January 20, 1969

That's one small step for a man, one giant leap for mankind.—Neil Armstrong, as he stepped on the moon, Sunday, July 20, 1969

It is the best of times, yet the worst of times: we live in unparalleled prosperity, yet have starvation; modern science can perform miracles to save lives, yet we have war; we balance ourselves delicately on the moon, yet destroy the delicate balance of the earth. Young people search for meaning in life, yet are confused, demoralized, frustrated.—Jesse E. Hobson and Martin E. Robbins, from an article in *America,* December 27, 1969

By the time it's empty, life will be full.—Caption for a magazine ad picturing a bottle of Canoe, a men's cologne by Dana, May 31, 1969

It was the unknown author of *Rhetorica ad Alexandrum* who most clearly pointed up the fact that the opposition in an *antithesis* can reside either in the words or in the ideas or in both:

> An antithesis occurs when both the wording and the sense, or one or other of them, are opposed in a contrast. The following would be an antithesis both of wording and sense: "It is not fair that my opponent should become rich by possessing what belongs to me, while I sacrifice my property and become a mere beggar." In the following sentence we have a merely verbal antithesis: "Let the rich and prosperous give to the poor and needy"; and an antithesis of sense only in the following: "I tended him when he was sick, but he has been the cause of very great misfortune to me." Here there is no verbal antithesis, but the two actions are contrasted. The double antithesis (that is, both of sense and of wording) would be the best to use; but the other two kinds are also true antitheses. (From *Rhetorica ad Alexandrum,* Ch. 26, trans. E. S. Forster.)

Nicely managed, antithesis can produce the effect of aphoristic neatness and can win for the author a reputation for wit. Antithesis is obviously related to the topic of dissimilarity and the topic of contraries. (See the analysis of antithesis in Clark Kerr's sentence.)

2. *Schemes of unusual or inverted word order* (hyperbaton)

Anastrophe—inversion of the natural or usual word order.

Examples: Backward run the sentences, till reels the mind. (From a parody of the style of *Time* Magazine.)

> The question between preaching extempore and from a written discourse, it does not properly fall within the province of this treatise to discuss on any but what may be called rhetorical principles.—Richard Whately, *Elements of Rhetoric* (1828)

> The emotional isolation, the preoccupation with God and themselves, the struggles for freedom, which seem to have possessed many of my friends at the same age, I knew almost nothing of.—C. P. Snow, *The Search*

> Puffed-up asses Arcangeli and Bottini unquestionably are.—Richard D. Altick and James F. Loucks, *Browning's Roman Murder Story* (1968)

> I got, so far as the immediate moment was concerned, away.—Henry James, *The Turn of the Screw*

> Rich, famous, proud, a ruling despot Pope might be—but he *was* middle class!—V. S. Pritchett, from a review in the *New York Review of Books,* February 27, 1969

> Good musicians of their type they are. Clean and neat in appearance they are. Needed, we might say, they are.—Student paper

> People that he had known all his life he didn't really know.—Student paper

> One ad does not a survey make.—Caption from an ad for Peugeot automobiles

Perfectly does *anastrophe* conform to our definition of a scheme as "an artful deviation from the ordinary pattern or arrangement of words." Because such deviation surprises expectation, anastrophe can be an effective device for gaining attention. But its chief function is to secure emphasis. It is a commonplace that the beginning and end of a clause are the positions of greatest emphasis. Words placed in those positions draw special attention, and when those initial or terminal words are not normally found in those positions, they receive extraordinary emphasis.

Parenthesis—insertion of some verbal unit in a position that interrupts the normal syntactical flow of the sentence.

Examples: But wherein any man is bold—I am speaking foolishly—I also am bold. . . . Are they ministers of Christ? I—to speak as a fool —am more.—St. Paul, 2 Cor. 11, 21 and 23

But when Savage was provoked, and very small offences were sufficient to provoke him, he would prosecute his revenge with the utmost acrimony till his passion had subsided.—Samuel Johnson, *Life of Richard Savage*

All that remained for the moment was to decide where I would go to graduate school, and that question was settled—the "snobs" had been right—by a Kellett Fellowship and then a Fulbright Scholarship to boot.—Norman Podhoretz, *Making It* (1967)

Any theory of post-historical society—our sense of being "in history" is largely determined by the pressure of political and social conflicts —will have to consider the dilemma of human motivations in the just city.—George Steiner, *Language and Silence* (1967)

However far the interpreters alter the text (another notorious example is the Rabbinic and Christian "spiritual" interpretations of the clearly erotic Song of Songs), they must claim to be reading off a sense that is already there.—Susan Sontag, *Against Interpretation* (1966)

He said he supervised ten editors—another euphemism—in his department, which clears 90% of NBC's entertainment programming, including movies.—Joan Barthel, from an article in *Life,* August 1, 1969

There is even, and it is the achievement of this book, a curious sense of happiness running through its paragraphs.—Norman Mailer, from a book review in *Cannibals and Christians* (1966)

The distinguishing mark of *parenthesis* is that the interpolated member is "cut off" from the syntax of the rest of the sentence. A parenthesis abruptly —and usually briefly—sends the thought off on a tangent. Although the parenthetical matter is not necessary for the grammatical completeness of the sentence, it does have a pronounced rhetorical effect. For a brief moment, we hear the author's voice, commenting, editorializing, and, for that reason, the sentence gets an emotional charge that it would otherwise not have. Note, for instance, the difference in effect if the parenthetical element in St. Paul's first sentence is synactically integrated with the rest of the sentence: "But I am speaking foolishly if I claim that wherein any man is bold, I also am bold."

Apposition—placing side by side two co-ordinate elements, the second of which serves as an explanation or modification of the first.

Examples: John Morgan, the president of the Sons of the Republic, could not be reached by phone.

Men of this kind—soldiers of fortune, pool-hall habitués, gigolos, beachcombers—expend their talents on trivialities.—Student paper

Apart from the association of Latin with rhetoric as an art, this last mentioned fact, that Latin was totally controlled by writing no matter how much it was used for speech, produced other special kinds of drives toward the oral within the academic world.—Walter J. Ong, from an article in *PMLA,* June 1965

So we would have gone together, the Orthodox and I.—George Steiner, from an article in *Commentary,* February, 1965

A miscellaneous list, this, but all of the items on it are characterized by the same misunderstandings and misconceptions of the nature of American power; and all have this in common, that they defy solution so long as the energies and resources of the nation are monopolized by the war in Vietnam.—Henry Steele Commager, from a book review in the *New York Review of Books,* December 5, 1968

Apposition is such a common method of expansion in modern prose that it hardly seems to conform to our definition of a scheme as "an artful deviation from the ordinary patterns of speech." But if one reflects upon his own experience, he will have to acknowledge that appositional structures seldom occur in impromptu speech. Apposition may not be the exclusive property of written prose, but it certainly occurs most frequently in written prose—in a situation, in other words, where we have time to make a conscious choice of our arrangement of words. So there is something *artful* about the use of the appositive. And there is something out-of-the-ordinary about the appositive, too. Although the appositive does not disturb the natural flow of the sentence as violently as parenthetical expressions do (mainly because the appositive is grammatically co-ordinate with the unit that it follows), it does interrupt the flow of the sentence, interrupts the flow to supply some gratuitous information or explanation.

3. *Schemes of Omission*

Ellipsis—deliberate omission of a word or of words which are readily implied by the context.

Examples: And he to England shall along with you.—*Hamlet,* III, iii, 4

> Kant, we may suppose, was more startled by Hume's apparent de-
> struction of all basis for philosophical certainty; Reid, by the remoter
> consequences to morality and theology.—Sir Leslie Stephen, *History
> of English Thought in the Eighteenth Century* (1876)

> So singularly clear was the water that when it was only twenty or
> thirty feet deep the bottom seemed floating in the air! Yes, where it
> was even *eighty* feet deep. Every little pebble was distinct, every
> speckled trout, every hand's-breadth of sand.—Mark Twain, *Rough-
> ing It*

> As with religion, so with education. In colonial New England,
> education was broad-based, but nevertheless elitist; and in its basic
> assumptions, intellectualist.—David Marquand, from an article in
> *Encounter,* March 1964

> Rape is the sexual sin of the mob, adultery of the bourgeoisie, and
> incest of the aristocracy.—John Updike, from a book review in the
> *New Yorker,* August 2, 1969

> So let the class invent its own assignments. If it wants more sophis-
> tication, fine.—Peter Elbow, from an article in *College English,*
> November 1968

> The Master's degree is awarded by seventy-four departments, and
> the Ph.D. by sixty.—Student paper

Ellipsis can be an artful and arresting means of securing economy of expression. We must see to it, however, that the understood words are grammatically compatible. If we wrote, "The ringleader was hanged, and his
accomplices imprisoned," we would be guilty of a solecism, because the
understood *was* is not grammatically compatible with the plural subject
(*accomplices*) of the second clause. And we produce a "howler" if we say,
"While in the fourth grade, my father took me to the zoo."

Asyndeton—deliberate omission of conjunctions between a series of related
clauses.

Examples: I came, I saw, I conquered.

> They may have it in well-doing, they may have it in learning, they
> may have it even in criticism.—Matthew Arnold

> The infantry plodded forward, the tanks rattled into position, the big guns swung their snouts toward the rim of the hills, the planes raked the underbrush with gunfire.

The Tudor rhetoricians had a special name for the omission of conjunctions between single words or phrases. They would have labelled the following as instances of *brachylogia*:

> . . . and that government of the people, by the people, for the people, shall not perish from the earth.—Abraham Lincoln

> . . . that we shall pay any price, bear any burden, meet any hardship, support any friend, oppose any foe to assure the survival and the success of liberty.—John F. Kennedy

But there seems to be no good reason why we cannot use the single term *asyndeton* for all these instances of omission of conjunctions. The principal effect of asyndeton is to produce a hurried rhythm in the sentence. Aristotle observed that asyndeton was especially appropriate for the conclusion of a discourse, because there, perhaps more than in other places in the discourse, we may want to produce the emotional reaction that can be stirred by, among other means, rhythm. And Aristotle concluded his *Rhetoric* with an instance of asyndeton that is noticeable even in translation: "I have done. You have heard me. The facts are before you. I ask for your judgment."

The opposite scheme is *polysyndeton* (deliberate use of many conjunctions). Note how the proliferation of conjunctions in the following quotation slows up the rhythm of the prose and produces an impressively solemn note:

> And God said, "Let the earth bring forth living creatures according to their kinds: cattle and creeping things and beasts of the earth according to their kinds." And it was so. And God made the beasts of the earth according to their kinds and the cattle according to their kinds and everything that creeps upon the ground according to its kind. And God saw that it was good.—Genesis, 1:24-25

Ernest Hemingway uses polysyndeton to create another effect. Note how the repeated *and*'s in the following passage suggest the flow and continuity of experience:

> I said, "Who killed him?" and he said, "I don't know who killed him but he's dead all right," and it was dark and there was water standing in the street and no lights and windows broke and boats all up in the town and trees blown down and everything all blown and I got a skiff and went out and found my boat where I had her inside Mango Key and she was all right only she was full of water.—Hemingway, "After the Storm"

Polysyndeton can also be used to produce special emphasis. Note the difference in effect of these two sentences:

> This semester I am taking English, history, biology, mathematics, sociology, and physical education.

> This semester I am taking English and history and biology and mathematics and sociology and physical education.

4. Schemes of Repetition

Alliteration—repetition of initial or medial consonants in two or more adjacent words.

Examples: A sable, silent, solemn forest stood.
>   —James Thomson, "The Castle of Indolence," l. 38

> Progress is not proclamation nor palaver. It is not pretense nor play on prejudice. It is not the perturbation of a people passion-wrought nor a promise proposed.—Warren G. Harding nominating William Howard Taft in 1912

> Already American vessels had been searched, seized, and sunk.—John F. Kennedy, *Profiles in Courage*

> A moist young moon hung above the mist of a neighboring meadow.—Vladimir Nabokov, *Conclusive Evidence*

> I should hear him fly with the high fields
> And wake to the farm forever fled from the childless land.
>   —Dylan Thomas, "Fern Hill," ll. 50–51

> Tart, tingling, and even ticklish.—Caption from an ad for Sprite

> We double-distill a dram at a time, instead of taking the faster big batch away.—Caption from an ad for Old Grand-Dad bourbon

In Anglo-Saxon poetry, *alliteration* rather than rhyme was the device to bind verses together. Because it contributes to the euphony of verse or prose, alliteration became a conspicuous feature of Euphuistic prose and Romantic poetry. Because it is such an obvious mannerism, alliteration is rarely used in modern prose. It is sometimes used today, however, for special effects—as a mnemonic device for slogans (Better Business Builds Bigger Bankrolls) and advertising catch-lines (Sparkling . . . Flavorful . . . Miller High Life . . . The Champagne of Bottle Beer . . . Brewed only in Milwaukee. Sometimes alliteration is deliberately used for humorous effect: He was a preposterously pompous proponent of precious pedantry.

Assonance—the repetition of similar vowel sounds, preceded and followed by different consonants, in the stressed syllables of adjacent words.

Example: An old, mad, blind, despised, and dying king—
>   Princes, the dregs of their dull race, who flow
>   Through public scorn—mud from a muddy spring—
>   —Shelley, "Sonnet: England in 1819"

> Had Gray written often thus, it had been vain to blame and useless to praise him.—Samuel Johnson, *Life of Thomas Gray*

> Under a juniper-tree the bones sang, scattered and shining
> We were glad to be scattered, we did little good to each other
> Under a tree in the cool of the day, with the shining sand
>   —T. S. Eliot, "Ash Wednesday"

> Whales in the wake like capes and Alps
> Quaked the sick sea and snouted deep
>   —Dylan Thomas, "Ballad of the Long-Legged Bait"

> Refresh your zest for living
>   —Caption from an ad for French Line Ships

Assonance, a device of sound, like alliteration, is used mainly in poetry. A prose writer might deliberately use assonance to produce certain onomatopoetic or humorous effects. The danger for the prose writer, however, lies in the careless repetition of similar vowel-sounds, producing awkward jingles like this: "He tries to revise the evidence supplied by his eyes."

Anaphora—repetition of the same word or group of words at the beginnings of successive clauses.

Examples: The Lord sitteth above the water floods. The Lord remaineth a
>   King forever. The Lord shall give strength unto his people. The
>   Lord shall give his people the blessing of peace.—Psalm 29

> We shall fight on the beaches, we shall fight on the landing-grounds, we shall fight in the fields and in the streets, we shall fight in the hills.—Winston Churchill, speech in the House of Commons, June 4, 1940

> We are moving to the land of freedom. Let us march to the realization of the American dream. Let us march on segregated housing. Let us march on segregated schools. Let us march on poverty. Let us march on ballot boxes, march on ballot boxes until race baiters disappear from the political arena, until the Wallaces of our nation

tremble away in silence.—Martin Luther King, Jr., on a civil-rights march from Selma to Montgomery, Alabama, 1965

They are common just as theft, cheating, perjury, adultery have always been common. They were common, not because people did not know what was right, but because people liked to do what was wrong. They were common, though prohibited by law. They were common, though condemned by public opinion. They were common, because in that age law and public opinion united had not sufficient force to restrain the greediness of powerful and unprincipled magistrates.—Thomas Babington Macaulay, "Francis Bacon," 1837

Why should white people be running all the stores in our community? Why should white people be running the banks of our community? Why should the economy of our community be in the hands of the white man? Why?—Speech by Malcolm X

It is a luxury, it is a privilege, it is an indulgence for those who are at their ease.—Edmund Burke, "Letter to a Noble Lord," 1796

It is 1969 already, and 1965 seems almost like a childhood memory. Then we were the conquerors of the world. No one could stop us. We were going to end the war. We were going to wipe out racism. We were going to mobilize the poor. We were going to take over the universities.—Jerry Rubin, from an article in the *New York Review of Books*, February 13, 1969

Whenever anaphora occurs, we can be sure that the author has used it deliberately. Since the repetition of the words helps to establish a marked rhythm in the sequence of clauses, this scheme is usually reserved for those passages where the author wants to produce a strong emotional effect. Note how Reinhold Niebuhr combines anaphora with plays on words to produce this neat aphorism: "Man's capacity for justice makes democracy possible; but man's inclination to injustice makes democracy necessary."

Epistrophe—repetition of the same word or group of words at the ends of successive clauses.

Examples: Shylock: I'll have my bond! Speak not against my bond!
                 I have sworn an oath that I will have my bond!
                     —*The Merchant of Venice*, III, iii, 3-4

To the good American many subjects are sacred: sex is sacred, women are sacred, children are sacred, business is sacred, America is sacred, Mason lodges and college clubs are sacred.—George Santayana, *Character and Opinion in the United States*

But to all those who would be tempted by weakness, let us leave no doubt that we will be as strong as we need to be for as long as we need to be. . . . We cannot learn from one another until we stop shouting at one another.—Richard M. Nixon, Inaugural Address, January 20, 1969

Perhaps this is the most important thing for me to take back from beach-living: simply the memory that each cycle of the tide is valid, each cycle of the wave is valid, each cycle of a relationship is valid.
—Anne Lindbergh, *Gift from the Sea*

As long as the white man sent you to Korea, you bled. He sent you to Germany, you bled. He sent you to the South Pacific to fight the Japanese, you bled.—Speech by Malcolm X

In a cake, nothing tastes like real butter, nothing moistens like real butter, nothing enriches like real butter, nothing satisfies like real butter.—Caption from a Pillsbury ad

He's learning fast. Are you earning fast?—Caption from an ad for Aetna Life Insurance

Epistrophe not only sets up a pronounced rhythm but secures a special emphasis, both by repeating the word and by putting the word in the final position in the sentence.

Epanalepsis—repetition at the end of a clause of the word that occurred at the beginning of the clause.

Examples: Blood hath bought blood, and blows have answer'd blows:
          Strength match'd with strength, and power confronted power.
                              —Shakespeare, *King John,* II, i, 329-30

Year chases year, decay pursues decay.—Samuel Johnson, "The Vanity of Human Wishes"

Possessing what we still were unpossessed by,
Possessed by what we now no more possessed.
                              —Robert Frost, "The Gift Outright"

And when the shadow fades and is no more, the light that lingers becomes a shadow to another light.—Kahlil Gibran, *The Prophet*

A nut nut is a person who is nuts about the fun of eating nuts.
—Caption from an ad for Skippy Peanut Butter

Business forms are as various as people forms.—Caption from an ad for Nekoosa Paper Company

Epanalepsis is rare in prose, probably because when the emotional situation arises that can make such a scheme appropriate, poetry seems to be the only form that can adequately express the emotion. It would seem perfectly natural for a father to express his grief over the death of a beloved son in this fashion: "He was flesh of my flesh, bone of my bone, blood of my blood." But would the father be speaking prose or poetry? Perhaps the only answer we could give is that it is heightened language of some sort, the kind of language which, despite its appearance of contrivance, springs spontaneously from intense emotion. Repetition, we know, is one of the characteristics of highly emotional language. And in this instance what better way for the father to express the intimacy of the relationship with his son than by the repetition of words at the beginning and end of successive groups of words?

Perhaps the best general advice about the use of epanalepsis—in fact of all those schemes that are appropriate only to extraordinary circumstances—would be, If you find yourself consciously deciding to use epanalepsis, don't use it." When the time is appropriate, the scheme will present itself unbidden.

Anadiplosis—repetition of the last word of one clause at the beginning of the following clause.

Examples: Labor and care are rewarded with success, success produces confidence, confidence relaxes industry, and negligence ruins the reputation which diligence had raised.—Dr. Johnson, *Rambler* No. 21

They point out what is perfectly obvious, yet seldom realized: That if you have a lot of things you cannot move about a lot, that furniture requires dusting, dusters require servants, servants require insurance stamps. . . . It [property] produces men of weight. Men of weight cannot, by definition, move like the lightning from the East unto the West.—E. M. Forster, "My Wood," *Abinger Harvest*

The crime was common, common be the pain.—Alexander Pope, "Eloisa to Abelard"

The laughter had to be gross or it would turn to sobs, and to sob would be to realize, and to realize would be to despair.—John Howard Griffin, *Black Like Me*

Having power makes it [totalitarian leadership] isolated; isolation breeds insecurity; insecurity breeds suspicion and fear; suspicion and fear breed violence.—Zbigniew K. Brzezinski, *The Permanent Purge, Politics in Soviet Totalitarianism*

Queeg: "Aboard my ship, excellent performance is standard. Standard performance is sub-standard. Sub-standard performance is not permitted to exist."—Herman Wouk, *The Caine Mutiny*

Climax—arrangement of words, phrases, or clauses in an order of increasing importance.

Examples: More than that, we rejoice in our sufferings, knowing that suffering produces endurance, endurance produces character, and character produces hope, and hope does not disappoint us, because God's love has been poured into our hearts through the Holy Spirit which has been given to us.—St. Paul, Romans, 5, 3-5

Let a man acknowledge obligations to his family, his country, and his God.—Student paper

Renounce my love, my life, myself—and you.—Alexander Pope, "Eloisa to Abelard"

I think we've reached a point of great decision, not just for our nation, not only for all humanity, but for life upon the earth.—George Wald, "A Generation in Search of a Future," speech delivered at M.I.T. on March 4, 1969

When a boy lays aside his tops, his marbles, and his bike in favor of a girl, another girl, and still another girl, he becomes a youth. When the youth discards his first girl and his second girl for *the* girl, he becomes a bachelor. And when the bachelor can stand it no longer, he turns into a husband.—Alan Beck, from an article in *Good Housekeeping,* July 1957

It shreds the nerves, it vivisects the psyche—and it may even scare the living daylights out of more than a few playgoers.—A review in *Time,* January 7, 1966

Climax can be considered a scheme of repetition only when, as in the first example quoted above, it is a continued anadiplosis involving three or more members. Otherwise, as in the second and third examples, it is simply a scheme which arranges a series in an order of gradually rising importance. This latter variety of climax can be looked upon as a scheme related to the topic of degree, and it is the kind of climax that the student will most often find in modern prose and that he will probably find occasion to use in his own prose.

Antimetabole—repetition of words, in successive clauses, in reverse grammatical order.

Examples: One should eat to live, not live to eat.—Molière, *L'Avare*

> It ought to be the first endeavor of a writer to distinguish nature from custom, or that which is established because it is right from that which is right only because it is established.—Samuel Johnson, *Rambler* #156

> This man [Lord Chesterfield] I thought had been a lord among wits; but, I find, he is only a wit among lords.—Samuel Johnson, as quoted in Boswell's *Life of Johnson*

> Mankind must put an end to war—or war will put an end to mankind.—John F. Kennedy, United Nations Speech, 1961

> Ask not what your country can do for you; ask what you can do for your country.—John F. Kennedy, Inaugural Address

> The Negro needs the white man to free him from his fears. The white man needs the Negro to free him from his guilt.—Martin Luther King, Jr., from a speech delivered in 1966

> You can take Salem out of the country. But you can't take the country out of Salem.—Caption from a Salem cigarette ad

> You like it, it likes you.—Advertising slogan for Seven-Up

All of these examples have the air of the "neatly turned phrase"—the kind of phrasing that figures in most memorable aphorisms. Would the sentence from President Kennedy's Inaugural Address be so often quoted if it had read something like this: "Do not ask what America can do for you. You would do better to ask whether your country stands in need of *your* services"? The "magic" has now gone out of the appeal. It would be a profitable exercise for the student to take several of the schemes presented in this section and convert them into ordinary prose. Such an exercise would undoubtedly reveal what the schemes add to the expression of the thought.

Chiasmus ("the criss-cross")—reversal of grammatical structures in successive phrases or clauses

Examples: By day the frolic, and the dance by night.—Samuel Johnson, "The Vanity of Human Wishes"

His time a moment, and a point his space.—Alexander Pope, *Essay on Man*, Epistle I

Exalts his enemies, his friends destroys.—John Dryden, "Absalom and Achitophel"

It is hard to make money, but to spend it is easy.—Student paper

Language changes. So should your dictionary.—Caption from ad for *Webster's Seventh New Collegiate Dictionary*

Chiasmus is similar to *antimetabole* in that it too involves a reversal of grammatical structures in successive phrases or clauses, but it is unlike *antimetabole* in that it does not involve a repetition of words. Both *chiasmus* and *antimetabole* can be used to reinforce *antithesis*.

Polyptoton—repetition of words derived from the same root.

Examples: The Greeks are *strong*, and *skilful* to their *strength*,
         Fierce to their *skill*, and to their *fierceness* valiant;
                    —Shakespeare, *Troilus and Cressida*, I, i, 7-8

But alas . . . the gate is narrow, the threshold high, few are *chosen* because few *choose* to be *chosen*.—Aldous Huxley, from *Collected Essays* (1955)

Let me assert my firm belief that the only thing we have to *fear* is *fear* itself.—Franklin Delano Roosevelt, First Inaugural Address, March 1933

But in this desert country they may see the land being rendered *useless* by *overuse*.—Joseph Wood Krutch, *The Voice of the Desert* (1955)

We would like to *contain* the *uncontainable* future in a glass.—Loren Eiseley, from an article in *Harper's*, March 1964

Not as a call to *battle*, though *embattled* we are.—John F. Kennedy, Inaugural Address

Their *blood bleeds* the nation of its sanguine assurance.—Student paper

Please, Please Me.—Title of a Beatles' song

Polyptoton is very much akin to those plays on words that we will investigate in the next section on tropes.

The Tropes

Metaphor and Simile

Metaphor—an implied comparison between two things of unlike nature that yet have something in common.
Simile—an explicit comparison between two things of unlike nature that yet have something in common.

Examples (all from student themes):

> He had a posture like a question-mark. (simile)

> On the final examination, several students went down in flames. (metaphor)

> Like an arrow, the prosecutor went directly to the point. (simile)

> The question of federal aid to parochial schools is a bramble patch. (metaphor)

> Silence settled down over the audience like a block of granite. (simile)

> Birmingham lighted a runaway fuse, and as fast as the headlines could record them, demonstrations exploded all over the country. (metaphor)

We shall treat of metaphor and simile together because they are so much alike. The difference between metaphor and simile lies mainly in the manner of expressing the comparison. Whereas metaphor says, "David was a lion in battle," simile says, "David was *like* a lion in battle." Both of these tropes are related to the topic of similarity, for although the comparison is made between two things of unlike nature (*David* and *lion*), there is some respect in which they are similar (e.g., they are courageous, or they fight ferociously, or they are unconquerable in a fight). The thing with which the first thing is compared is to be understood in some "transferred sense": *David* is not literally a *lion*, but he is a lion in some "other sense."

An extended or continued metaphor is known as an *allegory*. We see one of these sustained metaphors in *The Battle of the Books*, where Jonathan Swift compares the classical writers, not to the spider, which spins its web out of its own entrails, but to the far-ranging bee:

> As for us the ancients, we are content with the bee to pretend to nothing of our own, beyond our wings and our voices, that is to say, our flights and our language. For the rest, whatever we have got has been by infinite labor and search, and ranging through every corner of nature; the difference is that instead of dirt and poison, we have chosen to fill our hives with honey and wax, thus furnishing mankind with the two noblest of things, which are sweetness and light.

Closely allied to this form of extended metaphor is *parable,* an anecdotal narrative designed to teach a moral lesson. The most famous examples of parable are those found in the New Testament. In the parable of the sower of seeds, for instance, our interest is not so much in the tale of a man who went out to sow some seeds as in what each detail of the anecdote "stands for," in what the details "mean." Whenever the disciples were puzzled about what a particular parable meant, they asked Christ to interpret it for them.

And while we are talking about these analogical tropes, we should warn the student to be on his guard against the "mixed metaphor," which results when he loses sight of the terms of his comparison. When Joseph Addison said, "There is not a single view of human nature which is not sufficient to extinguish the seeds of pride," it is obvious that he is mixing two different metaphors. We could say "to extinguish the *flames* of pride" or "to *water* the seeds of pride," but we cannot mix the notion of extinguishing with that of seeds. The rhetoricians sometimes called such "wrenching of words" *catachresis.*

Synecdoche—a figure of speech in which a part stands for the whole.

Examples:

> genus substituted for the species:
> *vessel* for *ship, weapon* for *sword, creature* for *man, arms* for *rifles, vehicle* for *bicycle*
>
> species substituted for the genus:
> *bread* for *food, cutthroat* for *assassin*
>
> part substituted for the whole:
> *sail* for *ship, hands* for *helpers, roofs* for *houses*
>
> matter for what is made from it:
> *silver* for *money, canvas* for *sail, steel* for *sword*

In general, we have an instance of *synecdoche* when the part or genus or adjunct that is mentioned suggests something else. It is an *oblique* manner of speaking. All of the following illustrate this trope: "Give us this day our daily *bread.*" "All *hands* were summoned to the quarter-deck." "Not *marble,* nor the gilded monuments of princes, shall outlive this powerful *rhyme.*" "They braved the *waves* to protect their fatherland." "Brandish your *steel*, men." "Are there no *roofs* in this town that will harbor an honorable man?" "It is pleasing to contemplate a *manufacture* rising gradually from its first mean state by the successive *labors* of innumerable *minds.*"—Johnson, *Rambler* No. 9. "The door closed upon the extempore surgeon and midwife, and *Roaring Camp* sat down outside, smoked its pipe, and awaited the issue."— Bret Harte, "The Luck of Roaring Camp."

Metonymy—substitution of some attributive or suggestive word for what is actually meant.

Examples: crown for *royalty, mitre* for *bishop, wealth* for *rich people, brass* for *military officers, bottle* for *wine, pen* for *writers*

Metonymy and synecdoche are so close to being the same trope that George Campbell, the eighteenth-century rhetorician, wondered whether we should make any great effort to distinguish them. Those rhetoricians who did make the effort to discriminate these tropes would label the following as examples of metonymy:

> If the nearness of our last necessity brought a nearer conformity into it, there were happiness in *hoary hairs* and no calamity in *half senses.* . . . and Charles the Fifth can never hope to live within two *Methuselahs* of Hector.—Sir Thomas Browne, *Urn-Burial* (1658)

> I have nothing to offer but *blood, toil, tears,* and *sweat.*—Sir Winston Churchill, speech in the House of Commons May 13, 1940

> . . . and with firm confidence in justice, freedom, and peace on earth that will raise the hearts and the hopes of mankind for that distant day when no one *rattles a saber* and no one *drags a chain.* —Adlai Stevenson, acceptance speech, July 21, 1952

> In Europe, we gave the *cold shoulder* to De Gaulle, and now he gives the *warm hand* to Mao Tse-tung.—Richard M. Nixon, campaign speech, 1960

> You can't read the history of the United States, my friends, without learning the great story of those thousands of unnamed women. And if it's ever told straight, you'll know it's the *sunbonnet* and not the *sombrero* that has settled the country.—Edna Ferber, *Cimarron* (1930)

Capital has learned to sit down and talk with *labor*.—George Meany, speech in 1966

Breaching the *White Wall* of Southern Justice.—Title of article in *Time*, April 15, 1966

In another song written by [Bob] Dylan and sung by the Turtles, he lectures *clinging vines* who only want a *strong shoulder* to lean on.—Review in *Time*, September 17, 1966

Puns—generic name for those figures which make a play on words.
   (1) **Antanaclasis**—repetition of a word in two different senses.

But lest I should be condemned of introducing *license*, when I oppose *licensing*, . . . —John Milton, *Areopagitica* (1644)

If we don't *hang* together, we'll *hang* separately.—Benjamin Franklin

Your argument is *sound*, nothing but *sound*.—Benjamin Franklin

Although we're *apart*, you're still *a part* of me.—Lyrics of the song "On Blueberry Hill"

Nothing is closer to the supreme *commonplace* of our *commonplace* age than its preoccupation with *Nothing*.—Robert Martin Adams, *Nil* (1966)

You may not find this *Scotch* as smooth as Barrymore, of course, but then Barrymore wasn't *Scotch*.—Ad for Seagram's Scotch Whiskey

The *long* cigarette that's *long* on flavor.—Ad for Pall Mall cigarettes

We make the traveler's *lot* a *lot* easier.—Ad for Overseas National Airways

   (2) **Paronomasia**—use of words alike in sound but different in meaning.

Neither hide nor hair of him had been seen since the day that Kwame Nkrumah had been *ostrichized*, accused of being the biggest *cheetah* in Ghana, but *safaris* anyone knew, no *fowl* play was involved.—Article in *Time*, April 8, 1966

The Bustle: A *Deceitful Seatful*.—Vladimir Nabokov, *Lolita*

Casting my *perils* before *swains*.—Marshall McLuhan

Fran [Elizabeth Taylor] is a chorine waiting for her paramour to obtain a divorce and *altar* her situation.—Movie review in *Time,* March 9, 1970

The end of the *plain plane, explained.*—Ad for Braniff International

One's metaphoric *retch* exceeds one's metaphoric *gasp.*—John Leonard, column in *Esquire,* February 1969

Independence is what a boy feels when all he wants from father is to be left *a loan.*—Minneapolis *Star,* April 26, 1966

The "in" idea in business travel—Hilton Inns.—Ad for Hilton Inns

(3) **Syllepsis**—use of a word understood differently in relation to two or more other words, which it modifies or governs

Here thou, great Anna! whom three realms obey
Dost sometimes counsel *take*—and sometimes tea.
—Alexander Pope, *The Rape of the Lock*

The play is armed with irascible wit, and Nicol Williamson's whip-lash acting *raises* laughs as well as welts.—Review in *Time,* April 1, 1966

There is a certain type of woman who'd rather *press* grapes than clothes.—Ad for Peck & Peck suits

Lights are as likely to *attract* a Viet Cong bullet as a mosquito.—Article in *Time,* September 10, 1966

Who was the first to *wrap up* a case: Scotland Yard or Alexander Gordon?—Ad for Gordon's Whiskey

The ink, like our pig, keeps *running* out of the pen.—Student paper

The figure of *zeugma* is somewhat like syllepsis, but whereas in *syllepsis* the single word is grammatically and idiomatically compatible with both of the other words that it governs, in a zeugma the single word does not fit grammatically or idiomatically with one member of the pair. If we say, "Jane *has murdered* her father, and may you too" or "He maintained a *flourishing* business and racehorse," we would be producing an instance of zeugma, because in both sentences the underlined word is either grammatically or idiomatically incongruous with one member (in these examples, the second member) of the pair it governs. Those two lines from Pope's *Rape of the Lock* which are often classified as zeugma—"Or stain her honour, or her new brocade" and "Or lose her heart, or necklace, at a ball"—would, according to our definition, be examples of syllepsis. Syllepsis is the only one of these two figures which can be considered a form of pun. Zeugma, if skill-fully managed, could be impressive as a display of wit, but often enough, zeugma is nothing more than a faulty use of the scheme of ellipsis.

Anthimeria—the substitution of one part of speech for another.

Examples: I'll *unhair* thy head.—Shakespeare, *Antony and Cleopatra,* II, v, 64

> A mile before his tent fall down, and *knee*
> The way into his mercy.—Shakespeare, *Coriolanus,* V, i, 5

> The thunder would not *peace* at my bidding.—Shakespeare, *King Lear,* IV, vi, 103

> That ghastly thought would drink up all your joy,
> And quite *unparadise* the realms of light.
> —Edward Young, *Complaint, or Night Thoughts*

> George Rogers Clark may have camped under that tree; buffalo may have *nooned* in its shade, switching flies.—Aldo Leopold, *A Sand County Almanac* (1949)

> They whack-whacked the white horse on the legs and he *kneed* himself up.—Ernest Hemingway, *in our time*

> Me, *dictionary-ing* heavily, "Where was the one they were watch-ing?"—Ernest Hemingway, *Green Hills of Africa*

> *Gift* him with *Playboy.*—Promotional letter for *Playboy* magazine

Dozens of other examples of anthimeria could be quoted from Shakespeare's plays. If a word was not available for what he wanted to express, Shake-speare either coined a word or used an old word in a new way. Today's writer must use anthimeria seldom and with great discretion unless he is truly a master of the existing English language. On the other hand, an apt creation can be pungent, evocative, witty, or memorable. English today is a rich, flexible language, because words have been borrowed, changed, and created. Think of all the ways in which a word like *smoke* has been used since it first came into the language:

> The smoke rose from the chimney.
> The chimney smokes.
> He smoked the ham.
> He smokes.
> He asked for a smoke.
> He objected to the smoke nuisance.

He noticed the smoky atmosphere.
He tried smoking on the sly.
He smoked out the thief.
His dreams went up in smoke.
The Ferrari smoked along the wet track.

Someday someone will say, if it hasn't been said already, "He looked at her smokily."

Periphrasis (antonomasia)—substitution of a descriptive word or phrase for a proper name or of a proper name for a quality associated with the name.

Examples: The *Splendid Splinter* hit two more *round-trippers* today.

> In his later years he became in fact the most scarifying of his own creatures: a *Quixote* of the Cotswolds who abdicated his century and thereafter lived in quasi-medieval delusions that degenerated at last into melancholia.—Article on Evelyn Waugh in *Time,* April 22, 1966

> They do not escape *Jim Crow;* they merely encounter another, not less deadly variety.—James Baldwin, *Nobody Knows My Name*

> Disney's *Pollyanna* is looking more like an aging *Lolita* now, but it's perfectly all right.—Article in *Time,* April 1, 1966

> Pale young men with larded and *Valentino-black* side whiskers.—Dylan Thomas, "Memoirs of an August Bank Holiday"

> When you're out of *Schlitz,* you're out of beer.—Advertising slogan for Schlitz beer

> She may not have been a *Penelope,* but she was not as unfaithful as the gossips made her out to be.—Student paper

The frequency with which we meet this trope, even in modern prose, is evidence of the urge in man to express familiar ideas in uncommon ways. Circumlocutions and tags can become tiresome clichés (as they often do on the sports page), but when they display a fresh, decorous inventiveness, they can add grace to our writing. It is the trite or overly ingenious oblique expression that wearies the reader.

Personification (prosopoeia)—investing abstractions or inanimate objects with human qualities or abilities.

Examples: The ground thirsts for rain.—Student paper

He glanced at the dew-covered grass, and it winked back at him.—
Student paper

A tree whose hungry mouth is prest
Against the earth's sweet-flowing breast.

—Joyce Kilmer, "Trees"

And indeed there will be time
For the yellow smoke that slides along the street,
Rubbing its back upon the window panes.
    T. S. Eliot, "The Love Song of J. Alfred Prufrock"
        —T. S. Eliot, "The Love Song of J. Alfred Prufrock"

Mother Tongue is a self-reliant female.—Charlton Laird, *The Miracle of Language*

The handsome houses on the street to the college were not fully awake, but they looked very friendly.—Lionel Trilling, "Of This Time, Of That Place"

Personification is such a familiar figure that there is no need to multiply examples of it. This is one of the figures that should be reserved for passages designed to stir the emotions. Another emotional figure, closely allied to personification, is *apostrophe* (addressing an absent person or a personified abstraction). Here is an example of apostrophe from Sir Walter Raleigh's *History of the World:*

> O eloquent, just, and mighty Death! whom none could advise, thou hast persuaded; what none hath dared, thou hast done; and whom all the world has flattered, thou only hast cast out of the world and despised. Thou hast drawn together all the far-stretched greatness, all the pride, cruelty, and ambition of man, and covered it all with these two narrow words, *Hic jacet.*

Hyperbole—the use of exaggerated terms for the purpose of emphasis or heightened effect.

Examples: His eloquence would split rocks.

It's really ironical . . . I have gray hair. I really do. The one side of my head—the right side—is full of millions of gray hairs.—Holden Caulfield in *Catcher in the Rye*

My left leg weighs three tons. It is embalmed in spices like a mummy. I can't move. I haven't moved for five thousand years. I'm of the time of Pharaoh.—Thomas Bailey Aldrich, "Marjorie Daw"

"Rozelle's right," pitched in the only man in New York still wearing a 1951 crew cut.—Rex Reed, article in *Esquire,* October 1969

What he does not like is the press, which he tells us misrepresents him ninety percent of the time, by which we must understand, in a world of hyperbole which so naturally accentuates in a world of sport (how excruciating it must be for the sportswriter who cannot report that Joe Namath ran two hundred yards for a touchdown!) that occasionally we have got him wrong.—William F. Buckley, Jr., article in *Esquire,* October 1969

I will buy anything—ANYTHING—that has been reduced to one third its original price.—Jean Kerr, *The Snake Has All the Lines*

We walked along a road in Cumberland and stooped, because the sky hung so low.—Thomas Wolfe, *Look Homeward, Angel*

Hyperbole is so steadily droned into our ears that most of us have ceased to think of it as a figure of speech. Advertisers and teenagers can hardly talk without using superlatives. Perhaps we would not be so much amused by the Oriental greeting, "We welcome you, most honorable sir, to our miserable abode," if we stopped to consider how exaggerated many of our forms of greeting, address, and compliment are.

Hyperbole can be a serviceable figure of speech if we learn to use it with restraint and for a calculated effect. Under the stress of emotion, it will slip out naturally and will then seem appropriate. If we can learn to invent fresh hyperboles, we will be able to produce the right note of emphasis (as in the first example above) or humor (as in the quotation from Aldrich).

Being related to the topic of degree, hyperbole is like the figure called *auxesis* (magnifying the importance or gravity of something by referring to it with a disproportionate name). So a lawyer will try to impress a jury by referring to a scratch on the arm as "a wound" or to pilfering from the petty-cash box as "embezzlement." We can accept Mark Antony's reference to the wound that Brutus inflicted on Caesar as "the most unkindest cut of all," but the occasion seemed not to warrant Senator Joseph McCarthy's classic remark, "That's the most unheard of thing I ever heard of."

Litotes—deliberate use of understatement, not to deceive someone but to enhance the impressiveness of what we say.

Examples: I am a citizen of no mean city.—St. Paul

To write is, indeed, no unpleasing employment.—Samuel Johnson, *Adventurer,* No. 138

Last week I saw a woman flayed, and you will hardly believe how much it altered her appearance for the worse.—Jonathan Swift, *A Tale of a Tub*

With its oratorical blast, the session filled more than 33,250 pages of the *Congressional Record,* another record which cost the taxpayers only some $3,000,000.—Article in *Time,* October 29, 1965

Dick was awake. He was rather more than that; he and Inez were making love.—Truman Capote, *In Cold Blood*

Entertainer Frank Sinatra isn't the slow-burn type.—Article in *Newsweek,* November 15, 1965

It isn't very serious. I have this tiny little tumor on the brain.—J. D. Salinger, *The Catcher in the Rye*

For four generations we've been making medicines as if people's lives depended on them.—Ad for Eli Lilly Drug Company

Litotes is a form of *meiosis* (a lessening). The same lawyer whom we saw in the previous section using *auxesis* might represent another of his clients by referring to a case of vandalism as "boyish highjinks." A rose by any other name will smell as sweet, but a crime, if referred to by a name that is not too patently disproportionate, may lose some of its heinousness.

Rhetorical Question (erotema)—asking a question, not for the purpose of eliciting an answer but for the purpose of asserting or denying something obliquely.

Examples: What! Gentlemen, was I not to foresee, or foreseeing was I not to endeavor to save you from all these multiplied mischiefs and disgraces? . . . Was I an Irishman on that day that I boldly withstood our pride? or on the day that I hung down my head and wept in shame and silence over the humiliation of Great Britain? I became unpopular in England for the one, and in Ireland for the other. What then? What obligation lay on me to be popular? —Edmund Burke, *Speech in the Electors of Bristol*

Wasn't the cult of James a revealing symbol and symbol of an age and society which wanted to dwell like him in some false world of false art and false culture?—Maxwell Geismar, *Henry James and His Cult*

How can the poor feel they have a stake in a system which says that the rich may have due process but the poor may not? How can the uneducated have faith in a system which says that it will take advantage of them in every possible way? How can people have hope when we tell them that they have no recourse if they run afoul of the state justice system?—Senator Edward Kennedy, Senate debate on the Omnibus Crime Control and Safe Streets Act, 1968

A good student-body is perhaps the most important factor in a great university. How can you possibly make good wine from poor grapes?—Student paper

The *rhetorical question* is a common device in impassioned speeches, but it can be used too in written prose. It can be an effective persuasive device, subtly influencing the kind of response one wants to get from an audience. The manner in which the question is phrased can determine either a negative or an affirmative response. If we say, "Was this an act of heroism?" the audience will respond, in the proper context, with a negative answer. By inducing the audience to make the appropriate response, the rhetorical question can often be more effective as a persuasive device than a direct assertion would be.

Irony—use of a word in such a way as to convey a meaning opposite to the literal meaning of the word.

Examples: For Brutus is an *honourable* man;
So are they all, *honourable* men.—Shakespeare, *Julius Caesar,* III, ii, 88-9

It is again objected, as a very absurd, ridiculous custom that a set of men should be suffered, much less employed and hired, to bawl one day in seven against the *lawfulness* of those methods most in use toward the pursuit of greatness, riches, and pleasure, which are the constant practice of all men alive on the other six. But this objection is, I think, a little unworthy of *so refined* an age as ours.—Swift, *Argument Against the Abolishing of Christianity*

By Spring, if God was good, all the *proud privileges* of trench lice, mustard gas, spattered brains, punctured lungs, ripped guts, asphyxiation, mud, and gangrene, might be his.—Thomas Wolfe, *Look Homeward, Angel*

Fielder smiled. "I like the English," he said. "That gives me a *nice warm* feeling," Leamas retorted.—John Le Carré, *The Spy Who Came in from the Cold*

Neither the union nor anyone else could persuade a single soul to

> move into this "model facility."—John Barron, article on the FHA
> in *Reader's Digest*, April 1966

> I was simply *overjoyed* at the thought of having to leave my guy
> and return to school for finals.—Student paper

> Sure you could live without Yellow Pages (or without newspapers
> or automobiles or clocks).—Bell Telephone ad

As a trope which quite definitely conveys a "transferred meaning," irony is related to the topic of contraries or the topic of contradiction. A highly sophisticated device, irony must be used with great caution. If one misjudges the intelligence of his audience, he may find that his audience is taking his words in their ostensible sense rather than in the intended opposite sense.

The Tudor rhetoricians had a special name for the kind of irony in which one proposed to pass over some matter, yet managed subtly to reveal the matter anyway. They called this kind of irony *paralipsis*. A notable example of paralipsis is found in Mark Antony's famous "Friends, Romans, countrymen" speech in *Julius Caesar:*

> Let but the commons hear this testament,
> Which (pardon me) I do not mean to read,
> And they would go and kiss dead Caesar's wounds . . .
> Have patience, gentle friends; I must not read it.
> It is not meet you know how Caesar lov'd you. . . .
> 'Tis good you know not that you are his heirs.
>
> (III, ii, 136-51)

A look at the entire speech will show how Antony, despite his disclaimers, managed to let the mob know what was in Caesar's last will.

Onomatopoeia—use of words whose sound echoes the sense.

Examples: 'Tis not enough no harshness gives offense,
The sound must seem an echo to the sense:
Soft is the strain when Zephyr gently blows,
And the smooth stream in smoother numbers flows;
But when loud surges lash the sounding shore,
The hoarse, rough verse should like the torrent roar:
When Ajax strives some rock's vast weight to throw,
The line too labors, and the words move slow;
Not so, when swift Camilla scours the plain,
Flies o'er the unbending corn, and skims along the main.
—Pope, *Essay on Criticism*, II, 364-73

Over the cobbles he clattered and clashed in the dark innyard.—
Alfred Noyes, "The Highwayman"

Strong gongs groaning as the guns boom far.—G. K. Chesterton,
Lepanto

My days have crackled and gone up in smoke.—Francis Thompson,
"The Hound of Heaven"

A talking twitter all they had to sing.—Robert Frost, "Our Singing
Strength"

The birds chirped away. Fweet, Fweet, Bootchee-Fweet.—Saul Bel-
low, "Masby's Memoirs," *New Yorker,* July 20, 1968

In the passage quoted above from Pope, some of the onomatopoetic effects
are produced by the rhythm of the lines as well as by the sounds of words.
Since onomatopoeia seeks to match sound with sense, it is easy to see why
this figure was commonly associated with the topic of similarity. Onomatopoeia will be used much less frequently in prose than in poetry, yet it still
has its appropriate uses in prose. Wherever sound-effects can be used to set
the emotional or ethical tone of a passage, onomatopoeia can make a contribution. In seeking to discredit a person or an act, we could reinforce the
effect of pejorative diction with cacophony. In a phrase like "a dastardly episode," we reveal our attitude toward the event not only by the unpleasant
connotations of the word *dastardly* but also by the harsh sound of the word.

Oxymoron—the yoking of two terms which are ordinarily contradictory.

Examples: expressions like *sweet pain, cheerful pessimist, conspicuous by his
absence, cruel kindness, thunderous silence, luxurious poverty, abject arrogance, make haste slowly.*

By thus combining contradictories, the writer produces a startling effect, and
he may, if his oxymorons are fresh and apt, win for himself a reputation for
wit. There is displayed in this figure, as in most metaphorical language,
what Aristotle considered a special mark of genius: the ability to see similarities. Here are some examples of oxymoron:

Here's much to do with hate, but more with love.
Why then, O *brawling love!* O *loving hate!*
O *anything* of *nothing* first create!
O *heavy lightness, serious vanity!*
Misshapen chaos of *well-seeming* forms!
Feather of lead, bright smoke, cold fire, sick health!

Still-waking sleep, that is not what it is!
This love I feel, that feel no love in this
　　　　　　　　—William Shakespeare, *Romeo and Juliet,* I, i

O *miserable abundance,* O *beggarly riches!*
　　　　　　　　—John Donne, *Devotions Upon Emergent Occasions*

A soul immortal, spending all her fires
Wasting her strength in *strenuous idleness.*
　　　　　　　　—Edward Young, *The Complaint, or Night Thoughts*

There is a sort of *dead-alive* hackneyed people about, who are scarcely conscious of living except in the exercise of some conventional occupation.—Robert Louis Stevenson, "An Apology for Idlers"

The new show at the Museum of Modern Art somehow manages to avoid *visual din.*—Aline Saarinen, a report on a showing of advertising posters on the Huntley-Brinkley show, January 24, 1968

. . . or, possibly, to a draft of Edward Kennedy, whose *absent presence* constituted one of the few phenomena here that were not familiar to those who had seen the Early Show at Miami Beach.—Richard H. Rovere, "Letter from Chicago," *New Yorker,* September 7, 1968

The *relaxed tenseness* of the Beatles' music reflects the restlessness of the teenage generation.—Student paper

These devices were calculated to stir his audience into a *rational hysteria.*—Student paper

Closely allied to oxymoron is *paradox,* an apparently contradictory statement that nevertheless contains a measure of truth. Paradox is like oxymoron in that both are built on contradictories, but paradox may not be a trope at all, because it involves not so much a "turn" of meaning in juxtaposed words as a "turn" of meaning in the whole statement. Here are some examples of paradox:

Art is a form of lying in order to tell the truth.—Pablo Picasso

The less we copy the renowned ancients, the more we shall resemble them.—Edward Young, *Conjectures on Original Composition*

Portnoy's Complaint, a novel in the form of a psychoanalytic monologue carried on by a guilt-ridden bachelor, is too funny not to be taken seriously.—Book review in *Time,* February 21, 1969

Professor [Harry] Levin has always in a sense suffered from the weakness of this strength.—Book review in the London *Times Literary Supplement,* September 1, 1966

He [Joseph K. in Kafka's *The Trial*] is guilty of being innocent.— J. Mitchell Morse, article in *College English,* May, 1969

But the essence of that ugliness is the thing which will always make it beautiful.—Gertrude Stein, "How Writing Is Written"

We know too much for one man to know much.—J. Robert Oppenheimer, *The Open Mind*

The past is the prologue.—Paul Newman, an NBC special "From Here to the Seventies," October 7, 1969

Concluding Remarks on the Figures of Speech

A knowledge of the figures that have been presented in this chapter will not insure that the student will be able to invent his own figures or that when he uses figures he will use them aptly and efficaciously. The benefit from such an investigation is rather that having been made aware of the various schemes and tropes the student may make a conscious effort to use figures when he sees that they will suit his purpose. In acquiring any skill, we must at first do consciously what experts do automatically; or, as Dr. Johnson said, "What we hope ever to do with ease, we must learn first to do with diligence." And during this period of apprenticeship, we can expect to do awkwardly what experts do smoothly. With practice, however, we will arrive at that happy state of naturalness that Longinus spoke of in *On the Sublime:*

> Wherefore a figure is at its best when the very fact that it is a figure escapes attention. . . . For art is perfect when it seems to be nature, and nature hits the mark when she contains art hidden within her.

Exercise

Directions: Find illustrations in twentieth-century prose or poetry of the following: (Page numbers refer to section in *Classical Rhetoric for the Modern Student* where the figure is discussed and illustrated.)

Schemes

Parallelism—similarity of structure in a pair or series of related words, phrases, or clauses (p. 463)

Isocolon—similarity not only of structure but of length (p. 464)

Antithesis—the juxtaposition of contrasting ideas, often in parallel structure (p. 464)

Anastrophe—inversion of the natural or usual word order (p. 466)

Parenthesis—insertion of some verbal unit in a position that interrupts the normal syntactical flow of the sentence (p. 467)

Apposition—placing side by side two co-ordinate elements, the second of which serves as an explanation or modification of the first (p. 468)

Ellipsis—deliberate omission of a word or of words which is readily implied by the context (p. 469)

Asyndeton—deliberate omission of conjunctions between a series (p. 469)

Polysyndeton—deliberate use of many conjunctions (p. 470)

Alliteration—repetition of initial or medial consonants in two or more adjacent words (p. 471)

Assonance—the repetition of similar vowel sounds, preceded and followed by different consonants, in the stressed syllables of adjacent words (p. 472)

Anaphora—repetition of the same word or group of words at the beginnings of successive clauses (p. 472)

Epistrophe—repetition of the same word or group of words at the ends of successive clauses (p. 473)

Epanalepsis—repetition at the end of a clause of the word that occurred at the beginning of the clause (p. 474)

Anadiplosis—repetition of the last word of one clause at the beginning of the following clause (p. 475)

Climax—arrangement of words, phrases, or clauses in an order of increasing importance (p. 476)

Antimetabole—repetition of words, in successive clauses, in reverse grammatical order (p. 477)

Chiasmus—reversal of grammatical structures in successive clauses (but no repetition of words) (p. 478)

Polyptoton—repetition of words derived from the same root (p. 478)

Tropes

Metaphor—implied comparison between two things of unlike nature (p. 479)

Simile—explicit comparison between two things of unlike nature (p. 479)

Synecdoche—figure of speech in which a part stands for the whole (p. 480)

Metonymy—substitution of some attributive or suggestive word for what is actually meant (p. 481)

Antanaclasis—repetition of a word in two different senses (p. 482)

Paronomasis—use of words alike in sound but different in meaning (p. 482)

Syllepsis—use of a word understood differently in relation to two or more other words, which it modifies or governs (p. 483)

Anthimeria—the substitution of one part of speech for another (p. 484)

Periphrasis (antonomasia)—substitution of a descriptive word or phrase for a proper name or of a proper name for a quality associated with the name (p. 485)

Personification (prosopesis)—investing abstractions for inanimate objects with human qualities or abilities (p. 485)

Hyperbole—the use of exaggerated terms for the purpose of emphasis or heightened effect (p. 486)

Litotes—deliberate use of understatement (p. 487)

Rhetorical question—asking a question, not for the purpose of eliciting an answer but for the purpose of asserting or denying something obliquely (p. 488)

Irony—use of a word in such a way as to convey a meaning opposite to the literal meaning of the word (p. 489)

Onomatapoeia—use of words whose sound echoes the sense (p. 490)

Oxymoron—the yoking of two terms which are ordinarily contradictory (p. 491)

Paradox—an apparently contradictory statement that nevertheless contains a measure of truth (p. 492)

Imitation

Up to this point we have been dealing with the precepts of style. Now we will move on to the second of the ways in which one learns to write or to improve his writing—imitation. Classical rhetoric books are filled with testimonies about the value of imitation for the refinement of the many skills involved in effective speaking or writing. Style is, after all, the most imitable of the skills that co-operate to produce effective discourse.

Rhetoricians recommended a variety of exercises to promote conscious imitation. Roman schoolboys, for example, were regularly set the task of translating Greek passages into Latin and vice versa. In some of the Renaissance schools in England, schoolboys worked back and forth between Greek and Latin and English. Schoolmasters—the better ones anyway—were aware that grammatical differences among these three languages necessitated certain stylistic adjustments in the translation from one language to another. Despite these differences, however, students did learn from this exercise many valuable lessons about sentence structure.

Another exercise imposed on schoolboys was the practice of paraphrasing poetry into prose. Here again many adjustments in style had to be made. Besides teaching students the salient differences between the poetic medium and the prose medium, this exercise made students pay close attention to the potentialities of precise, concrete diction, of emphatic disposition of words, and of figures of speech. Even today there are those who maintain that the best way to improve one's prose style is to study or write poetry.

Another common practice was to set the students the task of saying something in a variety of ways. This process usually started out with a model sentence, which had to be converted into a variety of forms each retaining the basic thought of the original. Erasmus, for instance, in Chapter 33 of his widely-used little book, *De duplici copia verborum ac rerum,* showed the students 150 ways of phrasing the Latin sentence, *Tuae literae me magnopere delectarunt* (Your letter has delighted me very much). This variety was achieved partly by the choice of different words, partly by different collocations of words. Here is a sampling of Erasmus's reworkings:

> Your epistle has cheered me greatly.
>
> Your note has been the occasion of unusual pleasure for me.
>
> When your letter came, I was seized with an extraordinary pleasure.
>
> What you wrote to me was most delightful.
>
> On reading your letter, I was filled with joy.
>
> Your letter provided me with no little pleasure.

Obviously, not all of the 150 sentences were equally satisfactory or appropriate; in fact, some of them were monstrosities. But by artificially experimenting with various forms, the student becomes aware of the flexibility of the language in which he is working and learns to extend his own range. Ultimately he learns that although there is a variety of ways of saying something, there is a "best way" for his particular subject matter, occasion, or audience. What was "best" for one occasion or audience, he discovers, is not "best" for another occasion or audience.

This text will give the student the opportunity to practice two kinds of imitation—copying passages of prose and imitating various sentence patterns. But before we get into those exercises, we will present the testimony of some famous writers about how they learned to write. The student will see as he reads these testimonies how basic imitation is to the formation of style.

Testimonies about the Value of Imitation

Malcolm X

I saw that the best thing I could do was get hold of a dictionary—to study, to learn some words. I was lucky enough to reason also that I should try to improve my penmanship. It was sad. I couldn't even write in a straight line. It was both ideas together that moved me to request a dictionary along with some tablets and pencils from the Norfolk Prison Colony school.

I spent two days just riffling uncertainly through the dictionary's pages. I'd never realized so many words existed! I didn't know *which* words I needed to learn. Finally, just to start some kind of action, I began copying.

In my slow, painstaking, ragged handwriting, I copied into my tablet everything printed on that first page, down to the punctuation marks.

I believe it took me a day. Then, aloud, I read back, to myself, everything I'd written on the tablet. Over and over, aloud, to myself, I read my own handwriting.

I woke up the next morning, thinking about those words—immensely proud to realize that not only had I written so much at one time, but I'd written words that I never knew were in the world. Moreover, with a little effort, I also could remember what many of these words meant. I reviewed the words whose meanings I didn't remember. Funny thing, from the dictionary first page right now, that "aardvark" springs to my mind. The dictionary had a picture of it, a long-tailed, long-eared, burrowing African mammal, which lives off termites caught by sticking out its tongue as an anteater does for ants.

I was so fascinated that I went on—I copied the dictionary's next page. And the same experience came when I studied that. With every succeeding page, I also learned of people and places and events from history. Actually the dictionary is like a miniature encyclopedia. Finally the dictionary's A section had filled a whole tablet—and I went on into the B's. That was the way I started copying what eventually became the entire dictionary. It went a lot faster after so much practice helped me to pick up handwriting speed. Between what I wrote in my tablet, and writing letters, during the rest of my time in prison I would guess I wrote a million words.

Benjamin Franklin

About this time I met with an odd volume of the *Spectator*. It was the third. I had never before seen any of them. I bought it, read it over and over, and was much delighted with it. I thought the writing excellent, and wished, if possible, to imitate it. With this view I took some of the papers, and, making short hints of the sentiment in each sentence, laid them by a few days, and then, without looking at the book, try'd to compleat the papers again, by expressing each hinted sentiment at length, and as fully as it had been expressed before, in any suitable words that should come to hand. Then I compared my *Spectator* with the original, discovered some of my faults, and corrected them. But I found I wanted a stock of words, or a readiness in recollecting and using them, which I thought I should have acquired before that time if I had gone on making verses; since the continual occasion for words of the same import, but of different length, to suit the measure, or of different sound for the rhyme, would have laid me under a constant necessity of searching for variety, and also have tended to fix that variety in my mind, and make me master of it. Therefore I took some of the tales and turned them into verse; and, after a time, when I had pretty well forgotten the prose, turned them back again. I also sometimes jumbled my collections of hints into confusion, and after some weeks endeavored to reduce them into the best order, before I began to form the full sentences and compleat the paper. This was to teach me method in the arrangement of thoughts. By comparing my work afterwards with the original, I discovered many faults and amended them; but I sometimes had the pleasure of fancying that, in certain particulars of small import, I had been lucky enough to improve the method or the language, and this encouraged me to think I might possibly in time come to be a tolerable English writer, of which I was extreamly ambitious.

From *The Autobiography of Benjamin Franklin*, 1771.

Winston S. Churchill

I continued in this unpretentious situation for nearly a year. However, by being so long in the lowest form [at Harrow] I gained an immense advantage over the cleverer boys. They all went on to learn Latin and Greek and splendid things like that. But I was taught English. We were considered such dunces that we could learn only English. Mr. Somervell—a most delightful man, to whom my debt is great—was charged with the duty of teaching the stupidest boys the most disregarded thing—namely, to write mere English. He knew how to do it. He taught it as no one else has ever taught it. Not only did we learn English parsing thoroughly, but we also practised continually English analysis. Mr. Somervell had a system of his own. He took a fairly long sentence and broke it up into its components by means of black, red, blue, and green inks. Subject, verb, object: Relative Clauses, Conditional Clauses, Conjunctive and Disjunctive Clauses! Each had its colour and its bracket. It was a kind of drill. We did it almost daily. As I remained in the Third Form (β) three times as long as anyone else, I had three times as much of it. I learned it thoroughly. Thus I got into my bones the essential structure of the ordinary British sentence—which is a noble thing. And when in after years my schoolfellows who had won prizes and distinction for writing such beautiful Latin poetry and pithy Greek epigrams had to come down again to common English, to earn their living or make their way, I did not feel myself at any disadvantage. Naturally I am biased in favour of boys learning English. I would make them all learn English: and then I would let the clever ones learn Latin as an honour, and Greek as a treat. But the only thing I would whip them for is not knowing English, I would whip them hard for that.

Somerset Maugham

IX

As it is, I have had to teach myself. I have looked at the stories I wrote when I was very young in order to discover what natural aptitude I had, my original stock-in-trade, before I developed it by taking thought. The manner had a superciliousness that perhaps my years excused and an irascibility that was a defect of nature; but I am speaking now only of the way in which I expressed myself. It seems to me that I had a natural lucidity and a knack for writing easy dialogue.

When Henry Arthur Jones, then a well-known playwright, read my first novel, he told a friend that in due course I should be one of the most successful dramatists of the day. I suppose he saw in it directness and an effective way of presenting a scene that suggested a sense of the theatre. My language was commonplace, my vocabulary limited, my grammar shaky and my phrases hackneyed. But to write was an instinct that seemed as natural to me as to breathe, and I did not stop to consider if I wrote well or badly. It was not till some years later that it dawned upon me that it was a delicate art that must be painfully acquired. The discovery was forced upon me by the difficulty I found in getting my meaning down on paper. I wrote dialogue fluently, but when it came to a page of description I found myself entangled in all sorts of quandaries. I would struggle for a couple of hours over two or three sentences that I could in no way manage to straighten out. I made up my mind to teach myself how to write. Unfortunately I had no one to help me. I made many mistakes. If I had had someone to guide me like the charming don of whom I spoke just now I might have been saved much time. Such a one might have told me that such gifts as I had lay in one direction and that they must be cultivated in that direction; it was useless to try to do something for which I had no aptitude. But at that time a florid prose was admired. Richness of texture was sought by means of a jewelled phrase and sentences stiff with exotic epithets: the ideal was a brocade so heavy with gold that it stood up by itself. The intelligent young read Walter Pater with enthusiasm. My common sense suggested to me that it was anaemic stuff; behind those elaborate, gracious periods I was conscious of a tired, wan personality. I was young, lusty and energetic; I wanted fresh air, action, violence, and I found it hard to breathe that dead, heavily scented atmosphere and sit in those hushed rooms in which it was indecorous to speak above a whisper. But I would not listen to my common sense. I persuaded myself that this was the height of culture and turned a scornful shoulder on the outside world where men shouted and swore, played the fool, wenched and got drunk. I read *Intentions* and *The Picture of Dorian Gray*. I was intoxicated by the colour and rareness of the fantastic words that thickly stud the pages of *Salome*. Shocked by the poverty of my own vocabulary, I went to the British Museum with pencil and paper and noted down the names of curious jewels, the Byzantine hues of old enamels, the sensual feel of textiles, and made elaborate sentences to bring them in. Fortunately I could never find an opportunity to use them, and they lie there yet in an old notebook ready for anyone who has a mind to write nonsense. It was generally thought then that the Authorized Version of the Bible was the greatest piece of prose that the English language has produced. I read it diligently, especially the Song of Solomon, jotting down for future use turns of phrase that struck me and making lists of unusual or beautiful words. I studied Jeremy Taylor's *Holy Dying*. In order to assimilate his style I copied out passages and then tried to write them down from memory.

The first fruit of this labour was a little book about Andalusia called *The Land of the Blessed Virgin*. I had occasion to read parts of it the other day. I know Andalusia a great deal better now than I knew it then, and I have changed my mind about a good many things of which I wrote. Since it has continued in America to have a small sale it occurred to me that it might be worth while to revise it. I soon saw that this was impossible. The book was written by someone I have completely forgotten. It bored me to distraction. But what I am concerned with is the prose, for it was as an exercise in style that I wrote it. It is wistful, allusive and elaborate. It has neither ease nor spontaneity. It smells of hothouse plants and Sunday dinner like the air in the greenhouse that leads out of the dining-room of a big house in Bayswater. There are a great many melodious adjectives. The vocabulary is sentimental. It does not remind one of an Italian brocade, with its rich pattern of gold, but of a curtain material designed by Burne-Jones and reproduced by Morris.

x

I do not know whether it was a subconscious feeling that this sort of writing was contrary to my bent or a naturally methodical cast of mind that led me then to turn my attention to the writers of the Augustan Period. The prose of Swift enchanted me. I made up my mind that this was a perfect way to write, and I started to work on him in the same way as I had done with Jeremy Taylor. I chose *The Tale of a Tub*. It is said that when the Dean re-read it in his old age he cried: 'What genius I had then!' To my mind his genius was better shown in other works. It is a tiresome allegory, and the irony is facile. But the style is admirable. I cannot imagine that English can be better written. Here are no flowery periods, fantastic turns of phrase or high-flown images. It is a civilized prose, natural, discreet and pointed. There is no attempt to surprise by an extravagant vocabulary. It looks as though Swift made do with the first word that came to hand, but since he had an acute and logical brain it was always the right one, and he put it in the right place. The strength and balance of his sentences are due to an exquisite taste. As I had done before, I copied passages and then tried to write them out again from memory. I tried altering words or the order in which they were set. I found that the only possible words were those Swift had used and that the order in which he had placed them was the only possible order. It is an impeccable prose.

But perfection has one grave defect: it is apt to be dull. Swift's prose is like a French canal, bordered with poplars, that runs through a gracious and undulating country. Its tranquil charm fills you with satisfaction, but it neither excites the emotions nor stimulates the imagination. You go on and on and presently you are a trifle bored. So, much as you may admire Swift's wonderful lucidity, his terseness, his naturalness, his lack of affectation, you find your attention wandering after a while unless his matter peculiarly interests you. I think if I had my time over again I would give to the prose of Dryden the close study I gave to that of Swift. I did not come across it till I had lost the inclination to take so much pains. The prose of Dryden is delicious. It has not the perfection of Swift nor the easy elegance of Addison, but it has a springtime gaiety, a conversational ease, a blithe spontaneousness that are enchanting. Dryden was a very good poet, but it is not the general opinion that he had a lyrical quality; it is strange that it is just this that sings in his softly sparkling prose. Prose had never been written in England like that before; it has seldom been written like that since. Dryden flourished at a happy moment. He had in his bones the sonorous periods and the baroque massiveness of Jacobean language, and under the influence of the nimble and well-bred felicity that he learnt from the French he turned it into an instrument that was fit not only for solemn themes but also to express the light thought of the passing moment. He was the first of the rococo artists. If Swift reminds you of a French canal Dryden recalls an English river winding its cheerful way round hills, through quietly busy towns and by nestling villages, pausing now in a noble reach and then running powerfully through a woodland country. It is alive, varied, windswept; and it has the pleasant open-air smell of England.

The work I did was certainly very good for me. I began to write better; I did not write well. I wrote stiffly and self-consciously. I tried to get a pattern into my sentences, but did not see that the pattern was evident. I took care how I placed my words, but did not reflect that an order that was natural at the beginning of the eighteenth century was most unnatural at the beginning of ours. My attempt to write in the manner of Swift made it impossible for me to achieve the effect of inevitable rightness that was just what I so much admired in him. I then wrote a number of plays and ceased to occupy myself with anything but dialogue. It was not till five years had passed that I set out again to write a novel. By then I no longer had any ambition to be a stylist; I put aside all thought of fine writing. I wanted to write without any frills of language, in as bare and unaffected a manner as I could. I had so much to say that I could afford to waste no words. I wanted merely to set down the facts. I began with the impossible aim of using no adjectives at all. I thought that if you could find the exact term a qualifying epithet could be dispensed with. As I saw it in my mind's eye my book would have the appearance of an immensely long telegram in which for economy's sake you had left out every word that was not necessary to make the sense clear. I have not read it since I corrected the proofs and do not know how near I came to doing what I tried. My impression is that it is written at least more naturally than anything I had written before; but I am sure that it is often slipshod, and I daresay there are in it a good many mistakes in grammar.

Since then I have written many other books; and though ceasing my methodical study of the old masters (for though the spirit is willing, the flesh is weak), I have continued with increasing assiduity to try to write better. I discovered my limitations, and it seemed to me that the only sensible thing was to aim at what excellence I could within them. I knew that I had no lyrical quality. I had a small vocabulary, and no efforts that I could make to enlarge it much availed me. I had little gift of metaphor; the original and striking simile seldom occurred to me. Poetic flights and the great imaginative sweep were beyond my powers. I could admire them in others as I could admire their far-fetched tropes and the unusual but suggestive language in which they clothed their thoughts, but my own invention never presented me with such embellishments; and I was tired of trying to do what did not come easily to me. On the other hand, I had an acute power of observation, and it seemed to me that I could see a great many things that other people missed. I could put down in clear terms what I saw. I had a logical sense, and if not great feeling for the richness and strangeness of words, at all events a lively appreciation of their sound. I knew that I should never write as well as I could wish, but I thought with pains I could arrive at writing a well as my natural defects allowed. On taking thought it seemed to me that I must aim at lucidity, simplicity, and euphony. I have put these three qualities in the order of the importance I assigned to them.

Rollo Walter Brown: How the French Boy Learns to Write

As soon as an American teacher comes into direct contact with the French educational system, he marvels at the large place writing holds in the schools and their routine life. First, it matters not in what classroom a small boy may be seen, he is never without his general notebook, in which he records all assignments, all problems, all experiments, all quotations to be learned, all geographical and historical notes and maps, as well as many special exercises; and the language he employs in this work is carefully marked and graded by the teacher. In the second place, compositions are numerous. From the time the boy is regarded as mature enough to think consecutively, he prepares compositions at regular intervals. In some classes he writes two

From Rollo Walter Brown, *How the French Boy Learns to Write: A Study in the Teaching of the Mother Tongue*, Cambridge, Mass.: Harvard University Press, 1915. Reprinted by permission of the publishers.

short exercises every three or five days. In the elementary primary schools, even up to the time the boy is thirteen or fourteen years old, the shorter themes once or twice a week seem to stand in great favor. These vary in length, usually, from a hundred and fifty to four hundred words—they are rather longer than the average American daily theme—and the less frequent, longer compositions range ordinarily from six hundred to fifteen hundred words. Then, in the upper grades, there are, in addition, many papers in history, civics, philosophy, and literature. So it may be seen that a boy is provided with much opportunity to write. It is, in fact, scarcely an exaggeration to say that he writes all the time. In any event, his practice is so continuous that he sooner or later comes to do the work in a perfectly normal frame of mind, just as he performs his other schoolday labors.

The volume of required writing, however, is regarded as less important than its quality. If a boy thinks and writes poorly, he is looked upon as an unfortunate who deserves either pity or contempt. If, on the other hand, he is able to think and write skillfully, he is held in great honor by his teachers and his classmates. And this interest in ability to write is evident outside the recitation-room. Authors of books and articles discuss the perils of the pure mother tongue as seriously as if they were dealing with a question of ethics or of grave national policy. Parents, I found when I was securing compositions for the purposes of this book, are usually desirous of preserving the written work of their children. Moreover, when pupils distinguish themselves in examinations—which in France are always largely a matter of composition—they receive prizes and public mention very much as if they were the winners of athletic trophies. Now I would not have anyone make the hasty inference that intellectual contests are substituted for athletics. The French boy loves the open just as much as the American boy does, and outdoor sports are steadily taking a larger place in school life. But the ideal of writing well has been held up before the schoolboy so long, and with such seriousness, that he attaches more importance to ability of this kind than the average American boy could at present be led to comprehend.

When so much importance is everywhere attached to ability to write, it is not surprising to find that in both the primary and secondary school systems the course in the mother tongue gives large place to systematic training in composition. It is the conviction of the great body of teachers, as well as the Ministry, that work in grammar, rhetoric, and literature is in most respects lost unless it contributes to the pupil's ability to give full, intelligent expression to his thought. Moreover, theories of teaching, and all the proposed changes in the course of study, seem to be considered first in respect to their influence on this ability of the pupil. Expression is not the sole end, but in all the lower schools it is the primary end. And, taking the other point of view, the chief responsibility for the pupil's manner of expression rests upon the teacher of the mother tongue. As we shall see later, the writing that the boy does in history, geometry, and his other subjects is made to contribute its full share to his skill; yet upon the teacher of the native language rests the largest responsibility and the greatest burden of labor. He accepts his task as difficult, very expensive in time and energy, but extremely important. Without going into any examination of exceptional aims or of intricate personal devices, let us see what he attempts to accomplish and how he pursues his way.

Two groups of exercises are everywhere regarded as essential preliminaries to work in original composition. Those in the first group are intended to enlarge and organize the pupil's vocabulary. Now, I am aware that when one stands apart and looks at exercises designed to improve the vocabulary, they are likely to appear very artificial and ineffective. And, in truth, they may be. In the hands of a poorly trained teacher, or one who lacks the all-important teaching instinct, it would be difficult to imagine an exercise that could be more dismally futile. But this possibility seems to be disregarded by French educators. They are ready to admit that the lessons may become valueless, or even harmful, when directed by a poor teacher—and what exercise may not?—but they do not spring to the conclusion that such lessons should for that reason be cast aside. They have taken the good teacher as the norm, and have given themselves earnestly to the task of obviating the dangers and developing the advantages of a kind of instruction which at its best appears to them to have unquestioned value.

The theory upon which this instruction is based is not the individual hasty inference that intellectual contests are substituted for athletics. The French boy loves the open just as much as the American boy does, and outdoor sports are steadily taking a larger place in school life. But the ideal of writing well has been held up before the schoolboy so long, and with such seriousness, that he attaches more importance to ability of this kind than the average American boy could at present be led to comprehend.

When so much importance is everywhere attached to ability to write, it is not surprising to find that in both the primary and secondary school systems the course in the mother tongue gives large place to systematic training in composition. It is the conviction of the great body of teachers, as well as the Ministry, that work in grammar, rhetoric, and literature is in most respects lost unless it contributes to the pupil's ability to give full, intelligent expression to his thought. Moreover, theories of teaching, and all the proposed changes in the course of study, seem to be considered first in respect to their influence on this ability of the pupil. Expression is not the sole end, but in all the lower schools it is the primary end. And, taking the other point of view, the chief responsibility for the pupil's manner of expression rests upon the teacher of the mother tongue. As we shall see later, the writing that the boy does in history, geometry, and his other subjects is made to contribute its full share to his skill; yet upon the teacher of the native language rests the largest responsibility and the greatest burden of labor. He accepts his task as difficult, very expensive in time and energy, but extremely important. Without going into any examination of exceptional aims or of intricate personal devices, let us see what he attempts to accomplish and how he pursues his way.

Two groups of exercises are everywhere regarded as essential preliminaries to work in original composition. Those in the first group are intended to enlarge and organize the pupil's vocabulary. Now, I am aware that when one stands apart and looks at exercises designed to improve the vocabulary, they are likely to appear very artificial and ineffective. And, in truth, they may be. In the hands of a poorly trained teacher, or one who lacks the all-important teaching instinct, it would be difficult to imagine an exercise that could be more dismally futile. But this possibility seems to be disregarded by French educators. They are ready to admit that the lessons may become valueless, or even harmful, when directed by a poor teacher—and what exercise may not?—but they do not spring to the conclusion that such lessons should for that reason be cast aside. They have taken the good teacher as the norm, and have given themselves earnestly to the task of obviating the dangers and developing the advantages of a kind of instruction which at its best appears to them to have unquestioned value.

The theory upon which this instruction is based is not the individual abstract or figurative. It is taken for granted that if a word is to be of much value to a boy, it must represent an idea clearly established in his mind, and it must have its individual flavor.

. . . .

In the exercises designed primarily to sharpen feeling for words, one is sure to be impressed with the many means by which a word is brought into the pupil's life. He defines it, he finds examples of its accepted uses, he learns its original significance—its literal meaning when the word is predominantly figurative—he compares it with other words of similar meaning, and above all, he contrasts it with words that are essentially its opposite. It is scarcely too much to say that the basis of all word-teaching is contrast rather than likeness. If a given word is used chiefly as a noun, the teacher does not let the pupil form the notion that synonymous adjectives may be attached to it indiscriminately, but helps him to learn what adjectives are or may be used appropriately with it. If the word is an adjective or verb, he shows how it normally takes certain adverbs, and how others, as soon as they are brought into close relation with it, seem awkward and unidiomatic. In a similar manner he guides the pupil to see the distinctions that usage has established between nouns which in general meaning are the same. To take a very simple example, if the word *stem* appeared in a lesson, he would be extremely careful to bring out the difference between *stem* and *stalk,* *stem* and *trunk,* and *stalk* and *trunk,* so that the pupil would never fall into the error of using them as if they were convertible terms. Through numerous exercises of this kind the pupil is made to see that words do not have the same value, and that the choosing of them is not merely a question of finding approved dictionary definitions when occasion arises, but of possessing a word sense.

Concerning the exercises in calling words to mind quickly, little need be said. Their character has already been suggested. They usually consist of rapid-fire questions about the word itself, its use, its likes and opposites, and of oral or written practice in composition on subjects likely to call words of a given class into use. I saw no turning of verse into prose, but I did see many exercises that required the pupils to turn one kind of prose into another. In most instances the teacher simply read a story or an essay to the class and then called upon pupils to repeat it in language of their own. After a little practice of this kind, a boy unconsciously adopts many words that he has well understood but has not made a part of his working vocabulary. He does not surrender his individuality, as he must do—momentarily, at least—in writing imitations, yet he is in a state of open-mindedness that encourages a definite impression of what he reads or hears read.

The scope of the lessons in vocabulary is wide. By the time a boy has reached the age of twelve he not only has had practice in calling simple objects by their right names, but he has reached out into the world around him and made acquaintance with words belonging to a great variety of activities. He can speak intelligently about the professions, the occupations of workingmen, the farm, social life, political life; he can discuss the more familiar phenomena of the atmosphere, the physical qualities of his friends, their moral virtues and their moral faults; he can use accurately the words that spring from such relations as commerce, war, colonization, life in the city or the small village; and he can talk or write about such means of communication as railways, steamships, street-railways, and the telegraph and telephone. This ability he gains not by sporadic or blind plunging about, but by means of orderly, systematic study. The instruction is not overrigid or mechanical; one might visit classrooms for months without feeling that the instruction was organized in any large way. Yet it is the careful organi-

zation that makes the wide scope of the work possible. The simplicity is
not that of isolated, individual effort, but of well-designed plan.

.   .   .   .

The second of the preliminary exercises universally employed by the French
teacher of the mother tongue is dictation. In America, dictation seems to have
been put aside to make way for something new. French teachers, however,
do not hesitate to use an old-fashioned method or device if they believe it
is good. Instead, therefore, of dropping dictation from the programme of
studies, they have emphasized it and developed it until it is now a very
important and thoroughly established part of their educational procedure.
It is based on the conviction that a child can acquire skill before he develops
the power of profound or sustained thought. He has much practice, then,
in writing the thoughts of others while he is yet too young to write his own.
Teachers admit that dictation has its dangers, but since they regard these
as incomparable to its possible value, they employ it, just as they employ
exercises in vocabulary, with the confidence that though they are risking
small dangers, they are following the direction of a larger common sense.

French teachers usually dwell upon four or five specific values of dictation.
It gives the pupil much practice in the handling of the sentence; it directs
his attention to grammatical constructions; it helps him to learn to spell,
to punctuate, and to capitalize; it enlarges his vocabulary and gives him
practice in the use of words already known to him; and it fills his mind with
good standards of speech. To these should be added one value that the
thoughtful teacher must regard as greatest of all; namely, that dictation
prevents the pupil from separating spoken language and writing. One of the
objections almost invariably made by the young pupil to practice in original
composition is that writing seems an artificial process quite unlike anything
he has ever before attempted. In making this objection, he is, of course,
merely giving expression to the fact that language is naturally a matter of
speech rather than writing, and the additional fact that he has not felt a
close relation between what he says by word of mouth and what he writes
on paper. If then, before he begins composition, and later while he is practicing it in an elementary manner, he has drill in writing down what he
hears, the relation between speech and writing is much less likely to be
weakened. While he is listening carefully to his teacher's reading, catching
the words in their natural thought groups, and putting them down one by
one in his exercise-book, he is not only learning much about the mechanics
of composition, but he is saving himself from the error of looking upon
theme-writing as something far removed from normal existence.

In giving dictations, the teacher exercises great care. After the very earliest
classes, where the work must of necessity be simple, he does not give isolated

or detached sentences, but instead, a complete, interesting paragraph. More-over, he always explains the paragraph fully before he asks the pupil to write it down. This precaution is regarded as so important that a teacher is prohibited from requiring a pupil to write down anything that is mean-ingless or vague. Again, he reads a paragraph that contains material suited to keep the pupil's attention. That is to say, the ideas and the words in which they are expressed must be just within the pupil's reach. And finally, the teacher guards against letting the exercise become monotonous. It is never long—usually it is a short, crisp paragraph—the corrections are made immediately while interest is warm, and the pupil is not asked to rewrite the dictation unless he has been exceedingly careless. The ten or fifteen min-utes are so full of pleasant activity that the time passes quickly, and the boy seems never to dream that he is doing something that might, under a thoughtless teacher, become a dreary, useless punishment.

.   .   .   .

Summary

The attention, then, that the actual business of writing receives in the French schools is a matter not only of adequate instruction, but of full and definite practice under stimulating circumstances. Composition is held up as a very important part—in fact, the most important part—of the course in the mother tongue. Studies in vocabulary and practice in dictation are carried on con-stantly in the lower grades in order that the boy may express himself with-out hindrance when he is once old enough to have something of his own to say in organized compositions. The material assigned is regarded as a matter of great moment. It is intended to develop, in order, the powers of attention and observation, the imagination, and habits of reflection. This material, moreover, is almost invariably discussed in the classroom until the pupil is awakened and interested; and when he writes upon it, he must give the most thoughtful care to organization and general good form. In the criticism of themes, oral discussion holds a large place. Furthermore, the teacher makes his critical suggestions distinctly constructive; that is, he emphasizes the difference between poor work and good, and he leads the pupils to reflect upon the possibilities that the subject-matter possesses, rather than upon the magnitude of their own shortcomings. And finally, the training that pupils receive in the study of the mother tongue is re-enforced to no small degree by the work in other subjects.

Exercises in Imitation

Copying Passages

The first exercise in imitation that we will recommend to the student consists of copying passages, word for word, from admired authors. This may strike the student as being a rather brainless exercise, but it can teach the student a great deal about the niceties of style. Earlier in this chapter, we pointed out a number of features one looks for when he makes a close study of style. These features will strike the student as he carefully transcribes the passage.

If the student is to derive any benefit from this exercise, he must observe a few simple rules:

1. He must not spend more than fifteen or twenty minutes copying at any one time. If he extends this exercise much beyond twenty minutes at any one sitting, his attention will begin to wander, and he will find himself merely copying words.

2. He must do this copying with a pencil or pen. Typing is so fast and so mechanical that the student can copy off whole passages without paying any attention to the features of an author's style. Copying by hand, he transcribes the passage at such a pace that he has time to observe the choice and disposition of words, the patterns of sentences, and the length and variety of sentences.

3. He must not spend too much time with any one author. If the student concentrates on a single author's style, he may find himself falling into that "servile imitation" that rhetoricians warned of. The aim of this exercise is not to acquire someone else's style but to lay the groundwork for developing one's own style by getting the "feel" of a variety of styles.

4. He must read the entire passage before starting to copy it so that he can capture the thought and the manner of the passage as a whole. When he is copying, it is advisable to read each sentence through before transcribing it. After the student has finished copying the passage, he should read his transcription so that he once again gets a sense of the passage as a whole.

5. He must copy the passage slowly and accurately. If he is going to dash through this exercise, he might as well not do it at all. A mechanical way of insuring accuracy and the proper pace is to make his handwriting as legible as he can.

The student will derive the maximum benefit from this copying exercise if he will practice it over an extended period of time. Transcribing a single different passage every day for a month will prove more beneficial to the student than transcribing several different passages every day for a week. The student must have time to absorb what he has been observing in this exercise; and he will not have time to absorb the many lessons to be learned from this exercise if he crams it into a short period.

Specimen Passages for Imitation

The Bible

I returned and saw under the sun that the race is not to the swift, nor the battle to the strong, neither yet bread to the wise, nor yet riches to men of understanding, nor yet favour to men of skill; but time and chance happeneth to them all. For man also knoweth not his time: as the fishes that are taken in an evil net, and as the birds that are caught in the snare; so are the sons of men snared in an evil time, when it falleth suddenly upon them. This wisdom have I seen also under the sun, and it seemed great unto me. There was a little city, and few men within it; and there came a great king against it, and besieged it, and built great bulwarks against it. Now there was found in it a poor wise man, and he by his wisdom delivered the city; yet no man remembered that same poor man. Then said I, Wisdom is better than strength: nevertheless the poor man's wisdom is despised, and his words are not heard. The words of wise men are heard in quiet more than the cry of him that ruleth among fools. Wisdom is better than weapons of war: but one sinner destroyeth much good.

(From Ecclesiastes, IX, 11-18, King James Version, 1611.)

And so it was, that, while they were there, the days were accomplished that she should be delivered. And she brought forth her firstborn son and wrapped him in swaddling clothes and laid him in a manger; because there was no room for them in the inn. And there were in the same country shepherds abiding in the field, keeping watch over their flock by night. And, lo, the angel of the Lord came upon them, and the glory of the Lord shone round about them: and they were sore afraid. And the angel said unto them, Fear not: for, behold, I bring you good tidings of great joy, which shall be to all people. For unto you is born this day in the city of David a Saviour, which is Christ the Lord. And this shall be a sign unto you; Ye shall find the babe wrapped in swaddling clothes, lying in a manger. And suddenly there was with the angel a multitude of the heavenly host praising God and saying, Glory to God in the highest, and on earth peace, good will toward men.

(From St. Luke, II, 6-14, King James Version, 1611.)

Jeremy Taylor

By the Cross of Christ stood the holy Virgin Mother, upon whom old Simeon's prophesy was now verified. For now she felt a sword passing through her very soul; she stood without clamour and womanish noises, and, silent, and with a modest grief, deep as the waters of the abyss, but smooth as the face of a pool, full of love and patience and sorrow and hope. Now she was put to it to make use of all those excellent discourses her holy Son had used to build up her spirit and fortify it against this day. Now she felt the blessings and strengths of Faith, and she passed from the griefs of the Passion to the expectation of the Resurrection, and she rested in this death as in a sad remedy; for she knew it reconciled God with all the World. But her hope drew a veil before her sorrow, and though her grief was great enough to swallow her up, yet her love was greater and did swallow up her grief. But the sun also had a veil upon his face and taught us to draw a curtain before the passion, which would be the most artificial expression of its greatness, whilst by silence and wonder we confess it great, beyond our expression, or which is all one, great as the burden and baseness of our sins; and with this veil drawn before the face of Jesus let us suppose him at the gates of Paradise, calling with his last words in a loud voice to have them opened: *That the King of glory might come in.*

(From *The Great Exemplar . . . the History of the Life and Death of . . . Jesus Christ*, 1649.)

Thomas Hobbes

By this it appears how necessary it is for any man that aspires to true Knowledge to examine the Definitions of former Authors; and either to correct them, where they are negligently set down; or to make them himself. For the errors of Definitions multiply themselves, according as the reckoning proceeds; and lead men into absurdities, which at last they see, but cannot avoid, without reckoning anew from the beginning; in which lies the foundation of their errors. From whence it happens that they which trust to books do as they that cast up many little sums into a greater, without considering whether those little sums were rightly cast up or not; and at last finding the error visible, and not mistrusting their first grounds, know not which way to clear themselves; but spend time in fluttering over their books; as birds that entering by the chimney and finding themselves inclosed in a chamber flutter at the false light of a glass window, for want of wit to consider which way they came in. So that in the right Definition of Names lies the first use of Speech; which is the acquisition of Science; and in the wrong, or no Definitions, lies the first abuse, from which proceed all false and senseless Tenets; which make those men that take their instruction from the authority of books, and not from their own meditation, to be as much below the condition of ignorant men, as men endued with true Science are above it. For between true Science and erroneous doctrines, ignorance is in the middle. Natural sense and imagination are not subject to absurdity. Nature itself cannot err, and as men abound in copiousness of language, so they become more wise or more mad than ordinary.

(From *Leviathan*, Part I, Chapter 4, 1651.)

Sir Thomas Browne

If the nearness of our last necessity brought a nearer conformity into it, there were a happiness in hoary hairs, and no calamity in half-senses. But the long habit of living indisposeth us for dying; when avarice makes us the sport of death, when even David grew politicly cruel, and Solomon could hardly be said to be the wisest of men. But many are too early old, and before the date of age. Adversity stretcheth our days, misery makes Alcmena's nights, and time hath no wings unto it. But the most tedious being is that which can unwish itself, content to be nothing, or never to have been, which was beyond the malcontent of Job, who cursed not the day of his life, but his nativity; content to have so far been, as to have a title to future being, although he had lived here but in an hidden state of life, and as it were an abortion.

(From *Hydriotaphia, Urn-Burial*, 1658.)

John Bunyan

Now therefore I went on in sin with great greediness of mind, still grudging that I could not be so satisfied with it as I would. This did continue with me about a month or more; but one day, as I was standing at a neighbor's shop-window, and there cursing and swearing and playing the madman, after my wonted manner, there sat within the woman of the house, and heard me, who, though she was a very loose and ungodly wench, yet protested that I swore and cursed at that most fearful rate that she was made to tremble to hear me; and told me further that I was the ungodliest fellow for swearing that ever she heard in all her life; and that I, by thus doing, was able to spoil all the youth in the whole town, if they came but in my company.

At this reproof I was silenced and put to secret shame, and that too, as I thought, before the God of heaven; wherefore, while I stood there, and hanging down my head, I wished with all my heart that I might be a little child again, that my father might learn me to speak without this wicked way of swearing; for, thought I, I am so accustomed to it that it is in vain for me to think of a reformation, for I thought it could never be.

But how it came to pass, I know not; I did from this time forward so leave my swearing that it was a great wonder to myself to observe it; and whereas before, I knew not how to speak unless I put an oath before and another behind, to make my words have authority, now I could, without it, speak better, and with more pleasantness, than ever I could before. All this while I knew not Jesus Christ, neither did I leave my sports and play.

(From *Grace Abounding to the Chief of Sinners*, 1688.)

Sir William Temple

I know very well that many, who pretend to be wise by the forms of being grave, are apt to despise both poetry and music as toys and trifles too light for the use or entertainment of serious men. But whoever find themselves wholly insensible to these charms would, I think, do well to keep their own counsel, for fear of reproaching their own temper, and bringing the goodness of their natures, if not of their understandings, into question. It may be thought at least an ill sign, if not an ill constitution, since some of the Fathers went so far as to esteem the love of music a sign of predestination, as a thing divine, and reserved for the felicities of Heaven itself. While this world lasts, I doubt not but the pleasure and request of these two entertainments will do so too; and happy those that content themselves with these or any other so easy and so innocent, and do not trouble the world or other men, because they cannot be quiet themselves, though nobody hurts them.

When all is done, human life is, at the greatest and the best, but like a froward child, that must be played with and humoured a little to keep it quiet till it falls asleep, and then the care is over.

(From "Of Poetry," 1690.)

John Dryden

'Tis a vanity common to all writers, to overvalue their own productions; and 'tis better for me to own this failing in myself, than the world to do it for me. For what other reason have I spent my life in so unprofitable a study? why am I grown old in seeking so barren a reward as fame? The same parts and application which have made me a poet might have raised me to any honours of the gown, which are often given to men of as little learning and less honesty than myself. No Government has ever been, or ever can be, wherein time-servers and blockheads will not be uppermost. The persons are only changed, but the same jugglings in State, the same hypocrisy in religion, the same self-interest and mismanagement, will remain for ever. Blood and money will be lavished in all ages, only for the preferment of new faces, with old consciences. There is too often a jaundice in the eyes of great men; they see not those whom they raise in the same colours with other men. All whom they affect look golden to them, when the gilding is only in their own distempered sight. These considerations have given me a kind of contempt for those who have risen by unworthy ways. I am not ashamed to be little, when I see them so infamously great; neither do I know why the name of poet should be dishonourable to me, if I am truly one, as I hope I am; for I will never do anything that shall dishonour it.

(From the Dedication to *Examen Poeticum*, 1693.)

Daniel Defoe

I must confess myself to have been very much dejected just before this happened; for the prodigious number that were taken sick the week or two before, besides those that died, was such, and the lamentations were so great everywhere, that a man must have seemed to have acted even against his reason if he had so much as expected to escape; and as there was hardly a house but mine in all my neighbourhood but what was infected, so had it gone on it would not have been long that there would have been any more neighbours to be infected. Indeed it is hardly credible what dreadful havoc the last three weeks had made, for if I might believe the person whose calculations I always found very well grounded, there were not less than 30,000 people dead and near 100,000 fallen sick in the three weeks I speak of; for the number that sickened was surprising; indeed it was astonishing, and those whose courage upheld them all the time before, sank under it now.

In the middle of their distress, when the condition of the City of London was so truly calamitous, just then it pleased God, as it were, by His immediate hand to disarm this enemy; the poison was taken out of the sting. It was wonderful; even the physicians themselves were surprised at it. Wherever they visited they found their patients better; either they had sweated kindly, or the tumors were broke, or the carbuncles went down, and the inflammations round them changed color, or the fever was gone, or the violent headache was assuaged, or some good symptom was in the case; so that in a few days everybody was recovering, whole families that were infected and down, that had ministers praying with them, and expected death every hour, were revived and healed, and none died at all out of them.

(From *A Journal of the Plague Year*, 1722.)

Gilbert White

Though large herds of deer do much harm to the neighbourhood, yet the injury to the morals of the people is of more moment than the loss of their crops. The temptation is irresistible; for most men are sportsmen by constitution: and there is such an inherent spirit for hunting in human nature, as scarce any inhibitions can restrain. Hence, towards the beginning of this century all this country was wild about deer-stealing. Unless he was a *hunter,* as they affected to call themselves, no young person was allowed to be possessed of manhood or gallantry. The *Waltham blacks* at length committed such enormities that government was forced to interfere with that severe and sanguinary act called the *black act,* which now comprehends more felonies than any law that ever was framed before. And, therefore, a late bishop of Winchester, when urged to re-stock Walthamchase, refused, from a motive worthy of a prelate, replying that "it had done mischief enough already."

Our old race of deer-stealers are hardly extinct yet: it was but a little while ago that, over their ale, they used to recount the exploits of their youth; such as watching the pregnant hind to her lair and, when the calf was dropped, paring its feet with a penknife to the quick to prevent its escape, till it was large and fat enough to be killed; the shooting at one of their neighbours with a bullet in a turnip-field by moonshine, mistaking him for a deer; and the losing a dog in the following extraordinary manner:—Some fellows, suspecting that a calf new-fallen was deposited in a certain spot of thick fern, went, with a lurcher, to surprise it; when the parent-hind rushed out of the brake and, taking a vast spring with all her feet close together, pitched upon the neck of the dog and broke it short in two.

(From *The Natural History of Selborne,* 1789.)

Edward Gibbon

The renewal, or perhaps the improvement, of my English life was embittered by the alteration of my own feelings. At the age of twenty-one I was, in my proper station of a youth, delivered from the yoke of education, and delighted with the comparative state of liberty and affluence. My filial obedience was natural and easy; and in the gay prospect of futurity, my ambition did not extend beyond the enjoyment of my books, my leisure, and my patrimonial estate, undisturbed by the cares of a family and the duties of a profession. But in the militia I was armed with power; in my travels, I was exempt from control; and as I approached, as I gradually passed, my thirtieth year, I began to feel the desire of being master in my own house. The most gentle authority will sometimes frown without reason, the most cheerful submission will sometimes murmur without cause; and such is the law of our imperfect nature that we must either command or obey; that our personal liberty is supported by the obsequiousness of our own dependents. While so many of my acquaintances were married or in parliament, or advancing with a rapid step in the various roads of honour and fortune, I stood alone, immovable and insignificant; for after the monthly meeting of 1770, I had even withdrawn myself from the militia, by the resignation of an empty and barren commission. My temper is not susceptible of envy, and the view of successful merit has always excited my warmest applause. The miseries of a vacant life were never known to a man whose hours were insufficient for the inexhaustible pleasures of study. But I lamented that at the proper age I had not embraced the lucrative pursuits of the law or of trade, the chances of civil office or India adventure, or even the fat slumbers of the church; and my repentance became more lively as the loss of time was more irretrievable.

(From *Memoirs of My Life and Writings*, 1796.)

Francis Jeffrey

A man who has been for twenty years at work on such matter as is now before us and who comes complacently forward with a whole quarto of it, after all the admonitions he has received, cannot reasonably be expected to "change his hand or check his pride," upon the suggestion of far weightier monitors than we can pretend to be. Inveterate habit must now have given a kind of sanctity to the errors of early taste; and the very powers of which we lament the perversion, have probably become incapable of any other application. The very quantity, too, that he has written, and is at this moment working up for publication upon the old pattern, makes it almost hopeless to look for any change of it. All this is so much capital already sunk in the concern, which must be sacrificed if that be abandoned; and no man likes to give up for lost the time and talent and labour which he has embodied in any permanent production. We were not previously aware of these obstacles to Mr. Wordsworth's conversion; and, considering the peculiarities of his former writings merely as the result of certain wanton and capricious experiments on public taste and indulgence, conceived it to be our duty to discourage their repetition by all the means in our power. We now see clearly, however, how the case stands; and, making up our minds, though with the most sincere pain and reluctance, to consider him as finally lost to the good cause of poetry, shall endeavour to be thankful for the occasional gleams of tenderness and beauty which the natural force of his imagination and affections must still shed over all his productions, and to which we shall ever turn with delight, in spite of the affectation and mysticism and prolixity, with which they are so abundantly contrasted.

(From a review, in the *Edinburgh Review,* of Wordsworth's *Excursion,* 1814.)

Samuel Taylor Coleridge

To these defects which, as appears by the extracts, are only occasional, I may oppose, with far less fear of encountering the dissent of any candid and intelligent reader, the following (for the most part correspondent) excellences. First, an austere purity of language both grammatically and logically; in short a perfect appropriateness of the words to the meaning. Of how high value I deem this, and how particularly estimable I hold the example at the present day, has been already stated: and in part, too, the reasons on which I ground both the moral and intellectual importance of habituating ourselves to a strict accuracy of expression. It is noticeable how limited an acquaintance with the masterpieces of art will suffice to form a correct and even a sensitive taste, where none but masterpieces have been seen and admired: while, on the other hand, the most correct notions, and the widest acquaintance with the works of excellence of all ages and countries, will not perfectly secure us against the contagious familiarity with the far more numerous offspring of tastelessness or of a perverted taste. If this be the case, as it notoriously is, with the arts of music and painting, much more difficult will it be to avoid the infection of multiplied and daily examples in the practice of an art which uses words, and words only, as its instruments. In poetry, in which every line, every phrase, may pass the ordeal of deliberation and deliberate choice, it is possible, and barely possible, to attain that ultimatum which I have ventured to propose as the infallible test of a blameless style— its *untranslatableness* in words of the same language without injury to the meaning. Be it observed, however, that I include in the *meaning* of a word not only its correspondent object but likewise all the associations which it recalls. For language is framed to convey not the object alone, but likewise the character, mood, and intentions of the person who is representing it.

(From *Biographia Literaria,* Ch. XXII, 1817.)

Washington Irving

The dominant spirit, however, that haunts this enchanted region and seems to be commander-in-chief of all powers of the air, is the apparition of a figure on horseback without a head. It is said by some to be the ghost of a Hessian trooper, whose head had been carried away by a cannon-ball, in some nameless battle during the revolutionary war; and who is ever and anon seen by the country folk, hurrying along in the gloom of night, as if on the wings of the wind. His haunts are not confined to the valley, but extend at times to the adjacent roads, and especially to the vicinity of a church at no great distance. Indeed, certain of the most authentic historians of those parts, who have been careful in collecting and collating the floating facts concerning this spectre, allege that the body of the trooper having been buried in the churchyard, the ghost rides forth to the scene of battle in nightly quest of his head; and that the rushing speed with which he sometimes passes along the Hollow, like a midnight blast, is owing to his being belated and in a hurry to get back to the churchyard before daybreak.

(From "The Legend of Sleepy Hollow," *The Sketch-Book*, 1819-20.)

William Hazlitt

Any one may mouth out a passage with a theatrical cadence, or get upon stilts to tell his thoughts; but to write or speak with propriety and simplicity is a more difficult task. Thus it is easy to affect a pompous style, to use a word twice as big as the thing you want to express: it is not so easy to pitch upon the very word that exactly fits it. Out of eight or ten words equally common, equally intelligible, with nearly equal pretensions, it is a matter of some nicety and discrimination to pick out the very one, the preferableness of which is scarcely perceptible, but decisive. The reason why I object to Dr. Johnson's style is that there is no discrimination, no selection, no variety in it. He uses none but "tall, opaque words," taken from the "first row of the rubric"—words with the greatest number of syllables, or Latin phrases with merely English terminations. If a fine style depended on this sort of arbitrary pretension, it would be fair to judge of an author's elegance by the measurement of his words, and the substitution of foreign circumlocutions (with no precise associations) for the mother-tongue. How simple it is to be dignified without ease, to be pompous without meaning! Surely, it is but a mechanical rule for avoiding what is low to be always pedantic and affected. It is clear you cannot use a vulgar English word, if you never use a common English word at all. A fine tact is shewn in adhering to those which are perfectly common, and yet never falling into any expressions which are debased by disgusting circumstances, or which owe their significance and point to technical or professional allusions. A truly natural or familiar style can never be quaint or vulgar, for this reason, that it is of universal force and applicability, and that quaintness and vulgarity arise out of the immediate connection of certain words with coarse and disagreeable, or with confined, ideas.

(From "On Familiar Style," 1821.)

Charles Lamb

I am by nature extremely susceptible of street affronts; the jeers and taunts of the populace; the low-bred triumph they display over the casual trip, or splashed stocking, of a gentleman. Yet can I endure the jocularity of a young sweep with something more than forgiveness. In the last winter but one, pacing along Cheapside with my accustomed precipitation when I walk westward, a treacherous slide brought me upon my back in an instant. I scrambled up with pain and shame enough—yet outwardly trying to face it down, as if nothing had happened—when the roguish grin of one of these young wits encountered me. There he stood, pointing me out with his dusky finger to the mob, and to a poor woman (I suppose his mother) in particular, till the tears for the exquisiteness of the fun (so he thought it) worked themselves out at the corners of his poor red eyes, red from many a previous weeping, and soot-inflamed, yet twinkling through all with such a joy, snatched out of desolation that Hogarth—but Hogarth has got him already (how could he miss him?) in "The March to Finchley," grinning at the pie-man—there he stood, as he stands in the picture, irremovable, as if the jest was to last for ever—with such a maximum of glee, and minimum of mischief, in his mirth—for the grin of a genuine sweep hath absolutely no malice in it—that I could have been content, if the honour of a gentleman might endure it, to have remained his butt and his mockery till midnight.

(From "The Praise of Chimney-Sweepers," 1822.)

Walter Savage Landor

Let those who look upon style as unworthy of much attention ask themselves how many, in proportion to men of genius, have excelled in it. In all languages, ancient and modern, are there ten prose-writers at once harmonious, correct, and energetic? Harmony and correctness are not uncommon separately, and force is occasionally with each; but where, excepting in Milton, where, among all the moderns, is energy to be found always in the right place? Even Cicero is defective here, and sometimes in the most elaborate of his orations. In the time of Milton it was not customary for men of abilities to address to the people at large what might inflame their passions. The appeal was made to the serious, to the well-informed, to the learned, and was made in the language of their studies. The phraseology of our Bible, on which no subsequent age has improved, was thought to carry with it solemnity and authority; and even when popular feelings were to be aroused to popular interest, the language of the prophets was preferred to the language of the vulgar. Hence, amid the complicated antagonisms of war there was more austerity than ferocity. The gentlemen who attended the court avoided the speech as they avoided the manners of their adversaries. Waller, Cowley, and South were resolved to refine what was already pure gold, and inadvertently threw into the crucible many old family jewels deeply encased within it. Eliot, Pym, Selden, and Milton reverenced their father's house and retained its right language unmodified. Lord Brougham would make us believe that scarcely a sentence in Milton is easy, natural, and vernacular. Nevertheless, in all his dissertations, there are many which might appear to have been written in our days, if indeed any writer in our days were endowed with the same might and majesty.

(From *Imaginary Conversations,* 1829.)

Thomas Carlyle

Here, too, may we not pause for an instant and make a practical reflection? Considering the multitude of mortals that handle the Pen in these days, and can mostly spell, and write without glaring violations of grammar, the question naturally arises: How is it, that no Work proceeds from them, bearing any stamp of authenticity and permanence; of worth for more than one day? Shiploads of Fashionable Novels, Sentimental Rhymes, Tragedies, Farces, Diaries of Travel, Tales by flood and field, are swallowed monthly into the bottomless Pool: still does the Press toil; innumerable Paper-makers, Compositors, Printers' Devils, Book-binders, and Hawkers grown hoarse with loud proclaiming, rest not from their labour; and still, in torrents, rushes on the great array of Publications, unpausing, to their final home; and still Oblivion, like the Grave, cries, Give! Give! How is it that of all these countless multitudes, no one can attain to the smallest mark of excellence, or produce aught that shall endure longer than "snowflake on the river," or the foam of penny-beer? We answer: Because they *are* foam; because there is no *Reality* in them. These Three Thousand men, women and children, that make up the army of British Authors, do not, if we will well consider it, *see* anything whatever; consequently *have* nothing that they can record and utter, only more or fewer things that they can plausibly pretend to record. The Universe, of Man and Nature, is still quite shut up from them; the "open secret" still utterly a secret; because no sympathy with Man or Nature, no love and free simplicity of heart has yet unfolded the same. Nothing but a pitiful Image of their own pitiful Self, with its vanities, and grudgings, and ravenous hunger of all kinds, hangs forever painted in the retina of these unfortunate persons; so that the starry ALL, with whatsoever it embraces, does but appear as some expanded magic-lantern shadow of that same Image—and naturally looks pitiful enough.

(From "Biography," *Fraser's Magazine,* April, 1832.)

Ralph Waldo Emerson

There is a time in every man's education when he arrives at the conviction that envy is ignorance; that imitation is suicide; that he must take himself for better for worse as his portion; that though the wide universe is full of good, no kernel of nourishing corn can come to him but through his toil bestowed on that plot of ground which is given to him to till. That power which resides in him is new in nature, and none but he knows what that is which he can do, nor does he know until he has tried. Not for nothing one face, one character, one fact, makes much impression on him and another none. This sculpture in the memory is not without pre-established harmony. The eye was placed where one ray should fall, that it might testify of that particular ray. We but half express ourselves, and are ashamed of that divine idea which each of us represents. It may be safely trusted as proportionate and of good issues, so it be faithfully imparted, but God will not have his work made manifest by cowards. A man is relieved and gay when he has put his heart into his work and done his best; but what he has said or done otherwise shall give him no peace. It is a deliverance which does not deliver. In the attempt his genius deserts him; no muse befriends; no invention, no hope.

Trust thyself: every heart vibrates to that iron string. Accept the place the divine providence has found for you, the society of your contemporaries, the connection of events. Great men have always done so, and confided themselves childlike to the genius of their age, betraying their perception that the absolutely trustworthy was seated at their heart, working through their hands, predominating in all their being. And we are now men, and must accept in the highest mind the same transcendent destiny; and not minors and invalids in a protected corner, not cowards fleeing before a revolution, but guides, redeemers, and benefactors, obeying the Almighty effort and advancing on Chaos and the Dark.

(From "Self-Reliance," 1841.)

Henry David Thoreau

I have paid no poll-tax for six years. I was put into a jail once on this account, for one night; and, as I stood considering the walls of solid stone, two or three feet thick, the door of wood and iron, a foot thick, and the iron grating which strained the light, I could not help being struck with the foolishness of that institution which treated me as if I were mere flesh and blood and bones, to be locked up. I wondered that it should have concluded at length that this was the best use it could put me to, and had never thought to avail itself of my services in some way. I saw that, if there was a wall of stone between me and my townsmen, there was a still more difficult one to climb or break through before they could get to be as free as I was. I did not for a moment feel confined, and the walls seemed a great waste of stone and mortar. I felt as if I alone of all my townsmen had paid my tax. They plainly did not know how to treat me, but behaved like persons who are underbred. In every threat and in every compliment there was a blunder; for they thought that my chief desire was to stand the other side of that stone wall. I could not but smile to see how industriously they locked the door on my meditations, which followed them out again without let or hindrance, and *they* were really all that was dangerous. As they could not reach me, they had resolved to punish my body; just as boys, if they cannot come at some person against whom they have a spite, will abuse his dog. I saw that the State was half-witted, that it was timid as a lone woman with her silver spoons, and that it did not know its friends from its foes, and I lost all my remaining respect for it, and pitied it.

(From *Civil Disobedience*, 1849.)

John Stuart Mill

The object of this Essay is to assert one very simple principle, as entitled to govern absolutely the dealings of society with the individual in the way of compulsion and control, whether the means used be physical force in the form of legal penalties, or the moral coercion of public opinion. That principle is that the sole end for which mankind are warranted, individually or collectively, in interfering with the liberty of action of any of their number, is self-protection. That the only purpose for which power can be rightfully exercised over any member of a civilized community, against his will, is to prevent harm to others. His own good, either physical or moral, is not a sufficient warrant. He cannot rightfully be compelled to do or forbear because it will be better for him to do so, because it will make him happier, because, in the opinions of others, to do so would be wise or even right. These are good reasons for remonstrating with him, or reasoning with him, or persuading him, or entreating him, but not for compelling him, or visiting him with any evil in case he do otherwise. To justify that, the conduct from which it is desired to deter him must be calculated to produce evil to some one else. The only part of the conduct of any one, for which he is amenable to society, is that which concerns others. In the part which merely concerns himself, his independence is, of right, absolute. Over himself, over his own body and mind, the individual is sovereign.

(From *On Liberty*, 1859.)

Abraham Lincoln

Fourscore and seven years ago our fathers brought forth on this continent a new nation, conceived in liberty and dedicated to the proposition that all men are created equal.

Now we are engaged in a great civil war, testing whether that nation, or any nation so conceived and so dedicated, can long endure. We are met on a great battle-field of that war. We have come to dedicate a portion of that field as a final resting-place for those who here gave their lives that that nation might live. It is altogether fitting and proper that we should do this.

But, in a larger sense, we cannot dedicate—we cannot consecrate—we cannot hallow—this ground. The brave men, living and dead, who struggled here, have consecrated it far above our poor power to add or detract. The world will little note nor long remember what we say here, but it can never forget what they did here. It is for us, the living, rather, to be dedicated here to the unfinished work which they who fought here have thus far so nobly advanced. It is rather for us to be here dedicated to the great task remaining before us—that from these honored dead we take increased devotion to that cause for which they gave the last full measure of devotion; that we here highly resolve that these dead shall not have died in vain; that this nation, under God, shall have a new birth of freedom; and that government of the people, by the people, for the people, shall not perish from the earth.

(From *The Gettysburg Address*, 1863.)

John Ruskin

And therefore, first of all, I tell you earnestly and authoritatively (I *know* I am right in this), you must get into the habit of looking intensely at words and assuring yourself of their meaning, syllable by syllable—nay, letter by letter. For though it is only by reason of the opposition of letters in the function of signs, to sounds in the function of signs, that the study of books is called "literature," and that a man versed in it is called, by the consent of nations, a man of letters instead of a man of books, or of words, you may yet connect with that accidental nomenclature this real fact: that you might read all the books in the British Museum (if you could live long enough) and remain an utterly "illiterate," uneducated person; but that if you read ten pages of a good book, letter by letter—that is to say, with real accuracy—you are for evermore in some measure an educated person. The entire difference between education and non-education (as regards the merely intellectual part of it) consists in this accuracy. A well-educated gentleman may not know many languages—may not be able to speak any but his own—

may have read very few books. But whatever language he knows, he knows precisely; whatever word he pronounces, he pronounces rightly; above all, he is learned in the *peerage* of words; knows the words of true descent and ancient blood, at a glance, from words of modern canaille; remembers all their ancestry, their intermarriages, distant relationships, and the extent to which they were admitted, and offices they held, among the national noblesse of words at any time and in any country. But an uneducated person may know, by memory, many languages, and talk them all, and yet truly know not a word of any—not a word even of his own.

(From "Of Kings' Treasuries," *Sesame and Lilies,* 1864.)

Walter Bagehot

History, it is said, is of no use; at least a great critic, who is understood to have in the press a very elaborate work in that kind, not long since seemed to allege that writings of this sort did not establish a theory of the universe, and were therefore of no avail. But whatever may be the use of this sort of composition in itself and abstractedly, it is certainly of great use relatively and to literary men. Consider the position of a man of that species. He sits beside a library-fire, with nice white paper, a good pen, a capital style, every means of saying everything, but nothing to say; of course he is an able man; of course he has an active intellect, beside wonderful culture; but still one cannot always have original ideas. Every day cannot be an era; a train of new speculation very often will not be found; and how dull it is to make it your business to write, to stay by yourself in a room to write, and then to have nothing to say! It is dreary work mending seven pens and waiting for a theory to "turn up." What a gain if something would happen! then one could describe it. Something has happened, and that something is history. On this account, since a sedate Greek discovered this plan for a grave immortality, a series of accomplished men have seldom been found wanting to derive a literary capital from their active and barbarous kindred. Perhaps when a Visigoth broke a head, he thought that that was all. Not so; he was making history; Gibbon has written it down.

(From "Edward Gibbon," *Literary Studies,* 1879.)

Mark Twain

Once a day a cheap, gaudy packet arrived upward from St. Louis, and another downward from Keokuk. Before these events, the day was glorious with expectancy; after them, the day was a dead and empty thing. Not only the boys, but the whole village, felt this. After all these years I can picture that old time to myself now, just as it was then: the white town drowsing in the sunshine of a summer's morning; the streets empty, or pretty nearly so; one or two clerks sitting in front of the Water Street stores, with their splint-bottomed chairs tilted back against the walls, chins on breasts, hats slouched over their faces, asleep—with shingle-shavings enough around to show what broke them down; a sow and a litter of pigs loafing along the sidewalk, doing a good business in watermelon rinds and seeds; two or three lonely little freight piles scattered about the "levee"; a pile of "skids" on the slope of the stone-paved wharf, and the fragrant town drunk-ard asleep in the shadow of them; two or three wood flats at the head of the wharf, but nobody to listen to the peaceful lapping of the wavelets against them; the great Mississippi, the majestic, the magnificent Mississippi, rolling its mile-wide tide along, shining in the sun; the dense forest away on the other side; the "point" above the town, and the "point" below, bound-ing the river-glimpse and turning it into a sort of sea, and withal a very still and brilliant and lonely one. Presently a film of dark smoke appears above one of those remote "points"; instantly a negro drayman, famous for his quick eye and prodigious voice, lifts up the cry, "S-t-e-a-m-boat a-comin'!" and the scene changes! The town drunkard stirs, the clerks wake up, a furious clatter of drays follows, every house and store pours out a human contribution, and all in a twinkling the dead town is alive and moving. Drays, carts, men, boys, all go hurrying from many quarters to a common center, the wharf. As-sembled there, the people fasten their eyes upon the coming boat as upon a wonder they are seeing for the first time.

(From *Life on the Mississippi*, 1883.)

Henry James

The house of fiction has in short not one window, but a million—a number of possible windows not to be reckoned, rather; every one of which has been pierced, or is still pierceable, in its vast front, by the need of the indi-vidual vision and by the pressure of the individual will. These apertures, of dissimilar shape and size, hang so, all together, over the human scene that we might have expected of them a greater sameness of report than we find. They are but windows at the best, mere holes in a dead wall, dis-connected, perched aloft; they are not hinged doors opening straight upon life. But they have this mark of their own that at each of them stands a figure with a pair of eyes, or at least with a field-glass, which forms, again and again, for observation, a unique instrument, insuring to the person making use of it an impression distinct from every other. He and his neighbours are watching the same show, but one seeing more where the other sees less, one seeing black where the other sees white, one seeing big where the other sees small, one seeing coarse where the other sees fine. And so on, and so on; there is fortunately no saying on what, for the particular pair of eyes, the window may *not* open; "fortunately" by reason, precisely, of this incalculability of range. The spreading field, the human scene, is the "choice of subject"; the pierced aperture, either broad or balconied or slit-like and low-browed, is the "literary form"; but they are, singly or together, as nothing without the posted presence of the watcher—without, in other words, the consciousness of the artist. Tell me what the artist is, and I will tell you of what he has *been* conscious. Thereby I shall express to you at once his boundless freedom and his "moral" reference.

(From the Preface to *The Portrait of a Lady*, 1915.)

Ernest Hemingway

Sometimes in the dark we heard the troops marching under the window and the guns going past pulled by motor-tractors. There was much traffic at night and many mules on the roads with boxes of ammunition on each side of their packsaddles and gray motor-trucks that carried men, and other trucks with loads covered with canvas that moved slower in the traffic. There were big guns too that passed in the day drawn by tractors, the long barrels of the guns covered with green branches and green leafy branches and vines laid over the tractors. To the north we could look across a valley and see a forest of chestnut trees and behind it another mountain on this side of the river. There was fighting for that mountain too, but it was not successful, and in the fall when the rains came the leaves all fell from the chestnut trees and the branches were bare and the trunks black with rain. The vineyards were thin and bare-branched too and all the country wet and brown and dead with the autumn. There were mists over the river and clouds on the mountain and the trucks splashed mud on the road and the troops were muddy and wet in their capes; their rifles were wet and under their capes the two leather cartridge-boxes on the front of the belts, gray leather boxes heavy with the packs of clips of thin, long 6.5 mm. cartridges, bulged forward under the capes so that the men, passing on the road, marched as though they were six months gone with child.

(From *A Farewell to Arms*, 1929. Reprinted by permission of Charles Scribner's Sons, New York, Jonathan Cape, Ltd., London, and the Executors of the Ernest Hemingway Estate.)

E. M. Forster

In the first place, [my wood] makes me feel heavy. Property does have this effect. Property produces men of weight, and it was a man of weight who failed to get into the Kingdom of Heaven. He was not wicked, that unfortunate millionaire in the parable, he was only stout; he stuck out in front, not to mention behind, and as he wedged himself this way and that in the crystalline entrance and bruised his well-fed flanks, he saw beneath him a comparatively slim camel passing through the eye of a needle and being woven into the robe of God. The Gospels all through couple stoutness and slowness. They point out what is perfectly obvious, yet seldom realized: that if you have a lot of things you cannot move about a lot, that furniture requires dusting, dusters require servants, servants require insurance stamps, and the whole tangle of them makes you think twice before you accept an invitation to dinner or go for a bathe in the Jordan. Sometimes the Gospels proceed further and say with Tolstoy that property is sinful; they approach the difficult ground of asceticism here, where I cannot follow them. But as to the immediate effects of property on people, they just show straight-forward logic. It produces men of weight. Men of weight cannot, by definition, move like the lightning from the East unto the West, and the ascent of a fourteen-stone bishop into a pulpit is thus the exact antithesis of the coming of the Son of Man. My wood makes me feel heavy.

(From "My Wood," *Abinger Harvest,* 1936. Reprinted by permission of Harcourt, Brace & World, Inc., New York, and Edward Arnold Ltd., London.)

D. H. Lawrence

We have our very individuality in relationship. Let us swallow this important and prickly fact. Apart from our connections with other people, we are barely individuals, we amount, all of us, to next to nothing. It is in the living touch between us and other people, other lives, other phenomena that we move and have our being. Strip us of our human contacts and of our contact with the living earth and the sun, and we are almost bladders of emptiness. Our individuality means nothing. A skylark that was alone on an island would be songless and meaningless, his individuality gone, running about like a mouse in the grass. But if there were one female with him, it would lift him singing into the air, and restore him his real individuality.

And so with men and women. It is in relationship to one another that they have their true individuality and their distinct being: in contact, not out of contact. This is sex, if you like. But it is no more sex than sunshine on the grass is sex. It is a living contact, give and take: the great and subtle relationship of men and women, man and woman. In this and through this we become real individuals, without it, without the real contact, we remain more or less nonentities.

(From *Phoenix: The Posthumous Papers,* 1936. Reprinted by permission of The Viking Press, Inc., New York, and A. Watkins, Inc., New York.)

James Agee

I must excuse myself this apparent digression because you of whom I write are added to the meaning of this song, and its meaning to yours: for here, here, in this time; on this vast continental sorrowful clay it is I see you, encamped, imprisoned, each in your pitiably decorated little unowned ship of home, ten million, patient, ignorant, grievous, ruined, so inextricably trapped, captured, guarded; in the patience of your lives; and though you cannot know it you like these prisoners are constantly waiting; and though you cannot hear it yet like them you do hear; how on the stone of this planet there is a marching and resonance of rescuing feet which shall at length all dangers braved, all armies cut through, past, deliver you freedom, joy, health, knowledge like an enduring sunlight: and not to you alone, whose helpless hearts have been waiting and listening since the human world began, but to us all, those lovable and those hateful all alike. And whether this shall descend upon us over the steep north crown I shall not know, but doubt: and after how many false deliverances there can be no hopeful imagining: but that it shall come at length there can be no question: for this I know in my own soul through that regard of love we bear one another: for there it was proved me in the meeting of the extremes of the race.

(From *Let Us Now Praise Famous Men,* 1939. Reprinted by permission of Houghton Mifflin Company, Boston.)

William Faulkner

This time the bear didn't strike him down. It caught the dog in both arms, almost loverlike, and they both went down. He was off the mule now. He drew back both hammers of the gun but he could see nothing but moiling spotted houndbodies until the bear surged up again. Boon was yelling something, he could not tell what; he could see Lion still clinging to the bear's throat and he saw the bear, half erect, strike one of the hounds with one paw and hurl it five or six feet and then, rising and rising as though it would never stop, stand erect again and begin to rake at Lion's belly with its forepaws. Then Boon was running. The boy saw the gleam of the blade in his hand and watched him leap among the hounds, hurdling them, kicking them aside as he ran, and fling himself astride the bear as he had hurled himself onto the mule, his legs locked around the bear's belly, his left arm under the bear's throat where Lion clung, and the glint of the knife as it rose and fell.

It fell just once. For an instant they almost resembled a piece of statuary: the clinging dog, the bear, the man astride its back, working and probing the buried blade. Then they went down, pulled over backward by Boon's weight, Boon underneath. It was the bear's back which reappeared first but at once Boon was astride it again. He had never released the knife and again the boy saw the almost infinitesimal movement of his arm and shoulder as he probed and sought; then the bear surged erect, raising with it the man and the dog too, and turned and still carrying the man and the dog it took two or three steps toward the woods on its hind feet as a man would have walked and crashed down. It didn't collapse, crumple. It fell all of a piece, as a tree falls, so that all three of them, man dog and bear, seemed to bounce once.

James Baldwin

Negroes want to be treated like men: a perfectly straightforward statement, containing only seven words. People who have mastered Kant, Hegel, Shakespeare, Marx, Freud, and the Bible find this statement utterly impenetrable. The idea seems to threaten profound, barely conscious assumptions. A kind of panic paralyzes their features, as though they found themselves trapped on the edge of a steep place. I once tried to describe to a very well-known American intellectual the conditions among Negroes in the South. My recital disturbed him and made him indignant; and he asked me in perfect innocence, "Why don't all the Negroes in the South move North?" I tried to explain what *has* happened, unfailingly, whenever a significant body of Negroes move North. They do not escape Jim Crow: they merely encounter another, not-less-deadly variety. They do not move to Chicago, they move to the South Side; they do not move to New York, they move to Harlem. The pressure within the ghetto causes the ghetto walls to expand, and this expansion is always violent. White people hold the line as long as they can, and in as many ways as they can, from verbal intimidation to physical violence. But inevitably the border which has divided the ghetto from the rest of the world falls back bitterly before the black horde; the landlords make a tidy profit by raising the rent, chopping up the rooms, and all but dispensing with the upkeep; and what has once been a neighborhood turns into a "turf." This is precisely what happened when the Puerto Ricans arrived in their thousands—and the bitterness thus caused is, as I write, being fought out all up and down those streets.

Susan Sontag

This is why so many of the objects prized by Camp taste are old-fashioned, out-of-date, *démodé*. It's not a love of the old as such. It's simply that the process of aging or deterioration provides the necessary detachment—or arouses a necessary sympathy. When the theme is important, and contemporary, the failure of a work of art may make us indignant. Time can change that. Time liberates the work of art from moral relevance, delivering it over to the Camp sensibility. . . . Another effect: time contracts the sphere of banality. (Banality is, strictly speaking, always a category of the contemporary.) What was banal can, with the passage of time, become fantastic. Many people who listen with delight to the style of Rudy Vallee revived by the English pop group The Temperance Seven, would have been driven up the wall by Rudy Vallee in his heyday.

   Thus, things are campy, not when they become old—but when we become less involved in them, and can enjoy, instead of be frustrated by, the failure of the attempt. But the effect of time is unpredictable. Maybe "Method" Acting (James Dean, Rod Steiger, Warren Beatty) will seem as Camp some day as Ruby Keeler's does now—or as Sarah Bernhardt's does in the films she made at the end of her career. And maybe not.

Tom Wolfe

The first good look I had at customized cars was at an event called a "Teen Fair," held in Burbank, a suburb of Los Angeles beyond Hollywood. This was a wild place to be taking a look at art objects—eventually, I should say, you have to reach the conclusion that these customized cars *are* art objects, at least if you use the standards applied in a civilized society. But I will get to that in a moment. Anyway, about noon you drive up to a place that looks like an outdoor amusement park, and there are three serious-looking kids, like the cafeteria committee in high school, taking tickets, but the scene inside is quite mad. Inside, two things hit you. The first is a huge platform a good seven feet off the ground with a hully-gully band—everything is electrified, the bass, the guitars, the saxophones—and then behind the band, on the platform, about two hundred kids are doing fantastic dances called the hully-gully, the bird, and the shampoo. As I said, it's noontime. The dances the kids are doing are very jerky. The boys and girls don't touch, not even with their hands. They just ricochet around. Then you notice that all the girls are dressed exactly alike. They have bouffant hairdos—all of them—and slacks that are, well, skin-tight does not get the idea across; it's more the conformation than how tight the slacks are. It's as if some lecherous old tailor with a gluteous-maximus fixation designed them, striation by striation. About the time you've managed to focus on this, you notice that out in the middle of the park is a huge, perfectly round swimming pool; really rather enormous. And there is a Chris-Craft cabin cruiser in the pool, going around and around, sending up big waves, with more of these bouffant babies bunched in the back of it. In the water, suspended like plankton, are kids in Skuba-diving outfits; others are tooling around underwater, breathing through a snorkel. And all over the place are booths, put up by shoe companies and guitar companies and God knows who else, and there are kids dancing in all of them—dancing the bird, the hully-gully, and the shampoo —with the music of the hully-gully band piped all over the park through loudspeakers.

James Dickey

(*The man described in these paragraphs has just been shot through the breast with an arrow*)

I got up with the gun and the power, wrapping the string around my right hand. I swung the barrel back and forth to cover everything, the woods and the world. There was nothing in the clearing but Bobby and the shot man and me. Bobby was still on the ground, though now he was lifting his head. I could understand that much, but something kept blurring the clear idea of Bobby and myself and the leaves and the river. The shot man was still standing. He wouldn't concentrate in my vision; I couldn't believe him. He was like a film over the scene, gray and vague, with the force gone out of him; I was amazed at how he did everything. He touched the arrow experimentally, and I could tell that it was set in him as solidly as his breastbone. It was in him tight and unwobbling, coming out front and back. He took hold of it with both hands, but compared to the arrow's strength his hands were weak; they weakened more as I looked, and began to melt. He was on his knees, and then fell to his side, pulling his legs up. He rolled back and forth like a man with the wind knocked out of him, all the time making a bubbling, gritting sound. His lips turned red, but from his convulsions—in which there was something comical and unspeakable—he seemed to gain strength. He got up on one knee and then to his feet again while I stood with the shotgun at port arms. He took a couple of strides toward the woods and then seemed to change his mind and danced back to me, lurching and clog-stepping in a secret circle. He held out a hand to me, like a prophet, and I pointed the shotgun straight at the head of the arrow, ice coming into my teeth. I was ready to put it all behind me with one act, with one pull of a string.

But there was no need. He crouched and fell forward with his face on my white tennis shoe tops, trembled away into his legs and shook down to stillness. He opened his mouth and it was full of blood like an apple. A clear bubble formed on his lips and stayed there.

From *Deliverance* by James Dickey. Copyright © 1967 by James Dickey. Reprinted by permission of Houghton Mifflin Company.

Imitating Sentence Patterns

After the student has spent some time merely copying passages, he might attempt another kind of imitation. He can take individual sentences as patterns on which to devise sentences of his own. This is a more difficult exercise than the verbatim copying, but it pays high dividends to the student who uses it conscientiously.

How closely should the student follow the model? As closely as he cares to, is the most sensible answer. But he will find this exercise most fruitful if he will observe at least the same *kind, number,* and *order* of clauses and phrases. If the model sentence has an adverb clause, he should write an adverb clause. If the model sentence is introduced by a participial phrase, he should put a participial phrase in the lead-off position. If the model sentence has three noun clauses arranged in parallel structure, he should write a sentence containing three noun clauses in a similar structure.

The aim of this exercise is not to achieve a word-for-word correspondence with the model but rather to achieve an awareness of the variety of sentence structures of which the English language is capable. The reason why many students never venture outside their puerile, monotonous sentence structure is that they have never attempted sophisticated sentence patterns. Writing such patterns according to models will increase the student's syntactical resources. And with more resources at his command, he will acquire more confidence in his writing ability.

No one, of course, says to himself while he is writing, "I just wrote a compound sentence interspersed with gerund phrases. This time I think I'll begin my sentence with an adverb clause and use a series of noun clauses as the object of the main verb." Such a self-conscious approach to writing would undoubtedly result in some monstrous prose.

No, our prose must come as naturally as—to use Keats's words—"the leaves to the trees." The kind of prose we write cannot be arbitrary; it is governed by the subject matter, the occasion, the purpose, the audience, and the personality of the writer. If it is true that matter and form are intimately related, then there must be one best way in which to say a particular thing for a given audience and purpose. But as a practical matter, what we manage to achieve most of the time is one of a number of *better* ways to say something. Coleridge once said that the infallible test of a perfect style was "its *untranslatableness* in words of the same language without injury to the meaning." Only seldom, perhaps, do we achieve this kind of "inevitable prose." What we achieve most of the time is, at best, an adequate prose.

A great deal of the writing the student may be called upon to do in the future will be impromptu, spur-of-the-moment writing. While he is still in school, he will have to write essay-type examinations, where he has little time for reflection and almost no time for revision. In his job someday, he will have to dash off memos, directives, and letters. As a private citizen, he will have to scribble off notes to send to school with his children, pen a hurried letter to his parents, pound out a letter to the editor of the local newspaper. The more practice he has had in writing, the better will be this one-draft prose.

But he may also be called upon at times to do some writing that entails a great deal of reflection, research, organization, and revision. He may have to write a report to be read to the board of governors or prepare a speech to be delivered before the Chamber of Commerce. It is this kind of deliberate writing that will call upon all the inventive and stylistic resources at his command. This will necessarily be slow writing, but it does not have to be labored writing for being slow. Someone once said that "hard writing makes for easy reading." And Quintilian once said, "Write quickly and you will never write well; write well and you will soon write quickly."

So with these cautions and objectives in mind, let the student now try his hand at imitating the sentence patterns of practiced writers. The student may never in his life have occasion to write a sentence like some of those that he has mechanically imitated in this exercise, but he will be none the worse for having gone through the paces.

As examples of how to imitate sentence patterns, a few samples of the method are printed below. For models, the student can select sentences from his favorite authors, or he can use sentences from the specimen passages reproduced in this chapter.

Sample Imitations

MODEL SENTENCE: The gallows stood in a small yard, separate from the main grounds of the prison and overgrown with tall prickly weeds.— George Orwell, *Burmese Days*

IMITATION: The dog shivered in the background, wet from nosing his way through the early-morning grasses and covered with damp cockle-spurs.

(Write a sentence according to the pattern of the model sentence.)

MODEL SENTENCE: He went through the narrow alley of Temple Bar quickly, muttering to himself that they could all go to hell because he was going to have a good night of it.—James Joyce, "Counterparts"

IMITATION: They stood outside on the wet pavement of the terrace, pretending that they had not heard us when we called to them from the library.

MODEL SENTENCE: To regain the stage in its own character, not as a mere emulation of prose, poetry must find its own poetic way to the mastery the stage demands—the mastery of action. Archibald MacLeish, "The Poet as Playwright"

IMITATION: To discover our own natures, not the personalities imposed on us by others, we must honestly assess the values we cherish—in short, our "philosophy of life."

MODEL SENTENCE: If one must worship a bully, it is better that he should be a policeman than a gangster.—George Orwell, "Raffles and Miss Blandish"

IMITATION: Since he continued to be belligerent, it was plain that cajoling would prove more effective than scolding.

MODEL SENTENCE: I went to the woods because I wished to live deliberately, to front only the essential facts of life, and see if I could learn what it had to teach, and not, when I came to die, discover that I had not lived.—Henry David Thoreau, *Walden*

IMITATION: I greeted him politely, although I planned to challenge him repeatedly, to assess his erudition, to test whether he could discriminate what was expedient in each situation, and, after I had probed him thoroughly, to announce that we had no place for him in our organization.

MODEL SENTENCE: To have even a portion of this illuminated reason and true philosophy is the highest state to which nature can aspire, in the way of intellect.—John Henry Newman, *The Idea of a University*

IMITATION: To win a measure of his affection and esteem was the most difficult task that I had ever assigned myself.

MODEL SENTENCE: As most of these old Custom House officers had good traits and as my position in reference to them, being paternal and protective, was favorable to the growth of friendly sentiments, I soon grew to like them all.—Nathaniel Hawthorne, *Scarlet Letter*

IMITATION: When he offered me the gift and when his classmates, perceiving his embarrassment, discreetly withheld their applause, I gratefully accepted his gesture of friendship.

MODEL SENTENCE: The real art that dealt with life directly was that of the first men who told their stories round the savage camp-fire.—Robert Louis Stevenson, "A Humble Remonstrance"

IMITATION: The man who insists on perfection in others is the man who is most tolerant of imperfection in himself.

MODEL SENTENCE: The most important Indian grouping on the continent, north of Mexico, from the very beginning of European conquest on through and after the American Revolution was the Confederacy of the Iroquois.—John Collier, *Indians of the Americas*

IMITATION: The foremost alliance in Europe, amenable to expansion, during the eighteenth century and again after the collapse of the three-nation concordat, was the pact among the Big Four.

MODEL SENTENCE: This brings us to that growing army of "publicity men" and women who sometimes do not—but frequently do—give the best of their years and their vitality to pushing causes in which they have no faith and to becoming personalities whom privately they designate as stuffed shirts.—Stuart Chase, "The Luxury of Integrity"

IMITATION: He presented a startling conglomeration of statistics and testimonies that confirmed—or allegedly confirmed—the general's capacity for subverting causes of which he was suspicious and toward minimizing faults that he considered "politically innocent."

Another exercise that can be worked off this concentration on a single sentence is to vary the pattern of the model sentence or to devise an alternate way of expressing it. At the beginning of this section on imitation, we mentioned the 150 variations that Erasmus worked off a single Latin sentence. Besides making the student aware that style is the result of choices that a writer makes from among the available lexical and syntactical resources, such an exercise forces the student to discover the options that are available to him. Varying the sentence pattern usually calls for nothing more than a reordering of the words in the original sentence. Devising an alternate expression, however, often involves the choice of different words and different syntactical structures. Let us take the first three model sentences that we worked with earlier and show how they might be varied and altered.

MODEL SENTENCE: The gallows stood in a small yard, separate from the main grounds and overgrown with tall prickly weeds.—George Orwell, *Burmese Days*

VARIATION OF THE PATTERN: In a small yard, separate from the main grounds and overgrown with tall prickly weeds, stood the gallows.

ALTERNATE EXPRESSIONS: Located in a small yard, which was overgrown with tall prickly weeds, the gallows was separated from the main grounds.

The gallows was situated outside the main grounds, in a small yard that was overgrown with tall prickly weeds.

(Transformational grammar can be a help in suggesting alternate ways of phrasing a sentence. Reducing the model sentence to its "kernel sentences" can reveal how the "deep structure" was transformed into the "surface structure" that the author actually wrote. These are some of the "kernel sentences" of Orwell's sentence:

> The gallows stood in a yard.
> The yard was small.
> The yard was separate from the main grounds.
> Or: The gallows was separate from the main grounds.
> The yard was overgrown with weeds.
> Or: The gallows was overgrown with weeds.
> The weeds were tall.
> The weeds were prickly.

There is some ambiguity of structure in the Orwell sentence, because the two adjectival phrases "separate from . . ." and "overgrown with . . ." could modify *gallows* or *yard*. By reducing the original sentence to its kernels, however, the student can see how Orwell transformed them into different grammatical combinations and can see what other combinations are possible.)

MODEL SENTENCE: He went through the narrow alley of Temple Bar quickly, muttering to himself that they could all go to hell because he was going to have a good night of it.—James Joyce, "Counterparts"

VARIATION OF THE PATTERN: Muttering to himself that they could all go to hell because he was going to have a good night of it, he went quickly through the narrow alley of Temple Bar.

ALTERNATE EXPRESSIONS: As he went quickly through the narrow alley of Temple Bar, he muttered to himself that they could all go to hell, for he was going to have a good night of it.

"You can all go to hell," he muttered to himself as he went quickly through the narrow alley of Temple Bar. "I am going to have a good night of it."

MODEL SENTENCE: To regain the stage in its own character, not as a mere emulation of prose, poetry must find its own poetic way to the mastery the stage demands—the mastery of action.—Archibald Mac-Leish, "The Poet as Playwright"

VARIATION OF THE PATTERN: Poetry must find its own poetic way to the mastery the stage demands—the mastery of action—if it is to regain the stage in its own character, not as a mere emulator of prose.

ALTERNATE EXPRESSIONS: Poetry can regain the stage in its own character, not as a mere emulator of prose, only if it can master the kind of action that the stage peculiarly demands.

If poetry is to regain the stage in its own character, it must master the kind of action that the stage peculiarly demands; otherwise it will remain a mere emulator of prose.

All of these exercises in imitation—copying passages, writing original sentences according to pattern, varying the pattern of a model sentence, and devising alternate expressions for the same thought—can teach the student a number of valuable lessons: (1) they can make him aware of the variety of lexical and syntactical resources which his language offers; (2) they can afford him practice in choosing apt words and collocating them in various ways; (3) they can teach him that not every variation is equally clear, graceful, or appropriate; (4) they can teach him that variation of the pattern of the sentence often results in a different *effect* and that an alternate expression often results in a different *meaning*. The ultimate goal of all imitation exercises, however, is eventually to cut the student loose from his models, equipped with the competence and resources to go it on his own.

Readings

Hugh Blair: Critical Examination of the Style of Mr. Addison in No. 411 of "The Spectator" *

In 1759, Dr. Hugh Blair began teaching rhetoric at the University of Edinburgh, and in 1762, he was appointed the first Regius Professor of Rhetoric and Belles Lettres at Edinburgh. In 1783, upon his retirement from this post, Blair published the forty-seven lectures on rhetoric and literature that he had presented for twenty-four years to packed classrooms. This text Lectures on Rhetoric and Belles Lettres *became a widely used book in the English and American schools in the late eighteenth and early nineteenth century.*

* Lecture XX of Blair's *Lectures on Rhetoric and Belles Lettres,* first published in 1783.

Midway in the course of lectures Blair presented detailed stylistic analyses of four of Addison's Spectator *essays (Nos. 411–14) and an analysis of Jonathan Swift's "A Proposal for Correcting, Improving, and Ascertaining the English Tongue." These analyses represent one of the few instances in English of a stylistic analysis of an entire essay.*

Blair comments on points of grammar, usage, and style in Addison's essays. From the reprinting of Blair's first analysis, the student will learn one technique of analyzing, pointedly and concretely, English prose sentences and may become more conscious of his own prose style. Some of Blair's strictures on Addison's style, such as his views on the relative pronouns which *and* that, *are delivered from the standpoint of eighteenth-century usage. And while some of Blair's comments may strike a modern audience as being somewhat captious, most students will find Blair's criticism judicious. In almost every case where Blair has rewritten Addison's sentences, the student will remark an improvement in the neatness and clarity of the prose.*

Occasionally, Blair's style of punctuation has been silently changed.

I have insisted fully on the subject of language and style, both because it is, in itself, of great importance and because it is more capable of being ascertained by precise rule, than several other parts of composition. A critical analysis of the style of some good author will tend further to illustrate the subject, as it will suggest observations which I have not had occasion to make and will show, in the most practical light, the use of those which I have made.

Mr. Addison is the author whom I have chosen for this purpose. *The Spectator,* of which his papers are the chief ornament, is a book which is in the hands of every one and which cannot be praised too highly. The good sense and good writing, the useful morality and the admirable vein of humour which abound in it, render it one of those standard books which have done the greatest honour to the English nation. I have formerly given the general character of Mr. Addison's style and manner as natural and unaffected, easy and polite, and full of those graces which a flowery imagination diffuses over writing. At the same time, though one of the most beautiful writers in the language, he is not the most correct; a circumstance which renders his composition the more proper to be the subject of our present criticism. The free and flowing manner of this amiable writer sometimes led him into inaccuracies which the more studied circumspection and care of far inferior writers have taught them to avoid. Remarking his beauties, therefore, which I shall have frequent occasion to do, as I proceed, I must also point out his negligences and defects. Without a free, impartial discussion, of both the faults and beauties which occur in his composition, it is evident this piece of criticism would be of no service; and from the freedom which I use in criticising Mr. Addison's style, none can imagine that I mean to depreciate his writings, after having repeatedly declared the high opinion which I entertain of them. The beauties of this author are so many and the general character of his style is so elegant and estimable that the minute imperfections I shall have occasion to point out are but like those spots in the sun, which may be discovered by the assistance of art but which have no effect in obscuring its lustre. It is, indeed, my judgment that what Quintilian applies to Cicero, *"Ille se profecisse sciat, cui Cicero valde placebit,"* may, with justice, be applied to Mr. Addison: that to be highly pleased with his manner of writing is the criterion of one's having acquired a good taste in English style. The paper on which we are now to enter is No. 411, the first of his celebrated Essays on the Pleasures of the Imagination in the sixth volume of *The Spectator*. It begins thus:

(1) Our sight is the most perfect and most delightful of all our senses.

This is an excellent introductory sentence. It is clear, precise, and simple. The author lays down, in a few plain words, the proposition which he is going to illustrate throughout the rest of the paragraph. In this manner, we should always set out. A first sentence should seldom be a long, and never an intricate, one.

He might have said, *"Our sight is the most perfect and the most delightful."* But he has judged better in omitting to repeat the article *the*. For the repetition of it is proper, chiefly when we intend to point out the objects of which we speak, as distinguished from, or contrasted with, each other; and when we want that the reader's attention should rest on that distinction. For instance, had Mr. Addison intended to say that our sight is at once the most *delightful* and the most *useful* of all our senses, the article might then have been repeated with propriety, as a clear and strong distinction would have been conveyed. But as between *perfect* and *delightful* there is less contrast, there was no occasion for such repetition. It would have had no other effect but to add a word unnecessarily to the sentence. He proceeds:

(2) It fills the mind with the largest variety of ideas, converses with its objects at the greatest distance, and continues the longest in action, without being tired or satiated with its proper enjoyments.

This sentence deserves attention, as remarkably harmonious and well constructed. It possesses, indeed, almost all the properties of a perfect sentence. It is entirely perspicuous. It is loaded with no superfluous or unnecessary words. For *tired or satiated* towards the end of the sentence are not used for synonymous terms. They convey distinct ideas and refer to different members of the period: that this sense *continues the longest in action without being tired,* that is, without being fatigued with its action; and also, without being *satiated with its proper enjoyments.* That quality of a good sentence which I termed its unity is here perfectly preserved. It is *our sight* of which he speaks. This is the object carried through the sentence and presented to us, in every member of it, by those verbs, *fills, converses, continues,* to each of which it is clearly the nominative. Those capital words are disposed of in the most proper places; and that uniformity is maintained in the construction of the sentence which suits the unity of the object.

Observe, too, the music of the period; consisting of three members, each of which, agreeable to a rule I formerly mentioned, grows and rises above the other in sound, till the sentence is conducted, at last, to one of the most melodious closes which our language admits—*without being tired or satiated with its proper enjoyments. Enjoyments* is a word of length and dignity, exceedingly proper for a close which is designed to be a musical one. The harmony is the more happy, as this disposition of the members of the period which suits the sound so well is no less just and proper with respect to the sense. It follows the order of nature. First, we have the variety of objects mentioned, which sight furnishes to the mind; next, we have the action of sight on those objects; and lastly, we have the time and continuance of its action. No order could be more natural and happy.

This sentence has still another beauty. It is figurative, without being too much so for the subject. A metaphor runs through it. The sense of sight is, in some degree, personified. We are told of its *conversing* with its objects; and of its not being *tired or satiated* with its *enjoyments;* all which expressions are plain allusions to the actions and feelings of men. This is that slight sort of personification which, without any appearance of boldness and without elevating the fancy much above its ordinary state, renders discourse picturesque and leads us to conceive the author's meaning more distinctly, by clothing abstract ideas, in some degree, with sensible colours. Mr. Addison abounds with this beauty of style beyond most authors; and the sentence which we have been considering is very expressive of his manner of writing. There is no blemish in it whatever, unless that a strict critic might perhaps object that the epithet *large,* which he applies to *variety—the largest variety of ideas*—is an epithet more commonly applied to extent than to number. It is plain that he here employed it to avoid the repetition of the word *great,* which occurs immediately afterwards.

(3) The sense of feeling can, indeed, give us a notion of extension, shape, and all other ideas that enter at the eye, except colours; but, at the same time, it is very much straitened and confined in its operations to the number, bulk, and distance of its particular objects.

This sentence is by no means so happy as the former. It is, indeed, neither clear nor elegant. *Extension* and *shape* can, with no propriety, be called *ideas;* they are properties of matter. Neither is it accurate, even according to Mr. Locke's philosophy (with which our author seems here to have puzzled himself), to speak of any sense *giving us a notion of ideas;* our senses give us the ideas themselves. The meaning would have been much more clear if the author had expressed himself thus: "The sense of feeling can, indeed, give us the idea of extension, figure, and all the other properties of matter which are perceived by the eye, except colours."

The latter part of the sentence is still more embarrassed. For what meaning can we make of the sense of feeling being *confined in its operation to the number, bulk, and distance, of its particular objects?* Surely, every sense is confined, as much as the sense of feeling, to the number, bulk, and distance of its own objects. Sight and feeling are, in this respect, perfectly on a level; neither of them can extend beyond its own objects. The turn of expression is so inaccurate here that one would be apt to suspect two words to have been omitted in the printing, which were originally in Mr. Addison's manuscript, because the insertion of them would render the sense much more intelligible and clear. These two words are *with regard—it is very much straitened and confined in its operations, with regard to the number, bulk, and distance of its particular objects.* The meaning then would be that feeling is more limited than sight *in this respect*—that it is confined to a narrower circle, to a smaller number of objects.

The epithet *particular,* applied to *objects,* in the conclusion of the sentence, is redundant and conveys no meaning whatever. Mr. Addison seems to have used it in place of *peculiar,* as indeed he does often in other passages of his writings. But *particular* and *peculiar,* though they are too often confounded, are words of different import from each other. *Particular* stands opposed to *general; peculiar* stands opposed to what is possessed in *common with others. Particular* expresses what, in the logical style, is called *species; peculiar,* what is called *differentia. Its peculiar objects* would have signified, in this place, the objects of the sense of feeling, as distinguished from the objects of any other sense and would have had more meaning than *its particular objects,* though, in truth, neither the one nor the other epithet was requisite. It was sufficient to have said simply, *its objects.*

(4) Our sight seems designed to supply all these defects, and may be considered as a more delicate and diffusive kind of touch, that spreads

itself over an infinite multitude of bodies, comprehends the largest figures, and brings into our reach some of the most remote parts of the universe.

Here again the author's style returns upon us in all its beauty. This is a sentence distinct, graceful, well arranged, and highly musical. In the latter part of it, it is constructed with three members, which are formed much in the same manner with those of the second sentence, on which I bestowed so much praise. The construction is so similar that if it had followed immediately after it, we should have been sensible of a faulty monotony. But the interposition of another sentence between them prevents this effect.

> (5) It is this sense which furnishes the imagination with its ideas; so that by the pleasures of the imagination or fancy (which I shall use promiscuously) I here mean such as arise from visible objects, either when we have them actually in our view or when we call up their ideas into our minds by paintings, statues, descriptions, or any the like occasion.

In place of, *It is this sense which furnishes,* the author might have said more shortly, *This sense furnishes.* But the mode of expression which he has used is here more proper. This sort of full and ample assertion, *it is this which,* is fit to be used when a proposition of importance is laid down to which we seek to call the reader's attention. It is like pointing with the hand at the object of which we speak. The parenthesis in the middle of the sentence, *which I shall use promiscuously,* is not clear. He ought to have said, *terms which I shall use promiscuously;* as the verb *use* relates not to the pleasures of the imagination but to the terms of fancy and imagination, which he was to employ as synonymous. *Any the like occasion.* To call a painting or a statue *an occasion* is not a happy expression, nor is it very proper to speak of *calling up ideas by occasions.* The common phrase, *any such means,* would have been more natural.

> (6) We cannot indeed have a single image in the fancy that did not make its first entrance through the sight; but we have the power of retaining, altering, and compounding those images which we have once received into all the varieties of picture and vision that are most agreeable to the imagination; for, by this faculty, a man in a dungeon is capable of entertaining himself with scenes and landscapes more beautiful than any that can be found in the whole compass of nature.

It may be of use to remark that in one member of this sentence, there is an inaccuracy in syntax. It is very proper to say, *altering and compounding those images which we have once received into all the varieties of picture and vision.* But we can with no propriety say, *retaining them into all the varieties;* and yet, according to the manner in which the words are ranged, this construction is unavoidable. For *retaining, altering,* and *compounding* are participles, each of which equally refers to, and governs, the subsequent noun, *those images;* and that noun again is necessarily connected with the following preposition, *into.* This instance shows the importance of carefully attending to the rules of grammar and syntax; when so pure a writer as Mr. Addison could, through inadvertence, be guilty of such an error. The construction might easily have been rectified by disjoining the participle *retaining* from the other two participles in this way: "We have the power of retaining, altering, and compounding those images which we have once received and of forming them into all the varieties of picture and vision." The latter part of the sentence is clear and elegant.

> (7) There are few words in the English language which are employed in a more loose and uncircumscribed sense than those of the fancy and the imagination.

There are few words—which are employed. It had been better if our author here had said more simply, *few words in the English language are employed.* Mr. Addison, whose style is of the free and full, rather than the nervous, kind, deals, on all occasions, in this extended sort of phraseology. But it is proper only when some assertion of consequence is advanced, and which can bear an emphasis, such as that in the first sentence of the former paragraph. On other occasions, these little words, *it is,* and *there are,* ought to be avoided as redundant and enfeebling. *Those of the fancy and the imagination.* The article ought to have been omitted here. As he does not mean the powers of *the fancy and the imagination* but the words only, the article certainly had no proper place; neither, indeed, was there any occasion for the other two words, *those of.* Better if the sentence had run thus: "Few words in the English language are employed in a more loose and uncircumscribed sense than fancy and imagination."

> (8) I therefore thought it necessary to fix and determine the notion of these two words, as I intend to make use of them in the thread of my following speculations, that the reader may conceive rightly what is the subject which I proceed upon.

Though *fix* and *determine* may appear synonymous words, yet a difference between them may be remarked, and they may be viewed, as applied here, with peculiar delicacy. The author had just said that the words of which he is speaking were *loose* and *uncircumscribed.* *Fix* relates to the first of these, *determine* to the last. We *fix* what is *loose;* that is, we confine the word to its proper place that it may not fluctuate in our imagination and pass from one idea to another; and we *determine* what is *uncircumscribed;* that is, we ascertain its *termini* or limits, we draw the circle round it that we may see its boundaries. For we cannot conceive the meaning of a word, or indeed of any other thing, clearly, till we see its limits and know how far it extends. These two words, therefore, have grace and beauty as they are here applied, though a writer more frugal of words than Mr. Addison would have preferred the single word *ascertain,* which conveys, without any metaphor, the import of them both.

The *notion of these words* is somewhat of a harsh phrase, at least not so commonly used as the *meaning of these words. As I intend to make use of them in the thread of my speculations.* This is plainly faulty. A sort of metaphor is improperly mixed with words in the literal sense. He might very well have said, *as I intend to make use of them in my following speculations.* This was plain language; but if he chose to borrow an allusion from *thread,* that allusion ought to have been supported; for there is no consistency in *making use of them in the thread of speculations;* and indeed, in expressing anything so simple and familiar as this is, plain language is always to be preferred to metaphorical. *The subject which I proceed upon* is an ungraceful close of a sentence; better, *the subject upon which I proceed.*

> (9) I must therefore desire him to remember that, by the pleasures of the imagination, I mean only such pleasures as arise originally from sight, and that I divide these pleasures into two kinds.

As the last sentence began with, *I therefore thought it necessary to fix,* it is careless to begin this sentence in a manner so very similar, *I must therefore desire him to remember*—especially as the small variation of using, *on this account* or *for this reason,* in place of *therefore* would have amended the style. When he says, *I mean only such pleasures,* it may be remarked that the adverb *only* is not in its proper place. It is not intended here to qualify the word *mean* but *such pleasures,* and therefore should have been placed in as close a connexion as possible with the word which it limits or qualifies. The style becomes more clear and neat when the words are arranged thus: "By the pleasures of the imagination, I mean such pleasures only as arise from sight."

> (10) My design, being first of all to discourse of those primary pleasures of the imagination, which entirely proceed from such objects as are before our eyes; and, in the next place, to speak of those secondary pleasures of the imagination, which flow from the ideas of visible objects, when the objects are not actually before the eye but are called up into our memories or formed into agreeable visions of things that are either absent or fictitious.

It is a great rule in laying down the division of a subject to study neatness and brevity as much as possible. The divisions are then more distinctly apprehended and more easily remembered. This sentence is not perfectly happy in that respect. It is somewhat clogged by a tedious phraseology. *My design being first of all, to discourse—in the next place, to speak of—such objects as are before our eyes—things that are either absent or fictitious.* Several words might have been spared here; and the style made more neat and compact.

> (11) The pleasures of the imagination, taken in their full extent, are not so gross as those of sense, nor so refined as those of the understanding.

This sentence is distinct and elegant.

> (12) The last are indeed more preferable, because they are founded on some new knowledge or improvement in the mind of man; yet it must be confessed that those of the imagination are as great and as transporting as the other.

In the beginning of this sentence, the phrase *more preferable* is such a plain inaccuracy that one wonders how Mr. Addison should have fallen into it, seeing *preferable,* of itself, expresses the comparative degree and is the same with "more eligible" or "more excellent."

I must observe farther that the proposition contained in the last member of this sentence is neither clear nor neatly expressed—*it must be confessed that those of the imagination are as great and as transporting as the other.* In the former sentence, he had compared three things together—the pleasures of the imagination, those of sense, and those of the understanding. In the beginning of this sentence, he had called the pleasures of the understanding *the last;* and he ends the sentence with observing that those of the imagination are as great and transporting *as the other.* Now, besides that *the other* makes not a proper contrast with *the last,* he leaves it ambiguous whether, by *the other,* he meant the pleasures of the understanding or the pleasures of the sense; for it may refer to either, by the construction; though, undoubtedly, he intended that it should refer to the pleasures of the understanding only. The proposition reduced to perspicuous language runs thus: "Yet it must be confessed that the pleasures of the imagination, when compared with those of the understanding, are no less great and transporting."

> (13) A beautiful prospect delights the soul as much as a demonstration; and a description in Homer has charmed more readers than a chapter in Aristotle.

This is a good illustration of what he had been asserting and is expressed with that happy and elegant turn, for which our author is very remarkable.

(14) Besides, the pleasures of the imagination have this advantage above those of the understanding, that they are more obvious and more easy to be acquired.

This is also an unexceptionable sentence.

(15) It is but opening the eye, and the scene enters.

This sentence is lively and picturesque. By the gayety and briskness which it gives the style, it shows the advantage of intermixing such a short sentence as this amidst a run of longer ones, which never fails to have a happy effect. I must remark, however, a small inaccuracy. A *scene* cannot be said to *enter;* an *actor* enters, but a scene *appears* or *presents itself.*

(16) The colours paint themselves on the fancy, with very little attention of thought or application of mind in the beholder.

This is still beautiful illustration, carried on with that agreeable floweriness of fancy and style which is so well suited to those pleasures of the imagination of which the author is treating.

(17) We are struck, we know not how, with the symmetry of anything we see, and immediately assent to the beauty of an object, without inquiring into the particular causes and occasions of it.

There is a falling off here from the elegance of the former sentences. *We assent* to the truth of a proposition but cannot so well be said *to assent to the beauty of an object. Acknowledge* would have expressed the sense with more propriety. The close of the sentence too is heavy and ungraceful—*the particular causes and occasions of it;* both *particular* and *occasions* are words quite superfluous; and the pronoun *it* is in some measure ambiguous, whether it refers to beauty or to object. It would have been some amendment to the style to have run thus: "We immediately acknowledge the beauty of an object, without inquiring into the cause of that beauty."

(18) A man of polite imagination is let into a great many pleasures that the vulgar are not capable of receiving.

Polite is a term more commonly applied to manners or behaviour than to the mind or imagination. There is nothing farther to be observed on this sentence, unless the use of *that* for a relative pronoun, instead of *which*—an usage which is too frequent with Mr. Addison. *Which* is a much more definitive word than *that,* being never employed in any other way than as a relative, whereas *that* is a word of many senses—sometimes a demonstrative pronoun, often a conjunction. In some cases we are indeed obliged to use *that* for a relative, in order to avoid the ungraceful repetition of *which* in the same sentence. But when we are laid under no necessity of this kind, *which* is always the preferable word and certainly was so in this sentence. *Pleasures which the vulgar are not capable of receiving* is much better than *pleasures that the vulgar etc.*

> (19) He can converse with a picture and find an agreeable companion in a statue. He meets with a secret refreshment in a description; and often feels a greater satisfaction in the prospect of fields and meadows than another does in the possession. It gives him, indeed, a kind of property in every thing he sees; and makes the most rude, uncultivated parts of nature administer to his pleasures: so that he looks upon the world, as it were, in another light and discovers in it a multitude of charms that conceal themselves from the generality of mankind.

All this is very beautiful. The illustration is happy and the style runs with the greatest ease and harmony. We see no labour, no stiffness or affectation; but an author writing from the native flow of a gay and pleasing imagination. This predominant character of Mr. Addison's manner, far more than compensates all those little negligences which we are now remarking. Two of these occur in this paragraph. The first, in the sentence which begins with *it gives him indeed a kind of property.* To this *it* there is no proper antecedent in the whole paragraph. In order to gather the meaning, we must look back as far as to the third sentence before, the first of the paragraph, which begins with *a man of a polite imagination.* This phrase, *polite* imagination, is the only antecedent to which this *it* can refer; and even that is an improper antecedent, as it stands in the genitive case, as the qualification only of *a man.*

The other instance of negligence is towards the end of the paragraph, *so that he looks upon the world, as it were in another light.* By *another* light, Mr. Addison means a light different from that in which other men view the world. But though this expression clearly conveyed this meaning to himself when writing, it conveys it very indistinctly to others and is an instance of that sort of inaccuracy, into which, in the warmth of composition, every writer of a lively imagination is apt to fall and which can only be remedied by a cool, subsequent review. *As it were* is upon most occasions no more than an ungraceful palliative; and here there was not the least occasion for it, as he was not about to say anything which required a softening of this kind. To say the truth, this last sentence, *so that he looks upon the world,* and what follows had better been wanting altogether. It is no more than an unnecessary recapitulation of what had gone before—a feeble adjection to the lively picture he had given of the pleasures of the imagination. The paragraph would have ended with more spirit as the words immediately preceding—*the uncultivated parts of nature administer to his pleasures*.

> (20) There are, indeed, but very few who know how to be idle and innocent, or have a relish of any pleasures that are not criminal; every diversion they take is at the expense of some one virtue or another, and their very first step out of business is into vice or folly.

Nothing can be more elegant or more finely turned than this sentence. It is neat, clear, and musical. We could hardly alter one word or disarrange one member without spoiling it. Few sentences are to be found more finished or more happy.

> (21) A man should endeavour, therefore, to make the sphere of his innocent pleasures as wide as possible that he may retire into them with safety and find in them such a satisfaction as a wise man would not blush to take.

This is also a good sentence and gives occasion to no material remark.

> (22) Of this nature are those of the imagination, which do not require such a bent of thought as is necessary to our more serious employments, nor, at the same time, suffer the mind to sink into that indolence and remissness, which are apt to accompany our more sensual delights; but like a gentle exercise to the faculties awaken them from sloth and idleness, without putting them upon any labour or difficulty.

The beginning of this sentence is not correct and affords an instance of a period too loosely connected with the preceding one. *Of this nature,* says he, *are those of the imagination*. We might ask, of what nature? For it had not been the scope of the preceding sentence to describe the nature of any set of pleasures. He had said that it was every man's duty to make the sphere of his innocent pleasures as wide as possible, in order that, within that sphere, he might find a safe retreat and a laudable satisfaction. The transition is loosely made by beginning the next sentence with saying, *of this nature are those of the imagination*. It had been better if, keeping in view the governing object of the preceding sentence, he had said, "This advantage we gain" or "This satisfaction we enjoy by means of the pleasures of imagination." The rest of the sentence is abundantly correct.

> (23) We might here add that the pleasures of the fancy are more conducive to health than those of the understanding, which are worked out by dint of thinking and attended with too violent a labour of the brain.

On this sentence, nothing occurs deserving of remark, except that *worked out by dint of thinking* is a phrase which borders too much on vulgar and colloquial language to be proper for being employed in a polished composition.

> (24) Delightful scenes, whether in nature, painting, or poetry, have a kindly influence on the body, as well as the mind, and not only serve to clear and brighten the imagination but are able to disperse grief and melancholy and to set the animal spirits in pleasing and agreeable motions. For this reason, Sir Francis Bacon, in his Essay upon Health, has not thought it improper to prescribe to his reader a poem or a prospect, where he particularly dissuades him from knotty and subtile disquisitions and advises him to pursue studies that fill the mind with splendid and illustrious objects, as histories, fables, and contemplations of nature.

In the latter of these two sentences, a member of the period is altogether out of its place—which gives the whole sentence a harsh and disjointed cast and serves to illustrate the rules I formerly gave concerning arrangement. The wrong-placed member which I point at is this: *where he particularly dissuades him from knotty and subtile disquisitions;* these words should undoubtedly have been placed not where they stand but thus: *Sir Francis Bacon, in his Essay upon Health, where he particularly dissuades the reader from knotty and subtile speculations, has not thought it improper to prescribe to him etc.* This arrangement reduces every thing into proper order.

> (25) I have in this paper, by way of introduction, settled the motion of those pleasures of the imagination, which are the subject of my present undertaking, and endeavoured, by several considerations, to recommend to my readers the pursuit of those pleasures; I shall, in my next paper, examine the several sources from whence these pleasures are derived.

These two concluding sentences afford examples of the proper collocation of circumstances in a period. I formerly showed that it is often a matter of difficulty to dispose of them in such a manner as that they shall not embarrass the principal subject of the sentence. In the sentences before us, several of these incidental circumstances necessarily come in—*By way of introduction—by several considerations—in this paper—in the next paper.* All which are with great propriety managed by our author. It will be found, upon trial, that there were no other parts of the sentence, in which they could have been placed to equal advantage. Had he said, for instance, "I have settled the notion (rather, *the meaning*) of those pleasures of the imagination, which are the subject of my present undertaking, by way of introduction, in this paper, and endeavoured to recommend the pursuit of those pleasures to my readers, by several considerations," we must be sensible that the sentence, thus clogged with circumstances in the wrong place, would neither have been so neat nor so clear, as it is by the present construction.

John F. Kennedy: Inaugural Address

(January 20, 1961)

1 We observe today not a victory of party but a celebration of freedom, symbolizing an end as well as a beginning, signifying renewal as well as change. For I have sworn before you and Almighty God the same solemn oath our forebears prescribed nearly a century and three-quarters ago.

2 The world is very different now. For man holds in his mortal hands the power to abolish all forms of human poverty and all forms of human life. And yet the same revolutionary belief for which our forebears fought is still at issue around the globe, the belief that the rights of man come not from the generosity of the state but from the hand of God.

3 We dare not forget today that we are the heirs of that first revolution. Let the word go forth from this time and place, to friend and foe alike, that the torch has been passed to a new generation of Americans, born in this century, tempered by war, disciplined by a hard and bitter peace, proud of our ancient heritage, and unwilling to witness or permit the slow undoing of those human rights to which this nation has always been committed, and to which we are committed today at home and around the world.

4 Let every nation know, whether it wishes us well or ill, that we shall pay any price, bear any burden, meet any hardship, support any friend, oppose any foe to assure the survival and the success of liberty.

5 This much we pledge—and more.

6 To those old allies whose cultural and spiritual origins we share, we pledge the loyalty of faithful friends. United, there is little we cannot do in a host of co-operative ventures. Divided, there is little we can do, for we dare not meet a powerful challenge at odds and split asunder.

7 To those new states whom we welcome to the ranks of the free, we pledge our word that one form of colonial control shall not have passed away merely to be replaced by a far more iron tyranny. We shall not always expect to find them supporting our view. But we shall always hope to find them strongly supporting their own freedom, and to remember that, in the past, those who foolishly sought power by riding the back of the tiger ended up inside.

8 To those peoples in the huts and villages of half the globe struggling to break the bonds of mass misery, we pledge our best efforts to help them help themselves, for whatever period is required, not because the Communists may be doing it, not because we seek their votes, but because it is right. If a free society cannot help the many who are poor, it cannot save the few who are rich.

9 To our sister republics south of our border, we offer a special pledge: to convert our good words into good deeds, in a new alliance for progress, to assist free men and free governments in casting off the chains of poverty. But this peaceful revolution of hope cannot become the prey of hostile powers. Let all our neighbors know that we shall join with them to oppose aggression or subversion anywhere in the Americas. And let every other power know that this hemisphere intends to remain the master of its own house.

10 To that world assembly of sovereign states, the United Nations, our last best hope in an age where the instruments of war have far outpaced the instruments of peace, we renew our pledge of support: to prevent it from becoming merely a forum for invective, to strengthen its shield of the new and the weak, and to enlarge the area in which its writ may run.

11 Finally, to those nations who would make themselves our adversary, we offer not a pledge but a request: that both sides begin anew the quest for peace, before the dark powers of destruction unleashed by science engulf all humanity in planned or accidental self-destruction.

12 We dare not tempt them with weakness. For only when our arms are sufficient beyond doubt can we be certain beyond doubt that they will never be employed.

13 But neither can two great and powerful groups of nations take comfort from our present course—both sides over-burdened by the cost of modern weapons, both rightly alarmed by the steady spread of the deadly atom, yet both racing to alter that uncertain balance of terror that stays the hand of mankind's final war.

14 So let us begin anew, remembering on both sides that civility is not a sign of weakness, and sincerity is always subject to proof. Let us never negotiate out of fear, but let us never fear to negotiate.

15 Let both sides explore what problems unite us instead of belaboring those problems which divide us.

16 Let both sides, for the first time, formulate serious and precise proposals for the inspection and control of arms, and bring the absolute power to destroy other nations under the absolute control of all nations.

17 Let both sides seek to invoke the wonders of science instead of its terrors. Together let us explore the stars, conquer the deserts, eradicate disease, tap the ocean depths and encourage the arts and commerce.

18 Let both sides unite to heed in all corners of the earth the command of Isaiah to "undo the heavy burdens ... [and] let the oppressed go free."

19 And if a beachhead of co-operation may push back the jungle of suspicion, let both sides join in creating a new endeavor, not a new balance of power, but a new world of law, where the strong are just and the weak secure and the peace preserved.

20 All this will not be finished in the first one hundred days. Nor will it be finished in the first one thousand days, nor in the life of this Administration, nor even perhaps in our lifetime on this planet. But let us begin.

21 In your hands, my fellow citizens, more than mine, will rest the final success or failure of our course. Since this country was founded, each generation of Americans has been summoned to give testimony to its national loyalty. The graves of young Americans who answered the call to service surround the globe.

22 Now the trumpet summons us again—not as a call to bear arms, though arms we need; not as a call to battle, though embattled we are; but a call to bear the burden of a long twilight struggle, year in and year out, "rejoicing in hope, patient in tribulation," a struggle against the common enemies of man: tyranny, poverty, disease and war itself.

23 Can we forge against these enemies a grand and global alliance, North and South, East and West, that can assure a more fruitful life for all mankind? Will you join in that historic effort?

24 In the long history of the world, only a few generations have been granted the role of defending freedom in its hour of maximum danger. I do not shrink from this responsibility; I welcome it. I do not believe that any of us would exchange places with any other people or any other generation. The energy, the faith, the devotion which we bring to this endeavor will light our country and all who serve it, and the glow from that fire can truly light the world.

25 And so, my fellow Americans, ask not what your country can do for you; ask what you can do for your country.

26 My fellow citizens of the world, ask not what America will do for you, but what together we can do for the freedom of man.

27 Finally, whether you are citizens of America or citizens of the world, ask of us here the same high standards of strength and sacrifice which we ask of you. With a good conscience our only sure reward, with history the final judge of our deeds, let us go forth to lead the land we love, asking His blessing and His help, but knowing that here on earth God's work must truly be our own.

The Editors of the "New Yorker": John F. Kennedy's Inaugural Address

As rhetoric has become an increasingly dispensable member of the liberal arts, people have abandoned the idea, held so firmly by the ancient Greeks

From the *New Yorker*, XXXVI (Feb. 4, 1961), 23-24; © 1961, The New Yorker Magazine, Inc. Reprinted by permission of the publisher.

and Romans, that eloquence is indispensable to politics. Perhaps President Kennedy's achievements in both spheres will revive a taste for good oratory of the Inaugural Address ("To that world assembly of sovereign states, the United Nations...") is appropriate to the subject; the language ("In your hands, my fellow-citizens, more than mine, will rest the final success or failure of our course") is clear and direct. Cicero's ideal orator was able to speak in all three styles, in accordance with the demands of his subject, and in that respect Mr. Kennedy filled the role by speaking plainly on the practical ("All this will not be finished in the first one hundred days"), by speaking formally but directly on the purpose of national defense ("For only when our arms are sufficient beyond doubt can we be certain beyond doubt that they will never be employed"), and by speaking grandly on the potential accomplishments of the movement toward the New Frontier ("The energy, the faith, the devotion which we bring to this endeavor will light our country and all who serve it—and the glow from that fire can truly light the world").

The address, however, is largely in the grand style, which is characterized by Cicero as the ultimate source of emotional persuasion, through figures of speech and a certain degree of dignified periodic rhythm, not iambic ("The world is very different now. For man holds in his mortal hands the power to abolish all forms of human poverty, and all forms of human life"). The oration is so rich in figures of speech—the many metaphors include a torch, a beachhead, jungles, a trumpet, a tiger—that we can imagine students of the future studying it for examples of antithesis ("If a free society cannot help the many who are poor, it cannot save the few who are rich"), personification ("...the hand of mankind's final war"), and anaphora ("Not as a call to bear arms, though arms we need; not as a call to battle, though embattled we are..."). "Battle" and "embattled"—an excellent example of paronomasia.

And so we leave the speech to the students of rhetoric, having invoked for Mr. Kennedy the blessings of Aristotle and Cicero, and for ourself the hope that he has re-established the tradition of political eloquence.

Analysis of the Style of John F. Kennedy's Inaugural Address

> "If, in the effective use of language, style is the man, style is the nation too; men, countries, and entire civilizations have been tested and judged by their literary tone."—John F. Kennedy

General Situation for the Speech

If we are to relate the style of the Inaugural Address to its content, we must take into account the subject matter, the occasion, the audience, and the ethos

of the speaker. An inauguration is a solemn, ceremonial event, attended by
—a taste that has been alternately frustrated by inarticulateness and dulled
by bombast. There have been a few notable orators in our day—most
recently Adlai Stevenson—but they have been the exceptions, and it has
taken Mr. Kennedy's success as a politician to suggest that the power to
"enchant souls through words" (Socrates) may soon be at a premium once
more. Whatever the impact of the Inaugural Address on contemporary
New Frontiersmen, we find it hard to believe that an Athenian or Roman
citizen could have listened to it unmoved, or that Cicero, however jealous
of his own reputation, would have found reason to object to it.

We are all familiar by now with the generally high praise the President
received for his first speech, but before the responsibility for a final judgment is yielded to Time it would be a shame not to seek the opinion of a
couple of true professionals. Both Aristotle and Cicero, the one a theorist
and the other a theorizing orator, believed that rhetoric could be an art
to the extent that the orator was, first, a logician and, second, a psychologist
with an appreciation and understanding of words. Cicero felt further, that
the ideal orator was the thoroughly educated man. (He would be pleased
by Mr. Kennedy's background, with its strong emphasis on affairs of state:
the philosopher-orator-statesman.) Of the three types of oratory defined by
the ancients—political, forensic, and display (in which audience participation was limited to a judgment of style)—the political was esteemed most
highly, because it dealt with the loftiest of issues; namely, the fate of peoples,
rather than of individuals. ("Now the trumpet summons us again . . . against
the common enemies of man. . . .") The ideal speech was thought to be one
in which three kinds of persuasion were used by the speaker: logical, to
present the facts of the case and construct an argument based on them;
emotional, to reach the audience psychologically; and "ethical," to appeal
to the audience by establishing one's own integrity and sincerity. The
Inaugural Address, being a variation on the single theme of man's rights
and obligations, is not primarily logical, although it contains no illogic; it
is an appeal to men's souls rather than to their minds. During the Presidential campaign, Mr. Kennedy tested and patented an exercise in American
psychology that proved to be all the emotional appeal he required for the
inaugural speech: "And so, my fellow-Americans, ask not what your country can do for you, ask what you can do for your country." His ethical
persuasion, or indication of his personal probity, consisted of an extension
of that appeal: ". . . ask of us here the same high standards of strength and
sacrifice which we ask of you."

Aristotle recognized only one (good) style, while Cicero thought that
there were three styles—the plain, the middle, and the grand. To Aristotle,
who considered it sufficient for a style to be clear and appropriate, avoiding

undue elevation (whence bombast) and excessive lowliness, it would have seemed that Mr. Kennedy had achieved the Golden Mean. The formality certain traditions and rituals. A speech delivered on such an occasion is usually of the ceremonial variety, although there may be deliberative elements in it. What the people have come to expect is not so much a speech that lays down a specific program as a speech that sets a mood. In striking the keynote of the coming administration, the speaker will try to heal the wounds that may have been inflicted during the campaign, to remind the audience of a common heritage and a common purpose, to set forth, in a general way, the policies and objectives of the new administration, and to reassure the international community of the continuity and determination of the nation.

Since a ceremonial speech like this deals in generalities rather than in particulars, it can very easily slip off into platitude and pious cant. In seeking to please everyone with a "safe" speech, the speaker runs the risk of pleasing no one. In striving for that happy mean between the general and the specific, between the trite and the bizarre, and between the offensive and the fulsome, the speaker will have to draw on all his ingenuity to come up with a content and a form that will impress his audience without boring them.

Having characterized the kind of speech that is usually delivered at an inauguration, we might consider now the special situation that faced President Kennedy on that January morning in 1961. John Fitzgerald Kennedy was the youngest man and the first Catholic to be elected to the highest office in America, and he had been elected by a narrow margin of votes. His youth, his religious affiliation, and his narrow victory at the polls—all these combined to establish some doubts about him in the minds of his own people and the people of other countries. Having created an image, during the campaign, of enormous vitality and considerable political shrewdness, this leader of the New Frontier had to fulfill his promise to push the country forward. Clearly, this was an occasion when a powerful ethical appeal would have to be exerted if the confidence and initiative of the people were to be aroused.

What about the audience for this address? There would be the immediate audience—the high dignitaries on the platform and the thousands of people gathered in the plaza in front of the Capitol building. Then there were the millions of people who would see and hear the speaker through the medium of television. And finally there would be the millions of people in foreign lands who would read accounts of the speech in their newspapers the next day. Taken together, this was a vast, heterogeneous audience, posing special problems for the speaker. As we have remarked before, the larger and more heterogeneous the audience is, the more difficult it is to adjust the discourse to fit the audience. In his content and his style, the President must strike some common denominator—but a common denominator that does not fall below the dignity that the occasion demands.

Having looked at the general situation that prevailed for the speech, let us now see how the President accommodated his means to his end. In this analysis, of course, we are going to investigate only the way in which the President accommodated his *style* to the subject matter, occasion, audience, and his own personality.

The Speech as a Whole

One of the first things that strikes the reader is the relative brevity of the speech—1343 words, which at the normal rate for public address would take between nine and ten minutes to deliver. When the President wrote this speech he could not have known that the "live" audience for the speech would be standing in the biting cold that followed a heavy snowstorm in the Washington area on the day before the inauguration. So the President had not made his speech brief out of consideration for his wind-chilled audience. In preparing the speech, however, he might have taken into consideration that it would be delivered at the end of some lengthy preliminary speech-making. But perhaps the consideration that mainly determined the brevity of the speech was the traditional nature of inaugural addresses. As we have observed, inaugural addresses usually deal in broad, undeveloped generalities. Principles, policies, and promises are enunciated without elaboration.

Paragraphs

The relative brevity of the speech is reflected in the paragraph and sentence structure. A glance at the printed text of the speech reveals a succession of short paragraphs. Of the twenty-seven paragraphs in the speech, ten have only one sentence; seven paragraphs are two sentences long; and another seven are three sentences long. The longest paragraphs (9 and 24) contain only four sentences. In terms of averages, there are 49.3 words per paragraph and 1.92 sentences per paragraph.

The President is trying to cover a lot of ground in this short speech. In order to do this, he enunciates his principles, promises, and policies in a litany of capsule paragraphs. The effect of these unelaborated paragraphs would have been slight if the President had not rendered many of those paragraphs memorable by the brilliance of his style.

Sentences: Length

Descending to the next smallest unit of discourse, the sentence, we note some interesting facts about the length and kinds of sentences. The two extremes of sentence length are represented by the sentence of eighty words (second sentence of paragraph 3) and the sentence of four words (third sentence of paragraph 20). The average length of the President's sentences is 25.8 words. But what is more revealing about the President's style is the variation above and below this average. Fourteen of the fifty-two sentences (27 per cent) in the speech are ten words or more *above* the average; but twenty-three sentences (44 per cent) are five words or more *below* the average. Although the President has a number of unusually long sentences—66 words (paragraph 10), 64 words (paragraph 22), 54 words (paragraphs 8 and 13) —an unusually high proportion of his sentences are composed of twenty words or less. Even by modern journalistic standards, a twenty-word sentence is short. This high proportion of short sentences matches the over-all brevity of the speech and the short paragraphs. Although the President displays an admirable variety in sentence-length, his heavy use of the short sentence does suggest that he had his *listening* audience in mind when he composed his speech. Another consideration that may have influenced the President in the use of short sentences is that short sentences help to create the effect of sententiousness that is appropriate for a ceremonial speech.

Sentences: Grammatical Types

Having noted a high proportion of relatively short sentences, we might expect that a majority of the sentences would be of the simple or compound type. But a close investigation of the grammatical types reveals that this is not so. Twenty (38.4 per cent) of the sentences are simple; only six (11.6 per cent) sentences are compound. But twenty-six sentences (exactly 50 per cent) are complex. Taken together, the simple and compound sentences constitute 50 per cent of the whole, but the predominant grammatical type is the complex sentence. What this reveals is that the President manages the expansion of his sentences mainly through the sophisticated pattern of subordination. A study of the sequence of sentences, however, shows how well the President has mixed the grammatical types in order to avoid monotony of structure. Only in a half dozen or so places in the speech does he string together two or more sentences of the same grammatical type.

Sentences: Rhetorical Types

When we study the rhetorical patterns of the speech, we note another interesting feature of President Kennedy's style. The predominant rhetorical structure is antithesis. This recurring structure was perhaps dictated by the fact that the speech deals mainly with comparisons of opposites (end–beginning, old–new, rich–poor, friend–enemy). He strikes the theme of the speech and the antithetical keynote in the first sentence: "We observe today *not a victory of party/ but a celebration of freedom*—symbolizing *an end/* as well as *a beginning*—signifying *renewal/* as well as *change.*" Additional examples of antithesis are not hard to find:

> to friend and foe alike (paragraph 3)
> United ... Divided (paragraph 6)

Contrast the effect of this with the following:

> We dare not tempt them with weakness, for only when our arms are sufficient beyond doubt can we be certain beyond doubt that they will never be employed.

The content and rhetorical scheme of both sentences is exactly the same, and perhaps if one were *reading* the second sentence aloud he could produce the same effect as the first sentence has. But on the printed page, a special emphasis is achieved by setting off the second clause in a sentence by itself and by signaling the syllogistic relationship of the two clauses by the capitalized initial *For*. If the student analyzes the other uses of initial co-ordinating conjunctions, he will usually find some rhetorical purpose being served.

Sentences: Functional Types

The overwhelming majority of the sentences are declarative. This proportion is appropriate in a speech that is designed to inform and reassure the world about the objectives of the new administration. Occasionally, however, the President uses some other functional types of sentence. In paragraph 23, he uses two rhetorical questions ("Can we forge against these enemies a grand and global alliance, North and South, East and West, that can assure a more fruitful life for all mankind? Will you join in that historic effort?"). These questions occur at the point in the speech when the President is about to launch into his peroration. Up to this point the President has been declaring what he will do, what the American people will do. Now he wants to suggest what the international community can do to support his program of peace and prosperity. But he can only suggest—he cannot dictate or predict —what other countries will do. The rhetorical questions are phrased in such a way, however, that the natural answer to them is a resounding *Yes*.

The President groups together two other types of functional sentences— imperatives and hortatives. In paragraphs 25, 26, 27 (the concluding paragraphs of the speech), we see three sharp imperatives, using the verb *to ask*, which leave the citizens with a call to action. Up to this point, the audience have been mere listeners to this ceremonial discourse. Now the audience must be engaged actively. The imperatives point to the general line of action that they must take.

The series of fourteen hortative sentences ("Let us ... Let both sides ...") in paragraphs 14 through 20 also lays down a program of action, but the directives are softened by being cast in a hortatory form. (The Latin and Greek languages would have used the subjunctive mood of the verb to create this effect.) The President here is seeking to induce action, not command it In other words, he wants to persuade rather than coerce.

> To those old allies ... To those new states (paragraphs 6, 7)
>
> If a free society cannot help the many who are poor, it cannot save few who are rich. (paragraph 8)
>
> What problems unite us ... those problems which divide us (p graph 15)

And the most memorable line of the speech is cast in the form of an tithesis:

> ... Ask not what your country can do for you—ask what you can do your country.

Most of these antitheses of thought are laid out in parallel gramma structure. The recurring parallelism is appropriate here because althougl President is pointing up opposites by his antitheses he wants to suggest these opposites can be reconciled. Opposites can be reconciled only if are co-ordinate, and one way to emphasize the co-ordinate value of oppc is to juxtapose them in a parallel grammatical structure.

The other use that the President makes of parallelism is for the pur of specification or enumeration, as in these three examples:

> born in this century, tempered by war, disciplined by a hard and | peace, proud of our ancient heritage (paragraph 3)
>
> pay any price, bear any burden, meet any hardship, support any fr oppose any foe (paragraph 4)
>
> Together let us explore the stars, conquer the deserts, eradicate di and encourage the arts and commerce (paragraph 17)

As we shall see when we come to study the figures of speech, there are tional schemes intertwined in many of these parallel and antithetical pat

Before concluding this section on rhetorical patterns, we shall poin some other features of style. If the student needed any evidence to j his use of a co-ordinating conjunction at the beginning of the senten could cite this speech. The President begins fourteen of his sentences 25 per cent) with a co-ordinating conjunction. There is, of course, a precedent for this usage in modern prose and the prose of earlier cent But it is interesting to note how effective rhetorically this means of arti ing sentences is in the President's speech. Let us look at just one examp this usage:

> We dare not tempt them with weakness. For only when our arr sufficient beyond doubt can we be certain beyond doubt that the never be employed. (paragraph 12)

Diction

The diction of the speech unobtrusively but unmistakably exerts an influence on the effect of the speech. The simplicity of the diction is perhaps not immediately noticeable, but when one studies it, one notes that there is almost no word that a moderately intelligent high-school graduate would have to look up in a dictionary. A closer study of the diction reveals a high proportion of monosyllabic words: some 951 words in the speech (71 per cent) are monosyllabic. In paragraphs 19 and 20, the proportion of monosyllabic words is as high as 80 per cent. Even in the peroration of the speech, where one might expect the orator to make use of the sonorous cadence that can be achieved with polysyllabic diction, one finds a high proportion of one-syllable words. This monosyllabism helps to account not only for the impression of simplicity but also for the note of strength in the speech—a note that people had come to associate with the vigor of this youthful public figure. In working over the drafts of the speech, the President must consciously have sought out simple, Anglo-Saxon words.

Having noted the high proportion of monosyllabic words, one might expect to find also a high proportion of concrete words. But this is not the case. Investigation of the nouns in the speech turns up many abstract words—words like *freedom, poverty, tyranny, loyalty, devotion, responsibility, aggression, subversion*. And most of this abstract diction is Latinate and polysyllabic. Aside from the figures of speech—which we will investigate later—there are surprisingly few concrete words—*huts, villages, stars, deserts, graves*. Whatever air of concreteness the speech has is created by the figures of speech. Perhaps the high proportion of abstract words is the natural consequence of the brief, unelaborated character of the speech. Once the President had decided to enunciate only the broad, general policy of his administration, it was almost inevitable that most of his substantive words would be abstract. What we have in this short speech really is a series of undeveloped topic sentences.

Another thing that accounts for the formal quality of this ceremonial speech is the occasional use of slightly archaic diction. We find the President using such words as *forebears* (twice), *host, anew, asunder, foe, adversary, writ*. Besides echoing the tone of Lincoln's *Gettysburg Address* ("Fourscore and seven years ago," "our fathers," "final resting-place," "hallow"), this quaint diction has Biblical overtones and a certain appropriateness to the old-new motif. The President reinforced the effect of this kind of diction by two quotations from the Old Testament and the folksy adage about riding the back of the tiger. The repetition of certain honorific key terms, like *pledge, citizens, peace* also helps to reinforce the reverential tone of the speech.

Figures of Speech: Schemes

First of all, let us look at some of the schemes—those patternings of words which represent departures from the ordinary way of speaking. Since we have already remarked about the pervasive parallelism and antithesis in the speech, we will concentrate here on some of the other schemes.

There are a number of schemes of repetition. The most notable of these is anaphora—repetition of the same words at the beginning of successive clauses. Anaphora is conspicuous in two key passages in the speech: the section (paragraphs 6-11) in which the President is making a series of pledges ("To those ..."); and the section (paragraphs 15-18) in which the President is suggesting a course of action ("Let both sides ..."). We have previously observed that these two sections make use of parallelism. The addition of *anaphora* to these passages performs two functions: it combines with the parallelism to mark off and emphasize the co-ordinateness of the series, and it helps to establish the rhythm of the passages. The speech has no example of the opposite scheme, epistrophe (repetition of the same word at the end of successive clauses), but it does have two examples of repetition of similar words in a medial position: "bear *any* burden, meet *any* hardship, support *any* friend, oppose *any* foe" (paragraph 4); "sufficient *beyond doubt* ... certain *beyond doubt*" (paragraph 12).

The most remembered sentence in the speech—"ask not what your country can do for you—ask what you can do for your country"—contains a figure of repetition known as antimetabole (repetition of words in converse order). Another memorable utterance—"Let us never negotiate out of fear. But never fear to negotiate"—appears to be another example of antimetabole, but it is more accurately classified as polyptoton (repetition of words derived from the same root). Here we have different conjugates of the word *fear*—serving as a noun in the first clause and as an infinitive in the second clause. There is another example of polyptoton in paragraph 22 ("Not as a call to *battle*, though *embattled* we are")—although, as the editors of the *New Yorker* observed, there is a suggestion here too of the trope called paronomasia (play on words).

President Kennedy made sparing use of the scheme of repetition known as alliteration. There are only two instances of noticeable alliteration in the speech—"the *a*rea in which its *w*rit may *r*un" (paragraph 10); "to *l*ead the *l*and we *l*ove" (paragraph 27). Perhaps in accord with his personality, the President avoided frequent use of alliteration because of the soft, effeminate sound-effect often produced by this figure; the President was striving for a note of strength and vigor. One wonders, though, whether the President did not intend some sound-effect of appropriate harshness in the succession of *s* and *d* sounds in "before the dark powers of destruction unleashed by science engulf all humanity in planned or accidental self-destruction" (paragraph 11).

Let us look briefly at a few more schemes. In most of his parallel series, the President shows a preference for the hurried rhythms that can be achieved with asyndeton (omission of conjunctions)—e.g. "born in this century, tempered by war, disciplined by a hard and bitter peace, proud of our ancient heritage" (paragraph 3). The President makes little use of the scheme called anastrophe (unusual word order). In the entire speech, there is only one structure that is inverted: *"United,* there is little we cannot do in a host of co-operative ventures. *Divided,* there is little we can do" (paragraph 6). It is easy to see the special emphasis the President achieves here by placing the past participles in the initial position, even though these participles do not modify, as they normally do in this position, the subject of the main clause. One could regard this structure, however, as ellipsis rather than anastrophe. The closest the President comes to the figure known as climax is in paragraphs 25, 26, 27; but even here we have to strain a bit to find any element of rising importance in the series.

Figures of Speech: Tropes

Although the President makes rather skillful use of the schemes, he is less satisfactory in his use of tropes. There are a number of metaphors in the speech, and those metaphors represent, as we remarked earlier, the chief way in which the President introduces concreteness into the speech. But many of these metaphors—"the torch," "bonds of mass misery," "the chains of poverty," "corners of the earth," "the trumpet," "the glow from that fire"—are rather hackneyed. He achieves a little more freshness in some of his more subtle metaphors, like "iron tyranny," "destruction unleashed," "twilight struggle," "forge." Perhaps his most successful metaphor is the one in paragraph 19—"And if a beachhead of co-operation may push back the jungle of suspicion." By themselves, *beachhead* and *jungle* are rather shopworn metaphors, but they acquire a certain freshness by being combined in a complex metaphor.

The several uses of "hands" (part for the whole) and "arms" (genus for the species) can be looked upon as examples of synecdoche, but those tropes too are fairly trite. The use of "hand" in paragraph 13—"that uncertain balance of terror that stays the hand of mankind's final war"—should be classified as an instance of personification rather than of synecdoche. Perhaps the only other expression in the speech which might be read as an instance of personification is found in the last paragraph—"with history the final judge of our deeds."

Style of Delivery

Undoubtedly, a good deal of the effect of this speech was produced by the "style" of delivery. Those who watched the inauguration ceremonies on television may recall the President's clear, crisp voice, the distinctive Bostonian accent, the mannerisms of the jabbing finger, the pauses, the inflections, the stresses. All of these features of voice and gesture helped to put the speech across; combined with the carefully worked-out style, they helped to communicate the President's message to the electorate and to the world. And perhaps it would be well for the student who has read this close analysis of the style to put the speech together again by listening to it on one of the many memorial records that were issued shortly after the President's assassination. Listening to a recording of the speech will make the student aware that this was a discourse designed for oral delivery, and it might prove interesting to note how much of the highly refined style of the speech comes through to the student once he has had the devices of style pointed out to him.

Concluding Remarks

The various stylistic devices we have been observing may be looked upon by some people as the ornamentation of the speech. These devices do "dress up" the speech, but if they are regarded as no more than ornamentation, they have failed to perform the functions that rhetoricians traditionally assigned to them. These formal devices should be one of the carriers of meaning. If the diction, the composition of words, and the figures of speech are not functioning to clarify, enliven, and emphasize the thought, if they are not exerting an ethical, emotional, or logical appeal, then indeed the style of a piece is so much sounding brass and tinkling cymbals, so much sound and fury signifying nothing.

It is not so important that the style of the speech be recognizable as the "Kennedy style" as it is that the style be seen as appropriate to the subject matter, the occasion, the purpose, and the audience. Just as Lincoln's *Gettysburg Address* was not particularly impressive to the audience who heard it in the National Cemetery on November 19, 1863, so Kennedy's Inaugural Address was not—if we may judge from the restrained applause that greeted it while it was being delivered—notably impressive to the audience who heard it in the snow-packed Capitol Plaza on January 20, 1961. It is only when we get a chance to read and reread Lincoln's and Kennedy's speeches that we realize what splendid performances they were. Only a close analysis such as we have engaged in can make us aware of the great care and deliberation President Kennedy devoted to the "expression" of his speech. So much eloquence did not come by chance. It had to come from calculated choices from among a number of possibilities.

We should now be in a better position to judge whether the President's choices were judicious. And we should be in a better position to predict whether future generations will judge this Inaugural Address to be one of the noblest utterances to issue from the lips of an American statesman.

John Illo: The Rhetoric of Malcolm X

If the Reverend Martin Luther King, Jr. was the hero of the early civil-rights movement in America, the hero of the more militant phase of the civil-rights movement, especially among young whites and blacks, is Malcolm X. His rise to international fame is one of the most remarkable stories in the annals of American history. Malcolm Little was born in Omaha, Nebraska, on May 19, 1925, the seventh child of a poor Baptist minister, a dedicated disciple of Marcus Garvey, the man who preached that the Negroes' best hope lay in a return to their African homeland. Soon after their house in Omaha was burned down by Ku Klux Klanners, the Littles moved to Lansing, Michigan. When Malcolm was six years old, his father was mysteriously murdered, and soon after, his mother was consigned to a mental hospital, where she remained for twenty-six years. Malcolm finished the eighth grade, but having been discouraged by one of his teachers from aspiring to a career as a lawyer, he went to live with his sister Ella in Boston. From there he went to Harlem, where he ran the gamut of employment as a shoeshine boy, pimp, dope-peddler, and burglar. He was arrested in 1946 and sentenced to ten years in prison. The turning-point of his life came while he was in the Norfolk Prison Colony. He read omnivorously, he learned to write by copying the dictionary, and he came under the spell of Elijah Muhammad, the leader of the Black Muslim movement. After working tirelessly and loyally for the movement for twelve years, Malcolm X broke with the Black Muslims in 1964, when after his first trip to Mecca, he saw the need to broaden his mission to include the whole of the Islamic world. On February 21, 1965, while delivering a speech in the Audubon Ballroom in New York City, he was assassinated. Thus was stilled the most powerful and influential voice in the black-militancy movement.

Malcolm X's major speeches have been published by the Grove Press under the title Malcolm X Speaks. *In the following article, John Illo, who received his M.A. degree from Columbia University and who teaches English*

From *The Columbia University Forum*, IX (Spring 1966), 5-12. Reprinted by permission of the author.

at Monmouth College, analyzes the rhetoric of those amazingly effective speeches.

1 In a nation of images without substances, of rehearsed emotions, in a politic of consensus where platitude replaces belief or belief is fashioned by consensus, genuine rhetoric, like authentic prose, must be rare. For rhetoric, like any verbal art, is correlative with the pristine idea of reason and justice which, if it decays with the growth of every state and jurisprudence, now has developed into an unreason that aggressively claims the allegiance of the national mind.

2 Jurisprudence is the prudent justification of an absurd society, of institutionalized inequity and internal contradiction. Law, and juridical logic, and grammar conspire to frustrate the original idea of a just and good society, in which all men may freely become the best that they may be. Rhetoric, like the Shelleyan poetic, returns us to primal intelligence, to the golden idea and the godly nature whose mirror is unspoiled reason. The critical and reformist function of rhetoric, apparent in processes like irony and paradox, is perceptible in the whole range of tropes and syntactic and tonal devices. Repetitions and transposals of syntax recall the emphases of nature, before civil logic; and metaphor recalls the true relations, resemblances, predications, that we have been trained to forget. Love is not a fixation but a fire, for it consumes and cleanses; and man is not a rational animal so essentially as he is dust and breath, crumbling, evanescent, and mysterious because moved invisibly.

3 To use schemes, figures, tropes, in a plan or plot that corresponds with the broad proceeding of the juridically logical mind, is to make an oration. Within the grammatical frame of his society, the orator, using the language of primordial reason and symbol, restores to his audience the ideas that have been obscured by imposed categories that may correspond to institution but not to reality. Rhetoric, Aristotle taught, is analogous to logic because enthymeme is related to syllogism; but, more significantly, rhetoric is related to logic as logic is related to reality. And rhetoric is also related to poetry, as Cicero observed, his prosaic Roman mind reducing poetry to ornamented language, as the lyric mind of Plato had reduced rhetoric to "cookery." Cicero and Aristotle were each half right. Rhetoric is in fact poeticized logic, logic revised by the creative and critical imagination recalling original ideas. Rhetoric, the art that could grow only in a *polis* and a system of judicature, is the art that restores the primitive value of the mystical word and the human voice. With a matured craft and a legalist's acuteness, orators contrive the free language of childlike reason, innocently reproving the unnatural and perverse, which institution, custom, law, and policy ask us to accept as the way of the world.

4 And so great orators, when great, have spoken for absolute justice and reason as they perceived it, in defiance of their governments or societies, accusing tyrants, protesting vicious state policies that seduced the general will, execrating the deformation of popular morality. We think of an Isaiah prophesying against the corruption of ancestral religion, of a Demosthenes against Philip, a Cicero against Antony, a Burke against a colonial war, a Garrison against slavery. At the summit of their art they recalled the language of primal intelligence and passion in defense of elemental truth; and their symbols and transposed syntax, though deliberated, were no more spurious or obtrusive than in poetry. But unlike the pure poet, the orator always holds near enough to the juridical logic, grammar, and semantic of the institution to be able to attack the institution. He never yields his reformist responsibility for the private vision that may be illusive, and may be incommunicable. The orator unlinks the mind-forged manacles, but refashions them into an armor for the innocent intelligence, the naked right.

5 Lesser oratory, venal, hypocritical, in defense of the indefensible, is patently factitious, its free language a cosmetic, a youthful roseate complexion arranged on an old, shrewd and degenerated visage, as in the forced prosopopoeias of Cicero appealing for a criminal Milo, or in the tediously predictable alliterated triads of Everett McKinley Dirksen. Bad morals usually produce bad rhetoric, and such is the dureful weight of institutions and their parties that *rhetoric* had been pejorated, generally, into *bad rhetoric*. Even Henry Steele Commager can regard oratory like Senator Long's as "eloquent but shameless," attributes ideally exclusive. The swelling anaphoras of a Southern Congressman are not eloquent but ludicrous, raising irrepressible images of toads and swine. Little else but bad rhetoric is possible to those within the establishment, so far from original reason, so committed to the apologetics of unreason. And those outside are conditioned by established styles, or are graceless, or are misdirected in eccentric contrariety. The poetry of Bob Dylan veers in its metaphoric texture between the more lyrical ads and the *Daily New* editorials; the new left sniffles and stumbles into the unwitting anacolutha of *uh* and *you-know;* the old left tends to rant and cant, persuasive only to the persuaded. There are clear teachers like Allen Krebs and Staughton Lynd, but as good teachers they are probably not orators.

6 The achievement of Malcolm X, then, though inevitable, seems marvelous. Someone had to rise and speak the fearful reality, to throw the light of reason into the hallucinatory world of the capitalist and biracial society that thinks itself egalitarian, that thinks itself humanitarian and pacific. But it was unexpected that the speaking should be done with such power and precision by a russet-haired field Negro translated from conventional thief to zealot and at the end nearly to Marxist and humanist.

7 For the rhetoric of the American black outsider in this age has seldom been promising; this is not the century of Toussaint L'Ouverture or the nation of Frederick Douglass. The charismatic strength of Father Divine, or of Elijah Muhammad, did not derive from rhetoric. The language of one was hypnotically abstruse, if not perfectly unintelligible, related not to oratory or to religion but to New Thought. The oratory of the other is diffuse and halting, unornamented, solecistic, provincial, its development over-deliberate, its elocution low-keyed though rising to an affecting earnestness. Robert Williams has force but not majesty or art. Men like James Baldwin and Le Roi Jones are primarily writers, and each is deficient in the verbal and vocal size and action required in oratory, which is neither writing nor talking. The young Negro radicals are beyond criticism, the gloomy product not so much of the ghetto as of TV and the American high school. The Nobel Laureate and the Harlem Congressman have different oratorical talents, but neither is an outsider.

8 The rhetoric of Malcolm X was in the perennial traditions of the art, but appropriate to his audiences and purpose—perennial because appropriate. A Harlem rally is not the Senate of the Roman Republic, but Cicero would have approved Malcolm's discourses as *accommodatus, aptus, congruens,* suitable to his circumstances and subject. His exordia were properly brief, familiar, sometimes acidly realistic (". . . brothers and sisters, friends and enemies: I just can't believe everyone in here is a friend and I don't want to leave anybody out."), and he moved to his proposition within the first minute, for his audience needed relevant ideas and theses, not dignity and amplitude. His perorations were similarly succinct, sometimes entirely absorbed into the confirmations. His personal apologiae, negative or self-depreciatory, contrary to those of a Cicero or a Burke, assured his hearers that he was on the outside, like them: "I'm not a politician, not even a student of politics; in fact, I'm not a student of much of anything. I'm not a Democrat, I'm not a Republican, and I don't even consider myself an American," an ironic gradation or augmentative climax that was, in the world of Malcolm and his people, really a kind of declination or reversed climax.

9 His narration and confirmation were densely analytical, but perspicuous because of their familiar diction and analogies, and their catechetical repetitions: "And to show you what his [Tshombe's] thinking is—a hired killer —what's the first thing he did? He hired more killers. He went out and got the mercenaries from South Africa. And what is a mercenary? A hired killer. That's all a mercenary is. The anti-Castro Cuban pilots, what are they? Mercenaries, hired killers. Who hired them? The United States. Who hired the killers from South Africa? The United States; they just used Tshombe to do it."

10 Instruction was the usual purpose of Malcolm's oratory; he was primarily a teacher, his oratory of the demonstrative kind, and his speeches filled with significant matter. It was the substantive fullness and penetration, the honesty and closeness to reality of Malcolm's matter that imparted much of the force to his oratory.

11 A representative political speech in the United States is empty of content. What did President Kennedy's Inaugural Address contain that a commencement address does not? Indeed, the Inaugural displayed the meaningless chiasmus, the fatuous or sentimental metaphor, the callow hyperbaton of a valedictory. President Johnson's speeches on foreign affairs vitiate reason and intelligence as his foreign policy violates international morality: temporarily not to attack a neutral nation is a positive beneficence that should evoke gratitude and concessions, and one is ready to negotiate with any party under any conditions except the party and conditions that are relevant. But such is the tradition of vacant and meaningless political oratory in America, and such the profusion of the universally accepted and discredited rhetoric of advertising, that the public nods and acquiesces, not believes. We expect truth and substance not in open oration, but in secret conference or in caucus, "on the inside"—where we can't hear it. We assume that rhetoric is a futile and deceptive or self-deceived art, because rhetoric should persuade through rational conviction, but business and government are ruled by power and interest. And perhaps Congressional or party oratory is a facade, the votes having been decided not by analogies and metonymies but by the Dow-Jones averages.

12 Yet the people, closer to reason than their legislators, may still be moved by rhetoric, and popular oratory may still be a political force. We wonder how a crowd in Havana can listen to the Premier for three hours. A revolution needs people, and to explain a revolution needs time, and three hours is little enough. To explain a self-maintaining American polity and economy while evading its real problems needs very little time, and three hours of Hubert Humphrey would be unconscionable.

13 Malcolm's speeches, if not so complex, not so informed or copious as those of an accomplished revolutionary, were not vacuous. The man whose secondary education began painstakingly and privately in the Norfolk Prison Colony was able to analyze for his people their immediate burden, its maintenance in a system of domestic power and its relation to colonialism, more acutely than the white and black Ph.D.'s with whom he debated. A man about whose life it is difficult not to sentimentalize was seldom sentimental in his oratory, and though he simplified he did not platitudinize.

14 Malcolm's simplifications, sometimes dangerous, though commonplace in popular oratory and less sophistic than those in establishment rhetoric, derived from the simplicity of his central message: that colored people have

been oppressed by white people whenever white people have been able to oppress them, that because immediate justice is not likely ("Give it to us yesterday, and that's not fast enough"), the safest thing for all is to separate, that the liberty to "sit down next to white folks—on the toilet" is not adequate recompense for the past 400 years. Like Robert Owen or John Brown or William Lloyd Garrison, Malcolm spent the good years of his life asserting one idea and its myriad implications and its involved strategies in a society in which the black is often a noncitizen even *de jure*. And because what he said was as intelligible and obvious as a lynching, his rhetorical content was not embarrassed by the tergiversations, the sophisms, the labored evasions, the empty grandiloquence of American political oratory.

15   The American press attributed the preaching of violence to a man who was no political activist, who moved in the arena of words and ideas, and who usually described a condition of violence rather than urged a justifiably violent response. The *New York Times* obituary editorial, magisterially obtuse, was representative. At worst, Malcolm X, like St. Alphonsus Liguori, taught the ethic of self-defense. *Méchant animal!* The weakness of Malcolm, in fact, and of Elijah Muhammad, is that they were not activists; unlike Martin Luther King, neither had a "movement," for neither went anywhere. Malcolm's success in enlarging the Nation of Islam from 400 to 40,000 and in drawing "well-wishers" by the hundreds of thousands was from the ideas and the words, not from an appeal to action, and not from an appeal to license: the call to moral responsibility and the perpetual Lent of the Muslims repelled most Negroes as it would repel most whites.

16   But Malcolm's essential content was so simple and elemental, his arguments, like Thoreau's, so unanswerable, that the American press, even when not covertly racist, could not understand him, accustomed as it is to the settled contradictions of civil logic in a biracial country.

17   What answer is there to the accusations that in a large part of America, a century after the 14th Amendment, some kinds of murderers cannot be punished by law, that the law is the murderer? Is it an answer that we must tolerate injustice so that we may enjoy justice? Contemning such deformed logic, and adhering to obvious moral truths, Malcolm, like the Bogalusa Deacons, had little difficulty in understanding and explaining to his audiences the Thomistic conception of law better than the Attorney General of the United States understands it. Malcolm was always disconcerted when the powers that be and their exponents refused to recognize the legality of humanity. His strongest vocal emphases were on words like law and right: "They don't use *law*," he exclaimed of the United States Government, which, he asserted, directed the Central Congolese Government, which was directed by outside interests, and the lawfulness of the Eastern Government was more valid, he thought, because it was of its own people.

18   Justice and equity and emancipation, not violence, not hatred, not retribution, and not the theology of the Muslims were the central matter of Malcolm's oratory, though that theology was useful as a repudiation of American white Christianity. He had entered the stream of sane and moral social teaching before his parting from Elijah Muhammad, and was deepening his knowledge and expression of it at the moment of the death he expected each day, ἔρχεται νὺξ [the night comes].

19 If his theses were terrible, it was because they were asserted without compromise or palliation, and because the institutional reality they challenged was terrible. How else to indicate reality and truth if not by direct challenge? Indirection is not workable, for the state has stolen irony; satire is futile, its only resource to repeat the language of the Administration. To say that the American tradition beckons us onward to the work of peace in Vietnam, or that they who reject peace overtures are great servants of peace, is to speak not ironically but authoritatively. The critical efficacy even of absurd literature is threatened by real reductions toward the absurd and beyond, and when usable, absurd statement cannot be at once terse, clear, complex, and unequivocal. The only useful attack is directness, which, opposed to outrage, is outraged and, to apologists of outrage, outrageous.

20 Malcolm's challenge soon implied anticolonialism, in which was implied anticapitalism. Not a doctrinal Marxist when he died, Malcolm had begun to learn a relation between racism and capitalism during his first African journey, and a relation between socialism and national liberation. Rising above the ethical limitations of many civil rights leaders, he rejected a black symbiosis in the warfare state. The black housewife may collect Green Stamps or dividends, the black paterfamilias may possess an Impala and a hi-fi, the black student an unimpeachable graduate degree and a professorship, but what moral black or white could be happy in the world of color TV and Metrecal and napalm? If a rising Negro class could be contented by such hopes and acquirements, if it yearned for the glittering felicities of the American dream, for the Eden of *Life* and *Ebony*, Malcolm had finer longings, and so his following was small: his vision was more intense, more forbidding than that of King or Wilkins or Farmer. They preached integrated Americanism; Malcolm taught separation for goodness, the co-existence of morally contrary cultures in a geographic unit, in "America."

21 Because the black had been always alien in America, had been always taught to hate himself in America ("We hated our heads . . . the shape of our nose . . . the color of our skin. . . ."), he now had the freedom to despise, not embrace, a society that had grown alien to humanity, and whose profound alienation had been intimated for the black first in slavery, then in racism. Separation promised not the means to make a black image of Beverly Hills or Westchester, but the liberty to build a new Jerusalem. How might such an evangel be grasped by a social worker or a Baptist minister?

22 Malcolm's earlier expressions of racism, sometimes augmented or dis-

torted in the misreporting, were a means or an error that receded after his Islamic-African pilgrimage, qualified into renouncement. Their white counterparts have been the political hardware of thousands of local American statesmen and scores of United States Congressmen, and how many have not outgrown them, are legislators because of them? An American President can admit to prior racism with little embarrassment, with becoming repentance.

23 It is the growth and maturing that matter, and Malcolm's ideological journey, truncated after beginning late, was leftward, enlightened, and opening toward humanitarianism and unsentimental fraternalism, contrary to that of some British lords and some Yale graduates, contrary to that of the young American Marxists of the 1930s, now darkening into polarized anticommunism. There were no saner, more honest and perspicuous analyses of the racial problem than Malcolm's last speeches and statements, beside which the pronouncements of most administrations and civic officials are calculated nonsense. Only from the outside can some truths be told.

24 In the rhetoric of Malcolm X, as in all genuine rhetoric, figures correspond to the critical imagination restoring the original idea and to the conscience protesting the desecration of the idea. Tropes and schemes of syntax are departures from literal meaning, *abusiones,* "abuses" of a grammar and semantic that have themselves grown into abuses of original reason. As Shelley saw, the abusion, or trope, like revolutionism, destroys conventional definitions to restore original wholeness and reality. Rhetoric, like revolution, is "a way of redefining reality."

25 The frequent repetitions in Malcolm's rhetoric, like those of Cicero or St. Paul, are communications of the passion that is not satisfied by single statement, but that beats through the pulses. Good rhetorical repetition is viscerally didactic.

26 But it is an especially dangerous device, its potential of fraudulence proportionate to its elemental power to persuade. It may reinforce truths, it may add stones to build great lies. The anaphoras of Administration rhetoric lead successive clauses each further from reality. Abstractions in repetitions, like the "peace" and "freedom" of the Presidential addresses, are usually doubtful, because ambiguous and inaccessible to testing. War may very well be peace, and slavery freedom, if the predications are repeated often enough.

27 The substantives and verbs in Malcolm's repetitions were usually concrete, exposing themselves to empirical judgment:

> As long as the white man sent you to Korea, you bled. He sent you to Germany, you bled. He sent you to the South Pacific to fight the Japanese, you bled. You bleed for white people, but when it comes to seeing your own church being bombed and little black girls murdered, you haven't got any blood. You bleed when the white man says bleed;

you bite when the white man says bite; and you bark when the white man says bark.

28 Malcolm here began with epistrophe for reinforcement of a repeated reality, combined it with anaphora to shift focus to "the man," moved to epanastrophe in the third and fourth sentences, in which "the man" and the black man share the repeating emphasis, and to epanadiplosis in the fourth for a doubled emphasis on *bleed,* while a tolling alliteration of labials and liquids instructs the outer ear, while asyndeton accelerates a tautness and indignation, and while the fullness of emotion evokes a pathetic-sardonic syllepsis on *blood.*

29 His rhetorical questions and percontations with repetition, here anaphora and epistrophe, have the urgency of a Massillon convincing a noble audience of the probability of their damnation:

> Why should white people be running all the stores in our community?
> Why should white people be running the banks of our community?
> Why should the economy of our community be in the hands of the white
> man? Why?

30 The orator may redirect as well as repeat his syntactic units. Malcolm used chiasmus, or crossing of antithetic sets, not deceptively, not to confound realities, but to explore the calculated fantasies of the American press, to untangle the crossing of image and reality:

> . . . you end up hating your friends and loving your enemies . . . The press is so powerful in its image-making role, it can make a criminal look like he's the victim and make the victim look like he's the criminal.
> . . . If you aren't careful, the newspapers will have you hating the people who are being oppressed and loving the people who are doing the oppressing.

31 Malcolm was attracted to chiasmus as an economy in dialectic. In the Oxford Union Society debate of December 1964, he explicated and defended Senator Goldwater's chiasmus of *extremism* and *moderation,* converting the memorable assault upon radical reform into an apology for black militancy.
32 As the strict clausal scheme may be varied to represent emotional thought, strict demonstration may be relieved by paradox and analogy. Paradox, here climactic and with repetitions, writes itself into any narrative of American Negro history since 1863:

> How can you thank a man for giving you what's already yours? How then can you thank him for giving you only part of what's already yours?

33 With an analogy Malcolm dismissed Roy Wilkins' quaver that though the black may be a second-class American, he is yet an American, with his little part of the affluent dream:

> I'm not going to sit at your table and watch you eat, with nothing on my plate, and call myself a diner. Sitting at the table doesn't make you a diner, unless you eat some of what's on that plate. Being here in America doesn't make you an American. Being born here in America doesn't make you an American.

34 We see a black man with half the income of a white, and think of other hungers, and the analogy works as symbol and image, like Bacon's winding stair to great place or Demosthenes' Athenian boxer defending himself from multiple blows.

35 Metaphor and metonymy are the symbolic image condensed and made freer from customary logic than the more explicit analogy. Like repetitions and analogies they may be recognizably fraudulent, for symbolic language is not dissociated from truth. We must know or imagine the referent before we can judge and be moved by the symbol. When an American President now says, "The door of peace must be kept wide open for all who wish to avoid the scourge of war, but the door of aggression must be closed and bolted if man himself is to survive," he is disquieting tame, weary metaphors, long since grown insipid and moribund, into a defiance of meaning, and the very antithesis emphasizes the inanity of the ghostwritten rhetoric in a linguistic culture that has not finally adopted Newspeak. If the figures are initially suspect because of the designed, limitless ambiguity and abstractness of the referents, they are contemptible when related to the realities they profess to clarify. Such metaphor is not the discovery of truth but its concealment. "When I can't talk sense," said the eighteenth-century Irish orator, John Curran, "I talk metaphor."

36 The metaphors of Malcolm X, sometimes ethnically conventional, sometimes original, sometimes inevitable ("I don't see an American dream. I see an American nightmare."), were rarely ambiguous in the abstract member, and were often concrete in both, lending themselves to the touch of common experience. They were infrequent, less frequent than in the elevated tradition of Pitt and Burke and Webster. Malcolm's oratory resembled rather that of the self-educated reformer Cobden in its simple, unornamented vigor, in its reduction to essential questions, in its analytic directness and clarity. In Malcolm's oratory as in Cobden's, metaphor was exceptional in a patter of exposition by argumentation in abstract and literal diction.

37 And because Malcolm wished to demonstrate rather than suggest, he preferred the more fully ratiocinative structure, the analogy, to the more condensed and poetic metaphor: he had wished to be not a poet but a lawyer when his elementary school English teacher advised him to turn to carpentry. So also, Malcolm composed in the larger grammatical unit, the paragraph, which corresponds to analogy, rather than in the sentence, which corresponds to metaphor. In answering questions he often prefaced his extended expositions with the request not for one more word or one more sentence, but for "one more paragraph"—and a paragraph indeed was what he usually produced, extemporaneous and complete with counterthesis, thesis, development, synthesis and summary.

38 The metaphors and metonymies, restricted in number, often suggested truth, like the analogies, by fusing image and symbol, as in poetry: Blake's little black thing amid the snow is sensuously and spiritually black, the snow sensuously and spiritually white. Malcolm used the same deliberate indetermination of perception in the image by which he characterized white immigrants in America:

> Everything that came out of Europe, every blue-eyed thing is already an American.

Synecdoche and tmesis combine to refocus on generic essentials for a black audience.

39 In quick answer to an immoderating Stan Bernard and an uncivil Gordon Hall, and trying to defend the thesis that the Muslims were a force in the Negro movement though numerically insignificant, Malcolm compared them with the Mau Mau, then condensed an implicit analogy to a metaphor and, with characteristically temerarious simplification, expanded and explicated the metaphor into analogy:

> The Mau Mau was also a minority, a microscopic minority, but it was the Mau Mau who not only brought independence to Kenya, but— . . . but it brought it—that wick. The powder keg is always larger than the wick. . . . It's the wick that you touch that sets the powder off.

40 By a folk metonymy in one pronoun, more convincing than the usual rhethorical patriotic genealogies, Malcolm enlarged to their real dimension the time and space of the Negro's misfortune:

> many of us probably passed through [Zanzibar] on our way to America 400 years ago.

41 The identification of Malcolm with his audience, not merely through the plural pronoun, was so thorough that he affected the desired harmony or union in which the speaker can disregard his audience as an object and speak his own passion and reason, when between himself and his hearers there is no spiritual division. The great orator does not play upon his audience as upon a musical instrument; his verbal structures are artful but urged from within.

42 Malcolm's composition and elocution were remarkable in their assimilative variety. Before the mixed or white audiences, as at college forums, the composition was more abstract and literal, austerely figured, grammatically pure, and the elocution sharper, somewhat rapid and high-pitched, near his speaking voice, enunciated precisely but not mimetic or over-articulated. Before the great black audiences Malcolm adopted a tone and ornament that were his and his audience's but that he relinquished before the white or the academic. The composition of the black speeches was rich in ethnic figuration and humor, in paronomasia, alliteration, and rhyme (the novocained patient, blood running down his jaw, suffers "peacefully"; if you are a true revolutionary "You don't do any singing, you're too busy swinging"; the Negroes who crave acceptance in white America "aren't asking for any nation—they're trying to crawl back on the plantation"). The elocution of this, Malcolm's grand style, was deeper, slower, falling into a tonal weighting and meiosis, wider in its range of pitch, dynamics, emphasis.

43 Always exhibiting a force of moral reason, never hectic or mainly emotional, Malcolm changed from *homo afer* to *homo europaeus* as the ambience and occasion required. In the mosques he employed the heavy vocal power of impassioned Negro discourse; in academic dialogue and rebuttal his voice sometimes resembled that of Adlai Stevenson in its east-north-central nasality, and in its hurried, thoughtful pauses, its wry humor, its rational rather than emotional emphases.

44 It is understandable that he was correct, intelligible, lucid, rational, for few public orators in our time have been as free as Malcolm from the need to betray their own intelligence. John Kennedy, who in January pledged a quest for peace and a revulsion from colonialism, in one week of the following April repudiated the Cuban invasion he was then assisting, in another week of the same April pugnaciously justified the intervention, and, having been rebuked by reality, reproached reality with a dialectic from the Mad Tea-Party. His audience was appropriate: American newspaper editors. Later, waving a flag in the Orange Bowl, he would promise the émigré landlords warfare and their restored rents with melodramatic and puerile metonymy. Adlai Stevenson, who twice had talked sense to the American people, denied his government's aggression in Cuba with juridical solemnity, with the noble anaphoras, the poignant metaphors, the sensitive ironies of the campaign speeches, and, fatally drawn to display *expertise,* derisively censured the oratory of Raul Roa. His indignant exposure of revolutionaries was submerged in the laughter of the black galleries of the world; he indulged himself, during the Congo debates, in the pointless metonymies of Independence Day addresses; and his recurrent denunciations of colonialism were freaks of unintended irony.

45 "Who would not weep, if Atticus were he?"

46 Malcolm, more fortunate than these, was not ordained by history to be the spokesman or the apologist of violence and unthinkable power, and so was not forced to violate reason. In his last years he was in the great tradition of rational and moral speech, consanguineous with Isaiah, with Demosthenes and Cicero, with Paine and Henry, Lincoln and Douglass, as they were allied to the primitive idea of goodness. He was not an emotionalist or a demagogue, but an orator who combined familiarity with passion, with compelling ideas and analytic clarity, and with sober force of utterance, and with a sense, now usually deficient except when depraved, of rhetoric as an art and a genre.

47 His feeling for the art was probably the benefit of his old-fashioned verbal and literary education in prison. As the rhetoric of Frederick Douglass, then a young slave, originated in his readings of Sheridan's oratory, so Malcolm's alma mater, he said, was "books." The methodical longhand copying of thousands of logical definitions, his nightly labor with the dictionary in prison, left an impress of precision in diction and syntax, later tested and hardened in hostile debate. As he learned the science and the habits of grammar, Malcolm learned the unfamiliar subtleties of the art of rhetoric within a few years. As late as 1961 he prevailed in debate more by conviction than by linguistic accuracy, and the solecisms were embarrassing to his literate admirers and probably to himself, as were the parochial pronunciations, atavistic traces of which could be heard very rarely in the last year ("*influence*"). But this sense of rhetoric derived also from his perception of the ideas that antedate rhetoric and that inform all moral language. His teaching, because elemental and unsophisticated in its morality, was more sane, more philosophic than the wisdom of many an academician who, detached from the facts of human pain, has the institutionalized intelligence to devise a morality to fit his institution, who can make policy his morality: Arthur Schlesinger, Jr. can regard the genocidal war in Vietnam as "an experiment, . . . something you have to try."

48 In his maturity, Malcolm was always aware of the centrally ethical and honest enough not to elude it, and so he soon outgrew what was doctrinally grotesque in the Nation of Islam (what native American religious movement is without such grotesqueness?). But he retained the religious commitment and the wholesome ascesis of the Muslims, and thus was helped in the exhausting work of the last years, the weeks of eighteen-hour days. A mixed seed fell in good soil.

49 He emerged from dope, prostitution, burglary, prison, and a fanciful sectarianism to enter a perennial humanist art, to achieve a brilliant facility in oratory and debate, in less time than many of us consume in ambling through graduate school. His developing and accomplishment in the last year was, as a *New York Times* reporter exclaimed but could not write, "incredible." The Oxford Union Society, venerable, perceptive, and disinterested because unAmerican, adjudged him among the best of living orators after his debate there months before his death, a pleasant triumph ignored by the American press. Though he may be diluted, or obliterated, or forgotten by the established civil rights movement, which is built into the consensus, Malcolm was for all time an artist and thinker. In the full Aristotelean meaning he was a rhetorician, who, to be such, knew more than rhetoric: ethics, logic, grammar, psychology, law, history, politics; and his best speeches might be texts for students of that comprehensive science and art.

50 His controlled art, his tone of pride without arrogance, have followers if not a school, in his own Muslim Mosque and among the Nation of Islam, audible in the rational and disdainful replies of Norman 3X in the murder trial. But Malcolm is distinct rhetorically from his admirers among the surly school of Negro speakers, the oratorical equivalent of *Liberator,* who have little to offer their mixed auditory but insolence and commonplaces in broken and frenetic, in monotonous or ill-accented language. And he was remote from the misanthropic and negativist among the alienated. Malcolm, a religionist, could not be "bitter," or descend to scatology in expressing moral outrage. The laughter or chuckling, in his several oratorical styles, was, in motive and in sound, not embittered, or malicious, or frustrated, but apodictic; it was the laughter of assured rectitude, and amusement at the radical unreason of the opposition. For not he but the established structures were the opposition, dissentient to godly reason and justice, which were the authority for his teaching. Hearing Malcolm was an experience not morbid or frightening, but joyous, as Mark Van Doren said of reading *Hamlet.* Though the drama and the man were tragic, in each the confident and varied movement of language and moral ideas told us something superb about our humanity. Malcolm combined magnificence and ethnic familiarity to demonstrate what he asserted: the potential majesty of the black man even in America, a majesty idiosyncratic but related to all human greatness. And so his last ten years tell us that a man can be more fully human serving a belief, even if to serve it requires that he borrow from the society that his service and belief affront. If he and his people illustrate that the grand primal ideas and their grand expression can be spoiled for men by institutions, the whole work and life of Malcolm X declare that the good man, if he has the soul to resist the state and its courts and senates, can restore the ideal world of art and justice.

Leonard R. N. Ashley: A Guided Tour of Gobbledygook

As many of us have learned to our embarrassment or frustration, choice of words has consequences. If chosen with a sensitivity for their meaning and appropriateness, words can convey our thoughts and feelings lucidly, gracefully, and cogently. Chosen ineptly, they either block communication entirely or create an effect that is the opposite of what we intended. The term gobbledygook *is a coinage that designates a wide range of insensitive, inept word-choices, but originally it was used to label the kind of bureaucratic jargon that often appears in government, military, business, academic, or advertising prose. With wit and humor, but with a fine sense for the nuances of language, Leonard Ashley makes skillful use of the rhetoric of ridicule to expose occurrences of gobbedygook in several areas of modern life. The author, who took his Ph.D. degree at Princeton University and who now teaches English at Brooklyn College, originally delivered this as an address to the conference of District II of the American Alumni Council on January 31, 1963.*

1 Some intelligent person has said—I may have said it myself—that the most important skill a student acquires in college is the ability to express himself in words. Well, perhaps that isn't what he actually acquires, but that's what he pays for. (Education is one of the very few things in this country that people are willing to pay for and not get.)

2 Seriously, though (as the comedians are beginning to say today) ... seriously, though, the most fundamental and the most universally applicable skill a student can develop is the ability to communicate: to write and speak, to inform and explain and persuade.

3 To change tires or to jerk sodas or deliver groceries not much skill in expression is necessary. But at all levels beyond that, in both business and the professions, success, recognition, and advancement go to those (and only to those) who can convey their ideas. Men, even in the most technical specialties, must work together. No one makes a product alone any more: it seems that even executives (who manufacture decisions) are being compelled to work in teams. And even those who still enjoy the luxury of thinking for themselves and making their own decisions have to transmit their ideas— straight-forwardly, forcefully, accurately, convincingly, even inspiringly.

4 Part of my job as a college teacher is to teach students how to think and

From *The American Alumni Council News*, XXX (June 1963), 11-16. Reprinted by permission of the author and the American Alumni Council, Washington, D.C.

to write. (We prefer it when the two abilities coincide.) And one of the biggest difficulties encountered by those of us who teach English is the rapid and alarming collapse of the American language under an ever increasing load of gobbledygook and jargon.

5   As Duffy used to say in the dear, dead days of radio: "Leave us face it." The American language, a comparatively youthful and obstreperous offspring of English, is even more vigorous than its parent and (like many children today) even more confused. We are a nation that delights in misquoting the Chinese proverb that "one picture is worth a thousand words." Writing started with pictures, and it looks as if there is a real danger that we might revert. We don't read magazines any more; we look at pictures. We don't talk to each other any more; we watch pictures of other people talking to each other on television. When we get tired of television we don't read a book; we go to the cinema and look at pictures, bigger ones. Have you noticed that people no longer "give you the word"? Now they "put you in the picture."

6   We can understand pictures fairly well now—even the complicated anatomical ones in the TV commercials—but we are no longer so good at using words.

7   To make matters worse, America's highest-paid and most widely-published authors (I mean the advertising boys) are far more often determined to confuse you rather than tell you something clearly and simply. They bombard you with meaningless statistics, pseudo-scientific jargon, empty phrases studded with vague terms such as "additives" and "conditioners." They're taking the logic out of language. What's the "regular" size of soap? Why the one you don't regularly buy. (It's too small.) What's the "economy" size? The one that costs more.

8   Advertising ballyhoo has made us all insensitive to superlatives. A Hollywood producer is asked about his latest picture: "How is it?" "It's colossal, magnificent," he replies, "but it's improving." A 21-inch TV screen is described as "huge." If it is, what's a 9' x 12' rug? (I must admit that even the advertising boys are embarrassed about calling a 21-inch screen "huge"— by the way, that's the *diagonal* measurement!—and now they give the area in square inches, relying on the fact that, if there's anything the American public knows less about than its native language, it's mathematics.)

9   The politicians are adding to the confusion. "Nationalization" has become "public ownership." A "bust" has become "deflation," "retrenchment," or "downward readjustment." The word "free" has lost nearly all meaning, now that the "Free World" includes South Africa, Spain, and the vilest governments of South America. "Peace" has become a dirty word. Preparations for war are called "defence programmes." Hydrogen bombs are "thermonuclear deterrents"—which sounds as if they were protections

against hydrogen bombs. We even have "clean" bombs. The Ultimate Detergent?

10 The fact that more than a million young thugs are hauled before the courts every year doesn't sound nearly so bad if you'll call young criminals "juvenile delinquents." A "delinquent," by definition, *hasn't* done something. These kids *have!*

11 All this fuzzy expression reflects either plain dishonesty or mental incapacity. People who listen to this sort of thing day in and day out become the victims of Stupidity Fallout. We shop in "superettes" (a word formed from the Latin for "big" and the French for "small"). We say "A-OK." Our leaders talk of "future planning," as if we could plan for the past or this instant. I'd better get off this one. As a writer of occasional articles on military history I have been guilty of "past planning": telling the generals how to fight the last war. But, speaking of generals, I once met a janitor whom I thought to be a major-general because he told me he was the "superintendent" of West Point.

12 No wonder Emery Jacobs, a largely illiterate official of the Agriculture Department testifying before a Congressional Committee that was trying (I think) to nominate Billie Sol Estes as Farmer of the Year, could say: "The state to which the situation has been definitized is uncertain." No wonder the chief of staff of the United States Air Force burbles about the "globility" of Strategic Air Command. No wonder Peter de Vries can satirize people who complain of a charge that is "nominal in name only." No wonder Sonny Liston's manager announces that he won't let his fighter fly because on airlines today "people are dying who never died before." No wonder I personally have picked up a printed matchbook in a cafeteria at 1600 Pennsylvania Avenue, Washington, D.C., as a souvenir of "The White House Mess." No wonder I saw a sign in New Rochelle, New York, that read "Eyes Examined While You Wait."

13 Even our bright young men and women in the colleges have been infected. Pick up anything they've written: a note, a term paper, an examination. What do you find? Very often you find weak logic, vague language, blatant inaccuracy in more than orthography, and so little imagination that you seldom find an adjective in bed with a noun to which it has not been married for centuries.

14 Frequently those that are imaginative are deliriously so. Here are some gems of purest ray serene from the dark, unfathomed caves of my student files:

> Entrance requirements have gone so high that nobody can get into college, and the reason that nobody can get in is that everybody is going.

> Abstinence is a good thing if practised in moderation.

It was the painter Donatello's interest in the female nude that made him The Father of the Renaissance.

(Examination question: Identify "Skylark.") Skylark is the merchant of Shakespeare's play. When we first see him he is on the Rialto, which is the business end of Venus.

An active verb shows action, and a passive verb shows passion.

(If *pro* is the opposite of *con*, give examples.) Progress and Congress.

In Bernard Shaw's play *Mrs. Warren's Profession* her profession is the Oldest Profession but she is not really a Lost Woman. She is just mislaid.

The food in the cafeteria is absolute poison and they give you such small portions. It's about time the students spoke up about this unspeakable situation.

In Shakespeare's comedies every Tom, Dick and Harry is named Sebastian.

Socrates died from an overdose of wedlock, but before he went he had the crowned heads of Athens shaking in their shoes. It was a good thing for them he was determined to stay and die even if it killed him.

The world's greatest problem today is the H-Bomb. That's dynamite!

A virgin forest is a place where the hand of man has never set foot.

All these atrocities clearly demonstrate the connection between fuzzy writing and fuzzy thinking, and the student's explanation only makes matters worse: "I may be wrong, but I'm not far from it." As they say in businesses: "Here is creeping stagnation on a high plateau."

15 Some Americans, of course, write brilliantly, vividly, concretely, memorably. There are those who can say what they mean—and mean to say something. But there's a strange thing about our American civilization. (I believe we do have an American civilization, despite the charges of my European friends who claim that America is the only nation in the history of the world that has moved from barbarism to decadence without passing through civilization.) The strange thing here is that a number of Americans are called upon to speak when they have nothing to say—and they get up and say it!

16 Pity the poor president—and my example is drawn from history, not the current administration—inarticulate by nature and by military training, largely ungrammatical and faced by a battery of reporters who fire questions —many of which should not be asked or cannot be answered—and expect replies then and there. In a press conference the chief executive cannot use any of these sensible replies, however appropriate: "I don't know," "I've

never understood it," "They don't tell me these things," "That's a secret," "God only knows," "We don't know yet," etc. He has to say something. Moreover, he must begin now and go on until he thinks of something: he must start the mouth before the brain is engaged. He has to hem and haw and sound like a fool and know all the while that every inanity will be copied *verbatim* and reported in full in the *New York Times*. He cannot obey the first rule of communication: when you have nothing to say, say nothing. He goes on, "verbosing it up," stalling, stumbling, obfuscating, hiding behind words, embroidering with meaningless clichés, decorating any idea that may be there with a fringe of dangling modifiers.

17 To quote from a press conference transcript would be too painful, but here are some remarks (from an *ex tempore* address at West Point, June 5, 1960) which demonstrates the effect the presidency can have on a man's prose:

> It is indeed, difficult, in the circumstances in which I find myself, to dis-cover words that seem appropriate to the situation. . . .
>
> Now tonight we meet at a time of bewilderment. I don't like this term or the using of the term that we are living always in crisis. We are not. There is no nation in this world that dares at this moment to attack the United States, and they know it.
>
> But we wonder what is the outcome of every decent, proper gesture we make to those that live in the other camp. They live in a closed so-ciety, secrecy of intent—which we try to penetrate, and in my opinion properly, but we are certain of this: our problem is not only keeping ourselves strong, and by strong I don't mean merely militarily. I mean spiritually, intellectually, scientifically, economically and militarily; and then, we must make certain that all of those people who live with us, in the hope that those concepts of human dignity and freedom and liberty are going to prevail in the world, will always stand by our side in the determination that freedom and liberty will eventually triumph over tyranny.

Dwight MacDonald, who quotes this speech as well as Oliver Jensen's bril-liant *New Republic* parody of Eisenhower delivering The Gettysburg Ad-dress (*Parodies,* Random House, 1960), is not certain which is funnier, fact or fiction.

18 William H. Whyte, Jr. (*Is Anybody Listening,* Simon and Schuster, 1957) tells us about the executives in business who have to speak when they have nothing to say (annual meetings) or don't wish to say anything accurate (retiring employees). He defines their diction on these occasions as *reverse* gobbledygook:

> Where the traditional jargon is multisyllabic, longwinded, and pas-sive, it [reverse gobbledygook] is filled with short, terse words; its sen-

tences are short and the construction of them so much more active than passive that exclamation marks are as frequent as periods. Heavy on personification, homely analogies, and a rigid glossary of hard-hitting words, it lends a powerful straight-from-the-shoulder effect to ambiguity and equivocation.

Whyte and the editors of *Fortune* studied 200 business speeches, identified the 60 most characteristic expressions, and constructed an hilarious composite address. Look it up in Mr. Whyte's book (pages 55–58). You'll vastly enjoy reading it—and, if some day you're stuck for something to say, you can always steal it and deliver it at a board meeting, business convention, Rotary club gathering, academic convocation, etc. They'll love it. But you must deliver it with a straight face, like the ship captain in the Conrad novel who tended to "enunciate platitudes, not with a desire to dazzle, but from honest conviction."

19 Some people are deliberately hiding behind words or thinly veiling their meaning. Thus one British parliamentarian says that another "seldom deviates into accuracy," so Churchill describes Attlee as "a sheep in sheep's clothing," so Sam Goldwyn says, "The best I can give you is a definite maybe" and John Foster Dulles at the Washington airport (on one of his infrequent visits to the United States) said to a reporter: "No comment. And don't quote that." Subtlety is commendable. But what about other motives for being unclear or devious? What about the undertakers who call themselves "morticians," the carpenters who are "construction consultants" when they are simply driving nails ("interfibrous friction fastener installation")? Aren't things getting confused when a man employed to cut things *out* of TV scripts is called a "continuity *acceptance* man" instead of a "censor"? Why is the garbage man ashamed of his work to the point where he calls himself a "sanitary engineer"? And what happens to people who really are sanitary engineers? Must every man who cleans toilets prettify it into "restroom attendant employment"? Must every Billy Goat Hill become Angora Heights? What's wrong with "rat-catchers" (now "rodent operatives") and "watchmen" ("surveillance personnel")?

20 This kind of elegant variation can lead to a man whose father was hanged as a horse thief explaining the death by saying that "my father was taking part in a public ceremony when the platform collapsed." (If the father were electrocuted one could make him sound like a deceased professor: "My father occupied the chair of Applied Electricity at a large institution in one of the western states.")

21 It's only silly when pompous people talk about their "residences" instead of their homes and wear "suitings" and "shirtings" instead of suits and shirts, "creations" instead of dresses. But it may indicate a deep dishonesty when the Army purchases 2000 portable showers, for the use of laborers ("Missilemen Fourth Class"?) who spill rocket fuel on themselves, and calls them "Rocket Propellant Personnel Neutralizers."

22 It's the same unwillingness to call a spade a spade that lies behind this next example, an extract from an imaginary lecture by an Army sergeant who is compelled to "gobbledygook it up" because he is ordered (and ashamed) to lecture 50 minutes on an ordinary whistle:

> Awright, you men! Now today we introduce the U.S. missile whistle, Model M-1. This is a self-repeating, shoulder-strap, general personnel model issued to relevant ranks. It is lung-operated, reverberating-blast, and air-type cooled.
>
> The whistle itself proper weighs in the neighborhood of about an ounce and the attached chain (which you see attached) adds about another half an ounce or so to the overall weight. The whistle is divided up into two component related parts: these are the whistle-cylinder blowing assembly and the whistle-retaining chain assembly mechanism.
>
> At the blowing aperture there are two raised sections—the men in the back better stand up to see this—one on each side. They are called the upper-teeth guard lug and the lower-teeth guard lug, respectively.
>
> The opening from the blowing end into the main cylinder is termed the compressing blow channel. The remaining component part of the whistle is known as the chamber-cylinder operating assembly complex. *That* consists of the opening sound-emission slot, the cylinder-butt lock (onto which the whistle-retaining chain assembly part is attached on), and the cylinder-reverberating operating cork pellet device (which in this case is a common garden variety pea.)

The "disassembly" procedure is pretty funny too. But that's for ordnance only and will not be included in the final examination. We'll finalize this example here. ("Finalize," you'll have noticed, means "we haven't finished with it but to hell with it.")

23 Executives in the "Armed Forces" are prone to ape business. They, too, never begin anything—they "initiate action." They don't collect information —they "assemblize imponderables." Then they make these imponderables as ponderous as possible, "process" them, and "phase them in" with other "factors."

24 My own experience (in the Royal Canadian Air Force, among the paragraph troopers at a chairborne headquarters) includes a Wing Commander who advised me, in writing, to "get behind this thing and lead." There are other good examples of the military mind at work (or not working). Take my "opposite number" in the Navy when I was a staff officer at AFHQ. He belonged in the Navy, where he could use flags and heliographs to communicate, because he couldn't use prose. One day he telephoned me to say that he couldn't give me, over the 'phone, the information

I needed. It was secret. It was still secret, to me, after I read his subsequent memorandum, which I quote in part:

> In the referenced period under review, brought to your liaison for the cross-fertilization of ideas in a recent telephonic communication with the undersigned, the following SECRET situation, uncommunicable thereby, is hereby adumbrated in detail:
>
> Our sea/air strikes against the enemy realized a very real improvement in results relative to fighter forces and, while the reverse might obtain for the enemy, the steady rise in blanket cover of the opposing fighter effort (as disclosed by the figures in Appendix "A") is not materially altered when due allowance is made for this possibility.

This shows what can happen when you stop using human intelligence and start using military intelligence. It's the sort of thing that creates the "climate" in which a high-ranking officer can put this "minute" (the official term for a jotting in a margin) on a junior officer's "dossier":

> Flight Lieutenant A_____ is not recommended for this liaison duty as I consider him inexperienced. He has little Air Force experience and no naval.

Add jargon to gobbledygook and the result is horrendous. The officer who barks in trenchant monosyllables writes like this:

> We have locked on to operationally significant quantities of practicable equipment to zero in on optimum capabilities if the aforementioned philosophy materializes. Conceptual imponderables will be minimized by programming on the mach so as to firm it up and cream it off.

That's swashbuckling prose that buckles where it ought to swash! The deleterious effect of advertising jargon is apparent. Advertising jargon! I can just see General George Washington showing Betsy Ross's new American flag to the Continental Congress. "I'm just talking off the top of my head, of course," he says, "but what do you fellows say we run it up the pole and see if anybody salutes it?"

25 Advertising men and promotion men and public relations men! The PR people will soon make their "undertaker accounts" acceptable. I can see the black-bordered signs around the city: DIG WE MUST FOR A GREATER NEW YORK. The copywriters will begin to peddle "the only coffins with a lifetime guarantee." Supraliminally, liminally, and subliminally we'll be sold death. "Death: It's Only Nature's Way of Telling You To Slow Down." "Why not? Everybody's doing it." "Eventually—Why Not Now?"

26 Not only advertising jargon but the cant of other closed groups—thieves,

dope addicts, teenagers—has permeated all levels of American life. Low-level people imitate their middle-class betters. High-level people use it to be arch or funny, to avoid having to choose words, to be "democratic" (as stupid as everybody else). You know what I mean, I mean meaningwise? Like man, it's the *least!*

27 Then there's the pedant. He's capable of being polysyllabically stupid in sesquipedalian vocabulary. He writes:

> Individuals domiciled, perforce constrained to be resident, in vitrious structures of patent frangibility should desist absolutely from employing petrous formations as projectiles.

At least this means something—people who live in glass houses shouldn't throw stones—while jazz musicians, for example, can talk for hours without meaning anything or meaning to mean anything. They just dig each other and bury communication.

28 Many critics of literature—not the good ones, the ones John O'Hara so aptly calls "the professional pipe-smokers"—write this way. So do many other people who ought to know better, especially historians who want to impress rather than to inform. Political scientists and economists use (sorry, "utilize") more clichés and are more apt to split an infinitive and end with prepositions when they have nothing else to end with. (No matter what lengths they go to.) That's something which the more consciously literary pedant won't ... ah, *up with which* he will not put.

29 Here's what the political scientist or the sociologist might do with a pithy piece of prose from the King James Version. First, here's *Ecclesiastes:*

> I returned and saw under the sun that the race is not to the swift, nor the battle to the strong, neither yet bread to the wise, nor yet riches to men of understanding, nor yet favour to men of skill; but time and chance happeneth to them all.

Now here's the same passage as translated by George Orwell (whose *1984* warned us, perhaps too late, against "doublethink" and "doublespeak"):

> Objective consideration of contemporary phenomena compels the conclusion that success or failure in competitive activities exhibits no tendency to be commensurate with innate capacity, but that a considerable element of the unpredictable must be taken into account.

That's torturous, but it does mean something, and it does say it, if only "as in a glass, darkly." But what about the bad writers who have nothing to say? And what about the professors of education (always the laughing-stocks of any faculty) who have something to say but are immensely embarrassed because it's so simple a child could understand it (or have thought it up)? The typical education course, I sometimes think, starts with nothing and is continually taking up class time with review. Most of these education experts are renowned for their intolerable lectures and unreadable textbooks and so incompetent, indeed, that even the other pendants notice it. (Of course not *all* professors of education are laughable. You can easily identify the sensible ones: they occasionally speak hesitantly in favor of a little less "methodology" and a modicum of "subject-matter content," and they call themselves "teachers." The others call themselves "educators" or even "educationalists." Some are disguised as psychologists, student advisers, and so on, but they aren't fooling anybody.)

30   In the soft (or "social") sciences the writers most ridiculed (not always most deservedly) are the sociologists, so I suppose we'd better have a sample of their language. The story of the Good Samaritan. Brace yourselves, for such people are literate only in clichés.

> And behold, a certain Socialite stood up and tempted Him, saying, "Master, what shall I do to be socially acceptable?"
> And He said unto him, "Thou shalt love thy in-group as thyself."
> But he, willing to justify himself, said unto Him, "And who is my in-group?" And He, answering, said:
> "A certain fellow travelling down from Aix to Ghent fell among traditionalists, who stripped him of his pretense, offended him, and departed, leaving him half mortified. And by chance there came down a certain realist that way: and, looking upon him as an out-group, he passed him by on the other side. And likewise an idealist, when he was at the place and also looked upon him as an out-group, he passed him by on the other side. But a certain man with a rounded personality, as he journeyed, came where he was: and when he saw him, he adjusted himself to the social situation. And he went to him and took him to an inn and associated with him. Now which of these three, thinkest thou, was in-grouped with him who fell upon hard times?"
> And he said, "He that acted *democratically* towards him." Then He said unto him: "Go, and adjust thyself."

No wonder there's a rumor going around that sociologists are defining *orgy* as "sexual educational group dynamics."

31   Our college students see enough bad writing in the newspapers they read (if any) and in the pretentious as well as the shoddier magazines. They shouldn't find it in the textbooks we force them to buy and read in college. There's an ever-present danger that if they don't fall into one trap (impairing their minds by aping the slangy and inexact dialect of the common man) they may fall into another and plump for padded pedantry.

32   It's all right to write like Henry James if you're struggling with some-

thing subtle and involved, for even Henry James was doing his best to present the complexities lucidly and not consciously attempting to compound the difficulty, but it's pompous foolishness to take a phrase like "there was mob rule at this time" or "you can't concentrate when you are distracted" or "small business is failing in Utica" and make it utterly incomprehensible. There's something radically wrong when a great university cannot turn out a readable catalogue of courses, when students cannot read their psychology textbooks on "the learning process," when professional writers cannot use our language to produce simple income-tax instructions.

33 I once taught at a university whose president issued a Parents' Letter with so little feeling for the language that the one memorable sentence made him the butt of jokes for months. It seems that the university was offering, at the students' request, a course "on the subject of preparation for marriage" (read "sex"). It was to be given, said the announcement, by the chaplain and "three noted lay authorities."

34 I suggest that colleges hide their catalogues and, if necessary, their presidents. Tender minds ought not to be exposed to things like:

> The initiation of a beginning looking toward the commencement of a foundation for the establishment of an opening of a channel for communication of our day-to-day problem-solving activities is, in the writer's opinion, an important tool in the provision of a step forward in the right direction, and should eventually so alter the total university silhouette as to produce a maturation of the striving for the higher echelons of excellence which we are all involved in . . . in which we all have involvement.

Give us freedom from that sort of baleful influence, and we can educate your sons and daughters in their native language, a language which, incidentally, is spoken by 300 million other people. We can equip them with the essential, the fundamental, ability to understand, manipulate, and express ideas. We would even offer a guarantee: we shall succeed, or we shall cheerfully refund your child. The young person must be given something to say and taught how to say it. He must be cautioned that when he has nothing to say he must say nothing. He must be admonished never to use two words where one will suffice, to avoid sloppiness and imprecision. He must be reminded that it is hard to read and painful to listen, that he must have the good manners to make whatever he has to communicate as worthwhile, as accurate, as easy to assimilate as possible.

35 I try to teach my students to make all sentences as long as they have to be and as short as they can be. I tell them to bundle their ideas into packages worth carrying and, at the same time, light enough to be lifted. I tell them to write with distinction if they can—but with distinctness, at any rate. Clarity covers a multitude of sins. A good style may be dramatic and beautifully rhythmic and nicely balanced and euphonious—but above all it is clear, concise, concrete. I encourage them to be as adventurous in their expression as in their ideas—but sound.

36 I invite you as parents to assist in the home, to set an example and teach your children to speak simply, to think clearly, to write logically. Improve their manner of expression: teach them honest English and you will be giving them a great legacy, one that will gain them acceptance in college or professional schools or in life.

37 I invite (exhort) you as executives and administrators and people who deal in communication to speak and write simply yourself. Astound your colleagues. Don't begin letters with "Yours of the 16th *inst.* received and contents duly noted and beg to state...." Get to the point. Resolve that the next dozen letters you write will be only 50 words long each—and watch the results. Build the vocabulary you need—and begin by throwing away all the words you now have that are bent, broken, or worn out. Use what's left (supplemented by new words if necessary) to say honestly and straight-forwardly exactly what you mean, to inform rather than to impress or confuse. The ability to handle that vocabulary (and the ideas it represents and contains) is your greatest asset in handling your important jobs, your associates, and your lives.

Time Essay: Violent Protest: A Debased Language

The following essay discusses the new tactics and the new style that characterize much of the rhetoric of dissent in the second half of this century. Whereas the kind of rhetoric with which this book has been mainly concerned sought to effect its purpose through an expenditure of words that were carefully chosen to conciliate an audience and to appeal primarily to the reason or reasonableness of an audience, the new rhetoric has made extensive use of non-verbal means of communication, and when it has used words, the words chosen have often been notable for their capacity to arouse violent emotion and to alienate, rather than conciliate, at least some members of the audience. It is significant that the tactics of the new rhetoric have been adopted largely by the disenfranchised members of modern society—poor people, students, minority groups—people who normally do not have ready access to the regular channels of communication with the establishment. Unquestionably, the strategies of the new rhetoric have had a measure of

From a Time Essay, *Time*, XCV (May 18, 1970), p. 15. Reprinted by permission of *Time*, The Weekly Newsmagazine; Copyright Time, Inc.

success in getting people to listen, in changing attitudes, and in prompting beneficial actions, and in situations where these strategies are likely to prove appropriate and effective, they must be regarded as additional "available means of persuasion." But just as George Orwell, in his widely reprinted essay "Politics and the English Language" (see p. 000), warned us about the disastrous consequences of man's abuse of his language, so the author of the following essay sounds an ominous note about the potentialities of a deliberate neglect or debasement of the language.

1   Words, like trees, bend with the prevailing winds. In the climate of opinion of the past few years, the word *dissent* has undergone a decided transformation. For most of U.S. history, it clearly meant speech—the unorthodox opinion, the challenging idea. Then, during the 1960s, civil rights protesters took to the streets to fight segregation, and the word became associated with demonstrations as much as with speech. As protests have continued to broaden and increase, *dissent* has come to be used to describe and defend a wide variety of physical acts, including violence toward property and even toward people.

2   The explanation many protesters offer for their switch from verbal to physical dissent is that no one pays attention to words alone any longer. However eloquent it has been, however imaginative its uses, language has not succeeded in eliminating racial discrimination or ending the war in Indochina. So the protesters have resorted to what Social Psychologist Franklyn Haiman of Northwestern University calls "body rhetoric"—sit-ins, lie-ins, marches—and more and more bodies have started colliding. Such public confrontations are an expression of gathering frustration over a society that no longer seems to respond to more traditional forms of dissent.

Communication of Feeling

3   This argument contains a measure of truth. It is also true that in many cases the massed forces of dissent—as at most of last week's rallies mourning the Kent State four—have demonstrated a commendable restraint in not letting verbal protest build into violence. The fact remains, however, that all too often these days dissent is a matter of arson and rock throwing. The reason may be that protesters have despaired of the efficacy of words before they have really mastered them. It is significant that this generation of dissenters has failed to produce a literature, or even a polemic that is likely to endure. On the contrary, it has been persistently, even proudly, nonverbal. It has emphasized a communication of feeling rather than of words. The vocabulary of protest, often weighted down with an outmoded Marxism, is relentlessly conventional and conformist. The same phrases—"up against the

wall," "get the pigs," "tell it like it is"—are endlessly repeated, less for their intrinsic eloquence than for their emotive and symbolic value. And that sort of thing gets tiresome; to borrow from the jargon, it "turns people off." Even the most outrageous obscenities lose their impact when they are used ad nauseam.

4   There is often a disconcerting inexactness about today's rhetoric of dissent. To denounce the Establishment in blanket terms makes little sense in a society composed of several establishments, each with its own ideology and set of mores—many of them surprisingly competitive. "Power to the people" is an admirable democratic slogan—except that, as used presently, what it really seems to mean is power to the leftist radicals who seek to control any revolution in America. It is verbal overkill to describe every mild demurral by whites against the most bluntly radical of black-militant demands as nothing but "racism." And the case for political dissent is weakened when almost any attempts, however peaceful, by college authorities to restore law and order on campus are automatically condemned by militant radicals as proof that the U.S. is a "fascist Amerika." Taken at face value, many protest slogans suggest that the dissenters have seriously misestimated U.S. society and its possibility for evolutionary change.

5   The ultimate debasement of language, of course, is violence. Except for protesters who simply want to destroy—and there are more than a few— most dissenters turn to violence in a desperate effort to communicate their profound feelings of grievance. Yet surely this is too crude a way to get their message across. A bomb, for example, lacks specificity; its meaning is as scattered as its debris. Some people may interpret such an act as a signal to pay more attention to the protester and his cause; many more are likely to read into it a need to make life a lot tougher for the protester. Violence is, essentially, a confession of ultimate inarticulateness.

6   Throughout history, dissent has been more effectively expressed by the word than by the weapon. The French Revolution was betrayed by the ruthless masters of the Terror who silenced all opposition with the guillotine. The enduring importance of the revolution lies, rather, in the principles enunciated on its behalf by the philosophers of the Enlightenment, who bequeathed the notion of human equality to the modern world. During its bleakest hours, the American Revolution was resuscitated not so much by brilliant military strategy as by brilliant words—those of Tom Paine in the "times that try men's souls." Even less persuasive and more recondite words can have an impact that dramatic acts do not. Wrote Lord Keynes: "Madmen in authority, who hear voices in the air, are distilling their frenzy from some academic scribbler of a few years back. I am sure that the power of vested interests is vastly exaggerated compared with the gradual encroachment of ideas."

7 Debasement of the language cannot be blamed on protesters alone. The news media, the advertising agencies, the Government—even President Nixon himself—have all helped flatten and attenuate the English tongue. When radicals misuse language, they are only applying the lesson they have been so well taught by their society. That lesson has been reinforced by philosophers now in fashion—Marshall McLuhan, for instance, who says that pictures are more important than words and contemplates a society of inarticulate tribal emotions based on instant sight and sound. Or Herbert Marcuse, who teaches that protesting words are as empty as air in a technological society where power is concentrated in a few hands. Such a contempt for language makes people impatient with the orderly processes of thought. No sooner is something glimpsed or considered than it is demanded. Not only is dialogue destroyed, but so is rationality, when protesters insist upon immediate capitulation to their "nonnegotiable demands." This is what infants demand—and totalitarians.

Example of Agnew

8 Reactionary as the thought may seem, words are still as powerful a force as ever, when they are cogently used. It was, after all, language alone that catapulted Spiro Agnew from a political nonentity to a national figure with an enthusiastic personal following. Agnew, to be sure, can be accused of appealing to the raw emotions of the body politic in his now-famous attacks on "effete snobs" and "tomentose exhibitionists." On the other hand, a protester would have a hard time telling the Vice President that mere speech is not capable of stirring people. Unwittingly, he has shown his antagonists on the left that it can still be done.

9 During a period of national turmoil and self-doubt, it is all the more imperative for protesters to put down their rocks and find their voices again. As a commentary on the Kent State tragedy, President Nixon's remark that "when dissent turns to violence it invites tragedy" is callously inadequate. His warning, however, carries the weight of history: in a general unleashing of violence, dissent is the first casualty. Today the nation is in considerable need of healing, as well as elevating, language; often in the past that need has been filled by protesters whose perspective on society matched their passionate commitment to its improvement. Now is the time for dissenters to assert their own dignity and maintain their tradition by upholding the ultimate value of the word.

A SURVEY OF RHETORIC

The history of classical rhetoric covers more than two thousand years, from the fifth century B.C. until the first quarter of the nineteenth century. During most of that time, rhetoric was a prominent, and for long stretches the dominant, discipline in the schools, and some of the most famous men in history were involved in either the teaching or the practice of rhetoric. In view of this long and honorable tradition, it is presumptuous of anyone to think that he could present a satisfactory, not to speak of an adequate, survey of rhetoric in a few dozen pages. The article that R. C. Jebb wrote for the Ninth Edition of the *Encyclopaedia Britannica* was devoted almost entirely to Aristotle. Because of the formidableness of the task, most historians of rhetoric have sensibly confined themselves to a coverage of individual rhetoricians or to limited periods. The Bibliography appended to this survey directs the student's attention to some of the best of these limited histories. But to date, no one has attempted to write a history of rhetoric on the scale of George Saintsbury's *History of Criticism and Literary Taste in Europe* or even of René Wellek's more recent *A History of Modern Criticism, 1750–1950.*

Despite the impossibility of presenting an adequate survey of rhetoric in a few pages, an attempt will be made here to introduce the student to at least some of the key figures and some of the significant developments in rhetoric. Occasionally, authors and rhetoric texts will be mentioned, not because of their enduring worth or influence, but because they were historically important (the first of a kind, for instance) or representative of an especially important type.

594

Classical Rhetorics

The "art" or "science" of any discipline is almost always formulated inductively from a study of the long-standing practice of that discipline. This is certainly true of all the verbal arts—grammar, logic, poetics, and rhetoric. In the case of these language arts, the codification of principles did not come until several centuries after the practice had become a conspicuous feature of a national culture. There is ample evidence in extant Greek literature that rhetoric, conceived of as persuasive oratory, figured prominently in Hellenic society many hundreds of years before the first handbook of rhetorical precepts was compiled. One has only to note the prominence of speeches and debates in the Homeric epics, in the plays of the Greek dramatists, in the histories of Herodotus and Thucydides, and in the philosophical treatises of Hesiod, to be convinced that persuasive discourse exerted a continuing influence upon the ancient Greeks almost from the dawn of their civilization.

Although the practice of an art antedates its codification, there comes a time when men feel the urge to derive a set of "rules" from the study of accepted practice. The art of rhetoric was first formulated, in Sicily, during the second quarter of the fifth century B.C. Corax of Syracuse is commonly designated as the first formulator of the art of rhetoric. Certain political and social changes taking place at the time prompted him to establish some system of rhetoric. When Thrasybulus, the tyrant of Syracuse, was deposed and a form of democracy established, the newly enfranchised citizens flooded the courts with litigations to recover property that had been confiscated during the reign of the despot. The "art" that Corax formulated was designed to help ordinary men plead their claims in court. Since, understandably enough, no documentary evidence was available to prove their claims, they had to rely on inferential reasoning and on the general topic of probability (*eikos*) to establish their proprietary rights. Perhaps the chief contribution that Corax made to the art of rhetoric was the formula he proposed for the parts of a judicial speech—proem, narration, arguments (both confirmation and refutation), and peroration—the arrangement that becomes a staple of all later rhetorical theory.

There are references in Plato, Aristotle, Cicero, and Quintilian to the part that Corax and his pupil Tisias played in formulating rhetorical theory, but none of their handbooks survive. All we know of Tisias from the scattered references to him is that his theory was concerned exclusively with the rhetoric of the courtroom, that he wrote some judicial speeches for others to deliver, and that he may have been one of the teachers of at least two of the Attic orators—Lysias and Isocrates.

If modern students have heard the name of Gorgias at all, it is probably in connection with the Platonic dialogue that bears his name. In the history of rhetoric, however, Gorgias of Leotini is notable, first of all, for having stirred up interest in oratorical theory and practice among the Athenians. As an ambassador from Sicily to Athens in 427 B.C., he dazzled the Athenians with the brilliance of his speech-making. Thereafter he was, for several years, the most successful teacher and practitioner of oratory in Athens. Although he was one of the first rhetoricians to recognize the persuasiveness of emotional appeals, he distinguished himself mainly by the attention he paid to the cultivation of an ornate style. He placed great emphasis on the value of figures of speech, especially antithesis and parallelism. All the later rhetoricians who concentrated on the cultivation of a highly literary style of address could, for the sake of convenience, be placed in the Gorgianic school, but it is unfair to blame Gorgias for all the excesses of those rhetoricians who were concerned more with the flowers of style than with the substance. If some of Gorgias' speeches had survived, we would be better able to judge just how much the gaudy, mannered style known in Renaissance England as "Euphuism" owed to his influence.

Gorgias may well lay claim to being the *first* of the successful Sophists in Athens, but Isocrates competes with Aristotle for the title of the most influential of the Greek rhetoricians. Judging from the length of his reign as a renowned teacher of rhetoric (he lived to be 98 years old) and from the number of skillful orators who emerged from his school, it would probably be safe to say that Isocrates was the most influential Greek rhetorician among his contemporaries. Aristotle, with his more philosophical treatise on rhetoric, wins the title for long-range influence.

A word needs to be said here about the term *Sophist,* since it applies to men like Gorgias and Isocrates and since it figures in the views that Plato and Aristotle entertained toward the art of rhetoric. Among the Athenians of the fifth century B.C., the term *Sophist* carried no invidious connotations. It was a rather neutral term applied to professors who lectured on the "new learning" in literature, science, philosophy, and especially oratory. The Sophists set up small private schools and charged their pupils a fee for what amounted in many cases to tutoring. These schools eventually proved to be so lucrative that they attracted a number of charlatans into the teaching profession, and it was men like these who eventually gave Sophists an unsavory reputation and made "sophistry" a synonym for deceitful reasoning.

But men like Isocrates were highly ethical, with noble ideals and unimpeachable standards of intellectual integrity. We have already mentioned that he may have studied under Tisias, and there are hints in some of the early histories of rhetoric that he also studied under Gorgias and Socrates. He began his professional career as a *logographos,* the Greek term for a hired writer of courtroom speeches—a beginning that he later wanted to forget. About 392, he set up a school of oratory, and although he charged unusually high fees, he soon had more students than any other Sophists. During his lifetime he amassed a considerable fortune from his teaching.

Although some twenty-one discourses and nine letters of Isocrates have survived, the *Art of Rhetoric* that Isocrates is said to have compiled has been lost; hence we are forced to abstract his rhetorical theory from such autobiographical works as his *Antidosis* or his educational works like *Against the Sophists.* One of his major contributions to rhetoric was his development of an artistic prose style. He took the rather artificial style of Gorgias, tempered it, refined it, and made it an elegant vehicle for both written and spoken discourse. Whereas the structural units that Gorgias was most interested in were antithesis and parallelism, Isocrates, with his great interest in the rhythm of prose, centered his attention on the sonority of the periodic sentence—certainly one of Cicero's debts to him. His concept of the proper training for the ideal orator also had a marked influence on Cicero and Quintilian. He preached that the whole man must be brought to bear in the persuasive process, and so it behooved the aspiring orator to be broadly trained in the liberal arts and securely grounded in good moral habits. In all his discourses, he stressed the Greek ideals of freedom and autonomy, and perhaps as much as any other ancient humanist, he preached the value of the supreme Greek virtue, *sophrosyne* (that we may translate as "self-control," for want of a more adequate English equivalent).

Despite the high ideals that Isocrates set for his pupils and the exemplary eloquence of his discourses, he did not succeed in allaying Plato's suspicions of rhetoric. We should look briefly at what Plato (through his spokesman Socrates) had to say about rhetoric, because all the derogatory things that men have said about this art down through the ages have their roots in Plato's strictures.

Remarks about rhetoric are scattered through several of Plato's dialogues, but the two dialogues in which he concentrated his attacks were the *Gorgias* and the *Phaedrus.* Ironically, in the very act of depreciating rhetoric, Plato shows himself to be a masterful rhetorician; and equally ironic is the fact that some of the charges he made against the Sophists (e.g. that they corrupted young people and accepted fees for their teaching) were indictments later made against Socrates—as we see in the *Apology.* Students who read *The Republic* are often shocked to find that Plato would exclude poets from his ideal commonwealth. Basically, Plato's objections to poets are the same as those he made against the teachers of rhetoric. For one thing, rhetoric could not be considered a true art because it did not rest on universal principles. Moreover, rhetoricians, like poets, were more interested in opinions, in appearances, even in lies, than in the transcendental truth that the philosopher sought. They made the "worse appear the better reason." They were mere enchanters of the soul, more interested in dazzling their audience than in instructing it. Rhetoric—to bring it down to its lowest terms—was a form of flattery, like cosmetics.

Toward the end of the *Phaedrus,* Plato concedes the possibility of a true art of rhetoric. But it could be a true art only if the speaker made an effort to learn the truth about the subject he was going to talk about; if he would seek out essential definitions of key terms in his discourse; if he learned to make the proper divisions of his subject; and if he made an effort to fashion his speech to suit the nature of his audience. There are a lot of *if*'s here, and it is apparent that Plato does not have much confidence that rhetoricians, in their great eagerness to please the ignorant multitudes, will devise and teach such a rhetoric.

Certainly one of Aristotle's purposes in composing his *Rhetoric* was to counteract his former teacher's low estimate of the persuasive art. Even while he was still a pupil at Plato's Academy, he opened a school of rhetoric in competition with Isocrates. It is not known precisely when Aristotle first started to write his *Rhetoric,* but it is known that his treatise was not published until the second period of Aristotle's residence in Athens, sometime around 333 B.C. From internal evidence alone, we know that he completed his *Poetics* before he wrote Book Three of his *Rhetoric.* The late composition of Book Three, which deals mainly with style and arrangement, may suggest that this book was an afterthought, a concession to the interest taken in style by the other schools of rhetoric. But we must remember that he devoted several chapters of his *Poetics* to a discussion of language and style, and it is believed that the *Theodectea,* one of his lost rhetorical works, treated in great detail the subject matter of Book Three of the *Rhetoric.* Nevertheless, it is true that Aristotle was not as much interested in style as he was in the invention of arguments. And it is this primary interest in invention that indicates how he sought to counteract the bad opinion that many of his contemporaries had of rhetoric.

By concentrating in the first two books of his *Rhetoric* on the discovery of arguments, Aristotle sought to answer those who accused rhetoricians of being more concerned with words than with matter. And by abstracting first principles from the practice of oratory, he hoped to show that rhetoric was not, as Plato had accused it of being, a mere "knack," but was a true art, a teachable and systematic discipline that could guide men in adapting means to an end. With his philosophic treatise, Aristotle became the fountainhead of all later rhetorical theory. As Lane Cooper has said, "...the

Rhetoric not only of Cicero and Quintilian, but of the Middle Ages, of the Renaissance, and of modern times, is, in its best elements, essentially Aristotelian."

Perhaps the key to understanding Aristotle's approach to rhetoric is the recognition that *probability* is the basis of the persuasive art. The orator often based his arguments on opinions, on what men *believed* to be true rather than on what was demonstrably and universally true. But whereas Plato found this to be a defect in the art, Aristotle saw it as a necessity. Discoverable, verifiable truth fell within the province of science or logic. But in dealing with contingent human affairs, men soon learned that universal truths were not always discoverable or verifiable. It was in this area that dialectic and rhetoric had a part to play. "Rhetoric is the counterpart of Dialectic," Aristotle said in the very first sentence of his *Rhetoric*. It is significant that the Greek word that Aristotle used for rhetorical proofs was *pisteis*, which has its roots in the word *pistis*, "belief." *Belief*, Aristotle perceived, is often the highest degree of certainty to which we can attain in dealing with the everyday affairs of men.

This recognition of probability as the essence of the persuasive art lies behind most of Aristotle's contributions to rhetorical theory: the three modes of proof—the appeal to reason (*logos*), the appeal to emotion (*pathos*), the ethical appeal (*ēthos*); the enthymeme as the rhetorical equivalent of the syllogism, the example as the rhetorical equivalent of logical induction; the topics as a system of discovering available arguments; his stress on the audience as the chief informing principle in persuasive discourse. Another of his contributions was the removal of the success-at-any-price emphasis that had brought rhetoric into bad repute. By stressing the notion of "the available means of persuasion in any given case," he emphasized the virtuosity of the effort rather than the success of the results. This stress also tended to make rhetoric a morally indifferent activity. Another of his unique contributions was his analysis, in Book Two, of the more common emotions or passions. One of the three modes of appeal that Aristotle explores is the emotional, and he was trying to show his students how to evoke the appropriate emotional response. This was the beginning, admittedly primitive but amazingly perceptive, of psychology.

There is a great temptation to follow out all the ramifications of Aristotle's rhetorical theory, but this brief survey will not permit such an intriguing excursion. In fact, this textbook is so much indebted to Aristotle's theory that it can be regarded as a mere restatement, with some modifications and extensions, of the *Rhetoric*. So brilliant is Aristotle's treatise—it is certainly one of the great books of the Western world—that we can only regret the loss of the aforementioned *Theodectea* and of his history of rhetoric, *Gryllus,* named after Xenophon's son. For many years, the anonymous

Rhetorica ad Alexandrum was thought to be another of Aristotle's rhetorical works. But scholars today are convinced that Aristotle is not the author of this sprawling work, and they are inclined to attribute it to Anaximenes of Lampsacus, an older contemporary of Aristotle. It was never an influential work in the history of rhetoric.

Another Greek rhetorical treatise that deserves mention here is a text that has come to bear the English title *On Style.* The date and authorship of this work are uncertain. For a long time it was attributed to Demetrius Phalereus, who governed Athens from 317 to 307 B.C. and who was invited by Ptolemy Soter to help collect books for the great library at Alexandria. On the basis of internal and external evidence, however, W. Rhys Roberts, who has made an English translation of *On Style* for the Cambridge University Press, concludes that Demetrius Phalereus did not write this text, that it was written sometime in the first century B.C. or the first century A.D. This text, which deals exclusively with the *elocutio* (style) division of rhetoric, is notable for being one of the first to analyze the "kinds" of style. Whereas most later rhetorics discussed only three styles (the elevated or high style; the elegant or middle style; and the plain or low style), the author of this text discusses a fourth type, the forcible style. Throughout his discussion of style, the author is interested particularly in the choice and arrangement of words.

Until the end of the fifteenth century, the *Rhetorica Ad Herennium* was thought to have been written by Cicero. Whether Cornificius is the author of this text, as some modern scholars maintain, is still being debated, but the *Ad Herennium,* written probably between 86 and 82 B.C., has the distinction of being the earliest extant Latin work on rhetoric and the earliest treatment of prose style in Latin. Futhermore, as Harry Caplan, who translated the treatise for the Loeb Classical Library, points out, the *Ad Herennium* offers "the oldest extant division of the kinds of style into three and the oldest extant formal study of figures." It should also be pointed out that the treatise presents the most complete treatment of *delivery* and *memory* that we have in any of the surviving classical rhetorics. Although virtually unknown in the ancient world, the *Ad Herennium* enjoyed wide currency in the Middle Ages and the Renaissance. Professor T. W. Baldwin reveals that it was the basic elementary text in the English grammar-school curriculum when rhetoric had its great revival during the Tudor Age.

Although Cicero was not the author of the *Ad Herennium,* he has enough titles under his name to assure his place in the history of rhetoric. Among his minor rhetorical works, written between 84 and 45 B.C., are *De Inventione, De Optimo Genere Oratorum, Topica,* and *De Partitione Oratoria.* His major rhetorical works are the *De Oratore,* the *Brutus,* and the *Orator.*

There is no room here for an exposition of any of these works, but some general word can be said about Cicero's contribution to rhetoric. Cicero was a skillful orator as well as an esteemed teacher of rhetoric; some literary historians hold that he gave more effective instruction by the example of his orations and epistles (*rhetorica utens*) than he did by his theoretical treatises (*rhetorica docens*). His works played a great part in mediating the controversy between the "Asiatics" (the exponents of the florid, highly mannered style) and the "Atticists" (the exponents of the plain, neat, severe style). Cicero's chief contribution, however, is probably his extension of the scope of rhetoric. Unlike Aristotle, who held that rhetoric had no proper subject matter, Cicero felt that the perfect orator had to be conversant with many subjects. In order to invent his arguments, the perfect orator must have a command of a wide range of knowledge. Accordingly, under the Ciceronian system the study of rhetoric really became a liberal-arts course. This broadening of the scope of rhetoric helps to explain Cicero's appeal for the English and Continental Humanists when the study of rhetoric was revived during the Renaissance.

A later rhetorician whose name is invariably coupled with Cicero's is M. Fabius Quintilianus. Born in Spain about A.D. 35, Quintilian eventually went to Rome, where after completing his education he became a successful pleader in the law courts. In time he acquired such a great reputation that Vespasian established a chair of rhetoric for him at Rome. The prestige of this imperial endowment made him the supreme authority on rhetoric even after his death, about A.D. 96. About the year 88, he retired from his teaching post to write his great work on the training of the orator, the *Institutio Oratoria*. Fragments of this work seem to have been available throughout the Middle Ages, but after a complete text was discovered in the monastery of St. Gall in 1416, the *Institutes of Oratory* steadily gained popularity and firmly established itself in the European educational network. Between about 1475 and 1600, more than one hundred editions of the *Institutes* were published.

The twelve books of the *Institutio Oratoria* are divided as follows: Book I deals with the preliminary education necessary for a study of rhetoric. Book II defines the nature, aims, and scope of rhetoric. Books III-VII treat of oratory itself, with emphasis on the finding (*inventio*) and arranging (*dispositio*) of material. Books VIII-X treat of style (*elocutio*). Book XI deals with memory (*memoria*) and delivery (*pronuntiatio*). Book XII deals with the requirements for a perfect orator.

As the subject matter of Book I might suggest, Quintilian, like Cicero, regarded the broadly educated man as the fittest candidate for a course in rhetoric. Quintilian, moreover, emphasized a qualification that earlier rhetoricians had hinted at but did not belabor. Having accepted Marcus Cato's definition of the perfect orator as "a good man skilled in speaking" (*vir bonus dicendi peritus*), Quintilian insisted that in addition to being intellectually fortified for his office the orator must be trained to be a man of strong moral character. It was this insistence on the intellectual and moral training of the aspiring orator that made Cicero and Quintilian the two most potent classical influences on rhetorical education in England and America. The moral bias was especially important, because from the seventeenth through most of the nineteenth century the English and American school systems were dominated largely by clergymen.

Although the influence of the Roman rhetoricians had become dominant by the first century B.C., a few Greek works exercised a significant influence on the development of rhetoric. Dionysius of Halicarnassus, a Greek contemporary of Horace, taught rhetoric at Rome from 30 to 8 B.C. He wrote a monumental history and criticism of the great Attic orators and some minor rhetorical works which deal for the most part with a study of the style of such Greek luminaries as Plato, Thucydides, Herodotus, and Xenophon. But the work of his that influenced—or plagued—schoolboys was a work which bears the English title *On the Arrangement of Words*. Dionysius treated only one aspect of rhetorical style, the order of words. Although he realized that eloquent expression involves a due regard for *arrangement* and *choice* of words, he decided to confine himself to a study of arrangement because he felt that other rhetoricians had adequately dealt with the choice of words. Dionysius' particular contribution is that he made schoolboys aware of the inherent beauty of words and of the possibility of producing pleasing effects even with ordinary words if they were skillfully arranged.

Hermogenes and Aphthonius did not exercise as much influence on their contemporaries as they did on European schoolboys of the fifteenth and sixteenth centuries. Both of them published rhetorical texts entitled *Progymnasmata*. The *progymnasmata* were the first writing exercises, the "themes," that schoolboys attempted after they had learned their elementary rhetorical precepts. In addition to supplying technical rules for the construction of these minor forms of composition, the texts provided illustrations of the dozen or so common forms. These texts were clearly in the tradition of "formulary rhetoric"—the kind of rhetoric that taught by models. The *Progymnasmata* by Hermogenes and Aphthonius went through an astounding number of editions, in both Greek and Latin versions.

The mention of one more Greek text will end this survey of the more important classical rhetorics. This text is the famous *On the Sublime* by Longinus. Today, *On the Sublime* is for most students one of the cardinal documents of literary criticism. But one must not forget that this work was written by a rhetorician (earlier, about A.D. 260, he had written a now lost *Art of Rhetoric*) and that it has made a contribution to rhetoric as well as to literary criticism. "The object of the author," says W. Rhys Roberts, who has made one of the modern English translations of this treatise, "rather is to indicate broadly the essentials of a noble and impressive style." Three of the five sources of the sublime that Longinus discusses concern style: the appropriate use of figures of speech (chs. 16-29); nobility of diction (chs. 30-38); and dignity and elevation of word order (chs. 39-40). By making *enthusiasm* a respectable resource, Longinus encouraged the exploitation of emotional appeal in the suasive process, and by insisting that sublimity was "the echo of a great soul," he abetted the moralistic trend in later rhetorical education.

Rhetoric During the Middle Ages

Under the aegis of Hadrian and the Antonines (A.D. 117-80), the teachers of rhetoric attained a prestige and an immunity that they were never to enjoy again. These second-century Sophists acquired their unsavory reputation because they eventually abused their privileged office and adulterated their discipline. The object of the Sophists was to amaze an audience rather than persuade it. To effect this end, they encouraged all the flashy tricks of style and delivery. The schools of rhetoric during this period had two curricula: the "sophistic," which designated the academic study of rhetoric as an art; and the "political," which was concerned with the practical applications of the art. But because the "sophistic" school enjoyed greater prestige and higher emoluments, rhetoric took a turn that debased it.

Under the influence of the second-century Sophistic, rhetoric in the Middle Ages ceased to be pursued primarily as a practical art and became rather a scholastic exercise guided by the *compendia* of such medieval rhetoricians at Cassiodorus, Capella, and Isidore. Grammar, logic, and rhetoric constituted the *trivium*, the four-year undergraduate course of studies leading to the degree of bachelor of arts. Music, arithmetic, geometry, and astronomy made up the *quadrivium*, the three-year graduate course that led to the degree of master of arts. Scholastic logic held a decidedly superior position in the *trivium*. The province of rhetoric became principally a study of the art of letter writing (*ars dictaminis*) and of preparing and delivering sermons (*artes praedicandi*). True, the students were exercised in two forms of scholastic declamation—*suasoriae*, discourses on some historical or legendary subject, and *controversiae*, discourses on some classic legal question—but these declamations were conducted so much in the spirit of epideictic or ceremonial display that the product of such training was usually a glib, clever "entertainer" rather than a resourceful orator in command of all the available means of persuasion. Accordingly, the art of rhetoric stood still, if it actually did not retrogress, despite the prominent position that rhetoric held in the curriculum. As Richard McKeon has said in his essay "Rhetoric in the Middle Ages" (*Speculum,* 1942): "Yes, if rhetoric is defined in terms of a single subject matter—such as style, or literature, or discourse—it has no history during the Middle Ages."

Although St. Augustine (A.D. 353-430) is not chronologically of the Middle Ages, we might look at him as a representative figure in the development of rhetoric during the medieval period. Anyone who has read *The Confessions* knows that during the period of his "flaming youth" Augustine was a student of, and later a teacher of, the "pagan" rhetoric that derived largely from the second Sophistic of Rome. After his conversion, Augustine made a significant contribution to rhetoric in the Fourth Book of his *De Doctrina Christiana* (A.D. 426-27). Augustine was interested in rhetoric as a means of persuading Christians to lead a holy life. With that exclusive interest he can be said to have narrowed the province of rhetoric. But by rejecting the sophists' preoccupation with style and the other elements of display and by returning to the more comprehensive rhetoric of Cicero he can be said to have extended the province of rhetoric once again. He concentrated on Biblical texts and especially on the Epistles of that masterful rhetorical artist, St. Paul. Augustine's analyses of these texts, however, were concerned not so much with the "message" as with the rhetorical craftsmanship. Somewhat surprisingly, Augustine rejected Quintilian's notion that the rhetor must be a morally good man. He did not deny that a preacher's reputation for a virtuous life would have a persuasive effect on an audience, but he recognized that even a vicious preacher could induce his audience to follow Christ if he were skillful enough in the manipulation of his suasive resources.

Augustine's rhetoric laid the groundwork for the rhetoric of the sermon, the branch of study known today as homiletics—a science that was to command a great deal of attention during, and for many years after, the Renaissance and the Reformation. None of the classical rhetoricians, of course, had discussed the art of preaching, but the foundations for such an art lay in the epideictic variety of rhetoric.

Kenneth Burke, in his discussion of Augustine in *The Rhetoric of Motives,* pointed out that Augustine had noted the instructional function of rhetoric. Burke says that "once you treat instruction as an aim of rhetoric you introduce a principle that can widen the scope of rhetoric beyond persuasion. It is on the way to include also works on the theory and practice of exposition, description, *communication* in general." Following this lead, some modern students of rhetoric, like Donald C. Bryant, have seen the possibility of adapting classical rhetoric to cover at least two of the four forms of discourse—argumentation and exposition. As a matter of fact, there seems to be no reason why we could not develop a rhetoric of description and a rhetoric of narration too. As a case in point, Wayne C. Booth in his book *The Rhetoric of Fiction* (University of Chicago Press, 1961), has provided us with an excellent study of the rhetorical technique of non-didactic fiction.

Some Continental Rhetoricians

For the history of rhetoric on the European continent after the Middle Ages, we shall mention only a few Continental rhetoricians, confining our attention to the four or five who had a marked influence on the development of rhetoric in England.

The most influential rhetorician was Erasmus. Although this illustrious scholar spent only five years in England (1509-14), he set the pattern for the English grammar-school curriculum and for rhetorical training in the schools. He happened to be in England just at the time Dean Colet was founding St. Paul's school, and at the request of Colet he prepared a number of textbooks. Among these were *De Ratione Studii* and *De Duplici Copia Verborum ac Rerum*. Originally published in 1512, both of these texts went into an astounding number of editions in subsequent years. (The *De Copia,* for instance, had at least 150 editions—only a few of those, it should be pointed out, issuing from presses in England.) The *De Ratione Studii* is more a treatise on pedagogy than a rhetoric, but it is of interest to students of rhetoric for its incidental remarks about the language arts. It was not by endless drilling in rules that students learned to write and speak well, Erasmus maintained, but by discriminating reading and much practice. Erasmus is one of the early enunciators of that sanest of all precepts about writing: "write, write, and again write." He also recommends the exercise of keeping a commonplace book; of paraphrasing poetry into prose, and vice versa; of rendering the same subject in two or more styles; of proving a proposition along several different lines of argument; and of construing from Latin into Greek.

The *De Copia,* which became a widely used textbook of rhetoric in the Tudor schools, was designed to assist grammar-school students in acquiring elegance and variety of expression in Latin composition. This text was based on the traditional *res-verba* distinction (literally, the *thing* and *words;* more broadly, *matter* and *form*). The first book of *De Copia* showed the student how to use the schemes and tropes (*elocutio*) for the purpose of variation; the second book instructed the student in the use of topics (*inventio*) for the same purpose.

The matter of *copia* became one of the major concerns of Tudor education. The Latin word *copia* meant literally "plenty, abundance"; in a more particular sense, the phrase *copia dicendi* or *copia orationis* meant "fullness of expression." One achieved this fullness of expression by accumulating a number of things to say on a subject and by being able to say the same thing in a variety of ways. So *copia* was partly a matter of fertile invention and partly a matter of stylistic resourcefulness. By way of illustrating *copia,* Erasmus in Chapter 33 of Book One presents 150 variations of the sentence "Tuae literae me magnopere delectarunt" and 200 variations of "Semper dum vivam tui meminero."

The only other rhetorical work by Erasmus that we shall mention is his text on letter writing, *Modus Conscribendi Epistolas,* published in 1522. As we have seen, letter writing had been one of the favorite rhetorical exercises during the Middle Ages. During the Renaissance, it dropped to an inferior, but not insignificant, position in the curriculum. For Erasmus, letters became the first extended form of composition that the student wrote after he had mastered the fundamental rules of rhetoric. In that age which lacked our means of rapid communication and transportation, diplomatic and business affairs were promoted principally through letters. Accordingly, the man skilled in letter writing was as much sought after as the man skilled in oratory. And the number of letter writing manuals, both in Latin and in the vernacular, attests to the demand for this training in the sixteenth and seventeenth centuries. Today we also cannot afford to neglect formal training in this form of written discourse. Letters—friendly letters, business letters, promotional letters, letters to the editor—are the major form of written discourse that many of us will be called upon to produce after we leave school. There is as much rhetoric involved in some kinds of letters (the "begging letter," for instance) as there is in the most elaborate campaign oratory.

Along with Erasmus, Juan Luis Vives (1492–1540) stands in the forefront of those Continental scholars who spent only a few years in England but exercised an influence on the English grammar school that endured for well over a century. Born in Spain (and, for that reason, sometimes called the "second Quintilian"), educated in Paris and Flanders, he was appointed by Cardinal Wolsey in 1523 to the Lectureship of Rhetoric at Oxford. King Henry VIII entrusted the education of his daughter Mary to the joint tutorship of Vives and Thomas Linacre. Vives became *persona non grata* when Henry VIII was seeking a divorce from his compatriot, Catherine of Aragon, and he left England, never to return, in 1528.

Vives exercised an influence on English rhetoric, not so much from his textbooks as from his treatise on education, by which he helped to set the pattern of the rhetorical curriculum. Unlike Erasmus, Vives did not publish any rhetorical works during his sojourn in England, and none of his rhetoric texts that he later produced were widely used in the schools. Vives published the *De Disciplinis,* his major work on education, at Antwerp in 1531, three years after he left England. Three works on rhetoric followed soon after: *Rhetoricae, sive De Ratione Dicendi, Libri Tres* (Louvain, 1533); *De Consultatione* (Louvain, 1533), a short treatise on rhetoric that he had composed while he was teaching at Oxford; and *De Conscribendis Epistolas* (Basel, 1536), his contribution to the rhetoric of letter writing.

The *De Ratione Dicendi* and the companion *De Consultatione* provided a rich mine of material for Ben Jonson when he composed his own rhetorical work *Timber or Discoveries,* and it is highly probable that Shakespeare too was exposed to these works in his grammar school. But an examination of the statutes of the various grammar schools of the period shows that where Erasmus's textbooks are frequently recommended for the curriculum, Vives's textbooks are seldom mentioned. In his monumental study of Tudor grammar schools, *William Shakespere's Small Latine & Lesse Greeke,* Professor T. W. Baldwin accounts for the pre-eminence of Erasmus on the ground that he was the true Renaissance champion, whereas men like Vives and Colet belonged to the Catholic Reformation rather than to the Renaissance. Vives and Colet, he maintained, were more interested in moral reform than in literary polish.

Three other Continental rhetoricians who had a noticeable influence on English rhetoric deserve brief mention here. The first of these is Petrus Mosellanus or, to use his family name, Pierre Schade (1493–1524), a German professor of Greek at Leipzig University. He published a rhetoric text entitled *Tabulae de Schematibus et Tropis Petri Mosellani.* As early as 1530 the boys at Eton were using Mosellanus's text in the sixth form, and during the first half of the sixteenth century Mosellanus became the standard author on *elocutio* in the English grammar schools.

Philippus Melanchthon or Philip Schwartzerd (1497–1560), a professor of classics at Wittenberg and a close associate of Martin Luther, published three rhetoric texts: *De Rhetorica Libri Tres* (Wittenberg, 1519); *Institutiones Rhetoricae* (Hagenow, 1521); and *Elementorum Rhetorices Libri Duo* (Wittenberg, 1531). Whereas Mosellanus had concentrated on style, Melanchthon gave only a minimum treatment of the schemes and tropes, referring his readers, for a fuller treatment, to such rhetoricians as Cicero, Quintilian, Erasmus, and Mosellanus; he devoted most of his attention to *inventio* and *dispositio.* Melanchthon tended to relegate *invention* and *arrangement* to the province of logic, and by doing so, he laid the groundwork for the revolution that Ramus and Talaeus were to effect in rhetoric later on in the sixteenth century.

Joannes Susenbrotus's *Epitome Troporum ac Schematum* (Zurich, 1540) was an amalgam of Mosellanus and Melanchthon. The *Epitome,* with its collection of 132 schemes and tropes, had a printing in England in 1562, and thereafter, for the remainder of the sixteenth century, it replaced Mosellanus as the standard grammar-school text for the figures and served as the model for the later vernacular treatments of these stylistic devices.

English Vernacular Rhetorics of the Sixteenth Century

All of the rhetorics mentioned so far in this survey were written in either Greek or Latin, and most of the compositions by English schoolboys up to the second decade of the sixteenth century were in Latin. With the Renaissance, which began in Italy, spread to France, and eventually made its influence felt in England through the apostleship of Humanists like Roger Asham, Sir John Cheke, and Sir Thomas Elyot, there came a revival of interest in the pagan literature produced by the classical authors. When Aldus, in 1503, published the works of the chief Greek rhetoricians, classical rhetoric was assured of its share of this renewed interest. The cause of rhetoric was further aided, as we have seen, by the direction that men like Erasmus and Vives gave to the curriculum of the English schools. It was not long before rhetoric became the dominant discipline in the Tudor grammar schools and universities.

Although the rhetoric taught in the schools was basically Aristotelian, Aristotle's *Rhetoric* was never a prominent textbook. It was the Latin rhetoricians, especially Cicero, Quintilian, and the anonymous author of the *Ad Herennium,* who dominated the early teaching of rhetoric in the English schools. As the pride of the English people in the status and achievements of the nation grew, pride in their native language grew correspondingly, and it was natural that schoolmasters should begin to think of composing textbooks, and of getting their students to orate and write, in the vernacular.

It is common to classify the vernacular rhetorics produced during the English Renaissance into three main groups: (1) the Traditionalists—those who taught a full-fledged rhetoric, with attention given to the five parts: invention, arrangement, style, memory, and delivery; (2) the Ramists—those who assigned invention and arrangement to the province of logic and allocated only style and delivery to rhetoric; (3) the Figurists—those whose primary, if not exclusive, interest centered on the study of the schemes and tropes. Actually, these three groups differ more in their pedagogical approaches than in their fundamental conception of the art of rhetoric. The Ramists, for instance, believed as strongly in the importance of invention and arrangement as the Traditionalists did, but they believed that these subjects were more properly studied under logic. The Ramists may not have considered as many schemes and tropes as the Figurists did, but many figures that the Figurists studied under the aspect of style, the Ramists studied in connection with the topics of invention. Even from the brief exposition of the vernacular textbooks that follows, the reader should be able to determine into which of these three groups the books fall.

Leonard Cox, a schoolmaster at Reading, has the distinction of having written the first rhetoric textbook in English, *Arte or Crafte of Rhetoryke* (1530). It is perhaps appropriate that this first English rhetoric should be of the traditionalist school. F. I. Carpenter, in a modern edition of Cox's text, demonstrates quite convincingly that it was based upon, even partly translated from, the first book of Melanchthon's *Institutiones Rhetoricae*. Like Melanchthon, Cox was interested primarily in *inventio*.

In 1550, Richard Sherry, a headmaster at Magdalen College School, published through J. Day's press *A Treatise of Schemes and Tropes*, which has sometimes been called "the second book on rhetoric in English." It can certainly lay claim to being the first English textbook on the schemes and tropes. Five years later, Sherry printed a Latin-English revision of the earlier text, changing the title to *A Treatise of the Figures of Grammar and Rhetorike* and treating about 120 figures. Sherry produced his text in the hope of capturing the grammar-school trade. But his hopes proved futile, for Mosellanus and Susenbrotus were at the time too firmly entrenched in the curriculum to be dislodged. The *Treatise of Schemes and Tropes* had only one edition.

Although the compilers of vernacular rhetorics found the competition with Latin texts disheartening, they continued to produce them, and although their texts did not at first replace the classical texts in the schools, English rhetorics eventually superseded the older texts, in sales if not in prestige.

The first of the vernacular rhetorics to gain wide currency was Thomas Wilson's *The Arte of Rhetorique* (1553). G. H. Mair, who has published a handsome modern edition of this rhetoric, says of Wilson that he was one of the Cambridge men "who ... did much to mould the course of the Renaissance in England on its pedagogic side and who had no inconsiderable influence on the development of English prose." Wilson's text is a "Ciceronian" rhetoric, in that it treats of the five parts, but as Russell H. Wagner, perhaps the chief modern authority on the *Rhetorique*, has pointed out, Wilson appropriated some of his rhetorical doctrines from Erasmus, Cox, and Sherry.

The *Arte of Rhetorique* has the careful organization and schematic form that characterized the best of the classical and medieval texts. Book I considers such matters as the five elements of rhetoric ("Inuention, Disposition, Elocution, Memorie, Utteraunce"); the seven parts of an oration ("Enterance, Narration, Proposition, Division, Confirmation, Confutation, Conclusion"); the three kinds of oratory ("Demonstrative, Deliberative, Judiciall"); and, in connection with these three kinds of oratory, the matter of Invention.

Book II treats of Disposition and the Figures of Amplification. Book III deals mainly with Elocution (style) but gives also a summary treatment of Memory and Delivery. The chief appeal of the *Rhetorique* stemmed from the fact that Wilson had collected a great mass of sound classical doctrine and stitched it all together with his own observations, expositions, and illustrations, in an appealing English prose style. For native Englishmen there was something appealing too in Wilson's strictures on what he called "strange inkhorn terms."

Many vernacular rhetorics appeared in England from this point on, but the most popular were not necessarily the soundest rhetorics or the most venturesome ones. We will mention some representative texts of several kinds to show the vigor and variety of the rhetorical tradition in English schools (and later in American schools) up to about the end of the eighteenth century.

The rhetoric of letter writing, originating in the Middle Ages and continuing with the popular treatises of Erasmus and Vives, received another impetus late in the sixteenth century with the publication of Angel Day's *The English Secretorie* (1586). Day discusses some thirty different kinds of letters under four main headings: demonstrative, deliberative, judicial, and familiar. In the second edition of 1592, Day added a section on the figures of speech and provided marginal glosses identifying the various tropes and figures in the illustrative letters.

George Puttenham's *The Arte of English Poesie* (1589) is remembered by students of English literature as one of a group of Elizabethan treatises that attempted a defense of, or an apology for, poetry; but it also made a contribution to rhetorical theory. The third book of the *Arte of English Poesie*, with its elaborate treatment of figures, is operating in the tradition of Susenbrotus, Mosellanus, Erasmus, and Sherry. Puttenham made two contributions to English rhetoric: he invented vernacular names for the Greek and Latin figures, and, seeking a more rational basis for the classification of the figures, he decided to classify them according to the nature of their appeal. So we have the *auricular,* those figures which depend for their effect on alterations of "sound, accent, time" and therefore appeal primarily to the ear; the *sensable,* those figures which depend upon alterations of sense and therefore appeal primarily to the mind; the *sententious,* those that appeal both to the mind and to the ear. All in all, Puttenham treats 107 figures. George Saintsbury is not entirely right when he said of the *Arte of English Poesie* that it contained "the most elaborate treatment of rhetorical figures to be found, up to its time, in English literature," for Henry Peacham in his *The Garden of Eloquence* of 1577 distinguished 184 figures.

Richard Rainolde's *Foundacion of Rhetorike* (1563) was an English adaptation of Hermogenes and Aphthonius's *progymnasmata* exercises that proved so popular in the early Tudor schools. Rainolde, in fact, considers the same fourteen types of elementary compositions that Aphthonius treated, with examples that Rainolde himself had supplied. Rainolde's hope of replacing Aphthonius was doomed to disappointment, since only one edition of his text was published, and that has approached so close to oblivion that only five copies of the original edition exist today.

About this time a revolution in rhetorical studies was effected by the French scholar, Peter Ramus. Dissatisfied with the repetitiveness and vagueness that prevailed in the teaching of the subjects of the *trivium,* Ramus distributed the traditional parts of rhetoric between logic and rhetoric. *Inventio* and *dispositio*—that is, the discovery and arrangement of matter—he assigned to the province of logic. Rhetoric had a franchise only on *elocutio* (style) and *pronuntiatio* (delivery). The fifth office of rhetoric, *memoria*—the memorization of the speech—Ramus simply ignored. Style would confine itself to a study of schemes and tropes, leaving to grammar the study of etymology and syntax. Ramus was working for a strict departmentalization of knowledge, for he felt that a great deal of the error and confusion that had sprung up in the arts was the result of scholars' mistaking the proper subject matter of the arts. Although the teaching of the two arts would be kept separate, logic and rhetoric in practice would combine and work together. As Karl Wallace has pointed out, the effect of this Ramistic dichotomy was that henceforth such processes as discovery, arrangement, and judgment tended to be assigned exclusively to the intellect, while the "dress" or "ornament" that style gave to matter fell to the lot of the imagination. We shall see later what Francis Bacon is to make of this division of labor between the reason and the imagination.

Although Ramus himself never published a rhetoric text, he did inspire a number of rhetorics based on his philosophy. His most fervent disciple and propagator was Audomarus Talaeus (Omer Talon). Talaeus published in Paris in 1544 his *Institutiones Oratoriae* (or, as it is more familiarly known, *Rhetorica*) as a companion to Ramus's logic text, *Dialecticae Libri Duo.* As John Brinsley tells us in his *Ludus literarius; or The Grammar Schoole* (1612)—one of the most valuable primary sources of information about English schools in the late sixteenth and early seventeenth centuries—Talaeus's *Rhetorica* soon became the rhetoric text "most used in the best Schooles." The main reason for the popularity of Talaeus's text with schoolmasters seems to have been its brevity and simplicity.

In his extensive treatment of the Ramistic revolution (see *Logic and Rhetoric in England, 1500-1700,* pp. 146-281), Wilbur Samuel Howell has pointed out that it was Gabriel Harvey who first introduced Ramistic rhetoric to his countrymen, when he became praelector in rhetoric at Christ's College, Cambridge, in the spring of 1574, just about the time that Roland MacIlmaine was publishing in London the Latin text of Ramus' *Dialecticae Libri Duo*. Thereafter Talaeus and Ramus served as the model for the rhetoric and logic texts of Dudley Fenner (*The Artes of Logike and Rethorike*, 1584), Abraham Fraunce (*The Lawiers Logike* and *The Arcadian Rhetorike*, both in 1588), Charles Butler (*Rameae Rhetoricae Libri Duo*, 1597), and Thomas Farnaby (*Index Rhetoricus*, 1625; the fifteenth edition of this appeared as late as 1767). The appearance and success of these texts lend support to Professor Baldwin's contention that by the end of the sixteenth century the French-Calvinistic school of Ramus and Talaeus had scored a complete triumph over the German-Lutheran school of Melanchthon and Sturm.

English Rhetorics of the Seventeenth Century

During the course of the seventeenth century, we find English criticism gradually making the passage from the broad Humanistic ideals of the Italian Renaissance to the more rationalistic, stringent attitudes of the French critics. Renaissance critics had drawn eclectically from classical, medieval, and contemporary theory. No one authority or system was accepted as final or all-inclusive. It was the French critics of the second half of the century who induced the English to write and judge by a single, settled canon of rules. Since most of the French criticism of the seventeenth century was concerned with the epic and drama (largely as a result of the importation of the neo-Aristotelianism of such sixteenth-century Italian critics as Scaliger, Castelvetro, and Robortello), poetics began to absorb more attention than rhetoric. Furthermore, the line of demarcation between poetics and rhetoric began to blur. Consequently, it is sometimes difficult to point to a seventeenth-century textbook and say with any finality, "This is a rhetoric book" or "This is a treatise on poetics." One is just as likely to find rhetorical theory in Spingarn's collection of seventeenth-century critical essays as in a textbook whose title explicitly designates it as a rhetoric book. Another result of the shift in emphasis is that fewer rhetoric books were produced in the seventeenth century than in the previous period, and none of those that were produced exercised the influence or enjoyed the popularity of some Renaissance texts.

Besides the growing preoccupation with the rules, the seventeenth century exhibits some concern for the development of a simple, utilitarian style. The incipient interest in science—an interest created largely by Francis Bacon and fostered, after the close of the anti-science regime of the Puritans, by members of the Royal Society—encouraged the development of a "scientific" style. Coupled with this growth of the scientific spirit was the reaction against

"Ciceronianism," the movement that fostered the development of an ornate, highly mannered style by proposing Cicero as the principal, if not the sole, model for imitation. Morris Croll and George Williamson (see Bibliography) have traced out for us the counter development of the so-called "Senecan style," characterized by the relative brevity of the sentences, looseness of structure, succinctness and pithiness of phrasing, and jerkiness of rhythm. It was this movement that prepared the way for the development of the easy, colloquial style that graced so many eighteenth-century compositions. As might be expected, the growing interest in the "plain style" resulted in a diminishing concern for the schemes and tropes. But as we shall see in the discussion of the Royal Society's proposal for the development of a suitable expository style, John Dryden's development of an impressive "middle style" prevented the development of a prose style that would be as severely barren and denotative as mathematical symbols.

Our discussion of seventeenth-century rhetoric might well begin with Francis Bacon (1561–1626). Although Bacon wrote no systematic work on rhetoric, there are scattered throughout his writings remarks and discourses that throw light not only on his own literary practice but on the direction that rhetorical theory was to take in the seventeenth century. The chief loci for Bacon's rhetorical theory are *The Advancement of Learning* and the expanded Latin translation of this work, *De Augmentis Scientiarum*. Complementary material can be found in his *Colours of Good and Evil* and *Apophthegms, New and Old*. The best guide to Bacon's rhetorical theory is Karl R. Wallace's *Francis Bacon on Communication and Rhetoric* (University of North Carolina Press, 1943). Our discussion must be limited to two or three points.

"The duty and office of Rhetoric," Bacon says in *The Advancement of Learning*, "is to apply Reason to Imagination for the better moving of the Will." In a later work, Bacon says, "Rhetoric is subservient to the imagination, as Logic is to the understanding; and the duty and office of Rhetoric, if it be deeply looked into, is no other than to apply and recommend the dictates of reason to imagination, in order to excite the appetite and will." By viewing the imagination and reason as definitely distinct faculties, Bacon lays the groundwork for the great amount of subsequent discussion about the separate provinces and the separate cultivation of these faculties; and of course he is thereby fostering the Ramistic dichotomy between logic and rhetoric.

The view that imagination and reason were distinct and yet had to work together constituted the basis for Bacon's observations on style. Because he considered imagination subservient to reason, he advocated the precedence of *res* over *verba*. He took issue with the Renaissance school of rhetoric—the

Ciceronians especially—that was more concerned with words than with matter. As a result of this preoccupation with style,

> men began to hunt more after words than matter; and more after the choiceness of the phrase, and the round clean composition of the sentence, and the sweet falling of the clauses, and the varying and illustration of their works with tropes and figures, than after the weight of matter, worth of subject, soundness of argument, life of invention, or depth of judgment. (From *The Advancement of Learning.*)

Though preferring *res* to *verba,* Bacon did not entirely neglect the matter of style. The three stylistic features that he concentrates on were the conformity of the style to the subject matter, the use of simple words, and the cultivation of "agreeableness." Bacon's insistence on the integral relationship between style and content is one expression of his revolt against the Ciceronians, who tended to employ the copious style for all forms of address. Closely connected with this idea of style suiting the matter is Bacon's admonition that the style should be so adapted to the audience that "if a man should speak of the same thing to several persons, he should nevertheless use different words to each of them."

One of the seventeenth-century rhetoricians obviously influenced by Baconian doctrines was the Roman Catholic lawyer Thomas Blount (1618–79). In 1654, Blount published *The Academie of Eloquence.* As Professor Hoyt Hudson has demonstrated, the first forty-eight pages of this 232-page book are copied, without acknowledgment, from *Directions for Speech and Style,* a little book produced earlier in the century by another lawyer, John Hoskins, but never published under his name until the 1930's. Blount was one of the first English rhetoricians to draw his illustrative material from contemporary English writers, such as Sir Philip Sidney, Ben Jonson, and Edmund Spenser.

For Blount, the four virtues of style are brevity, perspicuity, "life" or wit, and "respect" or propriety. Note the premium that Blount placed on *brevity* (what other rhetoricians called *conciseness*). This emphasis and Blount's discussion of *sententia* and other figures connected with the "curt style" indicate that the Senecan manner was beginning to gain some attention. Blount was undoubtedly referring to the "pointed style" when he says in the section of the book dealing with commonplaces: "Eloquence is a way of speech prevailing over those whom we design it to prevail; That is, if we will take it in the short or Laconick way, a distilling our notions into a quintessence, or forming all our thoughts in a Cone and smiting with the point." Blount treats of only twenty-five figures (for the most part, those treated by Talaeus in his *Rhetorica*) and devotes about thirty pages of his book to amplification.

Blount's text concentrates on style, but it was style held under the tight checkrein of the reason. In the thirty years after the original publication of his work, five editions appeared. George Williamson, who has given us one of the most valuable studies of seventeenth-century rhetoric in his book *The Senecan Amble,* attests that "no other rhetoric of that time seems to have been quite so popular."

A number of rhetorics made use of the Scriptures. The most popular of these was *The Mysteries of Rhetorique Unvail'd* (1657) by John Smith, which defined rhetorical figures with special reference to the Scriptures; by 1709 nine editions of the work had appeared. With the ascendancy of the Puritans in the seventeenth century, rhetoric came more and more to serve as the tool of the sermon-writer and the expositor of the Scriptures. The sub-title of *Centuria Sacra* (1654) by Thomas Hall, a Puritan clergyman and schoolmaster at King's Norton, reveals the use to which rhetoric was being put during the Commonwealth period:

> About one hundred Rules for the expounding and clearer understanding of the Holy Scriptures. To which are added a Synopsis or Compendium of all the most materiall Tropes and Figures contained in the Scriptures.

John Prideaux, who was, successively, Rector of Exeter College, Oxford University, Regius Professor of Divinity at Oxford, and Bishop of Rochester, published a rhetoric in 1659 entitled *Sacred Eloquence: or, The Art of Rhetoric as It Is Laid Down in the Scriptures.* The names of John Smith, John Prideaux, and Thomas Hall have all but passed into oblivion, and although John Smith's book alone of these three enjoyed a spurt of success, neither the popularity nor the influence of these Scriptural rhetorics was ever widespread or long-lived.

One section of Thomas Hobbes's *Answer to Davenant's Preface to Gondibert* (1650), the section dealing with the "natural" style, has some pertinence to rhetoric and to the easy, colloquial style that Dryden was to "father" later in the century. True and natural expression is based, according to Hobbes, on two things, *to know well* and *to know much.* Hobbes goes on to examine the psychological effects of these two qualities:

> A signe of the first is perspicuity, property, and decency, which delight all sorts of men, either by instructing the ignorant or soothing the learned in their knowledge. A signe of the latter is novelty of expression, and pleaseth by excitation of the minde; for novelty causeth admiration, and admiration curiosity, which is a delightful appetite of knowledge.

To know much was taken care of by *inventio,* that part of rhetoric concerned with finding things to say. The invention of matter, however, eventually had its effect on style when there developed a great interest in amplification. *Copia* resulted in that variety of expression which pleased because of its novelty and ingenuity. *To know well* was originally more the concern of logic than of rhetoric. But here too the quality of one's knowledge was seen to have some effect on style. Many rhetoricians, both before and after Hobbes, insisted that an idea could not be *expressed* clearly if it were not *apprehended* clearly.

The natural style must also avoid words that are high-sounding but hollow (those "windy blisters") and phrases that express either "more than is perfectly conceived, or perfect conception in fewer words than it requires." Since Hobbes's consistent aim is to chasten the exuberance of a kind of prose that had been fashionable, one is not surprised to find that he devotes little attention to the figures and tropes. In general, his feeling is that while figures of speech add a certain grace and charm to writing they should be used sparingly and discreetly.

Although Hobbes may seem bent on undermining the classical tradition, he was in fact thoroughly steeped in the classics. He wrote several of his works in Latin, translated Thucydides and Homer, and published a helpful digest of Aristotle's *Rhetoric*. In his efforts to bridle rampant fancy, he may be said to be operating under the great classical principle of moderation. With his rationalistic aesthetics he is laying the groundwork for the "temperate" prose of the neo-classical period and for the psychological approach that was to figure in eighteenth-century rhetoric and criticism.

Another spur to the development of restrained prose was given by the activities of the Royal Society. In December 1664, two years after its founding, the Royal Society named a committee for the improvement of the English language. Among those named to the committee were John Dryden, John Evelyn, Thomas Sprat, and Edmund Waller. Their hope was that the authority of the Royal Society would help to refine, augment, and fix the English language. Although this project never advanced much beyond the planning stage, the Royal Society was to have some influence on the kind of prose written in the neo-classical period. The encouragement that Bacon had given to the formation of a "scientific" prose was to be supported by the Royal Society and given a new impetus. One section of Thomas Sprat's *History of the Royal Society* (1667) contains the manifesto of this reform.

The "superfluity of talking," Sprat said, had had such a devastating effect on the arts and professions that he could not help concluding that *"eloquence ought to be banish'd out of all civil Societies,* as a thing fatal to Peace and good Manners." The only remedy for this disease of "fine speaking" is "to reject all amplifications, digressions, and swellings of style; to return back to the primitive purity and shortness, when men deliver'd so many things almost in an equal number of words." In "An Account of the Life and Writings of Mr. Abraham Cowley" (1668), Sprat proposed Cowley as an exemplar of this "proper style." In his choice of words, Cowley "neither went before nor came after the use of the Age," and he "forsook the Conversation, but never the Language, of the City and Court." Cowley, Sprat goes on to say, had mastered "the hardest secret of good Writing, to know when he has done enough." Despite the "new comliness" that Cowley achieved in his expression, he did not lose sight of *decorum:* "But it seems all to arise out of the Nature of the subject, and to be justly fitted for the thing of which he speaks."

It is regrettable that Cowley did not live long enough to write his projected "Discourse Concerning Style." Undoubtedly he would have said many sensible things about the plain style, for he was himself an admirable prose-stylist, one whom John Dryden himself took as a model. This "metaphysical" poet distrusted metaphysics, because he felt that the schoolmen had reduced philosophy to a matter of mere words. Scattered throughout his poems are several instances of the sort of comment that might have figured in his proposed treatise on style.

Many of the same ideas about the plain style as those advanced by Sprat were presented by John Wilkins (1614–72), one of the pillars of the Royal Society and later Bishop of Chester, in his *Ecclesiastes* (1646) and *An Essay Towards a Real Character and a Philosophical Language* (1668). In the former essay he maintains that style should be "plain and natural, not being darkened with the affectation of *Scholastical* harshness, or *Rhetorical* flourishes." Obviously influenced by the doctrines of style in Seneca's *Epistles,* Wilkins recommends a style that follows a happy medium. Style, he says, "must be *full* without empty and needless Tautologies"; our expressions "should be so close, that they may not be obscure; and so plain, that they may not seem vain and tedious."

The extreme to which the Royal Society's advocacy of a plain, utilitarian style could be pushed is discovered in Wilkins's *Essay* where he proposes "a Real universal Character, that should not signify words, but things and notions." In other words, a series of symbols would be established, each symbol having a univocal, universal, and constant meaning. Literary symbols would thus approach the precision and stability of mathematical symbols. Fortunately for literature, this project never crystallized. Instead of words with rich associations and many-leveled meanings, our literary vocabulary might have been made up of "useful," universal ideographs.

Perhaps it was John Dryden, as much as anyone, who prevented the English language from taking that turn. Dryden preserved our language from taking on this mathematical character as much by his practice as by the rhetorical pronouncements scattered throughout his writings. He made *propriety* the central doctrine of his views on style. The propriety that Dryden called for is threefold: the language and style must fit "the occasion, the subject, and the persons." Closely allied to this concern for propriety is his discouragement of a "foreign" bias in our language. Dryden condemned Ben

Jonson because "he did a little too much to Romanize our tongue." It is Dryden's move "to English" contemporary prose that has been largely responsible for his reputation as the father of modern English prose style. His advocacy of native words and his encouragement of the use of vernacular, rather than Latinate, syntax are part of his program to refine the language and to attain more naturalness, more ease, more spontaneity in writing. And in his recognition of the "beauties" and the "spirits" of writing he is preparing the way for the triumphant re-entry of the Longinian "transport" into the rhetorical criticism of the eighteenth century.

The documents we have been considering over the last few pages have not been, strictly speaking, rhetoric texts at all. They reflect rather the intellectual currents that contributed to the development and to the eventual decay of the rhetorical tradition in the eighteenth century. In their preoccupation with style, these texts indicate how much the Ramistic program had caught on: the province of rhetoric seemed more and more to be restricted to style alone. But these documents also indicate how the groundwork was laid for the development of the kind of easy, natural, colloquial prose style that prevails today. The kind of prose style that is most admired today is not the Euphuistic prose of the Renaissance nor the Ciceronian prose of the nineteenth century but rather the plain but elegant prose found in such magazines as the *New Yorker* and the *Reporter* and exemplified in such writers as E. B. White, James Thurber, and George Orwell. And this kind of writing had its origin during the Restoration period with writers like Dryden, Bunyan, and Temple and its development during the Queen Anne period through writers like Defoe, Swift, and Addison.

English Rhetorics of the Eighteenth Century

As we pass to the eighteenth century, we confront the last full century in which rhetoric, in all its classical complexion, occupied a prominent position in the academic programs of the schools. During at least the first half of the eighteenth century, the influence of French critics, especially of Boileau, Rapin, and Le Bossu, was even more dominant than it had been in the last half of the previous century. The lamentable feature of this adulation for classical precepts was the uncritical manner in which they were accepted as absolute, inviolable law.

The questioning of Aristotelian and Horatian canons came with the appearance of editions and translations of Longinus. With the gradual emergence during this century of Longinus's *On the Sublime,* judgment came to be more a thing of taste and less a thing of rule. The new temper was displayed in such works as Leonard Welsted's *Dissertation Concerning the Perfection of the English Tongue and the State of Poetry* (1724), Robert Lowth's *De Sacra Poesi Hebraeorum* (1753), and Edward Young's *Conjectures on Original Composition* (1759). With the freer, more subjective type of criticism gradually claiming more and more adherents, the stage was being set for the appearance of the "romantic" writers.

These shifts in the perspective of criticism were reflected in the rhetoric books of the period. The eighteenth-century rhetoricians still paid allegiance to the classical precepts, but at the same time they urged their pupils to strike out on their own, to discover a style that was natural to themselves, to submit to the dynamic force of *enthusiasm*. They no longer felt it necessary to classify, define, and illustrate multitudes of figures and tropes. Delivery, that aspect of rhetoric which had been so long neglected in the schools, began to receive attention again, largely as a result of the elocutionary programs of such mentors as Sheridan and Walker. Pulpit oratory continued to be assiduously cultivated, inspired by the elegant practice of such famous English preachers as Tillotson, Barrow, Atterbury, and of the even more famous French preachers, Bossuet, Bourdaloue, and Massillon. By the end of the century, collections of sermons sold on the scale of popular novels today.

It can be said to the credit of eighteenth-century teachers that for the most part they regarded rhetoric as a practical art, much as Aristotle had conceived of it, rather than as a more speculative art. As in the seventeenth century, the line between poetics and rhetoric was hard to ascertain. Critics and rhetoricians drew on native belles-lettres for their illustrations. "In fact," George Saintsbury says, "Rhetoric, new dubbed as Eloquence, becomes the Art of Literature, or in other words Criticism." This merger of poetics and rhetoric helps to explain why the eighteenth century was the last great age of a serious academic interest in rhetoric.

At least fifty rhetoric texts produced during the eighteenth century are important enough to deserve being mentioned, but we shall have to content ourselves with a look at only six or seven. Although a number of informative books have been published in recent years about English rhetoric in the sixteenth and seventeenth centuries (see the Bibliography), no survey has yet been published about English rhetoric in the eighteenth century. A fairly exhaustive survey, but that only of the latter half of the century, is the unpublished doctoral dissertation that Harold F. Harding wrote at Cornell University in 1937, *English Rhetorical Theory, 1750–1800*. A number of books, monographs, articles, and dissertations have been done, however, on individual rhetoricians of this period.

John Stirling's very popular rhetoric, *A System of Rhetoric* (1733), only thirty pages long, contains in the first part a listing of ninety-seven figures and tropes. The Greek or Latin terms for the figures and tropes are translated into their English equivalents, and all are simply defined and briefly illustrated. The second part, entitled *Ars Rhetorica,* is nothing more than a Latin translation of the first part (apparently a concession to those schoolmasters who refused to use vernacular rhetorics in the classroom).

With its list of ninety-seven figures and tropes, *A System of Rhetoric* has the distinction of providing a catalogue of more figures than was given by any other rhetoric book in the eighteenth century—a century in which rhetoricians generally were defining and illustrating fewer and fewer figures. Among eighteenth-century rhetorics, only John Holme's *The Art of Rhetoric* (1739), with eighty-three figures and tropes, approaches this abundance.

Lectures Concerning Oratory was published in 1758 by John Lawson (1712–59), a Master of Arts from Trinity College, Dublin, and the first librarian of the University library. Lawson's book is firmly based on Aristotle's *Rhetoric* and is pieced out by examples, mainly from Cicero and Quintilian. The first six lectures give a short history of classical and modern rhetoric. Lecture 7 presents "some thoughts concerning Imitation." The remaining lectures treat of eloquence in relation to reason (chs. 8-9), to passion (chs. 10-11), and to the senses (chs. 12-18). It is in the seven lectures devoted to eloquence and the senses that Lawson treats of style "as it comprehendeth Ornament, Composition, Figures."

Lawson is a sensible, sometimes original, scholar, one who had absorbed a good deal of the learning of the past without closing his mind to the excellences of the present and the promises of the future. Following Aristotle as he did, he was deviating from the Longinian direction that criticism and rhetoric were taking in the eighteenth century. The encouragement Lawson gave to the cultivation of a simple, jargonless prose is remarkably akin to Jonathan Swift's pronouncements on style in *A Letter to a Young Clergyman* (1720).

John Ward served as professor of rhetoric at Gresham College in London from 1720 until his death in 1758. In the year after his death there appeared a two-volume collection of lectures on rhetoric, *A System of Oratory,* that Harold Harding in his survey of eighteenth-century rhetoric has called "the most elaborate and detailed synthesis of Greek and Roman rhetorical theory published in English." Although his greatest debt is to Quintilian, Ward acknowledges early in the first volume that he has borrowed "the finest precepts of Aristotle, Cicero, Quintilian, Longinus, and other celebrated authors, with proper examples taken from the choicest parts of purest antiquity." The fifty-four lectures cover 863 pages—a bulk which indicates the thoroughness of the work but which helps to explain why it never became a widely used school text. Ward's text is, however, the only English rhetoric published in

the eighteenth century which came anywhere near matching the comprehensiveness of Hugh Blair's *Lectures on Rhetoric,* a text that we shall discuss
presently.

Ward's chief preoccupation is with style. Exactly one half of the lectures
are devoted to *elocutio.* The other parts of rhetoric receive adequate, but less
thorough, treatment. Disposition rates eight lectures; six lectures treat invention; four lectures are spent on delivery; memory is the subject of only
one lecture. The last eight lectures deal with imitation, the nature of the
passions, the character of the orator, and a brief history of oratory. This collection of lectures shows how seriously and exhaustively rhetoric was still
being taught as late as the mid-eighteenth century.

We shall turn now to a consideration of two men who were most responsible in the eighteenth century for quickening an interest in *pronuntiatio* or
the delivery aspect of rhetoric. The most successful of these speech teachers
(he might be called the Dale Carnegie of the eighteenth century) was
Thomas Sheridan, the father of the dramatist Richard Brinsley Sheridan.
Sheridan's works fall into three categories: those dealing with (1) reading
and speaking; (2) pronunciation; and (3) education.

The most popular and probably the most representative of his printed
works was *Lectures on Elocution* (1762). This book, which is a compilation
of seven of his public lectures, deals exclusively with the problems of delivery
—articulation, pronunciation, accent, emphasis, tone, pause, pitch, voice control, and gesture. His *Lectures on Reading* (1775) gives directions for reading prose and for reading verse. Archbishop Whately, in his rhetoric text
published in the nineteenth century, lauded and recommended Sheridan's
system of marking passages to be read aloud. Sheridan's success as an actor
lent great weight to his pronouncements on matters of delivery. He is the
chief figure in the late-eighteenth century elocutionary movement which
resulted in the shift of meaning of *elocution* from *style* to *delivery* and in the
later vogue of the "elocution contest" in the schools.

John Walker (1732–1807), the other eighteenth-century promoter of the
art of delivery, was, like Sheridan, an Irish actor. In 1769, he gave up the
dramatic stage, and after teaching for a time at Kensington Gravel-Pits
School, he began a career of lecturing, at which he continued, with signal
success, for the next thirty-five years.

Walker's first appearance in print came in 1777 when he published *The
Exercises for Improvement in Elocution,* which was nothing more than a
collection of readings from select authors for those seeking to acquire the
art of reading or speaking in public. Perhaps the best and most popular of
Walker's works was *Elements of Elocution* (1781). This two-volume work
covered such matters as rhetorical punctuation, voice inflections, gesture,

accent, emphasis, and pronunciation. The similarity of this work with Sheridan's *Lectures on Elocution* is apparent.

It should not be surprising that it was professional actors who gave a special impetus to a study of delivery, for all the spell-binding orators in history (men like Demosthenes, Churchill, William Jennings Bryan, Bishop Sheen, Billy Graham) have been, in a sense, great actors. Walker had the acting skill to qualify him as a teacher of delivery, but he lacked the grounding in the classics that Sheridan had and accordingly did not have the reserves to draw upon when it came to citing collaborative or illustrative material.

The history of British rhetoric in the second half of the eighteenth century is dominated by three Scottish rhetoricians. With the great cultural renascence that took place in Scotland after its union with England, Edinburgh soon came to be known as "the Athens of the North." During this period, in such fields as philosophy, aesthetics, psychology, history, economics, there are more eminent Scottish names than English names. And in rhetoric during this period, men like Kames, Campbell, and Blair had no serious rivals.

Henry Home, Lord Kames (1696–1782), a Scottish jurist and psychologist, published in 1762 the three-volume *Elements of Criticism,* a work that was frequently reprinted and that exercised a marked influence on subsequent poetical and rhetorical theory. The scope of *The Elements of Criticism* is much broader than that of most texts considered in this survey. Kames's book, as a matter of fact, makes its major contribution to aesthetics. In that regard, it is of a piece with three other Scottish works—Francis Hutcheson's *Original of Our Ideas of Beauty and Virtue* (1725), David Hume's *Of the Standard of Taste* (1757), and Alexander Gerard's *Essay on Taste* (1758). Only a small part of Kames's book deals with rhetoric in the traditional sense of that word. His purpose, he tells us, is "to examine the sensitive branch of human nature, to trace the objects that are naturally agreeable, as well as those that are naturally disagreeable; and by these means to discover, if we can, what are the genuine principles of the fine arts." Kames hoped that by probing human psychology he could find an immutable standard of taste by which to assess all works of art.

Despite its undeniable influence on literature, Kames's *Elements* was never widely used in the schools. His book was bulky, involved, and written in a rather ponderous style. Kames's influence was exercised indirectly, through the medium of those more popular Scottish rhetoricians whom he helped to form. As Helen Randall, who wrote a full-length study of Kames's critical theory, says: "If one may consider the direct influence of Blair as a secondary influence of Kames, one may almost say that the textbooks on this subject for about a hundred years owed their main outline and many of their rules to the *Elements of Criticism.*"

The second of the noted Scottish rhetoricians whom we are considering was George Campbell (1709–96). No less a critic than George Saintsbury has called Campbell's *The Philosophy of Rhetoric* (1776) "the most important treatise on the New Rhetoric that the eighteenth century produced." Campbell was at once more readable than Lord Kames and more profound than the other member of this Scottish triumvirate, Dr. Hugh Blair.

What was Campbell's peculiar contribution to the art of rhetoric? For one thing, he ventured the notion that rhetoric could have an end other than to persuade. In the first two paragraphs of his treatise, he defines *eloquence* (the term he prefers to *rhetoric*) as the "art or talent by which the discourse is adapted to its end," and he says that a speech may have any one of four ends: "to enlighten the understanding, to please the imagination, to move the passions, or to influence the will." This is reminiscent of Cicero's notion of the tripartite function of rhetoric: to teach (*docere*), to persuade (*movere*), to delight (*delectare*). Reversing the notion advanced by Aristotle and his followers that rhetoric was a mere offshoot of dialectic, Campbell proposed that logic be regarded merely as the tool of rhetoric. Campbell is perhaps best known to students of the English language as the one who proposed as the criterion of good usage the norm that locutions be *reputable, national,* and *present.*

Campbell's probing of the "philosophy" of rhetoric was so adventurous and original that his book exerted a fascination for students of rhetoric for many years after its original publication. More than twenty editions of *The Philosophy of Rhetoric* were demanded during the eighteenth and nineteenth centuries, and it was regularly used in American colleges until about 1870. His book might have proved even more popular if it had not been for the formidable competition it received from one of the most widely reprinted rhetorics ever written, Hugh Blair's *Lectures on Rhetoric and Belles-Lettres.*

By 1783, when Blair published his book, he had been delivering lectures to the students at the University of Edinburgh for twenty-four years. It was in 1759, at the urging of Lord Kames, that he agreed to deliver, without salary, a series of lectures on rhetoric. This series was so enthusiastically received that a group of his friends proposed to George III that he establish an endowed Chair of Rhetoric at the University and that Blair be installed as the first holder of the post. The reputation of the celebrated preacher of St. Giles in Edinburgh was already so high that the English monarch had no hesitation about commissioning Blair in 1762 as the first Regius Professor of Rhetoric. Blair was finally prompted to publish his lectures because for years handwritten copies of them had circulated freely among enthusiastic students and had been boldly offered for sale in the bookshops.

We shall probably never get an accurate count of the number of editions and reprints of Blair's *Lectures,* but by 1835 there were at least fifty editions. Later this text was translated into such languages as French, Italian, and

Russian. It continued to be used in English and American schools until almost the end of the nineteenth century. William Charvat, a historian of American critical thought, has said that at one time Blair's *Lectures* was a text "which half the educated English-speaking world studied."

Why was Blair's text such a popular rhetoric? One reason was the amazing comprehensiveness of the forty-seven lectures in this one-volume text. In addition to the thirteen lectures devoted to belles-lettres, there were discussions of taste, beauty, and sublimity (three of the key terms in eighteenth-century criticism); a survey of philology and a review of classical and English grammar; a detailed exposition of the principles of style, with special attention to the major figures of speech, and a detailed analysis of several pieces of prose composition; a history of oratory; and instructions for the composition of various kinds of speeches; discourses on poetry; and a compilation of the best classical and contemporary rhetorical doctrines. The marked religious tone of the *Lectures* also played a part in recommending Blair's text to schoolmasters. Blair's insistence that a man of eloquence must be a man of virtue became the warp upon which his lectures were woven. The mode and style of presentation also contributed to the popularity of the *Lectures*. Besides being clearly and systematically organized, the lectures were presented on an elementary level. Presuming in his students no previous training in rhetoric, Blair took great pains to define his terms, to elaborate on what might strike us as commonplaces, and to supply whatever background he deemed necessary for an understanding of the topic under discussion. As a result, Blair's *Lectures* could be used on several levels of the school curriculum.

The history of English rhetoric might well terminate with the end of the eighteenth century, but it is customary to carry the history one step further to include Richard Whately's *Elements of Rhetoric* (1828). Whately was one of that brilliant group of Oxford reformers that gravitated to Oriel College in the 1820's. Eventually he was made Archbishop of Dublin. In 1826, with some help from John Henry Newman, he published his *Elements of Logic,* which had grown out of an article he wrote earlier for the *Encyclopaedia Metropolitana.*

Whately's rhetoric has a strong Aristotelian flavor. Agreeing with Aristotle that rhetoric was "an offshoot of logic," Whately treated rhetoric as the art of "argumentative composition." His book is organized under four heads: (1) the appeal to the reason or understanding (this was the equivalent of Aristotle's logical proofs); (2) the appeal to the will (Aristotle's ethical and pathetic appeals); (3) style; (4) delivery. Among the notable features of Whately's *Rhetoric* were his elaboration of such Aristotelian concepts as sign, example, and probability, his brilliant analyses of argumentative fallacies, and his development of the function of presumption and burden of proof in the conduct of an argument.

Throughout the first three-quarters of the nineteenth century, Campbell, Blair, and Whately were the three modern rhetoricians most often used in the English and American schools wherever rhetoric continued to be taught. Although Blair proved to be the most popular of this trio, modern teachers of rhetoric speak with most respect of Campbell and Whately. Neither of them was a particularly original thinker, but both of them based their rhetorics on sound principles of logic and psychology. If their texts had come somewhat earlier, the tenure of rhetoric in the schools might have been extended for several more years.

Rhetoric in the Nineteenth and Twentieth Centuries

A review of the first hundred years of the Boylston Professorship of Rhetoric at Harvard University reveals what happened to rhetorical training during the nineteenth century and the early years of the twentieth century.* The Boylston Professorship, the most famous and influential chair of rhetoric in America, was made possible by a grant from Nicholas Boylston, a wealthy Boston merchant, in 1771 and was formally activated in 1806. The first two holders of the chair, John Quincy Adams (1806–1809) and Joseph McKean (1809–1818), adhered closely to the prescriptions of the original statutes, which charged that the training offered be solidly rooted in the classical tradition and that it be primarily concerned with eloquence in persuasive oratory. Edward T. Channing during his thirty-two-year tenure (1819–51) broadened the purview of his office to include lectures on literary criticism and abandoned the exclusively classical orientation of his lectures on rhetoric. The influence of Blair, Whately, and Campbell is especially evident in his exploration of psychological processes, in his concern with terms like *genius* and *taste,* and in his alliance of rhetoric with belles lettres. Having little interest in students' declamations, he gradually shifted the emphasis from speaking to writing.

The changes in scope and emphasis introduced by Channing were confirmed and extended by Francis James Child, who occupied the Boylston

* This account of nineteenth-century rhetoric is adapted from my article "What Is Being Revived?" *College Composition and Communication,* XVIII (October 1967), 166-72. For the account of the Boylston Professorship, I am heavily indebted to Ronald F, Reid, "The Boylston Professorship of Rhetoric and Oratory, 1806–1904: A Case Study of Changing Concepts of Rhetoric and Pedagogy," *Quarterly Journal of Speech,* XLV (October 1959), 239-57.

chair for twenty-five years, from 1851 to 1876. While doing graduate work at the University of Göttingen, Child became enamored of German research in early English linguistics, literature, and folklore, and this philological interest profoundly affected the cast of his lectures and led eventually to the production of his great work, *The English and Scottish Popular Ballads* (1882–98). He used his podium to expound on Chaucer and to introduce his students to Anglo-Saxon, delegating instruction in oratory, for which he had no relish, to his assistants. When Charles William Eliot introduced the elective system at Harvard about 1875, Child found further encouragement for his slighting of composition, written and spoken, and for his concentration on philology and literary criticism. When Johns Hopkins, the first American university to be founded on the German model, tried to woo Child, the only way Harvard could keep him was to create for him the new office of Professor of English and to assign John Richard Dennett as his assistant to take over the rhetoric lectures. It was in the school-term of 1874–75 that Harvard established its first course in Freshman English, a course dealing with matters that previously had been taught only to sophomores, juniors, and seniors.

Adams Sherman Hill's twenty-eight-year tenure, from 1876 to 1904, rounds out the first century of the Boylston Professorship. During Hill's term, the Boylston Professorship was incorporated into the English department and the term *rhetoric* fell out of fashion, being replaced by the term *composition;* rhetoric's association with oratory was once and for all severed, and composition now dealt exclusively with written discourse; and the abandonment of textbooks in the rhetoric course reflected the shift from the theoretical approach to writing to the methods of imitation and practice. It was Hill too who introduced the use of literature to teach freshman composition and who resorted to the four forms of discourse—exposition, argumentation, description, and narration—as his way of approaching the process of composition. He paid a great deal of attention to style, but he made such a fetish of grammatical correctness that he soon reduced rhetoric to a set of "do and don't" prescriptions.

Part of the nineteenth-century development in the teaching of rhetoric, though not associated primarily with the Boylston Professorship, was the doctrine of the paragraph, stemming from Alexander Bain's *English Composition and Rhetoric* (1866) and fostered by such teachers as Fred Scott, Joseph Denney, John Genung, George Carpenter, Charles Sears Baldwin, and Barrett Wendell. Barrett Wendell's successful rhetoric texts helped to establish the pattern of instruction that moved from the word to the sentence to the paragraph to the whole composition. Henry Seidel Canby reversed that sequence, moving from the paragraph to the sentence to the word. It is to these men that we owe the system of rhetoric that most students were exposed to in the first half of the twentieth century—the topic sentence, the various methods of developing the paragraph (which were really adaptations of the classical "topics"), and the holy trinity of unity, coherence, and emphasis.

But even this kind of rhetorical approach to writing disappeared from our classrooms and our textbooks sometime in the 1930's. With the clamor from parents, businessmen, journalists, and administrators for correct grammar, correct usage, and correct spelling, rhetoric books began to be replaced with handbooks. By 1936 the study of rhetoric had sunk to such an estate in our schools that I. A. Richards, in his *The Philosophy of Rhetoric,* could say of it that it was "the dreariest and least profitable part of the waste that the unfortunate travel through in Freshman English," and W. M. Parrish, reviewing the situation in 1947, could say, in an article addressed to teachers of speech, "English teachers . . . have almost abandoned the very name of rhetoric, and the classical tradition is now completely in our hands."

It was the Speech Department at Cornell University that fostered the resuscitation of classical rhetoric in our time. In the fall semester of 1920–21, Alexander Drummond and Everett Hunt established a seminar at Cornell in which the students read and discussed Aristotle's *Rhetoric,* Cicero's *De Oratore,* and Quintilian's *Institutio Oratoria.* The effects of this classically oriented program began to be felt when graduates of Cornell's Speech Department took posts at universities in various parts of the country. The place to find articles on classical rhetoric during the '30's and '40's was not the journals directed to teachers of English but the *Quarterly Journal of Speech* and *Speech Monographs.* English teachers began to take notice when studies appeared of the rhetorical training of some of the great English writers— studies like T. W. Baldwin's *William Shakespere's Small Latine and Lesse Greeke,* Donald L. Clark's *John Milton at St. Paul's School,* and Karl Wallace's *Francis Bacon on Communication and Rhetoric.* The renewed interest in classical rhetoric was given another boost by the vogue of Mortimer Adler's *How to Read a Book* and by the post-war popularity of the New Criticism, for both Adler and the New Critics were applying rhetorical techniques to the reading process. In recent years, a number of books and articles have appeared which subject some of the literary masterpieces to a rhetorical analysis.

There has been sporadic talk during the last thirty years or so of a "new rhetoric." This "new rhetoric" is said to have profited by what it appropriated from the modern refinements in psychology, semantics, motivational research, and other behavioral sciences. Two of the names commonly mentioned in connection with the "new rhetoric" are I. A. Richards and Kenneth Burke. The roots of Richards's interest in rhetoric can be found in the book on semantics that he wrote with C. K. Ogden in 1923, *The Meaning of Meaning.* In 1936 he published *The Philosophy of Rhetoric.* One of his purposes in this work was to point up the limitations of the rhetoric of persuasion as it was taught by the ancients. To confine oneself to the persuasive aspect of language, he maintained, was to cut oneself off from some of the other uses of language. It was just because Bishop Whately had announced in his *Elements of Criticism* in 1828 that he was going to confine his study to "argumentative composition, generally and exclusively" that Richards chose him as the chief target of his strictures on the old rhetoric. George Campbell's *The Philosophy of Rhetoric,* with its concern for the psychology of the audience and its broadening of the function of rhetoric to include enlightening the understanding, pleasing the imagination, moving the passions, and influencing the will, represented for Richards a more desirable model for a twentieth-century rhetoric. We can epitomize Richards's approach to rhetoric by saying that he is interested mainly in how language *in any kind of discourse* works to produce understanding (or misunderstanding) in an audience. Something of this concern can be seen in the four terms he uses in his study of human utterances—sense, feeling, tone, and intention.

Kenneth Burke has more reverence for the classical rhetoricians than I. A. Richards does, but like Richards, he sees the possibility of extending the scope of rhetoric. In an article in the *Journal of General Education* in 1951, a year after the publication of his *A Rhetoric of Motives,* Burke said: "If I had to sum up in one word the difference between the 'old' rhetoric and a 'new' (a rhetoric re-invigorated by fresh insights which the 'new Science' contributed to the subject), I would reduce it to this: The key term for the old rhetoric was 'persuasion' and its stress was upon deliberate design. The key term for the new rhetoric would be *'identification,'* which can include a partially 'unconscious' factor in appeal." "Appeal" is the essence of communication for Burke. When men use symbols to induce co-operation in other human beings, they must *identify* themselves with the audience, must, in Burke's term, become *consubstantial* with them. Rhetoric becomes for Burke a study of the various modes of achieving identification. *Structure* of any kind is a mode of identification. The way we structure or arrange our discourse, for instance, could be one of the ways in which we adjust our discourse to fit the needs of our audience. Style, too, can be a mode of identification, since it can be a conscious or an unconscious attempt on our part to suit our language to the level of the audience. Burke's "dramatistic pentad"—name, agent, agency (means), scene (background), purpose—constitutes his critical apparatus for analyzing the motivation of human acts.

Another significant contributor to the "new rhetoric" is the Belgian philosopher Chaim Perelman.* Although Perelman has been publishing books and articles in continental Europe for over thirty years, he has only lately

* For a convenient summary of Perelman's "new rhetoric," see Ray D. Dearin, "The Philosophical Basis of Chaim Perelman's Theory of Rhetoric," *Quarterly Journal of Speech,* LV (October 1969), 213-24.

come to wide attention in America, mainly through the pages of a new journal, *Philosophy and Rhetoric,* founded at Pennsylvania State University in 1968 under the editorship of Henry W. Johnstone, Jr., and Carroll C. Arnold. Now English-speaking students of rhetoric can get a firsthand acquaintance with Perelman's major rhetorical work, *The New Rhetoric: A Treatise on Argument,* a translation of *La Nouvelle Rhétorique: Traité de l'Argumentation,* which Perelman and his colleague Madame L. Olbrechts-Tyteca published in France in 1958.

Like the English philosopher Stephen Toulmin, Perelman has been dissatisfied with the applicability of formal logic to the problems of decision-making in human affairs. Perelman contends that the development of a theory of argumentation suitable to the practical deliberations and decisions of public life has been hampered by the rigid allegiance in the Western world to Descartes's concept of reason and reasoning. "It was this philosopher," says Perelman in his Introduction, "who made the self-evident the mark of reason, and considered rational only those demonstrations which, starting from clear and distinct ideas, extended, by means of apodictic proofs, the self-evidence of the axioms to the derived theorems." But most things about which men argue exist in the realm of the contingent, the probable, the plausible, and in this realm, absolute, "scientific" demonstration based on self-evident premises is not always possible or effective. Perelman saw that the kind of "dialectical" proofs which Aristotle dealt with in the *Topics* and utilized in the *Rhetoric* provided the mode of nonformal logic which could "induce or increase the mind's adherence to theses presented for its assent."

Perelman, who also holds an advanced degree in law, found an effective model for this non-formal mode of reasoning in jurisprudence. In his book *The Idea of Justice and the Problem of Argument* (1963), Perelman says, "A thorough investigation of proof in law, of its variations and evolution, can, more than any other study, acquaint us with the relations existing between thought and action." He points, for example, to the use in courtroom trials of precedents, "the rationality of which is linked with the observance of the *rule of justice,* which demands equal treatment for similar situations." He goes on to say, "Now, the application of the rule of justice assumes the existence of precedents to teach us how situations similar to the one confronting us now have been dealt with in the past." Precedents, in other words, produce something less than conclusive proof, but they do constitute a *reasonable* basis for making crucial decisions. So do a host of other psychological, social, and cultural conditions, and it is with those operative conditions that the bulk of *The New Rhetoric* deals.

Chaim Perelman claims that "only the existence of an argumentation that is neither compelling nor arbitrary can give meaning to human freedom, a state in which a reasonable choice can be exercised. . . . The theory of argumentation will help to develop what a logic of value judgments has tried in vain to provide, namely the justification of the possibility of a human community in the sphere of action when this justification cannot be based on a reality of objective truth."

There are other developments in the "new rhetoric" that we might explore. We might look at the exciting work now being done in style and stylistics (the application of linguistics to literature), involving such men as Roger Fowler, Geoffrey Leech, and M. A. K. Halliday in England and Roman Jakobson, Seymour Chatman, Richard Ohmann, Louis Milic, and Francis Christensen in America. Noam Chomsky's transformational grammar and B. F. Skinner's psycholinguistics also have bearings on the "new rhetoric." The growing literature in communications theory has certainly put rhetorical behavior on a more scientific basis. Nor can we neglect the rhetorical dimensions of Marshall McLuhan's pronouncements about how the electronic media are altering the way in which we perceive, structure, and communicate our experiences. We must further explore all those manifestations of non-verbal rhetoric or "body rhetoric," as Franklyn Haiman terms it— marches, demonstrations, sit-ins in the political arena; music, the film, light-shows in the cultural sphere. We are even beginning to speak now of "the rhetoric of alienation" and "the rhetoric of black power" as new and distinctive styles of persuasive discourse. And not enough attention has been paid yet to the rhetoric of advertising, that pervasive influence on all our lives. But the mere mention of these "stirrings" should convince us that rhetoric —although perhaps of a different brand from what we have been studying in this book—is still very much alive.

This survey of rhetoric, abbreviated and hurried as it is, has probably left the student's head swirling with names and titles and dates. It is not so important that the student be able to recall and place all these details as it is that he be aware, in a general way, of the long and honorable tradition that classical rhetoric has enjoyed. His being aware of the history of rhetoric should make this book's approach to the problems of composition more meaningful and fruitful. The tradition of classical rhetoric may currently be dormant, but the discipline itself was not and is not moribund. What was once so vital cannot be, even with the passage of time and the creation of a new world, entirely irrelevant and ineffectual.

BIBLIOGRAPHY

This selective bibliography will serve as a guide for those who may want to pursue further the study of rhetoric. The primary texts are listed chronologically; the secondary texts are listed alphabetically. The listing of primary texts has been limited to those which are available in modern editions.

Bibliographies

Albert R. Kitzhaber, *A Bibliography on Rhetoric in American Colleges, 1850-1900* (Denver: Bibliographical Center for Research, Denver Public Library, 1954).

J. F. McGrew, "Bibliography of the Works on Speech Composition in England during the 16th and 17th Centuries," *Quarterly Journal of Speech,* XV (1929), 381–412.

Lester Thonssen, "Recent Literature in Rhetoric," *Quarterly Journal of Speech,* XXXIX (December 1953), 501-5. Good commentary on most of the significant modern work on rhetoric.

Karl R. Wallace, "Books on Rhetorical Theory, 1500-1700," in *Francis Bacon on Communication and Rhetoric* (Chapel Hill, N.C., 1943), pp. 231–55.

The annual bibliography of rhetoric ("Bibliography of Rhetoric and Public Address") was carried from 1947 to 1950 in the *Quarterly Journal of Speech;* since 1951, it has been in the periodical *Speech Monographs.* The first fifteen of these annual bibliographies have been accumulated under an author-title index and a subject index in *Rhetoric and Public Address: A Bibliography, 1947-1961,* ed. James W. Cleary and Frederick W. Haberman (Madison, Wis., 1964).

631

Primary Texts

Isocrates, Vol. I and II trans. George Norlin; Vol. III trans. Larue Van Hook. Loeb Classical Library (London, 1928-29, 1945). All the Loeb Classical Library editions have the Greek (or Latin) and English on facing pages.

Plato, *Phaedrus,* trans. W. C. Helmbold and W. G. Rabinowitz, Library of Liberal Arts paperback ed. (Indianapolis, 1956).

——, *Gorgias,* trans. W. C. Helmbold, Library of Liberal Arts paperback ed. (Indianapolis, 1952).

Aristotle, *Rhetoric,* trans. W. Rhys Roberts (Oxford, 1924)—this is the translation reproduced in the Modern Library edition of the *Rhetoric* and *Poetics.* Trans. John H. Freese, Loeb Classical Library (Cambridge, Mass., 1947). Trans. Lane Cooper, Appleton-Century-Crofts paperback ed. (New York, 1960)—this is a helpful version for the student because Lane Cooper provides, within brackets in the text, definitions of terms and amplifications of cryptic and elliptical passages.

Ad Herennium, trans. Harry Caplan, Loeb Classical Library (Cambridge, Mass., 1954).

Cicero, *De Oratore,* Books I and II trans. E. W. Sutton and H. Rackham; Book III trans. H. Rackham, 2 vols., Loeb Classical Library (Cambridge, Mass., 1942).

——, *De Inventione; De Optimo Genere Oratorum; Topica,* all three texts trans. H. M. Hubbell, Loeb Classical Library (Cambridge, Mass., 1949).

——, *Brutus; Orator,* both texts trans. G. L. Hendrickson, Loeb Classical Library (Cambridge, Mass., 1939).

Demetrius, *On Style,* trans. W. Rhys Roberts (Cambridge, 1902).

Demosthenes, *On the Crown,* ed. James J. Murphy, with a new translation by John J. Keaney (New York, 1967).

Dionysius, *On Literary Composition,* trans. W. Rhys Roberts (London, 1910).

Longinus, *On the Sublime,* the Greek text ed. and trans., with Notes and Introduction, W. Rhys Roberts, 2nd ed. (Cambridge, 1907). Trans. G. M. A. Grube, Library of Liberal Arts (Indianapolis, 1957). *Longinus on Sublimity,* trans. D. A. Russell, paperback ed. (Oxford, 1966).

Quintilian, *Institutio Oratoria,* trans. H. E. Butler, 4 vols., Loeb Classical Library (London, 1920-22).

——, *On the Early Education of the Citizen-Orator,* ed. James J. Murphy and trans. Rev. John Selby Watson, Library of Liberal Arts paperback ed. (Indianapolis, 1965)—translation of Book I and Chapters 1-10 of Book II of *Institutio Oratoria.*

St. Augustine, *On Christian Doctrine* (*De Doctrina Christiana*), trans. D. W. Robertson, Jr., Library of Liberal Arts paperback ed. (Indianapolis, 1958). Book IV of this text is St. Augustine's contribution to the rhetoric of the sermon.

Desiderius Erasmus, *On Copia of Words and Ideas* (*De duplici copia verborum ac rerum*), ed. and trans. Donald B. King and H. David Rix (Milwaukee, Wis., 1963).

Leonard Cox, *The Arte or Crafte of Rhetoryke* (1530), ed. F. I. Carpenter (Chicago, 1899).

Richard Sherry, *A Treatise of Schemes and Tropes* (1550), with his translation of *The Education of Children* by Desiderius Erasmus, a facsimile reproduction with an Introduction and Index by Herbert W. Hildebrant (Gainesville, Fla., 1961).

Thomas Wilson, *Arte of Rhetorique* (1553), ed. George H. Mair (Oxford, 1909).

Richard Rainolde, *The Foundacion of Rhetorike* (1563), a facsimile reproduction with an Introduction by Francis R. Johnson (New York, 1945).

Henry Peacham, *The Garden of Eloquence* (1577, 1593), a facsimile reproduction with an Introduction by William G. Crane (Gainesville, Fla., 1954).

Abraham Fraunce, *The Arcadian Rhetorike* (1588), ed. Ethel Seaton (Oxford, 1950).

George Puttenham, *The Arte of English Poesie* (1589), ed. Gladys Dodge Willock and Alice Walker (Cambridge, 1938); also in *Elizabethan Critical Essays*, ed. G. Gregory Smith (Oxford, 1904), II, 1–193.

John Hoskins, *Directions for Speech and Style* (1600), ed. Hoyt H. Hudson (Princeton, N.J., 1935); for another edition of this, see Louise Brown Osborn, *The Life, Letters, and Writings of John Hoskyns, 1566–1638* (New Haven, Conn., 1937).

François de la Mothe Fénelon, *Fénelon's Dialogues on Eloquence,* trans. Wilbur Samuel Howell (Princeton, N.J., 1951).

George Campbell, *The Philosophy of Rhetoric* (1776), ed. Lloyd F. Bitzer (Carbondale, Ill., 1963).

Hugh Blair, *Lectures on Rhetoric and Belles-Lettres* (1783), ed. Harold Harding (Carbondale, Ill., 1966).

Richard Whately, *Elements of Rhetoric* (1828), ed. Douglas Ehninger (Carbondale, Ill., 1963).

The Rhetoric of Blair, Campbell, and Whately, ed. James L. Golden and Edward P. J. Corbett (New York, 1968)—substantial excerpts from these three rhetorics.

Joseph Priestley, *A Course of Lectures on Oratory and Criticism,* ed. Vincent M. Bevilacqua and Richard Murphy (Carbondale, Ill., 1965).

Secondary Texts

Paul Abelson, *The Seven Liberal Arts: A Study in Medieval Culture* (New York, 1906).

Bower Aly, *The Rhetoric of Alexander Hamilton* (New York, 1965).

J. W. H. Atkins, *Literary Criticism in Antiquity,* 2 vols. (Cambridge, 1934); *English Literary Criticism: The Renascence* (London, 1951); *English Literary Criticism: 17th and 18th Centuries* (London, 1951).

J. L. Austin, *How to Do Things with Words,* ed. J. O. Urmson, Galaxy Paperback (New York, 1968).

A. Craig Baird, *Rhetoric: A Philosophical Inquiry* (New York, 1965).

Sheridan Baker, *The Practical Stylist* (New York, 1962).

Charles Sears Baldwin, *Ancient Rhetoric and Poetic* (New York, 1924); *Medieval Rhetoric and Poetic* (New York, 1928); *Renaissance Literary Theory and Practice* (New York, 1939).

T. W. Baldwin, *William Shakespere's Small Latine & Lesse Greeke,* 2 vols. (Urbana, Ill., 1944).

Charles Allen Beaumont, *Swift's Classical Rhetoric* (Athens, Ga., 1961).

Edwin Black, *Rhetorical Criticism: A Study in Method* (New York, 1965).

Wayne C. Booth, *The Rhetoric of Fiction* (Chicago, 1961).

———, *Now Don't Try To Reason with Me* (Chicago, 1970).

John Brinsley, *Ludus Literarius: or The Grammar Schoole,* ed. E. T. Campagnac (Liverpool, 1917). This and Charles Hoole's book (see below) are the best contemporary accounts of the teaching of rhetoric in the Tudor grammar schools.

Cleanth Brooks and Robert Penn Warren, *Modern Rhetoric,* 3rd ed. (New York, 1970).

Donald C. Bryant, ed., *Ancient Greek and Roman Rhetoricians: A Biographical Dictionary* (Columbia, Mo., 1969).

Kenneth Burke, *A Rhetoric of Motives* (New York, 1950).

Donald L. Clark, *John Milton at St. Paul's School: A Study of Ancient Rhetoric in English Renaissance Education* (New York, 1948).

———, *Rhetoric and Poetic in the Renaissance* (New York, 1922).

———, *Rhetoric in Greco-Roman Education* (New York, 1957). Perhaps the best introductory book on classical rhetoric.

Martin Lowther Clarke, *Rhetoric at Rome: A Historical Survey* (London, 1953).

Francis Connolly, *A Rhetoric Case Book,* 3rd ed. revised by Gerald Levin (New York, 1969).

Francis Connolly and Gerald Levin, *The Art of Rhetoric* (New York, 1968).

E. M. Cope, *An Introduction to Aristotle's Rhetoric* (London, 1867). Long out of print, this valuable commentary on the *Rhetoric* was reprinted in 1965 by the William C. Brown Co. of Dubuque, Iowa.

Jim W. Corder and Lyle H. Kendall, Jr., *A College Rhetoric* (New York, 1962).

William G. Crane, *Wit and Rhetoric in the Renaissance: The Formal Basis of Elizabethan Prose Style* (New York, 1937).

Harry H. Crosby and George F. Estey, *College Writing: The Rhetorical Imperative* (New York, 1968).

Donald Davidson, *American Composition and Rhetoric,* 5th ed. (New York, 1968).

Hugh M. Davidson, *Audience, Words, and Art: Studies in Seventeenth-Century French Rhetoric* (Columbus, Ohio, 1965).

Jacques Ellul, *Propaganda: The Formation of Men's Attitudes,* trans. Konrad Kellen and Jean Lemer (New York, 1966).

Daniel Fogarty, *Roots for a New Rhetoric* (New York, 1959).

Wallace C. Fotheringham, *Perspectives on Persuasion* (Boston, 1966).

Paul Fussell, *The Rhetorical World of Augustan Humanism: Ethics and Imagery from Swift to Burke* (Oxford, 1965).

Mary Amelia Grant, *The Ancient Rhetorical Theories of the Laughable: The Greek Rhetoricians and Cicero* (Madison, Wis., 1924).

Hans P. Guth, *Words and Ideas,* 3rd ed. (Belmont, Calif., 1969).

Elbert W. Harrington, *Rhetoric and the Scientific Method of Inquiry: A Study of Invention,* University of Colorado Studies (Boulder, Colo., 1948).

S. I. Hayakawa, *Language in Thought and Action* (New York, 1949).

Marvin T. Herrick, *The Poetics of Aristotle in England* (New Haven, Conn., 1930). See also, Lee S. Hultzén, "Aristotle's *Rhetoric* in England to 1600," unpub. diss., Cornell University, 1932.

Laura Virginia Holland, *Counterpoint: Kenneth Burke and Aristotle's Theories of Rhetoric* (New York, 1959).

Charles Hoole, *A New Discovery of the Old Art of Teaching Schoole,* ed. E. T. Campagnac (Liverpool, 1913).

Carl I. Hovland, Irving L. Janis, and Harold H. Kelley, *Communication and Persuasion* (New Haven, Conn., 1953).

Wilbur Samuel Howell, *Logic and Rhetoric in England, 1500–1700* (Princeton, N.J., 1956).

——, *The Rhetoric of Alcuin and Charlemagne* (Princeton, N.J., 1941).

Richard Hughes and P. Albert Duhamel, *Rhetoric: Principles and Usage,* 2nd ed. (Englewood Cliffs, N.J., 1967).

James W. Johnson, *Logic and Rhetoric* (New York, 1962).

William Powell Jones, *The Rhetoric of Science* (London, 1966).

John E. Jordan, *Using Rhetoric* (New York, 1965).

Sister Miriam Joseph, *Shakespeare's Use of the Arts of Language* (New York, 1947). Now available, in a slightly condensed form, in a Harbinger paperback, under the title *Rhetoric in Shakespeare's Time* (New York, 1962).

Sister Miriam Joseph, *The Trivium,* 3rd ed. (South Bend, Indiana, 1948).

Martin Kallich, *Heav'n's First Law: Rhetoric and Order in Pope's Essay on Man* (DeKalb, Ill., 1967).

Thomas S. Kane and Leonard J. Peters, *A Practical Rhetoric of Expository Prose* (New York, 1966).

George Kennedy, *The Art of Persuasion in Greece* (Princeton, N.J., 1963). The first really adequate history of Greek rhetoric in English.

Sister Joan Marie Lechner, *Renaissance Concepts of the Commonplaces* (New York, 1962).

Charles Osborne McDonald, *The Rhetoric of Tragedy: Form in Stuart Drama* (Amherst, Mass., 1966).

John H. Mackin, *Classical Rhetoric for Modern Discourse* (New York, 1969).

James M. McCrimmon, *Writing with a Purpose,* 4th ed. (Boston, 1967).

Marshall McLuhan, *Understanding Media: The Extensions of Man* (New York, 1964).

——, *The Gutenberg Galaxy: The Making of Typographic Man* (Toronto, 1962).

H. I. Marrou, *A History of Education in Antiquity,* trans. George Lamb (London, 1956). Reprinted as a Mentor paperback, 1964.

Harold C. Martin, Richard M. Ohmann, and James H. Wheatley, *The Logic and Rhetoric of Exposition,* 3rd ed. (New York, 1969).

Wayne Minnick, *The Art of Persuasion* (Boston, 1957).

W. F. Mitchell, *English Pulpit Oratory* (London, 1932).

Robert Hamilton Moore, *Effective Writing,* 3rd ed. (New York, 1966).

Maurice Natanson and Henry Johnstone, *Philosophy, Rhetoric, and Argumentation* (University Park, Pa., 1965).

Marie Hochmuth Nichols, *Rhetoric and Criticism* (Baton Rouge, La., 1963).

Walter J. Ong, *Ramus, Method, and the Decay of Dialogue* (Cambridge, Mass., 1958). See also the chapter on Ramism in Howell's *Logic and Rhetoric in England,* pp. 146–281.

———, *Ramus and Talon Inventory* (Cambridge, Mass., 1958).

———, *The Presence of the Word: Some Prolegomena for Cultural and Religious History* (New Haven, Conn., 1967).

Vance Packard, *The Hidden Persuaders* (New York, 1957). A study of modern advertising techniques.

Louis John Paetow, *The Arts Course at Medieval Universities with Special Reference to Grammar and Rhetoric* (Urbana, Ill., 1910). See also Richard McKeon, "Rhetoric in the Middle Ages," in *Critics and Criticism,* ed. R. S. Crane (Chicago, 1952), pp. 260–96.

Chaim Perelman and L. Olbrechts-Tyteca, *The New Rhetoric: A Treatise on Argument* (Notre Dame, Ind., 1969), a translation by John Wilkinson and Purcell Weaver of *La Nouvelle Rhétorique: Traité de l'Argumentation* (Presses Universitaires de France, 1958).

Chaim Perelman, *The Idea of Justice and the Problem of Justice,* trans. John Petrie (London, 1963).

Porter G. Perrin, *Writer's Guide and Index to English,* 4th ed. revised by Karl W. Dykema and Wilma R. Ebbitt (Glenview, Ill., 1965).

Irving J. Rein, *The Relevant Rhetoric* (New York, 1969).

I. A. Richards, *The Philosophy of Rhetoric* (New York, 1936). Available in a Galaxy Books paperback (New York, 1965).

Herbert David Rix, *Rhetoric in Spenser's Poetry* (State College, Pa., 1940).

W. Rhys Roberts, *Greek Rhetoric and Literary Criticism* (New York, 1928).

James E. Robinson, *The Scope of Rhetoric* (Glenview, Ill., 1970).

Leo Rockas, *Modes of Rhetoric* (New York, 1964).

Alexander H. Sackton, *Rhetoric as a Dramatic Language in Ben Jonson* (New York, 1948).

William F. Sandford, *English Theories of Public Address, 1530–1828* (Columbus, Ohio, 1931).

Izora Scott, *Controversies over the Imitation of Cicero as a Model for Style* (New York, 1910).

Jerrold E. Seigel, *Rhetoric and Philosophy in Renaissance Humanism: The Union of Eloquence and Wisdom, Petrarch to Valla* (Princeton, N.J., 1968).

W. David Shaw, *The Dialectical Temper: The Rhetorical Art of Robert Browning* (Ithaca, N.Y., 1968).

Lester Thonssen and A. Craig Baird, *Speech Criticism: The Development of Standards of Rhetorical Appraisal* (New York, 1948).

A. M. Tibbetts, *The Strategies of Rhetoric* (Glenview, Ill., 1969).

Wesley Trimpi, *Ben Jonson's Poems: A Study of the Plain Style* (Palo Alto, Calif., 1962).

Rosemond Tuve, *Elizabethan and Metaphysical Imagery: Renaissance Poetic and Twentieth-Century Critics* (Chicago, 1947).

Brian Vickers, *Classical Rhetoric in English Poetry* (London, 1970).

Karl R. Wallace, *Francis Bacon on Communication and Rhetoric* (Chapel Hill, N.C., 1943).

———, *Understanding Discourse: The Speech Act and Rhetorical Action* (Baton Rouge, La., 1970).

William M. Watt, *An American Rhetoric,* 4th ed. (New York, 1970).

Winston Weathers and Otis Winchester, *The Attitudes of Rhetoric* (Englewood Cliffs, N.J., 1970).

Richard M. Weaver, *The Ethics of Rhetoric* (Chicago, 1953). Now available in a Gateway paperback edition.

———, *Rhetoric and Composition,* 2nd ed. revised by Richard S. Beal (New York, 1967).

Bernard Weinberg, *A History of Literary Criticism in the Italian Renaissance* (Chicago, 1961).

John F. Wilson and Carroll C. Arnold, *Public Speaking as a Liberal Art,* 2nd ed. (Boston, 1968).

W. Ross Winterowd, *Rhetoric: A Synthesis* (New York, 1968).

———, *Rhetoric and Writing* (Boston, 1965).

———, *Structure, Language, and Style* (Dubuque, Iowa, 1969).

Richard E. Young, Alton L. Becker, and Kenneth L. Pike, *Rhetoric: Discovery and Change* (New York, 1970).

Some Collections of Articles on Rhetoric

To list even the better articles on rhetoric in the modern journals of the humanities would swell this Bibliography to twice its size. Some collections of valuable articles on rhetoric, however, are given below. A good starting point to find articles on rhetoric would be the *Index to Quarterly Journal of Speech, Volumes I–XL (1915–1954),* compiled by Giles W. Gray (Dubuque, Iowa, 1956).

The Art of Victorian Prose, ed. George Levine and William Madden (New York, 1968).

Dimensions of Rhetorical Scholarship, ed. Roger E. Nebergall (Norman, Okla., 1963).

Essays from Select British Eloquence by Chauncey Allen Goodrich, ed. A. Craig Baird (Carbondale, Ill., 1963).

Essays on Rhetoric, ed. Dudley Bailey (New York, 1965).

Essays on Rhetorical Criticism, ed. Thomas R. Nilsen (New York, 1968).

The Ethics of Controversy: Politics and Protest (Lawrence, Kansas, 1968).

Forms of Rhetoric: Ordering Experience, ed. Tom E. Kakonis and James C. Wilcox (New York, 1969).

Historical Studies of Rhetoric and Rhetoricians, ed. Raymond F. Howes (Ithaca, N.Y., 1961).

History and Criticism of American Public Address, Vols. I and II ed. William Norwood Brigance (New York, 1943); Vol. III ed. Marie K. Hochmuth (New York, 1955).

History of Speech Education in America, ed. Karl R. Wallace (New York, 1954).

Language Is Sermonic: Richard M. Weaver on the Nature of Rhetoric, ed. Richard L. Johannesen, Rennard Strickland, and Ralph T. Eubanks (Baton Rouge, La., 1970).

New Rhetorics, ed. Martin Steinmann, Jr. (New York, 1967).

Oratory of the Old South, 1828–1860, ed. Waldo W. Braden (Baton Rouge, La., 1970).

Papers in Rhetoric and Poetic, ed. Donald C. Bryant (Iowa City, 1965).

The Prospect of Rhetoric, ed. Edwin Black (Englewood Cliffs, N.J., 1971). Position Papers, Responses, and Reports from the National Developmental Project in Rhetoric at the Wingspread and Pheasant Run Conferences held in January and May, 1970.

The Province of Rhetoric, ed. Joseph Schwartz and John A. Rycenga (New York, 1965).

Readings in Classical Rhetoric, ed. Thomas W. Benson and Michael H. Prosser (Boston, 1969).

Readings in Rhetoric, ed. Lionel Crocker and Paul A. Carmack (Springfield, Ill., 1965).

Rhetoric, ed. Richard L. Larson (Indianapolis, 1968).

The Rhetoric of Black Power, ed. Robert L. Scott and Wayne Brockriede (New York, 1967).

Rhetoric of Black Revolution, ed. Arthur L. Smith (Boston, 1969).

The Rhetoric of Christian Socialism, ed. Paul H. Boase (New York, 1969).

The Rhetoric of the Civil-Rights Movement, ed. Haig A. Bosmajian and Hamida Bosmajian (New York, 1969).

The Rhetoric of Our Times, ed. J. Jeffery Auer (New York, 1969).

Rhetorical Analyses of Literary Works, ed. Edward P. J. Corbett (New York, 1969).

The Rhetorical Idiom: Essays in Rhetoric, Oratory, Language and Drama, Presented to Herbert August Wichelns, ed. Donald C. Bryant (Ithaca, N.Y., 1958).

Selected Readings in Rhetoric and Public Speaking, ed. Lester Thonssen (New York, 1942).

Studies in Rhetoric and Public Speaking in Honor of James Albert Winans (New York, 1925).

Studies in Speech and Drama in Honor of Alexander M. Drummond (Ithaca, N.Y. 1944).

Some Books on Style

If available, inexpensive reprint editions of the following books have been cited rather than the original editions. For a more extensive bibliography of books and articles on style, consult the following: Louis T. Milic, *Style and Stylistics: An Analytical Bibliography* (New York, 1967); Richard W. Bailey and Dolores M. Burton, *English Stylistics: A Bibliography* (Cambridge, Mass., 1968); R. C. Alston and J. L. Rosier, "Rhetoric and Style: a Bibliographical Guide," *Leeds Studies in English,* New Series I (1967), 137–59; James R. Bennett, "An Annotated Bibliography of Selected Writings on English Prose Style," *College Composition and Communication,* XVI (December 1965), 248–55; Paul C. Doherty, "Stylistics—A Bibliographical Survey," *The CEA Critic,* XXVIII (May 1966), 1, 3, and 4.

Robert Adolph, *The Rise of Modern Prose Style* (Cambridge, Mass., 1968).

Richard Bridgman, *The Colloquial Style in America* (New York, 1966).

Huntington Brown, *Prose Styles: Five Primary Types* (Minneapolis, Minn., 1966).

Rollo Walter Brown, *How the French Boy Learns to Write* (Cambridge, Mass., 1915). Special reprint ed., with Foreword by Harold C. Martin, for the National Council of Teachers of English, 1963.

Frederick Candelaria, ed., *Perspectives on Style* (Boston, 1968).

Seymour Chatman and S. R. Levin, *Essays on the Language of Literature* (Boston, 1967).

J. V. Cunningham, ed., *The Problem of Style,* Fawcett Premier Books (New York, 1966).

Bonamy Dobrée, *Modern Prose Style,* 2nd ed. (Oxford, 1964).

Lubomir Dolezel and Richard W. Bailey, eds., *Statistics and Style* (New York, 1969).

Richard M. Eastman, *Style: Writing as the Discovery of Outlook* (New York, 1970).

Rudolf Flesch, *The Art of Readable Writing,* Collier Books (New York, 1962).

H. W. Fowler and F. G. Fowler, *The King's English,* 3rd ed. (Oxford, 1931).

Donald C. Freeman, ed., *Linguistics and Literary Style* (New York, 1970).

Walker Gibson, *Tough, Sweet, and Stuffy: An Essay on Modern American Prose Styles* (Bloomington, Ind., 1966).

———, *Persona: A Style Study for Readers and Writers* (New York, 1969).

Ian A. Gordon, *The Movement of English Prose* (London, 1966).

Robert Graves and Alan Hodge, *The Reader over Your Shoulder: A Handbook for Writers,* Macmillan Paperbacks (New York, 1961).

Donald Hall, ed., *The Modern Stylists: Writers on the Art of Writing* (New York, 1968).

David King and Thomas Crerar, *A Choice of Words* (Toronto, 1969).

Carl H. Klaus, ed., *Style in English Prose* (New York, 1968).

George Philip Krapp, *The Rise of English Literary Prose* (London, 1966).

Richard A. Lanham, *A Handlist of Rhetorical Terms: A Guide for Students of English Literature* (Berkeley, Calif., 1968).

Jacob Leed, ed., *The Computer and Literary Style: Introductory Essays and Studies* (Kent, Ohio, 1967).

Edwin Herbert Lewis, *The History of the English Paragraph* (Chicago, 1894).

Glen A. Love and Michael Payne, eds., *Contemporary Essays on Style: Rhetoric, Linguistics, and Criticism* (Glenview, Ill., 1968).

F. L. Lucas, *Style,* Collier Books (New York, 1962).

Marsh H. McCall, Jr., *Ancient Rhetorical Theories of Simile and Comparison* (Cambridge, Mass., 1970).

Josephine Miles, *Style and Proportion: The Language of Prose and Poetry* (Boston, 1967).

Louis T. Milic, *Stylists on Style* (New York, 1969).

——, *A Quantitative Approach to the Style of Jonathan Swift* (The Hague, 1967).

J. Middleton Murry, *The Problem of Style,* Oxford Paperbacks (London, 1960).

John Nist, ed., *Style in English* (Indianapolis, 1969).

Raymond Queneau, *Exercises in Style,* trans. Barbara Wright (London, 1958).

Sir Arthur Quiller-Couch, *On the Art of Writing,* new ed. (New York, 1943).

Walter Raleigh, *Style* (London, 1897).

Herbert Read, *English Prose Style,* Beacon Paperback (Boston, 1955).

Roget's International Thesaurus, 3rd ed. (New York, 1962).

R. A. Sayce, *Style in French Prose: A Method of Analysis* (Oxford, 1958).

Bernard N. Schilling, ed., *Essential Articles for the Study of English Augustan Backgrounds* (Hamden, Conn., 1961). Contains the following articles on the development of English prose style in the seventeenth century: Morris Croll, "Attic Prose Style in the Seventeenth Century"; A. C. Howell, *"Res et Verba:* Words and Things"; R. F. Jones, "Science and English Prose Style in the Third Quarter of the Seventeenth Century"; R. F. Jones, "The Attack on Pulpit Eloquence in the Restoration"; George Williamson, "Senecan Style in the Seventeenth Century."

Thomas A. Sebeok, ed., *Style in Language* (Cambridge, Mass., 1960).

Lee A. Sonnino, *A Handbook to Sixteenth Century Rhetoric* (New York, 1968). Among other information, this handbook contains definitions and illustrations of the various schemes and tropes.

John Spencer, Nils Erik Enkvist, and Michael J. Gregory, *Linguistics and Style* (London, 1964).

William Strunk, Jr., and E. B. White, *The Elements of Style,* paperback ed. (New York, 1959).

Style, Rhetoric, and Rhythm: Essays by Morris Croll, ed. J. Max Patrick and Robert O. Evans, with John M. Wallace and R. J. Schoeck (Princeton, N.J., 1966).

James R. Sutherland, *On English Prose,* The Alexander Lectures, 1956 (Toronto, 1957).

Harry and Agathe Thornton, *Time and Style: A Psycho-Linguistic Essay in Classical Literature* (London, 1962).

Brian Vickers, *The Artistry of Shakespeare's Prose* (London, 1969).

————, *Francis Bacon and Renaissance Prose* (London, 1969).

Winston Weathers and Otis Winchester, *Copy and Compose: A Guide to Prose Style* (Englewood Cliffs, N.J., 1969).

Joan Webber, *Contrary Music: The Prose Style of John Donne* (Madison, Wis., 1963).

————, *The Eloquent "I": Style and Self in Seventeenth-Century Prose* (Madison, Wis., 1967).

Webster's New Dictionary of Synonyms (Springfield, Mass., 1968).

Paul C. Wermuth, ed., *Modern Essays on Writing and Style,* 2nd ed. (New York, 1969).

George Williamson, *The Senecan Amble: A Study in Prose from Bacon to Collier* (Chicago, 1951).

W. K. Wimsatt, Jr., *The Prose Style of Samuel Johnson,* Yale Paperbound (New Haven, Conn., 1963).

Warren Taylor, *A Dictionary of the Tudor Figures of Rhetoric* (Chicago, 1937).

Dictionaries of Usage

Bergen Evans and Cornelia Evans, *A Dictionary of Contemporary American Usage* (New York, 1957).

Wilson Follett, *Modern American Usage,* edited and completed by Jacques Barzun in collaboration with Carlos Baker, Frederick W. Dupee, Dudley Fitts, James D. Hart, Phyllis McGinley, and Lionel Trilling (New York, 1966).

H. W. Fowler, *A Dictionary of Modern English Usage* (Oxford, 1926, 1950); 2nd ed. revised and edited by Sir Ernest Gowers (Oxford, 1965).

Margaret Nicholson, *A Dictionary of American-English Usage* (New York, 1958).

INDEX

643